1995 Food & Wine

AN ENTIRE YEAR'S RECIPES FROM
AMERICA'S FAVORITE FOOD MAGAZINE

Racks of Pork with Cider-Pepper Glaze (p. 186)

1995 Food & Wine

AN ENTIRE YEAR'S RECIPES FROM AMERICA'S FAVORITE FOOD MAGAZINE

Food & Wine
BOOKS

American Express Publishing Corporation
New York

FOOD & WINE MAGAZINE
Editor in Chief: Dana Cowin
Food Editor: Tina Ujlaki
Art Director: Gwynne Truglio Bettencourt

FOOD & WINE BOOKS
Editorial Director: Judith Hill
Editor: Terri Mauro
Art Director: Nina Scerbo
Production Manager: Yvette Williams-Braxton

Vice President, Books and Information Services: John Stoops
Marketing Director: Mary V. Cooney
Marketing/Promotion Manager: Roni Stein
Operations Manager: Doreen Camardi

PHOTOGRAPHY

Cover Photo: **William Abranowicz** (Penne with Eggplant and Ricotta Salata, p. 246)
Back Photo: **Carin and David Riley** (Hot Chocolate Torte, p. 386)

William Abranowicz: 16 (*top left*), 74, 93, 244, 247, 249, 250, 251, 262, 276, 281, 286, 288, 289; **Melanie Acevedo:** 2, 20, 42, 55, 92, 97, 104, 110, 121, 156, 169, 173, 187, 194, 233, 254, 291, 326 (*top left*), 390, 395, 396, 402, 404, 407, 417, 418, 430, 431, 455, 458, 460 (*center*); **Christopher Baker:** 45, 49, 63, 91, 96, 200 (*bottom left*), 256, 270, 271, 272 (*top left*), 272 (*bottom left*), 273, 275, 278, 301, 316, 321 (*top right*), 437, 462; **Bruno Barbey:** 35, 72, 135, 180, 457; **Mary Ellen Bartley:** 153, 177, 231; **Antoine Bootz:** 144, 147, 149; **Langdon Clay:** 311, 338, 342, 433; **Fran Collin:** 78, 179, 190, 224, 295, 414, 424, 432; **Grey Crawford:** 230; **Reed Davis:** 209, 211, 212, 218; **John Reed Forsman:** 32, 76, 198, 206, 453, 459; **Dana Gallagher:** 53, 62, 99, 167, 208, 260, 265, 329, 345, 352; **Mauro Galligani:** 451; **Gentl & Hyers:** 25 (*bottom right*), 341, 343, 397; **Francis Hammond:** 219, 248, 349, 460 (*top*); **Ruedi Hofmann:** 25 (*top right*), 28, 31, 38, 75, 90, 429, 452; **Ilisa Katz:** 109, 132, 245, 344; **Ken Kochey:** 229; **Joshua McHugh:** 348; **Michael Mundy:** 59, 94, 227, 310, 420; **Gilles Peress:** 60, 61, 127, 158, 175, 220, 258; **Carin and David Riley:** 8, 12, 13, 23, 50, 52, 70, 83, 86, 100, 133 (*top right*), 134, 136, 168, 197, 203, 298, 304 (*top*), 304 (*bottom*), 312, 314, 323, 326 (*bottom left*), 340, 353, 360, 363, 366, 386, 391, 394, 408, 434, 454; **Maria Robledo:** 6, 44, 57, 68, 69, 84, 166, 232, 234, 253, 321 (*bottom right*), 334, 389; **Jeremy Samuelson:** 27, 221, 252, 392 (*bottom left*), 444; **Victor Schrager:** 46, 116, 228, 410, 419; **Neil Selkirk:** 216; **Tara Sgroi:** 133 (*bottom right*), 266; **Ellen Silverman:** 58, 73, 79, 81, 160; **Jerry Simpson:** 106, 107, 237, 238, 240, 371, 392 (*top left*); **Bill Steele:** 118, 125, 130, 264, 308, 332, 372, 421; **Ann Stratton:** 16 (*bottom right*), 82, 122, 123, 374, 377, 379, 387, 398, 405, 439, 443, 448, 460 (*bottom*), 464; **Mark Thomas:** 139, 164, 176, 184, 191, 200 (*top left*); **Lisa Charles Watson:** 112, 201, 293, 294.

American Express Publishing Corporation

Library of Congress Cataloging-in-Publication Data
1995 Food & wine : an entire year's recipes from America's favorite food magazine.
p. cm.
Includes index.
ISBN 0-916103-29-3 (hardcover)
1. Cookery. I. Food & wine (New York, N.Y.)
TX714.A198 1996
641.5--dc20 95-48206
CIP

Published by American Express Publishing Corporation
1120 Avenue of the Americas, New York, New York 10036

Manufactured in the United States of America

CONTENTS

Clockwise from bottom: Spaghetti Squash Salad with Lemon Dressing (p. 69), Roasted Buttercup Squash and Baked Apples (p. 329), Roti (p. 339), Spicy Thickened Yogurt (p. 355), and Smoky Black Beans (p. 332)

FOREWORD

I've heard the words "new" and "improved" applied to products so many times that I hesitate to utter them. However, just this once, I want to tell you that this book, which collects our FOOD & WINE recipes into one volume, is indeed new and improved. Here's why: We listened to your suggestions, and for the first time ever, we're putting an entire year's recipes between two covers. We've included 550 recipes, about 50% more than last year. Plus more than 100 tip boxes and menus.

For me, the annual serves two purposes: It's a space-saver and organizer—it allows me to move twelve FOOD & WINE magazines out of the kitchen into the study, where they stay for handy reference. But it also lets me relive the year that has just past. I remembered the moment I tasted Julia Child's Coq au Vin. It was as delicious a rendition as I've ever had. I was reminded of the foolproof soufflé from Anne Willan that I'd always wanted to give a go. And I promised myself to make a few of FOOD & WINE food editors' favorite recipes: Jerk Chicken, Roasted Pork Loin with Fennel, Linguine with Tomato Pesto, and Strawberry Spiral Pie.

I hope this annual will bring back memories for you and also spur you on to create new ones. And, as we say here, I hope you enjoy your food and wine!

DANA COWIN
Editor in Chief
FOOD & WINE Magazine

Lemon Flan with Lemon Sauce and Candied Zest (p. 433)

For your convenience, recipes that have appeared in our "Low-Fat Cooking" and "Good Food Fast" columns (or in articles specifically dealing with low-fat or quick cooking) have been marked:

LF for low-fat **Q** for quick

CHAPTER 1

BEVERAGES

The Martini, with a Crisp Pasta Bite (p. 34) and Garlic-Parmesan Puffs (p. 34)

THE MARTINI

The origin of the martini is much debated. Some claim that Jerry Thomas, while tending bar in San Francisco in the mid-19th century, created the prototype: the Martinez, made with Old Tom sweetened gin, lots of vermouth, bitters, and maraschino liqueur. Others cite early-20th-century New York City bartender Martini di Arma di Taggia as the first to marry gin with dry vermouth and call it a martini. The facts will probably never surface, so choose between these stories—and any others you may hear.

Martinis are perhaps the most idiosyncratic of all cocktails. Each recipe is a personal statement: a lot of vermouth, a little vermouth, no vermouth ("just wave the bottle over the glass"), one olive, three olives, shake or stir.

- 2½ ounces London dry gin
- 1½ teaspoons dry vermouth
- 1 pitted olive (stuffed with pimento if desired), for garnish

Chill a 4-ounce stemmed cocktail (martini) glass. Pour the gin and vermouth into a mixing glass half filled with ice cubes. Stir well to blend and chill. Strain into the cocktail glass; garnish with the olive.—GARY REGAN

THE MANHATTAN

This cocktail was created in the 1870s at New York City's Manhattan Club for an affair hosted by Lady Jennie Churchill, the Brooklyn lass who became Winston Churchill's mother. In my opinion, this is the cocktail that is most frequently made incorrectly. When properly fashioned, the Manhattan is a God-given creation.

I once used blended whiskey but have concluded that straight bourbon or rye whiskey is better. Whatever the whiskey you select, make sure you add a few dashes of Angostura bitters. Without them, a Manhattan is no more than a modest mixture; with them, it is a dazzling cocktail.

- 2½ ounces straight bourbon or rye whiskey
- ½ ounce sweet vermouth
- 3 dashes Angostura bitters
- 1 maraschino cherry, for garnish

Chill a 4-ounce stemmed cocktail (martini) glass. Pour the whiskey, vermouth, and bitters into a mixing glass half filled with ice cubes. Stir well to blend and chill. Strain into the cocktail glass; garnish the Manhattan with the cherry.—GARY REGAN

THE SAZERAC

According to Famous New Orleans Drinks & How to Mix 'Em *(Pelican) by Stanley Clisby Arthur, the drink we know as the Sazerac was first concocted in the mid-19th century by Leon Lamothe, a New Orleans bartender. The original formula called for brandy as its base. In time, rye whiskey replaced the brandy, and now the Sazerac is usually made with bourbon. Still, one ingredient hasn't changed: Peychaud's bitters. They are quite different from Angostura bitters and are absolutely indispensable if you are going to make a correct Sazerac.*

- 2 teaspoons absinthe substitute (Herbsaint, Ricard, or Pernod)
- 1 sugar cube (or ½ teaspoon superfine sugar)
- 3 dashes Peychaud's bitters (see Note)
- 1 teaspoon water
- 2½ ounces bourbon
- 1 lemon twist, for garnish

Pour the absinthe substitute into a 6-ounce old-fashioned glass and swirl it around to coat the glass; pour out any excess. In another old-fashioned glass, mix the sugar, bitters, and water with the back of a teaspoon until the sugar dissolves. Fill the first glass with crushed ice. Add the bourbon to the mixture and stir gently; pour into the ice-filled glass. Rub the outside of the lemon twist around the rim of the glass, twist it over the glass to release the oils, and drop it into the drink as a garnish.

NOTE: Peychaud's bitters can be ordered directly from the manufacturer. A 5-ounce bottle is $5.50 and 10 ounces are $7.50, including shipping and handling. Send checks to Sazerac Co., Peychaud's Consumer Purchase Orders, 803 Jefferson Hwy., New Orleans, LA 70121. Allow 4 to 6 weeks for delivery.—GARY REGAN

THE OLD-FASHIONED

This drink was created around the turn of the century at the Pendennis Club in Louisville, Kentucky, where one of the regular customers, a retired Civil War general, didn't care much for the taste of straight whiskey. (In Kentucky, disliking bourbon is tantamount to treason.) To accommodate him, the bartender added a little sugar, a couple of dashes of bitters, and a few drops of water to the veteran's whiskey, unknowingly creating the old-fashioned for the old-timer. Personally, I enjoy the version here, which calls for the addition of a maraschino cherry and a slice of orange.

- ½ orange slice, cut about ¼ inch thick
- 1 maraschino cherry, stem removed
- 3 dashes Angostura bitters
- 1 teaspoon water
- 1 sugar cube (or ½ teaspoon superfine sugar)
- 2½ ounces bourbon

In a 6-ounce old-fashioned glass, combine the orange slice, cherry, bitters, water, and sugar cube. Mix the ingredients with the back of a teaspoon to dissolve

The Manhattan, with Garlic-Parmesan Sticks (p. 34)

the sugar and mash the fruit somewhat. Fill the glass with ice cubes, add the bourbon, and stir gently.—GARY REGAN

THE ROB ROY

In his marvelous book, Straight Up or on the Rocks: A Cultural History of American Drink *(Simon & Schuster), William Grimes claims that the Rob Roy was named for a Broadway show that ran in the Thirties. The drink originally contained Angostura bitters, but they have not been used in most versions since the late Sixties. Recently, when I was leafing through* The Fine Art of Mixing Drinks *(Doubleday), I noticed that the author, David A. Embury, suggested substituting Peychaud's bitters. I tried them, and the resulting Rob Roy was a nectar fit even for Robert Burns himself.*

- 2½ ounces blended scotch
- 1 ounce sweet vermouth
- 1 dash Peychaud's bitters (see Sazerac Note, p. 13)
- 1 maraschino cherry, for garnish

Chill a 4-ounce stemmed cocktail (martini) glass. Pour the scotch, vermouth, and bitters into a mixing glass half filled with ice cubes. Stir well to blend and chill. Strain into the cocktail glass; garnish with the cherry.
VARIATION: For a Perfect Rob Roy, use ½ ounce sweet vermouth and ½ ounce dry vermouth. Garnish with a lemon twist.—GARY REGAN

WATERMELON MARGARITAS

Don't be afraid to put the watermelon seeds in the food processor; they won't get chopped up. If you use a blender, remove the seeds from the flesh before pureeing.

MAKES 6 MARGARITAS

- 6-pound piece of watermelon
- 1 cup sugar
- ¼ cup fresh lime juice
- 6 or more shots of tequila (at least ¾ cup)

1. Cut the watermelon into large chunks, discarding the rind. Put the melon in a food processor or blender and process until pureed. Strain the puree into a bowl. Pour all but 1 cup of the puree into a glass pitcher.
2. Combine the remaining 1 cup puree with the sugar in a small saucepan. Bring to a simmer over high heat, stirring, until the sugar dissolves, about 3 minutes. Pour the mixture into the puree in the pitcher and stir occasionally until cooled. (MAKE AHEAD: The puree can be refrigerated, covered, for up to 1 week.)
3. To make Margaritas, stir the lime juice and then the tequila into the watermelon puree. Fill tall glasses with ice, pour the Margarita mixture over, and serve.—MARCIA KIESEL

THE CHAMPAGNE COCKTAIL

Although there are many variations on this wonderful drink, the classic Champagne cocktail hasn't changed since pre-Prohibition days.

Many people like to make this drink with inexpensive Champagne, and to their credit the extra ingredients most definitely disguise that economy. However, although I wouldn't recommend using a super-premium bottle, I do believe that a decent bottling—one that you would buy for drinking on its own—improves the cocktail.

- 1 sugar cube (or ½ teaspoon superfine sugar
- 3 dashes Angostura bitters
- 5 ounces Champagne
- 1 lemon twist, for garnish

Place the sugar cube into a 6-ounce Champagne flute, sprinkle the bitters over the sugar, and add the Champagne. Garnish the cocktail with the lemon twist.—GARY REGAN

CHAMPAGNE PUNCH

This classic Champagne punch is made with a large block of frozen lemonade, which chills and flavors it. The punch must be served ice cold, so assemble it at the last moment.

MAKES ABOUT 3 DOZEN 3-OUNCE SERVINGS

- Frozen Lemonade (recipe follows)
- 1 pint Cognac or brandy
- 1 thin-skinned orange, thinly sliced crosswise
- 2 bottles cold semidry Champagne, Spanish Semi-Seco Cava or Italian Prosecco
- 1 quart cold soda water or seltzer

Remove the lemonade from its container and place it in a crystal or silver punch bowl. Pour the Cognac over the block of lemonade, add the sliced orange, Champagne, and soda water, and serve.

Frozen Lemonade

MAKES ABOUT 6 CUPS

- 6 large, heavy lemons, scrubbed clean of any oil or wax coating
- 1 cup sugar
- 6 cups boiling water

1. Halve the lemons and put them in a nonreactive heatproof bowl. Add the sugar. Pour the boiling water over the lemons and stir to dissolve the sugar. Set aside for 30 minutes.
2. Squeeze the juice from the lemons and strain into the bowl; discard the lemons. Pour the lemonade into an empty half-gallon milk carton, close the top, and freeze until solid or for up to 1 week.—JOHN MARTIN TAYLOR

STRAWBERRY RUM PUNCH

Overproof Jamaican rum, available in many liquor stores, adds an authentic wallop to this colorful festive drink. Other varieties of overproof rum or a regular Jamaican rum can be substituted.

MAKES 8 SERVINGS

- 2 cups Strawberry Syrup (recipe follows)
- 3 limes—2 halved, 1 thinly sliced
- 2 cups pineapple juice
- 1 to 2 cups overproof white Jamaican rum
- 1 tablespoon allspice berries
- 8 dashes Angostura bitters
- 1 cup fresh strawberries
- Fresh mint sprigs, for garnish

1. In a large bowl, combine the Strawberry Syrup with 2 cups of water. Squeeze the juice from the 2 halved limes into the bowl and add the pineapple juice, rum, allspice, and bitters. Mix well, cover, and refrigerate overnight.
2. Strain the punch into a glass bowl and add the sliced lime. Hull and halve the strawberries and add them to the punch. Serve over ice, garnished with sprigs of mint.

BEVERAGE BASICS

EQUIVALENTS: **To help you calculate how much you will need, keep these guidelines in mind.**

- **One 750-ml bottle of wine produces about five 5-ounce glasses of wine.**
- **One 750-ml bottle of liquor yields about 17 shots (a shot equals 1½ ounces).**
- **One 1-liter bottle of liquor yields about 22½ shots.**
- **One liter of soda tops off six to seven 12-ounce highball glasses that contain ice and one shot of liquor.**
- **5 pounds of ice fills twenty 12-ounce highball glasses.**

WHAT TO HAVE ON HAND: **Unless I were certain of their preferences, I would buy the following to offer sufficient variety for a group of 10.**

- **One 750-ml bottle bourbon**
- **One 750-ml bottle blended whiskey**
- **One 750-ml bottle blended scotch**
- **One 750-ml bottle London dry gin**
- **Two 750-ml bottles vodka**
- **One 375-ml bottle dry vermouth**
- **One 375-ml bottle sweet vermouth**
- **Three to four 750-ml bottles dry white wine**
- **Two 750-ml bottles dry red wine**
- **12 bottles beer**
- **1 liter lemon-lime soda**
- **1 liter cola**
- **1 liter diet cola**
- **1 liter ginger ale**
- **1 liter tonic water**
- **2 liters club soda**
- **2 quarts orange juice**
- **1 quart cranberry juice**
- **1 quart tomato juice**
- **1 bottle each of Angostura and Peychaud's bitters**
- **1 bottle Worcestershire sauce**
- **1 jar horseradish**
- **1 jar cocktail olives**
- **1 jar cocktail onions**
- **1 jar maraschino cherries**
- **15 to 20 pounds ice**

—GARY REGAN

Strawberry Syrup

Bottled strawberry syrup is available at Latin American markets. It has a stronger strawberry flavor than the homemade version that follows.

MAKES ABOUT 2 CUPS

- 3 pounds very ripe fresh strawberries, hulled and thinly sliced
- 2 cups sugar

1. In a large bowl, toss the strawberries and sugar. Let stand, stirring often, until the strawberries are swimming in liquid, about 1½ hours.
2. Pass the strawberries and their liquid through a colander or coarse strainer, pressing lightly to release as much syrup as possible. (MAKE AHEAD: The syrup can be refrigerated for up to 1 week.)—PAUL CHUNG

VERBENA-CITRUS COOLER

This refreshing beverage is a variation of a tisane, an herbal infusion. It's made with lemon verbena, which has an aromatic lemon flavor. A good

Verbena-Citrus Cooler

way to measure the herbs is to fill a pitcher to the top with three parts verbena sprigs and one part mint sprigs, then remove any woody stems and proceed with the recipe.

MAKES 2 QUARTS

- ⅔ cup sugar
- 6 loosely packed cups lemon verbena sprigs, plus more for garnish
- 2 loosely packed cups pineapple mint or spearmint sprigs
- 1 cup fresh orange juice
- ½ cup fresh lemon juice
- ½ cup fresh lime juice
- Orange slices, for garnish

1. In a large saucepan, combine the sugar with 6 cups of water and bring to a boil over moderately high heat. Cook, stirring occasionally, until the sugar is thoroughly dissolved, about 5 minutes.

2. Wash the lemon verbena and mint sprigs and drain well. Place in a large stainless steel bowl.

3. Pour the hot sugar syrup over the herbs and let steep until cooled to room temperature, about 30 minutes. Strain through a fine sieve into a half-gallon pitcher. Strain the orange, lemon, and lime juices into a pitcher and stir well.

4. To serve, fill tall tumblers with ice. Pour the drink over the ice and garnish with verbena sprigs and orange slices.—STEVE MELLINA

FRESH LEMON-LIMEADE Q

4 SERVINGS

- 1 cup plus 2 tablespoons sugar
- ¾ cup fresh lemon juice
- ¾ cup fresh lime juice
- Lemon and lime slices

In a medium saucepan, combine the sugar and 1½ cups of water over moderately high heat; stir to dissolve the sugar. Just before the mixture comes to a boil, remove from the heat. Stir in 3¾ cups of cold water, then pour into a pitcher. Stir in the lemon and lime juices and refrigerate. Serve in tall glasses over ice, garnished with lemon and lime slices.—TRACEY SEAMAN

CREOLE CAFE AU LAIT

For a delicious café au lait, the milk is boiled twice; this Creole technique actually makes the milk taste sweeter.

1. Take a head count of drinkers and prepare a pot of coffee, making it a bit stronger than you usually do. You'll need to figure on ½ cup freshly brewed strong coffee and ½ cup milk per person.

2. While the coffee is brewing, bring the milk to a boil over high heat in a large heavy saucepan. Watch the milk carefully and remove it from the heat the moment it comes to a full boil so that it doesn't boil over. When the bubbles have subsided, return the milk to the heat and allow it to come to a full boil for a second time, removing it from the heat again so that it doesn't boil over. Strain the hot milk into mugs, add equal parts of coffee, and serve the café au lait.—JOHN MARTIN TAYLOR

TRADITIONAL MINT TEA

6 SERVINGS

- 1 tablespoon plus 1 teaspoon Chinese green tea*
- 2 medium bunches of fresh mint, stems discarded, plus additional whole sprigs for garnish
- 10 sugar cubes

*Available at Asian markets and many supermarkets

1. Bring a large kettle of water to a boil. In a large teapot, cover

Caribbean Red Zinger Tea

the green tea with 1 cup of the boiling water to rinse the leaves and warm the pot. Quickly pour off the water without discarding the tea.

2. Return the remaining water to a rolling boil. Pack the mint leaves and sugar cubes into the teapot and add about 4 cups of the boiling water. Cover and let steep for 5 minutes.

3. Pour a little of the tea into a glass, then pour it back into the teapot. Repeat 3 times to mix the ingredients. Pour the tea into glasses or cups, garnish with mint sprigs, and serve warm or iced.—FATIMA HAL

CARIBBEAN RED ZINGER TEA

This hot rum-spiked drink, made with Red Zinger tea, is related to the Caribbean drink sorrel.

4 SERVINGS

Thickly slice 1 large scrubbed unpeeled orange; reserve 2 slices for garnish. In a large nonreactive saucepan, combine the remaining orange slices with 10 whole cloves, 2 cinnamon sticks, 6 allspice berries, and 2 quarts of water, and bring to a boil over high heat. Remove the saucepan from the heat, add 6 Red Zinger tea bags, and let steep, covered, for 5 minutes. Strain and stir in honey and dark rum to taste. Halve the 2 reserved orange slices and stick 1 or 2 cloves in each. Serve the tea hot or warm, garnished with the clove-studded oranges.—JESSICA B. HARRIS

CHAPTER 2

HORS D'OEUVRES

Pickled Vegetable-Eggplant Rolls

PICKLED VEGETABLE-EGGPLANT ROLLS LF

6 SERVINGS

PICKLED VEGETABLES:
- ¼ cup white wine vinegar
- 1 medium serrano chile, thinly sliced
- 1 garlic clove, peeled
- 1 tablespoon light brown sugar
- 2 fresh thyme sprigs
- 1 bay leaf
- ½ teaspoon mustard seeds
- ½ teaspoon fennel seeds
- ½ teaspoon kosher salt
- ½ medium carrot, cut into 2-by-⅛-inch matchsticks
- ½ medium red bell pepper, cut into 2-by-⅛-inch matchsticks
- ½ medium yellow bell pepper, cut into 2-by-⅛-inch matchsticks
- ½ medium jicama, peeled and cut into 2-by-⅛-inch matchsticks

Vegetable oil cooking spray
One 1¼ pound eggplant, trimmed and cut lengthwise into twelve ⅛-inch-thick slices
Kosher salt and freshly ground black pepper
- 6 large Swiss chard leaves
- 2 tablespoons Cilantro Puree (recipe follows)
- 2 tablespoons freshly grated aged Monterey Jack, Parmesan, or Asiago cheese

1. Make the pickled vegetables: In a small nonreactive saucepan, bring the vinegar, serrano chile, garlic, brown sugar, thyme, bay leaf, mustard seeds, fennel seeds, salt, and ¼ cup of water to a boil over moderate heat.

2. In a bowl, combine the carrot, red and yellow peppers, and the jicama. Pour the hot pickling liquid over the vegetables. Let cool. Cover and refrigerate overnight. Let the vegetables return to room temperature before proceeding.

3. Preheat the oven to 475°. Spray 2 baking sheets with the cooking spray. Arrange the eggplant slices on the prepared baking sheets and season with salt and pepper. Bake for about 12 minutes, or until the edges begin to brown. Brush the slices lightly with a moistened pastry brush so that they remain pliable; let cool.

4. Meanwhile, in a saucepan of gently boiling salted water, blanch the Swiss chard until wilted, about 1 minute. Drain, rinse, and pat dry. Cut out and discard the tough ribs.

5. Lay a 15-inch-long rectangle of plastic wrap on a work surface, long end toward you. Arrange half of the eggplant slices vertically in a row on the plastic, slightly overlapping, to make a 7-by-12-inch rectangle with a long end toward you. Lay 3 Swiss chard leaves on the eggplant. About 1 inch in from the closest long end, arrange half of the vegetable matchsticks in a 1-inch-wide strip across the width of the rectangle. Spread 1 tablespoon of the Cilantro Puree next to the vegetables and top with 1 tablespoon of the grated cheese.

6. Fold the nearest long end of the eggplant snugly over the vegetables and cheese and roll, pulling up on the plastic to help form a 12-by-1½-inch cylinder. Make a second roll with the remaining ingredients. (MAKE AHEAD: The rolls can be prepared up to 3 hours ahead; wrap tightly in plastic and let stand at room temperature.)

7. Unwrap the rolls. Using a thin sharp knife, slice each one crosswise into 9 equal pieces, trimming the ends if desired. Transfer to a platter or individual plates and serve.

Cilantro Puree

This herb paste can also be used as a spread on grilled vegetables or chicken sandwiches.

MAKES ABOUT ⅓ CUP

- ¼ cup fresh cilantro leaves
- 2 medium garlic cloves
- ½ medium jalapeño chile, seeded
- 2 tablespoons dried plain bread crumbs
- 3 tablespoons dry white wine

Kosher salt and freshly ground black pepper

Put the cilantro, garlic, and jalapeño in a mini-chopper or mortar and blend until well mashed. Work in the bread crumbs until incorporated. Gradually blend in the wine and season with salt and pepper. (MAKE AHEAD: The puree can be prepared up to 4 hours ahead; cover and refrigerate.) —CHARLES WILEY

HERB-ROASTED MUSHROOMS

MAKES ABOUT 30

Juice of 1 lemon
- 2 teaspoons *herbes de Provence* (see Note)
- 1 teaspoon hot pepper sauce
- 1 teaspoon salt
- ½ teaspoon freshly ground white pepper
- ½ cup olive oil
- 3 pounds large mushrooms, stems discarded

MIX-AND-MATCH SERVING SUGGESTIONS

Throwing a cocktail party is easiest when you can mix and match hors d'oeuvres. Consider the Sun-Dried Tomato and Mango Chutney Relish, as delicious with grilled shrimp as it is with fried wonton chips. Herb-Roasted Mushrooms (p. 21) are as tasty stuffed with French Green Lentil Dip (p. 24) as they are atop a toast point spread with cream cheese.

The marinade for the mushrooms is versatile, too. Try it on shelled and deveined medium shrimp, trimmed pork or lamb tenderloins, or chicken breasts. Marinate the meats or shrimp for a couple of hours, then grill or broil. Slice the meat or chicken into medallions or strips. Serve with the sun-dried tomato relish or lentil dip, the mushrooms, and the Oven-Dried Cherry Tomatoes.

The dilled cream cheese from the Smoked Salmon Roll-Ups (p. 26) can be blended with chopped oven-dried cherry tomatoes to make a dip for the Fried Wonton Triangles (p. 34).

Garlic-Parmesan Puffs (p. 34) can be topped with the oven-dried cherry tomatoes or dollops of lentil dip. Or halve them horizontally and make sandwiches with the cream cheese, the sun-dried tomato relish or lentil dip, and the grilled meat, poultry, or shrimp.—BOB CHAMBERS

1. Preheat the oven to 450°. In a medium bowl, combine the lemon juice with the *herbes de Provence*, hot pepper sauce, salt, and pepper. Stir in the olive oil. Add the mushrooms and toss until coated.
2. Spread the mushrooms on a large nonstick baking sheet, stemmed sides up. Bake for 30 minutes. Turn them over and continue baking for about 15 minutes longer, or until tender. Let cool completely before serving. (MAKE AHEAD: The mushrooms can be refrigerated, covered, for up to 4 days. Let return to room temperature before serving.)
NOTE: *Herbes de Provence* is a mixture of dried herbs—usually rosemary, thyme, savory, lavender, and fennel seeds—and is available at specialty food stores and in the spice section of some supermarkets.—BOB CHAMBERS

OVEN-DRIED CHERRY TOMATOES

MAKES ABOUT 100

6 pints firm cherry tomatoes, halved
2 tablespoons basil
1 tablespoon sugar
1½ teaspoons salt
1½ teaspoons freshly ground pepper

1. Preheat the oven to 300°. Line 2 heavy baking sheets with parchment paper. Spread the halved cherry tomatoes on the baking sheets, cut sides up. In a small bowl, combine the basil, sugar, salt, and pepper, and sprinkle evenly over the cherry tomatoes.
2. Put the tomatoes in the oven and immediately reduce the temperature to 250°. Bake for about 3 hours, or until dried and chewy, but still slightly moist. Let cool. (MAKE AHEAD: The tomatoes can be refrigerated for up to one week; layer them in an airtight container.) Serve chilled or at room temperature.—BOB CHAMBERS

ROASTED PEPPERS WITH ANCHOVIES

Peperoni e Acciughe

As the roasted peppers and anchovies steep together in olive oil, a powerful exchange of flavors is achieved: the peppers acquire spiciness while sharing their sweetness with the anchovies. I always use plump, salt-packed anchovies that I buy loose; then I rinse them, skin them, open them up flat, and pull out the bones. If you can't find them, you can use those packed in oil in a glass jar.

12 SERVINGS

12 red and yellow bell peppers
4 garlic cloves
24 large anchovy fillets
Salt and freshly ground black pepper
Oregano
4½ tablespoons capers, soaked and rinsed if packed in salt, drained if packed in vinegar
About ½ cup extra-virgin olive oil

1. Roast the red and yellow bell peppers directly over a gas flame or under a preheated broiler, as close to the heat as possible, until blackened all over. Transfer the roasted peppers to a plastic bag and close tightly. When the peppers are cool enough to handle, peel off the charred skins. Discard the cores and cut the roasted peppers lengthwise into broad strips about 2 inches wide. Discard all the seeds and

veins. Pat the strips as dry as possible with paper towels. (Do not ever rinse them.)
2. Crush the garlic cloves with a heavy knife handle just enough to split the skins. Peel the garlic.
3. Choose a serving dish that is deep enough to accommodate 6 layers of peppers. Line the bottom with a layer of pepper strips and top them with 4 anchovy fillets. Add a pinch of salt, black pepper, a light sprinkling of oregano, a few capers, and 1 garlic clove. Repeat the procedure until you have used all of the ingredients. Pour enough olive oil on top to just cover the peppers. Let the vegetables marinate at room temperature for at least 2 hours. (MAKE AHEAD: The marinated peppers can be refrigerated, covered, for up to 3 days. Bring to room temperature before serving.)—MARCELLA HAZAN

From left: **Crisp Pasta Bites (p. 34), Garlic Parmesan Puffs (p. 34) topped with Oven-Dried Cherry Tomatoes or French Green-Lentil Dip (p. 24), Smoked Salmon Roll-Ups (p. 26), and grilled shrimp with Sun-Dried Tomato and Mango Chutney Relish**

SUN-DRIED TOMATO AND MANGO CHUTNEY RELISH

For ideas on how to use this versatile relish, see "Mix and Match Serving Suggestions" (opposite page).

MAKES ABOUT 1½ CUPS

- ½ pound oil-packed sun-dried tomatoes, drained
- ½ cup Major Grey's chutney
- 2 medium scallions, minced
- 1 tablespoon finely chopped fresh flat-leaf parsley
- 2 teaspoons fresh lemon juice
- ¼ teaspoon freshly ground pepper

In a food processor, pulse the tomatoes and chutney until finely chopped. Transfer to a bowl and fold in the scallions, parsley, lemon juice, and pepper. (MAKE AHEAD: The relish can be refrigerated, covered, up to 1 week. Let return to room temperature before serving.) —BOB CHAMBERS

SWEET POTATO CAKES WITH FRESH CRANBERRY RELISH

These little cakes, from The Upper Crust in New York City, have a wheaty flavor and a refreshing citrus-spiked topping. Serve the leftover relish with roast poultry or pork or lamb chops.

MAKES ABOUT 6 DOZEN

CRANBERRY RELISH:

- 1 medium unpeeled orange—scrubbed, halved, seeded, and cut into 2-inch chunks
- 1 medium Granny Smith apple—peeled, cored, and cut into 2-inch chunks
- ¼ medium unpeeled lemon—scrubbed, seeded, and cut into 2-inch chunks
- 2 cups fresh or frozen cranberries (½ pound)
- ½ cup sugar
- ½ cup coarsely chopped walnuts

SWEET POTATO CAKES:

- 1 cup whole wheat flour
- 1 teaspoon baking powder
- 1 teaspoon salt
- ⅛ teaspoon cayenne pepper
- 1 medium sweet potato, peeled and coarsely grated

LOW-FAT TORTILLA CHIPS

Q: I'm watching my fat intake. Is there an easy way to make low-fat chips for dipping in salsas?

A: Steven Raichlen, author of the new *Caribbean Pantry Cookbook* (Artisan) and the award-winning *High-Flavor, Low-Fat* cookbook series (Viking), says bake, don't fry. Cut flour or corn tortillas (or pita bread) in even wedges and arrange them on a dry baking sheet. Bake them in a 350° oven for 8 to 10 minutes, until lightly browned and crisp. Transfer them to a rack to dry out and cool slightly.—ARLENE FELTMAN-SAILHAC

½ cup shredded sharp Cheddar cheese (about 2 ounces)
1 teaspoon finely chopped fresh thyme
1 large egg, lightly beaten
1½ cups milk
About ½ cup vegetable oil, for frying

1. Make the cranberry relish: In a food processor, combine the orange, apple, and lemon, and pulse until finely chopped. Add the cranberries and pulse until the berries are coarsely chopped. Transfer to a bowl and stir in the sugar and walnuts. (MAKE AHEAD: The relish can be refrigerated for up to 1 week.)
2. Make the sweet potato cakes: In a small bowl, sift together the flour, baking powder, salt, and cayenne. Add the sweet potato, cheese, and thyme, and toss. In a medium bowl, combine the egg and milk. Stir in the dry ingredients just until combined.
3. Heat 1 tablespoon of the vegetable oil in a large nonstick skillet. Working in batches, spoon rounded teaspoons of the batter into the skillet and flatten slightly to form 1½-inch cakes. Cook over moderately high heat until the bottoms are lightly browned and tiny bubbles form on the tops, about 2 minutes. Flip the cakes and cook until lightly browned, about 1 minute longer. Transfer to paper towels to drain and repeat with the remaining oil and batter. (MAKE AHEAD: The cakes can be layered between sheets of wax paper and refrigerated for 1 day. Reheat in a 350° oven.) Arrange the cakes on a platter, top each one with about ½ teaspoon of the relish and serve.—THE UPPER CRUST

FRENCH GREEN LENTIL DIP

You can substitute other types of lentils for the French Puy *lentils, but the cooking time may vary.*

MAKES ABOUT 3½ CUPS

1½ cups French *Puy*,* or green lentils, rinsed and picked over
1 medium onion, coarsely chopped
1 small carrot, halved lengthwise and sliced crosswise ⅛ inch thick
2 garlic cloves, minced
½ teaspoon thyme
Pinch of ground cloves or allspice
Salt and freshly ground pepper
1 8-ounce container plain low-fat (1%) yogurt
2 tablespoons finely chopped fresh flat-leaf parsley

*Available at specialty food stores

1. In a medium saucepan, combine the lentils, the chopped onion, the sliced carrot, the minced garlic, the thyme, cloves, and 3 cups of water. Bring to a boil over moderately high heat. Lower the heat, cover, and simmer until the lentils are just tender, about 30 minutes.
2. Add 1½ teaspoons salt and ½ teaspoon pepper to the lentils and cook over moderate heat, uncovered, until almost all the water has evaporated and the lentils are very tender, about 10 minutes. Transfer the lentils to a food processor and puree. Transfer to a bowl, cover, and refrigerate until chilled, at least 1 hour or up to 1 week.
3. Stir the low-fat yogurt and the chopped parsley into the lentil puree and season the dip with salt and pepper. Serve the dip chilled.—BOB CHAMBERS

YOGURT AND POMEGRANATE DIP WITH CILANTRO

A snap to assemble, this tangy and refreshing yogurt dip is perfect with warm pita bread or as an accompaniment for grilled meats or steamed vegetables.

MAKES 2½ CUPS

1 large ripe pomegranate
2 cups chilled plain yogurt
2 scallions, white and tender green, finely chopped
¼ cup finely chopped fresh cilantro
Fresh mint sprigs, for garnish

1. Cut the pomegranate in half crosswise and gently lift out the seeds in sections, being careful not to break them. Pull the pomegranate seeds off the yellow pithy membrane.
2. In a medium bowl, combine the chilled yogurt, the chopped scallions, and the chopped cilantro. Gently fold in all but 2 tablespoons of the pomegranate seeds. Transfer the yogurt dip to a glass bowl and garnish with fresh mint sprigs and the reserved pomegranate seeds.—JEFFREY ALFORD AND NAOMI DUGUID

GOAT CHEESE TOASTS WITH TRUFFLE OIL

For this recipe, you will need a small bottle of truffle oil, typically a little less than 2 fluid ounces.

MAKES 2 DOZEN TOASTS

1 baguette, cut into 24 slices about ¼ inch thick
1 medium garlic clove
8 ounces Montrachet goat cheese or Italian Robiola cheese
Truffle oil
Fresh thyme leaves
Freshly ground pepper

Toast the baguette slices on a baking sheet in a 375° oven for about 8 minutes, or until golden brown. Very lightly rub the toasts with the garlic clove. Spread each toast with a thin layer of cheese. Pour a small amount of truffle oil into a teaspoon and tilt the spoon to sprinkle 3 or 4 drops of truffle oil on each toast. Top with a few thyme leaves and a pinch of black pepper and serve immediately.—MARCIA KIESEL

PESTO AND BRIE CANAPES

Choose a wedge of ripe Brie that's soft in the center for these garlic-spiked bites from Word of Mouth caterers in New York City. You can toast the baguette slices to give the canapés a crisper base.

MAKES ABOUT 4 DOZEN

½ cup pine nuts (about 3 ounces)
8 oil-packed sun-dried tomato halves, drained and finely chopped
2 small garlic cloves, minced
½ cup freshly grated Parmesan cheese (about 2 ounces)
¼ cup olive oil
⅓ cup minced fresh flat-leaf parsley
1 tablespoon minced fresh basil
Freshly ground pepper
1 pound ripe Brie, rind removed, at room temperature
1 long baguette, sliced diagonally ¼ inch thick (about 50 slices)

1. Preheat the oven to 350°. Spread the pine nuts on a baking sheet and toast for about 8 minutes, shaking the pan occasionally, until golden. Transfer the nuts to a work surface and coarsely chop them.
2. In a small bowl, combine the sun-dried tomatoes with the minced garlic, the grated Parmesan, the olive oil, parsley, basil and pepper. In a medium bowl, vigorously beat the Brie. Spread 1 rounded teaspoon of Brie on each of the baguette slices. Top each with ½ teaspoon of the pesto, sprinkle with the pine nuts, and serve.—WORD OF MOUTH

Sweet Potato Cake with Fresh Cranberry Relish

Yogurt and Pomegranate Dip with Cilantro

SMOKED SALMON CANAPES ON BRIOCHE

Assemble these no more than an hour before serving, so they won't get soggy.

MAKES ABOUT 6 DOZEN

1 cup crème fraîche or sour cream

WINE WITH HORS D'OEUVRES

What to serve with hors d'oeuvres? Champagne, with its palate-tingling effervescence, is a classic choice. Consider appetizingly dry brut styles, such as the Bollinger Special Cuvée or the Deutz Classic Brut, or a California sparkling wine, such as the Roederer Estate or the 1991 Iron Horse Brut. Or punctuate the hors d'oeuvres with the cleansing bite of a small shot of straight spirits. Go for an increasingly popular, easy-to-sip high-end vodka, such as Absolut or Finlandia, or white (silver) tequila, such as Patrón or Porfidio—served ice cold.

¼ teaspoon finely grated lemon zest
One ¾-pound rectangular loaf of brioche, crusts removed, brioche sliced ⅜ inch thick
4 tablespoons unsalted butter, melted
½ pound sliced smoked salmon, cut into ¼-inch-thick strips
2 scallions, thinly sliced on the diagonal

1. In a small bowl, combine the crème fraîche and lemon zest. Transfer to a strainer lined with a paper coffee filter and set over a bowl. Let drain in the refrigerator until the crème fraîche is just stiff, about 2 hours. Transfer the lemon cream to a small bowl.
2. Meanwhile, preheat the oven to 350°. Lightly brush both sides of the brioche slices with the melted butter and cut each slice into 4 triangles. Arrange the triangles on 2 large baking sheets and bake for about 10 minutes, or until lightly golden and crisp. Let cool completely. (MAKE AHEAD: The recipe can be prepared to this point up to 2 days ahead. Cover and refrigerate the lemon cream; store the toasts in an airtight container at room temperature. Recrisp in a warm oven if desired.)
3. To assemble the canapés, spoon ¼ teaspoon of the lemon cream in the center of each toast. Mound the salmon strips on top and garnish with the scallions. Arrange the canapés on platters and serve.—GRACE PARISI

SMOKED SALMON ROLL-UPS WITH DILLED LIME CREAM CHEESE

Make the smoked salmon rolls at least one day ahead to allow the flavors to mellow before slicing. Garnish the sliced roll-ups with your favorite caviar; salmon or whitefish caviar are good inexpensive choices. You'll have plenty of dilled cream cheese left over, which can be used in combination with other hors d'oeuvres (see "Mix and Match Serving Suggestions," p. 22).

For an easy, tasty alternative to the salmon, make a roll with prosciutto (see variation that follows). Use imported prosciutto de Parma that has been trimmed of fat.

MAKES ABOUT 45

½ pound cream cheese, softened
3 large scallions, finely chopped
1½ tablespoons finely chopped fresh dill plus additional sprigs for garnish
1½ teaspoons fresh lime juice
½ teaspoon finely grated lime zest
¼ teaspoon freshly ground pepper
1 pound thinly sliced smoked salmon
Thinly sliced pumpernickel bread, cut into triangles, or water crackers, for serving
Caviar, for garnish (optional)

1. In a medium bowl, whip the softened cream cheese until fluffy. Add the chopped scallions, the chopped dill, the lime juice, lime zest, and pepper and beat until combined.
2. Spread a 2-foot-long sheet of plastic wrap on a work surface. Arrange the smoked salmon slices on the plastic, overlapping them slightly so that there are no gaps, to form a 15-by-8-inch rectangle. Spread ⅔ cup of the dilled lime cream cheese evenly over the salmon slices. Starting from a long end and using the plastic to help, roll up the salmon to form a log about 1 inch thick. Wrap the roll in the plastic, twist the ends tightly, and refrigerate the log overnight or for up to 2 days.
3. Using a very sharp knife, slice the smoked salmon and cream cheese log ⅓ inch thick. Arrange the salmon roll-ups on pumpernickel bread triangles, garnish with a little caviar and a dill sprig, and serve.

PROSCIUTTO ROLL-UPS VARIATION: Substitute ½ pound of thinly sliced imported prosciutto for the smoked salmon. Refrigerate overnight before serving. Omit the caviar and the dill-sprig garnish.—BOB CHAMBERS

Sesame-Coated Escarole Rolls (p. 33) and Smoked Salmon Canapés on Brioche

TUNA NICOISE CANAPES

This clever version of salade niçoise comes from Flavors Catering in New York City. Use potatoes about 1½ inches in diameter so that the hors d'oeuvres will be the same size. Thin green bean tips are used for garnish; the rest of them can be tossed into a green salad.

MAKES 2 DOZEN

- ½ pound tuna steak, 1 inch thick
- ¼ cup soy sauce
- 1 tablespoon tapenade (black olive paste)
- ¼ cup olive oil
- 6 Niçoise olives, pitted and coarsely chopped
- 3 tablespoons drained capers
- ¼ cup mayonnaise
- 1 pound small unpeeled red potatoes
- 24 *haricots verts* or thin green beans (about 4 ounces)
- 2 small plum tomatoes, seeded and cut into ½-inch dice

1. Cut the tuna against the grain into ½-inch-thick strips. Cut each strip into 1-inch-long pieces; you should have 24 pieces of tuna.

2. In a medium bowl, combine the soy sauce and the black olive paste. Add the pieces of tuna and gently stir to coat. Cover and let the tuna marinate in the refrigerator for at least 1 hour or up to 3 hours.

3. Heat the olive oil in a large skillet. Pat the tuna pieces dry with paper towels and add half the pieces to the skillet. Cook over high heat, turning once, until the tuna is well browned, about 15 seconds per side. Transfer the tuna to paper towels to drain. Sear the remaining

Tuna Niçoise Canapés

tuna pieces in the skillet. Let cool, then cover and refrigerate the tuna for at least 2 hours or up to 1 day.

4. Chop the olives with 1 tablespoon of the capers to form a chunky paste. Transfer to a small bowl and stir in the mayonnaise.

5. Cut the red potatoes crosswise into 24 rounds, about ¼ inch thick. Put the potato rounds in a medium saucepan of cold salted water and bring to a boil over high heat. Lower the heat to moderate and cook the potatoes until tender, 7 to 10 minutes. Using a slotted spoon, transfer the potato rounds to paper towels to drain.

6. Bring the cooking water back to a boil and add the *haricots verts*. Boil over moderately high heat until the beans are tender, about 1 minute. Drain the beans, rinse them with cold water, and transfer to paper towels to drain. Cut 1 inch from both tips of each of the beans and reserve for the garnish.

7. Spoon ½ teaspoon of the olive mayonnaise on each potato slice. Set a piece of tuna on top and garnish each with ½ teaspoon of the diced tomatoes, a few capers, and 2 *haricot vert* tips. (MAKE AHEAD: The hors d'oeuvres can be refrigerated for up to 8 hours.)—FLAVORS CATERING

PEPPER BISCUITS WITH CHEDDAR-PECAN SPREAD

This southern-style hors d'oeuvre is one of the bestsellers at Sage & Swift, a caterer in Durham, North Carolina. Serve any leftover cheese spread on white toast, wheat crackers, or celery.

MAKES ABOUT 4 DOZEN

CHEESE SPREAD:

- 4 ounces cream cheese
- ½ cup sour cream
- 2 cups shredded sharp Cheddar cheese (about 7 ounces)
- ½ cup finely chopped pecans (about 2 ounces)
- 2 medium scallions, white part only, finely chopped
- ¼ teaspoon salt
- ¼ teaspoon freshly ground black pepper
- ¼ teaspoon hot pepper sauce

BISCUITS:

- 2 cups all-purpose flour
- 1 tablespoon plus ¼ teaspoon baking powder
- 1 teaspoon sugar
- ½ teaspoon baking soda
- ½ teaspoon salt
- 2 teaspoons freshly ground black pepper
- 3 tablespoons finely chopped fresh chives
- 6 tablespoons cold unsalted butter
- 1 cup buttermilk

1. Make the cheese spread: In a food processor, blend the cream cheese and the sour cream. Add the Cheddar cheese and pulse until combined. Add the chopped pecans and scallions and pulse until incorporated. Add the salt, black pepper, and pepper sauce. (MAKE AHEAD: The spread can be refrigerated for up to 3 days. Let return to room temperature before serving.)

2. Make the biscuits: Preheat the oven to 425°. In a bowl, combine the flour, baking powder, sugar, baking soda, salt, pepper, and 1 tablespoon of the chives. Cut in the butter until the mixture resembles coarse meal. Add the buttermilk and stir until a soft dough forms; do not overmix.

3. Turn the dough out onto a floured surface and knead lightly until smooth. Roll out the dough ¼ inch thick. Using a 1½-inch biscuit cutter or Champagne glass, cut out rounds from the dough. Arrange the rounds on 2 large baking sheets and bake for about 10 minutes, or until golden brown on the bottom and top. Let cool. (MAKE AHEAD: The biscuits can be frozen for up to a month. Rewarm in a 350° oven before serving.)

4. Using a sharp knife, cut the biscuits in half horizontally. Spread the bottom half of each biscuit with about 1 rounded teaspoon of the cheese mixture. Cover with the top halves of the biscuits and transfer to a platter. Sprinkle the biscuits with the remaining 2 tablespoons chopped chives and serve.—SAGE & SWIFT

ROASTED EGGPLANT AND TOMATO BRUSCHETTA LF

MAKES 36

1. Cut a French baguette into 36 ¼-inch-thick slices and brush the slices lightly with 1 tablespoon olive oil. Toast in a 350° oven for about 7 minutes until golden. Rub the toasts with 2 halved garlic cloves.

2. Lightly coat 2 large baking sheets with vegetable oil cooking spray. Slice 1 medium eggplant lengthwise ¼ inch thick and arrange the slices on 2 baking sheets. Brush the eggplant slices with 2 tablespoons of olive oil and season them with salt and pepper. Roast for about 10 minutes, until softened. Cut the eggplant into ½-inch dice and transfer to a large bowl. Add 1 large seeded, diced (¼ inch) tomato, 1 tablespoon fresh lemon juice, 1 tablespoon olive oil, and 12 shredded fresh basil leaves. Season with salt and pepper.

3. Mound the eggplant-tomato mixture on the garlic-rubbed toasts and serve.—THE UPPER CRUST

PEPPER-CRUSTED BEEF CROSTINI WITH ARUGULA

MAKES 2 DOZEN

- 1½ teaspoons crushed black peppercorns
- ¾ pound trimmed beef tenderloin, tied
- ½ teaspoon salt
- 3 tablespoons olive oil
- 1 baguette, cut diagonally into 24 ¼-inch-thick slices
- 2 tablespoons tapenade (black olive paste)
- 12 medium arugula leaves, halved

1. Gently press the crushed pepper into the beef and sprinkle with the salt. Heat 1 tablespoon of the olive oil in a medium skillet. Add the beef and cook over high heat until well browned all over, about 10 minutes. Let cool, then refrigerate until chilled, at least 2 hours or for up to 2 days.

2. Preheat the oven to 350°. Brush the bread slices lightly on both sides with the remaining 2 tablespoons olive oil and arrange on a large baking sheet. Bake for about 7 minutes, turning once, until lightly browned.

3. Spread about ¼ teaspoon of the tapenade on each toast. Set a halved arugula leaf on top. Using a sharp, thin-bladed knife, cut the beef against the grain into 24 very thin slices. Arrange a slice on each crostini.—THE UPPER CRUST

EGGPLANT-TOMATO CROSTINI

6 TO 8 SERVINGS

- 1 eggplant (about 1 pound)
- Coarse salt
- 3½ tablespoons olive oil
- Freshly ground pepper
- 1 red onion, finely diced
- 3 medium tomatoes, seeded and cut into small dice
- 3 tablespoons aged red wine vinegar or sherry vinegar
- 1 tablespoon honey
- 2 teaspoons chopped fresh mint
- 1 long narrow loaf of bread, sliced ⅓ inch thick
- 1 garlic clove, halved
- 1 or 2 tablespoons crumbled feta or thinly sliced ricotta salata cheese (optional)
- Finely chopped fresh mint or flat-leaf parsley, for garnish

1. Slice the eggplant crosswise ½ inch thick, then cut the slices into 2-by-½-inch strips. Spread in a nonreactive dish and sprinkle with coarse salt. Let stand for an hour, then rinse and pat dry.

2. Heat 2½ tablespoons of the oil in a large nonstick skillet over moderately high heat. Add the eggplant and cook, stirring, until browned, about 15 minutes. Season with coarse salt and pepper; transfer to a bowl.

3. Add the remaining tablespoon oil and the onion to the skillet. Cook over moderate heat until the onion begins to color, about 3 minutes. Stir in the tomatoes, vinegar, and honey, increase the heat to moderately high, and cook, shaking the pan frequently, until the vinegar evaporates, 2 to 3 minutes. Stir in the eggplant and mint. Let cool completely.

4. Preheat the oven to 350°. Arrange the bread on a baking sheet. Toast in the oven about 10 minutes, or until lightly golden. Rub each slice with the cut garlic clove.

5. Stir the cheese into the eggplant mixture and spread on the croutons. Garnish with chopped mint or parsley.—DEBORAH MADISON

ARTICHOKE CROSTINI

A long, dense-textured baguette, about two inches in diameter, would be perfect for these tasty appetizers. Domestic provolone or mozzarella melts more readily than imported.

8 SERVINGS

- 2 red bell peppers
- Olive oil
- 4 tablespoons unsalted butter, at room temperature
- 2 tablespoons finely chopped fresh flat-leaf parsley
- 2 garlic cloves, crushed through a press
- Salt and freshly ground pepper
- Twenty-four ¼-inch-thick slices of French bread
- 1 lemon, halved
- 4 medium artichokes
- ¼ pound provolone or mozzarella cheese, thinly sliced or shaved into 24 pieces

1. Roast the bell peppers directly over a gas flame or under a broiler as close to the heat as possible, turning often until charred all over. Using tongs, transfer the peppers to a paper bag and set aside to steam for 10 minutes.

From left: **Pancetta-Wrapped Scallops (p. 38), Roasted Eggplant and Tomato Bruschetta, and Arancini (p. 39)**

Using a small sharp knife, scrape off the blackened skins and remove the stems, seeds, and ribs. Cut the peppers into 1-by-2-inch strips. Drizzle them with olive oil. (MAKE AHEAD: The peppers can be prepared to this point up to 2 days ahead; cover with plastic wrap and refrigerate.)

2. Preheat the oven to 400°. In a small bowl, combine the butter, parsley, garlic, and a pinch each of salt and pepper. Evenly spread the garlic butter on the bread slices. Arrange the slices on a baking sheet and toast for 8 to 10 minutes, or until golden brown. Do not turn off the oven.

3. Fill a medium bowl with water. Squeeze the juice from the lemon halves into the bowl. Reserve the lemon. Prepare 1 artichoke heart at a time. Trim the artichoke by first removing the 5 or 6 layers of tough outer leaves, bending them back at the base so that they snap off. Trim off the stem. Cut off the top half of the artichoke and discard; trim away all the dark green parts from the base. Pull off the sharp inner leaves. Scoop out the hairy choke with a spoon. Rub all cut surfaces with the reserved lemon halves and place the artichoke heart in the lemon water. Repeat with the remaining artichokes. Cut each artichoke heart into 6 slices, about ¼ inch thick. ➤

4. To assemble the crostini: Layer each toasted bread slice with 1 artichoke slice and one red pepper strip. Cover the red pepper completely with 1 slice of cheese. Place the crostini on a baking sheet and bake on the top shelf of the oven for 5 minutes, or until the cheese starts to bubble. Serve at once.—JOAN AND DICK ERATH

ROCKEFELLER TURNOVERS

These puff pastry turnovers are based on oysters Rockefeller, the traditional starter served at Antoine's restaurant in New Orleans. The turnovers can be assembled ahead of time and baked just before guests arrive, or baked earlier in the day and then reheated.

MAKES ABOUT 32

- 1 pint freshly shucked oysters, coarsely chopped
- 1 stick unsalted butter
- 1 celery rib, finely chopped
- 2 large shallots, finely chopped
- 1 garlic clove, finely chopped
- 1 pound fresh spinach—chopped, steamed, and drained, or one 10-ounce package frozen chopped spinach, well drained
- 1 teaspoon salt
- ¼ cup fresh lemon juice
- ¼ cup Herbsaint or Pernod, or ½ teaspoon ground fennel seeds
- ½ teaspoon Tabasco
- ½ cup fine dry bread crumbs
- 2 tablespoons finely chopped anchovy fillets
- One 17¼-ounce package frozen puff pastry or 18 ounces all-butter puff pastry, thawed but very cold
- 1 egg

Rockefeller Turnovers

1. Place the oysters in a strainer set over a bowl and let drain in the refrigerator for 1 hour.

2. Melt the butter in a large nonreactive skillet. Add the celery and shallots. Cook over moderate heat, stirring occasionally, until translucent, about 5 minutes.

3. Stir in the garlic, spinach, and salt. Increase the heat to moderately high. Add the lemon juice, Herbsaint, and Tabasco. Cook, stirring occasionally, until most of the liquid has evaporated and the spinach is a coarse puree, about 5 minutes. Remove from the heat and fold in the oysters, bread crumbs, and anchovies. Transfer to a large strainer to drain.

4. On a lightly floured surface, roll the pastry into two 14-inch squares or one 14-by-28-inch rectangle, about ⅛ inch thick. Cut the pastry into 3½-inch squares.

5. Place a rounded tablespoon of the oyster filling in the center of each square. Lightly moisten two adjacent edges of each square with water, then fold the opposite corner over to form triangular turnovers. Crimp the sealed edges with the tines of a fork. Arrange 1 inch apart on baking sheets.

6. Make a wash by beating the egg with 2 tablespoons of water. Lightly brush the top of each turnover with the egg wash; take care not to let it drip down the sides. Reserve the remaining egg wash. Cover the turnovers with plastic wrap and refrigerate until chilled or for up to 1 day.

7. Preheat the oven to 400°. Just before baking, lightly brush the tops of the turnovers with the egg wash again. Bake for 20 minutes, or until golden brown. Serve hot.—JOHN MARTIN TAYLOR

SESAME-COATED ESCAROLE ROLLS

MAKES ABOUT 5 DOZEN

- 2 tablespoons olive oil
- 2 small dried red chiles
- 1 large head of escarole, trimmed and coarsely chopped
- 1 large garlic clove, minced
- 2 teaspoons sherry vinegar or red wine vinegar
- 1 teaspoon salt
- ¼ teaspoon freshly ground pepper
- Pinch of sugar
- 1 ounce cream cheese, softened
- 3 ounces ricotta salata or feta cheese, coarsely crumbled (about ¾ cup)
- ¾ pound frozen puff pastry, preferably all butter, thawed
- 1 large egg, lightly beaten
- 3 tablespoons sesame seeds

1. Heat the oil in a large nonstick skillet. Add the chiles and cook over high heat until dark brown, about 1 minute. Discard the chiles. Add one-third of the escarole to the skillet and stir until wilted. Add the remaining escarole in 2 batches, stirring until wilted before adding more. Cook the escarole, stirring, until tender and just lightly browned, about 5 minutes. Add the garlic, vinegar, salt, pepper, and sugar, and cook, stirring, until the garlic is fragrant, about 1 minute. Transfer to a medium bowl, stir in the cream cheese and then the ricotta salata. Refrigerate until chilled, about 1 hour.

2. Line a large, heavy baking sheet with parchment paper. On a lightly floured work surface, roll out the puff pastry to a 16-by-10-inch rectangle, about ⅛ inch thick. Trim the edges so they're straight. Cut the dough crosswise into five 3-inch-wide strips. Arrange the strips side by side, long ends toward you.

3. Brush the strips with half the beaten egg. Spread the escarole filling evenly on the strips, leaving a 1-inch border on all sides. Fold the dough over to enclose the escarole and pinch the edges together to seal. Pinch the short ends closed and set the rolls, seam sides down, on the prepared baking sheet, leaving about 1½ inches between each roll. Brush with the remaining beaten egg and sprinkle with the sesame seeds. Using a skewer or toothpick, prick 5 or 6 holes along the top of each roll. Cover and refrigerate for at least 1 hour or overnight. (MAKE AHEAD: The uncooked rolls can be frozen for up to two weeks. Wrap each in plastic, then in foil. Let stand at room temperature for 30 minutes before baking.)

4. Preheat the oven to 400°. Bake the rolls for about 40 minutes, or until the pastry is browned and crisp. Let stand on the baking sheet for 20 minutes. Using a sharp knife, cut each roll into ¾-inch slices. Arrange the rolls on platters and serve.—GRACE PARISI

PECAN-CHEDDAR COINS

MAKES ABOUT 100

- ½ cup pecan halves (about 2 ounces)
- 1 cup all-purpose flour
- ½ teaspoon salt
- ½ teaspoon cayenne pepper
- 5 tablespoons unsalted butter, cut into ½-inch pieces
- ½ pound sharp Cheddar cheese, coarsely grated
- 2 tablespoons freshly grated Romano cheese
- 1 large egg yolk

1. Preheat the oven to 350°. Spread the pecans on a baking sheet and toast for about 7 minutes, or until fragrant. Let cool slightly, then finely chop.

2. Using an electric mixer at low speed, combine the flour, salt, and cayenne. Add the butter and blend on medium speed until the mixture resembles coarse meal. Add the Cheddar and Romano and the pecans and mix until the Cheddar is broken up into ¼-inch bits, about 2 minutes. Add the egg yolk and mix just until combined; the dough will be crumbly. Press the dough together to form a ball, then divide the ball in half. On a lightly floured work surface, shape each of the halves into a 12-inch log, about 1¼ inches in diameter. Wrap each log in plastic and refrigerate until firm, at least 2 hours or overnight.

3. Preheat the oven to 400°. Line 2 large baking sheets with parchment paper. Cut each log into ¼-inch slices and arrange the slices about 1 inch apart on the prepared baking sheets. Bake in the upper and lower thirds of the oven for about 9 minutes, switching the pans halfway through baking, until the coins are golden around the edges. Let cool completely. (MAKE AHEAD: The coins can be stored in an airtight container for 2 days or frozen for up to 1 month. Let return to room temperature before serving.) Serve the coins in bowls or baskets.—GRACE PARISI

GARLIC-PARMESAN PUFFS AND STICKS

Pastry puffs and sticks are an elegant and unusual alternative to standard chips and crackers; they're also very tasty on their own.

MAKES ABOUT 20 PUFFS AND 30 STICKS

- 1 cup milk
- 1 stick (4 ounces) unsalted butter
- 2 garlic cloves, minced
- 1 teaspoon thyme
- 1½ teaspoons salt
- ½ teaspoon freshly ground pepper
- 1 cup all-purpose flour
- 6 large eggs, 1 lightly beaten for brushing
- ¾ cup freshly grated Parmesan cheese (about 2 ounces)

1. Preheat the oven to 425°. In a heavy medium saucepan, combine the milk, butter, garlic, thyme, salt, and pepper. Bring just to a boil over moderately high heat. Remove the saucepan from the heat and let stand, covered, for 5 minutes.

2. Bring the mixture back to a boil over moderately high heat. Remove from the heat and stir in all the flour until combined. Cook over moderately high heat, stirring constantly, until the mixture comes together and forms a ball, about 1 minute. Transfer to a bowl and let cool slightly. Add 5 eggs, one at a time, stirring well after each addition; the mixture will separate, then come together after vigorous stirring. Stir in ½ cup of the Parmesan.

3. Divide the mixture between 2 pastry bags, 1 fitted with a ¼-inch star tip and 1 fitted with a ¼-inch round tip. On 1 baking sheet, using the star tip, pipe out puffs about 1 inch wide and ½ inch high, allowing about 1 inch of space between them. Using the round tip, pipe out 6-by-¼-inch sticks onto the second baking sheet, allowing about 1 inch of space between them. Brush the puffs and sticks with the beaten egg and sprinkle them with the remaining ¼ cup Parmesan.

4. Bake the puffs and sticks for about 15 minutes, or until golden brown and crisp and the puffs feel light when you pick them up. Transfer to a rack and let cool. Serve warm or at room temperature. (MAKE AHEAD: The baked puffs and sticks can be stored in plastic bags and frozen for up to 2 weeks. Rewarm in a low oven before serving.) —BOB CHAMBERS

CRISP PASTA BITES

Store-bought pasta stuffed with an intensely flavored filling, such as pesto or wild mushrooms, is best for these baked snacks. Serve on skewers for an attractive presentation.

MAKES ABOUT 90

- Salt
- 1 pound small stuffed fresh pasta, such as tortellini, agnolotti, or raviolini
- 1 tablespoon unsalted butter
- 3 tablespoons sesame seeds
- 3 tablespoons poppy seeds
- ¼ cup freshly grated Parmesan cheese

1. Preheat the oven to 450°. Bring a large saucepan of water to a boil. Line a medium baking sheet with parchment paper.

2. Add salt to the boiling water. Add the pasta and cook until just tender, about 3 minutes. Drain well. Divide the pasta between 2 bowls and add half the butter to each. Toss one bowl of pasta with the sesame seeds and the other with the poppy seeds. Let the pasta cool slightly.

3. Spread the pasta on the prepared baking sheet. Sprinkle the Parmesan over both batches of seeded pasta. Bake the pasta for about 5 minutes, or until nicely browned on the bottom. Turn the pasta over and bake for about 3 minutes longer, or until browned all over. Transfer to paper towels to drain, then transfer to a platter and serve warm.—BOB CHAMBERS

FRIED WONTON TRIANGLES

MAKES ABOUT 50

- Vegetable oil, for frying
- 1 package fresh wonton wrappers (12 ounces), cut in half diagonally

Heat 1 inch of oil in a large, heavy, high-sided skillet. Add 4 or 5 wonton triangles and cook over moderately high heat, turning once, until lightly browned, about 1 minute per side. Transfer to plates lined with paper towels and repeat with the remaining wonton skins. (MAKE AHEAD: The triangles can be kept in an airtight container at room temperature for up to two weeks. Rewarm before serving.) —BOB CHAMBERS

RATATOUILLE FRITTATA SQUARES

A thin pastry crust flavored with cheese and herbs forms the base for a variation on the frittata, an Italian-style omelet, making it easy to pick up with your hands.

MAKES 48

RATATOUILLE:

1 small eggplant, finely diced (about 2 cups)
Salt
3 tablespoons olive oil
½ cup finely chopped yellow onion
1 medium garlic clove, minced
6 medium plum tomatoes, peeled and finely diced
1 medium zucchini, finely diced
1 medium green bell pepper, finely diced
Freshly ground black pepper

CRUST:

4 tablespoons cold unsalted butter, cut into small pieces
1 cup all-purpose flour
1 tablespoon finely grated Parmesan cheese
1 teaspoon fennel seeds or caraway seeds
1 large egg yolk
1 tablespoon ice water

CUSTARD:

4 large eggs
¼ cup heavy cream
½ cup milk
¼ cup finely grated Parmesan cheese
½ cup mascarpone cheese or softened cream cheese

1. Make the ratatouille: Toss the eggplant with 1 teaspoon salt and place in a colander. Cover with a bowl or plate and weigh it down with some cans. Let drain at least 1 hour. Rinse, drain, and pat dry.
2. Heat the oil in a heavy, medium nonreactive saucepan. Add the onion and garlic. Cook over moderate heat until translucent, about 4 minutes. Add the eggplant, tomatoes, zucchini, and bell pepper. Stew over low heat until thick and reduced to about 2 cups, about 45 minutes. Stir frequently during the last 15 minutes. Season with salt and black pepper (enough to flavor the custard as well). Let cool. (MAKE AHEAD: The recipe can be made to this point up to 3 days ahead; cover and refrigerate.)
3. Make the crust: In a medium bowl, using a pastry cutter, two knives, or your fingers, cut or rub the butter into the flour until large crumbs form. Stir in the Parmesan and fennel seeds.
4. Stir together the egg yolk and ice water and drizzle over the flour. Toss together lightly until incorporated, then turn into a 13-by-9-inch baking dish. Using your fingertips, pat the mixture evenly into the pan. Cover with plastic wrap and refrigerate for 1 hour.
5. Preheat the oven to 350°. Bake the crust for 15 minutes; it will be pale and covered with cracks.
6. Make the custard: In a large bowl, whisk together the eggs, cream, milk, Parmesan, and mascarpone until blended.
7. Pour the custard over the crust, covering the surface as evenly as possible. Using a teaspoon, distribute the ratatouille all over the custard. Bake for 45 minutes, or until golden brown all over. Transfer to a rack to cool. (MAKE AHEAD: The frittata can be made up to 1 day ahead; cover and refrigerate. Return to room temperature before serving or reheat 10 minutes in a warm oven.) Using a very sharp knife, slice lengthwise into 4 strips, then cut each strip crosswise into 12 bite-size squares.—SUSAN SIMON

SAVORY MEAT PASTRIES

MAKES 2 DOZEN

½ pound ground chuck
1 small onion, finely chopped

Savory Meat Pastries

2 large eggs
2 tablespoons olive oil
½ cup finely chopped fresh cilantro
½ cup finely chopped fresh flat-leaf parsley
¾ teaspoon salt
½ teaspoon freshly ground pepper
Pinch of cinnamon
6 to 12 sheets of phyllo dough (see Note)
1 large egg white, lightly beaten
4 tablespoons unsalted butter, melted

PRESENTATION TIPS

Any caterer will tell you that the more appealing the presentation, the more popular the hors d'oeuvre. Here are a few ideas for making your appetizers disappear at record speed.

- **Add color to the rim of your favorite silver, glass, or porcelain platter by lightly buttering the edge, then dusting it with a brightly colored spice like sweet paprika or turmeric. Don't use a strong spice, such as cayenne pepper; it would flavor any food that touches it.**
- **Spread uncooked soba or flat rice sticks on a platter to create an attractive base that will help absorb grease from fried or buttery items.**
- **Make a rustic bed with shafts of wheat or large sprigs of fresh sturdy herbs, such as rosemary and thyme; replenish them if they begin to wilt. Or tie smaller bunches of herbs with twine and use them as a garnish.**

1. Preheat the oven to 350°. In a medium bowl, mix together the chuck, onion, eggs, olive oil, cilantro, parsley, salt, pepper, and cinnamon.
2. Stack the phyllo sheets on a work surface and cut them lengthwise into 4 long strips, about 3 inches wide. Set aside 1 strip (or 2 strips if they're fragile) and cover the rest with a damp cloth.
3. Lay the phyllo strip(s) on the work surface, short end toward you. Put a scant tablespoon of the meat mixture about 1 inch from the top of the strip. Fold the left-hand corner of the phyllo over the filling to enclose it and form a triangle. Then fold the right-hand corner down to form another triangle. Continue folding the triangle over in this manner until the filling is completely enclosed. Seal the edges with egg white. Set the triangle on a baking sheet and cover with a damp cloth. Repeat with the remaining strips and meat filling, using a second baking sheet for half of the pastries.
4. Brush the pastries with the melted butter. Bake, one sheet at a time, for 15 minutes. Brush with more melted butter and continue baking about 15 minutes longer, or until golden all over. Let cool slightly while you bake the remaining pastries. (MAKE AHEAD: The pastries can be refrigerated, covered, up to 1 day. Rewarm in a 400° oven before serving.)
NOTE: Some phyllo dough, such as Apollo, is especially fragile so that you'll need to use a double thickness to make the pastries. Other brands, such as Fantis, are sturdy enough to use only one layer.—FATIMA HAL

GARLIC HUMMUS WITH SPICY WONTON TRIANGLES LF

MAKES 40

9 unpeeled garlic cloves
19-ounce can chickpeas, drained and rinsed
2 tablespoons tahini (sesame paste)
3 tablespoons fresh lemon juice
1 teaspoon salt
¼ teaspoon ground cumin
Vegetable oil cooking spray
20 wonton wrappers
1 egg white, lightly beaten
Chili powder

1. Loosely wrap the garlic in foil. Bake in a 350° oven for about 30 minutes, or until soft. Let cool slightly. Leave the oven on.
2. In a food processor, combine the chickpeas, tahini, lemon juice, salt, cumin, and 2 tablespoons water. Add the pulp from the roasted garlic. Puree until smooth.
3. Lightly coat 2 baking sheets with cooking spray. Cut the wonton wrappers diagonally in half. Arrange the triangles on the baking sheets, brush with egg white, and dust with chili powder.
4. Bake about 5 minutes, or until golden. Gently turn over and bake about 2 minutes longer, or until crisp. Let cool. Serve with the hummus.—THE UPPER CRUST

COCONUT SHRIMP WITH CURRIED HUMMUS

You can substitute two pita breads for the pappadums, *which are available at Indian markets and specialty food stores. Split the pitas in half horizontally, then cut into wedges and toast.*

MAKES 2 DOZEN

¾ cup unsweetened shredded coconut* (about 2 ounces)
12 medium shrimp—shelled, halved lengthwise, and deveined
Salt and freshly ground pepper
3 tablespoons honey
½ cup prepared hummus (about 4 ounces)
2 teaspoons Madras curry powder
24 miniature *pappadums*
24 fresh cilantro leaves

*Available at health food stores

1. Preheat the oven to 350°. Toast the coconut for about 5 minutes, tossing occasionally, until golden and crisp. Transfer to a plate and let cool.
2. Season the shrimp with salt and pepper and brush with the honey. Toss the shrimp in the coconut and arrange them on a baking sheet. Bake for about 7 minutes, or until the shrimp are cooked through. Let cool.
3. In a small bowl, combine the hummus and the curry powder. Transfer to a pastry bag fitted with a small round tip and pipe a dime-size amount of curried hummus on each *pappadum*. Alternatively, dollop the hummus on the *pappadums*. Top each *pappadum* with a coconut shrimp, garnish with a cilantro leaf and serve.—FLAVORS CATERING

MINI BEEF WELLINGTONS

MAKES ABOUT 4 DOZEN

7 ounces frozen puff pastry, preferably all butter, thawed
⅓ cup Boursin cheese (about 2½ ounces), at room temperature
½ pound trimmed beef tenderloin, cut into ½-inch cubes
Salt and freshly ground pepper
1 large egg, lightly beaten

1. Preheat the oven to 400°. On a lightly floured sheet of parchment paper, roll out the puff pastry to a 7½-by-15-inch rectangle, about ⅛ inch thick. Cut the pastry into 1½-inch squares.
2. Spoon a scant ¼ teaspoon of the Boursin in the center of each square. Season the beef with salt and pepper and set a cube on each pastry square. Fold the pastry over the beef, neatly tucking in the corners. Arrange the pastries seam side down on a large baking sheet lined with parchment paper. (MAKE AHEAD: The recipe can be prepared to this point and frozen for up to 1 week.)
3. Lightly brush each pastry with the beaten egg. Bake for 10 to 12 minutes, or until puffed and golden brown. Let cool slightly, then transfer to a platter and serve.—FLAVORS CATERING

FIVE-SPICE CHICKEN SALAD IN WONTON SHELLS

At Creative Edge Parties Caterers in New York City, Asian-flavored chicken salad is served in simple baked wonton wrapper shells. Wonton wrappers are available in the produce department or freezer section of most supermarkets.

MAKES 4 DOZEN

48 wonton wrappers, thawed if frozen
Butter-flavored cooking spray
2 teaspoons five-spice powder*
1½ teaspoons salt
1 large whole skinless, boneless chicken breast
1 medium navel orange
1 large shallot, minced
1 tablespoon rice wine vinegar
1 tablespoon honey
1 tablespoon olive oil
½ cup finely chopped fresh cilantro

*Available at Asian markets

1. Preheat the oven to 350°. Trim the wonton wrappers to form 2-inch squares. Coat a nonstick mini-muffin tin with cooking spray and press a wonton square into each cup. Lightly coat the squares with cooking spray and bake for about 7 minutes, or until lightly browned. Let cool in the pan. Repeat the process with the remaining wrappers and more cooking spray. (MAKE AHEAD: The wonton shells can be stored in an airtight container at room temperature for up to 1 week.)
2. In a small bowl, combine the five-spice powder and salt and sprinkle on both sides of the chicken breast. Transfer the chicken to a lightly oiled baking sheet and bake for about 18 minutes, or until cooked through. Let cool and cut into ¼-inch dice.
3. Using a vegetable peeler, remove the zest from half the orange, leaving behind the bitter white pith. Cut the zest into very thin 1-inch-long strips. Measure 1 packed teaspoon of julienned zest and discard the rest. Using a sharp knife, peel the rest of the orange, removing all the white pith. Working over a bowl, cut in between the membranes to release the sections. Cut the sections into ¼-inch dice. Reserve 1 tablespoon of the accumulated orange juice. ➤

Five-Spice Chicken Salad in Wonton Shells

4. In a medium bowl, combine the diced orange with the shallot, reserved orange juice, vinegar, honey, and olive oil. Gently stir in the chicken, half of the orange zest, and half of the cilantro. (MAKE AHEAD: The chicken salad can stand at room temperature for 2 hours.)

5. Spoon 2 teaspoons of the chicken salad into each of the wonton shells. Garnish with the remaining orange zest and cilantro and serve.—CREATIVE EDGE PARTIES CATERERS

PANCETTA-WRAPPED SCALLOPS WITH LEMON

Pancetta lends a dash of saltiness to the sweet scallops and protects them from direct heat in this simple hors d'oeuvre recipe from Capers Catering in Chicago. You can substitute 8 to 10 strips of sliced bacon for the pancetta; cut each strip into three-inch lengths.

MAKES 2 DOZEN

6 large sea scallops (about ½ pound), membrane removed, scallops quartered
3 tablespoons extra-virgin olive oil
Four 3-inch-long strips of lemon zest plus 1 teaspoon finely grated zest for garnish
2 fresh rosemary sprigs plus 2 teaspoons finely chopped rosemary for garnish
Freshly ground pepper
12 thin slices of pancetta (about 4 ounces), halved

1. In a bowl, toss the scallops with the oil, zest strips, rosemary sprigs, and pepper. Let marinate in the refrigerator for 2 hours. In another bowl, soak 24 wooden toothpicks in water for 2 hours.

2. Preheat the broiler. Remove the scallops from the marinade and lightly pat dry. Drain the toothpicks. Wrap each piece of scallop in a slice of pancetta, secure with a toothpick, and transfer to a broiler pan. Broil for about 1 minute per side, turning once, until the pancetta sizzles and the scallops are firm but not rubbery.

3. In a small bowl, combine the grated zest and chopped rosemary. Dip one end of each wrapped scallop in the lemon-herb mixture, transfer to a platter, and serve.—CAPERS CATERING

ARANCINI

At parties catered by Jackson and Company in Houston, these deep-fried balls of risotto—known as arancini, *or little oranges, in Italy—are arranged on a bed of thinly sliced prosciutto and served garnished with bundles of fresh thyme and rosemary.*

MAKES ABOUT 7 DOZEN

- 5½ cups chicken stock or 4 cups canned broth mixed with 1½ cups of hot water
- 3 tablespoons unsalted butter
- ½ cup finely chopped onion
- 2¼ cups arborio rice (about 1 pound)
- ¾ cup dry white wine
- 4 ounces prosciutto, cut into ¼-inch dice
- 1 cup frozen baby peas
- 2 tablespoons finely chopped fresh rosemary
- 2 tablespoons finely chopped fresh thyme
- ¼ cup heavy cream
- 2¼ cups freshly grated Parmesan cheese (about 7 ounces)
- Salt and freshly ground pepper
- 1 cup all-purpose flour
- 5 large eggs, lightly beaten
- 2 cups plain dry bread crumbs
- 1 quart vegetable oil, for deep-frying

1. In a medium saucepan, heat the chicken stock until just boiling; keep warm. Melt the butter in a large nonreactive saucepan. Add the onion and cook over moderate heat, stirring, until translucent, about 3 minutes. Add the arborio rice and stir to coat. Add the white wine and cook, stirring, until absorbed, about 3 minutes.

2. Add ½ cup of the stock to the rice. Stir constantly over moderate heat until the liquid is completely absorbed, about 3 minutes. Continue adding the stock, ½ cup at a time, stirring constantly until absorbed before adding more. When half of the stock has been added, stir in the prosciutto, peas, rosemary, and thyme, and continue cooking. The rice is done when it's tender but still slightly firm to the bite. Remove from the heat, stir in the cream and ¼ cup of the Parmesan, and season with salt and pepper. Spread the risotto on a baking sheet and let cool. Cover and refrigerate until chilled, for at least 2 hours or up to 1 day.

3. Roll the risotto into 1-inch balls. Roll each ball in the flour, then dip in the beaten eggs and coat with the bread crumbs. (MAKE AHEAD: The balls can be prepared to this point and frozen for up to 1 month; spread on a baking sheet in a single layer and freeze until firm, then store in tightly sealed plastic bags. Let stand at room temperature for 30 minutes before frying.)

4. In a deep fryer fitted with a basket, heat 4 inches of oil to 360°. Working in batches of 8, fry the balls until golden, about 45 seconds; if they have been frozen, fry for about 4 minutes. Transfer to paper towels to drain. (MAKE AHEAD: The balls can be fried up to 1 hour ahead; let stand at room temperature. Rewarm in a 375° oven.) While the balls are hot, roll them in the remaining 2 cups Parmesan to lightly coat them. Transfer to platters and serve immediately.—JACKSON AND COMPANY

PECANS ON FIRE

MAKES 1 POUND

- 1½ teaspoons salt
- 2¼ teaspoons sweet paprika
- 1½ teaspoons cayenne pepper
- 1½ teaspoons freshly ground black pepper
- 1 pound extra-large pecan halves
- 1 cup confectioners' sugar
- 1 quart canola oil

1. Mix the seasonings in a large bowl. Blanch the pecans in boiling water for 5 minutes. Drain well. Coat with confectioners' sugar.

2. Heat the oil in a large pot over moderately high heat until it reaches 350°. Add the pecans. Fry until golden brown, about 4 minutes. With a slotted spoon, transfer the nuts to the seasoning mixture. Toss until well coated. Let cool completely before serving.—PAMELA HUBBELL

CHAPTER 3

FIRST COURSES

Fava Bean Succotash with Crisp Phyllo Rounds

FAVA BEAN SUCCOTASH WITH CRISP PHYLLO ROUNDS LF

You can substitute one cup of thawed frozen baby lima beans for the fava beans; proceed from Step 2.

6 SERVINGS

SUCCOTASH:

- 2 pounds fava beans, shelled
- 1 teaspoon unsalted butter
- 1 small red onion, finely diced
- 3 garlic cloves, minced
- 1 medium zucchini, cut into ¼-inch dice
- 1 medium yellow squash, cut into ¼-inch dice
- 1 cup fresh or frozen corn kernels
- Kosher salt and freshly ground pepper

CRISP PHYLLO AND SALAD:

- Vegetable oil cooking spray
- 3 sheets of phyllo dough
- ½ teaspoon moderately hot pure red chile powder, such as japone or New Mexico
- 1 teaspoon fresh lemon juice
- 1 teaspoon balsamic vinegar
- ½ teaspoon Dijon mustard
- Kosher salt and freshly ground pepper
- 1½ cups bite-size pieces of *frisée* lettuce

1. Make the succotash: In a medium saucepan of boiling salted water, blanch the fava beans over high heat for 1 minute. Drain, rinse with cold water, and drain again. Peel the favas, discarding the skins.

2. Melt the butter in a saucepan. Add the diced onion and minced garlic. Cook over moderate heat, stirring, until fragrant, about 1 minute. Stir in the peeled fava beans, the diced zucchini and yellow squash, and the corn kernels. Season with salt and pepper. Cover and cook, stirring, until the vegetables are tender, about 15 minutes; keep warm. (MAKE AHEAD: The fava bean succotash can be kept at room temperature for 4 hours; rewarm before serving.)

3. Make the crisp phyllo and salad: Preheat the oven to 400°. Spray a baking sheet with the vegetable oil cooking spray. Lay 1 phyllo sheet on a work surface, lightly spray with cooking spray, and dust with half the chile powder. Lay another phyllo sheet on top, spray lightly, and sprinkle with the remaining chile powder. Set the third phyllo sheet on top. Using a 4-inch round biscuit cutter or glass, cut out 6 circles and transfer them to the prepared baking sheet. Bake for about 7 minutes, or until the phyllo rounds are golden.

4. In a medium bowl, whisk the lemon juice, the balsamic vinegar, and the Dijon mustard. Season with salt and pepper. Add the *frisée* lettuce and toss to coat.

5. To serve, mound the warm fava bean succotash on 6 individual plates. Set the crisp phyllo rounds on top of the succotash and arrange the salad on top of the rounds.—CHARLES WILEY

FIVE LOW-FAT TIPS

- INTENSIFY FLAVOR **with techniques such as roasting or pickling ordinary vegetables, or marinating low-fat cuts of meat (like pork tenderloin) or poultry (like skinless chicken or turkey breasts).**
- IF THE RECIPE REQUIRES CHEESE, **use small amounts of aged or hard varieties. Their concentrated flavor means you won't need to use as much.**
- INSTEAD OF THE USUAL BUTTER AND CREAM, **thicken sauces with crumbled baked tortillas, pureed roasted vegetables, or a combination of bread crumbs and wine or stock.**
- MAKE USE OF VEGETABLE OIL COOKING SPRAYS **and nonstick pans to avoid the temptation to pour too much oil into a pan or over food.**
- TOAST SPICES, THEN GRIND THEM **for maximum impact. Choose pure chile powders and grind dried chiles yourself whenever possible.**—CHARLES WILEY

TORTA RUSTICA

Italian tortas are generally savory or sweet pies encased in pastry. Gary Danko's rustic version uses sliced baked eggplant as the top and bottom layers, with ricotta, Parmesan and mozzarella cheeses, tomato sauce, bell peppers, and olives as the filling.

Olives, basil, and green peppers find a distinct taste echo in the flavors of crisp, herbaceous Sauvignon Blanc. California examples, such as the 1994 Robert Pecota or the 1994 Rodney Strong Charlotte's Home Vineyard, work particularly well.

6 TO 8 SERVINGS

- 2 large eggplants, sliced crosswise ¼ inch thick
- ½ cup plus ½ tablespoon olive oil
- Salt
- 2 medium red, green, or yellow bell peppers, sliced crosswise into ¼-inch rings

Nori Rolls with Roasted Eggplant

1 pound ricotta cheese, preferably fresh
6 large egg whites, lightly beaten
1¼ cups freshly grated Parmesan cheese (about 4 ounces)
¼ cup finely chopped fresh basil
¼ cup finely chopped fresh flat-leaf parsley
¼ teaspoon cayenne pepper
2 cups tomato sauce
½ pound shredded mozzarella cheese
4 ounces Mediterranean brine-cured black olives, such as Calamata, pitted and thinly sliced (about ⅔ cup)

1. Preheat the oven to 400°. Line 2 baking sheets with parchment paper. Arrange the eggplant slices in a single layer, lightly brush them with ½ cup of the olive oil, and season lightly with salt. Bake for about 20 minutes, until tender and golden. Let cool slightly and transfer to a plate. Lower the oven temperature to 350°.

2. In a large bowl, toss the bell pepper rings with the remaining ½ tablespoon olive oil. Spread the rings on a baking sheet and bake for about 10 minutes, or until slightly softened.

3. In a large bowl, combine the ricotta cheese, egg whites, 1 cup of the Parmesan cheese, the basil, parsley, cayenne pepper, and 1 teaspoon salt.

4. Lightly brush a 9-by-13-inch nonreactive baking dish with olive oil. Arrange half of the eggplant slices in the dish. Spread the ricotta mixture evenly over the eggplant and drizzle with 1 cup of the tomato sauce. Top with the mozzarella cheese, the bell pepper rings, and the sliced olives, and drizzle with the remaining 1 cup tomato sauce. Arrange the remaining eggplant slices on top. Brush the eggplant with 1 tablespoon of water and sprinkle with the remaining ¼ cup Parmesan cheese.

5. Bake the torta for about 45 minutes, or until heated through. (MAKE AHEAD: The torta can be refrigerated, covered, for 1 day. Let return to room temperature, then rewarm in a 350° oven for about 20 minutes.) —GARY DANKO

NORI ROLLS WITH ROASTED EGGPLANT

These rolls get a kick from the Japanese horseradish known as wasabi. *It is available in powder or paste form at Japanese markets and can also be purchased at take-out sushi restaurants.*

MAKES 8

SUSHI RICE:

1 cup medium-grain rice
1 tablespoon white wine vinegar
1 teaspoon sugar
½ teaspoon salt

EGGPLANT AND EGG CAKE:

4 small Asian eggplants (5 ounces total), sliced lengthwise ⅓ inch thick
2 tablespoons soy sauce
1 tablespoon white wine
2 tablespoons vegetable oil
2 teaspoons sugar
1 teaspoon Asian sesame oil
6 large eggs
Salt and freshly ground black pepper
10 fresh shiitake mushrooms, stemmed

WASABI SAUCE:

1 tablespoon wasabi powder*
2 teaspoons white wine vinegar
1 teaspoon vegetable oil
1 teaspoon dry mustard
Pinch of salt

8 large sheets of nori (seaweed)*

*Available at Asian markets

1. Make the sushi rice: Put the rice in a medium saucepan and rinse it several times to remove surface starch. Cover the rice with 1½ cups of water and bring to a boil over high heat. Reduce the heat to low, cover, and cook for 15 minutes. Remove from the heat and let stand, covered, for 5 minutes. Transfer the rice to a bowl. With a wooden spoon, gently mix in the vinegar, sugar, and salt, then cover.

2. Make the eggplant and egg cake: Preheat the broiler. Arrange the eggplant slices on a large baking sheet. In a small bowl, combine the soy sauce, wine, 1 tablespoon of the vegetable oil, the sugar, and the sesame oil. Brush or rub both sides of the eggplant slices with the soy mixture and marinate for 5 to 20 minutes. Broil the eggplant for about 3 minutes per side, or until deep brown and crusty. Transfer the eggplant to a large plate.

3. In a medium bowl, lightly beat the eggs with ½ teaspoon salt and ¼ teaspoon pepper. Heat the remaining 1 tablespoon vegetable oil in a 7-inch nonstick skillet over moderate heat. When the oil is hot, season the mushroom caps with salt and pepper, add to the pan, and cook until lightly browned and softened, about 4 minutes per side. Cut the mushroom caps into ½-inch dice and add them to the eggs.

4. Return the skillet to moderately high heat. When it is hot, add the eggs and cook, stirring gently with a hard rubber spatula, until they seem set. Stop stirring and pat the eggs into a firm cake. When the eggs are cooked through, slide the cake onto a large plate. Let cool, then cut the cake into 8 strips.

5. Make the wasabi sauce: In a small bowl, mix together the wasabi powder, vinegar, vegetable oil, dry mustard, and salt. Cover with a small plate and let stand for a few minutes.

6. Spread ⅓ cup of the rice on a sheet of nori in a diagonal line from corner to corner. Spread 1 teaspoon of the wasabi sauce over the rice and top with 2 slices of eggplant and a strip of egg cake. Neaten the fillings and tightly pull one corner of the nori up and over the rice at an angle to make a cone shape. Tightly roll the nori over itself to make a hand roll that's open like a trumpet at one end and pointed at the other. Repeat with the remaining fillings and nori. Serve immediately or wrap the rolls in plastic and set aside for up to 2 hours.—MARCIA KIESEL

GREEN PEA CAKES WITH GINGERED SPINACH

Be sure to start these Indian-inspired pea cakes one day ahead to allow time for the peas to soak.

🍷 *The spices and jalapeños in the spinach make lager beer, such as Carlsberg, an obvious choice; alternatively, a crisp, dry-style white Zinfandel, such as the 1994 De Loach from California, would also balance the heat attractively.*

4 SERVINGS

PEA CAKES:

- 1 cup dried green split peas (about ½ pound)
- 1 small onion, coarsely chopped
- 1 small mild fresh green chile, such as Anaheim, seeded and coarsely chopped
- 1 tablespoon finely chopped fresh ginger
- ½ teaspoon salt
- ¾ cup vegetable oil, for frying

GINGERED SPINACH:

- 2 tablespoons vegetable oil
- 1 teaspoon mustard seeds
- ¼ teaspoon cumin seeds
- ¼ teaspoon turmeric
- ½ teaspoon *garam masala**
- 1 medium onion, thinly sliced
- 1 tablespoon finely chopped fresh ginger
- 3 large garlic cloves, thinly sliced
- 1 to 2 medium jalapeño chiles, halved lengthwise and thinly sliced crosswise

Green Pea Cakes with Gingered Spinach

- 1 pound fresh spinach, tough stems trimmed
- 1 tablespoon unsalted butter
- 4 medium tomatoes, peeled and coarsely chopped
- Salt and freshly ground black pepper
- ¼ cup fresh cilantro leaves
- Lemon wedges, for serving

*Available at specialty food stores and Indian markets

1. Make the pea cakes: In a large bowl, cover the dried green split peas with 4 cups of water and let soak overnight. Drain and rinse the split peas and transfer them to a food processor. Add the onion, fresh green chile, fresh ginger, salt, and ¼ cup of water, and process until pureed.

2. Make the gingered spinach: Heat the vegetable oil in a large saucepan. Stir in the mustard seeds and the cumin seeds and cook over moderately high heat, stirring, for 1 minute. Add the turmeric and the *garam masala* and cook for 1 more minute. Add the sliced onion and the

Fresh Tomato and Zucchini Tart

chopped fresh ginger and cook, stirring, until the onion is softened, about 3 minutes. Stir in the sliced garlic and jalapeño and continue cooking until fragrant, about 2 more minutes.

3. Add the fresh spinach to the pan in large handfuls, stirring until the leaves are wilted before adding another handful. Cook, stirring, until the exuded liquid has evaporated, about 2 minutes. Stir in the butter until melted, then add the chopped tomatoes. Lower the heat to moderate and simmer, stirring occasionally, until the mixture is thickened, about 10 minutes. Season the mixture with salt and pepper and keep warm.

4. To finish the pea cakes, heat the ¾ cup vegetable oil in a large skillet. For each cake, drop 2 tablespoons of the split pea mixture into the skillet, pressing down on them lightly to make 3-inch rounds. Fry the cakes over moderately high heat until browned on the bottom, about 4 minutes. Turn the cakes and brown the other side, 2 to 3 minutes longer. Transfer to paper towels to drain and keep warm while you fry the remaining cakes.

5. Arrange the green pea cakes on 4 large plates and spoon the gingered spinach alongside. Garnish the dish with the fresh cilantro leaves and serve with lemon wedges.—MARCIA KIESEL

FRESH TOMATO AND ZUCCHINI TART

8 TO 10 SERVINGS

PASTRY:

- 4 ounces cream cheese, softened
- 1 stick (4 ounces) unsalted butter, softened
- 1¼ cups all-purpose flour
- ⅛ teaspoon salt
- 1 tablespoon minced fresh chives

FILLING:

- ⅔ cup coarsely chopped pitted Calamata olives (from 4 ounces unpitted)
- 1 tablespoon plus 1 teaspoon chopped anchovy fillets
- 1 tablespoon drained capers
- 3 ripe large tomatoes, thinly sliced
- 2 tablespoons olive oil
- 1 tablespoon finely chopped garlic
- 2 small zucchini, shredded on the large holes of a grater (about 1½ cups)

Salt and freshly ground pepper
Fresh basil leaves, for garnish

1. Make the pastry: In a food processor, blend the cream cheese and the butter. Add the flour and salt and process just until the dough begins to form a ball. Sprinkle the chives on a work surface. Turn out the dough and knead lightly until the chives are incorporated. Pat the dough into a disk about ½ inch thick. Wrap and refrigerate for at least 30 minutes and up to 1 day.

2. Remove the dough from the refrigerator and let stand at room temperature to soften slightly. On a well-floured work surface, roll the dough into a 13- to 14-inch round. Roll the pastry onto the rolling pin and gently unroll it over an 11-inch fluted tart pan with a removable bottom. Fit the dough evenly into the pan without stretching. Trim the overhanging dough to 1 inch from the rim. Fold the excess dough over and press it into the side of the pan. Refrigerate for 20 minutes, or until firm. Meanwhile, preheat the oven to 400°.

3. Line the chilled tart shell with foil and weigh down with pastry weights, dried beans, or rice. Bake the shell for 15 minutes. Remove the foil and weights and bake for 10 minutes longer, or until just set and golden. Transfer to a rack to cool completely; then remove the fluted rim of the tart pan and place the shell on a serving platter.

4. Prepare the filling: In a medium bowl, stir together the olives, anchovies, and capers. Spread the mixture evenly over the bottom of the baked shell. Starting at the edge, layer the tomato slices in overlapping concentric circles.

5. In a medium nonreactive skillet, heat the olive oil. Add the garlic and stir over moderately high heat for 1 minute, or until fragrant. Add the zucchini, season with salt and pepper, and stir the mixture until softened slightly, about 1 minute.

6. Spoon the zucchini over the tomatoes and garnish with basil. Serve the tart at room temperature.—KATHY CARY

MUSHROOM TIMBALES WITH TOMATO COULIS

Dried cèpes, also known as porcini and King Boletes, intensify the mushroom flavor of these elegant timbales. If the water in the roasting pan boils during baking, add a few ice cubes to cool it down; boiling water will cause air bubbles to form, giving the timbales a rougher texture.

6 SERVINGS

TIMBALES:

- 1 ounce (about 1 cup) dried cèpes (porcini)
- ¾ pound assorted fresh wild and cultivated mushrooms, such as shiitakes, cremini, and oyster mushrooms
- 3 tablespoons unsalted butter
- 2 medium shallots, minced
- 2 small garlic cloves, thinly sliced
- 4 large eggs
- 1 cup half-and-half
- 1 teaspoon salt
- ½ teaspoon freshly ground pepper

TOMATO COULIS:

- 1½ pounds tomatoes, quartered
- 1 tablespoon tomato paste
- ½ teaspoon sugar
- ½ teaspoon salt

1. Make the timbales: In a small bowl, cover the dried cèpes with hot water and let soak until softened, about 15 minutes. Drain well and rub the cèpes in the soaking liquid to remove any grit. Discard any tough pieces. Strain the liquid and reserve to use in soups and stocks.

2. Preheat the oven to 325°. Butter six ½-cup ramekins and arrange them in a roasting pan so that they don't touch. Rinse the fresh mushrooms thoroughly in cool water. Lift the mushrooms from the water and drain well. Cut the larger mushrooms into 2-inch pieces.

3. Melt the butter in a large skillet. Add the minced shallots and sauté over high heat for 1 minute. Add the sliced garlic cloves and sauté for 10 seconds longer. Add the fresh mushrooms and the reconstituted cèpes, cover, and cook over moderate heat until the fresh mushrooms are tender, about 10 minutes. If necessary, continue cooking the mushrooms, uncovered, until all of the liquid has evaporated.

4. Transfer the mushroom mixture to a food processor and process until smooth. Add the eggs, half-and-half, salt, and pepper, and process just until incorporated. Spoon the mushroom puree into the prepared ramekins. Add enough hot water to the roasting pan to come halfway up the sides of the ramekins. Bake for 35 to 45 minutes, or until set. Remove the pan from the oven and keep the timbales warm in the pan.

5. Meanwhile, **make the tomato coulis:** In a medium saucepan, combine the quartered tomatoes, the tomato paste, and ¼ cup of water. Bring the mixture to a boil over moderately high heat, then reduce the heat to low, cover, and cook for 10 minutes. Transfer to the food processor and process until smooth. Pass the *coulis* through a fine strainer into a bowl and stir in the sugar and salt.

6. Just before serving, spoon about ¼ cup of the tomato *coulis* onto each of 6 individual plates. Unmold one of the mushroom timbales onto each pool of *coulis*. Spoon the remaining tomato *coulis* over the mushroom timbales and serve.—JACQUES PEPIN

GOAT CHEESE-STUFFED CHILES WITH ROASTED TOMATO-FENNEL SAUCE

🍷 *The flavors of the roasted chiles, tomatoes, and goat cheese all point to a medium-bodied red for balance. A Rioja from Spain, such as the 1990 Marqués de Murrieta Reserva or the 1989 Muga Reserva, would work nicely here.*

4 SERVINGS

TOMATO-FENNEL SAUCE:

- 2 medium onions—1 coarsely chopped and 1 finely chopped
- 4 garlic cloves, coarsely chopped
- 12 medium plum tomatoes
- ⅔ cup coarsely chopped fresh cilantro plus whole sprigs, for garnish
- 1 tablespoon olive oil
- 1 medium fennel bulb—trimmed, quartered, cored, and finely chopped
- 1½ teaspoons salt

STUFFED CHILES:

- 8 medium poblano chiles
- 1½ teaspoons olive oil
- 6 ounces soft goat cheese, cut into 8 equal pieces
- 4 ounces grated Monterey Jack cheese

CREAMY GRITS:

- 1½ teaspoons salt
- 1 cup grits (not instant)
- ¼ cup heavy cream

1. Prepare the tomato-fennel sauce: Preheat the broiler. Scatter the coarsely chopped onion and garlic in a large roasting pan. Spread the tomatoes on top and broil for about 20 minutes, turning the tomatoes every 5 minutes, until lightly charred all over. Let cool.

2. Discard any large pieces of excessively charred skin from the tomatoes. Transfer the broiled vegetables to a blender or food processor, add the chopped cilantro, and blend until smooth.

3. Heat the olive oil in a large skillet. Add the finely chopped onion and the fennel and cook over moderately high heat, stirring, until lightly browned and tender, about 8 minutes. Stir in the pureed tomato and the salt. (MAKE AHEAD: The tomato sauce can be refrigerated, covered, for up to 1 day.)

4. Make the stuffed chiles: Preheat the broiler. Lightly rub the poblanos with the olive oil and arrange them on a baking sheet. Broil the chiles for about 12 minutes, turning frequently, until lightly charred all over. Let cool. Peel the poblanos. Using scissors, cut each chile open lengthwise, leaving the stems intact; discard the seeds and cores. Tuck a piece of goat cheese into each chile, then fold the chile over to enclose the cheese.

5. Preheat the oven to 350°. Pack the stuffed chiles into a 9-inch square baking dish. Pour the tomato-fennel sauce over and sprinkle with the Monterey Jack. Bake for about 20 minutes, until heated through and the Monterey Jack is melted.

6. Meanwhile, **prepare the grits:** Bring 4 cups of water and the salt to a boil in a medium saucepan. Gradually whisk in the grits over high heat, then lower the heat and simmer, stirring frequently, until thickened and smooth, 15 to 20 minutes. Stir in the heavy cream.

7. Divide the grits among 8 large plates and spoon the chiles and tomato-fennel sauce on top. Garnish with cilantro sprigs and serve.—ROBERT DEL GRANDE

WHITE BEAN, SWISS CHARD AND WHEAT BERRY CROQUETTES

These little cakes are crisp on the outside and soft and chewy on the inside. They make a lovely first course or light main dish accompanied with a watercress salad dressed with a lemon vinaigrette. Or serve them with a simple, light tomato sauce.

🍷 *A lean dry white, such as a California Pinot Blanc, complements these crisp croquettes. Look for 1993 examples, such as Villa Mt. Eden or Murphy-Goode.*

MAKES ABOUT 32 (8 SERVINGS)

- ¾ cup dried medium to large white beans, such as cannellini or Great Northern, picked over and rinsed well, or 1½ cups canned white beans
- ¼ cup wheat berries, rinsed
- Salt
- 2 tablespoons extra-virgin olive oil
- 1 small onion, finely diced
- 1½ tablespoons chopped fresh sage or 1 teaspoon dried
- ¾ teaspoon oregano
- 1 bunch of Swiss chard, white stems trimmed, finely chopped (about 2 cups)
- 2 medium garlic cloves, minced
- Pinch of crushed red pepper
- 3 tablespoons freshly grated Dry Jack, Asiago, or Parmesan cheese

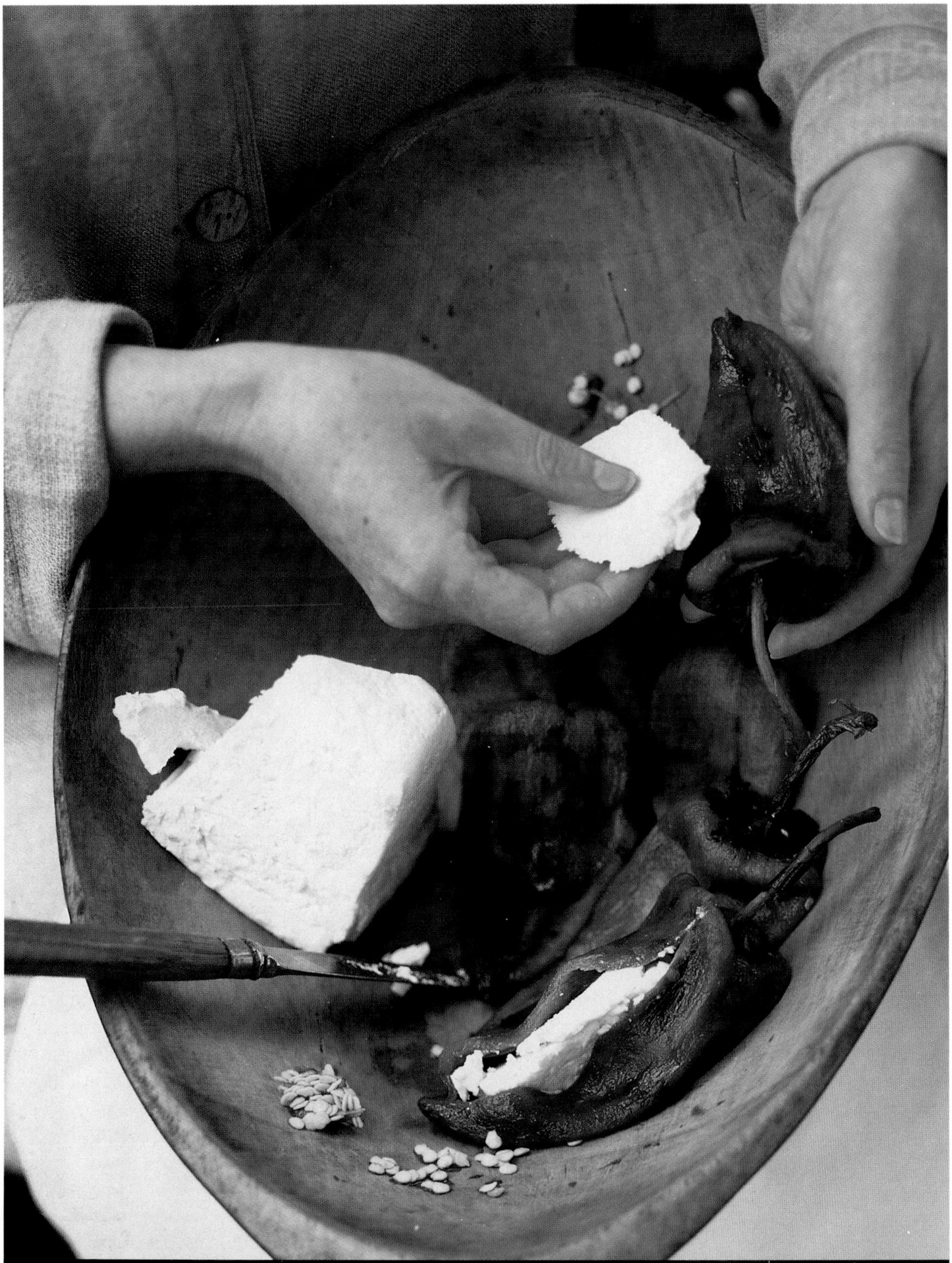

Making Goat Cheese-Stuffed Chiles with Roasted Tomato-Fennel Sauce

White Bean, Swiss Chard and Wheat Berry Croquettes

¼ cup finely chopped pecans or walnuts (about 1 ounce)
Freshly ground black pepper
1 large egg, lightly beaten
Olive oil, for frying
1 cup fine dry unseasoned bread crumbs
Lemon wedges, for garnish

1. If using dried white beans, place them in a large bowl, cover with water, and let soak for at least 6 hours or overnight. (Alternatively, in a large saucepan, cover the beans with water and boil over moderately high heat for 2 minutes. Remove from the heat, cover, and let soak for 1 hour.) Drain off the soaking liquid and rinse the beans well.
2. In a medium bowl, cover the wheat berries with water and let soak at least 6 hours or overnight. (Alternatively, in a medium heatproof bowl, cover the wheat berries with boiling water and let soak for 1 hour.) Drain well.
3. In a large saucepan, cover the beans with 2 to 3 inches of water. Simmer the beans over moderate heat until tender but not mushy, about 45 minutes. Skim the foam off the surface as necessary; taste the beans often to test for doneness. Let cool slightly in their liquid, then drain and transfer to a bowl. (Alternatively, drain and thoroughly rinse the canned white beans and put them in a bowl.)
4. In a medium saucepan, bring 1 cup of water to a boil over high heat and stir in the wheat berries. When the water returns to a boil, reduce the heat to moderately low, cover the pan, and simmer until the wheat berries are tender but still chewy, about 1 hour; drain well. Season with salt.
5. In a large nonstick skillet, heat the extra-virgin olive oil. Add the onion, sage, and oregano, and cook over moderately high heat until the onion starts to brown, about 3 minutes. Add the Swiss chard, garlic, and crushed red pepper, and cook until the chard is wilted, about 2 minutes. Add the white beans and mash them coarsely with a fork. Cook until the chard is tender, about 5 minutes. Remove from the heat and stir in the wheat berries, cheese, and nuts. Season well with salt and black pepper and let cool slightly. Stir in the egg. Let cool to room temperature.
6. In a large skillet, bring ½ inch of mild olive oil to 365° over moderate heat. Spread the bread crumbs on a plate and season with salt. Scoop out a heaping tablespoon of the croquette mixture, drop it into the crumbs, and roll to coat all over, gently shaping it into an oblong. Repeat to make the remaining croquettes.
7. In batches of 5, fry the croquettes in the hot oil, turning once, until they are browned and crisped, about 2 minutes on each side. Drain on paper towels. Serve the croquettes with the lemon wedges.—DEBORAH MADISON

PERFECT STEAMED ARTICHOKES

The ideal way to cook whole artichokes is to steam them upside down so that the hearts aren't exposed to direct heat; this will prevent them from overcooking. Also, since excess water won't get trapped in the leaves, the artichokes will not need to be drained after cooking.

Start by trimming the artichokes (see "Trimming a Whole Artichoke," p. 52). Arrange the artichokes in a steamer basket, tops down. Cover and steam over about 2 inches of simmering water until the leaves can be easily pulled out, about 40 minutes for large artichokes. Let cool slightly. Spread the artichoke leaves open and pull out the center cone of small, pale leaves. Using a melon baller or teaspoon, scrape out the hairy chokes. Serve the steamed artichokes with Saffron and Orange Aioli or Mint and Yogurt Dipping Sauce (recipes follow), or simple melted butter; or stuff them.

Saffron and Orange Aioli

For a particularly nice presentation, spoon the citrus-spiked aioli into the center of the steamed artichoke and arrange thin orange slices and sprigs of fresh oregano around the plate. This recipe makes enough to serve with six to eight artichokes.

MAKES 1½ CUPS

- ¼ teaspoon saffron threads
- 2 tablespoons dry white wine
- 2 tablespoons fresh orange juice
- 2 teaspoons finely grated orange zest
- 2 large egg yolks, at room temperature
- 2 garlic cloves, very finely minced
- 1 tablespoon fresh lemon juice
- 1 cup plus 2 tablespoons olive oil
- Salt and freshly ground pepper

1. In a small saucepan, crumble the saffron threads into the white wine and orange juice and warm over low heat, stirring, for 2 minutes. Remove from the heat. Stir in the orange zest. Let steep for 15 minutes.

2. In a food processor, combine the egg yolks, garlic, and lemon juice. With the machine on, add the olive oil in a thin steady stream and process until thickened and emulsified. Add the saffron-orange infusion and process until blended. Season with salt and pepper and serve.

Mint and Yogurt Dipping Sauce

This yogurt sauce makes a refreshing low-fat change of pace from oil-heavy vinaigrettes or rich egg-emulsified sauces such as hollandaise. The mint flavor is strongest when the sauce is just made and tends to fade after a few hours, so don't let the mixture stand for too long.

MAKES ABOUT 1 CUP

- 2 scallions, thinly sliced
- 1 tablespoon Dijon mustard
- 2 teaspoons red wine vinegar
- Salt and freshly ground pepper
- One 8-ounce container plain low-fat (1%) yogurt
- ¼ cup finely chopped fresh mint
- 2 tablespoons finely chopped fresh flat-leaf parsley
- 1 tablespoon extra-virgin olive oil

In a blender or food processor, combine the scallions, mustard, vinegar, 1 teaspoon salt, and ¼ teaspoon pepper. Add ¼ cup of the yogurt, the mint leaves, and the parsley, and process until

ARTICHOKE FACTS

● HOW THEY GROW: **There are three sizes of globe artichokes, all of which grow on the same stalk. The largest ones weigh about 10 ounces, ripen at the top of the plant, and are the first to be harvested. They are frequently stuffed or served with dipping sauces. Medium artichokes, about 7 ounces, tend to be ready a week after the large ones and are good for sautés; they often have pointy leaves. Baby artichokes grow where the leaf meets the stalk and ripen last. They are picked at their mature size and usually don't contain chokes.**

● PICKING THE RIGHT ONES: **Opt for firm, bright green artichokes with tightly packed leaves; avoid any that have withered, opened leaves, which indicate that the artichoke is old. Check the base of the plant for brown spots that might signal decay.**

● AVOIDING DISCOLORATION: **Artichoke flesh discolors after exposure to air, so be sure to rub it with lemon soon after cutting. Drop artichoke hearts into acidulated water when you finish preparing them; the hearts can be stored overnight in the same water. Use stainless steel or other nonreactive knives and cooking utensils to cut, pare, and cook the artichokes; cast-iron or aluminum will turn the artichokes black.**—ANN CHANTAL ALTMAN

Shrimp-Stuffed Artichokes

pureed. Add the remaining ¾ cup yogurt and process until combined. Stir in the olive oil, season with salt and pepper, and serve.—ANN CHANTAL ALTMAN

SHRIMP-STUFFED ARTICHOKES

6 SERVINGS

- ½ cup extra-virgin olive oil
- ¾ cup fresh bread crumbs
- 1 large onion, thinly sliced
- 1½ tablespoons minced garlic
- ⅓ cup capers, drained
- 1 teaspoon oregano
- 1 28-ounce can Italian peeled tomatoes, coarsely chopped, and their liquid
- Salt and freshly ground pepper
- 8 anchovy fillets, minced
- 1¾ pounds medium shrimp—shelled, deveined, and split in half lengthwise
- ¾ cup freshly grated Parmesan cheese (about 2 ounces)
- ⅓ cup minced fresh flat-leaf parsley
- 6 large Perfect Steamed Artichokes (p. 50)

1. Heat 1 tablespoon of the oil in a small skillet. Add the bread crumbs and cook over moderate heat, stirring, until golden, about 4 minutes. Transfer to a plate.

2. Heat 3 more tablespoons of the oil in a large nonreactive skillet. Add the onion and cook over moderate heat, stirring, until golden, about 10 minutes. Add ½ tablespoon of the garlic and cook, stirring, until softened, about 2 minutes. Stir in the capers and oregano and cook for 3 minutes. Add the tomatoes and their liquid, 1 teaspoon salt, and 1 teaspoon pepper, and bring to a boil, breaking up the tomatoes. Lower the heat and simmer until the sauce thickens, 25 to 30 minutes. Transfer the sauce to a bowl, reserving 1 cup separately. (MAKE AHEAD: The recipe can be prepared to this point up to 1 day ahead. Cover and refrigerate the sauce and let the bread crumbs stand, covered, at room temperature. Let the sauce return to room temperature before proceeding.)

3. Heat 3 more tablespoons of the oil in the skillet. Add the anchovies and the remaining 1 tablespoon garlic and cook over moderately high heat, stirring, until fragrant, about 1 minute. Add the shrimp, season with pepper, and cook, stirring, until the shrimp are pink but still translucent in the center, about 2 minutes. Add the shrimp to the bowl of tomato sauce with ½ cup of the bread crumbs, the Parmesan, and half the parsley, and mix well. Season with salt and pepper.

4. Spoon the shrimp stuffing into the hollowed out centers and between the leaves of the steamed artichokes. Spread the remaining 1 tablespoon oil in an enameled cast-iron casserole large enough to hold the artichokes in a single layer. Arrange the stuffed artichokes upright in the casserole and add ½ inch of water to the dish. Cover and bring to a simmer over moderately high heat. Lower the heat to moderate and cook until the artichoke bottoms are tender when pierced with a knife and a leaf can easily be pulled out, 20 to 25 minutes. Transfer the artichokes to individual plates and keep warm. Pour the cooking liquid into a small bowl.

5. Add the reserved 1 cup tomato sauce to the casserole. Add half of the artichoke cooking liquid and bring to a simmer over moderate heat. Stir in the remaining minced parsley and season with salt and pepper. To serve,

TRIMMING A WHOLE ARTICHOKE

Using a large, sharp knife, cut off the stem at the base of the artichoke. Then trim about 1 inch from the top of the artichoke leaves. Using kitchen scissors, trim approximately ½ inch from the artichoke's lower leaves. Rub the cut edges with a halved lemon.—ANN CHANTAL ALTMAN

sprinkle the remaining ¼ cup bread crumbs over the artichokes and spoon the tomato sauce around.—ANN CHANTAL ALTMAN

HAPPY PANCAKES WITH SPICY CUCUMBERS

Golden turmeric makes these crisp, thin pancakes look as though they're made with eggs. Spicy cucumber slivers are a fresh alternative to the meat and shrimp fillings usually found in happy pancakes. These cakes are best straight out of the pan, so serve them as they're made.

MAKES 6

- 1 cup Chinese or Latin American rice flour
- ½ teaspoon salt

Large pinch of turmeric

- 6 tablespoons plus 1 teaspoon vegetable oil
- ¼ cup fresh lime juice
- 2 tablespoons fish sauce (*nuoc mam*)
- 1 medium Thai, or bird, chile or 1 large serrano chile, minced
- 1 large garlic clove, minced
- 1 tablespoon sugar
- 1 large European cucumber—halved lengthwise, seeded, and sliced crosswise ¼ inch thick
- 6 large mushrooms, sliced ¼ inch thick
- 1 medium onion, thinly sliced

1. In a medium bowl or large measuring cup, combine the rice flour, salt, and turmeric. Whisk in 1¼ cups of water plus 1 teaspoon of the oil until smooth.

2. In a medium bowl, combine the fresh lime juice, the fish sauce, the minced chile and garlic clove, and the sugar. Fold in the cucumber slices and allow them to macerate for 5 minutes, stirring occasionally.

3. Heat 1 tablespoon of the vegetable oil in an 8-inch nonstick skillet. Scatter one-sixth of the mushroom and onion slices in an even layer in the skillet. Cook over high heat without stirring until well browned on the bottom, about 2 minutes. Stir the rice-flour batter and add ¼ cup to the skillet, tilting the skillet to distribute the batter evenly. Cover the skillet and cook over high heat without peeking until the pancake is browned and crisp on the bottom and around the edges, about 4 minutes. Remove from the heat and spoon about 3 tablespoons of the spicy cucumbers into the center of the pancake. Fold the pancake in half like an omelet, slide it onto a plate, and serve at once. Repeat with the remaining ingredients, serving the pancakes as soon as they are cooked.—MARCIA KIESEL

ASPARAGUS WITH RED PEPPER MAYONNAISE

4 SERVINGS

- 1 pound medium asparagus, trimmed
- ½ cup drained bottled roasted red peppers (pimentos)
- ½ cup mayonnaise

Salt and freshly ground black pepper

- 1 tablespoon olive oil

1. In a medium skillet, combine the trimmed asparagus and ½ cup of water. Bring to a boil over moderately high heat and cook until the water is evaporated, about 5 minutes.

Happy Pancakes with Spicy Cucumbers

2. Meanwhile, puree the red peppers in a food processor. Add the mayonnaise; process until blended. Season with salt and black pepper. Transfer to a small bowl.

3. Add the oil to the asparagus and sauté over moderately high heat, turning until lightly colored, about 2 minutes. Season with salt and pepper. Serve with the mayonnaise.—TRACEY SEAMAN

OLIVE AND CELERY ANTIPASTO

Look for an uncomplicated, not-too-heavy red, such as the 1991 Castellare di Castellina Chianti Classico from Italy or the 1992 Los Vascos Cabernet Sauvignon from Chile.

4 SERVINGS

- ½ pound plump Mediterranean black and green olives, such as Calamata or Gaeta

4 celery ribs, sliced diagonally ¼ inch thick
2 tablespoons olive oil
1 tablespoon fresh lemon juice
¼ teaspoon crushed red pepper
3 tablespoons minced fresh flat-leaf parsley
4 romaine lettuce leaves
Salt (optional)
4 thin slices of prosciutto
Breadsticks, for serving

1. In a medium bowl, toss the olives and celery with the olive oil, lemon juice, and crushed red pepper. Add the minced parsley and toss again. Let marinate at room temperature for at least 15 minutes, stirring occasionally.
2. Arrange the romaine on individual plates. Season the antipasto with salt, if necessary, and spoon over the lettuce. Garnish each serving with a slice of prosciutto and serve with breadsticks.—JUDITH SUTTON

GRILLED CHANTERELLES AND PROSCIUTTO-WRAPPED FIGS OVER ARUGULA

Black Mission figs are available from late June through October, depending on the weather. You can also use Calimyrna figs (their growing season is slightly shorter).

4 SERVINGS

4 ounces thinly sliced prosciutto di Parma
½ cup extra-virgin olive oil
3 tablespoons balsamic vinegar
½ teaspoon fine sea salt
¼ teaspoon freshly ground pepper
10 ripe but firm fresh black Mission figs, trimmed and halved lengthwise
4 ounces chanterelle or hedgehog mushrooms, wiped or brushed clean
8 loosely packed cups young arugula leaves
¼ cup mixed edible flowers (optional)

1. Using a small sharp knife, cut twenty 3-by-1-inch strips from the prosciutto di Parma. Cut the remaining prosciutto into 1-by-¼-inch strips.
2. In a small bowl, whisk together the olive oil, the balsamic vinegar, the fine sea salt, and the pepper. Reserve ¼ cup of this vinaigrette and set aside. Pour the remaining vinaigrette into a medium nonreactive bowl. Add the fig halves and the mushrooms and toss gently. Allow the figs and mushrooms to marinate for 30 minutes.
3. Light a grill or preheat the broiler. Remove the fig halves from the marinade one at a time and wrap individually in the large strips of prosciutto. Alternating with the marinated mushrooms, thread 5 of the wrapped fig halves onto each of four 10-inch-long wooden skewers. Grill or broil the figs and mushrooms for about 1 minute on each side, until lightly browned. Transfer to a plate.
4. In a large salad bowl, toss the arugula with the reserved dressing. Divide the arugula among 4 large salad plates. Arrange the grilled prosciutto-wrapped figs and mushrooms from 1 skewer on each salad. Garnish with the edible flowers and the remaining small slivers of prosciutto. Serve the salads at once.—MARGARET FOX AND CHRISTOPHER KUMP

GREEN LENTILS WITH SMOKED TROUT AND FRISEE SALAD

🍷 *The straightforward, supportive flavors of a dry, round white, such as an Alsace Pinot Blanc, are all that's required to play off against this salad. Look for the 1992 Pierre Sparr or the 1992 Léon Beyer.*

4 SERVINGS

1 tablespoon olive oil
1 small onion, finely diced
1 small carrot, finely diced
1 small celery rib, finely diced
1 cup French green lentils (*lentilles du Puy*),* picked over (about ½ pound)
Salt and freshly ground pepper
6 ounces skinless smoked trout fillets, coarsely flaked
½ cup Tarragon-Shallot Vinaigrette (recipe follows)
4 ounces *frisée*, torn into bite-size pieces

*Available at specialty food stores

1. Heat the olive oil in a heavy medium saucepan. Add the onion, carrot, and celery, and cook over moderate heat, stirring occasionally, until softened, about 5 minutes. Add the lentils and 2 cups of water, season with salt and pepper, and bring to a boil over high heat. Reduce the heat to moderately low, cover partially, and cook, stirring occasionally, until the lentils are tender but not mushy and the liquid is absorbed, about 1 hour.
2. Gently stir the smoked trout and Tarragon-Shallot Vinaigrette into the lentils and season with salt and pepper. Arrange the *frisée* on 4 plates, spoon the warm lentils on top, and serve.

Green Lentils with Smoked Trout and Frisée Salad

Tarragon-Shallot Vinaigrette

Use any extra vinaigrette to dress green salads.

MAKES ABOUT 1 CUP

2 tablespoons tarragon vinegar
1½ teaspoons minced shallot
1 teaspoon Dijon mustard
¼ cup plus 2 tablespoons olive oil
Salt and freshly ground pepper

In a bowl, combine the vinegar, shallot, and mustard. Whisk in the oil and season with salt and pepper. (MAKE AHEAD: The dressing can be refrigerated, covered, for up to 1 day; whisk before serving.)—RICK ROBINSON

GINGER-PICKLED SALMON

In this Asian-inspired starter, the salmon actually "cooks" in the ginger brine for one to three days; the longer it's left in, the more cooked it will be. At Chanterelle in New York City, it's served with a seaweed salad that's available at Japanese specialty shops.

> **CHEF'S MENU**
>
> COOL RED PEPPER SOUP WITH CUCUMBER RELISH (P. 92)
>
> GREEN LENTILS WITH SMOKED TROUT AND FRISEE SALAD (P. 54)
> *or*
> FRIED OYSTERS WITH PANCETTA AND LEEKS (P. 233)
>
> PORK RIB ROAST WITH PANCETTA
> SUMMER BEAN RAGOUT
>
> SPICED LEMON SORBET
>
> —RICK ROBINSON

8 FIRST-COURSE SERVINGS

FOR THE SALMON:

2 cups cider vinegar
½ pound fresh ginger, washed and thinly sliced crosswise
1¼ cups sugar
1½ tablespoons salt
1½ teaspoons whole black peppercorns
1½-pound piece of center-cut skinless salmon fillet

FOR SERVING:

¾ pound prepared Japanese green seaweed salad with sesame seeds, or Cucumber Salad (recipe follows)
Wasabi Sauce (recipe follows)
Chive Oil (recipe follows)

1. In a nonreactive medium saucepan, combine the vinegar, ginger, sugar, salt, and peppercorns. Add 2 cups of water and bring to a boil over high heat. Boil for 5 minutes. Let the brine cool to room temperature, then refrigerate overnight.

2. Put the salmon in a glass or ceramic bowl and pour the cold ginger brine on top. Soak a small clean kitchen towel in the brine; cover the salmon with the towel to keep it submerged. Cover the bowl with plastic wrap and refrigerate for at least 24 hours or up to 3 days.

3. Remove the salmon from the brine and pat dry. Using a sharp knife, slice the salmon fillet crosswise ⅛ inch thick.

4. Mound the seaweed salad or the Cucumber Salad on plates and arrange the sliced salmon alongside. Lightly drizzle each serving with the Wasabi Sauce and dot with drops of the Chive Oil. Serve at once.

Cucumber Salad

MAKES ABOUT 2½ CUPS

¼ cup soy sauce
¼ cup rice vinegar
1 scallion, green part only, finely chopped
1 tablespoon Oriental sesame oil
1 tablespoon sugar
1½ teaspoons sesame seeds
Pinch of crushed red pepper
2 large European cucumbers—peeled, halved lengthwise, seeded, and thinly sliced crosswise

Combine all the ingredients in a large nonreactive bowl. Set aside at room temperature for 1 hour, or cover and refrigerate for up to 6 hours. Serve the salad with a slotted spoon.

Wasabi Sauce

Wasabi is a hot, green Japanese horseradish that comes in powdered or paste form. The powdered version is more likely to taste fresh. In Chanterelle's kitchen, this sauce is put in squeeze bottles to make easy work of drizzling it over the salmon.

MAKES ABOUT 1 CUP

¼ cup wasabi powder
¼ cup rice vinegar
1 tablespoon Dijon mustard
¼ cup vegetable oil
½ teaspoon salt

In a food processor, combine the wasabi powder, rice vinegar, and Dijon mustard. Add ¼ cup of water and, with the machine on, slowly pour in the vegetable oil to form a lightly thickened sauce. Add the salt and process briefly. (MAKE AHEAD: The sauce can be refrigerated for up to 1 month. Shake or stir before using.)

Chive Oil

MAKES ABOUT ½ CUP

4 ounces fresh chives, coarsely chopped
½ teaspoon fresh lemon juice
¼ teaspoon salt
½ cup vegetable oil

1. In a food processor, mince the chives with the lemon juice and salt. With the machine on, slowly pour in the oil and blend until smooth. Transfer the oil to a jar and let steep overnight in the refrigerator.
2. The next day, allow the chive oil to return to room temperature, then strain it into a clean jar. (MAKE AHEAD: The chive oil can be refrigerated for up to 2 weeks.) —DAVID WALTUCK

RICE PAPER ROLLS WITH SMOKED SALMON

Rice paper spring roll wrappers are available at Asian markets in a variety of shapes and sizes. The thin, brittle sheets become thoroughly pliable after being moistened briefly.

MAKES 6

2 tablespoons sesame seeds
1 tablespoon soy sauce
1 tablespoon white wine vinegar
1 tablespoon finely slivered fresh ginger
½ teaspoon minced fresh chile, or more to taste
½ teaspoon Asian sesame oil
¼ teaspoon sugar
¼ teaspoon salt
4 cups finely shredded green cabbage
½ cup thinly sliced red bell pepper
½ cup thinly sliced onion
Six 8-inch round rice papers
¼ pound sliced smoked salmon, cut into long thin strips

1. In a small heavy skillet, toast the sesame seeds over moderate heat, shaking the pan frequently, until golden brown, about 5 minutes. Transfer the toasted seeds to a plate to cool.
2. In a small bowl, combine the soy sauce, vinegar, ginger, chile, sesame oil, sugar, and salt. In a large bowl, toss the shredded cabbage with the red bell pepper and the onion. Add the dressing and the toasted sesame seeds and toss well.
3. Dip a rice paper in a bowl of cool water to wet it thoroughly. Set the rice paper on a work surface to soften for about 2 minutes; the paper will turn opaque and be pliable and slightly stretchy. If there are still some dry spots, rub them with more water and wait another minute. Pat the rice paper dry with a paper towel so that it will be easier to roll.
4. Measure out ¼ cup of the cabbage salad and lightly squeeze it dry if necessary. Put the cabbage on the lower third of the rice paper and top with one-sixth of the salmon strips. Pull the rice paper up and over the filling and roll up tightly, folding in the ends as you go. Repeat with the remaining rice papers and fillings. (MAKE AHEAD: The rice paper rolls can be wrapped in plastic and refrigerated for up to one hour.) —MARCIA KIESEL

Rice Paper Rolls with Smoked Salmon

GLASS NOODLE SALAD WITH SHRIMP AND SHIITAKES

Thai salads such as this are best served on individual plates or in small bowls.

🍷 *What's needed is a sharply assertive dry wine that tolerates the bite of the dressing. Whites from France's Loire region would be ideal; look for the 1993 Sauvion Muscadet Sur Lie or the 1993 Pierre Archambault Sancerre Clos la Perrière.*

4 SERVINGS

4 dried Chinese black mushrooms
2 ounces bean thread noodles
1 tablespoon vegetable oil
2 large skinless, boneless chicken breast halves, coarsely chopped
4 thin asparagus spears
6 ounces medium shrimp, shelled and deveined

Glass Noodle Salad with Shrimp and Shiitakes.

Salt and freshly ground pepper
3 medium shallots, thinly sliced
3 tablespoons fresh lime juice
2 tablespoons Thai fish sauce (*nam pla*)
1 teaspoon sugar
¼ cup coarsely chopped fresh coriander (cilantro)
1 teaspoon finely shredded fresh mint plus whole sprigs for garnish
2 serrano chiles, preferably red, seeded and finely chopped
8 large red leaf lettuce leaves—4 leaves left whole, 4 leaves shredded
Crisp Shallots (recipe follows) made with 4 shallots, or ¼ cup packaged fried red onions

1. In a small bowl, cover the dried mushrooms with hot water and let stand until softened, about 20 minutes. Drain and squeeze out the excess water. Cut off and discard the stems and thinly slice the mushroom caps.
2. In a medium bowl, cover the noodles with hot water and let stand until softened, about 5 minutes. Drain and cut into 4-inch lengths.
3. Heat the oil in a wok. Add the chicken and stir-fry over moderately high heat, breaking up the lumps, until the meat is opaque throughout, about 3 minutes. Transfer the chicken to a bowl. Stir-fry the sliced mushroom caps in the wok for 30 seconds, then add them to the chicken.
4. In a medium saucepan of boiling salted water, blanch the asparagus until just tender, about 2 minutes. Using a slotted spoon, transfer the asparagus to a bowl of cold water, then drain. Cut the asparagus into 1½-inch lengths and add to the chicken.
5. Add the shrimp to the pan and poach until they turn pink, about 30 seconds. Drain, rinse with cold water, and drain again. Add to the chicken and season with salt and pepper. (MAKE AHEAD: The recipe can be prepared to this point up to 4 hours ahead. Set the salad components aside separately at room temperature.)
6. In a large bowl, combine the shallots, lime juice, fish sauce, sugar, coriander, and shredded mint. Add the chicken mixture, noodles, and chiles. Toss to mix.
7. Line 4 individual plates or bowls with the whole lettuce leaves. Scatter the shredded lettuce in the center and mound the noodle salad on top. Garnish with the Crisp Shallots and the mint sprigs.

Crisp Shallots

Fried shallots make a crunchy garnish for many Asian salads, as well as for soups and stir-fries.

MAKES ABOUT ¼ CUP

½ cup peanut oil
4 medium shallots, sliced ⅛ inch thick

In a wok or small skillet, heat the oil to 375°. Remove the pan from the heat, add the sliced shallots, and stir until golden and crisp, about 3 minutes. Transfer to paper towels. (MAKE AHEAD: The fried shallots can be refrigerated, covered, for up to 1 week. Recrisp before using.) —JOYCE JUE

CHESAPEAKE CRAB CAKES

There are hundreds of versions of crab cakes. Some are bound with eggs and others with mayonnaise, but there is always a little Worcestershire, Tabasco, and onion. Those are the givens, along with white meat from Maryland's famous blue crabs. I've made the cakes my own here by adding orange zest and my favorite spices. The crab cakes are loosely packed, light, and delicate; they therefore require careful handling.

6 SERVINGS

12 slices of best-quality white bread, crusts removed
¼ cup olive oil, or more if necessary
1 tablespoon Old Bay Seasoning
1 pound fresh lump crabmeat, picked over to remove any cartilage
Scant 1 cup mayonnaise
½ cup finely diced onion
½ cup diced celery (¼ inch)
½ cup diced red bell pepper (¼ inch)

- 1 tablespoon drained tiny capers
- 1 tablespoon chopped fresh flat-leaf parsley
- 2 teaspoons finely grated orange zest
- 1 teaspoon Worcestershire sauce
- ½ teaspoon dry mustard
- ⅛ teaspoon ground mace
- Dash of Tabasco, or more to taste
- 1 large egg, lightly beaten
- 2 tablespoons unsalted butter, or more if necessary
- Rosy Fruit Salsa and Tartar Sauce (recipes follow), for serving

1. Preheat the oven to 350°. Cut the bread into 1-inch cubes and toss with 2 tablespoons of the olive oil and the Old Bay Seasoning. Spread the bread cubes on a baking sheet in a single layer and bake for 10 to 12 minutes, or until toasted. Let cool for 30 minutes. Using a rolling pin, crush the bread cubes into medium-fine crumbs.

2. In a bowl, combine the crabmeat, mayonnaise, onion, celery, red bell pepper, capers, chopped parsley, orange zest, Worcestershire sauce, mustard, mace, Tabasco, and egg with ¼ cup of the bread crumbs.

3. Transfer the remaining bread crumbs to a shallow dish. Form the crabmeat mixture into 12 cakes about ¾ inch thick. Carefully dredge each of the cakes thoroughly in the bread crumbs. Arrange the cakes on a large platter and cover them with plastic wrap. Refrigerate the crab cakes for at least 1 hour and up to 8 hours.

4. In a large nonstick skillet, melt 1 tablespoon of the butter in the remaining 2 tablespoons olive oil over moderate heat. Fry the crab cakes in batches for about 3 minutes per side, or until golden brown. (Add more butter and olive oil as necessary.) Drain the crab cakes on paper towels. Serve immediately with the Rosy Fruit Salsa and Tartar Sauce.

Rosy Fruit Salsa

With its clean, fresh taste of melon, burst of sweet juice, and bite of jalapeño, this salsa is the perfect foil for the rich, highly seasoned crab cakes. You can prepare the ingredients early in the day, but don't toss them together more than an hour before serving.

MAKES 4 CUPS

- 1 cup diced ripe cantaloupe (¼ inch)
- 1 cup diced ripe watermelon (¼ inch)
- 1 cup diced peeled European cucumber (¼ inch)
- 4 ripe plum tomatoes, seeded and cut into ¼-inch dice
- ⅓ cup finely chopped red onion
- 2 tablespoons fresh lime juice
- 2 tablespoons coarsely chopped fresh flat-leaf parsley
- 1 teaspoon minced seeded jalapeño chile

Mix all the ingredients in a bowl and let rest at room temperature for up to 1 hour before serving.

Tartar Sauce

Tartar sauce originated in France, where it was made with hard-boiled egg yolks mashed into fresh mayonnaise and blended with onions, chives, or scallions. The sauce has now taken on a purely American flavor with the addition of sweet pickle relish. Its silky texture and slightly sweet, familiar taste make it the perfect choice for dolloping on everything from crab cakes to grilled trout.

MAKES 1¼ CUPS

- 1 cup mayonnaise
- 2 tablespoons drained sweet pickle relish
- 1 tablespoon fresh lemon juice
- 1 teaspoon finely grated lemon zest
- 1 teaspoon Dijon mustard
- Dash of Tabasco sauce
- 2 tablespoons chopped fresh flat-leaf parsley
- 2 tablespoons minced shallots
- 1 tablespoon drained tiny capers
- Salt and freshly ground pepper

In a bowl, combine the mayonnaise, relish, lemon juice, lemon zest, mustard, and Tabasco. Stir

Chesapeake Crab Cakes

in the parsley, shallots, and capers. Season with salt and pepper. Cover and refrigerate for at least 1 hour and up to 2 days before serving to allow the flavors to blend.—SHEILA LUKINS

SPINACH AND CRAB TARTS WITH FETA

🍷 *The crab, feta, spinach, and phyllo can all find a taste echo in a round, ripe-flavored Chardonnay, such as the 1993 Hess Select or the 1993 Napa Ridge Central Coast from California or the 1993 Rothbury Estate from Australia.*

6 SERVINGS

SPINACH AND CRAB TARTS:

- 2 tablespoons unsalted butter plus 3 tablespoons, melted, for the phyllo dough
- 1 small onion, finely chopped
- 1 tablespoon olive oil
- 1 pound fresh spinach, tough stems removed
- 2 garlic cloves, minced
- Salt
- ½ pound lump crabmeat, picked over
- 4 ounces feta cheese, preferably Bulgarian, crumbled
- 1 large egg
- 1 large egg white
- 1 tablespoon heavy cream
- ⅛ teaspoon paprika
- Pinch of cayenne pepper
- 6 sheets of phyllo dough

SAUCES:

- 2 large tomatoes, finely chopped
- ½ teaspoon red wine vinegar
- ½ teaspoon tomato paste
- Salt
- 2 cups fresh basil leaves
- ½ cup extra-virgin olive oil
- ⅓ cup mayonnaise
- ¼ cup flying fish roe*
- 1 teaspoon fresh lemon juice
- ½ teaspoon Dijon mustard
- About ¼ cup balsamic vinegar
- Fresh chervil sprigs (optional)

*Available at Asian markets

Spinach and Crab Tart with Feta

1. Make the spinach and crab tarts: Melt 1 tablespoon of the butter in a small saucepan. Add the chopped onion and cook over moderately low heat, stirring occasionally, until translucent, about 6 minutes.

2. In a large skillet, melt the remaining 1 tablespoon butter in the olive oil. Add the spinach and cook over high heat, stirring often, until wilted, about 2 minutes. Stir in the minced garlic and ¼ teaspoon salt. Spoon the spinach into a colander set over a bowl and press down to remove the excess liquid. Transfer the spinach to a large bowl; reserve ¼ cup of the liquid.

3. Add the reserved spinach liquid to the sautéed onion. Bring to a boil over high heat and boil for 2 minutes. Add the mixture to the spinach along with the crabmeat and feta. In a small bowl, beat the whole egg, egg white, heavy cream, paprika, cayenne, and ¼ teaspoon salt. Stir the mixture into the spinach.

4. Preheat the oven to 350°. Lightly butter six 3-ounce muffin cups in a 12-cup muffin tin. Spread 1 sheet of phyllo on a work surface; keep the remaining sheets covered with a damp towel. Brush the phyllo with some of the melted butter. Lay another sheet of phyllo on top, brush with butter, and repeat the process with 1 more sheet of phyllo and more butter. Cut the phyllo into three 6-inch squares and gently press a square into each of the buttered muffin cups; discard the trimmings. Repeat the process with the remaining phyllo and melted butter. Using scissors, trim the corners of the phyllo, then neatly fold in the overhanging edges.

5. Meanwhile, make the sauces: In a blender, combine the tomatoes, red wine vinegar, and tomato paste. Season with salt and puree until smooth. Strain the tomato *coulis* into a medium bowl.

6. Rinse and dry the blender. Add the basil and olive oil and puree until smooth. Scrape the basil oil into a small bowl and season with salt.

7. In another small bowl, combine the mayonnaise, fish roe, lemon juice, and mustard.

8. Spoon the crab filling into the phyllo-lined cups. Bake the tarts in the center of the oven for about 30 minutes, or until the phyllo is golden brown and the filling is set. Let cool slightly in the muffin tin.

9. Transfer the crab tarts to individual plates. Top each tart with a heaping teaspoon of flying fish roe mayonnaise. (Serve the remainder with sliced tomatoes, or stir it into tuna salad.) Drizzle the tomato *coulis*, basil oil, and balsamic vinegar around each tart, garnish with chervil sprigs, and serve.—CHARLES DALE

Sautéed Lobster with Ginger Vinaigrette

SAUTEED LOBSTER WITH GINGER VINAIGRETTE

🍷 *The abundance of rich, sweet, aromatic tastes calls for a crisp but fruity wine. Consider a California sparkling wine with complementary flavors, possibly a nonvintage Blanc de Noir, such as Mumm Cuvée Napa or Domaine Chandon. Their effervescence will also add contrast.*

4 SERVINGS

2-inch piece of vanilla bean, split
¼ cup canola oil
Two 1½-pound live lobsters
2 tablespoons unsalted butter
1 tablespoon olive oil
2 cups fresh corn kernels (from 3 medium ears)
Salt and freshly ground pepper
Ginger Vinaigrette (recipe follows)
Fresh rosemary sprigs and sunflower sprouts or bean sprouts, for garnish

1. Scrape the seeds from the vanilla bean into a small bowl and add the bean. Stir in the canola oil. Cover and let stand at room temperature for at least 1 hour or up to 2 days. Strain the vanilla oil. (MAKE AHEAD: The oil can be refrigerated, covered, for up to 1 month. Let return to room temperature before using.)

2. Bring a large pot of salted water to a boil. Add the lobsters head first, cover, and cook over high heat for 5 minutes. Transfer the lobsters to a large plate and let cool for 5 minutes.

3. Detach the lobster tails from the bodies. Twist off the claws and crack them; remove the meat, in one piece if possible, and transfer to a bowl. Using shears, cut along the underside of the tail shells and remove the meat. Discard the intestinal vein that runs along each lobster tail and cut the meat crosswise into ¾-inch-thick medallions. Add to the claw meat. ➤

4. In a heavy medium skillet, melt the butter in the olive oil. Add the corn and cook over moderately high heat for 1 minute, stirring occasionally. Add the lobster meat and cook, stirring often, until just cooked through, about 3 minutes. Season with salt and pepper.

5. Divide the lobster and the corn among 4 shallow bowls or plates. Drizzle each serving with ½ tablespoon of the vanilla oil and 2 tablespoons of the vinaigrette. Garnish with rosemary sprigs and sunflower sprouts and serve at once.

Ginger Vinaigrette

MAKES ABOUT ¾ CUP

- 1-inch piece of fresh ginger, peeled and coarsely chopped
- 1 small garlic clove
- ½ teaspoon coarsely chopped fresh rosemary
- ¼ cup rice wine vinegar
- 2 tablespoons soy sauce
- 1 tablespoon honey
- ½ cup peanut oil
- 2 drops of Asian sesame oil

In a mini-food processor, finely chop the ginger, garlic, and rosemary. Add the vinegar, the soy sauce, and the honey, and process until blended. Add the peanut oil and sesame oil and process until emulsified.—ANNE QUATRANO AND CLIFFORD HARRISON

Clams in Sherry and Black Bean Sauce

CLAMS IN SHERRY AND BLACK BEAN SAUCE

Fermented black bean and chili sauce is available under a variety of names, such as soy chilli sauce, black bean chili sauce, and soybean paste with chili. Just be sure the ingredient list includes fermented black beans (also called fermented soybeans) and chiles.

Baguettes are a standard accompaniment to many Vietnamese soups and sauced dishes, and they are ideal for sopping up the briny broth.

4 SERVINGS

- 1 tablespoon vegetable oil
- 1 large shallot, minced
- 1 large garlic clove, minced
- ¼ cup medium dry sherry
- 1 teaspoon sugar
- ¼ teaspoon freshly ground pepper
- 1 teaspoon fermented black bean and chili sauce
- 3 dozen littleneck clams, scrubbed
- 2 large scallions, thinly sliced
- Warm French bread, for serving

1. Heat the vegetable oil in a large nonreactive saucepan. Add the shallot and cook over high heat, stirring, for 10 seconds. Add the garlic and stir for 10 seconds longer. Add the sherry, sugar, and pepper, and boil for 1 minute. Stir in the fermented black bean and chili sauce and ¼ cup of water and bring to a boil.

2. Add the clams to the saucepan in an even layer. Cover and cook over high heat, shaking the pan occasionally, until most of the clams open, about 5 minutes. Using a slotted spoon, divide the opened clams among 4 shallow bowls and keep warm. Cover and continue cooking any remaining clams until they open. Ladle the cooking liquid over the clams, sprinkle with the scallions, and serve with warm French bread.—MARCIA KIESEL

TWO-CHEESE SOUFFLE

This cheese soufflé is special: it is wonderfully light in texture but rich in flavor. Because its base is thickened with potato starch, which thins after extended heating, it shouldn't be made ahead.

4 TO 6 SERVINGS

1 tablespoon unsalted butter
1 cup heavy cream
1 tablespoon potato starch*
5 large egg yolks
½ cup freshly grated Parmesan cheese (about 1½ ounces)
½ cup grated Gruyère cheese (about 2 ounces)
Salt and freshly ground pepper
Pinch of dry mustard
8 large egg whites, at room temperature

*Available at supermarkets and specialty food stores

1. Preheat the oven to 425°. Butter a 2-quart soufflé dish and freeze until set. Butter the soufflé dish again.

2. In a medium saucepan, melt the butter in the cream over low heat. Add the potato starch and whisk just until the sauce thickens, about 3 minutes; don't overcook the sauce or it will separate. Remove from the heat and whisk in the egg yolks one at a time, mixing well after each addition. Stir in the Parmesan cheese and all but 2 tablespoons of the Gruyère and stir over low heat until slightly thickened and just hot to the touch, about 1 minute. Do not overcook or the cheese will become stringy. Remove from the heat and season well with salt, pepper, and the dry mustard.

3. Meanwhile, in a large bowl, beat the egg whites with a pinch of salt until firm peaks form. Stir one quarter of the egg whites into the warm cheese mixture, then fold the mixture into the remaining whites just until combined.

4. Spoon the soufflé mixture into the prepared soufflé dish and sprinkle with the remaining 2 tablespoons of Gruyère cheese. Smooth the surface of the soufflé and run your thumb around the inside edge of the dish. Bake the soufflé in the lower third of the oven for about 20 minutes, until puffed, nicely browned on top, and set around the edges. Serve immediately.—ANNE WILLAN

ROASTED EGGPLANT AND GARLIC SOUFFLE

Roasted eggplant and garlic aren't exactly a classic soufflé combination, but they work beautifully here, especially with the tangy Parmesan.

6 SERVINGS

1 small eggplant (about ¾ pound), trimmed and sliced crosswise ⅜ inch thick
Salt
3 tablespoons olive oil
Freshly ground pepper
1 medium head of garlic, separated into unpeeled cloves
1 cup milk
2 tablespoons unsalted butter
2 tablespoons all-purpose flour
Pinch of freshly grated nutmeg
4 large egg yolks
¼ cup freshly grated Parmesan cheese (about ¾ ounce)
2 tablespoons plain dry bread crumbs
6 large egg whites, at room temperature

1. Spread the eggplant slices in a single layer on a large baking sheet. Sprinkle with salt and let stand for 15 minutes to draw out the bitter juices.

2. Preheat the oven to 375°. Rinse the eggplant slices and pat dry, then transfer to a lightly oiled baking sheet. Brush with 2 tablespoons of the olive oil and season with salt and pepper. Toss the garlic with the remaining 1 tablespoon oil and wrap loosely in foil. Roast the eggplant and garlic for about 30 minutes, until both are softened and golden. Remove them from the oven and increase the temperature to 400°.

3. Bring the milk just to a boil in a small saucepan; keep warm. In a medium saucepan, melt the butter. Add the flour and whisk over moderately high heat until foaming but not colored, 2 to 3 minutes. Remove the pan from the heat and whisk in the milk. Bring the sauce to a boil over moderately high heat and cook, whisking constantly, until thickened, about 2 minutes. Continue cooking the white sauce, whisking, until it thins slightly (indicating that the flour is cooked),

Two-Cheese Soufflé

about 2 minutes. Season with salt, pepper, and nutmeg.

4. Squeeze the roasted garlic cloves out of their skins. In a food processor, combine the garlic, eggplant, and white sauce, and puree until smooth. Add the egg yolks and process until combined. Transfer the mixture to a medium saucepan and cook over moderately low heat, stirring, until slightly thickened, about 5 minutes. Stir in the Parmesan cheese and season well with salt and pepper. (MAKE AHEAD: The recipe can be prepared to this point up to 4 hours ahead; press plastic wrap directly on the surface of the eggplant mixture and let stand at room temperature.)

5. Butter a 1½-quart soufflé dish and freeze until set. Butter the dish again and dust with the bread crumbs. Rewarm the eggplant mixture over moderately low heat, stirring, until just hot to the touch.

6. Meanwhile, in a medium bowl, beat the egg whites with a pinch of salt until firm peaks form. Stir one quarter of the egg whites into the eggplant mixture, then fold the mixture into the remaining whites just until combined.

7. Spoon the soufflé mixture into the prepared soufflé dish and smooth the surface. Run your thumb around the inside edge of the dish. Bake the soufflé in the lower third of the oven for 20 to 25 minutes, until puffed, nicely browned on top, and set around the edges.—ANNE WILLAN

ZUCCHINI AND SQUASH-BLOSSOM FRITTATA

Most farmers' markets have plenty of squash blossoms in the summer. You should use lots of them, since they cook down to almost nothing.

6 SERVINGS

- 6 eggs
- ¼ cup finely grated Parmesan cheese
- 1 tablespoon coarsely chopped fresh marjoram, flat-leaf parsley, or basil
- 1 medium garlic clove, minced
- Salt and freshly ground pepper
- 2 tablespoons olive oil, butter, or a mixture of the two
- 1 pound small green or golden zucchini, thinly sliced crosswise
- 12 squash blossoms, cleaned (see Note) and cut into lengthwise strips

1. Preheat the broiler. In a bowl, beat the eggs, Parmesan, marjoram, garlic, and a pinch of salt and pepper.

2. Heat 1 tablespoon of the oil in a large ovenproof skillet. Add the zucchini and cook over moderately high heat until tender and browned, about 10 minutes. Add the squash blossoms during the last five minutes. Season with salt and pepper.

3. Add the cooked vegetables to the eggs. Heat the remaining 1 tablespoon olive oil in the skillet. When the pan is hot, add the eggs, reduce the heat to moderately low, and cook until the frittata is mostly set, about 8 minutes. Slide the pan under the broiler for about 30 seconds to finish cooking the eggs and to brown the top. Slide the frittata out onto a serving plate.

NOTE: To prepare squash blossoms, peel the stem and pull out the filament that stands upright in each blossom. Open up the flower, give it a shake, then swish it around in a bowl of cold water. Shake dry.—DEBORAH MADISON

JULIA CHILD'S CHEESE AND BACON QUICHE

What lovely little luncheons and suppers we used to have in the Sixties, when real people ate quiche. Maybe you weren't around during its glory days, or you may not remember what a quiche is—it's all so long ago. To begin with, a quiche is an open-faced savory pie with a custard filling. The original, Quiche Lorraine, came to us from Alsace-Lorraine, that beautiful region of France bordering the Rhine, Germany, and Switzerland. The custard for that rich and famous mother of the quiche was simply heavy cream, eggs, and bits of bacon. Delicious!

Here's how to go about the quiche: Buy a preformed frozen shell or bake your own. Try my formula of 2½ sticks of unsalted butter and 4 tablespoons of shortening for 3½ cups of unbleached flour, 2 teaspoons of salt, and ⅔ to 1 cup of ice water. It makes enough dough for two 9-inch quiches plus leftovers for appetizers, since the dough freezes perfectly for months.

Prebaking the shell: Whatever raw shell you use, homemade or store-bought, prebake it briefly to prevent a soggy bottom. Set a buttered pie pan in the frozen store-bought shell, or press a sheet of buttered foil against the bottom and sides of a homemade shell and weigh it down with dried beans. Bake for about 10 minutes at 450° to set the crust, then remove the pie pan or foil and beans and bake for 7 to

8 minutes longer to brown it very lightly. Now you are ready to fill the quiche.

Making the custard: The proportions never vary. Every ½ cup of liquid includes 1 egg. For example, for a 9-inch quiche that will serve six a wedge of reasonable size, whisk 3 "large" eggs in a 4-cup measure and when blended, pour in enough milk to reach the 1½-cup mark. If, in the midst of battle, you find you need more custard, whisk 1 egg in a measure and pour in milk to the ½-cup mark. As to liquid, that's up to you—skim, 1%, 2%, or regular milk; or cream from half-and-half to heavy; or part sour cream and part milk or cream. Season nicely with salt, white pepper, and a pinch or two of nutmeg.

Heat the oven to 375°. Spread ½ cup of grated Swiss cheese in the crust and strew on 3 crumbled crisply cooked bacon strips. Pour in enough custard to reach within ¼ inch of the lowest part of the shell rim and strew an additional 2 tablespoons cheese on top. Slide the quiche onto the middle rack of the oven and bake for 30 to 35 minutes, or until the top is nicely browned. Let the quiche cool for 5 minutes before serving.

CHAPTER 4

SALADS

Clockwise from bottom: Spaghetti Squash Salad with Lemon Dressing, Roasted Buttercup Squash and Baked Apples (p. 329), Roti (p. 339), Spicy Thickened Yogurt (p. 355), and Smoky Black Beans (p. 332)

SPAGHETTI SQUASH SALAD WITH LEMON DRESSING

4 SERVINGS

Salt
One 3-pound spaghetti squash, halved lengthwise, seeds scraped out
½ teaspoon finely grated lemon zest
3 tablespoons fresh lemon juice
2 teaspoons olive oil

1. Bring a large pot of water to a boil over high heat. Add salt and the spaghetti squash and boil until slightly tender but still crunchy, about 8 minutes. Remove the squash with tongs and let cool slightly.
2. Using a fork, scrape the spaghetti squash to loosen and separate the strands, keeping them as long and as intact as possible. Scrape the squash strands into a large bowl, cover, and refrigerate until thoroughly chilled or for up to 1 day.
3. In a small bowl, combine the lemon zest, lemon juice, olive oil, and ¾ teaspoon salt. Just before serving, pour the dressing over the spaghetti squash strands and toss well.—MARCIA KIESEL

CHAYOTE SALAD

4 SERVINGS

2 medium chayote squash
1 large shallot, minced
2 teaspoons finely slivered fresh ginger
1 small garlic clove, minced
3 tablespoons fresh lime juice
2 teaspoons sugar
¼ teaspoon finely grated lime zest
¼ teaspoon freshly ground pepper
2 tablespoons chopped salted peanuts

1. Lay the chayote flat on a work surface and cut it in half horizontally. Discard the small flat pit. Slice the squash lengthwise into strips, then cut crosswise into small sticks.
2. Blanch the chayote sticks in boiling salted water just until the skin turns bright green, about 40 seconds. Drain and refresh under cold running water. Put the chayote in a bowl and dry lightly with a towel.
3. In a small bowl, stir the shallot, ginger, garlic, lime juice, sugar, lime zest, and pepper until the sugar dissolves. Pour the dressing over the chayote sticks, toss lightly, and sprinkle the chopped peanuts on top. Serve at once.—MARCIA KIESEL

BEET AND ORANGE SALAD

8 SERVINGS

3 pounds medium beets, scrubbed but not peeled
5 navel oranges
3 tablespoons white wine vinegar
1 tablespoon fresh lemon juice
Coarse salt and freshly ground pepper
½ cup olive oil
1 tablespoon minced fresh tarragon
1 medium red onion, thinly sliced crosswise

Clockwise from left: **Chayote Salad, Sweet Potato Bake (p. 280), Coconut Rice and Peas (p. 297), Allspice-Pickled Onions (p. 354), Fried Plantains (p. 332), and Mixed Roasted Peppers (p. 311)**

Beet and Orange Salad

3 medium bunches of arugula or watercress, stems trimmed

1. Preheat the oven to 375°. Divide the beets into groups of 3 or 4 and wrap them in foil, crimping the edges to seal tightly. Place the foil packets on a large baking sheet and bake for about 1 hour, or until the beets are tender when pierced. When cool enough to handle, peel the beets and slice them crosswise ¼ inch thick or cut into ½-inch dice.

2. Using a small, sharp knife, peel the oranges, removing the bitter white pith. Slice crosswise ¼ inch thick. (MAKE AHEAD: The recipe can be made to this point 1 day ahead. Cover and refrigerate the beets and oranges separately.)

3. In a medium bowl, whisk together the vinegar and lemon juice. Whisk in 1 teaspoon coarse salt and ½ teaspoon pepper. Gradually whisk in the olive oil. Add the tarragon. In a small bowl, toss the onion with 1 tablespoon of the dressing.

4. Toss the arugula with half of the remaining dressing and arrange on a large platter. Arrange the oranges and beets on the greens. Drizzle with the remaining dressing. Scatter the onion on top and serve.—DIANA STURGIS

SHREDDED BEET AND CELERY ROOT SALAD WITH APPLE VINAIGRETTE

You can embellish this tasty first course, from Sooke Harbor House in Sooke, British Columbia, with thin slices of smoked salmon, sablefish, or other smoked fish. Or serve the salad with toasted slices of whole-grain or sourdough bread.

4 SERVINGS

¼ cup hazelnuts
1 Granny Smith apple—peeled, cored, and coarsely chopped
¼ cup apple cider vinegar
¼ cup sparkling apple cider
1 garlic clove, minced
1 tablespoon grainy mustard
1 cup cold-pressed canola oil
Salt and freshly ground pepper
2 medium beets
8 ounces (½ bulb) celery root (celeriac)
1 cup walnuts (about 3½ ounces)
Whole fresh chives, for garnish

1. Preheat the oven to 425°. Spread the hazelnuts on a baking sheet and toast in the middle of the oven for about 8 minutes, until fragrant. Wrap the hot nuts in a kitchen towel and vigorously rub them together to remove most of the skins.

2. In a blender, combine the hazelnuts, apple, vinegar, cider, garlic, and mustard, and blend until almost smooth. Blend in the oil in a steady stream until thoroughly incorporated. Season the dressing with salt and pepper. (MAKE AHEAD: The dressing can be made to this point up to 6 hours ahead.)

3. In a small saucepan, cover the beets with water and bring to a boil over moderate heat. Cook until tender when pierced, about 45 minutes. Drain and let cool.

4. Meanwhile, peel the celery root and shred on the large holes of a box grater to yield 1 cup. Peel the beets and shred on the large holes of the box grater to yield 1 cup.

5. Preheat the oven to 375°. Spread the walnuts on a baking sheet and toast until fragrant, 8 to 10 minutes.

6. Place the shredded beets and celery root in separate bowls. Add ½ cup of the apple dressing to each bowl and stir well.

7. Evenly divide the beets and celery root among 4 plates. Distribute ⅔ cup of the walnuts on top. Drizzle the plates with a little of the dressing (reserve the rest for another use). Garnish each plate with chives and the remaining walnuts. Serve at once.—BILL JONES

BEET, ENDIVE AND GOAT CHEESE SALAD WITH WALNUT OIL VINAIGRETTE

As an alternative to boiling the beets, they can also be wrapped individually in foil and roasted in a 375° oven for about 1 hour, or until they are tender when pierced.

6 SERVINGS

- 4 large beets (2½ pounds), stem ends trimmed
- 1 cup walnuts (4 ounces)
- 1 tablespoon plus 1 teaspoon red wine vinegar
- 1 teaspoon Dijon mustard
- 1 shallot, minced
- ½ teaspoon salt
- ¼ teaspoon freshly ground pepper
- 2½ tablespoons walnut oil
- 2 tablespoons extra-virgin olive oil
- 6 heads of Belgian endive (2 pounds), 1 separated into whole spears and 5 sliced crosswise ½ inch thick
- 4 ounces soft goat cheese

1. Preheat the oven to 350°. In a large saucepan, cover the beets with cold water and bring to a boil over high heat. Reduce the heat to moderately high and boil the beets until fork-tender, about 25 minutes. Transfer the beets to a plate to cool.

2. Meanwhile, spread the walnuts on a baking sheet and toast in the oven for about 15 minutes, until evenly browned. Transfer to a plate.

3. In a small bowl, combine the vinegar, mustard, shallot, salt, and pepper, and mix with a fork. Beat in the walnut oil and olive oil. Set aside for 10 minutes to blend the flavors.

4. Peel the beets and cut them into 2-inch wedges. Decoratively arrange the whole endive spears around a small platter. In a large bowl, toss the sliced endives with 2 tablespoons of the dressing and mound on the platter. Add the beets to the bowl and toss with the remaining dressing. Scatter the beets over the endives and crumble the goat cheese on top. Garnish with the toasted walnuts and serve.—MARCIA KIESEL

ROASTED EGGPLANT AND ARUGULA SALAD WITH BALSAMIC VINEGAR

4 SERVINGS

- 5 tablespoons olive oil
- One 1-pound eggplant—peeled, sliced crosswise 1 inch thick, and each slice cut into 4 strips
- Salt and freshly ground pepper
- 2 tablespoons balsamic vinegar
- 8 cups bite-size pieces of arugula

Preheat the oven to 450°. Pour 2 tablespoons of the oil onto a baking sheet and dip each strip of eggplant into the oil to coat. Season the strips with salt and pepper. Roast the eggplant on the bottom shelf of the oven until tender and deep brown on the underside, about 25 minutes. Using a metal spatula, scrape up the eggplant and transfer to a plate. In a small bowl, combine the remaining 3 tablespoons olive oil with the balsamic vinegar, ½ teaspoon salt, and ¼ teaspoon pepper. In a large bowl, toss the arugula with 3 tablespoons of the dressing. Transfer the salad to a platter and arrange the roasted eggplant on top. Drizzle the eggplant with the remaining 2 tablespoons of dressing and serve.—MARCIA KIESEL

ROASTED EGGPLANT SALAD

6 TO 8 SERVINGS

- 2 medium eggplants (about 2¼ pounds total)
- ¼ cup plus 1 tablespoon olive oil
- 1 large ripe tomato—peeled, seeded, and finely chopped
- 2 garlic cloves, minced
- 1½ tablespoons fresh lemon juice
- 1 teaspoon sweet paprika
- 1 teaspoon salt
- 1 teaspoon freshly ground pepper
- Calamata olives, lemon wedges, and pita bread, for serving

1. Preheat the broiler. Pierce the eggplants all over with a fork and broil for about 25 minutes, turning often, until the skin is blackened and the eggplants are tender. Let cool. Slit the skins and scoop out the flesh. Finely chop the eggplant flesh.
2. Heat the oil in a large nonreactive skillet. Add the roasted eggplant, tomato, garlic, lemon juice, paprika, salt, and pepper, and simmer over low heat, stirring occasionally, until the mixture is slightly thickened, about 30 minutes. Transfer the eggplant salad to a bowl. (MAKE AHEAD: The salad can be refrigerated, covered, for up to 1 day.) Serve the eggplant salad warm, at room temperature, or chilled, with the olives, lemon wedges, and pita bread.—FATIMA HAL

ROASTED PEPPER SALAD

6 SERVINGS

- 2 medium green bell peppers
- 2 medium red bell peppers
- 1 ripe medium tomato—peeled, seeded, and very finely chopped
- 2 garlic cloves, minced
- ¼ teaspoon freshly ground black pepper
- Pinch of ground cumin
- Salt
- 2 tablespoons olive oil

Clockwise from top: Roasted Eggplant Salad, Chickpea Salad with Cumin (p. 85), and Roasted Pepper Salad

1. Roast the green and red bell peppers over a gas flame or under the broiler as close to the heat as possible, turning frequently, until charred all over. Transfer the peppers to a paper bag and let steam for 15 minutes. Peel off the charred skin and discard the cores, seeds, and ribs. Finely chop the peppers.
2. In a medium bowl, combine the roasted peppers and the tomato. Stir in the garlic, black pepper, and cumin. (MAKE AHEAD: The salad can be prepared to this point up to 1 day ahead; cover and refrigerate.) Season the roasted pepper salad with salt and drizzle with the olive oil. Serve chilled or at room temperature.—FATIMA HAL

SPICY THAI GREEN BEAN SALAD

If you're making the Crisp Shallots, you can use the same oil to fry the garlic slices.

6 SERVINGS

- ½ pound Chinese winged beans or yard-long beans or green beans
- 3 tablespoons shredded unsweetened coconut*
- ½ cup peanut oil
- 6 garlic cloves, sliced lengthwise ⅛ inch thick
- ¼ cup fresh lime juice
- ¼ cup canned unsweetened coconut milk (see Note)
- 1 tablespoon roasted chile paste (*nam prik pao*)
- 1 tablespoon Thai fish sauce (*nam pla*)
- 1 tablespoon sugar
- 12 whole radicchio leaves
- 4 ounces cooked small shrimp, cut into ¼-inch dice
- 1 cup finely diced cooked chicken breast meat
- 2 serrano chiles, preferably 1 red and 1 green, seeded and finely chopped
- Crisp Shallots (p. 58), made with 6 shallots, or ⅓ cup packaged fried red onions
- 3 tablespoons dry-roasted peanuts, coarsely chopped
- Fresh coriander (cilantro) sprigs, for garnish

*Available at health food stores

1. In a medium saucepan of boiling salted water, blanch the beans until they are tender but still crisp, about 3 minutes. Drain, rinse with cold water, and drain again. Cut the beans into ½-inch pieces (or longer if you prefer).
2. Heat a dry wok or a small skillet. Add the coconut and toss gently over moderate heat until golden, about 1 minute. Transfer to a plate.
3. In the wok, heat the peanut oil to 375°. Remove the wok from the heat, add the garlic slices, and stir until golden and crisp, about 1 minute. Transfer the garlic to paper towels to drain.
4. In a bowl, whisk the lime juice, 3 tablespoons of the coconut milk, the chile paste, fish sauce, and sugar. (MAKE AHEAD: The recipe can be prepared to this

point up to 4 hours ahead. Set the salad components aside separately at room temperature.)

5. Arrange the radicchio leaves on a platter or individual plates. In a large bowl, combine the beans, shrimp, chicken, serranos, toasted coconut, half of the Crisp Shallots, and half of the garlic. Toss with the dressing and mound the salad on the radicchio. Drizzle with the remaining 1 tablespoon coconut milk and garnish with the peanuts, coriander sprigs, and the remaining Crisp Shallots and fried garlic.

NOTE: Use the rich coconut cream that rises to the top as the can sits.—JOYCE JUE

Spicy Thai Green Bean Salad

SUMMER GREEN BEAN SALAD

8 SERVINGS

- ½ cup pine nuts
- 2 pounds green beans
- ¼ cup plus 2 tablespoons olive oil
- 8 large shallots (10 ounces), thinly sliced
- ¼ cup plus 1 tablespoon Champagne vinegar or white wine vinegar
- 1 teaspoon Dijon mustard
- 3 medium scallions, finely chopped
- ¼ cup finely chopped fresh dill
- 1 tablespoon finely chopped lemon zest

Salt and freshly ground pepper

1. Spread the pine nuts in a dry heavy skillet. Toast over moderate heat, shaking the pan, until golden, about 5 minutes.

2. Bring a large saucepan of salted water to a boil. Add the beans and cook over moderately high heat until tender, about 8 minutes. Drain and refresh under cold water; drain.

3. Meanwhile, in a medium nonreactive skillet, heat 2 tablespoons of the oil. Add the shallots and cook over moderate heat, stirring often, until caramelized, about 5 minutes. Add the vinegar and reduce by half, 1 to 2 minutes. Scrape the contents of the skillet into a large bowl.

4. Whisk in the mustard and the remaining 4 tablespoons olive oil. Add the green beans, scallions, dill, and lemon zest, and toss. Season with salt and pepper. (MAKE AHEAD: The salad can be made up to 3 hours ahead. Keep covered at room temperature.) Sprinkle the pine nuts on top and serve.—KATHY CARY

ZUCCHINI, MINT AND LEMON SALAD LF

4 SERVINGS

- 5 small zucchini (about 6 ounces each), cut into 1-by-⅓-inch sticks
- 3 scallions, thinly sliced
- 3 tablespoons thinly sliced fresh mint
- 2 teaspoons extra-virgin olive oil
- 1 teaspoon finely grated lemon zest
- 1 teaspoon fresh lemon juice

Heirloom Tomato Salad

¼ teaspoon freshly ground pepper
⅛ teaspoon coarse salt

1. In a steamer basket set over a saucepan of simmering water, steam the zucchini until just tender, about 3 minutes. Rinse with cold water and drain well. Pat dry with paper towels.
2. In a medium bowl, combine the scallions, mint, olive oil, lemon zest, lemon juice, pepper, and salt. Add the steamed zucchini and toss to coat. Serve with the pasta.—JEAN GALTON

HEIRLOOM TOMATO SALAD

The beauty of this simple salad from Mark's Place in North Miami, Florida, lies in the colors and sizes of the tomatoes used. There are some wonderful organic heirloom varieties you can grow yourself or buy at farmers' markets. Look for prime specimens, such as Brandywine, Lemon Boy, Green Zebra, Tigrella, Peach, Pink Grapefruit, and Yellow Pear.

6 SERVINGS

¼ cup balsamic vinegar
1 teaspoon whole black peppercorns
2½ pounds assorted tomatoes
1 large bunch of arugula, large stems discarded
⅓ cup extra-virgin olive oil
1 tablespoon finely chopped fresh marjoram leaves
Coarse sea salt
1½-ounce chunk of Parmesan cheese

1. In a small nonreactive saucepan, boil the vinegar over moderate heat until reduced by half, about 4 minutes. Set aside to cool.
2. In a small dry skillet, roast the peppercorns over moderate heat,

shaking the pan once or twice, until fragrant, about 2 minutes. Transfer the peppercorns to a mortar and crush coarsely.

3. Cut the tomatoes in slices, chunks, and wedges, depending on their size, and arrange on six large salad plates. Surround with the arugula leaves. Drizzle the oil over the salads and sprinkle the marjoram and crushed black pepper on top. Season the salads with coarse sea salt.

4. Using a vegetable peeler, shave the Parmesan cheese over the salads. Drizzle the balsamic vinegar around the edge of each plate and serve.—MARK MILITELLO

BUYING ORGANIC SEEDS

Amateur gardeners with a passion for the environment should know about Seeds of Change, a company that sells only organically grown seeds. Its mail-order catalog features hundreds of vegetables, fruits, and herbs, from arugula and basil to watermelon and zucchini. In an effort to promote biological diversity and prevent plant extinction, Seeds of Change also sells dozens of unusual heirloom varieties that have been carefully preserved by generations of gardeners. One such offering is the yellow intermediate mangel beet, which can weigh up to 10 pounds. For a catalog, call 800-957-3337, or write to Seeds of Change (P.O. Box 15700, Santa Fe, NM 87506).

CHERRY TOMATO SALAD

4 SERVINGS

- 2 tablespoons drained capers
- 1 tablespoon olive oil
- 1 tablespoon wine vinegar
- 1 medium garlic clove, minced
- 1 pint cherry tomatoes, halved
- Salt and freshly ground pepper

In a bowl, combine the capers, olive oil, wine vinegar, and garlic. Add the tomatoes and toss well. Season with salt and pepper and serve.—SARAH FRITSCHNER

RADISH SALAD

Cut about one inch off the tops of firm, nicely shaped yellow bell peppers. Remove the cores, seeds, and inner ribs. Cut red radishes into small dice, then toss with cider vinegar, safflower oil, sugar, sea salt, and freshly ground black pepper to taste. Spoon the salad into the bell peppers.—GENE MEYER

CUCUMBER SALAD

Prepare orange bell peppers as described in the Radish Salad, above. Halve European cucumbers lengthwise and scoop out the seeds. Cut the cucumbers into small dice and toss them with balsamic vinegar, olive oil, feta cheese, chopped oregano, salt, and freshly ground black pepper to taste. Spoon the salad into the bell peppers.—GENE MEYER

Radish Salad and Cucumber Salad

LEMONY CUCUMBER SALAD WITH BELL PEPPERS

4 SERVINGS

- 2 unpeeled European seedless cucumbers, halved lengthwise and sliced crosswise ¼ inch thick
- 1 medium red bell pepper, cut into 1-by-¼-inch matchsticks
- 1 medium yellow bell pepper, cut into 1-by-¼-inch matchsticks
- Salt
- 3 tablespoons fresh lemon juice
- 1 teaspoon Dijon mustard
- ⅓ cup olive oil
- 2 tablespoons minced fresh chives
- Freshly ground pepper

1. In a colander, toss the sliced cucumbers and bell pepper matchsticks with 1 teaspoon salt. Let stand at room temperature for 30 minutes to drain.

2. In a bowl, whisk the lemon juice with the mustard. Whisk in the oil and chives; season with salt and pepper.

3. Transfer the cucumbers and the bell peppers to a medium bowl. Add the lemon and mustard dressing and toss to combine.—BOB CHAMBERS

CUCUMBER, ONION AND PURSLANE SALAD

Purslane, a succulent weed, is sold at many farmers' markets. It grows along the ground and is often sandy, so be sure to wash it in a few changes of water. Dry, then break it into small clumps. You can eat the stems, which are as tender as the leaves. If the skin of the cucumber is unwaxed, taste a slice, and if it is sweet and tender, leave the skin on.

6 SERVINGS

3 small cucumbers, such as kirbys
2 very small white or red onions
1½ cups purslane or 1 cup watercress, ½ cup mâche, and 2 tablespoons mint leaves, washed thoroughly
2 tablespoons finely chopped fresh flat-leaf parsley
1 small garlic clove
Salt
2 teaspoons red wine vinegar
2 tablespoons extra-virgin olive oil

1. Halve the cucumbers lengthwise, scoop out and discard the seeds, and chop the flesh into bite-size pieces. Place in a bowl. Quarter the onions and thinly slice crosswise. Add to the cucumbers, along with the purslane and parsley. Refrigerate the salad while you proceed.

2. Using a mortar and pestle, mash the garlic with a few pinches of salt. Whisk in the vinegar and oil. Pour the dressing over the vegetables, toss well, and serve.—DEBORAH MADISON

Mixed Lettuces with Raspberry Vinaigrette

ONION SALAD WITH MINT AND POMEGRANATE

Throughout central Asia, pomegranates and sweet, mild yellow onions are used together in endlessly inventive ways; this pungent and refreshing dish, as much condiment as salad, is perfect with grilled beef or lamb.

MAKES ABOUT 2½ CUPS

1 large Spanish or Bermuda onion (1 pound), halved lengthwise and thinly sliced crosswise
1 tablespoon coarse salt
3 tablespoons fresh lemon juice
1 teaspoon pomegranate syrup
½ teaspoon sugar
Pinch of cayenne pepper
¼ cup finely chopped fresh mint leaves
½ cup fresh pomegranate seeds

1. In a medium bowl, toss the onion slices with the salt and let stand for 20 minutes. Rinse the onion in 2 changes of cold water and pat dry.

2. In a medium bowl, whisk together the lemon juice, pomegranate syrup, sugar, and cayenne. Add the onion and mint and toss well. Transfer the salad to a plate and garnish with the pomegranate seeds.—JEFFREY ALFORD AND NAOMI DUGUID

MIXED LETTUCES WITH RASPBERRY VINAIGRETTE

To give this salad a special kick, it's worth buying good-quality raspberry

vinegar, but you can substitute any vinegar you like. The edible flowers here add a whimsical, colorful touch and a peppery bite.

8 SERVINGS

- 3 tablespoons raspberry vinegar
- ¼ cup plus 2 tablespoons extra-virgin olive oil
- ½ teaspoon salt
- ¼ teaspoon freshly ground white pepper
- 2 bunches of arugula, large stems removed, leaves torn in half
- 1 medium head of butter lettuce, such as Boston or Bibb, torn into bite-size pieces
- 1 medium head of curly endive (frisée), torn into bite-size pieces
- 2 to 3 small heads of lamb's lettuce (mâche), large stems discarded
- 1 small head of radicchio, torn into bite-size pieces
- Nasturtiums or pansies, for garnish

1. Put the vinegar in a small bowl. Gradually whisk in the oil. Add the salt and pepper.
2. In a large bowl, combine all of the lettuces. Add the raspberry vinaigrette, toss, and arrange on salad plates. Garnish each salad with nasturtiums or pansies and serve.—JOAN AND DICK ERATH

MIXED GREEN CAESAR SALAD Q

4 SERVINGS

- ½ cup walnut halves (about 2 ounces)
- 1 large shallot, minced
- 1 large garlic clove, minced
- 2 anchovy fillets, mashed, plus ½ teaspoon anchovy oil
- 2 tablespoons fresh lemon juice
- 2 teaspoons Dijon mustard
- ½ teaspoon salt
- ¼ teaspoon freshly ground pepper
- ¼ cup olive oil
- 4 cups bite-size pieces of romaine lettuce (about ½ head)
- 4 cups bite-size pieces of arugula (about 2 bunches)
- ¼ cup freshly grated Parmesan cheese

1. Preheat the oven to 500°. Spread the walnuts on a baking sheet and toast in the oven for about 6 minutes, or until golden brown. Transfer to a plate and let cool.
2. In a small bowl, combine the shallot, garlic, anchovies and their oil, lemon juice, mustard, salt, and pepper. Using a fork, whisk in the olive oil until smooth.
3. Just before serving, combine the romaine and arugula in a large salad bowl. Pour the dressing over the greens and toss well. Add the toasted walnuts and the Parmesan cheese. Toss the salad again and serve.—MARCIA KIESEL

SALAD OF SMOKED TROUT, PINK GRAPEFRUIT AND RADICCHIO WITH WALNUTS

6 SERVINGS

- 1 cup cubed firm-textured white bread (½ inch)
- 1 garlic clove, minced
- 1 tablespoon olive oil or walnut oil
- 1 large pink grapefruit
- ⅓ cup heavy cream
- 2 tablespoons sherry vinegar
- Salt and freshly ground pepper
- ¾ pound radicchio, 12 large outer leaves reserved, the rest cut into ¼-inch strips
- One ¾-pound whole smoked trout—skinned, boned, and cut into ½-inch dice
- ½ cup coarsely chopped walnuts (about 2 ounces)
- 2 teaspoons chopped fresh coriander (cilantro), plus additional leaves for garnish
- 3 small scallions, white part only, thinly sliced crosswise

1. Preheat the oven to 350°. On a baking sheet, toss the bread cubes with the garlic and olive oil. Toast for about 7 minutes, or until golden.
2. Using a sharp stainless steel knife, peel the grapefruit, removing all the bitter white pith. Working over a bowl, cut in between the membranes to release the sections. Set aside 6 sections; cut the remaining sections into ½-inch pieces. ➤

VINAIGRETTE

Q: Is there any way to quickly emulsify a vinaigrette that has separated?

A: Jean-Georges Vongerichten, chef and co-owner of JoJo and Vong in New York City, mixes a tablespoon of boiling water into the dressing to emulsify it (this will keep for about five minutes).—ARLENE FELTMAN-SAILHAC

Salad of Smoked Trout, Pink Grapefruit and Radicchio with Walnuts

3. In a small bowl, combine the heavy cream and sherry vinegar. Season with salt and pepper. In a large bowl, toss the radicchio strips with three quarters of the dressing. Add the smoked trout, walnuts, chopped coriander, scallions, and the cut-up grapefruit sections. Season with salt and pepper and toss well.

4. On each of 6 plates, arrange 2 radicchio leaves. Mound the salad in the center. Garnish with the croutons, coriander leaves, and whole grapefruit sections. Drizzle with the remaining dressing and serve.—DANIEL BOULUD

PAN-SEARED MUSHROOMS ON ARUGULA WITH LEMON-SOY VINAIGRETTE

4 SERVINGS

LEMON-SOY VINAIGRETTE:

- 2 tablespoons fresh lemon juice
- 2 tablespoons olive oil
- 1 tablespoon soy sauce
- ¼ teaspoon finely grated lemon zest
- ¼ teaspoon salt

MUSHROOMS AND ARUGULA:

- 1 pound mixed white, shiitake, and oyster mushrooms, tough stems discarded, caps sliced ¼ inch thick
- 2 tablespoons fresh lemon juice
- 1 tablespoon olive oil
- Salt and freshly ground pepper
- 1 tablespoon soy sauce
- 2 bunches arugula, stemmed, leaves torn into large pieces (8 packed cups)

1. Make the vinaigrette: In a small bowl, whisk all the ingredients until blended. Set aside for up to 4 hours.

2. Prepare the mushrooms and arugula: Toss the mushrooms with 1 tablespoon of the lemon juice. Heat the olive oil in a large nonreactive skillet over moderately high heat. When very hot, add the mushrooms in an even layer and season with salt and pepper. Cook undisturbed until all the mushroom juices have evaporated and the mushrooms are browned on the underside, about 4 minutes. Stir and continue cooking until well browned, 4 minutes longer.

3. Add the soy sauce and stir to coat the mushrooms. Add 1 tablespoon of water and stir until the mushrooms are dry again. Add the remaining 1 tablespoon lemon juice and cook, stirring, until evaporated.

4. In a large bowl, toss the arugula with 1 tablespoon of the vinaigrette. Arrange the salad on plates and scatter the mushrooms on top.—MARCIA KIESEL

CABBAGE, CAULIFLOWER AND CARROT SLAW

Here's a hearty version of coleslaw.

MAKES ABOUT 5 CUPS

- 1¼ pounds cabbage, shredded (4 cups)
- ¼ head of cauliflower, broken into ½-inch florets
- ½ cup finely diced red bell pepper
- 1 medium carrot, peeled and shredded on the large holes of a grater
- 1 small zucchini, finely diced
- 1 small red onion, finely chopped
- ¼ cup finely chopped fresh flat-leaf parsley
- ¼ cup rice vinegar or tarragon vinegar
- ½ tablespoon salt
- ½ teaspoon freshly ground black pepper

½ teaspoon dried oregano, crushed
¼ cup olive oil

In a salad bowl, toss all of the vegetables and the parsley. In a small bowl, whisk together the vinegar, salt, black pepper, and oregano. Gradually whisk in the olive oil until incorporated. Pour the dressing over the slaw and toss. Cover and refrigerate overnight. Toss the salad again before serving.—KAREN LEE

RED CABBAGE SLAW WITH TURKEY CRACKLINGS

8 SERVINGS

Reserved skin from a 10-pound turkey
¼ cup olive oil
1 large head of red cabbage—halved, cored, and finely shredded
2 bunches of scallions, cut diagonally into 1-inch pieces
¼ cup balsamic vinegar
1 tablespoon honey
1 teaspoon fresh lemon juice
Coarse salt and freshly ground pepper
4 heads of Bibb lettuce, separated into leaves

1. In a large enameled cast-iron casserole, cook the turkey skin over moderately low heat, turning occasionally, until ¼ cup of fat has been rendered and the skin is browned and crisp, about 15 minutes. Using a slotted spoon, transfer the skin to paper towels to drain, then coarsely chop it.

2. Add the oil to the rendered fat in the casserole and raise the heat to high. Add the cabbage and cook, stirring occasionally, until wilted, about 4 minutes. Add the scallions, vinegar, honey, and lemon juice, and toss for 30 seconds; season with coarse salt and pepper. (MAKE AHEAD: The recipe can be prepared to this point up to 1 day ahead; cover and refrigerate the cabbage and cracklings separately. Reheat both on the stove before serving.)

3. Arrange the lettuce leaves on a large platter and spoon the red cabbage slaw on top. Sprinkle with the turkey cracklings and serve.—SANFORD D'AMATO

VIETNAMESE CABBAGE SLAW WITH CHICKEN AND GRAPEFRUIT

This salad is traditionally made with pomelos—a pear-shaped, yellow citrus fruit, also known as Chinese grapefruit, that has a sweeter and drier pulp than other citrus fruits. The oil-free dressing uses Vietnamese fish sauce, which is more delicate than the Thai version.

6 SERVINGS

1 large whole chicken breast on the bone
1 teaspoon salt
2 large pink grapefruits
2 serrano chiles, preferably red, seeded and minced
1 large garlic clove, minced
1 tablespoon sugar
3½ tablespoons Vietnamese fish sauce (*nuoc mam*)
3 tablespoons fresh lime juice
2 large carrots, cut into thin 2-inch-long julienne strips
½ pound red cabbage, finely shredded
½ pound green cabbage, finely shredded
⅓ cup coarsely chopped fresh mint plus whole sprigs for garnish
¼ cup coarsely chopped fresh coriander (cilantro) plus whole sprigs for garnish
2 tablespoons sesame seeds, toasted (see "How to Toast Sesame Seeds," p. 161)
2 tablespoons finely chopped dry-roasted peanuts
18 shrimp chips, fried (see Note)

1. In a large saucepan, cover the chicken with water and add the salt. Bring just to a boil over moderate heat, skimming the surface. Cover, lower the heat, and simmer the chicken until cooked through, about 15 minutes. Let cool in the broth.

2. Meanwhile, peel the grapefruits with a sharp knife, removing the bitter white pith. Cut between the membranes to release the sections. Using a fork, coarsely flake apart half of the

Vietnamese Cabbage Slaw with Chicken and Grapefruit

grapefruit sections; set aside the whole sections separately. (MAKE AHEAD: The recipe can be prepared to this point up to 6 hours ahead. Set the components aside separately at room temperature.)

3. Drain the chicken; reserve the broth for another use. Discard the skin and bone. Tear the chicken into ¼-inch-thick shreds.

4. In a mortar or mini-food processor, work the serranos, garlic, and sugar to a paste. Transfer to a small bowl, add the fish sauce and lime juice, and stir until the sugar is dissolved.

5. In a large bowl, toss together the carrots, cabbages, chicken, flaked grapefruit, chopped mint and coriander, and sesame seeds. Add the lime juice dressing, toss to combine, and let stand for 10 minutes to soften the vegetables.

6. To serve, transfer the salad to a large platter with tongs, shaking off the excess liquid. Garnish with the grapefruit sections, mint and coriander sprigs, and the chopped peanuts. Tuck the shrimp chips around the edge or serve separately.

NOTE: Shrimp chips, which look like puffy potato chips, act as spoons for the salad. They can be purchased dehydrated or already cooked. Dehydrated chips need only be fried briefly in about 2 inches of hot oil until puffed before serving.—JOYCE JUE

SPICY CABBAGE SALAD

8 SERVINGS

One 3½-pound green or Savoy cabbage, finely shredded
1 to 2 Scotch bonnet chiles, seeded and very thinly sliced lengthwise
3 medium tomatoes, cut into ½-inch dice
½ cup white wine vinegar
1 tablespoon olive oil
2 teaspoons salt
½ teaspoon freshly ground pepper

In a large bowl, combine the cabbage, chiles, and tomatoes. In a small bowl, combine the vinegar, olive oil, salt, and pepper. Pour the dressing over the salad, toss well, and serve.—PAUL CHUNG

CHINESE SUMMER NOODLE SALAD

6 SERVINGS

SESAME DRESSING:

¼ cup chunky peanut butter
1½ tablespoons sugar
1 teaspoon minced garlic
1 teaspoon finely grated fresh ginger
About ⅓ cup chicken stock or canned low-sodium broth or water
2½ tablespoons soy sauce
2 tablespoons peanut oil
1½ tablespoons red wine vinegar
1½ teaspoons Asian sesame oil
1 teaspoon hot chili oil
½ teaspoon salt

NOODLE SALAD:

1 medium red bell pepper
2 medium Japanese eggplants or 1 small standard eggplant
2 tablespoons peanut oil
2 ounces snow peas, strings removed
1 pound fresh thin Chinese egg noodles (see Note)
1½ teaspoons Asian sesame oil
1 cup shredded cooked chicken breast meat
1 medium scallion, thinly sliced
2 tablespoons sesame seeds, preferably black, toasted (see "How to Toast Sesame Seeds," p. 161)
Generous handful of fresh coriander (cilantro) leaves

1. Prepare the sesame dressing: Combine all of the ingredients in a bowl. If the dressing is too thick, stir in a little more stock.

2. Prepare the noodle salad: Light a grill or preheat the broiler. Roast the bell pepper on the grill or under the broiler, turning often, until the skin is charred all over. Transfer to a paper bag and let steam for 10 minutes. Peel the pepper and discard the stem, ribs, and seeds. Slice the pepper into ¼-inch strips.

3. Slice the eggplants ¼ inch thick and brush with the peanut oil. Grill or broil for 2 to 3 minutes per side, until the flesh is lightly charred. Transfer to a plate to cool. If using a standard eggplant, cut the slices into ¼-inch-thick strips.

4. In a large 4-quart saucepan of boiling salted water, blanch the snow peas until they turn bright green, about 30 seconds. Using a slotted spoon, transfer the snow peas to a bowl of cold water, then drain and pat dry.

5. Add the noodles to the boiling water and stir to separate the strands. Cook over moderate heat until tender, about 30 seconds. Drain and rinse with cold water; drain again. Transfer to a bowl and toss with the sesame oil. (MAKE AHEAD: The recipe can be prepared to this point up to 4 hours ahead. Set the salad components aside separately at room temperature.)

6. Add half of the shredded chicken, the scallion, snow peas, and half of the sesame seeds to the noodles. Pour on the dressing and toss to combine. Mound the noodles in a shallow serving bowl and scatter the eggplant slices, red pepper strips, and the remaining chicken over the top. Sprinkle with the remaining sesame seeds and the coriander and serve.

NOTE: You can substitute ¾ pound dried thin Chinese egg noodles or thin pasta such as angel hair for the fresh noodles. The cooking time will be about 3 minutes.—JOYCE JUE

Chinese Summer Noodle Salad

SUMMER GARDEN COUSCOUS SALAD Q

4 SERVINGS

Salt
1¾ cups couscous (one 10-ounce package)
⅔ cup fresh orange juice
2 tablespoons distilled white vinegar
2 teaspoons brown mustard
¾ teaspoon sugar
½ cup olive oil
3 scallions, thinly sliced
2 medium carrots, shredded
2 kirby cucumbers—halved, seeded, and finely diced
1 medium jalapeño chile, seeded and minced
Freshly ground black pepper

1. In a medium saucepan, combine 2¼ cups of water with a pinch of salt and bring to a boil over moderately high heat. Remove from the heat and stir in the couscous. Cover the saucepan and let stand for 5 minutes. Fluff the couscous with a fork and transfer to a large bowl to cool.

2. In a small bowl, whisk together the fresh orange juice, the distilled white vinegar, the brown mustard, and the sugar. Whisk in the olive oil in a fine stream. Stir in 1½ teaspoons salt. Pour the dressing over the couscous. Add the scallions, carrots, cucumbers, and jalapeño, and toss well. Season with salt and pepper.—TRACEY SEAMAN

SALMON AND POTATO SALAD WITH HORSERADISH DRESSING LF

You can ask your fishmonger to slice the salmon for you.

The horseradish dressing for this salad points to a simple but substantial dry white. Consider the 1993 Badia a Coltibuono Trappoline from Italy or the 1994 Bonny Doon Vineyard Big House White from California.

4 SERVINGS

1½ pounds small waxy potatoes, such as Yukon Gold
Salt
1 cup low-fat (1.5%) buttermilk
2 medium scallions, coarsely chopped
¼ cup prepared white horseradish, drained
Freshly ground pepper
1 large bunch of watercress, tough stems discarded
Olive oil cooking spray
¾-pound salmon fillet, cut into thin slices on the diagonal

Salmon and Potato Salad with Horseradish Dressing

LOW-FAT MENU

FRESH TOMATO SOUP WITH GUACAMOLE (P. 94)

SALMON AND POTATO SALAD WITH HORSERADISH DRESSING (P. 81)

DOUBLE DATE BARS (P. 368)

—MICHELE SCICOLONE

1. In a medium saucepan, cover the potatoes with cold water and add 1 teaspoon salt. Bring to a boil over moderately high heat and cook until tender, about 20 minutes. Drain and slice crosswise ¼ inch thick.

2. In a small bowl, stir together the buttermilk, scallions, and horseradish; season with salt and pepper.

3. In a bowl, combine the potatoes and watercress. Add half of the horseradish dressing and toss to coat. Arrange the salad on 4 large plates and drizzle with the remaining dressing.

4. Lightly coat a grill pan or large nonstick skillet with the olive oil cooking spray and heat. Season the salmon with salt and pepper, add it to the skillet, and sear over high heat, without turning, until browned on the bottom, about 30 seconds. Arrange the salmon slices, browned sides up, on the salad and serve immediately.—MICHELE SCICOLONE

ROASTED ARTICHOKE AND POTATO SALAD WITH GARLIC VINAIGRETTE

6 SERVINGS

¾ pound small red potatoes, quartered
Salt
8 fresh artichoke hearts (see "Preparing Artichoke Hearts," opposite page), sliced ¼ inch thick
3 medium red bell peppers
2 small red onions, cut lengthwise into eighths with root ends intact
1 medium head of garlic, separated into unpeeled cloves
½ cup extra-virgin olive oil
Freshly ground black pepper
1 medium tomato, seeded and coarsely chopped
2 tablespoons balsamic vinegar
1 teaspoon finely chopped fresh tarragon
2 bunches of arugula, large stems discarded

1. Preheat the oven to 350°. In a medium saucepan, cover the potatoes with water, add salt, and bring the water to a boil over moderate heat. Boil for 1 minute, then drain well.

2. Drain the artichoke slices well. In a large nonreactive roasting pan, combine the artichokes with the potatoes, bell peppers, onions, and garlic. Toss with ¼ cup of the oil, 1 teaspoon salt, and ½ teaspoon black pepper. Roast for about 30 minutes, or until the garlic is softened. Transfer the garlic to a plate, stir the remaining vegetables, and continue roasting for 20 to 25 minutes longer, or until golden brown and tender.

3. Slip the garlic cloves from their skins. In a blender, puree the garlic and tomato until smooth. Add the vinegar, ½ teaspoon salt, and ½ teaspoon black pepper, and blend until combined. With the machine on, add the remaining ¼ cup oil in a thin, steady stream until emulsified. (MAKE AHEAD: The recipe can be prepared to this point up to 1 day ahead; cover and refrigerate the vegetables and vinaigrette separately. Let both return to room temperature before proceeding.)

4. Peel the bell peppers, discarding the stems, seeds, and ribs, and cut into ⅜-inch strips. Put the roasted potatoes, artichokes, onions, and bell peppers in a large bowl. Add half the garlic vinaigrette and the tarragon and toss to coat.

5. In a medium bowl, toss the arugula with the remaining garlic vinaigrette and arrange on individual plates. Spoon the roasted vegetables on top and serve warm or at room temperature.—ANN CHANTAL ALTMAN

PREPARING ARTICHOKE HEARTS

Cut off the stem at the base of the artichoke. Remove the outer leaves from the artichoke by pulling them down so that they snap off. On a work surface, using a large sharp knife, cut the artichoke crosswise to remove the remaining leaves, leaving about a 1½ inch base. Using a small paring knife, trim the green leaf stubs from the bottom of the artichoke heart. Then trim the dark green leaf stubs from the top. Using a melon baller or teaspoon, remove the hairy choke from the artichoke bottom. Immediately transfer the artichoke hearts to a bowl of acidulated water.—ANN CHANTAL ALTMAN

CAPONATA RICE SALAD

4 MAIN-COURSE SERVINGS

Salt
1½ cups arborio or long-grain white rice
1 medium onion, cut into ¼-inch dice
¼ cup plus 2 tablespoons olive oil
1 small eggplant, cut into ½-inch dice (2 cups)
2 medium garlic cloves, minced
3 tablespoons balsamic vinegar
3 large ripe tomatoes, seeded and cut into ½-inch dice (2 cups)
2 tablespoons drained capers
¼ cup pitted green olives, coarsely chopped
¼ cup finely chopped mixed fresh herbs, such as basil, marjoram, mint, oregano, and parsley
Freshly ground pepper

1. In a large saucepan, bring 10 cups of water to a boil. Stir in 1 tablespoon salt. Add the rice and cook uncovered over moderate heat until al dente, about 15 minutes. Drain in a colander, rinse with cold water, and drain again.

2. Meanwhile, in a large nonreactive skillet, cook the onion in 2 tablespoons of the olive oil over moderately high heat until translucent, about 5 minutes. Add the eggplant, garlic, and another tablespoon of olive oil, and cook until the eggplant is soft, about 7 minutes.

3. In a large bowl, toss the rice with the remaining 3 tablespoons olive oil and the balsamic vinegar. Add the eggplant, tomatoes, capers, olives, and fresh herbs, and toss. Season with salt and pepper. Let stand for at least 20 minutes before serving. (MAKE AHEAD: The salad can be made 1 day ahead and refrigerated, covered. Serve at room temperature.)—ERICA DE MANE

RICE SALAD WITH ASPARAGUS AND PROSCIUTTO

Try an herbal California Sauvignon Blanc, such as the 1992 Grgich Hills Fumé Blanc or the 1993 Robert Mondavi Reserve Fumé Blanc.

6 SERVINGS

Salt
1½ cups arborio or long-grain white rice
12 thin asparagus
¼ cup plus 2 tablespoons olive oil
¼ cup finely chopped fresh basil
3 tablespoons red wine vinegar
3 tablespoons freshly grated Parmesan cheese
1 garlic clove, minced
2 small red bell peppers, cut into ¼-inch dice

Roasted Artichoke and Potato Salad with Garlic Vinaigrette

REMOVING PITS FROM OLIVES

Q: What's an easy way to remove pits from a large quantity of olives?

A: Terrance Brennan, chef and owner of Picholine in New York City, places the olives inside a folded kitchen towel and hits them gently with a mallet. The pits pop right out.

Matthew Kenney, chef and owner of Matthew's in New York City, suggests that those of us who don't keep mallets in the kitchen simply put the olives in a folded kitchen towel and press down hard with the heel of the hand to loosen the olive pits.—ARLENE FELTMAN-SAILHAC

Rice Salad with Asparagus and Prosciutto

½ pound prosciutto, cut into ¼-inch dice
Freshly ground black pepper

1. In a large saucepan, bring 10 cups of water to a boil. Stir in 1 tablespoon salt. Add the rice and cook uncovered over moderate heat until al dente, about 15 minutes. Drain in a colander, rinse with cold water, and drain again. Place the cooked rice in a large bowl.
2. In a large skillet of boiling salted water, cook the asparagus until crisp-tender, about 5 minutes. Drain in a colander, rinse with cold water, and drain. Cut into ½-inch lengths.
3. Dress the cooked rice with the olive oil, fresh basil, red wine vinegar, Parmesan, and garlic, and toss well. Add the asparagus, red bell peppers, and prosciutto, and toss. Season with salt and black pepper. Let stand for at least 20 minutes before serving. (MAKE AHEAD: The salad can be made 1 day ahead and refrigerated, covered. Serve at room temperature.) —ERICA DE MANE

CORN SALAD WITH ROASTED BELL PEPPER

Serve this side dish, from the vegetarian Greens Restaurant in San Francisco, with slices of ripe tomato drizzled with olive oil or grilled red onions and Japanese eggplant brushed with balsamic vinegar.

🍷 *California Sauvignon Blanc echoes the flavor of the bell pepper, making the wine an obvious choice to underscore this relatively mild salad. Look for lively, crisp examples, such as the 1993 Quivira or the 1993 Montevina Fumé Blanc.*

4 TO 6 SERVINGS

5 ears of fresh corn, shucked
1 medium red bell pepper
1 tablespoon mild olive oil
Salt and freshly ground black pepper
½ small red onion, cut into ¼-inch dice (about ½ cup)
2 teaspoons fresh lemon juice
2 to 3 teaspoons Champagne vinegar
2 tablespoons coarsely chopped fresh basil

1. Using a thin sharp knife, slice the corn kernels from each ear into a bowl, scraping the cobs with the back of the knife to extract any juices.
2. Roast the red pepper directly over a gas flame or under a broiler, turning often, until charred all over. Transfer the pepper to a paper bag and set aside to steam for 10 minutes. Using a small sharp knife, scrape off the blackened skin and remove the stem, seeds, and ribs. Cut the pepper into thin strips.
3. In a large skillet, heat the olive oil. Add the corn, ¼ teaspoon of salt, and a few pinches of black pepper, and cook over moderate heat for 5 minutes. Add the onion and cook until the onion is soft and the corn is tender, about 3 minutes. If the corn is still crisp, add up to ¼ cup of water to the skillet, cover, and cook until tender, 2 to 10 minutes longer, depending on the freshness of the corn.
4. Transfer the cooked corn and red onion to a bowl. Stir in the lemon juice, red bell pepper, ¼ teaspoon salt, a few pinches of black pepper, and 2 teaspoons of the vinegar. Cool to room

temperature, then add the basil and toss gently but thoroughly. Season with salt and pepper and, if desired, another teaspoon of vinegar.—ANNIE SOMERVILLE

CORN AND BLACK BEAN SALAD

The corn here isn't cooked, so be sure to choose tender young ears.

4 TO 6 SERVINGS

2½ cups fresh corn kernels (from 3 to 4 medium ears)
2 cups cooked black beans, rinsed and drained
½ cup minced red onion
⅓ cup finely diced red bell pepper
1 large jalapeño chile, finely chopped
3 tablespoons vegetable oil
2 tablespoons fresh lime juice
¼ cup finely chopped fresh coriander
Salt
Few drops of Tabasco (optional)

In a large bowl, combine the corn kernels, black beans, red onion, bell pepper, and jalapeño. Stir in the vegetable oil and lime juice. Add the cilantro, 1 teaspoon salt, and the Tabasco, and toss well. Cover and refrigerate for 1 to 2 hours. Season with more salt and Tabasco, if necessary, and serve chilled or at room temperature.—JUDITH SUTTON

BLACK BEAN SALAD LF

4 SERVINGS

1½ cups cooked black beans, rinsed if canned
½ pound jicama, peeled and finely diced
1 medium tomato, seeded and finely diced
1 medium cucumber—peeled, seeded, and finely diced
1 serrano chile, finely chopped
1 tablespoon minced onion
2 tablespoons fresh lime juice
2 teaspoons olive oil
1 teaspoon unseasoned rice vinegar
½ teaspoon finely grated lime zest
½ teaspoon ground cumin
Salt and freshly ground pepper
Pale center leaves from 1 large head of romaine lettuce
1 tablespoon coarsely chopped cilantro (fresh coriander) plus 4 sprigs for serving
1 tablespoon finely chopped fresh mint

1. In a large bowl, combine the beans, jicama, tomato, cucumber, serrano chile, and onion. In a small bowl, whisk together the lime juice, olive oil, vinegar, lime zest, and cumin. Toss the dressing with the beans and season with salt and pepper.
2. Arrange the romaine leaves on 4 plates. Stir the chopped cilantro and mint into the beans, mound the bean salad on top of the romaine leaves, and garnish the salads with the sprigs of cilantro.—MARGE POORE

CHICKPEA SALAD WITH CUMIN

The chickpeas require overnight soaking so plan accordingly.

6 SERVINGS

1⅓ cups dried chickpeas (about 9 ounces), rinsed and picked over (see Note)
Salt
4 medium scallions, finely chopped
1 large ripe tomato—peeled, seeded, and finely chopped
6 Calamata olives, pitted and finely chopped
1 garlic clove, minced
2 tablespoons olive oil
1½ tablespoons fresh lemon juice
½ teaspoon ground cumin
¼ teaspoon freshly ground black pepper
Pinch of cayenne pepper

1. In a large bowl, cover the dried chickpeas with water. Stir in 1 teaspoon of salt and let soak overnight. Drain the chickpeas and transfer to a large saucepan. Add water to cover by 2 inches and stir in 1 teaspoon salt. Bring the chickpeas to a boil over high heat, then lower the heat to moderate and simmer until tender, about 1 hour. Drain the chickpeas and discard any loose skins. ➤

MOROCCAN MAIL ORDER

If you don't have access to a Moroccan *souk*, or market, in your neighborhood, you can mail-order the dried chickpeas called for in the Chickpea Salad with Cumin, and other Moroccan ingredients, such as preserved lemons, phyllo dough, Moroccan olives, orange flower water, couscous, and good-quality spices like cinnamon and saffron, from Kalustyan in New York City; 212-685-3451. In addition to foodstuffs, Kalustyan sells cooking equipment such as *couscousiers* and tagine dishes.

Winter Salad of Black-Eyed Peas, Kidney Beans and Barley

2. In a serving bowl, combine the scallions, tomato, olives, garlic, olive oil, lemon juice, cumin, ¼ teaspoon salt, the black pepper, and cayenne. Add the chickpeas and toss well. Cover and refrigerate for at least 4 or up to 8 hours before serving.

NOTE: Canned chickpeas can be used in this salad, but nothing compares with the flavor and texture of freshly cooked chickpeas. Good-quality dried chickpeas are available at Middle Eastern specialty food stores and by mail order (see "Moroccan Mail Order," p. 85).—FATIMA HAL

WINTER SALAD OF BLACK-EYED PEAS, KIDNEY BEANS AND BARLEY

This festive-looking salad is full of contrasting soft and crunchy textures. A generous quantity of parsley gives it a fresh, clean taste. The dressing departs from the traditional 3 to 1 ratio of oil to vinegar since the beans and grains are enlivened by adding a little more acid.

MAKES 6 SIDE-DISH SERVINGS

- ¾ cup dried red kidney beans, picked over and rinsed well, or one 16-ounce can of red kidney beans, drained and rinsed well
- ½ cup dried or 1 cup frozen thawed black-eyed peas
- ½ cup pearl barley
- Salt
- 1½ cups fresh or frozen corn kernels
- ⅓ cup finely chopped fresh flat-leaf parsley
- 2 tablespoons finely chopped fresh coriander (cilantro)
- 2 tablespoons finely diced red onion
- ¼ to ½ teaspoon crushed red pepper
- 3 tablespoons olive oil
- Zest and juice of 2 large limes
- ½ teaspoon ground cumin

1. If using dried kidney beans and black-eyed peas, place in 2 separate large bowls, cover with water, and let soak for at least 6 hours or overnight. (Alternatively, in 2 medium saucepans, cover the beans with water and boil over moderately high heat for 2 minutes. Remove from the heat, cover, and let soak for 1 hour.) Drain off the soaking liquid and rinse the beans.

2. In 2 medium saucepans, cover the dried beans and peas with 2 to 3 inches of water. Cover the pans and simmer over moderate heat until tender but not mushy, 50 to 60 minutes for the kidney beans and 40 to 45 minutes for the black-eyed peas. Skim the foam off the surface as necessary; taste the beans often to test for doneness. Let cool slightly in their liquid, then drain well and transfer to a serving bowl. (Alternatively, if you are using canned kidney beans and frozen thawed black-eyed peas, combine them in a bowl.)

3. Meanwhile, in a saucepan, simmer the barley with 2 cups of water and ½ teaspoon of salt until tender but chewy, about 40 minutes. Drain well and add to the beans and peas.

4. In the same saucepan, cook the corn in a little water until crisp-tender, about 5 minutes for fresh corn and 2 minutes for frozen. Drain well and add to the beans, peas, and barley. (MAKE AHEAD: The recipe can be made to this point up to 2 days ahead; cover and refrigerate.) Stir in the parsley, fresh coriander, onion, and crushed red pepper.

5. In a small bowl, whisk together the oil, ½ teaspoon salt, lime zest, lime juice, and cumin. Pour over the salad, toss gently, and serve.—DEBORAH MADISON

CHILLED FRESH ORANGES, MANGOES AND JICAMA LF

6 SERVINGS

- 2 medium mangoes
- 6 medium navel oranges
- 1 small jicama, peeled and cut into ¾-inch dice
- 1 tablespoon coarsely chopped fresh cilantro
- ½ teaspoon pure moderately hot red chile powder, such as japone or New Mexico

1. Working with 1 mango at a time, peel half the mango and cut ¾-inch lengthwise slices down to the pit. Cut crosswise to release the slices. Repeat with the other side of the mango, then cut all the slices into ¾-inch dice. Transfer to a large bowl.

2. Using a sharp paring knife, peel the navel oranges, removing all the bitter white pith. Working over the bowl, cut between the membranes to release the orange sections. Add them to the mango slices with the diced jicama and chopped cilantro. Cover and refrigerate up to 4 hours. Sprinkle with the chile powder and serve ice cold.—CHARLES WILEY

CHAPTER 5

SOUPS

Maringouin Squash Bisque

MARINGOUIN SQUASH BISQUE

Maringouin is a small community in Louisiana that's known for its farm-fresh vegetables.

6 SERVINGS

- 2 medium onions, coarsely chopped
- 2 tablespoons unsalted butter
- 6 cups chicken stock or canned low-sodium broth
- 4 medium yellow summer squash, thinly sliced
- 2 small carrots, thinly sliced
- 2 medium potatoes, cut into ½-inch dice
- 2 tablespoons chopped fresh dill
- 2 teaspoons Worcestershire sauce
- Dash of Tabasco
- Salt and pepper
- ½ pound smoked or boiled shrimp

In a large saucepan, sauté the onions in the butter over moderately high heat until translucent. Add the chicken stock, squash, carrots, and potatoes, and cook until the vegetables are just tender, about 10 minutes. Let cool, then puree in a blender. Return the bisque to the saucepan and add the dill, the Worcestershire sauce, the Tabasco, and salt and pepper. Serve warm or at room temperature, garnished with the shrimp.—ANGELE PARLANGE

FRESH CORN SOUP WITH CHIVES

4 TO 6 SERVINGS

- 2 tablespoons unsalted butter
- 2 garlic cloves, minced
- 7 medium ears of corn, grated (about 3 cups)
- 2½ cups milk
- 1¼ teaspoons salt
- ½ teaspoon freshly ground pepper
- ¼ cup minced fresh chives
- 1 small tomato—peeled, seeded, and cut into ⅓-inch dice

1. Melt the unsalted butter in a large saucepan. Add the minced garlic and cook over moderately low heat, stirring occasionally, until softened, 2 to 3 minutes. Stir in the grated corn with all its juices, the milk, salt, and pepper, and raise the heat to moderate. Bring to a simmer and cook, stirring occasionally, until the soup thickens, 12 to 15 minutes.

2. Stir half of the chives into the soup and simmer for 1 minute. Ladle into shallow bowls and garnish with the diced tomato and the remaining chives—JUDITH SUTTON

FARMERS' MARKET CORN SOUP

Fresh sweet summer corn makes all the difference in this rich soup, from Odessa Piper of L'Etoile in Madison, Wisconsin.

8 SERVINGS

- 12 ears of fresh corn, shucked
- 3 tablespoons unsalted butter
- 2 large onions, thinly sliced
- 1 tablespoon sugar
- Coarse salt and freshly ground white pepper

Fresh Corn Soup with Chives

- ¼ teaspoon crushed red pepper
- 3 cups heavy cream
- 3 cups milk
- 2 tablespoons minced fresh herbs, such as basil, chives, and dill

1. Using a sharp knife, slice the kernels from each ear of corn into a bowl, scraping the cobs with the back of the knife to extract any juices.
2. In a large, heavy saucepan or dutch oven, melt the butter over moderate heat. Add the onions, sugar, 1 tablespoon coarse salt, ½ teaspoon white pepper, and the crushed red pepper, and cook, stirring occasionally, until the onions are softened and most of the moisture has evaporated, about 20 minutes.
3. Add the corn and its juices, the cream, and the milk, and bring to a boil. Simmer over moderately low heat until the corn is tender, about 20 minutes. Let cool to room temperature.
4. Puree the soup in a food processor, then strain it through a medium or coarse sieve. Season with coarse salt and white pepper. (MAKE AHEAD: The soup can be made to this point up to 1 day ahead; cover and refrigerate. To serve, rewarm the soup over low heat.) Ladle the soup into bowls and garnish with the minced fresh herbs.—ODESSA PIPER

Cool Red Pepper Soup with Cucumber Relish

COOL RED PEPPER SOUP WITH CUCUMBER RELISH

4 SERVINGS

- 6 medium red bell peppers
- 1 tablespoon olive oil
- 1 medium yellow onion, coarsely chopped
- 1 garlic clove, coarsely chopped
- 4 cups vegetable stock or canned vegetable broth, or 3 cups of water
- 1 teaspoon coriander seeds
- 1 teaspoon cumin seeds
- 1 teaspoon fennel seeds
- Salt and freshly ground black pepper
- 2 tablespoons finely chopped peeled and seeded cucumber
- 1 small jalapeño chile, seeded and finely chopped
- 1 tablespoon finely chopped red onion
- 2 tablespoons finely chopped fresh flat-leaf parsley
- 1½ tablespoons fresh lime juice
- ¼ cup fresh orange juice
- ¼ cup crème fraîche or sour cream
- 2 tablespoons red wine vinegar

1. Roast the bell peppers directly over a gas flame or under the broiler as close to the heat as possible until charred all over. Transfer to a large bowl, cover with plastic wrap, and let stand for 15 minutes. Working over a bowl to catch the juices, peel the peppers and discard the stems, ribs, and seeds. Coarsely chop the peppers; strain the juices and reserve.
2. Heat the olive oil in a medium saucepan. Add the yellow onion and garlic. Cook over moderately high heat, stirring, until translucent, about 3 minutes. Add the stock and the chopped red peppers and their juices and bring to a boil. Lower the heat and simmer for 20 minutes. Transfer to a blender and puree until smooth. Let cool.
3. In a small dry skillet, toast the coriander seeds, cumin seeds, and fennel seeds over high heat, shaking the pan, until fragrant, about 2 minutes. Transfer to a spice grinder or mortar and grind to a powder. Stir all but a pinch of the spice mixture into the soup and season with salt and black pepper. Cover the soup and refrigerate until chilled, at least 2 hours or up to 3 days.
4. In a small bowl, combine the cucumber, jalapeño, red onion, parsley, lime juice, and the reserved pinch of the spice mixture.
5. Just before serving, stir the orange juice, crème fraîche, and vinegar into the soup and season with salt and black pepper. Ladle the soup into bowls, garnish with the cucumber relish, and serve.—RICK ROBINSON

ROASTED GARLIC AND YELLOW PEPPER SOUP

A roasted garlic puree, swirled in at the end, accents this soup.

6 SERVINGS

- 30 medium garlic cloves, peeled (from 2 to 3 heads)

½ cup extra-virgin olive oil
1 teaspoon balsamic vinegar
Salt and freshly ground black pepper
3 pounds yellow bell peppers
2 large onions, thinly sliced
1½ cups half-and-half
Chive blossoms or chopped chives, for garnish

1. Preheat the oven to 350°. Put the garlic cloves in an ovenproof dish and pour the olive oil on top. Cover with foil and bake for about 35 minutes, or until very soft and golden. Reserve 10 of the garlic cloves and ¼ cup of the oil. Put the remaining garlic and oil in a blender. Add the balsamic vinegar and puree. Scrape the puree into a bowl and season with salt and black pepper.
2. Roast the yellow bell peppers directly over a gas flame or under the broiler as close to the heat as possible, turning often, until charred all over. Transfer the peppers to a large bowl, cover with plastic wrap, and set aside to steam for 5 minutes. Peel the peppers over a strainer set in a bowl and remove the stems, cores, seeds, and ribs. Cut the peppers into thin strips, reserving any accumulated pepper juices.
3. Heat the reserved ¼ cup garlic oil over moderate heat in a large nonreactive saucepan. Add the sliced onions and cook, stirring occasionally, until translucent, about 8 minutes. Add the roasted peppers and their juices, the reserved roasted garlic, the half-and-half, and 1 cup water. Bring to a simmer, cover, and cook over low heat until the vegetables are tender and the soup is slightly thickened, about 20 minutes.
4. Transfer the soup to the blender and puree, then pass it through a fine sieve. Season the soup with salt and black pepper. (MAKE AHEAD: The soup can be made to this point up to 5 hours ahead; cover and refrigerate the soup and the garlic puree separately.) To serve, ladle the soup into shallow bowls, swirl a rounded teaspoon of the garlic puree into each bowl, and scatter the chive blossoms or chopped chives on top.—ODESSA PIPER

ROASTED TOMATO-EGGPLANT SOUP

This soup, from John Ash of Fetzer Vineyards in Redwood Valley, California, makes the most of bountiful summer vegetables.

8 SERVINGS

1 large eggplant (1⅓ pounds), peeled and sliced crosswise ¼ inch thick
Coarse salt
½ cup loosely packed basil leaves
4 large garlic cloves
2 scallions, cut into 1-inch lengths
⅛ teaspoon crushed red pepper
½ cup olive oil
Roasted Tomato Stock (recipe follows)
2 medium red bell peppers, sliced lengthwise into thin strips
1 medium red onion, thinly sliced
2 ripe plum tomatoes—peeled, seeded, and chopped
Freshly ground black pepper
Shaved Parmesan or Asiago cheese and chopped fresh basil, for garnish

Roasted Tomato-Eggplant Soup

1. Preheat the oven to 375°. Layer the eggplant slices in a colander, sprinkling 1 tablespoon of coarse salt in between the layers. Let drain for 20 minutes. Rinse the slices and pat dry.
2. In a food processor, add the basil, the garlic, the scallions, and the crushed red pepper. Process until finely chopped, scraping down as necessary. With the machine on, incorporate 6 tablespoons of the oil in a fine stream.
3. On a large baking sheet, arrange the eggplant slices in a single layer, overlapping them slightly if necessary. Drizzle the basil oil on the eggplant; then spread with a rubber spatula to coat evenly. Bake the eggplant for 20 minutes, until soft and beginning to brown on the edges. Let cool, then coarsely chop.
4. Meanwhile, in a large nonreactive saucepan, warm the stock over moderately low heat, stirring occasionally.
5. In a medium nonreactive skillet, heat the remaining 2 tablespoons oil over moderately high heat. Add the bell peppers and

Sorrel Soup

onion and cook, stirring often, until the vegetables are softened and lightly browned, about 10 minutes. Transfer to a food processor along with the tomatoes and chopped eggplant. Process until pureed, gradually adding 2 cups of the warm stock. Stir the puree into the pot of warm stock and stir occasionally until heated through.

6. Season the soup with coarse salt and black pepper. (MAKE AHEAD: The soup can be made 1 day ahead; cover and refrigerate. Warm gently over low heat to serve. If you are making the soup ahead, there is no need to heat the stock in Step 2.) Serve hot, topped with cheese shavings and chopped basil.

Roasted Tomato Stock

MAKES 6 GENEROUS CUPS

- 2 pounds ripe plum tomatoes
- 2 tablespoons olive oil
- 2 medium carrots, coarsely chopped
- 1 medium red onion, coarsely chopped
- ½ cup chopped white mushrooms
- 2 small garlic cloves, smashed
- ¾ cup dry white wine
- 1 tablespoon tomato paste
- 1 bay leaf
- ½ teaspoon chopped fresh thyme
- ⅛ teaspoon fennel seeds
- Pinch of saffron threads (optional)

1. Preheat the oven to 400°. In a roasting pan, toss the plum tomatoes with 1 tablespoon of the olive oil to coat. Bake the tomatoes for about 45 minutes, until nicely charred.

2. Meanwhile, heat the remaining 1 tablespoon olive oil in a large nonreactive saucepan over moderate heat. Add the carrots, red onion, and mushrooms, and cook, stirring often, until slightly softened and beginning to color, about 5 minutes. Stir in the garlic and cook until fragrant, 1 minute longer. Stir in the white wine, tomato paste, bay leaf, thyme, fennel seeds, saffron, and roasted tomatoes. Pour in 6 cups of water and bring to a boil. Reduce the heat to moderately low, cover partially, and simmer for 30 minutes. Let cool completely. Then strain the stock, pressing on the solids with a large spoon to extract as much liquid as possible. (MAKE AHEAD: The tomato stock can be refrigerated for up to 3 days or frozen for up to 1 month.) —JOHN ASH

FRESH TOMATO SOUP WITH GUACAMOLE LF

4 SERVINGS

- ½ teaspoon cumin seeds
- 2 pounds ripe medium tomatoes, peeled and halved crosswise
- 1 medium onion, coarsely chopped

- 3 tablespoons minced fresh jalapeño chiles
- 1 tablespoon raw rice
- ½ teaspoon sugar or to taste
- Salt and freshly ground black pepper
- ½ small pitted Hass avocado (about 3 ounces)
- 1 large scallion, finely chopped
- 2 tablespoons finely chopped fresh cilantro plus whole leaves, for garnish
- 1 teaspoon fresh lime juice

1. In a small dry skillet, toast the cumin seeds over high heat, shaking the pan, until fragrant, about 1 minute. Transfer the seeds to a mortar or spice grinder and grind to a powder.

2. Squeeze the tomato halves into a sieve set over a nonreactive medium saucepan. Coarsely chop the tomato flesh and add it to the pan along with the strained tomato juices, the onion, one-third of the jalapeño, the rice, and the ground cumin. Cover and bring to a simmer over moderate heat. Reduce the heat to low and cook gently, stirring occasionally, until the rice is very soft, about 30 minutes. Let the tomato mixture cool slightly.

3. In a food processor or blender, puree the tomato mixture until smooth. Return the soup to the saucepan and add 2 cups of water. Season the soup with sugar, salt, and pepper, and bring to a simmer over moderate heat. Keep the soup warm.

4. In a small bowl, mash the avocado lightly with a fork. Stir in the chopped scallion and cilantro, the lime juice, and the remaining jalapeño. Season with salt and pepper.

5. Ladle the warm tomato soup into individual bowls. Dollop the guacamole in the center of each bowl, scatter the cilantro leaves around the soup, and serve.—MICHELE SCICOLONE

SORREL SOUP

Fresh sorrel is available in the spring at farmers' markets and specialty produce markets, although unfortunately not in most supermarkets. If you find beautiful fresh sorrel, use it quickly since it does not keep long. In this soup, which can be served hot or cold, I've balanced sorrel's characteristic tang with a touch of mace and complemented it with the addition of yogurt.

6 SERVINGS

- 2 tablespoons unsalted butter
- 4 medium leeks, white and tender green parts, thinly sliced
- 2 garlic cloves, minced
- 1½ pounds fresh sorrel, stemmed
- 4 cups Vegetable Stock (p. 299) or broth
- ½ teaspoon ground mace
- Salt and freshly ground pepper
- 1½ cups plain yogurt
- 3 tablespoons snipped fresh chives plus 6 whole chives with blossoms, for garnish

1. Melt the butter in a large nonreactive saucepan. Add the sliced leeks and the minced garlic and cook over moderately low heat, stirring occasionally, until wilted, about 10 minutes.

2. Add the sorrel and increase the heat to moderate. Cover and cook until wilted, 5 to 7 minutes. Add the Vegetable Stock and mace, season with salt and pepper, and bring to a boil. Reduce the heat slightly and simmer for 20 minutes. Let cool to room temperature.

3. In a food processor, puree the soup in batches, gradually adding 1 cup of the plain yogurt, until completely smooth. (MAKE AHEAD: The soup can be prepared to this point up to 1 day ahead. Cover and refrigerate. If serving hot, rewarm over moderately low heat.)

4. Serve the sorrel soup in shallow bowls, topped with a generous dollop of the remaining yogurt and a sprinkling of the snipped fresh chives. Lay a blossoming chive across the top if desired.—SHEILA LUKINS

DOUBLE MUSHROOM SOUP WITH SAUTEED SHIITAKES *LF*

This clear, elegant mushroom soup is enhanced with Marsala and garnished with sautéed sliced shiitakes. White mushrooms are used to flavor the stock and then are strained out.

4 SERVINGS

- 2 teaspoons olive oil
- 3 medium shallots, finely chopped
- ¼ cup dry Marsala
- 1 pound white mushrooms, finely chopped
- ½ pound fresh shiitake mushrooms, stems removed and reserved and caps thinly sliced
- 1 teaspoon minced fresh thyme or ⅓ teaspoon dried
- Salt and freshly ground pepper
- 2½ cups chicken stock or canned low-sodium broth, skimmed of fat
- 2 teaspoons minced fresh flat-leaf parsley

1. Heat 1 teaspoon of the olive oil in a heavy nonreactive medium saucepan. Add the shallots and cook over moderate heat, stirring, until slightly softened but not browned, about 4 minutes. Add the Marsala and cook just until evaporated, about 2 minutes.
2. Add the white mushrooms, the shiitake stems, the thyme, ½ teaspoon salt, and ¼ teaspoon pepper, and cook over moderately high heat for 10 minutes, stirring occasionally. Add the chicken stock and bring to a boil. Reduce the heat to low, cover, and simmer for 30 minutes. Strain the soup and return it to the saucepan; you should have about 3 cups. (MAKE AHEAD: The soup can be prepared up to 1 day ahead; cover and refrigerate. Rewarm the soup before serving.)

Wild Mushroom Soup

3. Heat the remaining 1 teaspoon oil in a large nonstick skillet. Add the sliced shiitake caps and season with salt and pepper. Cook over moderate heat, stirring occasionally, until softened and lightly browned, about 5 minutes.
4. Ladle the hot soup into shallow soup bowls and add the shiitakes. Garnish with the parsley and serve.—DIANA STURGIS

WILD MUSHROOM SOUP

Oyster, lobster, or enoki mushrooms are especially good substitutes for the ones used here.

6 SERVINGS

- ¾ pound assorted fresh wild mushrooms, such as yellow, red, and black chanterelles
- 2 quarts Chicken Stock (recipe follows) or canned low-sodium broth
- 1 teaspoon salt
- 8 medium scallions, coarsely chopped
- 2 ounces dried vermicelli
- 1 tomato—peeled, seeded, and cut into ½-inch pieces

1. Rinse the mushrooms thoroughly in cool water. Lift the mushrooms from the water and drain well. Cut the larger mushrooms into 1-inch pieces.
2. In a large pot, combine the mushrooms with the Chicken Stock and salt. Bring to a boil over high heat, then reduce the heat to low and simmer until the mushrooms are tender, 10 to 12 minutes.
3. Add the scallions and pasta to the soup and bring back to a boil over moderate heat. Cover and simmer until the pasta is tender, about 5 minutes. Stir in the tomato, ladle the soup into individual bowls, and serve at once.

Chicken Stock

Use chicken necks, backs, and gizzards as the base for the stock.

MAKES ABOUT 3 QUARTS

- 3 pounds chicken bones
- 1 large onion, quartered
- 12 whole cloves
- 4 bay leaves, preferably imported
- 1 tablespoon *herbes de Provence** or dried thyme
- 1 tablespoon soy sauce

*Available at specialty food stores

In a large stockpot, cover the chicken bones with 6 quarts of water. Bring to a boil over high heat. Lower the heat and simmer, skimming often, for 30 minutes. Add the onion, cloves, bay leaves, *herbes de Provence*, and soy sauce, and simmer for 2½ hours. Strain the stock into a large bowl. Let cool, then cover and refrigerate for up to 3 days. Skim off the fat before using. (MAKE AHEAD: The stock can be frozen for up to 1 month.) —JACQUES PEPIN

DUMPLING SQUASH SOUP WITH PANCETTA

The hollowed-out shells of individual squash, such as sweet dumpling, carnival, or delicata, make ideal bowls for serving the soup. Try to find squash that sit upright on the table, but if they don't, cut a thin slice from the bottom of each so that they are stable. Alternatively, you can make the soup with larger buttercup squash (about 3½ pounds) and serve it in traditional bowls.

Dumpling Squash Soup with Pancetta

8 SERVINGS

Eight 1¼- to 1½-pound sweet dumpling squash
6 ounces pancetta, finely chopped
2 medium onions, thinly sliced
Ham Stock (recipe follows)
Salt and freshly ground white pepper
2 tablespoons finely chopped fresh chives

1. Bring a large pot of salted water to a boil. Using a small sharp knife, carefully cut a 2-inch circle around the stems of the squash and pull them out. Discard any seeds that cling to the tops; reserve the tops. Scoop out and discard the remaining seeds inside the squash. Cook the squash and tops in the boiling water until the flesh is just tender when pierced, 10 to 15 minutes. Transfer the squash to a bowl of ice water to cool, then drain upside down on paper towels.

2. Carefully scoop the flesh from each squash into a bowl, leaving a ⅜-inch-thick shell; do not pierce the squash, or they will leak. You should have about 4 cups of squash flesh; if necessary, scoop the flesh from the tops.

3. In a large saucepan, cook the chopped pancetta over moderately high heat, stirring frequently, until lightly browned, about 5 minutes. Transfer the cooked pancetta to a plate.

4. Add the onions to the saucepan and cook over low heat, stirring occasionally, until transparent, about 6 minutes. Add the Ham Stock and bring to a boil over high heat. Stir in the squash flesh and bring back to a boil. Transfer the soup to a blender or food processor and puree until smooth. Strain into the saucepan and season with salt and white pepper. If necessary, stir in a little hot water to thin the soup; keep warm. (MAKE AHEAD: The recipe can be prepared to this point up to 2 days ahead; cover and refrigerate the soup, the squash shells, and the pancetta separately. Reheat the soup before serving.)

STOCK OPTIONS

Q: When making stock, does it matter whether I use cold or hot water? Is it better to start with a lot of water and reduce it or with a little and then add more as needed?

A: Many cookbooks claim that starting and replenishing a stock with small amounts of cold water produces a clearer stock because the meat proteins separate more readily into a skimmable scum. This is true at the beginning stage of the process, but after several hours or so of careful simmering and skimming, a hot-water stock is just as clear as a cold-water stock.

A more significant influence on clarity is gentle cooking. A violent boil churns proteins, fats, and water together. Whether you use hot water or cold, start with a small quantity, since boiling down drives off flavor as well as liquid.—HAROLD MCGEE

5. Preheat the oven to 350°. Arrange the squash shells on a baking sheet and spread the cooked pancetta alongside. Warm in the oven for about 5 minutes, or until the squash shells are heated through.

6. Set the squash shells on individual plates and ladle the hot soup into these "bowls." Garnish the soup with the pancetta and chives and serve with the squash lids on top of, or alongside, the shells.

Ham Stock

MAKES ABOUT 1 QUART

- 3 quarts chicken stock or canned low-sodium broth
- 2 pounds smoked ham hocks
- 2 medium celery ribs, coarsely chopped
- 1 medium onion, coarsely chopped
- 1 medium leek, coarsely chopped
- 5 fresh flat-leaf parsley sprigs
- 2 imported bay leaves
- 2 fresh thyme sprigs
- 1 tablespoon ground ginger
- ½ teaspoon crushed black peppercorns
- ¼ teaspoon cinnamon
- ¼ teaspoon mace

Combine all the ingredients in a stockpot and bring to a boil over moderately high heat. Lower the heat and simmer until reduced by two-thirds, about 1¼ hours. Strain the stock. Let cool. (MAKE AHEAD: The stock can be covered and refrigerated for up to 3 days or frozen for up to 1 month.) Skim off the fat before using.—SANFORD D'AMATO

JERUSALEM ARTICHOKE SOUP WITH GARLIC CROUTONS

12 SERVINGS

- 2½ pounds Jerusalem artichokes
- 2 tablespoons plus 2 teaspoons fresh lemon juice
- 2 tablespoons unsalted butter
- 1 large onion, coarsely chopped
- 3 garlic cloves—2 minced and 1 halved
- 2 quarts chicken stock or canned low-sodium broth
- Salt and freshly ground white pepper
- 1½ cups heavy cream
- Twelve ½-inch-thick diagonal slices from a sourdough baguette
- 1½ tablespoons vegetable oil
- 2 tablespoons minced fresh chives

1. Peel and thickly slice the Jerusalem artichokes and transfer to a large bowl of cold water mixed with 2 tablespoons of the lemon juice.

2. Melt the butter in a large enameled cast-iron casserole. Add the chopped onion and cook over moderately high heat, stirring often, until the onion is translucent, about 7 minutes. Add the minced garlic cloves and cook, stirring, for 1 minute longer. Drain the Jerusalem artichokes and add them to the casserole along with the chicken stock, ½ teaspoon salt, and ¼ teaspoon freshly ground white pepper. Bring the mixture to a boil over high heat. Lower the heat to moderate and simmer until the Jerusalem artichokes are very tender, about 35 minutes.

3. Working in batches, transfer the soup to a blender and puree until smooth. Return the soup to the casserole. (MAKE AHEAD: The soup can be refrigerated for up to 1 day.)

4. Bring the soup to a boil over high heat and cook until thickened slightly, about 5 minutes. Reduce the heat to low and stir in the heavy cream. Season the soup with the remaining 2 teaspoons lemon juice, salt, and white pepper; keep warm.

5. Meanwhile, preheat the oven to 350°. Brush the baguette slices with the vegetable oil and toast for about 5 minutes, or until lightly browned. Rub each crouton on one side with the halved garlic clove.

6. Ladle the soup into a tureen or shallow bowls. Garnish with the garlic croutons and minced chives.—PATRICK CLARK

Bean and Swiss Chard Soup

BEAN AND SWISS CHARD SOUP

This soup is excellent reheated. If you are making it in advance, put the pasta in only when you reheat it, or else it will become gluey.

4 SERVINGS

- ½ pound Swiss chard
- Salt
- 2 flat anchovy fillets
- ¼ teaspoon dried rosemary or a 2- to 3-inch fresh rosemary sprig
- ⅓ cup extra-virgin olive oil, plus more for drizzling
- 2 whole garlic cloves
- ½ cup dried white kidney beans, soaked and cooked (see "On Using Dried Beans," p. 102), or 2 cups canned cannellini beans, drained
- Freshly ground pepper
- ½ cup short tubular pasta (½ inch long or less)
- ¼ cup freshly grated Parmigiano-Reggiano cheese

1. Trim the ends of the Swiss chard stalks. Discard any bruised or discolored leaves. Wash the leaves in several changes of cold water until no trace of sand remains.

2. Put the Swiss chard leaves in a pot with ½ cup of water and at least 1 teaspoon of salt. Cover and bring to a boil over moderate heat. Cook until the chard is tender, 4 to 5 minutes. Drain the chard over a bowl, reserving all its cooking liquid. Coarsely chop the chard.

3. Mince the anchovy fillets with the dried rosemary. If using fresh rosemary, do not chop it.

4. Put the olive oil and the garlic cloves in a large heavy saucepan and turn on the heat to moderately high. Cook, stirring frequently with a wooden spoon, until the garlic becomes a pale gold color. Add the anchovies and rosemary, stir for a few seconds, and then discard the garlic. If using fresh rosemary, discard the sprig.

5. Put the Swiss chard in the pan and cook for 2 to 3 minutes, stirring to coat well with oil. Add the cooked white kidney beans and a liberal amount of salt and pepper. Cook for 2 to 3 minutes longer, stirring well. ➤

White Bean Soup with Spelt

6. Add the reserved cooking liquid from the Swiss chard and enough water to reach 3 inches from the top of the saucepan (about 4 cups). When the soup comes to a boil, add the pasta and cook, stirring occasionally, until it is al dente, about 8 minutes. Season the soup with salt and pepper to taste.

7. Turn off the heat and mix in the grated cheese. Ladle the soup into bowls and allow the heat of the soup to abate slightly. Serve with a few drops of olive oil drizzled on top.—MARCELLA HAZAN

WHITE BEAN SOUP WITH SPELT

Spelt, Kamut, or wheat berries can be used in this recipe. Spelt and Kamut (both ancient forms of wheat) are similar in taste and texture to wheat berries—all are buttery and chewy—but they are larger. Spelt is almost twice the size of wheat berries, and Kamut is three times the size. For the white beans, you can select everyday navy beans or larger varieties like cannellini or snowcaps. You can also vary the recipe in other ways. Corn kernels and millet make good additions to the soup.

🍷 *The earthy, savory flavors of cabbage and mushrooms can be attractively contrasted by a fruity Pinot Noir. Try a California bottling, such as the 1992 Robert Sinskey Vineyards or the 1992 Rodney Strong, or a red Burgundy, such as the 1992 Marquis d'Angerville Volnay.*

6 SERVINGS

- 1 cup dried white beans, picked over and rinsed well
- ½ cup spelt, Kamut, or wheat berries
- Boiling water
- 2 quarts Vegetable Stock (recipe follows)
- 1 bay leaf
- 4 garlic cloves—1 thinly sliced and 3 minced
- 3 tablespoons extra-virgin olive oil, plus more for drizzling
- ½ teaspoon thyme
- 1 large onion, finely diced
- 2 medium carrots, finely diced
- 1 medium celery rib, finely diced, plus 2 tablespoons chopped pale celery leaves
- Salt and freshly ground pepper
- 1 pound Savoy or green cabbage, finely shredded
- 2 tablespoons finely chopped fresh flat-leaf parsley or celery leaves
- Freshly grated Parmesan cheese, for serving

1. In a large bowl, cover the white beans with water and let soak for at least 6 hours or overnight. (Alternatively, in a large saucepan, cover the beans with water and boil over moderately high heat for 2 minutes. Remove from the heat, cover, and let soak for 1 hour.) Drain off the soaking liquid and rinse the beans well.

2. In a medium bowl, cover the spelt with boiling water and let soak for 1 hour. Drain.

3. In a large saucepan, combine the Vegetable Stock and spelt and bring to a boil. Cover and simmer for 30 minutes. Add the white beans, bay leaf, sliced garlic, 1 tablespoon of the oil, and ¼ teaspoon of the thyme. Simmer, covered, for 35 minutes.

4. Meanwhile, heat 2 tablespoons of the olive oil in a large nonreactive skillet. Add the onion, carrots, celery rib, celery leaves, minced garlic, and the remaining ¼ teaspoon thyme, and cook over moderate heat until the onion is completely soft, 12 to 15 minutes. Season with 2 teaspoons of salt and add to the spelt and bean mixture. Simmer, uncovered, until the beans are very tender, about 15 minutes longer. Season with salt and freshly ground pepper. Discard the bay leaf. (MAKE AHEAD: The soup can be made to this point up to 1 day ahead; cover and refrigerate.)

5. Just before serving, steam the shredded cabbage in a steamer basket over simmering water until tender and bright green, about 5 to 8 minutes.

6. Ladle the soup into bowls and sprinkle with the chopped parsley. Mound the steamed cabbage in the middle, drizzle lightly with olive oil, and dust with pepper. Sprinkle a little Parmesan cheese on top and serve at once.

Vegetable Stock

MAKES ABOUT 2 QUARTS

- 3 medium carrots, scrubbed and coarsely chopped
- 3 medium celery ribs with leaves, coarsely chopped
- 1 large all-purpose potato, scrubbed and coarsely chopped
- ¾ pound mushrooms, coarsely chopped
- 5 garlic cloves
- 1 bay leaf

In a large, heavy, nonreactive saucepan, combine all of the ingredients with 10 cups of cold water and bring to a boil over high heat. Reduce the heat to moderately low and simmer for 1 hour. Strain the stock. (MAKE AHEAD: The stock can be made up to 3 days ahead; cover and refrigerate. Or freeze for up to 1 week.) —DEBORAH MADISON

PASTA AND BEAN SOUP

Maltagliati Fatti in Casa con Fagioli di Lamon

The classic bean variety for pasta e fagioli *is the cranberry, or Scotch, bean, brightly marbled in white and pink or even deep red. When cooked, its flavor is unlike that of any other bean, subtly recalling that of chestnuts. Fresh cranberry beans can be frozen with great success, so when in season, buy a substantial quantity and freeze the shelled beans in tightly sealed sturdy plastic bags. Cook them exactly as you would fresh beans.*

When fresh cranberry beans are not available, dried ones are a satisfactory substitute; if necessary, you may even use canned.

I like to use homemade maltagliati pasta in this soup, but the dried tubular macaroni called for here works very well too.

12 SERVINGS

- ¼ cup chopped onion
- ½ cup extra-virgin olive oil
- ⅓ cup chopped carrot
- ⅓ cup chopped celery
- 5 pork ribs, a lean, meaty ham bone, or 4 little pork chops
- 1⅓ cups canned imported Italian plum tomatoes, cut up, with their juice, or peeled and chopped ripe fresh tomatoes
- 4 pounds fresh cranberry beans, shelled and rinsed, or 1 pound dried cranberry beans, soaked and cooked (see "On Using Dried Beans," left), or 6 cups drained and rinsed canned beans
- 6 cups homemade meat broth or 2 cups canned beef broth diluted with 4 cups water
- Salt and freshly ground black pepper
- ½ pound small tubular macaroni
- 2 tablespoons unsalted butter
- ¼ cup freshly grated Parmigiano-Reggiano cheese

1. In a large heavy pot, cook the onion in the olive oil over moderate heat, stirring, until very lightly colored. Stir in the carrot and celery to coat them with oil, then add the pork ribs. Cook for about 10 minutes, turning the meat and vegetables from time to time with a wooden spoon.

2. Add the tomatoes and their juice and simmer very gently for 10 minutes. If using fresh beans, add them now, stirring 2 or 3 times to coat them well. Add the broth. Cover the pot and adjust the heat so that the soup bubbles at a steady gentle boil; cook for 45 minutes to 1 hour, or until the beans are fully tender. (Alternatively, if using cooked dried beans or canned, cook the tomatoes for 20 minutes above. Add the beans, stirring them thoroughly to coat them well. Cook for 5 minutes, then add the broth, cover the pot, and bring the soup to a gentle boil.)

3. Scoop up about 1 cup of the beans and mash them through a food mill held over the pot. Season with salt and pepper and stir thoroughly. (MAKE AHEAD: Let the soup cool, then cover and refrigerate for up to 3 days. Reheat before proceeding.)

4. Check the soup for density. There should be enough liquid to cook the pasta. Add more homemade broth or water, if necessary, and bring to a boil. Remove the bones from the soup. Add the pasta and cook just until tender but firm to the bite. Swirl in the butter and the grated Parmigiano-Reggiano cheese.

5. Pour the pasta and bean soup into a tureen and allow it to settle for 10 minutes before serving. The soup tastes best when it is eaten warm rather than piping hot.—MARCELLA HAZAN

ON USING DRIED BEANS

Canned beans are conveniently ready to use, but reconstituted dried beans have a much better flavor and texture. To reconstitute, soak the dried beans for 6 hours or overnight in enough water to cover by at least 3 inches. Drain and rinse the beans, then put them in a pot and cover with at least 3 inches of water, cover, and bring to a boil over moderate heat. Reduce the heat and simmer the beans gently until tender, 45 minutes to 1 hour. To keep them from drying and cracking during cooking, salt the beans only when they are almost cooked through.—MARCELLA HAZAN

YOGURT-BARLEY SOUP

This thick soup made with yogurt, barley, and lots of parsley and mint is an Armenian dish called tanabour. *It is terrific served warm or cold.*

6 TO 8 SERVINGS

- 4 tablespoons unsalted butter
- 1 teaspoon olive oil
- 1 large yellow onion, finely chopped (1 cup)
- ¾ cup barley, soaked overnight in 1 quart water
- 4 to 5 cups chicken stock or canned low-sodium broth
- 3 cups plain yogurt
- 1 large egg
- ¾ cup finely chopped fresh flat-leaf parsley
- ½ cup finely chopped fresh mint
- Salt

1. In a large, heavy, nonreactive saucepan, melt 3 tablespoons of the butter in the olive oil over moderate heat. Add the onion and cook until very soft, about 7 minutes.

2. Drain the barley, then rinse and drain again. Add the barley to the saucepan with 4 cups of the chicken stock. Bring to a simmer and cook over low heat until the barley is tender, about 50 minutes.

3. In a medium bowl, whisk the plain yogurt with the egg until smooth. Stir the mixture into the soup. Cook over low heat for 10 minutes; do not boil. Add more of the chicken stock if the soup is too thick.

4. Meanwhile, in a small skillet, melt the remaining 1 tablespoon butter over moderate heat. Add the chopped fresh flat-leaf parsley and the chopped fresh mint and cook until the herbs are wilted, about 1 minute. Stir the parsley and mint into the soup and simmer for 2 minutes to blend the flavors. Season the soup with salt and serve either warm or cold. (MAKE AHEAD: The soup can be refrigerated for up to 5 days. Reheat the soup carefully over very low heat to avoid curdling the yogurt. Thin the soup with additional chicken stock if you wish.) —SUSAN SIMON

TUSCAN BREAD SOUP

6 SERVINGS

- 6-inch loaf of French bread, torn into 1-inch pieces
- 3 tablespoons olive oil
- 1 medium onion, finely diced
- 2 tablespoons minced garlic
- 3 pounds ripe tomatoes, cut into ½-inch wedges
- 1 cup dry white wine
- Crushed red pepper
- 6 cups chicken stock or canned low-sodium broth
- 2 bay leaves
- Salt and freshly ground black pepper
- ¼ cup distilled white vinegar
- 6 large eggs
- Ice water
- ½ cup (loosely packed) fresh basil leaves, torn into large pieces
- 1 cup shaved Asiago cheese (about 3 ounces)
- Extra-virgin olive oil, for garnish

1. Preheat the oven to 325°. Spread the pieces of French bread on a baking sheet and toast them for about 10 minutes, until golden. Drizzle the bread with 1 tablespoon of the olive oil and toss to coat.

2. Heat the remaining 2 tablespoons olive oil in a large nonreactive saucepan. Add the finely diced onion and the minced garlic and cook over moderate heat, stirring, until the vegetables are golden, about 8 minutes. Add half of the tomato wedges, the white wine, and a large pinch of crushed red pepper. Simmer until the liquid is reduced by half, about 15 minutes.

3. Add the chicken stock and the bay leaves to the pan and bring to a boil over moderately high heat. Lower the heat and simmer for 15 minutes. Strain the broth into another saucepan, pressing down on the tomatoes. Season with salt and black pepper and keep warm.

4. In a large skillet, bring 6 cups of water and the white vinegar to a simmer. Crack the eggs into the water and poach them until they are just set, about 3 minutes. Using a slotted spoon, transfer the poached eggs to a shallow bowl of ice water to cool. Place the cooled eggs on baking sheets lined with paper towels.

5. To serve, divide the toasted pieces of French bread, the uncooked tomato wedges, the basil leaves, and half of the shaved Asiago cheese among 6 bowls and add a poached egg to each. Pour the hot broth over the top and garnish each serving with

CHEF'S MENU

TUSCAN BREAD SOUP (P. 103)

ROASTED SALMON SALAD (P. 215)

SAUTEED BERRIES WITH ZABAGLIONE ICE CREAM (P. 418)

—BEN BARKER

Tuscan Bread Soup

the remaining Asiago cheese, a drizzle of extra-virgin olive oil, and a pinch of crushed red pepper.—BEN BARKER

HOT AND SOUR FISH SOUP

For flavor and appearance, serve this tart soup with the lemon grass pieces floating in it; but remember that the lemon grass is too woody to eat.

4 SERVINGS

- ¼ cup plus 2 teaspoons fish sauce (*nuoc mam*)
- 1 teaspoon minced fresh ginger
- ½ teaspoon turmeric
- Two 10-ounce halibut or codfish steaks, with skin and bones
- 2 fresh lemon grass stalks, grassy upper portions discarded, tender white bulbs cut into 1-inch lengths
- 1 medium tomato or 2 plum tomatoes, quartered
- ¼ cup fresh lime juice
- ½ teaspoon finely grated lime zest
- 1 small dried red chile, finely chopped, or about ½ teaspoon crushed red pepper
- 2 large scallions, thinly sliced
- 2 tablespoons fresh coriander (cilantro) leaves
- Freshly ground white pepper
- About 6 cups steamed long-grain white rice, preferably jasmine (see "Cooking Rice," right)

1. In a small bowl, combine 2 teaspoons of the fish sauce, the minced fresh ginger, and the turmeric. Rub the fish steaks on both sides with the mixture and let stand for 5 minutes.

2. In a medium dutch oven or large nonreactive saucepan, bring 5 cups of water and the lemon grass to a simmer over moderate heat. Add the fish steaks and simmer until the steaks are just cooked through, about 4 minutes. Transfer the fish to a plate and let cool slightly. Discard the fish skin and bones and separate each steak into 2 pieces.

3. Bring the soup back to a simmer over moderate heat. Stir in the tomato quarters, the lime juice, the lime zest, and the dried red chile, and simmer for 2 minutes. Add the remaining ¼ cup fish sauce and the fish. Remove from the heat, add the scallions and coriander leaves, and season with white pepper. Set a piece of fish in each bowl, ladle the soup over the top, and serve with the steamed long-grain white rice on the side.—MARCIA KIESEL

GENOVESE FISH SOUP

In the part of Liguria that is south of Genoa, where ciuppin *(known here as cioppino) originated, this fish preparation is often so thick and smooth that it can serve as a sauce for pasta. The more varied the fish, the more successful the* ciuppin *will be. Good choices include sea bass, black sea bass, red snapper, porgy, whiting, and halibut.*

6 SERVINGS

SOUP:

- ¼ cup olive oil
- 1 medium onion, coarsely chopped
- 1 medium carrot, coarsely chopped
- 1 celery rib, coarsely chopped
- 2 to 3 garlic cloves, minced
- 4 anchovy fillets, finely chopped
- 2 tablespoons finely chopped fresh flat-leaf parsley
- Salt
- ¼ teaspoon cayenne pepper
- 1 cup dry white wine
- 2 cups drained canned Italian peeled tomatoes, coarsely chopped
- Freshly ground pepper
- 6 pounds whole assorted non-oily fish—cleaned and filleted, with heads, bones and tails left intact and fillets cut into large chunks

COOKING RICE

LONG-GRAIN RICE is a staple of Asian cooking, accompanying everything from soups and stews to stir-fries and roast chicken. Fragrant and pleasantly sticky jasmine rice is the best choice, though basmati and Texmati rice make fine substitutes. After cooking, the rice should stand covered to allow the steam to separate the individual grains of rice.

TO MAKE ABOUT 6 CUPS of steamed rice, rinse 2 cups of long-grain rice several times in a heavy medium saucepan until the water runs clear, which indicates that excess surface starch has been removed. Add 1¼ cups of water; the rice should be covered by about 1 inch of water. Bring to a boil over high heat, cover, and reduce the heat to low. Cook the rice for 20 minutes without peeking, then remove from the heat and let stand covered for at least 5 minutes before fluffing with a fork and serving.

GARNISHES:

Twelve ½-inch-thick diagonal slices of Italian bread
¼ cup plus 1 tablespoon olive oil
1 garlic clove, halved
½ pound small shrimp, shelled and deveined (optional)
½ pound cooked lobster meat, cut into large pieces (optional)
¼ cup dry white wine

1. Make the soup: Heat the oil in a large nonreactive saucepan. Add the onion, carrot, celery rib, garlic, anchovies, parsley, ¼ teaspoon salt, and the cayenne, and cook over moderately high heat, stirring occasionally, until the vegetables are tender, about 7 minutes. Add the wine and cook until slightly reduced, about 5 minutes. Add the tomatoes, crushing them with a wooden spoon, and 7 cups of water. Season with salt and pepper, and bring to a boil over moderately high heat. Lower the heat and simmer for 25 minutes.

2. Add the fish to the broth and bring to a boil over moderately high heat. Lower the heat. Simmer gently until the fish fillets are falling apart, about 20 minutes. Let cool; then discard the fish heads, tails, and bones. Working in batches, pass the soup through a food mill into a large nonreactive saucepan. (MAKE AHEAD: The soup can be prepared to this point up to 1 day ahead; cover and refrigerate.)

3. Bring the soup to a simmer over moderate heat and cook until the consistency of heavy cream, about 3 minutes. Season the soup with salt and pepper and keep warm.

4. Meanwhile, **prepare the garnishes:** Preheat the oven to 350°. Arrange the Italian bread slices on a baking sheet and brush with 3 tablespoons of the olive oil. Toast the bread for about 20 minutes, until lightly browned. Rub the toasts on one side with the garlic.

5. Heat the remaining 2 tablespoons olive oil in a small nonreactive skillet. Add the shrimp and cook over high heat just until pink, about 2 minutes. Stir in the cooked lobster meat and the wine and simmer until heated through, about 2 minutes. Stir the pan juices into the soup.

6. Put 2 toasts in each of 6 soup plates and ladle the soup on top. Garnish with the shrimp and lobster.—G. FRANCO ROMAGNOLI

Baked Halibut Soup

BAKED HALIBUT SOUP

This is a southern Italian dish known as zuppa di rombo in tegame. Rombo *is a large local flounder for which halibut is an excellent substitute.*

🍷 *Look for an assertive Italian white, such as the 1992 Corvo Bianco from Sicily or the 1992 San Quirico Vernaccia di San Gimignano.*

6 SERVINGS

1 medium onion, halved and thinly sliced
4 pounds halibut steaks, about 1½ inches thick, cut into 2-inch chunks
24 black Sicilian or Greek olives, pitted
3 canned Italian peeled tomatoes, coarsely chopped, with their liquid
2 garlic cloves, coarsely chopped
Zest of ¼ orange, cut into thin strips
1 bay leaf
3 generous dashes of Tabasco
Salt and freshly ground pepper
1 cup dry white wine
½ cup olive oil
1 pound mussels, scrubbed and debearded
½ pound shrimp, shelled and deveined
½ pound cleaned squid, cut into ½-inch rings
Twelve ¾-inch-thick slices of Italian bread

1. Preheat the oven to 375°. Spread half the onion in a large enameled cast-iron casserole and top with the halibut. Add the olives, tomatoes with their liquid, the garlic, orange zest, and bay leaf, and cover with the remaining sliced onion. Season

Genovese Fish Soup

with Tabasco, salt, and pepper. Drizzle with the wine, olive oil, and ½ cup water, and tilt the casserole to distribute the liquids. Scatter the mussels, shrimp, and squid evenly over all. Cover and bake for 40 minutes.

2. Meanwhile, arrange the Italian bread slices on a baking sheet. Toast them in the oven for about 15 minutes, until crisp and lightly browned.

3. Discard the bay leaf from the soup. Put 2 toasts in each of 6 soup plates or large bowls. Spoon the halibut, shellfish, and broth on top.—G. FRANCO ROMAGNOLI

MUSSEL SOUP

Mussels are the kind of shellfish that seem to grow and multiply in all seas and oceans, although those found on the rocky shores of cold waters are particularly good.

Mussel Soup

6 SERVINGS

¼ cup olive oil
2 garlic cloves, crushed
1 small dried red chile or ½ teaspoon cayenne pepper
2 celery ribs, finely diced
1 medium green bell pepper, finely diced
¾ cup dry white wine
2 cups drained canned Italian peeled tomatoes, coarsely chopped
6 pounds mussels, scrubbed and debearded
Salt
Crusty Italian bread

1. Heat the olive oil in a large nonreactive saucepan. Add the garlic and the chile and cook over moderately high heat, stirring, until fragrant and browned, about 3 minutes. Discard the garlic and chile.

2. Add the diced celery ribs and green bell pepper to the saucepan and cook over moderately high heat, stirring occasionally, until the vegetables are tender, about 5 minutes. Raise the heat to high, stir in the white wine, and cook until slightly reduced, 3 to 4 minutes. Stir in the tomatoes, lower the heat, and simmer for 5 minutes, crushing the tomatoes with a wooden spoon. Raise the heat to high and bring the liquid to a boil. Stir in the mussels and cover the pot. Lower the heat and cook until all of the mussels have opened, 6 to 7 minutes.

3. Using a slotted spoon, transfer the mussels to individual bowls. Season the broth with salt and ladle it over the mussels, leaving any sediment behind. Serve with the bread.—G. FRANCO ROMAGNOLI

SHRIMP SOUP WITH CRISP TORTILLA STRIPS LF

4 SERVINGS

2 medium poblano chiles
Four 6-inch corn tortillas, halved lengthwise and cut crosswise into ¼-inch-thick strips
¾ pound medium shrimp—shelled and deveined, shells reserved and shrimp cut in half
½ cup dry white wine
3 scallions, cut into 1-inch pieces
1 cilantro (fresh coriander) sprig plus 3 tablespoons coarsely chopped cilantro for garnish
1 teaspoon oregano, preferably Mexican
1 bay leaf
1 teaspoon salt
2 teaspoons olive oil
1 medium onion, thinly sliced
4 garlic cloves, finely chopped
2 large tomatoes—peeled, seeded, and finely chopped
1 tablespoon hot paprika
1¼ cups chicken stock or canned low-sodium broth
1 cup fresh or frozen corn kernels
Lime wedges, for serving

1. Roast the poblanos over a gas flame or under the broiler, turning often, until charred all over. Transfer to a paper bag and let steam for 10 minutes. Peel the poblanos, discarding the stems, ribs, and seeds, and cut the chiles into thin strips.

2. Preheat the oven to 325°. Toast the tortilla strips on a baking sheet for about 10 minutes, or until crisp.

3. Combine the shrimp shells, 2 cups of water, the wine, scallions, cilantro sprig, oregano, bay leaf, and salt in a medium nonreactive saucepan and bring to a boil over high heat. Lower the heat, cover, and simmer for 15 minutes. Strain the stock into a bowl and discard the solids.

4. Heat the olive oil in a large nonreactive saucepan. Add the onion and garlic and cook over moderate heat, stirring, until softened, 3 to 4 minutes. Add the tomatoes, raise the heat to high, and cook, stirring frequently, until the liquid is almost completely evaporated, 4 to 5 minutes. Stir in the paprika and cook for 30 seconds. Stir in the shrimp stock and chicken stock. (MAKE AHEAD: The recipe can be prepared to this point up to 1 day ahead; cover and refrigerate the soup and poblanos separately. Store the tortilla strips in an airtight container.)

5. Bring the soup to a boil over moderately high heat. Add the shrimp, poblanos, and corn. Lower the heat and simmer until the shrimp turn pink, 2 to 3 minutes. Ladle the soup into 4 bowls. Sprinkle with the chopped cilantro, pile the tortilla strips on top, and serve the soup with lime wedges.—MARGE POORE

SHRIMP, SWEET POTATO AND LEEK CHOWDER

6 SERVINGS

STOCK:

- 1 tablespoon vegetable oil
- 1 medium onion, minced
- 1 tablespoon minced fresh red chile
- 4 cups bottled clam juice
- ¾ pound medium shrimp—shelled, halved lengthwise, and deveined, shells reserved
- 2 tablespoons tomato paste

SOUP:

- 4 slices bacon, minced
- 3 medium leeks, white portion plus 3 inches of green, cut into ½-inch pieces
- 1 small onion, minced
- 1 medium celery rib, minced
- 1 tablespoon minced garlic
- 1 large sweet potato, peeled and cut into ½-inch dice
- 3 cups milk
- 1 tablespoon paprika
- Salt and freshly ground black pepper
- ¼ cup snipped chives

1. Make the stock: Heat the oil in a heavy medium saucepan. Add the onion and chile and cook over moderately high heat, stirring occasionally, until softened, about 3 minutes. Add the clam juice, shrimp shells, tomato paste, and 1 cup of water, and bring to a boil over high heat. Reduce the heat to moderate and simmer for 20 minutes. Strain the stock into a large heatproof measuring cup. You should have 4 cups of stock; boil to reduce if necessary.

2. Make the soup: Set a large saucepan over moderately high heat until hot. Add the minced bacon and cook, stirring, until crisp, about 4 minutes. With a slotted spoon, transfer the bacon to paper towels to drain. Stir in the leeks, the onion, the celery rib, and the garlic, and cook, stirring occasionally, until the vegetables soften, about 5 minutes. Add the shrimp stock and the diced sweet potato and simmer over moderately low heat until the sweet potato is tender, about 20 minutes.

3. Add the shrimp and the bacon and cook for 2 minutes. Stir in the milk and the paprika, season with salt and black pepper, and heat through; do not let the

Shrimp Soup with Crisp Tortilla Strips

THE TORTILLA TASTE TEST

FOOD & WINE recently tasted several tortillas to find the best of the increasing number of available brands. Our picks:

- **MARIA & RICARDO white corn tortillas (available by mail order from Harbar Corporation, 617-524-6107) had the best flavor and texture.**
- **GARDEN OF EATING'S yellow corn version, found at health food stores, was a close runner-up.**
- **Of the supermarket varieties, MARIACHI yellow corn had good flavor and MISSION white corn had good texture.**

Bay Scallop Chowder

chowder boil or it will curdle. Ladle the chowder into warmed soup plates and garnish with the chives.—ANNE ROSENZWEIG

BAY SCALLOP CHOWDER

This light-tasting, subtly spicy chowder, made with small sweet bay scallops, is the ideal opener to a big dinner.

12 SERVINGS

- 3 tablespoons unsalted butter
- 2 ounces thickly sliced smoked bacon, finely chopped
- 1 large onion, finely chopped
- 1 large garlic clove, minced
- ½ teaspoon crushed red pepper
- 6 cups bottled clam broth
- 6 cups chicken stock or canned low-sodium broth
- Bouquet garni made with 2 bay leaves, 5 fresh parsley sprigs, 3 fresh thyme sprigs, and 8 black peppercorns, wrapped in cheesecloth
- 1½ pounds Yukon Gold potatoes, peeled and cut into ¼-inch dice
- 2¼ cups heavy cream
- 2 tablespoons cornstarch
- 2 large leeks, white and tender green, halved lengthwise and sliced crosswise ⅛ inch thick
- 1½ pounds bay scallops, membranes removed
- Salt and freshly ground pepper
- ¼ cup finely chopped fresh chives

1. Melt the butter in a large enameled cast-iron casserole. Add the bacon and cook over moderately high heat, stirring, until lightly browned, about 2 minutes. Add the onion. Cook, stirring occasionally, until softened, about 7 minutes. Stir in the minced garlic and the crushed red pepper and cook, stirring, until the garlic is fragrant, about 2 minutes.

2. Add the bottled clam broth, the stock, and the bouquet garni. Bring to a boil over high heat. Lower the heat to moderately high. Simmer for 20 minutes. (MAKE AHEAD: The recipe can be refrigerated for up to 2 days. Bring to a boil before proceeding.)

3. Add the potatoes and cook over moderately high heat until just tender, about 10 minutes. Discard the bouquet garni.

4. In a medium bowl, whisk ¼ cup of the cream with the cornstarch until smooth. Whisk in the remaining 2 cups cream, then whisk into the soup. Bring to a boil over moderately high heat. Add the leeks and cook until just tender, about 4 minutes. (MAKE AHEAD: The chowder can stand at room temperature for up to 3 hours. Rewarm before finishing.)

5. Stir the scallops into the chowder and cook over moderate heat just until opaque throughout, 2 to 3 minutes; don't let the soup boil. Season with salt and pepper. Ladle into a tureen or individual bowls. Garnish with the chives and serve at once.—PATRICK CLARK

JULIA CHILD'S CREAM OF CHICKEN SOUP PRINTANIERE

This cream of chicken soup gets its unbelievably velvety and smooth texture from the rice and onion puree, so the cream I add at the end is for flavor and enrichment alone. To make a fat-free version, cook the onions for the base in a little stock instead of butter, and omit the cream that finishes the soup.

🍷 *This soup is perfect with a dry, fruity, blush wine, such as the 1993 Sanford Pinot Noir-Vin Gris from California, or a hearty red, such as the 1993 Georges Duboeuf Syrah from France.*

Shrimp, Sweet Potato and Leek Chowder

Prepare the Rice and Onion Soup Base (recipe follows), using only 5 cups of the chicken stock. Meanwhile, peel and cut into thin slices or julienne (matchsticks) enough onions, carrots, white of leek, and tender celery stalks to make about 1 cup each. Arrange the vegetables in a stainless saucepan with 2 skinless, boneless chicken breast halves, ½ cup dry white French vermouth, and the remaining 3 cups chicken stock. Bring to the simmer and cook for 4 minutes, skimming as necessary, until the chicken is just lightly springy to the touch. Remove the chicken and let the vegetables simmer for 5 minutes or more until tender. Correct the seasoning and remove the pan from the heat.

While the vegetables cook, cut the chicken lengthwise into julienne. Add to the vegetables and let steep for several minutes or longer to pick up the aromatic

Cream of Chicken Soup Printanière

flavors. Add the soup base to the saucepan and bring just to the simmer. Taste very carefully and correct the seasoning. Remove from the heat. Ladle into warm bowls and top each serving with a dollop of sour cream or crème fraîche and a sprinkling of parsley if you wish.

Rice and Onion Soup Base
For about 2 quarts of soup, you will want 2 cups of thinly sliced onions, 2 tablespoons of butter, 8 cups of homemade chicken stock or canned broth, and ½ cup of raw white rice, plus seasonings.

In a 3-quart heavy stainless saucepan, cook the onions in the butter over moderately low heat 7 to 8 minutes, stirring frequently, until the onions are very tender and colored no more than a buttery yellow. Pour in 4 cups of the stock, stir in the rice, and simmer for 20 minutes or more until the rice is very tender. Puree the soup in the blender until very smooth and lightly thickened, adding a little more stock if needed. Return the puree to the pan, add the rest of the stock, and season to taste with salt and pepper.

PERSIAN POMEGRANATE SOUP WITH MEATBALLS

6 TO 8 SERVINGS

- 1 pound lean ground lamb
- 2 medium onions, grated on the coarse holes of a box grater
- ¼ teaspoon ground cinnamon
- ¼ teaspoon ground allspice
- Salt and freshly ground pepper
- 1 cup long-grain rice, such as basmati, Texmati, or Thai jasmine, rinsed
- 2 cups sour pomegranate juice (see "Sweet and Sour Pomegranates," opposite page)
- ¼ pound fresh spinach, large stems removed, leaves cut into 1-inch strips
- ½ cup chopped fresh parsley
- 1 tablespoon sugar
- 3 tablespoons dried spearmint

VARIATIONS

● CREAM OF MUSHROOM SOUP: **Make the Rice and Onion Soup Base with 1 cup chicken broth and 6 cups of milk. Meanwhile, dice 1 quart of fresh mushrooms. After pureeing the base, bring it to the simmer and fold in the mushrooms and 1 sprig of fresh tarragon (or ¼ teaspoon dried). Simmer for 10 minutes, stirring frequently. Stir in ½ cup or so of sour cream, simmer a moment more and carefully correct seasoning, adding drops of lemon juice if needed.**

● CREAM OF CUCUMBER SOUP: **Peel and roughly chop 4 large cucumbers and toss with 2 teaspoons each of salt and wine vinegar. Make the Rice and Onion Soup Base as directed and simmer for 15 minutes, then add the cucumbers and their juices. Simmer 5 minutes more and puree. Whisk in ½ cup or so of sour cream, which will whiten as well as enrich the soup.—JULIA CHILD**

2 limes, cut into wedges
Warm pita bread, for serving

1. In a large bowl, combine the lamb with the onions, cinnamon, allspice, and ½ teaspoon each of salt and pepper. Mix well with your hands. Roll teaspoons of the meat mixture into firm balls and place on a lightly oiled platter; you will have about 50 balls. (MAKE AHEAD: The meatballs can be refrigerated for up to 1 day or frozen for up to 1 week.)
2. Pour 10 cups of cold water into a large saucepan. Add 1½ teaspoons salt and bring to a boil. Stir in the rice and return to a boil. Reduce the heat to moderate and simmer for 5 minutes. Stir in the pomegranate juice, spinach, parsley, sugar, and meatballs, and bring to a boil. Reduce the heat to moderate and simmer, partially covered, until the rice is tender and the meatballs are cooked through, about 15 minutes.
3. Rub the mint between your fingers to form a fine powder. In a small bowl, combine the mint with 1 teaspoon each of salt and pepper. Ladle the soup into large bowls. Top with a generous sprinkling of the mint. Serve the remainder on the side, with the lime wedges and pita bread.—JEFFREY ALFORD AND NAOMI DUGUID

HARIRA SOUP WITH CARAWAY

6 TO 8 SERVINGS

½ cup all-purpose flour
1 teaspoon fresh lemon juice
3½ ounces dried chickpeas (about ½ cup), rinsed and picked over
3½ ounces dried fava beans (about ½ cup)
Salt and freshly ground black pepper
9 ounces boneless lamb shoulder or leg, well trimmed and cut into ½-inch pieces
1 small beef marrow bone (about 1 pound)
3 medium onions, very finely grated
1 medium celery rib
1 tablespoon dried green lentils
1 medium bunch flat-leaf parsley
4-inch cinnamon stick or ½ teaspoon ground cinnamon
1-inch piece of fresh ginger or ½ teaspoon ground ginger
1 teaspoon sweet paprika
1 teaspoon ground cumin
1 teaspoon turmeric
½ teaspoon ground allspice
1¾ pounds ripe tomatoes
1 generous teaspoon ground caraway
⅓ cup finely chopped fresh cilantro
Lemon wedges and dates, for serving

1. Put the flour in a small bowl. Gradually stir in 1½ cups of water and the lemon juice until smooth. Cover and let stand at room temperature for 2 days.
2. In separate medium bowls, cover the chickpeas and fava beans with 2 inches of water. Add a pinch of salt to each and let soak overnight. Drain the chickpeas and rinse them well. Drain the beans and peel off the tough skins with a small knife.
3. In a large saucepan, combine the chickpeas, beans, lamb, marrow bone, onions, celery, lentils, parsley, cinnamon, ginger, paprika, cumin, turmeric, and allspice, and season with salt and pepper. Add about 2½ quarts of water to cover and bring to a boil over high heat. Lower the heat to moderate and simmer until the chickpeas are tender, about 1½ hours. Discard the bone, parsley, cinnamon stick, and piece of ginger.
4. Meanwhile, peel and seed the tomatoes and finely chop until almost pureed. Stir into the soup along with the caraway. Simmer over moderate heat for 5 more minutes, skimming frequently.
5. Stir the flour mixture into the soup until incorporated. Bring back to a boil over moderately high heat, stirring frequently. Lower the heat to moderate; simmer, stirring constantly, 5 minutes. Stir in the cilantro, season with salt, and serve, passing lemon wedges and dates.—FATIMA HAL

SWEET AND SOUR POMEGRANATES

Sweet red pomegranates, grown in California, are eating pomegranates. Sweet pomegranate juice is available at health food stores and makes a refreshing drink. The yellow sour fruits are not sold here, but Middle Eastern groceries sell pomegranate syrup, or pomegranate molasses, made from juice of the sour kind cooked down with a little sugar. In recipes using sour pomegranate juice, dilute 1 tablespoon pomegranate syrup in 1 cup of warm water. Or use sweet pomegranate juice, soured with 1 tablespoon strained fresh lemon or lime juice per cup of pomegranate juice.—JEFFREY ALFORD AND NAOMI DUGUID

CHAPTER 6

CHICKEN

Grilled Bluegrass Chicken, with Summer Green Bean Salad (p. 73)

GRILLED BLUEGRASS CHICKEN

8 SERVINGS

- ¼ teaspoon cumin seeds
- ¼ cup plus 2 tablespoons olive oil
- 1 tablespoon finely chopped garlic
- ¼ cup red wine vinegar
- 2 tablespoons red currant jelly
- 1 tablespoon fresh lemon juice
- 1 teaspoon Dijon mustard
- 1 teaspoon soy sauce
- ½ teaspoon crushed red pepper
- ¼ teaspoon ground ginger
- 8 large skinless, boneless chicken breast halves, pounded evenly
- Salt and freshly ground black pepper
- ¼ cup finely chopped fresh cilantro

1. In a small dry skillet, toast the cumin seeds over moderate heat, stirring occasionally, until fragrant, 2 to 3 minutes. Using a mortar and pestle or a spice grinder, grind the seeds to a powder. Empty into a large bowl.
2. Heat 2 tablespoons of the oil in the skillet. Add the chopped garlic and cook over moderate heat, stirring, until golden, about 3 minutes. Add to the ground cumin seeds, then whisk in the red wine vinegar, red currant jelly, lemon juice, Dijon mustard, soy sauce, crushed red pepper, and ginger. Whisk in the remaining ¼ cup oil. Add the chicken breast halves, turning to coat. Cover and refrigerate for 1 to 2 hours.
3. Light a grill or preheat a cast-iron grill pan until hot. Remove the chicken breasts from the marinade and season on both sides with salt and pepper. Cook the chicken, skinned side down, until nicely seared with grill marks, rotating the pieces once or twice, about 4 minutes. Flip and cook the other side, rotating, until charred all over and cooked through, about 4 minutes longer. Transfer the grilled chicken to a platter and sprinkle the cilantro on top. Serve warm or at room temperature.—KATHY CARY

PIQUANT CHICKEN WITH LEMON AND CAPERS

4 SERVINGS

- 4 skinless, boneless chicken breast halves
- 4 tablespoons cold unsalted butter
- 1 tablespoon olive oil
- Salt and freshly ground pepper
- ⅓ cup dry white wine
- 1 teaspoon finely grated lemon zest
- 2 tablespoons fresh lemon juice
- 1 tablespoon drained capers
- 2 tablespoons finely chopped flat-leaf parsley
- Lemon slices, for garnish

1. Place the chicken breasts between 2 pieces of plastic wrap and pound to an even ⅛-inch thickness using a meat pounder.
2. In a large nonreactive skillet, melt ½ tablespoon of the butter in ½ tablespoon of the olive oil over moderately high heat. Lightly season the chicken with salt and pepper. When the butter stops foaming, add 2 pieces of chicken to the pan and sauté, turning once, until they are lightly browned and cooked through, 2½ to 3 minutes. Transfer the chicken to a platter and keep warm in a low oven. Heat the remaining olive oil and another ½ tablespoon of the butter in the skillet and sauté the remaining chicken; keep warm. Pour off the fat from the pan.
3. Add the wine to the skillet and boil over high heat until reduced by half, about 2 minutes. Reduce the heat to low and add the lemon zest, lemon juice, capers, and half the parsley. Cut the remaining 3 tablespoons cold butter into pieces and whisk them into the sauce.
4. Transfer the sautéed chicken to warmed plates and pour the sauce over the top. Sprinkle the

CHEF'S MENU

🍷 The herby, savory-rich vegetable tart and the grilled chicken suggest a dry rosé. Consider a 1993 Bandol rosé from France, such as the Domaines Ott Cuvée Marine or the Domaine Tempier; alternatively, try a dry California rosé, such as the 1994 Pedroncelli Zinfandel rosé or the 1993 Sanford Vin Gris de Pinot Noir.

FRESH TOMATO AND ZUCCHINI TART (P. 46)

GRILLED BLUEGRASS CHICKEN (P. 117)

SUMMER GREEN BEAN SALAD (P. 73)

JALAPENO GRITS IN RED PEPPER CUPS (P. 303)

OLD-FASHIONED MERINGUES WITH PEACH ICE CREAM (P. 415)

—KATHY CARY

remaining parsley on the chicken, garnish with the lemon slices, and serve.—DIANA STURGIS

TEQUILA-ALMOND CHICKEN

2 TO 4 SERVINGS

- 4 skinless, boneless chicken breast halves
- ½ teaspoon finely grated lime zest
- 2 tablespoons fresh lime juice
- 1 tablespoon tequila
- 1 large garlic clove, thinly sliced
- ½ cup blanched whole almonds (2½ ounces), chopped
- ¼ teaspoon ground cumin
- Salt
- 1 tablespoon minced fresh chile, such as poblano or jalapeño
- 1 small shallot, minced
- 1 tablespoon plus 1 teaspoon olive oil
- 2 medium tomatoes, cored and cut into 1-inch dice

Clockwise from top left: **Piquant Chicken with Lemon and Capers, Tequila-Almond Chicken, Asian-Style Chicken and Noodles with Star Anise (p. 120), and Chicken with Peach-Jalapeño Salsa**

1 Hass avocado, cut into 1-inch dice
2 tablespoons unsalted butter
Freshly ground black pepper

1. Using a meat pounder, lightly flatten the chicken breasts. In a large shallow dish, combine the lime zest and 1 tablespoon of the lime juice with the tequila and garlic. Add the breasts and turn to coat with the marinade; set aside for 10 minutes.
2. In a food processor, finely grind the almonds; do not overprocess or the nuts will form a paste. Transfer to a large plate. Add the cumin and ½ teaspoon salt and toss well.
3. In a medium bowl, combine the remaining 1 tablespoon lime juice with the chile, shallot, and 1 teaspoon olive oil. With a rubber spatula, gently fold in the tomatoes and avocado.
4. Remove the chicken from the marinade, making sure no garlic sticks to the pieces. Pat the almond mixture on both sides of each piece to coat thoroughly.
5. In a large nonstick skillet, melt 1 tablespoon of the butter in ½ tablespoon of the olive oil over high heat. Add 2 of the chicken breast halves, reduce the heat to moderate, and cook until golden brown on the bottom, about 5 minutes. Turn the chicken and cook until browned on the second side and cooked through, 3 to 4 minutes longer. Transfer the chicken to plates and wipe out the skillet. Repeat with the remaining butter, oil, and chicken. Season the tomato-avocado salad with salt and pepper, spoon it over the chicken, and serve.—MARCIA KIESEL

CHOOSING AND PREPARING CHICKEN BREASTS

BREAST QUARTERS (with wings) are ideal for grilling, broiling, and cooking in stews.
WHOLE BREASTS (on the bone with skin) are best for roasting whole, with stuffing under the skin or not, and for poaching.
BREAST HALVES (on the bone with skin) are great for grilling, broiling, and roasting, with stuffing under the skin or not, and for poaching. Trim the breast halves with shears to give them a nice, neat shape.
BONELESS BREASTS are the quick cook's dream; this tender cut is best cooked quickly over direct heat (sautéed, panfried, stir-fried, deep-fried, broiled, and grilled) or cooked gently and briefly in a moist preparation such as soup or stew. In supermarkets, these are usually available as skinless whole or half breasts. Either way, they need to be trimmed of fat, membranes, and pieces of cartilage. Instead of choosing these pre-cut pieces, it's most economical to cut the breast yourself from a whole bird. Simply cut around the wishbone at the rounded end of the chicken breast and remove it. Then slice against the breastbone and follow the ribs with your knife to release the meat. Repeat the same procedure on the other side of the bird.
BREAST TENDERS, or breast tenderloins, as their name implies, are the most delicate morsels of all. Cook them as you would boneless breasts, but very briefly. To remove the tough white tendon running along the length, hold the tendon with your fingers and scrape away from you with the back of a table knife.

CHICKEN WITH PEACH-JALAPENO SALSA

4 SERVINGS

2 large peaches—peeled, pitted, and cut into ⅓-inch dice
1 medium jalapeño chile, seeded and minced
1 tablespoon fresh lime juice
2 teaspoons sugar
⅓ cup all-purpose flour
⅓ cup plain dry bread crumbs
3 tablespoons yellow cornmeal
1 tablespoon salt
1 teaspoon dried thyme
¼ teaspoon cayenne pepper
4 large skinless, boneless chicken breast halves
6 tablespoons peanut oil, for frying

1. In a bowl, combine the diced peaches, the jalapeño, lime juice, and sugar.
2. In a large bowl, toss together the flour, bread crumbs, cornmeal, salt, thyme, and cayenne. Put the chicken in a bowl of cool water. Remove the breast halves one at a time, let the excess water drip off, and coat them thoroughly with the seasoned flour mixture.
3. Heat ¼ cup of the peanut oil in a large heavy skillet. Add the chicken breast halves, skinned side down, and cook over moderately high heat until golden on the bottom, about 5 minutes. Turn the chicken breasts and add the remaining 2 tablespoons

LOW-FAT COOKOUT

🍷 All this cookout needs is a cold, light-flavored beer, such as Carta Blanca, Lone Star, or Coors Extra Gold. Or try a fruity California Chenin Blanc, such as the 1993 Dry Creek or the 1992 Mirassou Dry.

FIRESIDE PINTO BEAN AND CHILE STEW (P. 333)

CITRUS-GRILLED CHICKEN WITH MESQUITE HONEY (P. 120)

BUTTERMILK-SCALLION BISCUITS (P. 340)

FIRE-ROASTED CORN WITH SPICY RED PEPPER PUREE (P. 315)

PEACH AND BLACKBERRY CRISP (P. 423)

—CHARLES WILEY

peanut oil. Cook, turning occasionally, until the chicken is browned and cooked through, about 11 minutes longer. Serve the chicken with the peach-jalapeño salsa.—TRACEY SEAMAN

ASIAN-STYLE CHICKEN AND NOODLES WITH STAR ANISE

4 SERVINGS

- 8 dried shiitake mushrooms
- 1 cup boiling water
- ½ egg white
- 2 teaspoons cornstarch
- ¼ teaspoon salt
- 2 large skinless, boneless chicken breast halves—very thinly sliced crosswise and cut into short strips
- 4 ounces dried cellophane noodles or bean threads
- 2 tablespoons dry white wine
- ¼ cup soy sauce
- 1½ tablespoons Chinese oyster sauce
- 1 tablespoon peanut oil
- 1 tablespoon sesame oil
- 1 large garlic clove, minced
- Pinch of sugar
- Four ¼-inch-thick slices of fresh ginger
- 2 large star anise pods, lightly crushed with a knife
- 4 Swiss chard leaves, stemmed and thinly sliced crosswise
- 2 scallions, thinly sliced
- Freshly ground white pepper
- Chili oil, for serving

1. Put the shiitake mushrooms in a bowl and cover with the boiling water. Set aside to soften for about 20 minutes. Rub the mushrooms in the soaking liquid to remove any grit. Discard the stems and thinly slice the caps. Set the soaking liquid and the sliced caps aside.

2. In a medium bowl, stir together the egg white, the cornstarch, the salt, and 1 tablespoon of water. Add the chicken breasts and stir well to coat. Set aside for 20 minutes.

3. Put the cellophane noodles in a bowl and cover with warm water. Set aside until pliable, about 10 minutes. Drain the noodles and set aside. In a small bowl, combine the wine, soy sauce, oyster sauce, peanut oil, sesame oil, garlic, and sugar.

4. In a large saucepan, combine 3 cups of water with the ginger and star anise. Slowly pour in the reserved mushroom liquid, stopping before you reach the grit at the bottom. Bring to a boil over high heat. Reduce the heat to low, cover, and simmer for 10 minutes. Add the soy sauce mixture and increase the heat to moderately high.

5. Add the chicken and cook until opaque, stirring with a large fork to separate the strips. Add the shiitakes and the cellophane noodles. Using tongs, lift and stir the noodles until they become transparent, about 3 minutes. Stir in the Swiss chard and scallions and transfer to 4 large bowls. Season with white pepper and a few drops of chili oil and serve.—MARCIA KIESEL

CITRUS-GRILLED CHICKEN WITH MESQUITE HONEY *LF*

Mesquite honey, widely available in the Southwest, adds a light, smoky flavor to the chicken. Any honey can be used in its place.

6 SERVINGS

- ½ teaspoon coriander seeds
- ¼ teaspoon aniseed
- ½ cup honey, preferably mesquite
- ¼ cup fresh lemon juice
- 3 tablespoons fresh orange juice
- 3 tablespoons fresh lime juice
- 2 medium scallions, finely chopped
- 1 teaspoon finely chopped fresh thyme
- 1 teaspoon finely chopped fresh rosemary
- 1 teaspoon finely chopped fresh sage
- 6 skinless, boneless chicken breast halves (about 5 ounces each), pounded to a ½-inch thickness
- Kosher salt and freshly ground pepper

1. In a small skillet, toast the coriander seeds and aniseed over moderate heat, tossing, until fragrant, about 4 minutes. Transfer the seeds to a mortar or spice grinder; grind them to a powder. In a large nonreactive dish, whisk the honey, the fresh lemon juice, orange juice and lime juice, the chopped scallions, thyme, rosemary and sage, and the ground coriander and aniseed mixture. Add the chicken breast halves to the marinade and turn to coat. Let stand at room temperature for 30 minutes.

2. Light a grill or heat a cast-iron skillet, preferably ridged, over moderately high heat. Remove the chicken breasts from the marinade and season with salt and pepper. Grill or sear the chicken breasts, in batches if necessary, for about 4 minutes, or until opaque around the edges. Turn and cook them for about 3 minutes longer, or until opaque throughout. Brush the chicken with the marinade occasionally while grilling. Transfer the grilled chicken to a platter and serve.—CHARLES WILEY

GRILLED CHICKEN WITH SUMMER FRUIT CHUTNEY

Serve this main dish from Lilly's in Louisville, Kentucky, with orzo and toasted pine nuts tossed in olive oil. The colorful chutney, which is chock-full of large pieces of seasonal fruit, also makes a great accompaniment for grilled pork tenderloin, roasted turkey, or baked ham.

🍷 *Just about any wine complements grilled chicken, but the sweet, tangy chutney points to an aromatic, fruity white as the best choice. A French or California Viognier would be perfect. Try the 1992 Fortant de France or the 1993 Joseph Phelps.*

4 SERVINGS

CHUTNEY:

- 2 cups sugar
- 1 cup cider vinegar
- 1 tablespoon finely grated fresh ginger
- 2 medium peaches or nectarines—halved, pitted, and sliced ¼ inch thick
- 4 medium dark plums, such as Santa Rosa—halved, pitted, and cut into eighths
- 1 pint blueberries
- ½ pint raspberries

- 2 tablespoons fresh lemon juice
- 1 teaspoon Dijon mustard
- 6 tablespoons olive oil
- Eight 4-ounce skinless, boneless chicken breast halves, lightly pounded
- Salt and freshly ground pepper
- ¼ cup finely chopped fresh coriander (cilantro), for garnish

1. Make the chutney: In a medium nonreactive saucepan, combine

Citrus-Grilled Chicken with Mesquite Honey

Roast Chicken with Mango Rum Glaze

the sugar, vinegar, and ginger, and bring to a boil over moderate heat. Let cool for 30 minutes.

2. In a large bowl, combine the peaches, plums, blueberries, and raspberries. Pour the sugar syrup on the fruit and let macerate for about 30 minutes. (MAKE AHEAD: The chutney can be made up to 1 day ahead. Omit the raspberries, cover, and refrigerate. Stir in the raspberries and let sit at room temperature for 1 hour before serving.)

3. Meanwhile, in a large nonreactive bowl, whisk the lemon juice and mustard. Whisk in the oil in a thin stream until incorporated. Add the chicken breasts and turn to coat. Let marinate for 30 minutes.

4. Heat a grill or cast-iron grill pan until very hot. Season the chicken breasts well on both sides with salt and pepper. Working in batches if necessary, arrange the chicken breasts, smooth side down, on the grill or in the pan without crowding, and cook over moderately high heat for 2 minutes. Rotate and cook to create crisscross grill marks, 2 minutes longer. Then flip the chicken and cook on the other side until opaque throughout, about 4 minutes longer. Transfer to a plate and keep warm while you cook the remaining chicken breasts.

5. To serve, place 2 chicken breast halves on each plate. Using a slotted spoon, scoop some of the summer fruit chutney onto the chicken. Garnish the dish with a sprinkling of the fresh coriander.—KATHY CARY

ROAST CHICKEN WITH MANGO RUM GLAZE Q

A glaze of mango nectar and Major Grey's mango chutney, available in supermarkets, adds sweet fruitiness to roast chicken and is equally good with roast pork.

4 SERVINGS

- 1 teaspoon poultry seasoning or a mixture of ½ teaspoon thyme, ¼ teaspoon sage, and ¼ teaspoon ground allspice
- 1 teaspoon salt
- ½ teaspoon freshly ground pepper
- 4 large skinless, boneless chicken breast halves
- 1 tablespoon olive oil
- ¼ cup Major Grey's chutney
- ¼ cup canned mango nectar
- 2 tablespoons dark rum

1. Preheat the oven to 500°. In a small bowl, combine the poultry seasoning, salt, and pepper. Rub the chicken with the oil and then the dry seasonings. Let stand for 30 minutes.

2. Set the chicken breast halves, skinned side up, in a baking dish and roast for 15 minutes.

3. Meanwhile, in a food processor or blender, puree the chutney, mango nectar, and rum. Brush the chicken with 3 tablespoons of the mango glaze and bake for about 10 minutes, until browned and cooked through. Transfer the chicken to plates and serve with the remaining glaze.—JESSICA B. HARRIS

BARBECUED CHICKEN STEW

Marinating, then stewing the chicken results in meltingly tender meat.

8 SERVINGS

- 2 pounds skinless, boneless chicken breasts
- 2 cups Orange Barbecue Sauce (recipe follows)
- 4 tablespoons unsalted butter
- 3 medium green bell peppers, cut into 1-inch dice
- 1 medium Spanish onion, thinly sliced
- 2 tablespoons flour
- 4 cups chicken stock or canned low-sodium broth
- 2 pounds sweet potatoes, peeled and cut into 1-inch chunks
- 1½ tablespoons salt
- 1 pound plum tomatoes—peeled, seeded, and coarsely chopped
- 1¼ cups fresh or thawed frozen corn kernels
- 1 cup fresh flat-leaf parsley leaves, coarsely chopped
- 1 teaspoon finely grated orange zest

1. Place the chicken breasts and 1 cup of the Orange Barbecue Sauce in a large nonreactive dish or bowl. Turn the chicken to coat well. Marinate for at least 2 hours or overnight.

2. Light a grill or preheat the broiler. Grill or broil the chicken breast halves, turning once, until opaque, about 4 minutes per side. Let cool, then cut into 1-inch chunks.

3. In a large enameled cast-iron casserole, melt the butter over moderately high heat. Add the bell peppers and onion and cook, stirring, until browned, about 8 minutes.

4. Sprinkle the flour over the vegetables and stir for 2 minutes. Stir in the chicken stock, the sweet potato chunks, salt, and the remaining 1 cup Orange Barbecue Sauce. Bring to a boil, then simmer until the potatoes are tender, about 35 minutes.

5. Stir in the plum tomatoes, corn, parsley, and orange zest. Return the chicken to the pot and cook for 5 minutes, stirring occasionally. Season with salt. (MAKE AHEAD: The stew can be made up to 3 days ahead; cover and refrigerate. Rewarm over moderately low heat.)

Orange Barbecue Sauce

Use this sauce, which doubles as a marinade, with meat or poultry.

MAKES ABOUT 3 CUPS

- 4 tablespoons unsalted butter
- 1 very large onion, coarsely chopped
- 6 garlic cloves, minced
- 1 cup honey
- ½ cup tomato paste
- 3 tablespoons hot pepper sauce
- 2 tablespoons molasses
- 2 tablespoons fresh lemon juice
- 2 teaspoons salt
- 1½ teaspoons freshly ground black pepper
- ½ teaspoon freshly ground white pepper
- ½ teaspoon cayenne pepper
- ½ teaspoon ground cumin
- 2 cups chicken stock or canned low-sodium broth
- ½ cup fresh orange juice

1. In a medium nonreactive saucepan, melt the butter over moderately high heat. Add the onion and cook, stirring often, until golden brown, about 8 minutes. Reduce the heat to low, add the garlic, and cook, stirring, for 1 minute. Whisk in the honey, tomato paste, hot pepper sauce, molasses, lemon juice, and salt. Stir in the black, white, and cayenne peppers and the cumin. Whisk in the stock and orange juice. Simmer, stirring, for 30 minutes. Let cool.

2. Puree the sauce in a blender or food processor. (MAKE AHEAD: The sauce can be refrigerated for up to 3 days.) —PAMELA MORGAN

HERB-CRUSTED CHICKEN WITH TOASTED ALMONDS LF

6 SERVINGS

CHICKEN AND ALMONDS:

- 2 tablespoons sliced almonds
- Salt and freshly ground black pepper
- ¾ cup fresh bread crumbs
- 1 teaspoon thyme, crumbled
- 1 teaspoon basil, crumbled
- ½ teaspoon marjoram, crumbled
- Pinch of crushed red pepper

Herb-Crusted Chicken with Toasted Almonds

6 medium skinless, boneless chicken breasts
1 large egg white, lightly beaten
Vegetable oil cooking spray
2 teaspoons olive oil

SALAD:
1 tablespoon plus 1 teaspoon olive oil
1 tablespoon balsamic vinegar
Salt and freshly ground pepper
6 ounces mesclun

1. Prepare the chicken and almonds: Preheat the oven to 400°. Spread the almonds on a baking sheet and season with salt and pepper. Toast for about 3 minutes, or until lightly browned.
2. On a plate, combine the bread crumbs with the thyme, basil, marjoram, and crushed red pepper, and season with salt and black pepper. Brush the chicken on both sides with the egg white, then press the skinned sides into the seasoned bread crumbs.
3. Lightly coat a baking sheet with cooking spray. Heat 1 teaspoon of the olive oil in a large nonstick skillet. Add half the chicken breasts to the skillet, breaded sides down, and cook over moderately high heat without turning until browned, about 1 minute. Set the chicken breasts, breaded sides up, on the prepared baking sheet and cook the remaining breasts in the remaining 1 teaspoon oil. Bake the chicken for about 10 minutes, or until cooked through.
4. Meanwhile, **prepare the salad:** In a large bowl, whisk the olive oil and vinegar and season with salt and pepper. Add the mesclun and toss.
5. Make a bed of the salad on 6 plates. Set the herb-crusted chicken breasts on top, breaded sides up, and garnish with the toasted almonds.—MATTHEW KENNEY

CHICKEN IN A PONCHO

Ancho chile powder, poblanos, cilantro, and lime give this sandwich a real southwestern flavor.

6 SERVINGS

3 garlic cloves, chopped
Salt
2 tablespoons ancho chile powder
1 teaspoon red wine vinegar
¼ cup olive oil
6 skinless, boneless chicken breast halves
2 medium red onions, halved lengthwise and thinly sliced
3 large poblano chiles—halved, cored, seeded, and thinly sliced lengthwise
2 ripe Hass avocados
2 tablespoons mayonnaise
¼ cup fresh lime juice (2 limes)
Three 12-inch flour tortillas, halved
1 bunch of fresh cilantro

1. In a mortar, mash the garlic with ½ teaspoon salt. Add the chile powder, red wine vinegar, 1 tablespoon of the olive oil, and 1 tablespoon of water and pound to form a smooth paste.
2. Lightly pound the chicken breasts to an even ½-inch thickness. Spread both sides of the chicken with the ancho-garlic paste and let marinate for about 30 minutes.
3. Meanwhile, heat 2 tablespoons of the olive oil in a heavy medium skillet. Add the onions and the poblano chiles and sauté over moderately high heat until softened, about 10 minutes.
4. Halve, pit, and peel the avocados. In a small bowl, mash one avocado half with the mayonnaise, 1 tablespoon of the lime juice, and ½ teaspoon salt. Cut the remaining 1½ avocados into fairly thin lengthwise slices and place in a small bowl. Add the remaining 3 tablespoons lime juice and toss gently.
5. In a large skillet, heat ½ tablespoon of the oil. Add 3 of the chicken breasts and cook over moderately high heat, turning once, until opaque throughout, about 8 minutes. Wipe out the pan and repeat with the remaining oil and chicken. Cut the chicken breasts crosswise into ½-inch strips.
6. Spread the halved flour tortillas with the avocado mayonnaise and mound the chicken strips, the sliced avocados, and the sautéed onions and poblano chiles in the middle. Top each mound with 8 fresh cilantro sprigs. Fold up the straight edge of each tortilla half to hold the filling, then fold the sides over to enclose it. Serve immediately or cover with plastic wrap for up to 4 hours.—DIANA STURGIS

BBQ CHICKEN SANDWICHES WITH NAPA SLAW

4 SERVINGS

½ cup plus 1 tablespoon ketchup
⅓ cup unsulphured molasses
¼ cup yellow mustard
1 tablespoon cider vinegar
1 teaspoon Worcestershire sauce
1 teaspoon soy sauce

- 4 large skinless, boneless chicken breast halves, trimmed
- 4 hamburger buns, split

SLAW:

- ⅓ cup mayonnaise
- 2 tablespoons cider vinegar
- 2 teaspoons sugar
- ½ medium onion, finely chopped
- ¼ cup minced chives
- 1 medium head of napa cabbage, quartered lengthwise and thinly sliced crosswise

Salt and freshly ground pepper

1. In a large bowl, whisk together the ketchup, molasses, mustard, vinegar, Worcestershire sauce, and soy sauce. Reserve ½ cup of this sauce for serving; add the chicken breasts to the remaining sauce in the bowl and turn to coat. Set aside. ➤

Clockwise from top left: **BBQ Chicken Sandwich with Napa Slaw, Chicken Fingers with Tomato-Jalapeño Sauce (p. 126), Raspberry Chicken (p. 128), and Spinach-Stuffed Chicken (p. 127)**

2. Make the slaw: In a large bowl, stir together the mayonnaise, cider vinegar, and sugar. Add the onion and chives, then add the napa cabbage and toss well. Season the slaw generously with salt and pepper and toss.
3. Light a grill or preheat the broiler. Grill or broil the chicken for about 10 minutes, turning once, until nicely charred and cooked through.
4. Slice the chicken crosswise on the diagonal. Spoon some of the reserved barbecue sauce on the bottoms of the buns and arrange the chicken on top. Spoon the remaining sauce over the chicken and mound the napa slaw on top.—TRACEY SEAMAN

CHICKEN FINGERS WITH TOMATO-JALAPENO SAUCE

4 SERVINGS

- 1 pound chicken breast tenders, white membrane removed
- 2 cups buttermilk
- 2 tablespoons hot pepper sauce
- 2 tablespoons olive oil
- 3 garlic cloves, finely chopped
- 1 to 2 jalapeño chiles, minced
- 4 medium tomatoes, peeled and chopped
- Salt
- ¼ cup vegetable oil
- 1 pound small okra, trimmed
- 1 cup cornmeal, preferably stone ground
- 2 tablespoons unsalted butter or rendered bacon fat
- Lemon wedges, for garnish

1. Put the chicken breast tenders in a large bowl and cover them with the buttermilk. Stir in the hot pepper sauce. Set the tenders aside to marinate for 10 minutes to 1 hour.
2. In a nonreactive medium skillet, heat the olive oil over moderately low heat. Add the garlic and cook until softened, about 4 minutes. Add the jalapeños, increase the heat to moderately high, and cook until the chiles wilt, about 2 minutes. Add the tomatoes and boil, stirring often, until the sauce thickens, about 5 minutes. Season with salt.
3. Heat a large cast-iron skillet over moderate heat for about 5 minutes. Add 1 tablespoon of the vegetable oil and increase the heat to moderately high. Add half of the okra and fry, shaking the pan, until the okra is bright green and just tender, about 4 minutes. Transfer the okra to a plate. Add an additional ½ tablespoon of vegetable oil to the pan and fry the remaining okra. Season with salt.
4. Put the cornmeal on a large, shallow plate. Remove the chicken tenders from the buttermilk and shake lightly. Season the tenders with salt and dredge them in the cornmeal.
5. In the same cast-iron skillet, melt 1 tablespoon of the butter in 2 more tablespoons vegetable oil over moderately high heat. Add the chicken breast tenders to the skillet without crowding and fry until lightly browned and crisp, about 3 minutes per side. Adjust the heat if the oil gets too hot. Drain the chicken on paper towels and fry the rest, using the remaining ½ tablespoon vegetable oil and 1 tablespoon butter.
6. Meanwhile, reheat the tomato sauce. Spoon the sauce onto plates and arrange the chicken and okra beside it. Garnish with the lemon wedges or pass them separately.—MARCIA KIESEL

CHICKEN BREASTS STUFFED WITH HERBED GOAT CHEESE

🍷 *A tart, fruity California Pinot Noir, such as the 1992 Davis Bynum Limited Edition or the 1992 Acacia Reserve St. Clair Vineyard, would echo the sweet, tangy flavors of this chicken dish.*

8 SERVINGS

- ⅓ cup pecan pieces (about 1½ ounces)
- 6 tablespoons unsalted butter, at room temperature
- 2 ounces fresh goat cheese, softened
- 5 large shallots—4 minced and 1 coarsely chopped
- 7 medium garlic cloves—1 minced and 6 smashed
- 2 tablespoons finely chopped fresh flat-leaf parsley
- 2 tablespoons finely chopped fresh cilantro
- 2½ tablespoons olive oil
- 1 pound chicken wings, halved at the joint
- 1 cup Madeira
- 2 cups chicken stock or canned low-sodium broth
- Salt and freshly ground pepper
- 8 boneless chicken breast halves, with the skin on

VEGETABLE GARNISHES:

- ½ cup canola oil or vegetable oil
- 1 medium leek, white and tender green, cut lengthwise into 2½-by-⅛-inch strips
- 1 tablespoon rice flour or all-purpose flour

2 tablespoons olive oil
2 pounds Swiss chard, coarsely chopped

1. In a large skillet, toast the pecans over moderate heat, shaking the pan occasionally, until lightly browned, about 5 minutes. Let the pecans cool slightly, then finely chop them.

2. In a medium bowl, blend the butter and goat cheese. Stir in the toasted pecans, the minced shallots and garlic, the parsley, and the cilantro. Wrap the goat cheese mixture in wax paper and shape it into a 4-inch-long cylinder. Twist the ends to seal, and refrigerate until firm.

3. Heat ½ tablespoon of the olive oil in a large nonreactive saucepan. Add half of the chicken wings and cook over moderately high heat, turning occasionally, until nicely browned, about 8 minutes. Transfer to a plate and repeat with the remaining wings. Pour off any fat from the saucepan. Return the wings to the pan and add the chopped shallot, smashed garlic cloves, and Madeira. Bring to a boil over moderately high heat. Add the stock and boil, skimming, until reduced to ¾ cup, about 45 minutes. Strain the sauce into a small saucepan and skim off any fat. Season with salt and pepper. (MAKE AHEAD: The recipe can be prepared to this point up to 2 days ahead; cover and refrigerate the sauce. Skim the fat from the sauce before rewarming.)

4. Preheat the oven to 400°. Using your fingers, loosen the skin from the chicken breasts without detaching it. Cut the goat cheese mixture into 8 even slices and insert a slice under the skin of each breast half. Season the breasts with salt and pepper.

5. Heat the remaining 2 tablespoons olive oil in the large skillet. Add half the chicken breasts to the skillet, skin side down, and cook over moderately high heat without turning until golden brown, about 5 minutes. Transfer the chicken breasts to a large baking dish, skin side up. Repeat with the remaining chicken. Bake the chicken breasts for about 15 minutes, until the juices run clear when the meat is pierced with a knife.

6. Meanwhile, **prepare the vegetable garnishes:** Heat the canola oil in a large saucepan. Dust the leek strips with the rice flour. Working in 3 batches, fry the leeks over moderately high heat until golden and crisp, about 2 minutes per batch. Transfer to paper towels to drain.

7. Heat the olive oil in a large skillet. Add the Swiss chard and cook over moderately high heat, stirring, until wilted, 2 to 3 minutes. Season the chard with salt and pepper.

8. Just before serving, rewarm the Madeira sauce. Mound the Swiss chard in the center of 8 large plates. Top with a chicken breast half and spoon the sauce around. Garnish with the fried leeks and serve.—PASCAL OUDIN

Chicken Breasts Stuffed with Herbed Goat Cheese

SPINACH-STUFFED CHICKEN WITH SUN-DRIED TOMATOES

4 SERVINGS

1¼ pounds fresh spinach
2 tablespoons unsalted butter
1 large garlic clove, minced

Salt and freshly ground pepper
- ¼ cup drained oil-packed sun-dried tomatoes, thinly sliced lengthwise
- 4 large boneless chicken breast halves, with skin, pounded to a ¼-inch thickness

Four 2½-by-½-inch sticks of Italian Fontina cheese
- 2 tablespoons all-purpose flour
- 2 tablespoons olive oil
- ¾ cup chicken stock or canned low-sodium broth
- 1 tablespoon fresh lemon juice

1. Place half of the fresh spinach in a large nonreactive ovenproof skillet. Cover the skillet and cook the spinach over moderately high heat, turning occasionally with tongs, until wilted, 2 to 3 minutes. Add the remaining spinach and cook, turning until wilted, 1 to 2 minutes more. Transfer the spinach to a colander and rinse with cold water until cool. Squeeze the spinach dry, then coarsely chop it.

2. Wipe out the skillet and return it to moderately high heat. Add 1 tablespoon of the butter and the garlic and cook, stirring, until the garlic is fragrant and softened, about 3 minutes. Add the spinach, season with salt and pepper, and stir for 3 minutes. Transfer the spinach to a bowl and let cool. Stir in the sliced sun-dried tomatoes.

3. Place the chicken breasts on a work surface, skin side down. Spoon the spinach mixture in a mound across each breast and press the Fontina cheese into the spinach. Roll the breasts around the stuffing and secure with 2 toothpicks; smooth the skin over the meat.

4. Preheat the oven to 400°. Season the chicken rolls with salt and pepper and dust with flour. Heat the olive oil in the skillet. Add the chicken rolls, seam side down, and cook over moderately high heat, turning, until they are browned all over, about 8 minutes. Transfer the skillet to the oven and roast the chicken rolls for about 15 minutes, or until the cheese is melted and the juices run clear when the meat is pierced with a knife. Place the chicken on a plate, discard the toothpicks, and cover loosely to keep warm.

5. Pour the pan drippings into a small heatproof bowl and skim off the fat. Set the skillet over moderate heat. Add the chicken stock, lemon juice, and the degreased pan drippings, and bring to a boil, scraping to dislodge any browned bits from the bottom of the pan. Boil until the liquid is reduced to ⅓ cup, 4 to 5 minutes. Remove from the heat and stir in the remaining 1 tablespoon butter.

6. Slice the chicken rolls crosswise ½ inch thick. Arrange on plates, spoon the sauce on top, and serve.—TRACEY SEAMAN

RASPBERRY CHICKEN WITH THYME

4 SERVINGS

- 1½ cups fresh raspberries
- 8 fresh thyme sprigs plus 1 teaspoon minced thyme
- 4 boneless chicken breast halves, with skin

Salt and freshly ground pepper
- 3 tablespoons cold unsalted butter, cut into pieces
- 1 teaspoon olive oil
- ⅓ cup dry white wine
- 2 tablespoons balsamic vinegar
- 1 shallot, minced
- ½ cup chicken stock or canned low-sodium broth

1. Press half of the fresh raspberries through a fine stainless steel strainer; reserve the puree.

2. Tuck one thyme sprig under the skin of each chicken breast, loosening the skin as little as possible. Season the chicken with salt and pepper.

3. In a large, heavy, nonreactive skillet, melt ½ tablespoon of the butter in the oil over high heat. When the butter stops foaming, add the chicken, skin side down, and cook for 1 minute. Reduce the heat to moderate and cook until the skin is nicely browned, about 5 minutes longer. Turn the chicken and brown the second side, about 6 minutes. Transfer the chicken to a plate and keep warm in a low oven. Pour the fat from the skillet.

4. Add the wine, vinegar, shallot, and minced thyme to the skillet and boil over moderately high heat for 2 minutes, stirring to deglaze the pan. Add the chicken stock and boil until reduced to ¼ cup, about 5 minutes. Stir in the reserved raspberry puree and cook until warmed through. Remove the skillet from the heat and whisk in the remaining 2½ tablespoons butter.

5. Slice the browned chicken breast halves crosswise or leave them whole. Transfer them to warmed plates and spoon the sauce on top or alongside. Garnish with the remaining thyme sprigs and whole raspberries and serve.—DIANA STURGIS

HONEY-ROSEMARY CHICKEN WITH CHERRY TOMATOES

4 SERVINGS

8 garlic cloves, sliced 1/8 inch thick
2 tablespoons olive oil
4 boneless chicken breast halves, with skin
Salt and freshly ground pepper
2 tablespoons honey
1 pint cherry tomatoes
Ten 4-inch fresh rosemary sprigs
1 or 2 small dried hot chiles
1 tablespoon red wine vinegar

1. Preheat the oven to 425°. In a 9-by-13-inch enameled cast-iron or glass baking dish, toss the sliced garlic cloves with 1 tablespoon of the olive oil. Bake the garlic in the oven for 5 minutes, or until it is sizzling but not browned.

2. Place the chicken breast halves on a sheet of wax paper, skin side down. Season with salt and pepper and spread with half of the honey. Remove the dish from the oven and push the garlic to the side. Arrange the chicken breasts in the hot dish, skin side up. Season with salt and pepper and spread with the remaining honey.

3. Surround the chicken with the cherry tomatoes, 6 of the rosemary sprigs, and the dried chiles. Drizzle the remaining 1 tablespoon olive oil on top and season with salt and pepper. Bake for about 25 minutes, occasionally basting with the pan juices, until the chicken is cooked through. Transfer the chicken, cherry tomatoes, and baked garlic to plates. Stir the red wine vinegar into the baking dish and spoon the sauce over the chicken. Garnish each serving with a rosemary sprig.—DIANA STURGIS

COCONUT-CURRIED CHICKEN WITH ROASTED EGGPLANT

4 SERVINGS

MARINADE:

2 tablespoons dry white wine
1 tablespoon peanut oil
1 tablespoon curry powder
1 tablespoon finely chopped fresh ginger
1 tablespoon soy sauce
1 garlic clove, minced
1 large shallot, minced
1 teaspoon finely grated lemon zest

4 boneless chicken breast halves, with skin
1½ tablespoons peanut oil
One 1¼-pound eggplant, peeled and cut into 3-by-1 inch sticks
Salt and freshly ground pepper
½ teaspoon sugar
1 teaspoon soy sauce
½ teaspoon lemon zest
½ cup unsweetened coconut milk
12 ounces freshly cooked egg noodles, for serving
¼ cup fresh cilantro leaves
2 tablespoons chopped unsalted peanuts

1. Make the marinade and marinate the chicken: In a large shallow glass or ceramic dish, combine the dry white wine with the peanut oil, the curry powder, the chopped ginger, the soy sauce, the minced garlic and shallot, and the grated lemon zest. Add the chicken breast halves to the marinade and turn to coat. Set aside for at least 20 minutes or overnight.

2. Preheat the oven to 450°. Spread a little of the peanut oil on a large baking sheet. Arrange the eggplant sticks on the baking sheet and season them with salt and pepper. Bake the eggplant on the bottom shelf of the oven until the sticks are well browned on the bottom, about 25 minutes. Using a metal spatula, scrape the eggplant sticks from the sheet and set aside.

3. In a large skillet, heat the remaining peanut oil over high heat until almost smoking. Add the marinated chicken breast halves, skin side down, and reduce the heat to moderately high. Cook the chicken breast halves until the skin is nicely browned, about 3 minutes. Turn the chicken breasts and add 1 cup of water and the sugar. Cover, reduce the heat to moderately low, and simmer until the chicken breasts are cooked through, about 8 minutes. Transfer the chicken to a plate.

4. Increase the heat to moderately high and add the soy sauce and the lemon zest to the skillet. Boil the cooking liquid to thicken it slightly and concentrate the flavor. Return the cooked chicken breasts to the skillet, add the unsweetened coconut milk, and simmer for 1 minute.

5. Transfer the chicken breast halves to plates. Toss the eggplant sticks with the egg noodles and arrange the mixture next to the chicken. Pour the sauce over the chicken and noodles and garnish with the cilantro leaves and peanuts.—MARCIA KIESEL

LOW-FAT CHICKEN WITH WATERCRESS PESTO *LF*

4 SERVINGS

1 medium celery rib, coarsely chopped
1 medium carrot, coarsely chopped
1 medium onion, coarsely chopped
4 whole black peppercorns
1 large bay leaf
Sprig of fresh thyme (optional)
4 large chicken breast halves on the bone, with skin

PESTO:

3 packed cups of stemmed watercress plus whole sprigs for garnish
1 tablespoon fresh lemon juice
1 tablespoon olive oil
½ tablespoon rice vinegar
Salt and freshly ground pepper

Clockwise from top left: **Honey-Rosemary Chicken (p. 129), Coconut-Curried Chicken (p. 129), Italian-Style Chicken with Prosciutto and Basil, and Low-Fat Chicken with Watercress Pesto**

TABBOULEH:

Salt
1 cup medium bulgur
2 medium tomatoes, cut into ⅓-inch dice
⅓ cup finely chopped flat-leaf parsley
2 tablespoons fresh lemon juice
2 tablespoons olive oil
Freshly ground pepper
1 cucumber, thinly sliced

1. In a large nonreactive saucepan, combine the celery, carrot, onion, whole peppercorns, bay leaf, thyme, and 8 cups of water. Bring to a boil over high heat. Reduce the heat to moderately low, cover, and simmer for 10 minutes. Add the chicken breast halves to the pan skin side down. Place a plate directly on top of the chicken to keep it submerged. Reduce the heat to low and poach very gently for 30 minutes. Remove from the heat and let rest for 15 minutes.

2. Using tongs, transfer the chicken to a plate and let cool completely. Reserve the broth for another use. (MAKE AHEAD: The chicken can be cooked up to 1 day ahead. Wrap and refrigerate overnight. Remove from the refrigerator about ½ hour before serving.)

3. Make the pesto: In a food processor, finely chop the watercress, scraping down the bowl as necessary. With the motor running, add the lemon juice, olive oil, vinegar, and 1 tablespoon of water. Transfer to a small bowl. Stir in ¼ teaspoon salt and season with pepper.

4. Make the tabbouleh: In a large saucepan, bring 3 cups of water to a boil. Add ½ teaspoon salt and stir in the bulgur. Cover, reduce the heat to low, and cook until tender, about 20 minutes. Drain the bulgur and rinse well with cool water. Drain again.

5. In a large bowl, toss the bulgur with the tomatoes, parsley, lemon juice, and olive oil. Season with salt and pepper.

6. Skin the chicken breast halves with a sharp knife and, using the breastbone as your guide, cut off the meat. Thinly slice the chicken on the diagonal. Fan out the cucumber slices in a semicircle on 4 large plates. Spoon the tabbouleh in the center. Fan the chicken slices on the other side and top them with the watercress pesto. Garnish with watercress sprigs and serve.—TRACEY SEAMAN

ITALIAN-STYLE CHICKEN WITH PROSCIUTTO AND BASIL

4 SERVINGS

1 tablespoon unsalted butter
2 teaspoons olive oil
2 medium shallots, finely chopped
2 large garlic cloves, finely chopped
Salt and freshly ground pepper
4 large chicken breast halves on the bone, with skin
4 thin slices of prosciutto, folded in half
12 large basil leaves plus 1 tablespoon minced basil
¼ cup dry white wine
½ cup chicken stock or canned low-sodium broth
2 tablespoons heavy cream

1. Preheat the broiler. In a small skillet, melt the butter in the olive oil over moderate heat. Add half of the finely chopped shallots and garlic and cook, stirring often, until softened and fragrant, 2 to 3 minutes. Season with a pinch of salt and pepper. Scrape the mixture into a small bowl and let cool.

2. Loosen the skin from the chicken breast halves without detaching it completely. Place a teaspoon of the cooked shallot and garlic mixture under the skin of each breast half and spread it over the meat. Top the mixture with a folded piece of prosciutto and 3 basil leaves. Smooth the chicken skin over the fillings and season lightly with salt and pepper.

3. Set the chicken in a medium roasting pan, skin side up. Broil for 5 minutes. Turn and broil for 5 minutes more, then turn again and broil for about 5 minutes longer, or until nicely crisped on top; take care not to burn the skin. Turn the oven temperature to 350° and bake the chicken for about 20 minutes, or until the juices run clear when the meat is pierced. Transfer the chicken to a plate and keep warm.

4. Pour the juices from the roasting pan into a small bowl; spoon off the fat and reserve the brown drippings. Place the roasting pan over moderate heat. Add the remaining chopped shallot and garlic and stir until the vegetables are softened and golden, about 2 minutes. Pour in the wine and bring to a boil. When the wine is nearly evaporated, pour in the chicken stock and heavy cream. Bring to a boil and simmer, stirring occasionally, until reduced to ½ cup, about 4 minutes. Stir in the reserved drippings and the minced basil, and season with salt and pepper.

5. Place one of the stuffed chicken breast halves on each of 4 dinner plates. Spoon the sauce over or around the chicken breasts and serve.—TRACEY SEAMAN

Peppery Chicken Wings, with Mixed Green Caesar Salad (p. 77)

QUICK DINNER

PEPPERY CHICKEN WINGS (P. 132)

MIXED GREEN CAESAR SALAD (P. 77)

GARLIC BREAD IN A BAG (P. 340)

FRESH BING CHERRIES

TIMETABLE:

- **Season the chicken wings and put them in the oven. Toast the walnuts at the same time.**
- **Prepare the greens and the Caesar salad dressing.**
- **Make the garlic bread and bake it as soon as the wings are done.**
- **Toss the Caesar salad and you're ready to eat.**

PEPPERY CHICKEN WINGS

The simple, fruity, tart taste of a chilled white Zinfandel, such as the 1993 Beringer or the 1993 De Loach, is ideal to counterbalance the hot pepper sauce of the chicken.

4 SERVINGS

- 4 pounds chicken wings
- 2 teaspoons balsamic vinegar
- 2 teaspoons olive oil
- 2 tablespoons hot pepper sauce
- Salt and freshly ground black pepper

Preheat the oven to 500°. Lightly oil a large rimmed baking sheet and spread the chicken wings out on it. Drizzle the balsamic vinegar and the olive oil over and toss lightly. Pour the hot pepper sauce over the chicken wings, season them with salt and pepper, and toss again. Roast the chicken wings for about 30 minutes on the top shelf of the oven, until they are well browned and crisp. Keep the wings warm until serving.—MARCIA KIESEL

PEANUT CHICKEN WITH MANGO PICKLE SALSA

Serve this sweet and tangy chicken with fragrant steamed rice, such as Thai jasmine or Texmati. Or slice the cooked chicken and roll it up in flour tortillas with the mango pickle salsa and a little sour cream.

Given the heat and spice in this dish, consider serving a cold lager beer, such as Harp, Kirin, or Carlsberg, to refresh the palate.

4 SERVINGS

- 8 boneless chicken thighs
- 3 tablespoons Mango Pickle juice (p. 353)
- 2 tablespoons creamy peanut butter
- 1 cup diced (1/4-inch) Mango Pickle (p. 353)
- 3 tablespoons finely chopped red onion
- 1 teaspoon minced fresh hot chile (optional)
- 2 tablespoons chopped fresh coriander (cilantro)
- Salt and freshly ground pepper

1. Preheat the oven to 500° or light a grill. Trim the boneless chicken thighs of fat and excess skin. In a shallow dish, blend the Mango Pickle juice with the peanut butter. Add the thighs; turn to coat. Set the chicken aside to marinate for at least 15 minutes or up to 1 hour.

2. In a bowl, combine the Mango Pickle, red onion, hot chile, and fresh coriander. Season with salt and pepper.

3. Arrange the chicken thighs on a baking sheet, skin side up, and season with salt and pepper. Roast on the top shelf of the oven for about 20 minutes, or until well-browned and crisp. Alternatively, grill the chicken thighs over a medium fire until browned and cooked through. Transfer the chicken to a platter or plates and serve with the mango pickle salsa.—MARCIA KIESEL

JULIA CHILD'S COQ AU VIN

Recently I had a real coq au vin cooked by a real French chef at the Château du Clos de Vougeot in Burgundy, where, it is presumed, this famous chicken braised in red wine with onions and mushrooms originated. It was a marvel of true chicken taste with a richly nuanced Burgundian sauce. I had forgotten how very good a dish it is when cooked by a pro in the real manner with all the right ingredients—including the coq's blood.

Determined to produce a reasonable facsimile of that coq au vin, I went to our best supermarket where they specialize in organic, all natural, and other such hopeful products. I knew that I would never find fresh *coq*'s blood, but I remembered from experiences with pressed duck in France that you could get much the same effect using chicken livers. I got myself 4 fine fresh chicken livers, 4 guaranteed free-range chicken leg-thighs (I prefer dark meat to the white, but a whole cut-up chicken would do just as nicely), a 4-ounce slab of fresh salt pork, ¼ pound of mushrooms, and ½ pound of white pearl onions about an inch in diameter. A Clos de Vougeot red wine would have been authentic, but I settled for a respectable native Merlot. I filled in with a few other ingredients I had on hand. Here's the procedure.

First, get the onions, salt pork, and liver out of the way by bringing 2 quarts of water to the boil in a saucepan. To make onion peeling easy, drop them into the boiling water and boil for exactly 10 seconds; transfer to a bowl of cold water with a slotted spoon. Keep the water at the slow boil. Cut off and discard the rind from the salt pork; cut the rest into ⅜-inch dice and boil slowly for 5 minutes. Meanwhile, peel the onions and cut a cross ⅜-inch deep in their root ends to discourage them from bursting when braised. Drain the salt pork, rinse in cold water, and pat dry. Puree the livers in a blender or processor with ½ teaspoon red wine vinegar and 4 tablespoons soft butter. Rub the puree through a fine sieve, cover, and refrigerate.

Brown the diced salt pork slowly in a casserole in 2 tablespoons of butter; remove and reserve. Add the pearl onions to the casserole and cook slowly for several minutes, turning until lightly colored. Remove the onions to a stainless steel skillet just large enough to hold them in one layer and pour in enough chicken stock to come halfway up. Cover the skillet and simmer slowly for 20 minutes or so, or until the onions are tender when pierced; set aside.

Meanwhile, separate the chicken legs from the thighs, pat dry, and season with salt and pepper. Brown the chicken nicely all over, rather slowly, in the casserole. Remove the chicken when browned and pour the excess fat out of the casserole; do not disturb the coagulated browning juices.

Return the chicken to the casserole, sprinkle with 2 tablespoons of flour, and bring to a sizzle over moderate heat. Turn the chicken to brown the flour lightly, then pour in ¼ cup Cognac. Averting your face, light the Cognac with a match and shake the casserole for a moment until the flames begin to die down. Douse with 3 cups of the red wine and 1 cup of strong chicken stock. Add 1 chopped medium onion, 1 chopped carrot, 1 chopped unpeeled plum tomato, and a bouquet garni. ➤

Peanut Chicken with Mango Pickle Salsa

Julia Child's Coq au Vin

Bring to a simmer and return the salt pork to the casserole. Cover the casserole and simmer slowly for about 25 minutes, turning and basting the chicken with the sauce several times. The chicken is done when the juices run clear yellow if the meat is pricked deeply.

Meanwhile, halve the mushrooms and sauté them with 2 tablespoons chopped shallots in ½ tablespoon each of butter and vegetable oil until the vegetables are lightly browned; set aside.

Remove the chicken to a plate and keep warm. Skim the fat from the cooking liquid in the casserole and rapidly boil down the liquid by half. Strain it into a saucepan; you should have about 1½ cups of lightly thickened sauce. Taste carefully, correct the seasoning, and return the chicken to the casserole. Scatter the mushrooms and onions all around it.

Bring the stew to the simmer, basting the chicken with the sauce. Stir 2 tablespoons of the sauce into the liver and butter mixture, then 2 more and 2 more. Pour the liver mixture back into the sauce and pour the sauce over the chicken. Set over low heat, basting the chicken with the sauce until warmed through; do not let the sauce boil. Taste again carefully to check seasoning and serve.

JAMAICAN JERK MENU

STRAWBERRY RUM PUNCH (P. 15)

JERK CHICKEN (P. 134)

JOHNNYCAKES (P. 340)

CHILE-PIMENTO CORN (P. 316)

SPICY CABBAGE SALAD (P. 80)

—PAUL CHUNG

Jerk Chicken, Spicy Cabbage Salad (p. 80), and Chile-Pimento Corn (p. 316)

JERK CHICKEN

Be sure to allow time for the chicken to marinate overnight.

8 SERVINGS

1 medium onion, coarsely chopped
3 medium scallions, coarsely chopped

JERKING MEAT AND SEAFOOD

The spicy seasonings that characterize jerk can be used on a variety of foods besides chicken. Other meats that can be jerked include pork chops and pork tenderloin, boneless turkey breast, and lamb shoulder chops. The jerk seasonings are also wonderful on firm, full-flavored fish fillets, such as bluefish, mackerel, pompano, and kingfish. The marinating time for fish is shorter—two to three hours—depending on the size and thickness of the fillet.

Large shrimp can be jerked in their shells. Cut through the shell down the back of each shrimp and remove the vein. Spread the marinade all over the shrimp under the shell, then let marinate for about three hours.

SCOTCH BONNET CHILES

Scotch bonnets, small chiles with a fruity flavor and intense heat, should be handled with care: touch them as little as possible and wash your hands well after chopping. The seeds make dishes even hotter, but they can be discarded.

2 Scotch bonnet chiles, coarsely chopped
2 garlic cloves, chopped
1 tablespoon five-spice powder
1 tablespoon allspice berries, coarsely ground
1 tablespoon coarsely ground black pepper
1 teaspoon thyme, crumbled
1 teaspoon ground nutmeg
1 teaspoon salt
½ cup soy sauce
1 tablespoon vegetable oil
Two 3½- to 4-pound chickens, quartered

1. In a food processor, combine the onion, scallions, chiles, garlic, five-spice powder, allspice, black pepper, thyme, nutmeg, and salt, and process to a coarse paste. With the machine on, add the soy sauce and oil in a steady stream until combined. Pour the marinade into a large shallow dish, add the chicken, and turn to coat. Cover and refrigerate overnight. Let the chicken return to room temperature before cooking.
2. Light a grill, preferably charcoal, or preheat the oven to 500°. Grill or roast the chicken: if grilling, cover the grill for a smokier flavor; if roasting, cook the chicken, skin side up, on the top shelf of the oven. Cook, turning occasionally, for 30 to 40 minutes, until well browned and cooked through. Cut each chicken quarter in half, transfer to a platter, and serve.—PAUL CHUNG

Chicken Tagine with Olives and Preserved Lemons

CHICKEN TAGINE WITH OLIVES AND PRESERVED LEMONS

The savory tang of classic Moroccan dishes calls for uncomplicated, refreshing wines with contrasting, light fruity flavors. A chilled dry rosé, such as the 1994 Preston Le Petit Faux from California, is a good option; another is a fruity white Zinfandel, such as the 1993 Kenwood or the 1994 De Loach.

6 SERVINGS

¼ cup olive oil
Two 3-pound chickens, each cut into 6 pieces
½ teaspoon salt
¼ teaspoon freshly ground pepper
2 small onions, finely grated
2 teaspoons minced fresh ginger or ¼ teaspoon ground ginger
3-inch cinnamon stick or ½ teaspoon ground cinnamon
¼ teaspoon saffron threads, crumbled
2 medium tomatoes—peeled, seeded, and coarsely chopped—or 1½ cups drained canned tomatoes
6 garlic cloves, finely chopped
1 cup finely chopped fresh flat-leaf parsley
1 cup finely chopped fresh cilantro
3 Preserved Lemons (recipe follows)
½ pound Mediterranean brine-cured olives, such as picholine or Calamata

Sauté of Chicken with Artichokes, Parsley and Lemon

1. Heat the oil in a large enameled cast-iron casserole. Season the chicken pieces with the salt and pepper and add them to the casserole along with the onions, ginger, cinnamon, and saffron. Cook over high heat, turning the chicken occasionally, until the pieces are browned all over, about 10 minutes. Add the tomatoes, garlic, parsley, cilantro, and 2 cups of water, and bring to a boil. Reduce the heat to low, cover, and simmer, stirring occasionally, until the chicken is tender, about 1 hour. (MAKE AHEAD: The recipe can be prepared to this point up to 2 days ahead; cover and refrigerate. Rewarm before continuing.)

2. Meanwhile, rinse the Preserved Lemons under running water; pat dry. Separate the lemons into quarters. Discard the pulp from one of the lemons and finely chop the peel. Reserve the quarters for garnish.

3. Transfer the chicken to a large plate. Strain the cooking liquid and return it to the casserole. Boil over high heat until slightly thickened, about 10 minutes. Add the chopped lemons and the olives and simmer over moderate heat for 2 minutes. Add the chicken pieces and simmer until heated through.

4. Arrange the chicken pieces in a serving dish. Pour the sauce on top and garnish with the lemon quarters.

Preserved Lemons

Be sure that the lemons are covered with liquid when they're packed into jars. If there's not enough liquid, boil some water, let it cool to lukewarm, and pour it over the lemons.

Allow at least 12 days for the lemons to cure. Preserved lemons provide a wonderfully tangy, salty counterpoint to lamb and rich fish as well as chicken.

Try to use untreated lemons for this recipe. Jarred preserved lemons, available at Middle Eastern markets, can be substituted for these lemons in the tagine *(see "Moroccan Mail Order," p. 85).*

MAKES ABOUT 1½ QUARTS

- 4½ pounds very small, thin-skinned organic lemons
- 1½ cups coarse or kosher salt

1. Scrub the lemons thoroughly under running water. Transfer the lemons to a bowl, cover with water, and let soak for 1 hour. Drain and pat the lemons dry. Cutting only three-fourths of the way through, quarter each lemon lengthwise. Put the lemons in a large glass or ceramic bowl and fill the centers with salt. Cover with a plate and weigh the plate down with cans. Let stand until the juices are exuded and the lemons are covered in liquid, 2 to 3 days.

2. Pack the lemons into large glass jars. Pour the exuded liquid over the lemons to cover them completely. Screw the jar lids on tightly and let stand in a cool place for at least 10 days or up to 1 month. (MAKE AHEAD: The lemons can be refrigerated for up to 6 months.) Before using, rinse the lemons well under running water.—FATIMA HAL

SAUTE OF CHICKEN WITH ARTICHOKES, PARSLEY AND LEMON

🍷 *The zip and bite of the olives and lemon here—and the fact that artichokes make all foods, and notably wines, taste sweeter—point to a simple crisp white that can provide a refreshing foil to the flavors. Look for a modest French country white, such as the 1992 Fortant de France Vin de Pays d'Oc Sauvignon Blanc or the 1992 La Vieille Ferme Côtes du Lubéron Blanc.*

6 SERVINGS

- 2 tablespoons extra-virgin olive oil
- Two 3½-pound chickens, cut into 6 pieces each
- Salt and freshly ground pepper
- 8 fresh artichoke hearts (see "Preparing Artichoke Hearts," p. 83), each cut into 6 wedges
- 8 large garlic cloves, thinly sliced
- ½ cup dry white wine
- Juice of ½ lemon
- Zest of ½ lemon, cut into thin strips
- ⅓ cup finely chopped fresh flat-leaf parsley

¼ cup halved pitted Gaeta or other brine-cured black olives

1. Heat the olive oil in a large nonreactive skillet. Season the chicken pieces with salt and pepper. Add the chicken legs and thighs to the skillet, skin side down, and cook over moderately high heat, turning once, until the meat is well browned, about 15 minutes. Transfer to a plate. Add the chicken breasts to the skillet, skin side down, and cook, turning once, until the meat is well browned, about 10 minutes. Add the chicken breasts to the legs and thighs on the plate.
2. Pour off all but 2 tablespoons of the fat from the skillet. Drain the artichoke wedges well and add them to the skillet with the sliced garlic cloves. Cook over moderate heat, stirring, until lightly browned, about 3 minutes. Add the wine, lemon juice, and lemon zest, and bring to a boil. Cook, stirring occasionally, until the liquid has reduced to a glaze, about 15 minutes.
3. Return the chicken pieces to the skillet, cover, and cook over low heat until the breasts are cooked through, about 15 minutes. Transfer the chicken breasts to a platter. Continue cooking, covered, until the chicken legs and thighs are cooked through and the artichoke wedges are browned, about 15 minutes longer. Stir in the chopped flat-leaf parsley and the pitted olives, add the chicken breasts, and cook until warmed through, about 2 minutes longer. Season with salt and pepper and serve immediately.—ANN CHANTAL ALTMAN

HUNTER'S STYLE CHICKEN

Cacciatora di Pollo al Pomodoro

To make this dish for 12, you will need two large skillets. Simply split the ingredients equally between them.

12 SERVINGS

Two 3½-pound chickens, each cut into 6 to 8 pieces
3 tablespoons extra-virgin olive oil
2 cups very thinly sliced onions
4 garlic cloves, very thinly sliced
Salt and freshly ground pepper
⅔ cup dry white wine
3 cups peeled and chopped firm, ripe tomatoes or chopped imported canned Italian plum tomatoes with their juice

1. Wash the chicken pieces in cold water and pat thoroughly dry. Put the olive oil and onions into 2 large nonreactive skillets and cook over moderate heat, stirring occasionally, until translucent. Push the onions to the side and add the garlic and the chicken, skin side down. Cook until the skin is golden brown, then turn the chicken pieces and brown them on the other side.
2. Season the chicken with salt and pepper and turn the pieces over 2 or 3 times. Add the wine and simmer until reduced by half. Add the tomatoes, lower the heat, and cover the skillets with lids set slightly ajar.
3. Cook the chicken at an intermittent simmer, turning and basting from time to time, until the thighs are very tender and the meat is almost falling off the bones, about 40 minutes. If the pans begin to look dry at any point, add 2 tablespoons of water. (MAKE AHEAD: Let the chicken cool, then cover and refrigerate for up to 1 day. Rewarm the chicken in covered pans at a gentle simmer, turning the pieces until heated through.) Transfer the chicken to a warmed platter, spoon the sauce on top, and serve.—MARCELLA HAZAN

CHICKEN AND SAUSAGE JAMBALAYA

Jambalaya, a Louisiana dish, is typical of the one-pot Creole meals of the African diaspora. It's great party food because it can be made ahead and feeds a lot of people.

12 SERVINGS

2 large chickens, weighing a total of 9 to 10 pounds
¼ cup vegetable oil
2 large onions, coarsely chopped
4 celery ribs, coarsely chopped
1 green bell pepper, coarsely chopped
1 red bell pepper, coarsely chopped
1 jalapeño pepper, minced
2 pounds chopped peeled tomatoes and their liquid
2 teaspoons *herbes de Provence*
Salt and freshly ground black pepper
1 pound smoked sausage, cut into ¾-inch slices
3 cups long-grain white rice

1. Place the chickens in a stockpot and add water to just cover. Bring to a simmer and cook for 45 minutes. Remove the chickens from the pot and let cool. Strain the broth into a large bowl.
2. Skin the birds and pull all the meat from the bones; discard the

skin and bones. Cut or shred the meat into large bite-size pieces.

3. Heat the oil in a large nonreactive casserole or dutch oven. Add the chopped onions, celery, green and red bell peppers, and jalapeño, and cook over moderate heat, stirring occasionally, until all the vegetables are tender, about 15 minutes.

4. Add the tomatoes and their liquid. Season with the *herbes de Provence* and salt and black pepper. Raise the heat to moderately high and cook until the mixture is thick, about 15 minutes. Stir in the chicken, sausage, and 6 cups of the chicken broth (reserve the remaining broth for another use). Add the rice, stir well, and bring to a boil. Reduce the heat to low and cover tightly. Simmer the jambalaya without lifting the lid until all the liquid has been absorbed and the rice is tender, about 30 minutes.

5. Remove the casserole from the heat. Fluff the rice with a large fork to make sure the ingredients are evenly distributed and the grains of rice are separate; do not stir with a spoon. Re-cover and set aside off the heat to steam for at least 15 minutes. (MAKE AHEAD: The jambalaya will stay warm in the casserole for an hour or more. It can also be made ahead of time and reheated in the oven.) Serve the jambalaya straight from the casserole.—JOHN MARTIN TAYLOR

Roast Chicken with Two Lemons

ROAST CHICKEN WITH TWO LEMONS

Don't be tempted to add cooking fat of any kind. This bird is self-basting, so you need not fear it will stick to the pan. Try not to puncture the skin at any time during cooking; if it is kept intact, the chicken will swell like a balloon, which makes for an arresting presentation at the table. Don't worry too much about it, however, because even if it fails to swell, the flavor will not be affected.

Keep any leftovers moist with some of the cooking juices and eat them at room temperature.

4 SERVINGS

A 3- to 4-pound chicken
Salt and freshly ground pepper
2 rather small, thin-skinned lemons, washed well and dried

1. Preheat the oven to 350°. Thoroughly wash the chicken inside and out in cold water. Remove any bits of loose fat. Let the bird stand on a slightly tilted plate for about 10 minutes so that all the water drains out of it. Pat the chicken dry all over.

2. Season the chicken generously inside and out with salt and pepper; rub in the seasonings.

3. Set the lemons on a counter and roll them back and forth, pressing with your palm. Puncture each lemon in at least 20 places, using a sturdy round toothpick or a fork.

4. Place both of the lemons in the cavity of the chicken. Seal the opening with toothpicks; close it well, but don't make an airtight job of it because the chicken may burst. Run kitchen string from one leg to the other and tie it at the knuckle ends; the string serves only to keep the thighs from spreading apart and splitting the skin.

5. Set the chicken breast side down in a roasting pan. Place it in the upper third of the oven and roast for 30 minutes. Carefully turn the chicken over onto its back and cook for another 30 to 35 minutes.

6. Turn the oven up to 400° and cook for an additional 20 minutes. (Calculate between 20 and 25 minutes total cooking time per pound.) Whether the bird has puffed up or not, bring it to the table whole and leave the lemons inside until the chicken is carved. The juices that run out are perfectly delicious, so be sure to spoon them over the roast chicken.—MARCELLA HAZAN

FIVE-SPICE CHICKEN Q

The cinnamon and anise flavors in this dish point to an aromatic dry white as the most complementary wine match. Consider bottlings such as the 1991 Ceretto Arneis Blange

from Italy, the 1993 King Estate Pinot Gris from Oregon, or the 1992 Hugel Sylvaner from Alsace.

4 SERVINGS

- 2 garlic cloves, minced
- 1 tablespoon dry white wine
- 1 tablespoon soy sauce
- 1 teaspoon Oriental sesame oil
- 1 teaspoon light brown sugar
- ¼ teaspoon five-spice powder
- One 3-pound chicken
- About 6 cups steamed long-grain white rice, preferably jasmine (see "Cooking Rice," p. 105)

1. Preheat the oven to 350°. In a small bowl, combine the garlic, wine, soy sauce, sesame oil, brown sugar, and five-spice powder. Spoon half of the marinade into the cavity of the chicken, then set the chicken, breast side up, in a medium roasting pan. Rub the remaining marinade over the chicken.
2. Roast the chicken in the center of the oven for 1¾ hours, basting occasionally with the pan juices. Increase the oven temperature to 500° and continue roasting for about 10 minutes longer, or until the chicken is well browned and the juices run clear when a thigh is pierced with a fork. Pour the juices from the cavity into the pan, then transfer the chicken to a platter and let stand for 5 minutes before carving.
3. Set the roasting pan on the stove over 2 burners at high heat. Add 2 tablespoons of water and boil for 1 minute, scraping up any browned bits from the bottom. Pour the pan juices into a sauceboat and skim the fat. Carve the chicken and serve with the pan juices and rice.—MARCIA KIESEL

INDIAN ROAST CHICKEN

A spicy yogurt marinade lends this bird the distinctive flavor and texture of classic Indian tandoori chicken. Serve it with saffron rice, roasted onions, and a creamy cucumber raita. *Marinating the chicken in a plastic bag allows the entire bird to be coated with the yogurt mixture.*

🍷 *A fruity, simple, straightforward California Chenin Blanc, such as the 1993 Simi or the 1992 Chapellet, would balance the added heat and spice that the ginger, pepper, and turmeric give to this dish.*

4 SERVINGS

- 1 cup plain yogurt
- 3 medium garlic cloves, minced
- 2 tablespoons finely grated fresh ginger
- 2 tablespoons fresh lemon juice
- 2 teaspoons finely grated lemon zest
- 2 teaspoons ground coriander
- ½ teaspoon cayenne pepper
- ¼ teaspoon turmeric
- Salt and freshly ground black pepper
- One 3½-pound chicken

1. In a medium bowl, combine the plain yogurt, the minced garlic, the grated ginger, the lemon juice, the lemon zest, the ground coriander, the cayenne pepper, the turmeric, ½ teaspoon of salt, and ¼ teaspoon freshly ground black pepper; mix well. Place the chicken in a gallon-size plastic bag, add the marinade, and turn to coat all over. Seal the bag. Refrigerate the chicken for at least 4 or up to 12 hours, turning it occasionally in the bag.

Indian Roast Chicken

2. Preheat the oven to 350°. While the oven heats, let the chicken come to room temperature. Lift the chicken from the marinade and transfer to a roasting pan; discard the remaining marinade. Season the chicken with salt and pepper and roast for 25 minutes. Rotate the pan and roast for another 25 minutes. Increase the temperature to 400° and roast the chicken for about 35 minutes longer, or until the juices run clear when a thigh is pierced with a fork.
3. Transfer the chicken to a platter, cover loosely with foil, and let rest for 15 to 20 minutes before carving. Skim the fat from the juices in the roasting pan and strain the juices through a coarse strainer; season with salt and pepper and serve with the chicken.—JAN NEWBERRY

Julia Child's All-American Chicken Salad

RICE SALAD WITH CHICKEN AND PISTACHIOS

4 SERVINGS

Salt
1½ cups arborio or long-grain white rice
4 to 5 tablespoons extra-virgin olive oil
Zest and juice of 1 large lemon
3 cups cubed cooked chicken
¾ cup shelled unsalted pistachios (about 4 ounces)
1 small red onion, finely diced
½ cup finely chopped fresh flat-leaf parsley
¼ cup finely chopped fresh basil
3 tablespoons drained small capers
Freshly ground pepper

1. In a large saucepan, bring 10 cups of water to a boil. Stir in 1 tablespoon salt. Add the rice and cook uncovered over moderate heat until al dente, about 15 minutes. Drain the rice in a colander, rinse with cold water, and drain again. Place the rice in a large bowl.

2. In a small bowl, mix ¼ cup of the oil with the lemon zest and lemon juice and pour the dressing over the rice. Add the chicken, pistachios, onion, parsley, basil, and capers; toss. Add up to 1 tablespoon of oil. Season with salt and pepper. Let stand for at least 20 minutes before serving. (MAKE AHEAD: The salad can be made 1 day ahead and refrigerated, covered. Serve at room temperature.) —ERICA DE MANE

JULIA CHILD'S ALL-AMERICAN CHICKEN SALAD

What a wonderfully satisfying dish old-fashioned chicken salad is, with its celery and cucumber crunch, pleasant whiff of scallion, and tender morsels of meat—all joined together with real homemade mayonnaise. It bespeaks happy picnics as well as elegant buffets where a beautiful chicken salad can be the star.

For a comfortable midsummer meal for family and good friends, you might start with jellied consommé (shades of the Fifties), then follow with the chicken salad, a platter of ripe red tomatoes ringed with leaves of fresh basil, perhaps warm garlic bread, a bit of fresh goat cheese, and a cool bottle of white wine, like a dry Alsatian Riesling.

Let us start with the mayonnaise, which needs special attention during hot weather so that it will resist the harmful bacteria that raw eggs may develop. You can, of course, use a good store-bought brand, but if you want to make your own, here is my special, fail-safe version that is made with cooked eggs.

Hard-Boiled Egg Mayonnaise For the cooked sauce base, measure 2 tablespoons of flour into a 6-cup saucepan and gradually whisk in ½ cup of cold water until perfectly smooth. Whisk the sauce slowly over moderate heat and reaching all over the bottom of the pan, bring the sauce to a boil. Boil gently for 30 seconds; if the sauce is stiff rather than very thick, beat in droplets of water. Remove the sauce from the heat, break in one whole raw egg, and rapidly whisk it in. Return the sauce to low heat and boil for 15 seconds, whisking constantly.

DRESSING IT UP

For a decorative presentation, garnish chicken salad with finely chopped yellow, red, and green bell peppers, minced olives, chopped hard-boiled egg whites or yolks, minced parsley, or strips of pimento. Apply them whimsically or in neat triangles. To make the triangles, fold a narrow strip of wax paper in half to form a V-shaped template. Lay the tip of the V on the middle point of the salad and sprinkle the garnish into it to form a pie-wedge shape. Repeat with alternating colors to form a pinwheel pattern.—JULIA CHILD

Scrape the sauce into the bowl of a food processor. Add 1 teaspoon each of salt, Dijon mustard, wine vinegar, and fresh lemon juice plus several grinds of white pepper. Then drop in the yolks of 2 hard-boiled eggs and process until the egg yolks are smoothly and fully incorporated, about 15 seconds. With the machine still running, begin adding, in a very thin stream at first, 1 cup of fine fresh olive oil or a mixture of vegetable oil and olive oil to the sauce. When it has begun to thicken, you may add the oil a little faster—but be careful, too much oil at once will break the emulsion and the sauce will thin out. When all the oil has been added, taste the mayonnaise for seasoning, adding more salt, pepper, mustard, vinegar, or lemon juice as you feel them needed. At this point, the mayonnaise can be transferred to a tightly covered container and refrigerated for up to one week. (You can lighten the mayonnaise by stirring in an equal amount of sour cream.)

Seasoning the Chicken

I'm a chicken salad buff, and I think that any cold chicken for a salad should be seasoned and allowed to marinate for at least an hour before the salad is assembled. It makes all the difference in the final result. To make the seasoning mixture, grate the zest of ½ lemon into a jar and add 1 tablespoon of fresh lemon juice, ½ tablespoon of Dijon mustard, ¼ teaspoon salt, several grinds of white pepper, and ¼ cup of vegetable oil. Shake vigorously. Taste and correct the seasoning.

Making the Salad

When you plan to serve the chicken salad, you might want to have a fine big roast chicken or capon dinner for four people a day or two beforehand; serve half the bird for dinner and save the rest for salad.

Cut the cold roast chicken meat into ⅜-inch dice—four cups will serve six people. Toss it in a bowl with ⅓ cup each of diced tender celery stalks, finely minced scallions, and diced peeled and seeded cucumbers. Fold in a tablespoon or two of the seasoning mixture—just enough to coat the ingredients lightly—and taste carefully for seasoning. Cover and let marinate for an hour or overnight in the refrigerator, tossing several times.

When you are nearly ready to serve the salad, drain any excess liquid from the chicken. At this point, you can fold in other ingredients, such as diced hard-boiled eggs, diced green pepper, roughly chopped walnuts or pecans, or finely chopped fresh herbs, such as parsley, chives, dill, basil, or tarragon. Then fold in just enough of the Hard-Boiled Egg Mayonnaise to coat the ingredients.

For the greens surrounding the salad, use any salad mix that pleases you—lettuces, watercress or arugula, or a small head of romaine sliced into chiffonade. (To make a chiffonade, stack washed and dried leaves and roll them up lengthwise, then cut crosswise with a knife into very thin strips.) Toss the greens with some of the remaining seasoning mixture that was used for the chicken. Ring a serving platter or individual plates with the dressed greenery and mound the chicken salad in the center.

You can substitute turkey, salmon, lobster, crab, or shrimp for the chicken.

CHAPTER 7

OTHER BIRDS

Garlic and Herb-Roasted Cornish Hens with Wheat Berries and Portobellos

GARLIC AND HERB-ROASTED CORNISH HENS WITH WHEAT BERRIES AND PORTOBELLOS

Richard Benz at Gautreau's in New Orleans serves his hens with chewy wheat berries, grilled sliced Portobellos, and coriander-accented spinach. The wheat berries need to soak overnight, so plan accordingly.

🍷 *An assertive, herby Sauvignon Blanc-based wine—such as the 1993 Vacheron Sancerre from France or the 1993 Buena Vista Sauvignon Blanc from California—would echo the garlicky, herby tastes of this dish.*

4 SERVINGS

WHEAT BERRIES:

1 cup wheat berries (about 7 ounces)*
2 cups chicken stock or canned low-sodium broth
¼ cup finely diced onion
Salt and freshly ground black pepper

HERBED HENS:

6 large garlic cloves, very thinly sliced
2 teaspoons finely chopped fresh thyme
2 teaspoons finely chopped fresh rosemary
2 teaspoons finely chopped fresh oregano
Salt and freshly ground black pepper
4 Cornish hens (about 1 pound each)
2 tablespoons olive oil

CORIANDER SPINACH:

2 tablespoons olive oil
¼ cup finely diced onion
2 pounds fresh spinach, stemmed
¼ teaspoon ground coriander
Salt and freshly ground white pepper

PORTOBELLOS:

2 large Portobello mushrooms (about 10 ounces each), stems discarded
3 tablespoons olive oil
Salt and freshly ground black pepper

*Available at health food stores

1. Prepare the wheat berries: In a medium bowl, cover the wheat berries with water and let them soak overnight.

2. Drain and transfer the wheat berries to a medium saucepan. Add the chicken stock, 1 cup of water, and the onion, and bring to a boil over high heat. Reduce the heat to moderately low, cover partially, and simmer for 1 hour. Add ½ teaspoon salt and simmer, partially covered, until the wheat berries are tender but still chewy, about 20 minutes longer. Drain and return to the saucepan. Season with salt and pepper and keep warm. (MAKE AHEAD: The wheat berries can be prepared up to 1 day ahead; cover and refrigerate. Rewarm before serving.)

3. Prepare the herbed hens: Preheat the oven to 400°. In a small bowl, combine the garlic, thyme, rosemary, and oregano, and season with salt and pepper. Loosen the breast skin of each hen with your fingers. Spread a quarter of the herb mixture under the skin of each bird, rubbing it over the breasts and thighs.

4. Heat the olive oil in a large heavy skillet. Add 2 of the herbed hens to the skillet and cook over moderately high heat, turning with tongs, until browned on all sides, about 8 minutes. Transfer the browned hens to a large roasting pan and brown the remaining 2 hens. Roast the hens in the oven for 10 minutes. Lower the oven temperature to 300° and continue cooking for about 30 minutes, or until the hens are golden and the juices run clear when a thigh is pierced with a fork. Cover the hens loosely with foil and keep warm.

5. Meanwhile, **prepare the coriander spinach:** Heat the olive oil in a large nonreactive skillet. Add the onion to the skillet and cook over high heat, stirring, until translucent, about 3 minutes. Add the spinach and cook, tossing, just until wilted, 2 to 3 minutes. Drain off any excess liquid and season the spinach with the coriander and the salt and white pepper; keep warm.

6. Prepare the Portobellos: Heat a grill pan or cast-iron skillet over moderately high heat. Brush the Portobello caps on both sides with some of the olive oil and season them with salt and pepper. Grill or panfry the Portobello caps, turning often, until the mushroom juices are exuded and the caps are browned, about 8 minutes; brush the Portobellos with the remaining oil from time to time. Thinly slice the caps and keep warm.

7. To serve, set a Cornish hen on each of 4 large warmed plates. Pile the wheat berries, the coriander spinach, and the sliced Portobello mushrooms around the hens, and spoon any pan drippings over the wheat berries and hens.—RICHARD BENZ

SOY-BRAISED CORNISH HENS WITH COCONUT-PINEAPPLE SWEET RICE

To complement her moist, flavorful Cornish hens, Susanna Foo, of Susanna Foo Chinese Cuisine in Philadelphia, serves spicy broccoli rabe sautéed with crushed red pepper, and sweet coconut sticky rice.

You can serve a little of the leftover soy braising liquid with the hens at the table. The balance of the liquid can be covered and refrigerated for up to one month and used in meat or poultry stir-fries and braises, or to flavor soups and stews.

🍷 *Soy flavors complement red wines, but the sweetness of the rice narrows the choice to a grapey, fruity red such as Beaujolais-Villages—best served slightly cool. Look for examples from 1993 or 1994 from Louis Jadot, Prosper Maufoux, or Georges Duboeuf.*

4 SERVINGS

- 3 tablespoons soybean oil or corn oil
- 2 scallions, cut into 1-inch pieces
- 3 garlic cloves, smashed
- One 2-inch piece of fresh ginger, cut into ⅛-inch slices
- 3 star anise pods*
- 1 teaspoon Szechwan peppercorns*
- 1 cup soy sauce
- ½ cup sake or dry sherry
- 1 tablespoon sugar
- 4 Cornish hens (about 1 pound each)
- Coconut-Pineapple Sweet Rice (recipe follows)

*Available at Asian markets

1. Heat the oil in a large enameled cast-iron casserole. Add the scallions, the smashed garlic, the ginger slices, the star anise, and the Szechwan peppercorns, and cook over moderately high heat until fragrant and the vegetables are golden, about 5 minutes. Add the soy sauce, sake, sugar, and 1 cup water, and simmer gently for 10 minutes.

2. Add the hens to the casserole, breast sides up. Cover, reduce the heat to moderately low, and simmer, turning the hens every 10 minutes, until the juices run clear when a thigh is pierced with a fork, about 40 minutes. Remove from the heat and let the hens stand covered in the casserole for 10 minutes. Transfer the hens to a platter; cover loosely with foil and keep warm. Strain the braising liquid and skim off the fat.

3. Set the hens on individual plates and mound the Coconut-Pineapple Sweet Rice alongside. Serve with a little of the soy braising liquid.

Coconut-Pineapple Sweet Rice

MAKES ABOUT 4 CUPS

- 2 cups sweet rice*
- 1 small butternut squash (about ¾ pound)—peeled, halved, seeded, and cut into ¼-inch dice
- ½ cup unsweetened coconut milk*
- ½ cup coarsely chopped fresh pineapple
- 1 tablespoon sugar
- 1 tablespoon unsalted butter

*Available at Asian markets

1. In a bowl, cover the rice with 4 cups of water and let it soak for 4 hours. Drain well. (MAKE AHEAD: The rice can be prepared to this point up to 1 day ahead; cover and let stand at room temperature.)

2. Line a large bamboo steamer with a double layer of moistened cheesecloth. Spread the drained rice in a thin layer in the steamer over plenty of water. Cover and steam over high heat until tender, about 27 minutes. Transfer to a large bowl.

3. Meanwhile, in a small steamer, steam the diced butternut squash until tender but still slightly firm, about 5 minutes. Add to the rice in the bowl.

4. In a small nonreactive saucepan, combine the coconut milk, pineapple, sugar, and butter, and bring just to a boil over high heat, stirring until the sugar is dissolved. Stir the pineapple-coconut milk into the rice and squash and serve hot.—SUSANNA FOO

ROASTED CORNISH HENS WITH CORN BREAD STUFFING AND CREAMY PAN GRAVY

Greg Sonnier, of Gabrielle in New Orleans, likes to serve his spicy stuffed hens with a gravy that includes, as a surprise ingredient, a dash of vanilla for a lightly sweet, fragrant flavor.

🍷 *This relatively rich dish needs a light red for contrast. The 1992 Oregon Pinot Noirs from Adelsheim, Ponzi, and Knudsen-Erath have the tart, cherrylike flavors needed.*

4 SERVINGS

CORN BREAD STUFFING:

- 2 tablespoons unsalted butter, softened
- 2 medium onions, finely chopped

5 medium celery ribs, finely chopped
1 large red bell pepper, finely chopped
1 large garlic clove, minced
1 bay leaf
Salt and freshly ground black pepper
½ pound spicy pork sausage, such as andouille, sliced ¼ inch thick
⅓ cup all-purpose flour
⅓ cup yellow cornmeal
½ teaspoon baking powder
2 tablespoons sugar
¾ cup milk
1 large egg, lightly beaten
1 large egg yolk

HENS AND CREAMY GRAVY:
4 Cornish hens (about 1 pound each)
Salt and freshly ground black pepper
⅔ cup dry white wine
⅔ cup chicken stock or canned low-sodium broth
⅔ cup heavy cream
¼ teaspoon pure vanilla extract

1. Make the corn bread stuffing: Preheat the oven to 350°. Melt 1 tablespoon of the butter in a large cast-iron skillet. Add half the onions, half the celery, the bell pepper, garlic, bay leaf, and ½ teaspoon each of salt and pepper. Cook over moderately high heat, stirring occasionally, until softened, about 5 minutes. Lower the heat to moderate, add the sausage slices, and cook, stirring, until browned, about 10 minutes. Add the remaining onion and celery and cook, stirring, until translucent, about 10 minutes. Transfer to a plate and discard the bay leaf.

Soy-Braised Cornish Hens with Coconut-Pineapple Sweet Rice

2. Butter a 9-inch round cake pan and a 5-by-8-inch loaf pan. In a medium bowl, combine the flour, cornmeal, baking powder, sugar, and ¼ teaspoon salt. Add ¼ cup of the milk, the beaten egg, and the remaining 1 tablespoon butter, and stir until just combined. Pour the batter into the prepared round cake pan, spreading it evenly to the edges. Bake for about 13 minutes, or until set. Invert the corn bread onto a rack and let cool slightly. Leave the oven on.

3. Crumble the corn bread into a medium bowl, breaking it into ½-inch pieces. Stir in the sausage mixture. In a small bowl, combine the remaining ½ cup milk and the egg yolk. Add to the corn bread and combine. Transfer the corn bread stuffing to the prepared loaf pan, pressing it in firmly. Bake for about 10 minutes, or just until set. Invert the stuffing onto a plate and let cool slightly. Break the stuffing into small pieces and let cool completely. (MAKE AHEAD: The corn bread stuffing can be prepared up to 1 day ahead; cover and refrigerate. Let return to room temperature before proceeding.)

4. Prepare the hens and creamy gravy: Preheat the oven to 375°. Season the hens with salt and pepper. Loosely fill the cavities with the corn bread stuffing and transfer the hens to a large roasting pan, breasts up. Roast for about 50 minutes, or until golden brown and the juices run clear when a thigh is pierced with a fork. Transfer to plates, cover loosely with foil, and keep warm.

5. Pour off the excess fat from the roasting pan and set the pan over 2 burners on moderately high heat. Add the white wine and cook, scraping, until the liquid is reduced by half, about 5 minutes. Add the chicken stock and the heavy cream and boil until thickened. Stir in the vanilla extract and season the gravy with salt and pepper. Spoon the gravy around the Cornish hens and serve.—GREG SONNIER

CORNISH HENS WITH COCONUT CURRY SAUCE AND BASMATI RICE CAKES

David Ruggerio, of Le Chantilly in New York City, suggests using a biscuit cutter as a ring mold for the basmati rice cakes. If you don't want to make the fried rice cakes, you can simply omit Steps 6 and 7 and serve the hens on a bed of the basmati rice. Be sure to allow time for the hens to marinate overnight.

🍷 *Look for 1992 German Spätlese Rieslings, such as Dr. Fischer Ockfener Bockstein or Dr. Bürklin-Wolf Wachenheimer Gerümpel.*

4 SERVINGS

MARINATED HENS:

- 4 Cornish hens (about 1 pound each)
- ½ cup olive oil
- 2 shallots, thinly sliced
- 2 garlic cloves, crushed
- 4 fresh thyme sprigs
- 1 teaspoon whole black peppercorns, crushed
- ½ teaspoon salt

CURRY SAUCE:

- 2 tablespoons olive oil
- ½ cup finely chopped onion
- ¼ cup finely chopped celery
- ¼ cup finely chopped carrot
- ¼ cup finely diced banana
- ¼ cup finely diced ripe pear
- ¼ cup Madras curry powder
- ¼ cup fresh orange juice
- 1 tablespoon fresh lemon juice
- 1 cup chicken stock or canned low-sodium broth
- 2 tablespoons unsweetened coconut milk*
- 1 tablespoon Major Grey's chutney
- ½ cup heavy cream

RICE CAKES:

- 1 tablespoon unsalted butter
- 2 shallots, finely chopped
- 1 cup basmati or Texmati rice
- 2 tablespoons finely chopped fresh coriander (cilantro)
- 1 tablespoon finely chopped chives
- 1¾ cups chicken stock or canned low-sodium broth
- Salt
- 2 tablespoons olive oil

*Available at most supermarkets and at Asian markets

1. Cut up and marinate the hens: Using kitchen shears, cut out the backbone from each hen. Then cut through the breastbone to divide each hen in half. Remove the whole legs from each bird by cutting through the hip joints; you should have 2 breast sections and 2 leg sections from each of the birds.

2. In a large dish, combine the oil, shallots, garlic, thyme, peppercorns, and salt. Add the hens; turn to coat. Cover and refrigerate overnight.

3. Make the curry sauce: Heat the olive oil in a medium nonreactive saucepan. Add the onion, celery, and carrot, and cook over high heat, stirring occasionally, until slightly softened, about 4 minutes. Add the banana and the pear to the saucepan and cook, stirring, until nearly disintegrated, about 3 minutes. Stir in the curry powder and cook until fragrant, about 2 minutes.

4. Add the orange and lemon juices to the saucepan and bring to a boil. Stir in the chicken stock, coconut milk, and chutney, and bring back to a boil. Add the cream and simmer for 5 minutes. Strain the sauce, pressing down on the solids, and return it to the saucepan. Boil over moderately high heat until reduced to ¾ cup, about 7 minutes.

5. Make the rice cakes: Melt the butter in a saucepan. Add the shallots and cook over moderate heat until translucent, about 2 minutes. Stir in the rice, coriander, and chives. Add the chicken stock and bring to a boil. Cover

Cornish Hens with Coconut Curry Sauce and Basmati Rice Cakes

and cook over moderate heat until the rice is tender and all the liquid has been absorbed, about 25 minutes. Season with salt.

6. Line a medium baking sheet with foil and brush lightly with olive oil. Brush the insides of 4 metal ring molds measuring about 3 inches across and 1 inch high with olive oil and set them on the baking sheet. Divide the rice evenly among the ring molds, packing it tightly so that it is flush with the top of the rings. (MAKE AHEAD: The recipe can be prepared to this point up to 1 day ahead; cover and refrigerate the curry sauce and the basmati rice cakes.)

7. Preheat the broiler. Heat the olive oil in a large nonstick skillet. Add the rice cakes in their rings and fry over moderate heat until the cakes are browned and crisp on the bottom, about 3 minutes. Turn the rice cakes over in their rings and brown the other side, about 3 minutes. Transfer the cakes to paper towels to drain; keep warm.

8. Remove the hens from the marinade and pat them dry with paper towels. Place the hen pieces, skin side down, on a baking sheet and broil for about 12 minutes, until well browned; shift the pan as necessary so that the pieces will brown evenly. Turn the hens skin side up and broil for about 10 minutes longer, or until the skin is browned and the juices run clear when a thigh is pierced with a fork.

9. To serve the Cornish hens, rewarm the curry sauce. Set each rice cake in the center of a large warmed plate and remove the ring mold. Spoon the curry sauce around the rice cakes. Arrange 2 legs and 2 breast halves around each of the rice cakes and serve at once.—DAVID RUGGERIO

QUICK CORNISH HENS

Here are four ways to prepare 1- to 1¼-pound Cornish hens. After applying one of the quick fixes below, roast in a preheated 375° oven for about 45 minutes, or until the juices run clear when a thigh is pierced with a fork.

- FOR A CRISP SKIN AND CITRUS ACCENT, **rub the hens with a cut lemon and brush with melted butter, then stuff each with a lemon half and a thyme sprig. Baste with pan juices during roasting.**
- FOR AN ASIAN TASTE, **brush the hens with a mixture of soy sauce, white wine, and sesame oil, and spoon a little into the cavity. Baste with pan juices during roasting.**
- FOR SPICY BIRDS, **brush the hens with a mix of grainy and Dijon mustards, vegetable oil, and a little Tabasco.**
- FOR A SAVORY TANG, **stuff the hens under the breast skin with goat cheese, chopped sun-dried tomatoes, and chopped fresh basil.**

CUMIN-ROASTED CORNISH HENS WITH BLACK BEAN STEW

At Chef Allen's Restaurant in Miami, Allen Susser adds Cuban flavor to his birds by rubbing them with dried spices, ginger, and lime juice, and serving them with a black bean stew.

4 SERVINGS

- 2 tablespoons ground cumin
- 1 tablespoon fresh lime juice
- 3 large garlic cloves, minced
- 1 teaspoon kosher salt
- ½ teaspoon finely chopped fresh ginger
- ½ teaspoon sage
- ½ teaspoon ground allspice
- ½ teaspoon freshly ground pepper
- 3 tablespoons olive oil
- 4 Cornish hens (about 1 pound each)

Black Bean Stew (recipe follows)

1. In a bowl, combine the cumin, lime juice, garlic, salt, ginger, sage, allspice, and pepper. Stir in the olive oil and rub the mixture over the hens. Set the hens, breasts up, on a rack in a roasting pan and let stand at room temperature for 1 hour.

2. Preheat the oven to 375°. Roast the hens for about 25 minutes, just until the breasts are golden. Carefully turn the hens over and roast for about 10 minutes, or until golden. Set the hens breasts up again and roast for about 10 minutes longer, or until the juices run clear when a thigh is pierced with a fork.

3. To serve, spoon the Black Bean Stew into 4 soup plates and set a Cornish hen on top.

Black Bean Stew

MAKES ABOUT 3 CUPS

- 1 cup dried black beans (about 7 ounces), rinsed and picked over
- 4 ounces bacon, finely chopped
- 1 medium poblano chile, seeded and cut into ½-inch dice

1 medium tomato, seeded and cut into ½-inch dice
1 small onion, finely chopped
1 large garlic clove, minced
Salt
1 small acorn squash (about ¾ pound)—peeled, halved, seeded, and cut into 1-inch cubes
2 tablespoons fresh lime juice

1. In a medium bowl, cover the dried black beans with water and let them soak overnight. Alternatively, in a medium saucepan, cover the dried beans with 1 inch of water and boil over high heat for 2 minutes. Remove the saucepan from the heat and let the beans stand for 1 hour.
2. Drain the beans and transfer to a medium saucepan. Cover with 1 inch of water and bring to a boil over high heat. Reduce the heat to moderately low, cover partially, and simmer until just tender, about 1¼ hours.
3. Meanwhile, in a medium skillet, cook the chopped bacon over moderately high heat, stirring occasionally, until lightly browned but not crisp, about 5 minutes. Add the poblano chile, the diced tomato, the chopped onion, and the minced garlic clove, season with salt, and cook for 5 minutes, stirring frequently.
4. Stir the acorn squash cubes and the bacon mixture into the black beans and simmer over moderately low heat, partially covered, until the squash is tender, about 25 minutes. Stir in the lime juice, season with salt, and serve hot. (MAKE AHEAD: The stew can be made up to 1 day ahead; cover and refrigerate. Rewarm before serving.) —ALLEN SUSSER

PANCETTA-STUFFED CORNISH HENS WITH GRAPE LEAVES AND CREMINI MUSHROOMS

Grape leaves add subtle flavor and enhance the presentation of these crisp hens from Tony Mantuano of Tuttaposto in Chicago. Flattening the hens is easy; you can also ask your butcher to do it for you, but be sure to reserve the backbones.

2 SERVINGS

2 Cornish hens (about 1 pound each)
1½ cups chicken stock or canned low-sodium broth
2 slices of pancetta (about 1 ounce total)
4 whole brined grape leaves,* rinsed well
1 teaspoon finely chopped fresh rosemary plus 2 rosemary sprigs
Salt and freshly ground pepper
¼ cup all-purpose flour
1 tablespoon olive oil
4 ounces cremini mushrooms, stems discarded, caps sliced ⅛ inch thick

*Available at specialty food markets

1. Preheat the oven to 425°. Using kitchen shears, cut out the backbone from each hen. Set the hens on a work surface, breasts up. Using the heel of your hand, press down on the breastbones to flatten them. Chop the backbones into 2-inch pieces.
2. In a small saucepan, cook the backbones over high heat, stirring occasionally, until browned, about 5 minutes. Add the chicken stock and boil until the liquid is reduced to ½ cup, about 10 minutes. Strain the stock into a bowl and keep warm.
3. Bring a medium saucepan of water to a boil. Add the pancetta and blanch for 1 minute. Transfer to paper towels and pat dry. Add the grape leaves to the boiling water and blanch for 30 seconds, stirring occasionally; drain well. Line the bottom of a 9-by-13-inch roasting pan with the leaves.
4. Loosen the breast skin of each hen with your fingers. Spread the chopped rosemary under the skin, rubbing it over the breast, and top with a pancetta slice. Season the hens all over with salt and pepper and dredge the skin side in the flour.
5. Heat the olive oil in a large nonstick skillet. Add the hens, breasts down, and cook over moderately high heat until the skin is browned and crisp, about 4 minutes. Transfer the hens to the roasting pan, breasts up, and add the cremini and the rosemary sprigs. Pour the strained chicken stock around the hens. Season lightly with salt and pepper and roast the hens in the middle of the oven for about 18 minutes, or until the juices run clear when a thigh is pierced with a fork. Transfer the hens to a platter with the mushrooms and grape leaves. Cover loosely with foil.
6. Strain the pan juices into a medium saucepan and boil until the liquid is reduced to ½ cup, about 4 minutes.
7. Spread the grapes leaves out on 2 plates. Set the flattened hens on top and spoon the mushrooms alongside. Drizzle a little pan sauce on the hens and pass the remaining pan sauce at the table.—TONY MANTUANO

FRIED TURKEY CUTLETS *LF*

🍷 *This dish could be matched with a light, fruity red, such as Beaujolais, but a rich, round California Chardonnay, such as the 1992 Simi or Silverado Limited Reserve, has enough depth to match the rich savory flavors of the cutlets and spaetzle with gravy.*

6 SERVINGS

- 2 cups low-fat (1%) buttermilk
- 2 teaspoons Worcestershire sauce
- 2 teaspoons dry mustard
- ½ teaspoon cayenne pepper
- ½ small onion, thinly sliced
- 1 garlic clove, thinly sliced
- 1½ pounds turkey breast cutlets
- ¾ cup fresh plain bread crumbs
- Salt and freshly ground black pepper
- ½ recipe warm Three-Mushroom Gravy (recipe follows)

1. Combine the buttermilk, Worcestershire, dry mustard, and cayenne in a shallow nonreactive baking dish. Stir in the onion and garlic and add the turkey cutlets, turning to coat. Cover and refrigerate for at least 4 hours or overnight.

2. Preheat the oven to 350°. Spread the bread crumbs on a baking sheet and toast for about 5 minutes, until lightly browned. Transfer to a plate and season with salt and pepper.

3. Drain the turkey cutlets and discard the marinade. Coat the cutlets with the seasoned bread crumbs, shaking off the excess. Coat a large nonstick skillet with olive oil cooking spray and warm over moderately high heat. Add one-third of the turkey cutlets and spray them lightly. Fry the cutlets, turning once, until cooked through and golden, about 3 minutes per side. Transfer to a platter, cover loosely with foil, and keep warm. Wipe out the skillet and repeat the process with more olive oil spray and the remaining turkey cutlets.

4. Transfer the turkey cutlets to warmed plates. Spoon the Three-Mushroom Gravy on top.

Three-Mushroom Gravy

Chicken wings, the tastiest and fattiest part of the chicken, are used to make the stock that is the basis for this richly flavored gravy. All the fat is skimmed from the chilled stock before using. If you can find them, skinned turkey or chicken necks can be substituted for the wings. They provide great taste and are less fatty.

Serve the gravy with any roasted meats or poultry, or use as a sauce for pasta or polenta.

MAKES ABOUT 2 CUPS

- 1 ounce dried wild mushrooms, such as shiitake, porcini, or morels, or a combination
- 2 pounds chicken wings
- ¾ pound fresh shiitake mushrooms, stems finely chopped, caps sliced ⅛ inch thick
- 10 ounces white mushrooms, stems finely chopped, caps sliced ⅛ inch thick
- ⅓ cup brandy
- 2 medium carrots, coarsely chopped
- 2 medium shallots, coarsely chopped
- 2 fresh thyme sprigs
- 1 bay leaf
- 8 whole black peppercorns
- ½ teaspoon olive oil
- 1 teaspoon arrowroot
- Salt and freshly ground pepper
- 2 tablespoons finely chopped fresh chives

1. In a small bowl, cover the dried mushrooms with 2 cups of very hot water. Let soak until softened, about 20 minutes. Drain the mushrooms, reserving the soaking liquid. Rinse the mushrooms and finely chop them, discarding any tough bits.

2. Warm a large deep skillet over high heat. Add the chicken wings and cook, turning once, until well browned, about 15 minutes. Transfer to a plate and pour off all the fat from the skillet. Add the reconstituted dried mushrooms, shiitake stems, and white mushroom stems, and cook, stirring occasionally, until beginning to brown, about 4 minutes. Add the brandy and boil until evaporated. Pour in the mushroom soaking liquid, stopping when you reach the grit. Bring to a boil, scraping up any browned bits. Add 4 cups of water, the chicken wings, carrots, shallots, thyme, bay leaf, and peppercorns to the skillet, and bring back to a boil. Cover partially, reduce the heat to moderately low, and simmer the stock for 1½ hours.

3. Strain the stock, pressing down on the solids. Skim off any fat. Wipe out the saucepan and pour in the stock. Boil over high heat until reduced to 1½ cups.

4. Heat the olive oil in a large nonstick skillet until smoking. Add the sliced shiitake and white mushroom caps and cook over high heat, stirring occasionally, until well browned, about 12 minutes. Stir the sliced mushrooms into the reduced stock and bring to a simmer over moderate heat. In a small bowl, mix the arrowroot with 2 tablespoons of water and stir the mixture into the gravy. Cook, stirring, just until thickened, about 3 minutes; do not let the gravy boil. Season with salt and pepper. (MAKE AHEAD: The gravy can be made ahead; cover and refrigerate. Rewarm gently over low heat before proceeding.) Stir in the chives and serve.—GRACE PARISI

HERBED TURKEY SAUSAGE PATTIES LF

To make this dish low in fat, be sure to use ground turkey breast meat and not a combination of ground light and dark meat, which has substantially more fat. If you can't find ground turkey breast, buy a one-pound piece of breast meat and chop it yourself.

4 SERVINGS

- 1 large red potato
- 2 teaspoons vegetable oil
- ¼ pound fresh shiitake mushrooms, stems discarded and caps finely chopped
- 1 small onion, finely chopped
- 2 garlic cloves, minced
- 1 pound ground turkey breast or 1 pound skinless turkey breast, cut into 1-inch cubes
- 2 ounces cured ham, such as prosciutto, trimmed of visible fat and finely chopped
- 1 tablespoon low-fat (1%) milk
- 1 tablespoon finely chopped fresh flat-leaf parsley
- 1 teaspoon finely chopped fresh sage
- ½ teaspoon finely chopped fresh thyme or pinch of dried
- 1 teaspoon salt
- ¼ teaspoon freshly ground black pepper

1. In a steamer basket set over simmering water, steam the potato until tender when pierced with a fork, about 18 minutes. Let cool slightly, then peel the potato and coarsely grate it.

2. Heat 1 teaspoon of the oil in a large nonstick skillet. Add the mushrooms and cook over high heat, stirring occasionally, until beginning to brown, about 4 minutes. Add the onion and garlic and cook, stirring, until translucent, about 3 minutes. Transfer to a bowl and let cool.

3. If using cubed turkey, pulse in a food processor until coarsely ground or mince by hand.

4. Add the turkey to the mushroom mixture with the potato, ham, milk, parsley, sage, thyme, salt, and pepper, and mix well. Shape the mixture into eight 3-inch patties. (MAKE AHEAD: The patties can be refrigerated, covered, for up to 2 days.)

5. Heat the remaining 1 teaspoon vegetable oil in the large nonstick skillet. Add the patties and cook over moderately high heat, turning once, until well browned and cooked through, about 3 minutes per side. Transfer to plates and serve.—GRACE PARISI

TURKEY ROULADES WITH SUN-DRIED TOMATOES AND PROSCIUTTO

The roulades should be set at least two inches apart in the roasting pan, or they'll steam instead of roast. You can use two medium-size roasting pans; be sure to deglaze them both.

MAKES 50 BUFFET SERVINGS

TURKEY ROULADES:

- ½ pound unpeeled shallots, trimmed
- 20 large garlic cloves, peeled
- 5 fresh thyme sprigs
- 2 tablespoons olive oil
- 1 large boneless turkey breast with the skin (about 9 pounds), halved
- 2 cups drained oil-packed sun-dried tomatoes, coarsely chopped
- ¾ pound thinly sliced prosciutto, coarsely chopped
- 6 ounces cream cheese, at room temperature

Fried Turkey Cutlets

LOW-FAT MENU

FRIED TURKEY CUTLETS (P. 152)
THREE-MUSHROOM GRAVY (P. 152)
HERBED SPAETZLE (P. 257)
LEMON AND GARLIC ROASTED BEETS (P. 325)

—GRACE PARISI

SPRING BUFFET FOR 50

This buffet features time- and work-saving recipes: dishes that can be made in advance; dishes that can be prepared in disposable cookware; and, of course, dishes that can be made in large quantities without sacrificing a bit of flavor or flair.

🍷 If the occasion calls for Champagnes, you'll want to look for nonvintage bruts such as the Pol Roger and the Taittinger La Française; among California sparkling wines, look for the nonvintage Roederer Estate Brut and the 1990 Iron Horse Wedding Cuvée. Offer your guests red or white wine as well, since either could go with the roasted salmon and the turkey roulades. Good choices for whites include the 1993 Meridian Chardonnay or the 1993 Robert Mondavi Woodbridge Chardonnay; for reds, try the 1993 Georges Duboeuf Beaujolais-Villages or the 1991 Ruffino Aziano Chianti Classico Riserva.

SESAME-COATED ESCAROLE ROLLS (P. 33)

SMOKED SALMON CANAPES ON BRIOCHE (P. 25)

PECAN-CHEDDAR COINS (P. 33)

ROASTED SALMON WITH A FENNEL-CRUMB CRUST AND CREAMY HERB SAUCE (P. 207)

TURKEY ROULADES WITH SUN-DRIED TOMATOES AND PROSCIUTTO (P. 153)

ORZO SALAD WITH WILD MUSHROOMS AND ASPARAGUS (P. 252)

SUGAR SNAP PEAS WITH WALNUTS (P. 310)

LEMON POUND CAKE WITH BERRIES IN POMEGRANATE SYRUP (P. 392)

LEMON-PEPPER BISCOTTI, CHOCOLATE-ALMOND BISCOTTI, AND PISTACHIO-ORANGE BISCOTTI (P. 380-81)

—GRACE PARISI

⅓ cup finely chopped fresh flat-leaf parsley
¼ cup finely chopped fresh basil
2 teaspoons finely chopped fresh rosemary
Freshly ground black pepper
Salt
6 tablespoons unsalted butter, softened
8 bunches of arugula, large stems discarded

ROASTED PEPPER DRESSING:
½ cup sherry vinegar
1 cup olive oil
5 large garlic cloves, peeled
1 medium red bell pepper
Salt and freshly ground black pepper

1. Prepare the turkey roulades: Preheat the oven to 425°. In a medium baking dish, toss the shallots, garlic, and thyme with the olive oil. Cover with foil and roast for about 1 hour, or until the vegetables are softened and caramelized. Discard the shallot skins and thyme sprigs.

2. Meanwhile, remove the tenderloins from each turkey breast half and set them on a work surface. Using a sharp knife, make a horizontal slice three-quarters of the way through each tenderloin, to create a flap. Spread the tenderloins open, set between 2 sheets of plastic, and pound until ½ inch thick, using a meat pounder or the side of a cleaver. Set aside.

3. Set one turkey breast half on the work surface, skin side down and pointed end toward you. Make a horizontal slice three-quarters of the way through the thickest portion of the breast half and open it like a book. Set the breast half between 2 sheets of plastic and pound until ½ inch thick. Set one of the pounded tenderloins on the thinnest part of the breast. Cover with plastic and pound to form a 15-inch square. Transfer to a large baking sheet. Repeat the process with the remaining turkey tenderloin and breast half.

4. In a food processor, pulse the roasted shallots and garlic and the sun-dried tomatoes until finely chopped but not pureed. Add the prosciutto and pulse until finely chopped. Transfer to a bowl and stir in the cream cheese, parsley, basil, rosemary, and ¾ teaspoon pepper.

5. Season the turkey breasts with salt and pepper and spread half of the sun-dried tomato stuffing over each one in an even layer all the way to the edges. Starting with the side closest to you, roll up the turkey so that the skin surrounds the rolls. Tie at 3-inch intervals with butcher's string. (MAKE AHEAD: The recipe can be prepared to this point up to 2 days ahead; cover and refrigerate. Let return to room temperature before roasting.)

6. Preheat the oven to 350°. Set the turkey roulades in a very large roasting pan, leaving at least 2 inches between the roulades and the pan sides. Brush with half of the softened butter and season well with salt and pepper. Roast, basting occasionally with the remaining butter and pan drippings, for about 1 hour, or until the roulades are browned and an instant-read thermometer inserted in the center registers 130°; they will continue to cook as they sit. Transfer the roulades to 1 or 2 large platters and let stand for at least 20 minutes or up to 3 hours.

7. Make the dressing: Pour the pan drippings into a bowl and skim off the fat. Set the roasting pan over 2 burners on high heat. Add the vinegar and bring to a boil, scraping up any browned bits; don't reduce the sauce. Add to the pan drippings and let cool.

8. In a small saucepan, combine the oil and garlic. Bring to a boil over moderate heat. Reduce the heat to moderately low and cook until golden, about 15 minutes. Let cool, then remove the garlic cloves and reserve separately.

9. Meanwhile, roast the bell pepper directly over a gas flame or under a broiler, turning often, until charred all over. Transfer to a paper bag and let steam for 10 minutes. Scrape off the blackened skin and discard the stem, seeds, and ribs. Transfer the pepper to a food processor or blender along with the pan drippings and garlic cloves and process until smooth. With the machine on, gradually add the garlic oil until incorporated. Season the dressing with salt and pepper and let stand for up to 2 hours.

10. To serve, make a bed of arugula on 2 large serving platters. Cut the turkey into ⅓-inch slices and arrange on the arugula. Whisk the dressing, pour into 2 sauceboats, and serve with the turkey.—GRACE PARISI

MAPLE-PEPPER ROASTED TURKEY

Cooking the perfect turkey is a tricky business that has challenged Thanksgiving cooks over the years. Because the breast is done before the legs, you usually have to sacrifice perfectly cooked white meat for thoroughly done dark meat. If your goal is to bring a whole, beautiful, well-cooked turkey to the table, roast the 10-pound bird for about three hours, or until the temperature in the thickest part of the thigh reaches 180° and the juices run clear. Let the turkey sit for 30 minutes before carving.

If you want perfectly cooked light and dark meat and don't mind presenting your guests with a carved turkey, follow Sandy D'Amato's method. He roasts the turkey until the breast is done, then removes the legs and wings and continues roasting them.

The turkey needs to be started a day ahead to allow time for it to marinate.

8 SERVINGS

MAPLE-PEPPER BUTTER AND GLAZE:

2 sticks (½ pound) unsalted butter, softened

FIVE TIPS FOR A PERFECT TURKEY

• CHECK YOUR INSTANT-READ OR TRADITIONAL MEAT THERMOMETER. If you place it in a pot of boiling water and it registers 212° (water's boiling point at sea level), you're all set. If it doesn't, buy a new one.

• SET THE TURKEY ON A RACK in a large roasting pan to promote maximum air and heat circulation and to ensure even cooking.

• PROTECT THE TURKEY BREAST FROM OVERCOOKING by roasting the bird on the lowest rack in the oven; this will keep it away from the top, the hottest part of the oven. Once the breast skin is browned, loosely cover it with foil to prevent it from becoming too dark.

• KEEP A CAREFUL EYE ON THE THERMOMETER during the last half hour of cooking; the temperature may rise rapidly toward the end.

• CHECK FOR DONENESS IN THE THICKEST, MEATIEST PARTS. With the thermometer, test the widest section of the breast near the wing joint; the temperature should be 165°. Test the legs at the top of the thigh, near the hip joint; the temperature should be 180°. Insert an instant-read thermometer deep enough to cover its heat sensor, the indentation about two inches from the tip. Check the juices, too. If they have a pinkish tinge, continue roasting; if they're clear, the turkey's done. Try to insert the thermometer as infrequently as possible, to prevent the precious juices from escaping.

Maple-Pepper Roasted Turkey

½ cup plus 2 tablespoons pure maple syrup
¼ cup fresh lemon juice
2 teaspoons finely grated lemon zest
1 tablespoon coarsely ground black pepper
2 teaspoons coarse salt
½ teaspoon finely ground black pepper

MARINATED TURKEY:

1 cup fresh lemon juice
¾ cup pure maple syrup
½ cup corn oil
6 medium shallots, thinly sliced
6 large garlic cloves, thinly sliced
4 fresh thyme sprigs
3 imported bay leaves
2 teaspoons finely grated lemon zest
1 teaspoon freshly ground black pepper
One 10-pound turkey, neck skin removed and reserved for Red Cabbage Slaw with Turkey Cracklings (p. 79)
3 medium onions, cut into 1-inch pieces
3 medium celery ribs, cut into 1-inch pieces

GRAVY:

1 tablespoon all-purpose flour
2 cups chicken stock or canned low-sodium broth
Coarse salt and freshly ground black pepper

1. Make the maple-pepper butter and glaze: In a food processor, combine the butter, 6 tablespoons of the maple syrup, 3 tablespoons of the lemon juice, the lemon zest, coarsely ground pepper, and salt. Process until blended and transfer to a bowl. In another bowl, combine the remaining ¼ cup syrup, 1 tablespoon lemon juice, and the finely ground black pepper. (MAKE AHEAD: The maple-pepper butter and glaze can be refrigerated, covered, for 1 day; let the butter return to room temperature before using.)

2. Marinate the turkey: In a sturdy 2-gallon plastic bag, combine the lemon juice, maple syrup, corn oil, shallots, garlic, thyme, bay leaves, lemon zest, and pepper. Add the turkey to the bag and seal. Distribute the marinade evenly over and inside the turkey. Set the turkey, breast side down, in a bowl in the refrigerator and marinate for 24 hours, turning occasionally.

3. Preheat the oven to 450°. Position the oven rack near the bottom of the oven. Wipe off the shallots and garlic from the turkey and pat dry. Strain the marinade into a bowl and reserve the herbs, garlic, and shallots. Skim off the oil and reserve both oil and marinade.

4. Using your fingers, carefully loosen the turkey skin over the breast and thighs. Put all but 3 tablespoons of the softened maple-pepper butter in a pastry bag fitted with a small round tube and pipe it under the breast and thigh skin, patting gently to spread the butter. Alternatively, spread it evenly with your fingers.

5. Put one-third each of the diced onions and celery in the cavity. Tie the legs together with

THANKSGIVING DINNER

🍷 The sweet and savory tastes found in this menu call for a fruity-tart, refreshing wine. For a white, choose a 1994 Dry Chenin Blanc from the West Coast, such as Hogue Cellars or Dry Creek Clarksburg. For a red alternative, choose a fruity 1995 Beaujolais Nouveau from France or the 1994 Simi Rosé of Cabernet Sauvignon from California. And to end the meal, serve a luscious dessert wine, such as the 1991 Swanson Late Harvest Napa Valley Sémillon.

DUMPLING SQUASH SOUP WITH PANCETTA (P. 96)

MAPLE-PEPPER ROASTED TURKEY (P. 155)

WILD RICE, ITALIAN SAUSAGE AND SHIITAKE STUFFING (P. 196)

CRANBERRY, GINGER AND PEAR CHUTNEY (P. 354)

ASIAGO AND SAGE SCALLOPED POTATOES (P. 277)

LEMON-LACQUERED RADISHES, SHALLOTS AND BRUSSELS SPROUTS (P. 325)

RED CABBAGE SLAW WITH TURKEY CRACKLINGS (P. 79)

DRIED CHERRY AND PEACH STEAMED PUDDING (P. 429)

HAZELNUT TART (P. 403)

—SANFORD D'AMATO

TIMETABLE:

ONE MONTH AHEAD

- **Make and freeze the ham stock for the soup.**

THREE DAYS AHEAD

- **Make the Cranberry, Ginger and Pear Chutney.**

TWO DAYS AHEAD

- **Make the Dumpling Squash Soup with Pancetta.**

ONE DAY AHEAD

- **Marinate the turkey.**
- **Make the Wild Rice, Italian Sausage and Shiitake Stuffing.**
- **Make the Lemon-Lacquered Radishes, Shallots and Brussels Sprouts.**
- **Make the Red Cabbage Slaw with Turkey Cracklings.**
- **Bake the pastry and toast the nuts for the Hazelnut Tart.**

UP TO EIGHT HOURS AHEAD

- **Make the Dried Cherry and Peach Steamed Pudding.**
- **Finish the tart.**

FIVE HOURS AHEAD

- **Make the Asiago and Sage Scalloped Potatoes.**

ABOUT THREE HOURS AHEAD

- **Roast the Maple-Pepper Roasted Turkey.**

SHORTLY BEFORE SERVING

- **Reheat the squash soup, wild rice stuffing, scalloped potatoes, lemon-lacquered vegetables, red cabbage slaw, and steamed pudding.**
- **Make the gravy for the turkey.**

kitchen string and set the turkey, breast side up, on a rack in a large roasting pan. Rub the breast and thigh skin with the remaining maple butter and roast for 30 minutes, basting twice. The skin may appear dark in patches because the maple syrup in the marinade and the butter caramelize as the turkey cooks; cover it loosely with foil to keep the skin from burning.

6. Lower the oven temperature to 350°. Spread the remaining onions and celery around the turkey and roast for about 1½ hours longer, or until an instant-read thermometer inserted in the thickest part of the breast just above the wing joint reaches 165° and the juices run clear. During the last 30 minutes, add the reserved shallots, garlic, and herbs to the pan, remove the foil from the turkey, and brush twice with the maple-pepper glaze. Transfer to a carving board and let stand, loosely covered with foil, for 30 minutes.

7. Remove the whole legs from the turkey, cutting them off at the hip joint. Cut off the wings from the breast. Return the legs and wings to the pan and roast for about 30 minutes longer, until an instant-read thermometer inserted in the thickest part of the thigh reaches 180° and the juices run clear. Transfer the legs and wings to the turkey on the carving board, cover with foil, and let stand for 15 minutes before carving.

8. Meanwhile, **make the gravy:** Set the roasting pan over 2 burners over high heat and cook the vegetables, stirring, until golden brown. Carefully pour off all but 2 tablespoons of the fat. Add the flour and whisk for 1 minute. Add the reserved marinade and the stock and bring to a boil, scraping up any browned bits. Simmer, whisking constantly, for 3 minutes. Strain the gravy into a saucepan and boil over high heat until reduced by half, about 10 minutes. Season with salt and pepper, pour into a sauceboat, and serve alongside the turkey.—SANFORD D'AMATO

Grilled Duck with Wild Rice-Tasso Dressing

GRILLED DUCK WITH WILD RICE-TASSO DRESSING

🍷 *The richness of duck needs a contrasting red with some acerbity. Look for a good Cabernet Sauvignon, such as the 1992 Vichon from California or the 1993 Los Vascos from Chile.*

4 SERVINGS

- ½ pound wild rice, rinsed
- 1 stick (4 ounces) unsalted butter
- 2 small celery ribs, cut into ½-inch dice
- 1 medium onion, cut into ½-inch dice
- ¼ red bell pepper, cut into ½-inch dice
- 5 ounces tasso or other spicy smoked ham or spicy sausage, finely diced
- ½ pound mushrooms, finely chopped
- 1 large plum tomato, peeled and coarsely chopped
- About 1 cup chicken stock or canned low-sodium broth
- 1 garlic clove, minced
- 1½ teaspoons fresh thyme leaves, coarsely chopped
- Salt and freshly ground pepper
- Tabasco
- ¼ cup Dijon mustard
- 2 tablespoons olive oil
- Four 6-ounce skinless duck breasts
- 4 medium scallions, coarsely chopped
- ¼ cup coarsely chopped fresh flat-leaf parsley

1. In a medium saucepan, cover the wild rice with 2 inches of water and bring to a simmer. Cook over moderate heat until tender, 30 to 45 minutes. Drain.
2. Melt the butter in a large skillet. Add the celery, onion, and red bell pepper, and cook over moderately high heat, stirring, until wilted, about 5 minutes. Add the tasso and cook, stirring, until lightly browned, about 3 minutes. Add the mushrooms and cook, stirring, until softened, about 5 minutes. Add the tomato and cook for 1 minute. Stir in the cooked wild rice and 1 cup of the chicken stock and bring to a simmer. Add the garlic and ½ teaspoon of the thyme and season the dressing with salt, pepper, and Tabasco. (MAKE AHEAD: The wild rice dressing can be prepared to this point up to 2 days ahead; cover and refrigerate.)
3. In a shallow baking dish, combine the mustard, olive oil, and the remaining 1 teaspoon thyme. Coat the duck breasts with the mixture and let marinate at room temperature for 20 to 30 minutes.
4. Light a grill or preheat the broiler. Grill or broil the duck breasts until nicely browned, about 3 minutes per side for medium-rare. Transfer to a cutting board and let stand for at least 3 minutes before slicing.
5. Stir the scallions and parsley into the wild rice dressing and rewarm over moderate heat; add a little more stock if the rice seems dry. Slice the duck breasts crosswise ¼ inch thick. Spoon the dressing onto 4 large plates, fan the duck slices on top and serve.—HALLMAN WOODS III

ORANGE DUCK SALAD WITH GINGER-PLUM SAUCE

Even today in China many kitchens don't have ovens, so the average cook buys roast meats from the local delicatessen. If there is an Asian community in your area, you can use the roast duck you often see hanging in store windows for this salad. If not, the marinated grilled duck breast that follows works beautifully.

🍷 *These complex flavors call for a fruity, crisp German Riesling Spätlese, such as the 1992 Dr. Bürklin-Wolf Wachenheimer Gerümpel or the 1992 Kerpen Bernkasteler Bratenhöfchen.*

6 SERVINGS

GRILLED DUCK SALAD:

1 medium scallion, coarsely chopped
1 garlic clove, crushed through a press
2 teaspoons finely grated fresh ginger
1 tablespoon hoisin sauce
1 tablespoon soy sauce (see Note)
1 tablespoon Chinese rice wine or dry sherry
1 teaspoon Asian sesame oil
1½ teaspoons sugar
½ teaspoon five-spice powder
½ teaspoon salt
Four 4-ounce skinless, boneless duck breast halves
½ cup slivered blanched almonds (about 2 ounces)
1 cup peanut oil plus 1 tablespoon if panfrying the duck
12 fresh wonton wrappers, cut into ¼-inch strips
3 medium navel oranges

GINGER-PLUM SAUCE:

1 teaspoon dry mustard
¼ cup fresh orange juice (from the sectioned oranges)
1½ tablespoons soy sauce
1 tablespoon Chinese plum sauce
1 tablespoon balsamic vinegar
1 teaspoon finely grated fresh ginger
1 teaspoon fresh lemon juice
½ teaspoon sugar
½ teaspoon salt
1 tablespoon peanut oil
1½ teaspoons Asian sesame oil

4 cups watercress, tough stems discarded
2 cups finely shredded red cabbage
1 pound jicama, peeled and cut into 1½-by-¼-inch matchsticks
4 medium scallions, white and tender green, cut lengthwise into 1½-by-⅛-inch strips
2 cups fresh coriander (cilantro) leaves
1 tablespoon sesame seeds, toasted (see "How to Toast Sesame Seeds," p. 161)

1. Prepare the grilled duck salad: In a shallow bowl, combine the scallion, garlic clove, ginger, hoisin sauce, soy sauce, rice wine, sesame oil, sugar, five-spice powder, and salt. Add the duck to the marinade and turn to coat. Cover and let marinate at room temperature for at least 2 hours, turning occasionally.
2. Preheat the oven to 375°. Toast the almonds on a baking sheet for about 5 minutes, or until golden.
3. In a wok or medium saucepan, heat the peanut oil to 375°. Add several wonton strips and fry over moderately high heat, stirring,

Orange Duck Salad with Ginger-Plum Sauce

until golden, about 30 seconds. Transfer to paper towels to drain and repeat with the remaining wonton strips.

4. Peel the oranges with a sharp knife, removing the bitter white pith. Working over a bowl, cut between the membranes to release the sections. Drain the sections, reserving ¼ cup of the juice for the sauce.

5. Prepare the ginger-plum sauce: In a small bowl, mix the dry mustard with 1 teaspoon of water; let stand for 10 minutes. In a medium bowl, whisk the reserved orange juice with the soy sauce, plum sauce, vinegar, ginger, lemon juice, sugar, and salt. Whisk in the peanut oil and sesame oil and then the mustard paste. (MAKE AHEAD: The recipe can be prepared to this point up to 6 hours ahead. Set the salad components aside separately at room temperature; refrigerate the duck.)

6. Light a grill or heat the 1 tablespoon peanut oil in a large skillet. Drain the duck, discarding the marinade. Grill the duck or panfry over moderately high heat for 3 to 4 minutes per side, or until well browned but still rare. Transfer to a plate and let stand for 5 minutes. Slice the duck crosswise ¼ inch thick.

7. In a large bowl, toss together the watercress, cabbage, jicama, scallions, coriander leaves, almonds, and two-thirds of the orange sections. Add half of the ginger sauce and toss to coat. Scatter the wonton strips around the edge of a platter or individual plates and mound the salad in the middle. Arrange the duck slices on top and brush with the remaining sauce. Garnish with the remaining orange and the sesame seeds.

NOTE: Choose naturally fermented Chinese soy sauce, which has a distinctive flavor.—JOYCE JUE

HOW TO TOAST SESAME SEEDS

Toasting sesame seeds enhances their nutty flavor. To toast them, set a small dry skillet over moderate heat. Add the sesame seeds and stir constantly until lightly browned and fragrant, about 2 minutes.—JOYCE JUE

RICE SALAD WITH DUCK, OLIVES AND RADICCHIO

🍷 *The meaty flavors of duck, accented by the bite of radicchio and black olives, demand a red with depth and a hint of acerbic tannins to match—that's Cabernet Sauvignon. Look for a lighter example from California, such as the 1992 Gundlach-Bundschu or the 1992 Hawk Crest.*

4 SERVINGS

- 6 tablespoons olive oil
- 3 boneless duck breast halves, with skin
- Salt
- 1½ cups arborio or long-grain white rice
- ¼ cup tarragon vinegar
- 1 tablespoon Dijon mustard
- ½ cup oil-cured black olives, pitted
- 1 small head of radicchio, cored and cut into ½-inch pieces
- 1 small red onion, finely diced
- Leaves from 2 fresh tarragon sprigs, finely chopped
- 1 tablespoon finely chopped fresh flat-leaf parsley
- Freshly ground pepper

1. Heat 1 tablespoon of the oil in a heavy skillet over moderately high heat. When the oil is hot, add the duck breasts, skin side down, and cook until the skin is crisp, about 5 minutes. Reduce the heat to moderate, flip the breasts, and cook until just done, 4 to 5 minutes longer for medium-rare. Do not overcook. Set aside to cool, then cut the duck into ½-inch pieces.

2. In a large saucepan, bring 10 cups of water to a boil. Stir in 1 tablespoon salt. Add the rice and cook uncovered over moderate heat until al dente, about 15 minutes. Drain in a colander, rinse with cold water, and drain again. Place the rice in a large bowl.

3. In a small bowl, mix the remaining 5 tablespoons oil with the vinegar and mustard. Pour the dressing over the rice and toss. Add the duck, olives, radicchio, onion, tarragon, and parsley. Toss well and season with salt and pepper. Let stand for at least 20 minutes before serving. (MAKE AHEAD: The salad can be made 1 day ahead and refrigerated, covered. Serve at room temperature.) —ERICA DE MANE

CHAPTER 8

BEEF, LAMB & VENISON

Beef Tenderloin with Mushrooms and Walnuts

BEEF TENDERLOIN WITH MUSHROOMS AND WALNUTS

Potatoes (roasted or in a creamy gratin) and a salad would complement this dish nicely.

🍷 *A deeply flavorful red, such as the 1989 Guigal Côtes du Rhône or the 1991 Foppiano Petite Sirah Reserve, would best match the rich, meaty flavors here.*

6 SERVINGS

- 2 tablespoons unsalted butter
- 2 pounds white mushrooms, sliced ¼ inch thick
- 1 medium garlic clove, minced
- 1 teaspoon fresh thyme or ½ teaspoon dried
- Salt and freshly ground pepper
- 2 pounds beef tenderloin, tied
- ½ cup coarsely chopped walnuts (3 ounces)
- 2 tablespoons finely chopped fresh flat-leaf parsley

1. Preheat the oven to 450°. In a heavy medium roasting pan placed over 2 burners, melt the butter over moderate heat. Add the mushrooms, garlic, thyme, ¼ teaspoon of salt, and ⅛ teaspoon of pepper, and cook, stirring occasionally, until the mushrooms begin to soften and release their liquid, about 5 minutes.

2. Season the beef with salt and pepper and set it on top of the mushrooms. Roast in the oven for 25 to 30 minutes, until an instant-read thermometer inserted in the center reads 120° (for rare). Transfer the beef to a carving board, cover loosely with foil, and let rest for 15 minutes.

3. In a small heavy skillet, toast the walnuts over moderate heat until golden, about 5 minutes.

4. Stir the walnuts and parsley into the mushrooms. Season with salt and pepper if desired. Slice the roast and serve with the mushrooms.—JAN NEWBERRY

BEEF TENDERLOIN WITH MORELS

8 SERVINGS

- ¾ pound fresh morel mushrooms or 3 ounces dried
- 3 cups boiling water (optional)
- 2 tablespoons unsalted butter
- ¾ cup beef stock (optional)
- ¼ cup brandy
- ¾ cup heavy cream
- 2 tablespoons *glace de viande*, optional (see Note)
- 2 tablespoons fresh lemon juice
- Salt and freshly ground pepper
- 2 tablespoons extra-virgin olive oil
- 2½ pounds well-trimmed beef tenderloin in 1 piece, tied
- Glazed Carrots and Asparagus (p. 309)

1. Preheat the oven to 400°. If using dried morels, put them in a bowl and cover with the boiling water. Cover and let soak until soft, about 30 minutes. Rub the morels in the soaking water to release any grit, then transfer them to a plate. Let the soaking liquid settle for a few minutes, then carefully pour it into a saucepan, leaving the grit behind. Boil the liquid until reduced to 1 cup, 7 to 8 minutes.

2. Melt 1 tablespoon of the butter in a large skillet over moderate heat. Add the fresh morels to the pan and cook until they release their juices. Pour the juices into a glass measure and add enough beef stock to equal 1 cup. ➤

SPRING DINNER AT CHANTERELLE

GINGER-PICKLED SALMON (P. 56)

🍷 1981 Domaine des Baumard Savennières Clos de Saint Yves

RAVIOLI OF SPRING GREENS (P. 252)

🍷 1992 Morey Blanc Meursault

BEEF TENDERLOIN WITH MORELS (P. 165)

🍷 1990 Bernard Amiot Chambolle-Musigny Premier Cru

RASPBERRY GRATIN WITH SAUTERNES SABAYON (P. 421)

CRISPY CHOCOLATE SOUFFLE CAKES (P. 388)

🍷 1985 Château Raymond-Lafon Sauternes

If the wines that accompany this menu tug too hard on your purse strings or are difficult to find in your area, here are some other recommendations from Roger Dagorn, the sommelier at New York City's Chanterelle:

- IN PLACE OF THE SAVENNIÈRES, **try the 1990 Hugel Gewürztraminer Reserve Personelle ($20) or the 1985 Vouvray Prince Poniatowsky Aigle Blanc ($18).**
- IN PLACE OF THE MEURSAULT, **look for the 1989 Olivier Leflaive St-Aubin Premier Cru en Remilly ($23), the 1991 Joseph Drouhin Pernand-Vergelesses Blanc ($20), or the 1990 Antonin Rodet Château de Rully ($16).**
- IN PLACE OF THE CHAMBOLLE-MUSIGNY, **try the 1988 Marquis d'Angerville Volnay Premier Cru ($24).**
- IN PLACE OF THE SAUTERNES, **look for the 1988 Château Doisy-Daëne Sauternes Deuxième Cru ($20).**

Beef Tenderloin with Morels

3. Add the remaining 1 tablespoon butter to the pan and cook the fresh morels over high heat until slightly crisped, about 4 minutes. Alternatively, sauté the reconstituted morels in the full 2 tablespoons butter.

4. Slowly pour the brandy into the pan and ignite carefully; swirl the pan until the flames subside. Using a slotted spoon, transfer the morels to a plate. Return the skillet to the heat and add the reserved morel liquid, the cream, *glace de viande*, and 1 tablespoon of the lemon juice. Boil until slightly thickened, 2 to 3 minutes. Season with salt and pepper and remove from the heat. (MAKE AHEAD: The sauce can be prepared to this point up to 1 day ahead. Cover and refrigerate the sauce and morels separately.)

5. Heat the olive oil in a cast-iron skillet. Generously season the meat all over with salt and pepper. When the oil is almost smoking, add the tenderloin and cook over high heat, turning, until the meat is richly browned all over, 4 to 5 minutes per side. Roast the meat in the oven for about 15 minutes for medium-rare, or until an instant-read thermometer inserted in the center registers 125°. Transfer the meat to a carving board, cover loosely with foil, and let rest for 5 to 8 minutes.

6. Bring the sauce to a simmer over moderate heat. Stir in the morels and any accumulated meat juices. Season the sauce with the remaining 1 tablespoon lemon juice and salt and pepper; keep warm.

7. Using a sharp knife, carve the meat into ⅓-inch slices; add any carving juices to the sauce. Spoon the sauce onto warmed plates, evenly distributing the morels. Arrange the meat on top and garnish with the Glazed Carrots and Asparagus.

NOTE: *Glace de viande* is highly concentrated meat stock that is frequently used in restaurants to give flavor and body to a wide range of sauces. It is available frozen in many specialty food shops.—DAVID WALTUCK

FILET MIGNON WITH SHALLOTS AND COGNAC Q

2 SERVINGS

Two 6-ounce filet mignon steaks, about 1¼ inches thick
¼ cup Cognac
1 tablespoon unsalted butter
1 tablespoon vegetable oil
½ teaspoon coarsely ground black pepper
2 large shallots, minced
¼ cup beef stock or canned broth
Salt

1. Sprinkle the steaks with 1 tablespoon of the Cognac and let stand at room temperature for 45 minutes.

2. In a heavy medium skillet, melt ½ tablespoon of the butter in ½ tablespoon of the oil. Rub the steaks on both sides with the pepper. When the skillet is very hot, add the steaks, cover partially, and cook over high heat until a crust forms on the bottom, about 2 minutes. Turn the steaks over and cook, partially covered, until nicely crusted on the other side, about 2 minutes. Continue cooking over moderate heat, turning once, for about 2 minutes per side for medium-rare. Transfer the steaks to a plate and keep warm.

3. Melt the remaining ½ tablespoon butter in the remaining ½ tablespoon oil in the skillet. Add the shallots and cook over moderately high heat, stirring frequently, until translucent, about 3 minutes.

4. Add the remaining 3 tablespoons Cognac to the skillet. Ignite with a match and cook over high heat until the flame burns out, about 30 seconds. Add the beef stock and boil until the liquid is reduced to ¼ cup, 2 to 3 minutes. Stir in any accumulated juices from the steaks.

5. Season the steaks with salt and transfer to individual plates. Spoon the pan sauce on top and serve.—BOB CHAMBERS

SHELL STEAK WITH HORSERADISH CREAM

The bone-in shell steak is part of the larger porterhouse, cut from the loin. Each steak yields about 10 ounces of cooked meat, which is just right for a very hungry eater. Grilled onions and tomatoes are a nice complement to the meat.

🍷 *Red meat, red wine—and in this case the accompanying grilled onions, tomatoes, and horseradish sauce, suggest a hearty Syrah-based wine, such as the 1991 Paul Jaboulet Aîné Crozes-Hermitage Domaine Thalabert from France or the 1990 Taltarni Shiraz from Australia.*

2 TO 4 SERVINGS

- 2 medium red onions, sliced crosswise ½ inch thick
- About ¼ cup olive oil
- 3 large plum tomatoes, halved lengthwise
- Two 1-pound shell steaks, trimmed of excess fat, at room temperature
- Coarse salt and freshly ground pepper
- Horseradish Cream (recipe follows)

1. Light a grill. Press the red onion slices against a work surface with your palm and thread 2 long skewers through them in lollipop fashion.

2. Brush both sides of the red onion slices with olive oil and grill, turning, for about 10 minutes until nicely browned. Brush the cut sides of the tomato halves with oil and grill, cut sides down, for about 6 minutes, or until browned.

3. Season the shell steaks on both sides with coarse salt and pepper. Grill them over a hot fire for 7 minutes, or until nicely browned and crusty. Turn with tongs and cook for 7 minutes longer for medium-rare. Dollop with Horseradish Cream and serve with the grilled onions and tomatoes.

Horseradish Cream

This piquant horseradish sauce is the perfect companion for roast beef as well as for steak. Or try it as a dip for crudités.

Filet Mignon with Shallots and Cognac

ROMANTIC DINNER FOR TWO

🍷 If there's a menu that calls for a seductive, full-flavored red, this is it. A Washington State Merlot, such as the 1992 Columbia Crest, or an elegant 1988 Bordeaux, such as the Château Calon-Ségur, with its classic heart label, are top choices.

OSETRA CAVIAR WITH SOUR CREAM AND TOAST POINTS

FILET MIGNON WITH SHALLOTS AND COGNAC (P. 166)

OVEN-ROASTED RED POTATOES WITH ROQUEFORT (P. 277)

SAUTEED SPINACH WITH GARLIC AND ORANGE (P. 321)

BOX OF CHOCOLATES

TIMETABLE:

- **Bake the potatoes.**
- **Prepare the ingredients for the filet mignon and spinach; cook no more than 10 minutes before serving.**

—BOB CHAMBERS

MAKES ABOUT 1 CUP

- 2 tablespoons drained prepared horseradish
- 1 cup sour cream

In a small bowl, stir the drained prepared horseradish into the sour cream.—DIANA STURGIS

SLICED SIRLOIN STEAK WITH FLAVORED BUTTER

Each butter recipe makes enough for two 2½-pound sirloin steaks. Tightly wrap any leftover butter and refrigerate for up to three days or freeze for up to one month. The butters and the garnishes of arugula and grilled mushrooms can be served with any cut of steak.

🍷 *The rich, fatty flavors here need a red with some youthful tannins for contrast, but one with meaty flavors of its own to match the steak. A California Cabernet Sauvignon, such as the 1991 Simi or the 1992 Carmenet Dynamite Cabernet, would be ideal.*

4 SERVINGS

- 3 tablespoons olive oil
- 2 tablespoons sun-dried tomato oil or olive oil
- 2 tablespoons plus 1 teaspoon fresh lemon juice
- ½ teaspoon minced fresh thyme
- Salt and freshly ground pepper
- 12 large shiitake mushrooms (¾ pound), stemmed
- One 2½-pound boneless top sirloin steak, about 2 inches thick
- Herbed Gorgonzola Butter or Sun-Dried Tomato Pesto Butter (recipes follow)
- 2 bunches of arugula

Sliced Sirloin Steak with Flavored Butter

1. Light a grill or preheat the broiler. In a large bowl, whisk 2 tablespoons of the olive oil with the sun-dried tomato oil, 2 tablespoons of the lemon juice, the thyme, ½ teaspoon salt, and ¼ teaspoon pepper. Add the shiitake mushrooms, turn to coat, and let marinate.

2. Meanwhile, generously season the steak on both sides with salt and pepper. Grill or broil for about 8 minutes per side for rare to medium-rare. Transfer to a carving board with grooves. Let the steak rest for 10 minutes. Slice half of one of the flavored butters into ¼-inch diagonal pats and place on the steak; reserve the remaining butter for later use.

3. Meanwhile, on a work surface, thread four 10-inch wooden skewers through the mushrooms in lollipop fashion. Reserve the mushroom marinade. Grill the mushrooms for about 3 minutes per side until soft, juicy, and nicely charred.

4. Slice the steak ¼ inch thick against the grain and arrange on 4 dinner plates. Toss the arugula in the bowl with the reserved mushroom marinade and the remaining 1 tablespoon olive oil and 1 teaspoon lemon juice. Place the arugula next to the steak and top with the shiitake caps. Spoon the meat juices and melted butter over the steak and serve immediately.

FIVE POPULAR STEAKS AND HOW TO COOK THEM

RIB EYE: **Grill, broil, or pan-broil. For even cooking, the steak should be about 1½ inches thick.**

PORTERHOUSE: **Grill, broil, or pan-broil. For even cooking, the steak should be about 1½ inches thick.**

BONELESS TOP SIRLOIN: **Grill, broil, or pan-broil. Best if about 1½ inches thick.**

SKIRT: **Marinate, then grill, broil, or cut into thin strips and stir-fry. Serve sliced thin on the diagonal.**

FLANK: **Marinate, cut into thin strips, and stir-fry; grill or broil the steak whole, then slice very thin on the diagonal.—TANYA WENMAN STEEL**

Herbed Gorgonzola Butter

For this butter, I used creamy Gorgonzola cheese from Wisconsin. If Gorgonzola, domestic or imported, is not available, Saga blue cheese is a fine substitute.

8 SERVINGS

- ⅓ cup (packed) fresh flat-leaf parsley leaves
- 1 teaspoon fresh thyme leaves
- 1 stick (4 ounces) unsalted butter, softened
- 3 ounces Gorgonzola cheese
- 3 tablespoons thinly sliced chives
- ½ teaspoon salt
- ¼ teaspoon freshly ground pepper

1. In a food processor, finely chop the parsley and thyme leaves, scraping down the bowl as necessary. Add the butter and process until smooth. Add the Gorgonzola cheese, chives, salt, and pepper, and process until thoroughly blended.

2. Using a rubber spatula, scrape the butter onto a 12-inch length of wax paper. Fold the paper over the butter and, using the spatula to help, form the butter into a 1½-by-5-inch log. Twist the ends of the paper to secure snugly and refrigerate for at least 2 hours.

3. To serve, let the butter stand at room temperature for a few minutes until it is soft enough to slice easily.

Sun-Dried Tomato Pesto Butter

8 SERVINGS

- ¼ cup (packed) fresh basil leaves
- 1 medium garlic clove
- ½ medium jalapeño chile, stems and seeds discarded
- ¼ cup (packed) drained, oil-packed sun-dried tomatoes
- 1 stick (4 ounces) unsalted butter, softened
- ½ teaspoon salt
- ¼ teaspoon freshly ground black pepper

1. In a food processor, finely chop the basil, garlic, and jalapeño, scraping down the bowl as necessary. Add the sun-dried tomatoes and pulse to coarsely chop. Add the butter, salt, and black pepper, and process until thoroughly blended.

2. Using a rubber spatula, scrape the butter onto a 12-inch length of wax paper. Fold the paper over the butter and, using the spatula to help, form the butter into a 1½-by-5-inch log. Twist the ends of the paper to secure snugly and refrigerate for at least 2 hours.

3. To serve, let the butter stand at room temperature for a few minutes until it is soft enough to slice easily.—TRACEY SEAMAN

ITALIAN-STYLE STEAK WITH BASIL AND SAGE

A smooth, medium-bodied red Rioja, such as the 1989 Marqués de Riscal or the 1989 Campo Viejo Reserva, would perfectly showcase the herbed, sautéed slices of beef.

4 SERVINGS

- 1¼ pounds boneless sirloin steak, about 1 inch thick
- Salt and freshly ground pepper
- 1 small bunch of arugula, tough stems discarded
- 1 to 2 tablespoons balsamic vinegar
- 2 tablespoons olive oil

Italian-Style Steak with Basil and Sage

¼ cup finely shredded fresh basil leaves
3 tablespoons finely shredded fresh sage leaves
1 tablespoon unsalted butter

1. Cut the sirloin diagonally against the grain into 12 even slices. Pound the steak slices between plastic wrap to a ¼-inch thickness. Generously season the meat on both sides with salt and pepper. Mound the arugula on 4 large plates and drizzle with the balsamic vinegar.

2. In a large heavy skillet, heat 1 tablespoon of the oil until almost smoking. Add half of the steak slices and cook over high heat until just browned, about 1½ minutes. Turn the meat, sprinkle with half of the basil and sage, and cook until browned but still very rare, about 1 more minute. Transfer the slices to a plate. Repeat the process with the remaining oil, steak, and herbs.
3. Add the butter to the skillet and melt, scraping up any browned bits. Return the steak, herbs, and accumulated juices to the pan, and warm over moderate heat, turning the slices once, for 1 minute. Arrange the steak on the arugula, spoon the pan juices over, and serve.—JUDITH SUTTON

QUICK DINNER

ITALIAN-STYLE STEAK WITH BASIL AND SAGE (P. 169)

CRISP PARMESAN POTATOES (P. 280)

CHERRY TOMATO SALAD

RICH CHOCOLATE MOUSSE (P. 451)

TIMETABLE:

- **Make the mousse. Refrigerate.**
- **Slice the potatoes and cook until golden, then lower the heat.**
- **Prepare and cook the beef.**
- **Add the cheese to the potatoes.**

TIME-SAVING TIPS:

- **Have your butcher slice and pound the steak for you, or prepare it yourself several hours ahead, cover with plastic, and refrigerate.**
- **Double the steak recipe and use the leftovers to make delicious steak and arugula sandwiches the next day.**
- **Make the chocolate mousse in the morning; whisk the cream for the garnish just before serving.**

—JUDITH SUTTON

CUMIN-RUBBED SKIRT STEAK FAJITAS

Skirt steak is a very tender cut. It's the classic choice for fajitas, the Tex-Mex specialty of grilled meat and trimmings rolled into tortillas.

🍷 *This flavorful main dish calls for a straightforward, flavor-packed fruity red, such as a California Zinfandel. Among possible choices, look for the 1993 Kendall-Jackson Vintner's Reserve or the 1993 De Loach.*

2 TO 3 SERVINGS

½ teaspoon cumin seeds
½ teaspoon coarsely ground black pepper
1 large garlic clove, quartered
2 teaspoons olive oil
One 1-pound skirt steak, trimmed of excess fat, at room temperature
4 poblano chiles
⅓ cup sour cream
Salt
Six 8-inch flour tortillas
1 small onion, thinly sliced
1 cup finely chopped red and yellow tomatoes
1 avocado, peeled and cut into ½-inch chunks

1. Light a grill or preheat a cast-iron grill pan over low heat for about 10 minutes. In a small skillet, toast the cumin seeds over moderately high heat until lightly browned and fragrant, about 30 seconds. Transfer to a mortar to cool; then, using a pestle, coarsely grind. Add the black pepper and garlic and pound to a paste. (Alternatively, using a chef's knife, chop the cumin seeds as fine as you can and put them in a small bowl along with the black pepper. Mince the garlic and add it to the spices.) Stir in the olive oil.
2. Rub the cumin oil on the skirt steak and marinate for at least 10 minutes or refrigerate overnight.
3. Roast the poblano chiles directly on the grill or over a gas flame, turning often, until blistered all over; do not overcook or the flesh will burn. Transfer the chiles to a paper bag and let steam for about 5 minutes. Using a small knife, remove the skin, stems, and seeds. Cut the chiles into thin strips.
4. In a small bowl, mix the chiles and sour cream. Season with salt.
5. Season the skirt steak with salt and grill over a very hot fire or in the grill pan over high heat for about 2½ minutes per side for medium-rare. Transfer to a carving board to rest for about 5 minutes. Using a very sharp knife, thinly slice the steak lengthwise against the grain.

6. Warm the tortillas on the grill for a few seconds until pliable.
7. Place the sour cream, onion, tomatoes, and avocado in bowls. Serve alongside the steak and tortillas and let each person assemble his own fajita.—MARCIA KIESEL

WARM GRILLED BEEF, TOMATO AND RED ONION SALAD

Typically, Southeast Asian salad dressings such as this are oil free with sweet, sour, and spicy flavors punctuated with fresh herbs.

6 SERVINGS

1 pound top round or flank steak
Salt and freshly ground pepper
3 garlic cloves, minced
1 tablespoon peanut oil
3 small firm tomatoes
1 serrano chile, preferably red, seeded and coarsely chopped
1 tablespoon sugar
3 tablespoons fresh lime juice
1½ tablespoons Thai fish sauce (*nam pla*)
2 teaspoons rice vinegar
1 medium red onion, thinly sliced
1 small cucumber, thinly sliced
¼ cup coarsely chopped fresh mint
¼ cup coarsely chopped fresh coriander (cilantro)
1 teaspoon dried shrimp powder (optional)
1 medium head of red leaf lettuce, large leaves left whole, inner leaves shredded

1. Season the steak with salt and pepper. Mix two-thirds of the minced garlic cloves with the peanut oil and rub the mixture all over the steak. Let the steak marinate at room temperature for at least 30 minutes or refrigerate overnight.
2. Light a grill or preheat the broiler. Grill or broil the tomatoes for about 1 minute, turning occasionally, until the skin is slightly charred; the tomatoes should still be firm. Transfer to a plate and let cool. Cut each tomato into 6 wedges.
3. Grill or broil the beef for about 5 minutes per side for medium-rare. Transfer to a plate and let stand for 5 minutes. Cut across the grain into very thin 2-inch-long slices.
4. Meanwhile, in a mortar or mini food processor, work the serrano, the remaining garlic, the sugar, and ¼ teaspoon salt to a paste. Transfer to a large bowl and stir in the lime juice, fish sauce, and rice vinegar until the sugar has dissolved. Add the meat and toss to coat. Add the tomatoes, onion, cucumber, mint, coriander, and shrimp powder, and toss again.
5. Arrange the lettuce leaves on a platter or individual plates. Scatter the shredded lettuce over and mound the beef salad on top.—JOYCE JUE

ROASTED RACK OF LAMB WITH FIELD PEA RELISH

🍷 *A 1988 Bordeaux, such as Château Grand-Puy-Lacoste or Château Meyney, would be an ideal match for the lamb here.*

4 SERVINGS

4 garlic cloves, minced
1 tablespoon minced fresh rosemary
½ teaspoon hot paprika
½ teaspoon kosher salt

CHARCOAL GRILLING

- **The easiest way to start a charcoal fire is with an old-fashioned chimney starter (available at hardware and kitchenware stores). Place the coals in the chimney cylinder and light them. Allow them to sit until hot, about 20 minutes. Then spread the hot coals in a single layer. If the coals are tightly packed, the temperature will be higher; but, cautions Marlys Bielunski, test kitchen director at the Meat Board, "carcinogens can form at high temperatures, so we recommend a more moderate heat."**
- **Let the coals burn until they are covered with gray ash, about half an hour after lighting. Some aficionados recommend adding wood chips to give an aromatic smoky flavor to the meat. If you want to use them, soak applewood or hickory chips in water for at least 30 minutes, shake off any excess water, and then place the wood chips on top of the hot coals.**
- **Place the grill rack four to five inches from the fire while the coals are heating. Place small and medium-size steaks directly over the hottest part of the fire. But grill larger steaks, which require longer cooking, over the hot part just until seared; then move them to the side, turning when necessary.—TANYA WENMAN STEEL**

MEAT THERMOMETERS

Q: What's the difference between a meat thermometer and a candy/deep-fry thermometer, and are the two kinds interchangeable?

A: Conventional candy/deep-fry thermometers and meat thermometers are not interchangeable. The former have a temperature range of from 100 degrees Fahrenheit to 400 degrees Fahrenheit, whereas most meat thermometers reach only about 200 degrees Fahrenheit, a reading that is too low for making candies and frying foods.

A CANDY/DEEP-FRY THERMOMETER has markings that show specific temperatures for making candy. The gadget comes in two general styles. One is a long glass tube; at its base is a small bulb containing a liquid that expands and rises as the heat increases. The other is a metal probe that is crowned with a dial gauge. Both of these models have an adjustable clip to secure the thermometer to the inside of the pan for continuous reading.

A CONVENTIONAL MEAT THERMOMETER also consists of a metal probe and a dial gauge, which shows temperatures for meat doneness. The probe is inserted into the meat at the outset and left in during cooking. Unfortunately, the probe creates a perfect pathway for the meat's juices to escape; choose one with a thin probe so that the hole in the meat will be small.

A better bet is AN INSTANT-READ THERMOMETER, which may someday make conventional models obsolete. You insert it into the meat toward the end of cooking time, thereby preventing an unnecessary loss of juice. It shows the temperature in just a few seconds. Instant-read thermometers with a maximum temperature of 200 degrees Fahrenheit were introduced primarily for meat, but their success has spawned new models, which are now available in kitchenware shops. A top temperature of 400 degrees Fahrenheit makes them suitable for candymaking and deep frying too.—SHARON TYLER HERBST

¼ teaspoon crushed red pepper
¼ teaspoon freshly ground black pepper
1 large rack of lamb with 8 bones, frenched (see Note)
1 teaspoon olive oil
Field Pea Relish (recipe follows)

1. In a small bowl, combine the garlic, rosemary, paprika, salt, crushed red pepper, and black pepper. Rub the spice mixture all over the rack of lamb. Cover and refrigerate for at least 4 hours or overnight. Let stand at room temperature for at least 15 minutes before cooking.

2. Preheat the oven to 350°. Heat the olive oil in a large skillet. Add the rack to the skillet, fat side down, and sear over high heat until browned all over, about 3 minutes per side. Transfer to the oven and roast for about 18 minutes, or until an instant-read thermometer reaches 125° for medium-rare meat. Transfer the lamb to a carving board and let stand for 5 minutes. Carve the rack and serve 2 chops per person with the Field Pea Relish.

NOTE: Frenching is a butcher's term for scraping the rib bones clean of meat, fat and gristle.

Field Pea Relish

4 SERVINGS

⅓ cup plus 2 tablespoons peanut oil
2 medium red bell peppers, finely chopped
2 medium celery ribs, finely chopped
1 medium onion, finely chopped
1 tablespoon minced garlic
1¼-pound smoked ham hock
1½ pounds fresh field peas or black-eyed peas, shelled, or one 10-ounce package frozen black-eyed peas
½ teaspoon hot paprika
¼ teaspoon crushed red pepper
Freshly ground black pepper
1 bay leaf
2½ cups chicken stock or canned low-sodium broth
⅓ cup cider vinegar
3 tablespoons finely chopped fresh flat-leaf parsley
2 teaspoons finely chopped fresh thyme
Salt

1. Heat 2 tablespoons of the peanut oil in a large saucepan. Add the red peppers, celery, and onion, and cook over moderately high heat, stirring occasionally, until softened, about 5 minutes. Add the garlic and cook, stirring, for 1 more minute. Stir in the ham hock, field peas,

Roasted Rack of Lamb with Field Pea Relish

CHEF'S MENU

CRAB CAKES WITH JAMBALAYA SAUCE

ROASTED RACK OF LAMB WITH FIELD PEA RELISH (P. 171)

WILTED GREENS

CHOCOLATE BOURBON-PECAN TART (P. 403)

—WALTER ROYAL

paprika, crushed red pepper, ¼ teaspoon black pepper, and bay leaf, and cook for 1 minute. Pour in the chicken stock and bring to a boil. Lower the heat to moderate and simmer until the peas are tender, about 15 minutes for either fresh or frozen. Drain, reserving the cooking liquid, and transfer the peas to a bowl. Discard the bay leaf.

2. Remove the meat from the ham hock, coarsely chop it, and stir it into the peas. Pour the reserved cooking liquid into a medium nonreactive saucepan and boil over high heat until reduced to ¼ cup, about 20 minutes. Let cool. Stir in the vinegar, parsley, and thyme, then whisk in the remaining ⅓ cup peanut oil. Fold the herb dressing into the peas and season with salt and black pepper. Serve warm or at room temperature.—WALTER ROYAL

LAMB WITH SAUCE NICOISE

🍷 *Lamb is best paired with reds that have enough depth and tannin to balance the rich flavor of the meat. Try a Rhône red, such as the 1991 Château de Beaucastel Châteauneuf de Pape or the 1992 McDowell Valley Syrah from California.*

6 SERVINGS

2 pounds fresh fava beans, shelled
½ pound *haricots verts* or thin green beans, trimmed
8 garlic cloves
¾ cup plus 1 tablespoon extra-virgin olive oil
4 medium plum tomatoes—peeled, seeded, and cut into small dice
4 oil-packed sun-dried tomato halves, cut lengthwise into thin strips
¼ cup Niçoise olives, pitted
Salt and freshly ground pepper
6 medium Idaho potatoes, peeled and quartered
3 boneless lamb loins (about ½ pound each)
4 large scallions, thinly sliced
1 cup fresh basil leaves, slivered
2 tablespoons balsamic vinegar
1 cup fresh flat-leaf parsley leaves, coarsely chopped

1. In a medium saucepan of boiling salted water, cook the fava beans over high heat until they turn bright green, about 3 minutes. Using a slotted spoon, transfer the favas to a colander and refresh with cold water. Peel off and discard the tough skins from the favas and transfer the beans to a bowl.

2. Add the *haricots verts* to the boiling water and cook until just tender, about 3 minutes. Using a slotted spoon, transfer the beans to a colander and refresh with cold water. Cut the beans into 1-inch lengths and add to the favas in the bowl.

3. Add the garlic cloves to the boiling water and boil for 30 seconds. Drain and rinse with cold water. Return the garlic to the saucepan and cover with cold water. Bring to a boil over moderately high heat, then drain and repeat the process once more. Thinly slice the garlic cloves lengthwise and set aside.

4. Heat 2 tablespoons of the olive oil in a large nonreactive saucepan. Add the plum tomatoes, sun-dried tomatoes, sliced garlic, and the olives, and simmer gently over moderately low heat for 5 minutes. Season with salt and pepper. (MAKE AHEAD: The recipe can be prepared to this point up to 1 day ahead. Cover and refrigerate the sauce and the beans separately.)

5. Bring a large saucepan of salted water to a boil. Add the potatoes and boil over moderately high heat until tender, about 20 minutes. Drain the potatoes, return them to the saucepan, and shake over high heat for 1 minute to dry them out. Mash the potatoes with ½ cup of the olive oil. Season with salt and pepper, cover, and keep warm.

6. Preheat the oven to 450°. Heat a large ovenproof skillet until very hot. Add 1 tablespoon of the olive oil and heat until just smoking. Season the lamb loins with salt and pepper and cook over high heat, turning, until well browned all over, about 3 minutes per side. Transfer the pan to the oven and roast the lamb for about 5 minutes, until an instant-read thermometer inserted in the center of a loin registers 125° for medium-rare. Transfer to a cutting board and let stand for 5 minutes.

7. Meanwhile, bring the Niçoise sauce to a simmer over moderate heat. Stir in the fava beans and *haricots verts*, the scallions, basil, balsamic vinegar, and the remaining 2 tablespoons olive oil and cook until heated through. Stir the parsley into the warm mashed potatoes.

8. Slice the lamb loins crosswise ¼ inch thick. Mound the mashed potatoes on 4 large plates and arrange the lamb on top. Spoon the Niçoise sauce around the lamb and serve.—TRACI DES JARDINS

LAMB ADOBADO WITH CHIPOTLE SAUCE

Adobado *is a Mexican term that refers to any meat that's spread with chile paste (an* adobo*) before roasting. This* adobo *is made with ancho chile powder. The lamb is also served with a sauce made from hot, smoky chipotle chiles. To continue the Mexican theme, serve the dish with warm flour tortillas.*

The spicy heat of this lamb dish narrows red wine choices to very spicy Zinfandels, such as the 1992 Haywood Rocky Terrace, or very fruity reds, such as the 1994 Preston Vineyards Gamay Beaujolais. A chilled glass of beer, such as Bass Ale, would go just as well.

8 SERVINGS

LAMB:

- ½ teaspoon coriander seeds
- ½ teaspoon cumin seeds
- ¼ teaspoon whole black peppercorns
- 4 medium garlic cloves
- 2 teaspoons salt
- 2 tablespoons ancho chile powder or other pure chile powder*
- ½ teaspoon oregano
- ½ teaspoon thyme
- ⅛ teaspoon cinnamon
- ¼ cup cider vinegar
- One 7- to 8-pound leg of lamb, trimmed of excess fat

CHIPOTLE SAUCE:

- 2 tablespoons olive oil
- 1 cup canned whole tomatoes
- ½ teaspoon salt
- 2 medium garlic cloves, smashed and peeled
- 2 canned chipotle chiles*

*Available at Latin markets

1. Prepare the lamb: Set a small heavy skillet over moderate heat for 2 minutes. Add the coriander seeds, the cumin seeds, and the peppercorns, and cook, stirring frequently, until the spices are fragrant and beginning to brown, 3 to 5 minutes. Transfer to a plate to cool.

2. Using a mortar and pestle, crush the toasted spices, garlic, and salt to make a coarse paste. Stir in the chile powder, oregano, thyme, and cinnamon. Stir in the vinegar until well blended.

3. Rub the spice mixture all over the lamb and let stand at room temperature for at least 4 hours or cover and refrigerate overnight. (Remove the meat from the refrigerator at least 1 hour before cooking.)

4. Preheat the oven to 450°. In a large roasting pan, roast the lamb for 10 minutes. Lower the temperature to 350° and cook for 50 minutes longer, until an instant-read thermometer inserted in the thickest part of the lamb without touching the bone reads 140° (for medium-rare). Transfer the lamb to a carving board, cover loosely with foil, and let rest for 15 minutes before slicing. ➤

Lamb with Sauce Niçoise

Lamb Adobado with Chipotle Sauce

5. Meanwhile, **make the chipotle sauce:** Heat the olive oil in a medium nonreactive skillet. Add the tomatoes, breaking them up with a spoon. Stir in the salt and cook over high heat, stirring occasionally, until the liquid has reduced to ⅔ cup, about 5 minutes. Transfer the mixture to a food processor or blender. Add the garlic and chipotles and puree. Season with salt.

6. Slice the lamb and serve with the chipotle sauce.—JAN NEWBERRY

LAMB CHOPS RIVIERA

Though this recipe calls for loin chops, either leg steaks or rib chops may be used in their place.

4 SERVINGS

- 2 tablespoons virgin olive oil
- 4 loin lamb chops, cut 1¾ inches thick, trimmed of fat
- Salt and freshly ground black pepper
- Four 1-inch-thick slices from a large eggplant, peeled
- 1 small onion, chopped
- 3 garlic cloves, minced
- 1½ pounds fresh spinach, stemmed and well washed
- 6 ripe plum tomatoes—peeled, seeded, and cut into ½-inch dice
- 16 oil-cured black olives

1. Preheat the oven to 175°. Light a grill or preheat a grill pan. Rub ½ teaspoon of the olive oil over the lamb chops and season them with ¼ teaspoon each of salt and pepper. Rub the eggplant slices on both sides with 2½ teaspoons of the oil and season them with ¼ teaspoon salt.

2. Grill the lamb and the eggplant over a medium-hot fire or in the hot pan, turning often, until the eggplant is tender and browned, about 6 minutes, and the lamb is medium-rare, about 15 minutes. Transfer the lamb and eggplant to a baking sheet and keep warm in the oven while you prepare the spinach.

3. In a large nonreactive skillet, warm the remaining 1 tablespoon of olive oil over high heat. When hot, add the onion and cook for 1 minute. Add the garlic and then the spinach and season with ½ teaspoon salt and ¼ teaspoon pepper. Cover and cook until the spinach wilts, about 1 minute. Mix well, cover, and cook for 4 minutes longer. Transfer the spinach to a bowl.

4. Add the tomatoes to the skillet and season them with ¼ teaspoon salt. Cook over moderately high heat, tossing, until just heated through, about 1 minute.

5. Spread the spinach on 4 warmed plates and sprinkle the tomatoes on top. Arrange a slice of eggplant in the center of each plate and top with a lamb chop. Garnish with the olives and serve.—JACQUES PEPIN

LEMON PEPPER LAMB CHOPS ≡Q

🍷 *Lamb practically demands a rich, flavorful red with a tannic edge to check the fattiness of the meat. A 1992 California Merlot, such as the Alexander Valley Vineyards or the Rutherford Hill, would complement the chops as well as the side dishes.*

4 SERVINGS

- 2 teaspoons finely grated lemon zest
- 2 teaspoons coarsely ground black pepper
- 2 teaspoons thyme
- ¾ teaspoon salt
- 2 tablespoons olive oil
- 8 loin lamb chops, cut 1 inch thick and trimmed of excess fat

1. In a small bowl, combine the lemon zest, pepper, thyme, and

TIME-SAVING TIP

When making the Lemon Pepper Lamb Chops, make extra lemon pepper oil to give yourself a head start on another meal. You can keep it covered in the refrigerator for up to three days. Use the lemon pepper oil for brushing on chicken, veal, fish, and vegetables before roasting.—SUSAN SHAPIRO JASLOVE

Lemon Pepper Lamb Chops

QUICK DINNER

LEMON PEPPER LAMB CHOPS (P. 177)

GIANT POTATO PANCAKE (P. 279)

GLAZED CARROTS (P. 326)

BARTLETT PEARS

TIMETABLE:

- **Peel and boil the potatoes. Meanwhile, prepare the lemon pepper oil and marinate the lamb chops.**
- **Cut up and start cooking the carrots.**
- **Shred the potatoes and brown them in a large skillet.**
- **Broil the lamb while the potatoes finish cooking.**

—SUSAN SHAPIRO JASLOVE

salt. Stir in the olive oil. Rub the lamb chops on both sides with the lemon pepper marinade and transfer to a plate. Let stand at room temperature for at least 30 minutes.

2. Preheat the broiler. Arrange the chops on a broiler pan. Broil for about 6 minutes per side, turning once and brushing with any remaining marinade during cooking, until the lamb chops are nicely browned outside and medium-rare inside. Let rest for 5 minutes, then transfer to plates and serve.—SUSAN SHAPIRO JASLOVE

POMEGRANATE-MARINATED LAMB SHANKS WITH TOASTED BARLEY AND KALE RAGOUT

Pomegranate juice tenderizes the meat and gives it a lovely flavor. It's available at health food stores and Middle Eastern groceries.

6 SERVINGS

LAMB SHANKS:

1 quart pure pomegranate juice
1 cup fresh mint leaves
4 large heads of garlic, 2 separated into peeled cloves and 2 halved crosswise
¼ cup grenadine
6 meaty lamb shanks (1 pound each), well-trimmed
2 tablespoons vegetable oil
Salt and freshly ground pepper
4 medium carrots, cut into ½-inch dice
3 medium onions, finely chopped
3 cups dry red wine
1 cup chopped canned tomatoes
2 cups chicken stock or canned low-sodium broth

BARLEY AND KALE RAGOUT:

1½ cups pearl barley (10 ounces)
Salt
1 pound kale, stemmed, leaves coarsely chopped
Freshly ground pepper
¼ cup chopped fresh flat-leaf parsley, for garnish

1. Prepare the lamb shanks: In a nonreactive medium saucepan, boil the pomegranate juice over high heat until reduced by half, about 15 minutes. Let cool to room temperature.

2. In a blender or food processor, puree the pomegranate juice with the mint, peeled garlic cloves, and grenadine. Put the lamb shanks in a large glass or ceramic dish and pour the marinade on top. Cover and refrigerate for at least 12 and up to 24 hours, turning the shanks occasionally.

3. Preheat the oven to 375°. Heat the vegetable oil in a large, heavy, nonreactive skillet. Drain the lamb shanks and pat dry. Season them liberally with salt and pepper. Add 2 or 3 shanks at a time to the skillet and cook over moderately high heat, turning, until well-browned all over. Transfer the shanks to a roasting pan just large enough to hold them all.

4. Reduce the heat under the skillet to moderate and stir in the carrots, onions, and halved garlic heads. Cook until the onions just soften, about 3 minutes. Add the wine, increase the heat to moderately high, and scrape up any browned bits that are stuck to the pan. Boil until the wine is reduced to 1 cup, about 7 minutes. Stir in the tomatoes and pour the mixture over the lamb shanks. Add the chicken stock and enough water to submerge the shanks by two-thirds. Season with salt and pepper. Cover the roasting pan with foil and braise the shanks in the oven until the meat is tender and pulling away from the bones, about 2 hours.

5. Meanwhile, **make the barley and kale ragout:** In a deep-sided medium skillet, toast the barley over moderate heat, stirring constantly, until golden brown, about 7 minutes. Add 4½ cups of water, season with salt and bring to a boil. Cover, reduce the heat to moderately low, and simmer until the barley is tender and all the water has been absorbed, about 40 minutes. Keep warm.

6. Transfer the lamb shanks to a platter. Cover with foil and keep warm. Squeeze the garlic cloves from the heads and add to the sauce in the roasting pan, or reserve them for another use.

Stir the kale into the sauce until wilted, then strain the sauce into a large nonreactive saucepan; cover the vegetables in the strainer to keep them warm.

7. Boil the sauce over high heat until reduced to about 4½ cups; set aside ¾ cup. Stir the vegetables and barley into the sauce in the saucepan and season with salt and pepper.

8. Spoon the barley and kale ragout onto 6 large plates and set a lamb shank on top. Spoon the reserved sauce over the meat and garnish with the chopped parsley.—ANNE ROSENZWEIG

LAMB AND SEVEN-VEGETABLE COUSCOUS

A couscousier, *available at most specialty kitchen equipment stores, is the standard vessel for cooking couscous. It has two parts: a large pot used for cooking the stew and a perforated insert that holds the couscous. As the stew simmers, the couscous cooks in the aromatic steam. A large standard pot and a colander or a large sieve can be substituted for the* couscousier.

Start the recipe one day ahead to allow time for the chickpeas to soak.

8 SERVINGS

- ¾ cup dried chickpeas (about 6 ounces), rinsed and picked over (see Note, p. 87)
- Salt
- 4 cups couscous (about 1½ pounds)
- 3 pounds boneless lamb shoulder, trimmed of excess fat and cut into 1½-inch cubes
- 3 large yellow onions, finely chopped
- 1 medium bunch of fresh cilantro plus ½ cup coarsely chopped cilantro, for garnish
- 1 medium bunch of fresh flat-leaf parsley plus ½ cup coarsely chopped parsley, for garnish
- ¼ cup canola oil
- 3-inch cinnamon stick or ½ teaspoon ground cinnamon
- 1 tablespoon minced fresh ginger
- ¼ teaspoon saffron threads
- Freshly ground black pepper
- 3 ripe medium tomatoes, peeled and quartered
- 3 medium zucchini, halved lengthwise and cut crosswise into 2-inch pieces
- 6 small turnips, peeled and quartered
- 6 medium carrots, cut into 2-inch pieces
- 1-pound piece of winter squash, such as butternut or Hubbard, peeled and cut into 2-inch cubes
- ½ pound Savoy cabbage, cut into 3 wedges
- 2 medium celery ribs, cut into 2-inch pieces
- 1 stick (4 ounces) unsalted butter, softened
- ½ cup golden raisins
- 2 jalapeño or serrano chiles, finely chopped

1. In a medium bowl, cover the chickpeas with water and add a large pinch of salt. Let soak overnight.

2. Put the couscous in a large sieve and rinse quickly with water, stirring to moisten all the grains. Drain the couscous and transfer to a large shallow bowl. Let stand for 10 minutes so the grains swell slightly. Gently roll the grains between your fingers to break up any lumps. Crumble the grains into the top of a *couscousier* or a colander.

Pomegranate-Marinated Lamb Shanks with Toasted Barley and Kale Ragout

$60 DINNER PARTY

🍷 1993 Kunde Viognier

SHRIMP, SWEET POTATO AND LEEK CHOWDER (P. 109)

🍷 1992 Steele Pacini Vineyard Zinfandel

POMEGRANATE-MARINATED LAMB SHANKS WITH TOASTED BARLEY AND KALE RAGOUT (P. 178)

FROZEN PINEAPPLE AND COCONUT PARFAITS (P. 415)

COCONUT TUILES (P. 415)

—ANNE ROSENZWEIG

3. Drain the chickpeas and put them in the bottom of the *couscousier* or in a large pot. Add the lamb, one-third of the onions, the bunches of cilantro and parsley, the oil, cinnamon stick, ginger, and saffron. Season with ½ teaspoon each of salt and black pepper. Add 6 cups of water and bring to a boil over moderate heat. Skim the surface and cover with the couscous-filled top of the *couscousier* or the colander. Cook uncovered until the steam from the lamb stew rises through the couscous, about 25 minutes.

4. Remove the top half of the *couscousier*; keep the stew simmering gently. Spread the couscous in the large shallow bowl or on a baking sheet. Sprinkle with 1 teaspoon salt and ½ cup of water. Fluff the grains with a fork to separate them, letting them cool slightly. Lightly oil the palms of your hands and again gently crumble the grains. Let the couscous dry for 10 minutes.

5. Skim the simmering stew. Add the remaining chopped onions, the tomatoes, zucchini, turnips, carrots, squash, cabbage, and celery. Season with ½ teaspoon salt and bring back to a boil over moderate heat. Return the couscous to the top of the *couscousier* and set it over the stew. Cook uncovered until the steam rises through the couscous and the grains are tender and fluffy, about 25 minutes more. Transfer the couscous to a large shallow serving bowl. Add the butter, season with salt, and fluff with a fork until the butter is melted. Keep warm.

6. Meanwhile, add the raisins to the stew and continue simmering over moderate heat until the meat, chickpeas, and vegetables are tender, about 10 minutes longer. Discard the cilantro, the parsley, and the cinnamon stick. Season the stew with salt and black pepper. Make a well in the center of the couscous and spoon in the lamb stew. Serve the chiles, cilantro, and parsley in small bowls alongside.—FATIMA HAL

Lamb and Seven-Vegetable Couscous

SPRING LAMB STEW WITH GLAZED VEGETABLES

Navarin, *or lamb ragout, is a traditional French dish. The flavor improves as it sits, so it's an ideal do-ahead dish. You can make the vegetables ahead, too; undercook them slightly so that they will finish cooking when you reheat them in a skillet before serving.*

8 TO 10 SERVINGS

LAMB STEW:

About ⅓ cup olive oil
1 cup all-purpose flour
Salt and freshly ground pepper
4 pounds boneless leg of lamb, cut into 1½-inch cubes
2 teaspoons sugar
1 pound ripe plum tomatoes—peeled, seeded, and coarsely chopped
2 large garlic cloves, peeled and lightly crushed
Bouquet garni made with 3 fresh thyme sprigs, 3 fresh parsley sprigs, and 1 large bay leaf tied in cheesecloth

GLAZED VEGETABLES:

4 tablespoons unsalted butter
2 bunches of baby carrots
½ pint pearl onions, peeled

2 teaspoons sugar
2 pounds fresh peas, shelled (2 cups), or one 10-ounce package of thawed frozen peas

1. Make the lamb stew: In a large heavy skillet, heat 2 tablespoons of the oil over moderately high heat. On a plate, toss the flour with ¼ teaspoon each of salt and pepper. Divide the lamb into 4 batches. Pat one batch dry, toss it in the seasoned flour, and shake off the excess. When the oil is shimmering, add the floured lamb and cook, turning with tongs, until evenly browned, about 8 minutes. Transfer the browned meat to a large enameled cast-iron casserole. Repeat with the remaining batches of lamb, using the remaining oil as necessary. When all the meat has been browned and added to the casserole, pour 1 cup of water into the skillet and scrape with a wooden spoon to loosen the browned bits. Set the skillet aside.
2. Sprinkle the sugar over the lamb in the casserole and cook over moderately high heat, stirring until the sugar caramelizes and the meat is glazed, about 2 minutes; don't let the sugar burn. Season with salt and pepper. Stir in the tomatoes, garlic, bouquet garni, and the reserved liquid from the skillet. Cover tightly and cook at barely a simmer, stirring occasionally, until the meat is very tender, about 2 hours.
3. Using tongs, transfer the meat to a plate. Spoon off and discard the fat from the cooking liquid; let cool. Return the meat to the casserole. (MAKE AHEAD: The recipe can be made to this point up to 2 days ahead. If so, just refrigerate the meat in the cooking liquid. Then scrape off the fat and rewarm the lamb over moderately low heat for about 30 minutes.)
4. Meanwhile, **prepare the glazed vegetables:** In a large nonreactive skillet, melt the butter over moderately high heat. Add the carrots and pearl onions and cook, shaking the pan, until they begin to brown, about 5 minutes. Stir in 1½ teaspoons of the sugar and ¼ cup of water, cover, and braise until tender, about 6 minutes. Transfer to a bowl.
5. In a saucepan, combine the peas with the remaining ½ teaspoon sugar and ½ cup of water. Cover and cook over low heat until tender, about 6 minutes. Add to the onions and carrots.
6. To serve, spoon the stew in the center of a large warmed platter and surround with the vegetables.—LYDIE MARSHALL

VENISON TENDERLOIN WITH LEMON-ROSEMARY JUS AND MASHED POTATOES

4 SERVINGS

3 large russet potatoes (1¾ pounds), peeled and cut into 2-inch chunks
1 stick (4 ounces) unsalted butter
1 cup milk
Salt and freshly ground pepper
1 tablespoon vegetable oil
Two 12-ounce venison tenderloins, silver skin removed
1 cup rich chicken stock
1 tablespoon fresh lemon juice
½ teaspoon finely chopped fresh rosemary
6 tablespoons coarsely chopped unsalted pistachios

1. Preheat the oven to 400°. In a medium saucepan, cook the potatoes in lightly salted boiling water until tender, about 15 minutes. Drain well. Pass through a ricer or a food mill back into the pan.
2. In a small saucepan, melt 4 tablespoons of the butter in the milk over moderate heat. Stir into the potatoes; season with salt and pepper. Cover and set aside.
3. Heat the vegetable oil in a medium skillet over high heat. Cut the tenderloins in half crosswise and season them with salt and pepper. When the pan is hot, add the tenderloins and sear them on all sides until browned and crusty. Transfer the meat to a small pan and roast in the oven for 4 to 5 minutes, or until an instant-read thermometer inserted in the center registers 120°. Transfer the meat to a cutting board and let rest, loosely covered with foil, while you make the sauce.
4. Return the skillet to high heat. Add the chicken stock and cook, scraping up the browned bits from the bottom of the pan, until the liquid is reduced by half, about 5 minutes.
5. Meanwhile, in a small nonreactive saucepan, cook the remaining 4 tablespoons butter over high heat until golden brown. Stir in the lemon juice and add to the skillet. Stir in the rosemary.
6. Rewarm the potatoes over moderate heat if necessary. Fold in the pistachios. Arrange 3 rounded spoonfuls of potatoes on each of 4 warmed dinner plates. Carve each piece of venison on the diagonal into 3 slices and arrange in between the mounds of potatoes. Spoon the sauce over and serve.—ROBERT WAGGONER

CHAPTER 9

PORK & VEAL

Roasted Pork Loin with Fennel

ROASTED PORK LOIN WITH FENNEL

Serve this peppery pork roast with a side dish of buttered orzo with peas.

6 SERVINGS

3 fennel bulbs—trimmed, quartered, and cored, feathery fronds reserved
3 medium garlic cloves
2 tablespoons fennel seeds
1 tablespoon whole black peppercorns
2 teaspoons finely grated lemon zest
Salt
4 teaspoons olive oil
2½ pounds center-cut boneless pork loin
2 tablespoons fresh lemon juice
Freshly ground black pepper
⅔ cup dry white wine

1. Preheat the oven to 400°. In a large saucepan of boiling salted water, cook the quartered fennel bulbs until just tender, about 10 minutes. Drain.
2. Meanwhile, using a mortar and pestle, crush the garlic, fennel seeds, peppercorns, lemon zest, and ½ teaspoon of salt to a coarse paste. Stir in 2 teaspoons of the oil. Rub the mixture all over the pork loin.
3. Set the pork in a medium nonreactive roasting pan with the fennel quarters. Season the fennel with the lemon juice, the remaining 2 teaspoons olive oil, salt, and black pepper. Roast in the oven for 15 minutes. Lower the temperature to 325° and roast for about 45 minutes longer, until an instant-read thermometer inserted in the center of the pork loin reads 140°. Transfer the pork to a carving board, cover loosely with foil, and let stand for about 10 minutes before slicing.
4. Discard any fat from the pan. Set the pan over 2 burners, add the wine, and bring to a boil over moderately high heat, scraping up any browned bits. Boil until the wine is reduced by half, about 3 minutes. Season with salt and pepper.
5. Slice the roasted pork loin and arrange the slices and the fennel on a platter. Garnish with the fronds. Pour accumulated meat juices into the pan gravy and pass separately.—JAN NEWBERRY

ROAST PORK LOIN WITH APPLE SALSA

8 SERVINGS

One 4-pound boneless pork loin roast
¼ cup mild pepper sauce or 1½ tablespoons hot pepper sauce
¼ cup cumin seeds
Salt and freshly ground black pepper
Apple Salsa (recipe follows)

1. Place the pork in a roasting pan. Rub the pepper sauce all over the pork, then sprinkle the cumin seeds all over, patting them to adhere. Arrange the pork roast fattiest side up and let stand until it reaches room temperature, about 2 hours. Season the roast all over with salt and freshly ground black pepper.
2. Preheat the oven to 475°. Roast the pork loin in the upper third of the oven for 25 to 30 minutes, then lower the temperature to 350° and continue to roast the pork for 1 hour and 15 minutes longer, or until an instant-read thermometer inserted into the meat measures 150° to 155°.
3. Transfer the pork roast to a carving board and let stand for 10 minutes. Skim off any fat from the pan juices. Using a sharp knife, slice the pork into thin slices, about ¼ inch thick. Arrange the pork slices on a warmed serving platter and spoon the pan juices on top. Serve the pork with the Apple Salsa.

Apple Salsa

This salsa needs to be made a few hours ahead to give the flavors time to combine. If you want a slightly milder version, remove the seeds from the jalapeño before adding it.

MAKES 6 CUPS

4 tart apples, such as Gala, Granny Smith, or Pippin, cored and cut into ¼-inch dice
1 medium red onion, cut into ¼-inch dice
1 medium red bell pepper, cut into ¼-inch dice
1 medium jalapeño chile, minced
⅓ cup dried currants (about 2 ounces)
1 tablespoon finely chopped cilantro
2 teaspoons finely grated orange zest
¾ cup fresh orange juice or reconstituted frozen
2 tablespoons Dijon mustard
1 tablespoon ground cumin
½ cup safflower or canola oil
1 tablespoon dark sesame oil
Salt

1. In a large bowl, combine the apples, red onion, bell pepper, jalapeño chile, dried currants, cilantro, and orange zest. ➤

VINTNER'S DINNER

🍷 1990 Dry Gewürztraminer

ARTICHOKE CROSTINI (P. 30)

🍷 1993 Pinot Gris
or 1992 Pinot Noir

SALMON WITH PINOT GRIS CAPER SAUCE (P. 207)

🍷 1991 Vintage Select Pinot Noir

ROAST PORK LOIN WITH APPLE SALSA (P. 185)

WHITE AND WILD RICE PILAF (P. 297)

SAUTEED LEAFY GREENS (P. 323)

🍷 1991 Dry Riesling

MIXED LETTUCES WITH RASPBERRY VINAIGRETTE (P. 76)

🍷 1989 Vintage Select Riesling

HAZELNUT ICE CREAM (P. 459)

CHOCOLATE-DRIZZLED SHORTBREAD (P. 375)

—JOAN AND DICK ERATH

2. In a food processor or blender, combine the orange juice, mustard, and cumin. Process until smooth. With the machine on, gradually add the safflower oil, then the sesame oil, in a very thin stream; the dressing will thicken. Pour the dressing over the apple mixture. Toss gently to combine. Season to taste with salt. Cover the salsa and refrigerate for at least 2 and up to 4 hours before serving.—JOAN AND DICK ERATH

RACKS OF PORK WITH CIDER-PEPPER GLAZE

Patrick Clark likes to serve generous double chops of pork—at least 10 ounces of meat per person. This recipe provides one chop per person, with a few leftover chops for seconds. To ensure that there's plenty of meat on each chop, use racks from the thicker loin end. Have your butcher french the racks (scrape the meat from the rib bones) for you. Start the recipe the day before to allow time for the racks to marinate. If you have a party of big eaters, you can add another rack of pork to the recipe; use the same amount of marinade.

12 SERVINGS

1 cup olive oil
1 tablespoon minced garlic
1 tablespoon minced fresh rosemary
1 tablespoon minced fresh thyme
1 tablespoon minced fresh sage
1 tablespoon minced fresh savory
2 loin-end racks of pork, each with 8 ribs, frenched
Salt
2 medium onions, coarsely chopped
4 medium shallots, coarsely chopped
Cider-Pepper Glaze (recipe follows)
1 quart chicken stock or canned low-sodium broth
2 tablespoons unsalted butter, softened
2 tablespoons all-purpose flour
Freshly ground pepper

1. In a large nonreactive baking dish or very large, sturdy plastic bag, combine the oil, garlic, rosemary, thyme, sage, and savory. Add the pork racks and turn to coat. Cover and marinate overnight in the refrigerator. Let the meat stand at room temperature for 1 hour before roasting.

2. Preheat the oven to 325°. Set a large skillet over high heat. Remove the pork from the marinade, pat dry with paper towels, and season with salt. Add one rack to the skillet, fat side down, and cook, turning once, until well browned, about 5 minutes per side. Set the rack, fat side up, in a large roasting pan. Pour off the rendered fat from the skillet and brown the second pork rack; add it to the roasting pan. Pour off the fat and reserve the skillet.

3. Scatter the chopped onions and shallots around the pork in the roasting pan. Roast for 40 minutes. Raise the heat to 350° and roast for about 1 hour longer, basting the pork generously with the Cider-Pepper Glaze, until an instant-read thermometer inserted in the thickest part of the meat registers 140°. Transfer the pork racks to a carving board, cover with foil, and let rest for 30 minutes.

4. Meanwhile, add the chicken stock to the reserved skillet and cook over high heat, scraping up any browned bits, until reduced by half, about 20 minutes. Skim off any fat.

5. Strain the pan drippings from the roasting pan into a bowl and skim off the fat. Set the roasting pan over 2 burners. Turn the heat to high, add the reduced chicken stock and strained pan drippings, and bring to a boil, scraping up any browned bits. Strain the gravy into a small saucepan and bring to a boil over moderately

Racks of Pork with Cider-Pepper Glaze

high heat. In a small bowl, combine the softened butter and flour to make a smooth paste. Whisk the paste into the gravy and boil, whisking constantly, until thickened, about 3 minutes. Season with salt and pepper and pour the gravy into a sauceboat.

6. Carve the pork racks and arrange the chops on a large platter. Serve the gravy alongside.

CHRISTMAS DINNER

🍷 1993 Rothbury Estate Reserve Chardonnay *or*
1993 Château Ste. Michelle Cold Creek Vineyard Chardonnay

BAY SCALLOP CHOWDER (P. 111) *or*
JERUSALEM ARTICHOKE SOUP WITH GARLIC CROUTONS (P. 98)

🍷 1992 Matanzas Creek Merlot *or*
1992 Sterling Three Palms Merlot

RACKS OF PORK WITH CIDER-PEPPER GLAZE (P. 186)
SWEET POTATO AND MUSHROOM HASH (P. 282)
BRAISED MIXED GREENS WITH GLAZED RUTABAGAS (P. 323)
FIG AND APPLE CHUTNEY (P. 354)

🍷 1990 Château Raymond-Lafon Sauternes *or*
1991 Far Niente Dolce

WHITE CHOCOLATE BANANA CREAM PIES (P. 406)
CRANBERRY-ORANGE CHEESECAKE (P. 455)

—PATRICK CLARK

TIMETABLE:

THREE DAYS AHEAD
- **Make the Fig and Apple Chutney.**

TWO DAYS AHEAD
- **Make the Cider-Pepper Glaze.**
- **Start the Bay Scallop Chowder.**
- **Make the pastry for the pies.**

ONE DAY AHEAD
- **Make the cheesecake.**
- **Make and puree the Jerusalem Artichoke Soup with Garlic Croutons.**
- **Cook the mushrooms for the Sweet Potato and Mushroom Hash.**
- **Cook the vegetables for the Braised Mixed Greens with Glazed Rutabagas.**
- **Marinate the pork racks.**

ABOUT EIGHT HOURS AHEAD
- **Make the filling for the White Chocolate Banana Cream Pies.**

ABOUT THREE HOURS AHEAD
- **Roast the pork racks.**
- **Cook the sweet potatoes and finish the hash.**

ABOUT TWO HOURS AHEAD
- **Fill the banana cream pies.**

SHORTLY BEFORE SERVING
- **Finish the chowder or the soup.**
- **Make the gravy for the pork.**
- **Finish the greens and rutabagas.**
- **Rewarm the hash.**
- **Finish the banana cream pies just before dessert.**

Cider-Pepper Glaze

MAKES 1 CUP

- 1 quart unsweetened apple cider
- 1 large Granny Smith apple, peeled and cut into ½-inch pieces
- ¼ cup cider vinegar
- ¼ cup honey
- 1 tablespoon minced garlic
- 2 fresh thyme sprigs
- 2 teaspoons mustard seeds
- 5 juniper berries,* crushed
- 1 tablespoon freshly ground pepper

*Available at specialty food stores

Combine all of the ingredients except the pepper in a nonreactive medium saucepan and bring to a boil over high heat. Lower the heat to moderate and simmer until the pieces of apple are tender, about 20 minutes. Strain the mixture into another nonreactive saucepan, add the pepper, and cook over high heat until the glaze is reduced to 1 cup, about 30 minutes. (MAKE AHEAD: The glaze can be refrigerated for up to 2 days.) —PATRICK CLARK

BRAISED PORK SHOULDER WITH ENDIVES AND GREEN LENTILS

The pork is rubbed with a spice mixture and left to cure overnight in the refrigerator, so plan accordingly.

6 SERVINGS

PORK AND ENDIVES:

- 2 teaspoons ground coriander
- 2 garlic cloves, minced

PATRICK CLARK'S TIPS FOR LARGE FAMILY DINNERS

- PLAN YOUR MENU ACCORDING TO YOUR FACILITIES. **You can't cook racks of pork and a last-minute dessert in one oven, so I make my desserts ahead and leave the oven free for the pork.**
- PREPARE AS MUCH AS POSSIBLE IN ADVANCE. **I always make the chutney three days ahead, which has the added benefit of improving the flavor as it sits.**
- INVOLVE FAMILY MEMBERS IN THE PREPARATION **of the meal so that they won't feel like guests. I like to make my sister-in-law, Valerie, peel the potatoes. The kids slice the bananas and whip the cream for the pies.**
- KEEP RELATIVES AND KIDS WHO AREN'T HELPING YOU OUT OF THE KITCHEN. **My rule is, no work means no snacking and no chitchat. Cooking is fun, but there's still a dinner to be prepared.**
- SERVE THE KIDS FIRST.

Freshly ground pepper
One 4-pound boned and tied pork shoulder roast
2 tablespoons kosher salt
4 large carrots, sliced on the diagonal ⅓ inch thick
1 medium onion, thinly sliced
4 fresh oregano sprigs or 1 teaspoon dried
2 bay leaves
12 medium Belgian endives
Table salt
6 slices of bacon, halved lengthwise

LENTILS:
1½ cups green French lentils (Le Puy)
1 small onion
1 small carrot
1 small celery rib
1 bay leaf
1 fresh thyme sprig
Kosher salt
1 tablespoon unsalted butter
Freshly ground pepper
2 tablespoons sherry vinegar
1 teaspoon honey
Dijon mustard, for serving

1. Prepare the pork and endives: In a small bowl, combine the ground coriander, the minced garlic, and 2 teaspoons of pepper, and mix well. Rub the pork roast all over with the kosher salt, then rub with 1 tablespoon of the seasoning mixture. Reserve the remaining seasoning mixture. Cover the pork roast and refrigerate overnight. Let return to room temperature before proceeding.

2. Put the pork in a snug-fitting heavy saucepan and add 12 cups of water. Add half of the carrots, onion, oregano, and bay leaves, and bring to a boil over high heat. Reduce the heat to low and simmer, skimming occasionally, until the meat is just cooked through, about 1½ hours. Remove the meat from the pan and strain the broth.

3. Preheat the oven to 400°. Season the Belgian endives with table salt and pepper. Wrap each one with a half slice of bacon. Arrange the bacon-wrapped endives in a large, heavy, deep-sided skillet. Cook over moderate heat, turning often, until the bacon fat is rendered and the endives are browned all over, about 10 minutes. Add the remaining carrots, onion, oregano, bay leaf, and seasoning mixture, and cook for 3 minutes, stirring gently.

4. Put the pork roast in the center of the endives and add 3 cups of the reserved strained broth. Season lightly with table salt and freshly ground pepper. Cover the pan with foil and braise the pork roast and the endives in the oven for 40 minutes, turning twice, until very tender.

5. Meanwhile, **cook the lentils:** In a medium saucepan, cover the green French lentils with 8 cups of cold water and bring to a boil over high heat. Add the onion, carrot, celery rib, bay leaf, thyme sprig, and 1 tablespoon kosher salt, and return to a boil. Reduce the heat to moderately low and simmer, skimming as necessary

$60 DINNER PARTY

🍷 1992 Alsace Pinot Blanc *or* 1993 Georges Duboeuf Viognier

SALAD OF SMOKED TROUT, PINK GRAPEFRUIT AND RADICCHIO WITH WALNUTS (P. 77)

🍷 1993 Georges Duboeuf Côtes du Rhône

BRAISED PORK SHOULDER WITH ENDIVES AND GREEN LENTILS (P. 188)

BREAD PUDDING WITH DRIED CRANBERRIES, VANILLA AND MINT (P. 431)

—DANIEL BOULUD

Braised Pork Shoulder with Endives and Green Lentils

and stirring occasionally, until the lentils are tender, about 35 minutes. Strain the lentils and discard the vegetables and herbs. Return the lentils to the saucepan and toss with the butter. Season the lentils with kosher salt and pepper. Cover the lentils and keep them warm.

6. In a small bowl, mix the sherry vinegar and the honey. Remove the meat from the oven and raise the temperature to 500°. Set the pork roast in an ovenproof skillet and brush with the honey-vinegar mixture. Return the meat to the oven and roast for about 8 minutes, or until well-browned and glazed. Remove the bacon from the endives and discard it along with the oregano sprigs and bay leaf. Arrange the pork, vegetables, and endives on a warmed platter and cover with foil.

7. Set the deep-sided skillet over high heat and boil the cooking juices until reduced to 1½ cups, about 5 minutes. Season with salt and pepper and pour them over the pork roast, endives, and lentils. Carve the pork roast and pass the Dijon mustard at the table.—DANIEL BOULUD

CUBAN ROAST PORK

Black beans and rice are the logical accompaniment to this hearty pork roast inspired by a traditional Cuban dish. A salad of orange slices, red onion, and arugula dressed with a tangy cilantro vinaigrette would make a refreshing counterpoint to the richness of the meat.

Marinating meat in a plastic bag is a great way to keep it well coated. If you have any pork left over, use it to make media noches, *the quintessential Cuban sandwiches, which are made with Swiss cheese, ham, and toasted egg bread in addition to the roast pork.*

🍷 *Pork is mild enough to pair with a white or red wine, but choose one that can check the fat of the roast. A dry, spicy Gewürztraminer from Alsace is just the ticket for pork. Look for the 1991 examples from Hugel or Lucien Albrecht.*

6 TO 8 SERVINGS

- 2 teaspoons cumin seeds
- ½ teaspoon whole black peppercorns
- 4 medium garlic cloves, coarsely chopped
- 2 teaspoons salt
- 1 teaspoon oregano
- ⅓ cup fresh orange juice
- ⅓ cup dry sherry
- 3 tablespoons fresh lemon juice
- 3 tablespoons fresh lime juice
- 2 tablespoons olive oil
- 4 pounds boneless pork shoulder, trimmed and tied

1. Set a small heavy skillet over moderate heat for 2 minutes. Add the cumin seeds and the whole black peppercorns and cook, stirring, until the spices are fragrant and beginning to brown, about 2 minutes. Transfer the spices to a plate to cool.

2. Using a mortar and pestle, crush the toasted cumin seeds and peppercorns, the garlic, salt, and oregano to make a coarse paste. Transfer the spices to a small bowl and stir in the orange juice, dry sherry, lemon juice, lime juice, and olive oil until thoroughly incorporated.

3. Place the pork in a gallon-size plastic bag, add the marinade, and turn to coat all over. Seal the bag. Refrigerate the pork overnight, turning it occasionally in the bag.

4. Preheat the oven to 325°. Transfer the pork and its marinade to a nonreactive medium roasting pan and roast for about 2½ hours, basting occasionally, until an instant-read thermometer inserted in the center reads 155°. (After about 2 hours, if the liquid has dried up, add ¼ cup of water to the pan.)

5. Transfer the roasted pork to a carving board, cover it loosely with foil, and allow it to rest for 15 minutes before slicing. If desired, you can skim the fat from the pan juices and serve them alongside the pork.—JAN NEWBERRY

PULLED PORK

To most southerners, pork is the only barbecued meat that matters. Pulled pork refers to the falling-off-the-bone cooked meat that is pulled apart, or shredded, and is usually served with a vinegar-based sauce on a white-bread bun as a sandwich.

Marinate a 6- to 7-pound bone-in Boston butt (part of the pork shoulder) overnight. Smoke the meat for 8 hours, or until the internal temperature registers at least 140°. Transfer the meat to a roasting pan and pour in 1 cup of water. Cover the pan with foil and bake the meat in a preheated 300° oven for 2 hours, or until the internal temperature reaches 180°. In a bowl, mix the pan juices with 1 minced garlic clove, 1 tablespoon tomato paste, a

Cuban Roast Pork

pinch of cayenne, 1 to 2 teaspoons hot pepper sauce, and salt and pepper to taste. Using two forks, pull the meat off the bone and continue to pull it into small shreds. Dip the meat into the sauce or saturate a soft bun with the sauce, and pile the pulled pork on top.—CHERYL ALTERS JAMISON AND BILL JAMISON

PORK STEAKS WITH ANCHO SAUCE Q

Serve any extra ancho sauce the next day with scrambled eggs and fried tortillas for a different take on the Mexican dish huevos rancheros.

🍷 *Chiles, vinegar, and pineapple juice point to a big, round Australian Chardonnay, such as the 1994 Lindemans Bin 65 or the 1993 Rothbury Estate Hunter Valley Reserve—wines with tropical fruit flavors to match the sauce.*

4 SERVINGS

- 4 large dried ancho chiles
- ¾ cup boiling water
- ¼ cup cider vinegar
- ⅓ cup plus 1 tablespoon vegetable oil

WHERE THERE'S SMOKE—THERE'S FLAVOR

Once upon a time, smoke-flavored food was predominantly the domain of the South and Midwest "Bar-B-Q Belt"—famous for its pulled pork, spareribs, and beef brisket—and specialty food stores selling provisions like smoked fish and cheese. No longer. Now real smoke cooking has taken root in America's backyards and kitchens, aided by a revolution in home equipment.

THE TRADITIONAL METHOD: **Enthusiasts like to build fires from wood alone, using hardwood logs in big metal pits to make a dense cloud of smoke. You can buy backyard models of these pits (prices range from $300 to $1,500). Or choose less expensive equipment that uses charcoal, gas, or electricity to maintain a wood fire.**

WATER SMOKERS: **Water smokers are upright, domed cookers about waist high. They get their name from a water pan that sits between the lower heat source and the upper cooking grates; the water ensures indirect, low heat. You add hardwood chips or chunks to generate a light but ample stream of smoke. Available in mail-order catalogs, warehouse clubs, and large hardware stores, water smokers cost between $30 and $150. The major manufacturers are Char-Broil (Grill Lover's Catalog, 800-241-8981) and The Brinkmann Corporation (800-468-5252).**

KETTLE GRILLS: **If you don't want to spend money on a new piece of equipment, you can adapt a standard kettle grill to do a manufactured smoker's job. Spread a small amount of charcoal (about 20 to 25 briquettes or 10 to 12 handfuls of lump charcoal) in a single layer on one side of the lower grate; heat the grill. Sprinkle soaked wood chips on top. Place a loaf pan filled with water next to the charcoal. Position the food directly above the pan on the upper grate, as far from the fire as possible. Cover with the lid so that the vent is over the food, and lodge a candy thermometer in the opening, with its head facing outside and its probe suspended in the air near the food. The thermometer lets you know if you are maintaining the proper temperature. Close the bottom vents most of the way to lower the heat and open them to raise it. Every hour, or whenever the temperature falls below 225 degrees, add charcoal that has been heated in a can (about one-third of the original amount) and extra wood chips.**

STOVETOP SMOKING: **If you don't have room outdoors, or if you want to cook with smoke year-round despite the weather, look into the clever new stovetop smokers introduced in recent years. Cameron (719-573-9932) and Burton (Grill Lover's Catalog, 800-241-8981) make similar stainless steel versions. You place wood dust or chips in the bottom of a rectangular metal pan, insert a drip tray and food grate, and cook over the stove. The smoldering wood produces a puff of smoke that's trapped inside the pan by a tight-fitting lid and absorbed by the food during the cooking process. The smoker does an excellent job with chicken breasts, pork tenderloin, fish fillets, and other ingredients of a similar size that respond well to a light smoky taste. It cooks at a higher temperature than most outdoor equipment, so adjust the cooking times accordingly.—CHERYL ALTERS JAMISON AND BILL JAMISON**

1 cup pineapple juice
4 large garlic cloves
Salt and freshly ground black pepper
Four 6-ounce boneless pork loin steaks, trimmed of fat
½ medium red onion, finely chopped

1. In a medium skillet, toast the dried ancho chiles over high heat, turning and pressing down on them with a metal spatula to flatten, until pliable, about 1 minute. Remove the seeds and veins from the anchos and rinse well. Transfer to a medium bowl, add the boiling water and vinegar, and let soak, keeping the chiles submerged, until softened, about 20 minutes.
2. Light a grill or preheat the broiler. Heat ⅓ cup of the vegetable oil in a medium nonreactive saucepan. In a blender, puree the softened anchos and their soaking liquid with the pineapple juice, the garlic cloves, and ½ teaspoon salt. Pass the sauce through a coarse strainer into the hot oil and cook over high heat, stirring constantly, until slightly thickened, about 7 minutes. Season the sauce with salt and pepper.
3. Rub the pork steaks with the remaining 1 tablespoon vegetable oil and season with salt and pepper. Grill or broil the steaks for about 4 minutes per side, turning once, until just cooked through. Transfer the steaks to a platter. Ladle half of the ancho chile sauce over the pork steaks, sprinkle with the red onion, and serve, with additional sauce on the side if you like.—CHATA DUBOSE

TAMARIND PORK CHOPS Q

In this Vietnamese recipe, the pork chops are traditionally thin; the meat cooks quickly, saving money on expensive fuel. The tamarind caramelizes to a sweet glaze during cooking. Chayote in Oyster Sauce (p. 332) is a flavorful accompaniment.

4 SERVINGS

1 teaspoon instant tamarind paste
1 teaspoon sugar
¼ cup finely chopped fresh or unsweetened canned pineapple
2 medium shallots, minced
2 garlic cloves, minced
1 medium Thai, or bird, chile or 1 large serrano chile, minced
2 anchovy fillets, mashed
Four 6-ounce bone-in loin pork chops, about ⅓ inch thick
1 tablespoon vegetable oil

1. In a small bowl, mash the instant tamarind paste with the sugar. Blend in the chopped pineapple, the minced shallots, garlic cloves and chile, and the mashed anchovy fillets. Spread the paste on both sides of the pork chops and let stand at room temperature for at least 15 minutes or up to 2 hours.
2. In a large skillet, heat the vegetable oil until almost smoking. Scrape most of the tamarind marinade from the pork chops, leaving a thin layer on the meat. Add the pork chops to the skillet and cook them over high heat, turning once, until the meat is well browned, about 4 minutes per side. Transfer the tamarind-glazed pork chops to plates and serve at once.—MARCIA KIESEL

QUICK DINNER

PORK STEAKS WITH ANCHO SAUCE (P. 192)

LIME-GRILLED VEGETABLES (P. 313)

GRILLED BANANAS WITH SWEETENED CREAM (P. 421)

TIMETABLE:

- **Toast and soak the ancho chiles for the pork. Meanwhile, parboil and marinate the vegetables.**
- **Make the ancho sauce.**
- **Season the pork and grill or broil with the vegetables.**
- **Just before dessert, make the sweetened cream and grill the bananas.**

VARIATIONS:

Try varying these dishes by substituting any of the following ingredients.

- **Boneless chicken breasts or 1-inch-thick beef tenderloin steaks for the pork loin steaks.**
- **New Mexico red, guajillo, or long, red cascabel chiles (3 ounces worth) for the ancho chiles.**
- **Orange juice for the pineapple juice to make a sweeter ancho sauce.**
- **Whipped heavy cream instead of sour cream as a topping for the grilled bananas.**

—CHATA DUBOSE

ACHIOTE PORK TENDERLOIN TOSTADAS WITH RED-ONION MARMALADE LF

6 SERVINGS

ACHIOTE-RUBBED PORK:

3 ancho chiles
½ teaspoon cumin seeds
2 garlic cloves
2 teaspoons annatto seed* (optional)

½ teaspoon kosher salt
¼ teaspoon ground allspice
¼ cup fresh orange juice
2 tablespoons white wine vinegar
1 teaspoon olive oil
Two ½-pound pork tenderloins

TOSTADAS:

1 small green bell pepper
1 small red bell pepper
1 small yellow bell pepper

Achiote Pork Tenderloin Tostada with Red-Onion Marmalade

LOW-FAT PICNIC

🍷 Try fruity Cabernet Sauvignon, such as the 1992 Rosemount Estate from Australia, or the 1992 Fetzer Bonterra from California.

PICKLED VEGETABLE-EGGPLANT ROLLS (P. 21)

ACHIOTE PORK TENDERLOIN TOSTADAS WITH RED-ONION MARMALADE (P. 193)

CHILLED FRESH ORANGES, MANGOES AND JICAMA (P. 87)

CHOCOLATE CAKE (P. 389)

—CHARLES WILEY

Kosher salt and freshly ground black pepper
Six 6-inch corn tortillas
1 small head of romaine lettuce, shredded
1 cup plain nonfat yogurt
½ cup canned black beans, rinsed
6 tablespoons Red-Onion Marmalade (recipe follows)
Lime wedges, for serving

*Available at Latin American or Asian markets

1. Make the achiote-rubbed pork: In a medium skillet, toast the ancho chiles over moderately high heat, tossing, until fragrant, 2 to 3 minutes; let cool. Tear the chiles into pieces, discarding the stems, cores, and seeds.

2. Add the cumin seeds to the skillet and toast over moderately high heat, tossing, until fragrant, 1 to 2 minutes. Transfer the toasted seeds to a blender with the toasted chiles, the garlic, annatto seed, salt, and allspice. Blend until finely chopped. Add the orange juice, vinegar, and olive oil, and puree. Put the pork tenderloins in a nonreactive baking dish and brush with the chile paste. Let marinate at room temperature for 2 to 4 hours.

3. Make the tostadas: Roast the bell peppers directly over a gas flame or under the broiler, turning often, until charred all over. Transfer to a paper bag and let steam for 10 minutes. Peel the skin and discard the stems, ribs, and seeds. Slice the peppers ¼ inch thick, transfer to a bowl, and season with salt and pepper.

4. Preheat the oven to 400°. Bake the corn tortillas on a baking sheet for 4 to 5 minutes, or until they are crisp.

5. Set the pork in a roasting pan and season with salt and pepper. Roast for about 12 minutes, or until the internal temperature reaches 140° on an instant-read thermometer. Let stand for 10 minutes. (MAKE AHEAD: The recipe can be prepared to this point up to 2 hours ahead. Cover the pepper strips, tortillas, and pork separately and let stand at room temperature.)

6. Just before serving, thinly slice the pork against the grain. Set a crisp tortilla on each of 6 plates and top with the lettuce, yogurt, beans, and pepper strips. Arrange the pork slices on top and garnish each serving with 1 tablespoon of the Red-Onion Marmalade. Serve the tostados with lime wedges.

Red-Onion Marmalade

Use leftover marmalade to top a hamburger or as an accompaniment to grilled meat or poultry.

MAKES ABOUT 1 CUP

Vegetable oil cooking spray
1 large red onion, thinly sliced
1 garlic clove, minced
1 cup port wine
1 cup full-bodied red wine, such as Burgundy
½ cup fresh orange juice
⅓ cup honey
¼ cup balsamic vinegar
1 teaspoon finely grated orange zest
½ teaspoon kosher salt

1. Spray a medium nonstick skillet lightly with the cooking spray and heat. Add the onion and cook over moderate heat until caramelized, about 6 minutes. Add the garlic and stir for 1 minute. Add the port and simmer, stirring, for 10 minutes.

2. Add the red wine, orange juice, honey, vinegar, orange zest, and salt, and simmer until the liquid is reduced and the onions are very soft, about 15 minutes. Let cool, cover, and refrigerate overnight or for up to 2 days. Let return to room temperature before serving.—CHARLES WILEY

GRILLED PORK IN A PITA WITH PEANUT SAUCE

4 SERVINGS

MARINADE:

- 1 small onion, thinly sliced
- 1-inch piece of fresh ginger, peeled and coarsely chopped
- 3 garlic cloves, smashed
- 3 tablespoons fresh lime juice
- 1 tablespoon soy sauce
- 2 teaspoons sugar
- ⅓ cup peanut oil or vegetable oil
- ¼ teaspoon crushed red pepper
- ⅛ teaspoon freshly ground black pepper
- 1¼-pound piece of lean boneless pork loin, cut into 8 slices and pounded very thin

PEANUT SAUCE:

- 2 tablespoons peanut butter
- 2 teaspoons soy sauce
- 2 teaspoons Asian sesame oil
- 2 teaspoons fresh lemon juice
- 1 teaspoon sugar
- ½ teaspoon minced garlic

- Eight 7-inch pita breads
- 1 medium Granny Smith apple—quartered, cored, and very thinly sliced lengthwise
- 1 tablespoon fresh lemon juice
- 2 bunches of watercress, thick stems removed
- 6 medium scallions, trimmed and thinly sliced on the bias

1. Make the marinade: In a large bowl, combine the onion, ginger, garlic, lime juice, soy sauce, and sugar. Whisk in the oil in a fine stream. Stir in the crushed red pepper and the freshly ground black pepper. Add the pork slices to the marinade, one slice at a time, turning to coat completely. Set aside for 30 minutes to 1 hour.

2. Preheat the oven to 350°. **Make the peanut sauce:** In a small bowl, stir together the peanut butter, soy sauce, sesame oil, lemon juice, sugar, and garlic. Whisk in 1½ tablespoons of water and set aside.

3. Light a grill or preheat a grill pan over moderately high heat. Wrap the pitas in foil and warm them in the oven for 5 to 10 minutes, until pliable. Remove the pitas from the oven but do not unwrap them.

4. Remove the pork from the marinade and grill the slices, in batches if necessary, until just cooked through, 1 to 2 minutes per side. Transfer the grilled pork to a plate. Toss the apple slices with the lemon juice.

5. Lay the pita breads on a work surface, concave sides facing up. Spread each of the pitas with about 2 teaspoons of the peanut sauce and cover generously with watercress. Place a slice of grilled pork off to one side on each pita. Top the slice of pork with the slices of apple and the sliced scallion. Fold the pitas in half and wrap them in foil. (MAKE AHEAD: The grilled pork pita sandwiches can be made up to 3 hours ahead.)—TRACEY SEAMAN

FRIED RICE WITH MANGO PICKLE, CHINESE SAUSAGE AND TOASTED ALMONDS

4 TO 6 SERVINGS

- 2 cups long-grain white rice
- ½ cup blanched whole almonds
- 2 large eggs
- Salt and freshly ground pepper
- 3 tablespoons vegetable oil
- 3 Chinese sausages (see Note), sliced crosswise ¼ inch thick (about 4 ounces)
- 1 rounded tablespoon finely chopped fresh ginger
- 1 small onion, coarsely chopped
- 1½ tablespoons Cognac or other brandy
- 1 teaspoon soy sauce
- 2 cups diced (½-inch) Mango Pickle (p. 353)
- 2 scallions, thinly sliced crosswise

1. In a medium saucepan, cover the rice with cold water and rinse well, rubbing the grains together to remove excess starch. Drain the rice and repeat the rinsing process until the water is clear. Drain the rice again.

2. Add 2 cups of water to the rice and bring to a boil over high heat. Reduce the heat to low, cover, and cook the rice for 12 minutes without peeking. Remove the saucepan from the heat and let the rice stand, covered, for 5 minutes. Spread the rice on a baking sheet and let cool completely, then cover and refrigerate until very cold. (MAKE AHEAD: The rice can be made to this point up to 3 days ahead; transfer to a bowl.) ➤

3. Preheat the oven to 400°. Toast the almonds in the oven for about 8 minutes, or until golden brown. Transfer to a plate to cool. In a bowl, lightly beat the eggs with a large pinch of salt and pepper.

4. Heat a wok over moderately high heat. Add ½ tablespoon of the oil and when it is hot, add the eggs. Cook, stirring with a metal spatula to break the eggs into small pieces. Scrape the eggs onto a plate. Add another ½ tablespoon of oil to the wok. Add the sausages and stir-fry just until heated through; do not let them brown, or they will become tough. Transfer to a plate.

5. Add the remaining 2 tablespoons oil and the ginger to the wok and stir-fry until fragrant, about 1 minute. Add the onion and stir-fry for 2 minutes. Add the cold rice to the wok and stir-fry until heated through, using the spatula to break up the rice, about 5 minutes. Add the Cognac and cook for 1 minute. Stir in 1¼ teaspoons salt, ½ teaspoon pepper, and the soy sauce. Add the eggs, almonds, and sausages along with the Mango Pickle and scallions, stirring well after each addition. Stir-fry until heated through. Spoon the rice onto a platter and serve.

NOTE: Chinese sausages are available fresh and frozen at Asian groceries. Look for those that are made of pork, pork fat, and seasonings.—MARCIA KIESEL

WILD RICE, ITALIAN SAUSAGE AND SHIITAKE STUFFING

This grain-based stuffing, a departure from the usual moist bread stuffing, combines Wisconsin wild rice with rich Italian sausage.

8 SERVINGS

- 4 cups chicken stock or canned low-sodium broth
- 1 pound fresh shiitake mushrooms, stems removed and reserved, caps thinly sliced
- 2 cups wild rice (about 11 ounces)
- 1 imported bay leaf
- Coarse salt
- 1 pound Italian sausage, casings removed and meat crumbled
- 2 tablespoons olive oil
- 2 medium onions, finely chopped
- Freshly ground pepper
- 1 large tart apple, such as Granny Smith, peeled and finely chopped
- 1 tablespoon fennel seeds, finely chopped

1. In a large saucepan, combine the chicken stock and shiitake stems, and bring to a boil over high heat. Remove from the heat, cover, and let steep for 30 minutes. Strain the stock and return it to the saucepan. Add the wild rice, bay leaf, and 1½ teaspoons coarse salt. Cover and bring to a boil over moderate heat, stirring occasionally, until the rice is tender, about 1 hour; add a little water during cooking if necessary.

2. In a large nonstick skillet, brown the sausage meat over moderate heat, breaking it up with a wooden spoon, until cooked through, about 8 minutes. Transfer to a plate and let cool slightly, then coarsely chop. Pour off the fat from the skillet and reserve 2 tablespoons.

3. Heat 1 tablespoon of the reserved fat and 1 tablespoon of the olive oil in the skillet. Add the onions and season with salt and pepper. Cook over moderately high heat, stirring often, until lightly browned, about 6 minutes. Add the apple and fennel seeds and cook for 3 minutes. Transfer the mixture to a large baking dish.

4. Heat the remaining 1 tablespoon fat and 1 tablespoon olive oil in the skillet. Add the sliced shiitakes and cook over high heat, stirring, until softened and browned, about 5 minutes. Season with salt and pepper, and add the shiitakes to the onion mixture. Stir in the wild rice and the browned sausage and season the stuffing again with salt and pepper. (MAKE AHEAD: The stuffing can be prepared to this point up to 1 day ahead; cover and refrigerate. Let return to room temperature before baking.)

5. Preheat the oven to 400°. Cover the dish with foil and bake for about 25 minutes, until heated through.—SANFORD D'AMATO

WILD RICE SALAD WITH GRAPES AND SAUSAGE

4 SERVINGS

- Salt
- ¾ cup wild rice
- ¾ cup arborio or long-grain white rice
- 3 tablespoons balsamic vinegar
- 1½ tablespoons Dijon mustard
- ¼ cup plus 1 tablespoon extra-virgin olive oil
- Freshly ground pepper

Fried Rice with Mango Pickle, Chinese Sausage and Toasted Almonds

1 pound sweet Italian fennel sausage, casings removed
¾ pound seedless red or green grapes, washed and halved
1 fennel bulb—trimmed, cored, and cut into ¼-inch dice, feathery fronds reserved for garnish
1 head of red oak leaf lettuce

1. In a large saucepan, bring 5 cups of water to a boil. Stir in ½ tablespoon salt. Add the wild rice and cook uncovered over moderate heat until cooked through but still somewhat firm to the bite, about 40 minutes. In another large saucepan, cook the arborio rice the same way until al dente, about 15 minutes. Drain the rices in a colander, rinse with cold water, and drain.

2. In a small bowl, mix 2 tablespoons of the balsamic vinegar and the Dijon mustard. Whisk in ¼ cup of the olive oil and season with salt and pepper. Mix the wild and arborio rices in a large

Baked Ham, with Chicken and Sausage Jambalaya (p. 137) and A Mess o' Greens (p. 324)

serving bowl, pour the dressing over, and toss well.

3. In a skillet, cook the sausage over moderately high heat, breaking it up with a spoon, until browned, about 5 minutes. (If the sausage is very oily, drain on paper towels, but leave a little oil for flavor.) Let cool.

4. Add the cooled sausage, the grapes, and the diced fennel to the rice. Toss well. Season with salt and pepper. Let the salad stand for at least 20 minutes before serving. (MAKE AHEAD: The salad can be made 1 day ahead and refrigerated, covered. Serve at room temperature.)

5. When ready to serve the salad, toss the red oak leaf lettuce with the remaining 1 tablespoon each of olive oil and balsamic vinegar. Line serving plates with several of the lettuce leaves and spoon the rice salad on top. Garnish the salad with fennel fronds.—ERICA DE MANE

BAKED HAM

Nothing could be easier than a baked ham for a buffet. It can be served hot, warm, or at room temperature. Look for a bone-in smoked ham with no water added. The butt end is more expensive and yields larger slices; the meat of the shank is more delicious.

Set the ham on a rack in a roasting pan and place in a cold oven. Do not season the ham, and do not cover it. Turn the oven to 325° and roast the ham for 15 minutes per pound, or until a meat thermometer inserted into the thickest part of the meat without touching the bone registers 160°. Remove the ham from the oven and let rest for at least 20 minutes before carving. Arrange the ham on a platter and cover with foil until serving time.—JOHN MARTIN TAYLOR

MEXICAN LASAGNA

Instead of the standard tomato sauce, Miguel Ravago of Fonda San Miguel in Austin, Texas, moistens his southwestern corn tortilla lasagna with a tangy, spicy green tomatillo sauce.

9 SERVINGS

- ½ pound ground chuck
- ½ pound ground pork
- 4 ounces chorizo sausage, casings removed and meat crumbled
- Salt and freshly ground pepper
- 1 tablespoon corn oil plus ¾ cup for frying the tortillas
- 3 medium zucchini, thinly sliced
- 1 cup fresh or thawed frozen corn kernels
- 18 corn tortillas
- 2 cups shredded Monterey Jack cheese (about ½ pound)
- 2 cups shredded yellow Cheddar cheese (about ½ pound)
- 6 cups Tomatillo Sauce (recipe follows)
- 2 cups sour cream
- 1 tablespoon milk

1. In a large nonstick skillet, cook the ground chuck, ground pork, and chorizo over moderately high heat, breaking up the meat with a wooden spoon, until cooked through, about 12 minutes. Transfer to a strainer and drain off the excess fat. Spoon the meat into a bowl and season with salt and pepper.

2. Wipe out the skillet, add 1 tablespoon of the corn oil, and heat. Add the zucchini and cook over moderate heat, stirring occasionally, until slightly softened, about 5 minutes. Add the corn to the skillet and cook until just tender, 2 to 3 minutes. Season with salt and pepper.

3. In a small skillet, heat the remaining ¾ cup corn oil over moderate heat until the oil is shimmering. Using tongs and working with 1 tortilla at a time, submerge the tortillas in the hot oil for 10 seconds; they should remain pliable. Transfer to a baking sheet lined with paper towels to drain.

4. Preheat the oven to 375°. Lightly oil a 9-by-13-inch nonreactive baking dish. Arrange 6 overlapping tortillas in the prepared dish. Cover with half of the meat mixture, half of the vegetables, ¾ cup each of the Monterey Jack and Cheddar cheeses, 1 cup of the Tomatillo Sauce, and ¾ cup of the sour cream. Repeat the layering process with another 6 tortillas, the remaining meat and vegetables, another ¾ cup each of the cheeses, 1 cup of the Tomatillo Sauce, and ¾ cup of the sour cream. Top with the remaining 6 tortillas. (MAKE AHEAD: The lasagna can be assembled up to 2 days ahead and refrigerated, covered. Refrigerate the remaining Tomatillo Sauce, cheeses, and sour cream separately. Let the lasagna stand at room temperature for 2 hours before baking.)

5. Drizzle the lasagna with 1 cup of the Tomatillo Sauce and sprinkle with the remaining Monterey Jack and Cheddar cheeses. Bake for about 50 minutes, until the lasagna is heated through. Meanwhile, warm the remaining Tomatillo Sauce in a small nonreactive saucepan over moderately low heat. ➤

MARDI GRAS MENU

CHAMPAGNE PUNCH (P. 14)

ROCKEFELLER TURNOVERS (P. 32)

🍷 1991 Guigal Red Côtes du Rhône

🍷 1993 Guigal White Côtes du Rhône

CHICKEN AND SAUSAGE JAMBALAYA (P. 137)

BAKED HAM (P. 199)

A MESS O' GREENS (P. 324)

BREAD PUDDING WITH WHISKEY SAUCE (P. 452)

CREOLE CAFE AU LAIT (P. 16)

—JOHN MARTIN TAYLOR

Veal Rib Roast with Pancetta and Rosemary

Veal Cocotte with Wild Mushrooms

6. In a small bowl, combine the remaining ½ cup sour cream with the milk and drizzle over the hot lasagna. Serve with the warm Tomatillo Sauce alongside.

Tomatillo Sauce

Leftover tomatillo sauce can be served with enchiladas or fajitas, or used as a dip for tortilla chips.

MAKES ABOUT 6 CUPS

- 3 pounds tomatillos—husked, rinsed, and coarsely chopped
- 10 fresh serrano chiles, seeded and coarsely chopped
- 5 medium garlic cloves, coarsely chopped
- ½ cup coarsely chopped fresh cilantro
- Salt

1. In a large nonreactive saucepan, combine the tomatillos and serranos with 4 cups of water and bring to a boil over moderate heat. Reduce the heat to moderately low and simmer until the tomatillos are tender, about 12 minutes. Drain, reserving ½ cup of the liquid.

2. Working in batches in a blender or food processor, puree the tomatillo mixture with the garlic and cilantro and transfer to a bowl. If necessary, stir in some of the reserved cooking liquid to thin the sauce to a pouring consistency. Season with salt. (MAKE AHEAD: The sauce can be prepared up to 1 day ahead; cover and refrigerate.)—MIGUEL RAVAGO

VEAL RIB ROAST WITH PANCETTA AND ROSEMARY

This veal roast is cut into individual chops when served. If you like, use thyme or sage instead of rosemary; they're also delicious with veal. Sautéed greens, such as Swiss chard or kale, and white rice are fine accompaniments for the roast.

🍷 *A medium-bodied red is all that's needed to play off the satisfying flavors of this herbed roast. Among the possible choices, consider the 1986 CVNE Imperial Rioja or the 1988 Château d'Angludet.*

4 SERVINGS

- 2 ounces pancetta,* coarsely chopped
- 1 medium garlic clove, coarsely chopped
- ⅓ cup fine dry unseasoned bread crumbs
- 1 tablespoon olive oil
- 1 teaspoon finely chopped fresh rosemary
- ½ teaspoon salt
- ¼ teaspoon freshly ground pepper
- One trimmed 4-chop veal rib roast (about 3 pounds)

*Available at specialty food markets

1. Preheat the oven to 375°. In a medium skillet, cook the pancetta over moderately high heat, stirring occasionally, until it begins to brown and render its fat, about 5 minutes.

2. Using a slotted spoon, transfer the pancetta to a cutting board. Discard all but 1 tablespoon of the fat in the skillet. Mince the pancetta and garlic together and transfer to a small bowl. Add the reserved pancetta fat, the bread crumbs, 1 teaspoon of the oil, and the rosemary, salt, and pepper.

3. Place the veal roast, meaty side up, in a roasting pan and spread the bread crumb mixture over the exposed meat, pressing firmly to adhere. Drizzle the remaining 2 teaspoons olive oil on the bread crumbs.

4. Roast the veal for about 1 hour, until the crumbs are golden brown and an instant-read thermometer inserted in the thickest part of the roast without touching the bone reads 125°. Cover the veal loosely with foil and let stand for about 15 minutes before carving into chops.—JAN NEWBERRY

VEAL COCOTTE WITH WILD MUSHROOMS

6 SERVINGS

- 1½ pounds assorted fresh wild mushrooms, such as cèpes (porcini) and black chanterelles
- 2 tablespoons unsalted butter
- 3-pound boneless veal shoulder roast, trimmed of most visible fat and tied
- 1 teaspoon salt
- ¼ teaspoon freshly ground pepper
- ¾ cup dry vermouth
- 8 medium shallots, sliced ¼ inch thick
- 4 medium garlic cloves, sliced ¼ inch thick
- 1 teaspoon *herbes de Provence** or dried thyme
- 2 tablespoons minced fresh chives

*Available at specialty food stores

1. Rinse the mushrooms thoroughly in cool water. Lift the mushrooms from the water and drain well. Cut the larger mushrooms into 2-inch pieces.

2. Melt the butter in a dutch oven or enameled cast-iron casserole. Season the veal with the salt and pepper and add it to the dutch oven. Cover partially and cook over moderately low heat, turning occasionally, until browned all over, about 30 minutes.

3. Add the dry vermouth, the sliced shallots, the sliced garlic, and the *herbes de Provence* to the dutch oven, cover tightly, and cook over low heat for 30 minutes, turning the roast once.

4. Transfer the veal to a large platter. Add the mushrooms to the dutch oven and set the roast on top. Raise the heat to high and cook until the mixture is boiling, about 5 minutes. Cover, reduce the heat to low, and cook, turning the veal once, until an instant-read thermometer inserted in the roast registers 145°, about 35 minutes. Transfer the veal to a carving board and let rest for 15 minutes.

5. Carve the roast into ½-inch-thick slices and arrange the slices on the platter. Spoon the mushrooms around the veal, spoon any juices over, and sprinkle with the chives.—JACQUES PEPIN

Cocotte Veal Shanks

COCOTTE VEAL SHANKS

Serve the stew with a light red wine, perhaps a Stonestreet Merlot from California, or a robust white Hermitage from the Rhône Valley.

6 SERVINGS

- 2 whole large, meaty veal shanks or 4 large, meaty, center-cut pieces of osso buco (about 4½ pounds)
- Salt and freshly ground pepper

2 tablespoons unsalted butter
18 small onions, about the size of Ping-Pong balls, peeled
2 medium garlic cloves, finely chopped
2 dozen baby carrots (about 10 ounces) with part of the green tops left on, peeled
1 tablespoon coarsely chopped flat-leaf parsley

1. Whether you are using whole shanks or precut pieces, slide a knife around the bones to release the meat. (If using whole shanks, break the bones with a hammer and freeze to use later in stocks.) Divide the meat into lengthwise pieces following the membranes and sinews. You should have about 3 pounds of meat. Trim off any visible fat. (Some sinews will remain; they will melt away during cooking and give body to the sauce.)

2. Sprinkle the meat with salt and freshly ground pepper. In a heavy dutch oven, melt the unsalted butter over high heat. When the foaming subsides, cook the meat in batches until browned on all sides, about 5 minutes per batch.

3. Return all the browned meat to the pan and cover tightly. Cook over low heat for 20 minutes, stirring once. Add the small onions and the chopped garlic, cover, and cook for 10 minutes. Add the baby carrots, cover, and cook until the meat and vegetables are tender, 15 to 20 minutes longer. (MAKE AHEAD: This stew can be made up to 2 days ahead and refrigerated, covered. Rewarm gently over low heat before proceeding.) Season to taste. Transfer the stew to warmed plates. Spoon the gravy on top, garnish with the chopped parsley, and serve.—JACQUES PEPIN

QUICK DINNER

Some menus that include an appetizer make it impossible for the cook to sit down and enjoy it. This meal, however, allows you to eat the sautéed asparagus starter with your guests while the pasta sauce simmers on the stovetop and the veal steaks finish in the oven. Last-minute tossing and plating are all that remain.

A crisp California white wine, such as the 1992 Dry Creek Fumé Blanc Reserve or the 1993 Ferrari-Carano Fumé Blanc Reserve, would underscore the richness of the veal.

ASPARAGUS WITH RED PEPPER MAYONNAISE (P. 53)

PAN-ROASTED VEAL STEAKS (P. 203)

ORECCHIETTE WITH LEMON-PARMESAN CREAM (P. 258)

DILLED BABY PEAS

STRAWBERRIES WITH RICOTTA AND HONEY

TIMETABLE:

- **Put on the water for the pasta.**
- **Cook the asparagus and whip up the red pepper mayonnaise.**
- **Cook the pasta while you make the lemon cream sauce.**
- **Season, then sear the meat in a skillet and transfer the pan to the oven.**
- **Cook the peas over gentle heat.**

BRAISED WHOLE VEAL SHANK, TRIESTE STYLE

Schinco

Schinco *is a whole veal shank braised slowly, then carved off the bone in very thin slices. It comes from the same part of the hind leg that's used in Milan for osso buco, whose succulent quality it shares. The anchovies dissolve and become undetectable, but they contribute subtly to the depth of flavor that is the distinctive feature of this dish.*

The shanks must come from the hind leg. Have the joint at the broad end of the shank sawed off flat so that the bone can be brought to the table standing up, surrounded by the carved meat. Also have the butcher saw off enough of the bone at the narrow end to expose the marrow, which is most delectable.

12 SERVINGS

2 whole veal shanks, about 4½ pounds
3 tablespoons vegetable oil
3 tablespoons unsalted butter
½ cup chopped onion
2 garlic cloves, lightly smashed and peeled
Salt and freshly ground pepper
⅓ cup dry white wine
6 flat anchovy fillets

1. Stand each shank on its broad end and, with a sharp knife, loosen the skin, flesh, and tendons at the narrow end. This will cause the meat to pull away from the bone as it cooks and to gather in a plump mass at the base. (If you find this difficult to do when the meat is raw, try it after the shanks have cooked for 10 minutes; it will be much easier.)

2. Put the vegetable oil and butter in a heavy oval casserole that

Pan-Roasted Veal Steak, with Orecchiette with Lemon-Parmesan Cream (p. 258)

will hold both shanks snugly. Turn the heat to moderately high; when the butter stops foaming, put in the shanks. Brown the meat deeply all over.

3. Reduce the heat to moderate and add the onion, nudging it in between the meat and the bottom of the casserole. Cook, stirring, until golden. Add the garlic, salt, pepper, and wine, and simmer for about 1 minute, turning the shanks once or twice. Add the anchovies, turn the heat down to very low, and cover the pot with the lid set slightly askew. Cook, turning the shanks from time to time, until the meat is fork-tender, about 2 hours. Whenever there is so little liquid left that the meat begins to stick, add ⅓ cup water and turn the shanks.

4. When the meat is done, transfer the shanks to a cutting board. Carve the meat at an angle into thin slices. Stand each bone upright on its broader end on a warm serving platter and arrange the slices of meat around the base.

5. Pour ⅓ cup water into the casserole and bring to a boil over high heat, stirring with a wooden spoon to loosen all the cooking residues from the bottom and sides. Pour the juices over the meat and serve at once. (MAKE AHEAD: This dish can be prepared several hours in advance. Return the sliced meat and the bones to the casserole and pour the juices on top. Rewarm over gentle heat just before serving, turning the slices in the juices. Arrange on the platter as described above and serve at once.)—MARCELLA HAZAN

PAN-ROASTED VEAL STEAKS

4 SERVINGS

Four 6-ounce boneless veal loin steaks, about 1¼ inches thick
2 teaspoons extra-virgin olive oil
2 large pinches *herbes de Provence* or dried thyme
Salt and freshly ground pepper

1. Preheat the oven to 375°. Heat a large cast-iron skillet over moderately high heat. Rub the veal with the oil and sprinkle with the *herbes de Provence* and salt and pepper. Add the veal to the skillet and cook, turning once, until well browned, about 1½ minutes per side. Transfer the skillet to the oven and roast for about 8 minutes for medium. Transfer the meat to a plate and keep warm.

2. Add ⅓ cup of water to the skillet and bring to a boil over moderate heat, scraping up any browned bits. Add any exuded juices from the veal and boil until slightly reduced, about 1 minute.

3. Just before serving, transfer the warm veal steaks to individual plates. Spoon the pan sauce on top.—TRACEY SEAMAN

CHAPTER 10

FISH & SHELLFISH

Salmon with Pinot Gris Caper Sauce

SALMON WITH PINOT GRIS CAPER SAUCE

This salmon dish goes equally well with a white Pinot Gris or red Pinot Noir wine. The salmon fillet needs to be marinated for an hour before it is cooked, so do that first before you start working on the vegetables.

8 SERVINGS

Eight 5-ounce pieces of salmon fillet with skin, preferably center cut, about ¾ inch thick
2 tablespoons soy sauce
4 large garlic cloves, thinly sliced lengthwise
½ cup olive oil
3 medium red bell peppers—peeled, seeded, and cut into ¼-inch dice
½ cup Pinot Gris or dry Riesling
2 cups heavy cream
¼ cup Dijon mustard
One 3-ounce jar of capers with brine (about ½ cup)

1. Rub the salmon pieces with the soy sauce and refrigerate for 1 hour to marinate. Let the salmon return to room temperature before cooking.
2. In a large, heavy, nonreactive skillet, cook the sliced garlic cloves in the olive oil over moderate heat until the garlic turns light brown, about 5 minutes; do not let the garlic burn. Using a slotted spoon, discard the garlic.
3. Add the red bell peppers to the oil, cover, and cook over low heat until tender, about 5 minutes. Add the wine and bring to a boil over moderately high heat. Boil until reduced slightly, about 3 minutes. Add the heavy cream and return to a boil. Reduce the heat to low and simmer the sauce until thickened, about 8 minutes.
4. Heat 1 or 2 large, dry, nonstick skillets over high heat. Working in batches, sear the salmon pieces, skin side down, for 2 minutes. Flip the salmon over and sear the other side for 2 minutes. Reduce the heat to low and cook until the salmon is opaque on the outside and still slightly translucent in the center, about 4 minutes longer. Remove and discard the salmon skin.
5. Rewarm the sauce over low heat. Stir in the mustard and capers with brine. To serve, spoon the sauce onto warmed plates and place a portion of salmon on top.—JOAN AND DICK ERATH

ROASTED SALMON WITH A FENNEL-CRUMB CRUST

MAKES 50 BUFFET SERVINGS

One 1-pound loaf of country white bread, crusts removed, bread sliced ½ inch thick
2 teaspoons fennel seeds
2 tablespoons unsalted butter, softened
2 tablespoons olive oil
Salt and freshly ground pepper
Four 3-pound skinless salmon fillets
Creamy Herb Sauce (recipe follows)

1. Preheat the oven to 350°. Line 2 rimmed baking sheets with parchment paper and brush them with butter.
2. Arrange the bread on a third baking sheet and toast in the oven for about 10 minutes, turning once, until dry but not browned. Tear the bread into 1-inch pieces and transfer to a food processor. Pulse until the largest crumbs are ¼ inch; they should vary from fine to coarse. Raise the oven temperature to 450°.
3. In a small skillet, toast the fennel seeds over high heat, stirring, until just golden, about 3 minutes. Transfer the seeds to a spice grinder or mortar and grind to a coarse powder.
4. In a large skillet, melt the butter in the olive oil. Add the bread crumbs and the ground fennel seeds and cook over moderately high heat, stirring, until golden, about 5 minutes. Season with salt and pepper and transfer to a plate. (MAKE AHEAD: The bread crumbs can be made up to 1 day ahead; cover and let stand at room temperature.)
5. Sprinkle each prepared baking sheet with 2 tablespoons of the bread crumbs. Lay 2 salmon fillets, skinned sides down, on each baking sheet. Remove any stray bones with tweezers. Using a knife, make ⅜-inch-deep crosswise slashes about 1 inch apart along each fillet. Sprinkle the salmon with the remaining crumbs. Bake for about 20 minutes in the upper and lower thirds of the oven, switching the pans halfway through baking, until the salmon is opaque but still slightly rare in the center. Remove the salmon from the oven and preheat the broiler. Broil the salmon, one sheet at a time, for about 15 seconds, until the crust is browned. Let stand on the baking sheets for 15 minutes.
6. Using 2 large metal spatulas, transfer the roasted salmon fillets to large serving platters. (MAKE AHEAD: The roasted salmon can be prepared up to 2

hours ahead and kept at room temperature.) Serve the salmon warm or at room temperature with the Creamy Herb Sauce.

Creamy Herb Sauce

MAKES ABOUT 4 CUPS

- 1 cup fresh flat-leaf parsley leaves
- ½ cup fresh basil leaves
- ¼ cup coarsely chopped fresh chives
- 1 cup mayonnaise
- 1 cup sour cream
- ¼ cup heavy cream
- ¼ cup Dijon mustard
- ¼ cup fresh lemon juice
- 1 tablespoon finely grated lemon zest
- 1 teaspoon sugar
- Salt and freshly ground pepper

In a food processor, pulse the flat-leaf parsley leaves, the basil leaves, and the chives until finely chopped. Transfer to a bowl and stir in the mayonnaise, the sour cream, the heavy cream, the Dijon mustard, the fresh lemon juice, the grated lemon zest, and the sugar. Season the sauce with salt and pepper. (MAKE AHEAD: The sauce can be refrigerated, covered, for up to 1 day.) Transfer the sauce to 1 or 2 serving bowls and serve it chilled or at room temperature.—GRACE PARISI

GINGER-GLAZED SALMON STEAKS Q

The mild bite of ginger and soy here points to a California Pinot Blanc, such as the 1993 Mirassou or the 1992 Benziger.

4 SERVINGS

- 2 tablespoons finely grated fresh ginger
- ¼ cup plus 2 tablespoons sake or dry sherry
- 1 tablespoon plus 1 teaspoon soy sauce
- 2 teaspoons vegetable oil
- 2 teaspoons dry mustard
- Salt and freshly ground pepper
- Four 6-ounce boneless salmon steaks (about 1 inch thick), with their skin
- Steamed short- or medium-grain white rice, for serving

1. Put the grated ginger in a fine strainer set over a small bowl. Press down on the ginger with the back of a spoon to extract the juice. Discard the ginger pulp. Stir the sake, soy sauce, vegetable oil, and dry mustard into the ginger juice, and season with salt and pepper.

2. Set the boneless salmon steaks in a broiler pan. Pour the ginger marinade over the salmon steaks and turn to coat. Cover and let stand at room temperature for 30 to 40 minutes, turning the salmon once more.

3. Preheat the broiler. Broil the salmon steaks for about 6 minutes, without turning, just until they are cooked through. Transfer the broiled salmon steaks to individual plates. Spoon the pan juices over the salmon steaks and serve them with the steamed rice.—KENNETH WAPNER

Ginger-Glazed Salmon Steaks, with Stir-Fried Snow Peas (p. 311)

SALMON ON BROCCOLI RABE WITH SAFFRON LIMA BEAN BROTH

Sanford D'Amato, of Sanford Restaurant in Milwaukee, uses square-shaped pieces of salmon to ensure that the fish cooks evenly. You can ask your fishmonger to cut the salmon fillets into squares, buy larger pieces of salmon and trim them yourself, or use regular fillets.

Look for a fruity-floral dry white, such as the 1992 Leon Beyer Alsace Gewürztraminer, or a California Viognier, such as the 1994 Callaway.

Salmon on Broccoli Rabe with Saffron Lima Bean Broth

4 SERVINGS

BEANS AND BROTH:

- 1 cup dried lima beans, picked over and rinsed
- 1 small celery rib
- ½ small leek
- ¼ small onion, root intact
- ½ teaspoon loosely packed saffron threads
- 6 garlic cloves, peeled
- 3 star anise pods*
- 2 fresh thyme sprigs
- 2 bay leaves
- 2 whole cloves
- 1 teaspoon whole black peppercorns, crushed
- 1½ cups chicken stock or canned low-sodium broth
- Salt and freshly ground black pepper
- 2 tablespoons finely chopped fresh flat-leaf parsley

GARNISHES:

- 2 tablespoons plus 1 teaspoon olive oil
- ¾ pound broccoli rabe—thick stems trimmed, peeled, and cut into ⅛-inch pieces; leafy tops cut into ½-inch pieces

FIVE SPECIES OF WILD PACIFIC SALMON

KING, OR CHINOOK: These are the largest, fattiest, and rarest of the five Pacific Ocean species. Their average weight is 18 to 20 pounds, although there are plenty of 40 pounders too. Depending on the color of the flesh, they're referred to as red or white kings. They're mainly available from March to October. Those from the upper reaches of Alaska's Yukon and Copper Rivers and those from the Columbia River (called chinooks) are prized for their high-fat content, which gives them a complex flavor and rich texture.

SOCKEYE, OR RED: These are the second fattiest and weigh 3 to 6 pounds. They are available from late May through July. Look for fish from British Columbia's Fraser River and Alaska's Copper River.

COHO, OR SILVER: Coho weigh from 2 to 12 pounds and are available from July through September. Small cohos, 1½ to 2 pounds, are farm raised in British Columbia and Chile.

PINK, OR HUMPBACK: These are the smallest, averaging about 4 pounds, and the most abundant. Some are marketed fresh during July and August, but most are canned.

CHUM, OR DOG: Their average weight is 8 to 10 pounds, and they are available from July through October. Look for fish with bright silver skins. Chum eggs are sold as salmon caviar.—STEPHANIE LYNESS

1 small shallot, minced
8 medium garlic cloves, cut lengthwise into thin julienne strips, plus 1 small garlic clove, minced
Salt and freshly ground pepper
1 medium navel orange
1 teaspoon sugar

SALMON:

¼ cup olive oil
Four 7-ounce squares of skinless salmon fillet (about 3½ inches across and 1 inch thick)
Salt and freshly ground pepper
2 tablespoons all-purpose flour

*Available at Asian markets

1. Prepare the beans and broth: In a large bowl, cover the dried lima beans with 1 quart of hot water. Let the beans stand overnight at room temperature.

2. Drain the lima beans, discarding the loose skins. Rinse the lima beans well, transfer them to a large saucepan, and add the celery, leek, onion, saffron, and 1 quart of water. Wrap the garlic cloves, star anise, thyme, bay leaves, cloves, and peppercorns in a 6-inch square of cheesecloth; tie with string. Add the spice bag to the saucepan and bring to a boil over moderately high heat. Lower the heat and simmer until the beans are tender but still hold their shape, about 20 minutes. Drain, reserving 1½ cups of the bean broth. Discard the celery, leek, onion, and spice bag and return the beans to the reserved broth. Stir in the chicken stock and season with salt and pepper. (MAKE AHEAD: The recipe can be prepared to this point up to 1 day ahead; cover and refrigerate.)

3. Prepare the garnishes: Heat 2 tablespoons of the olive oil in a large skillet. Add the broccoli rabe stems and cook over moderately high heat, stirring, for 1 minute. Add the shallot and minced garlic and stir for 30 seconds. Add the broccoli rabe tops and cook, stirring, until just tender, 1 to 2 minutes. Season with salt and pepper and keep warm.

4. Using a vegetable peeler, peel strips of zest from the orange, leaving behind the bitter white pith. Cut the orange zest into thin 1-inch-long strips. Put the zest and the julienned garlic in a small saucepan of water and bring to a boil over high heat. Boil for 10 seconds, drain, and rinse with cold water.

5. Heat the remaining 1 teaspoon oil in a small skillet. Add the orange zest and garlic, sprinkle with the sugar and a pinch of salt, and cook over moderately high heat, stirring, until lightly caramelized, about 45 seconds. Remove from the heat.

6. Prepare the salmon: Heat the olive oil in a large heavy skillet. Season the salmon with salt and pepper and dust with the flour. Cook the salmon over moderately high heat, turning once, until just cooked through, about 4 minutes per side.

7. Meanwhile, rewarm the lima beans and broth. Drain the beans, reserving the broth. Mound the broccoli rabe in 4 warmed shallow soup bowls. Set a salmon square on each mound of broccoli rabe and top with the orange zest and garlic. Stir the parsley into the lima beans, then spoon the beans around the salmon and ladle the broth into the bowls.—SANFORD D'AMATO

SALMON IN PARCHMENT WITH HERB VINAIGRETTE

Serge Falesitch's Provençal-flavored salmon, served at Eclipse in West Hollywood, is baked in a heart-shaped piece of parchment. You can use foil instead, and the fish will be just as moist and tasty, though the presentation isn't as elegant.

🍷 *This dish is best set off by a classic oak-aged Chardonnay, such as the 1992 Louis Latour Chassagne-Montrachet from Burgundy or the 1992 Beaulieu Vineyard Carneros Reserve Chardonnay from California.*

4 SERVINGS

Four 5-ounce skinless salmon fillets, about 1 inch thick
Salt and freshly ground pepper
¼ cup dry white wine
3 tablespoons fresh lemon juice
1 garlic clove, minced
1 tablespoon finely chopped fresh basil
1 teaspoon finely chopped fresh tarragon
¼ cup extra-virgin olive oil
2 large plum tomatoes—peeled, seeded, and finely diced
1 medium leek, white and tender green portion, sliced lengthwise into thin julienne strips

1. Set the skinless salmon fillets in an 8-inch square nonreactive baking dish and season with salt and pepper. Pour the white wine over, cover, and let the salmon marinate at room temperature for 30 minutes.

Salmon in Parchment with Herb Vinaigrette

2. In a small bowl, combine the lemon juice, garlic, basil, and tarragon. Whisk in the olive oil in a thin, steady stream. Stir in the tomatoes and season with salt and pepper.

3. Preheat the oven to 450°. Cut out four 12-by-18-inch rectangles of parchment paper. Fold each parchment sheet in half so you have 12-by-9-inch rectangles. Draw a large half heart on the crease of each rectangle, then cut out the hearts. Open the parchment hearts on a work surface. Spread one-quarter of the julienned leeks in a thin layer on half of each parchment heart, close to the center. Set a salmon fillet on the leeks and spoon the herb vinaigrette on top. Fold the parchment over to enclose the fish and, starting at one end, crimp the paper with tiny folds to seal each package.

4. Set the packages on a large baking sheet and bake for about 12 minutes, or until the parchment is puffed. Transfer each of the packages to a plate and serve at once, allowing each diner to slit the package open at the table.—SERGE FALESITCH

CAYENNE-RUBBED SALMON WITH TOMATILLO SALSA

Tom Douglas, of the Dahlia Lounge in Seattle, warns against overprocessing

Cayenne-Rubbed Salmon with Tomatillo Salsa

the tomatillo salsa, which will make it watery.

4 SERVINGS

SALSA:

- ½ pound tomatillos—husked, rinsed, cored, and quartered
- 1 garlic clove
- ½ teaspoon mustard seeds
- 1½ tablespoons rice vinegar
- 1 tablespoon fresh lime juice
- 2½ teaspoons hot pepper sauce, preferably green
- 2 teaspoons sugar
- 1½ teaspoons drained bottled white horseradish

SALMON:

- 1 tablespoon sweet paprika
- 2 teaspoons cayenne pepper
- 1 teaspoon salt
- ½ teaspoon freshly ground black pepper
- Four 7-ounce skinless salmon fillets, about 1 inch thick
- 2 tablespoons peanut oil

½ cup sour cream mixed with 1 tablespoon milk
Tomato wedges, avocado slices, fresh coriander sprigs, and lime wedges

1. Make the salsa: In a food processor, pulse the tomatillos with the garlic clove and the mustard seeds until very coarsely chopped. Add the rice vinegar, the fresh lime juice, the hot pepper sauce, the sugar, and the white horseradish and process to blend.
2. Prepare the salmon: Preheat the oven to 425°. In a bowl, combine the sweet paprika, cayenne pepper, salt, and black pepper, and pat the spice mixture on both sides of the salmon. Heat the peanut oil in a large ovenproof skillet. Add the salmon fillets and sear over moderately high heat, turning once, until they are nicely browned, about 1½ minutes per side. Transfer the skillet to the oven and bake for about 8 minutes, or until the salmon is just cooked through.
3. Set each salmon fillet on a warmed plate. Spoon the salsa over the fish and drizzle the sour cream around. Garnish with tomato, avocado, coriander, and lime.—TOM DOUGLAS

PESTO-CRUSTED SALMON WITH WILTED SPINACH

Philippe Boulot likes to add oven-dried tomatoes and a relish of red onions and fresh coriander to the crisp-crusted salmon that he serves at the Heathman Hotel in Portland.

🍷 *This rich crust calls for a tart but fruity Pinot Noir, such as the 1992 Knudsen-Erath from Oregon or the 1992 Meridian from California.*

6 SERVINGS

3 pounds young spinach, large stems removed
⅓ cup fresh basil leaves
⅓ cup plain dry bread crumbs
2 strips lean bacon, coarsely chopped
3 tablespoons pine nuts
3 tablespoons freshly grated Parmesan cheese
2 small garlic cloves
3 tablespoons extra-virgin olive oil
Salt and freshly ground pepper
Six 7-ounce skinless salmon fillets, about 1 inch thick
3 tablespoons plus 2 teaspoons olive oil
1 medium shallot, finely chopped
Lemon wedges, for serving

1. Bring 1 inch of water to a boil in a large saucepan. Add half of the spinach, cover, and cook over moderately high heat, stirring, until wilted, 2 to 3 minutes. Drain, rinse with cold water, and squeeze to extract the excess liquid. Transfer to a plate and repeat with the remaining spinach.
2. Preheat the oven to 400°. In a food processor, combine the basil, bread crumbs, bacon, pine nuts, Parmesan, and garlic, and finely chop. With the machine on, add the extra-virgin olive oil in a steady stream until smooth. Season with salt and pepper. Spread a rounded tablespoon of the pesto evenly on the skinned side of each salmon fillet.
3. Heat 2 teaspoons of the olive oil in a large nonstick skillet. Add 3 of the salmon fillets, pesto side down, and cook over moderately high heat without turning until the pesto is browned, 1 to 2 minutes. Carefully invert the fillets into a large baking dish. Repeat with the remaining 3 salmon fillets. Bake in the oven for about 10 minutes, or until the salmon is just cooked through.
4. Meanwhile, wipe out the skillet and heat the remaining 3 tablespoons olive oil. Add the shallot and cook over moderately high heat for 1 minute. Add the spinach, season with salt and pepper, and toss until heated through, about 3 minutes.
5. Set each salmon fillet in the center of a warmed plate, pesto side up. Arrange the spinach around the fish and serve with lemon wedges.—PHILIPPE BOULOT

SALMON WITH OLIVES, SUN-DRIED TOMATOES AND LEMON CONFIT

Eric Ripart uses the cooking juices from mussels to intensify the delicious sauce served with the salmon at Le Bernardin in New York City.

🍷 *Choose Sauvignon Blanc/Sémillon blends from California, such as the 1992 Simi Sendal or the 1993 Preston Vineyards Cuvée de Fumé.*

4 SERVINGS

LEMON CONFIT:

1 large lemon
1 tablespoon salt
1 teaspoon sugar

SAUCE AND GARNISH:

2 teaspoons olive oil
1 medium shallot, thinly sliced
2 pounds medium mussels, scrubbed and debearded
½ cup dry white wine
1 teaspoon whole black peppercorns
1 bay leaf

3 oil-packed sun-dried tomatoes, thinly sliced, plus 2 tablespoons oil from the jar
1 tablespoon white wine vinegar
1 tablespoon minced fresh fennel fronds or fresh dill
Squeeze of fresh lemon juice
Salt and freshly ground pepper
2 tablespoons thinly sliced pitted brine-cured black olives, such as Calamata or Niçoise
2 tablespoons thinly sliced pitted oil-cured black olives
1 tablespoon finely chopped fresh oregano

SALMON:
2 tablespoons olive oil
Four 7-ounce squares of skinless salmon fillet (about 3½ inches across and 1 inch thick)

1. **Make the lemon confit:** Using a vegetable peeler, peel thin strips of zest from the lemon, leaving behind the bitter white pith. In a bowl, toss the zest with the salt and the sugar. Cover and let stand overnight at room temperature. Rinse before using.
2. In a small saucepan of boiling water, blanch the lemon zest for 20 seconds. Drain well and let cool. Cut the zest into very thin 1-inch-long julienne strips.
3. **Make the sauce and garnish:** Heat the olive oil in a large nonreactive saucepan. Add the shallot and cook over moderate heat, stirring often, until translucent, about 4 minutes. Add the mussels, white wine, peppercorns, and bay leaf. Cover and bring to a boil over moderate heat; boil gently for 10 minutes. Remove from the heat and let stand, covered, for 10 minutes.
4. Strain the broth into a medium saucepan and discard the solids. Bring to a boil over moderately high heat. Boil until reduced to ¾ cup, about 15 minutes. Transfer to a nonreactive saucepan and stir in the sun-dried tomato oil, vinegar, fennel fronds, and lemon juice. Season with salt and pepper and keep warm.
5. In a small bowl, toss the sun-dried tomatoes with the olives. In another bowl, toss the oregano with the lemon confit.
6. **Prepare the salmon:** Heat the olive oil in a large nonstick skillet. Cook the salmon over moderate heat, turning once, until just cooked through, 3 to 4 minutes per side.
7. Set the salmon on warmed plates and top with the olive mixture and lemon zest. Spoon the sauce around the salmon and serve.—ERIC RIPART

TANDOORI SALMON WITH FRESH PEACH CHUTNEY AND MINTED YOGURT SAUCE

At Christer's in New York City, Christer Larsson balances the complex flavors of his Indian-spiced salmon and tangy chutney with steamed basmati or brown rice.

6 SERVINGS

SALMON:
1 tablespoon olive oil
1 garlic clove, finely chopped
Six 8-ounce skinless salmon steaks, about 1¼ inches thick
1 tablespoon Garam Masala (recipe follows)
Salt

PEACH CHUTNEY:
1 tablespoon sugar
¼ cup rice vinegar
4 medium peaches—peeled and cut into ¼-inch dice
2 tablespoons finely grated fresh ginger

YOGURT SAUCE:
1½ teaspoons honey
1½ teaspoons finely chopped fresh mint
Pinch of ground cumin
Pinch of turmeric
1 cup plain low-fat yogurt
Salt and freshly ground pepper

1. **Prepare the salmon:** In a bowl, combine the olive oil and the chopped garlic. Rub the mixture all over the salmon. Sprinkle with the Garam Masala and season lightly with salt. Cover and refrigerate for up to 2 hours.
2. **Make the peach chutney:** In a nonreactive saucepan, dissolve the sugar in the vinegar, stirring, over moderately high heat. Bring to a boil and cook for 1 minute. Stir in the peaches and ginger and return to a boil. Reduce the heat and simmer, stirring, until the fruit is softened, about 5 minutes. Transfer to a bowl.
3. **Make the yogurt sauce:** In a small bowl, combine the honey, mint, cumin, and turmeric. Whisk in the yogurt until blended. Season with salt and pepper, cover, and refrigerate.
4. Light a grill or preheat the broiler. Grill or broil the salmon steaks, turning once, for about 4 minutes per side, or until nicely charred and just cooked through.
5. Transfer each of the salmon steaks to a warmed plate and remove the central bone with a

fork. Serve with the peach chutney and yogurt sauce.

Garam Masala

You can substitute commercial garam masala, *available at specialty food stores, for this spice blend. Use leftover* garam masala *to stir into Indian curries or sprinkle on chicken or vegetables before roasting.*

MAKES ABOUT 6 TABLESPOONS

- 1 tablespoon ground coriander
- 1 tablespoon ground cumin
- 1 tablespoon freshly ground black pepper
- 1 tablespoon cayenne pepper
- 1 tablespoon ground fennel seeds
- 1 tablespoon ground ginger
- 1 tablespoon ground cardamom
- 1 teaspoon ground cloves
- 1 teaspoon grated nutmeg

Combine all the ingredients in a small jar. (MAKE AHEAD: Cover and store at room temperature for up to 1 month.)—CHRISTER LARSSON

ROASTED SALMON SALAD

🍷 *Salmon calls for wines with both crispness to check the fattiness and the requisite flavor to complement the sweet, rich fish. An assertive Italian white, such as the 1993 Ceretto Arneis or the 1993 San Quirico Vernaccia di San Gimignano, would offer an attractive contrast.*

6 TO 8 SERVINGS

VINAIGRETTE:

- ¼ cup red wine vinegar
- 2 teaspoons fresh lemon juice
- 2 tablespoons minced shallots
- 1½ tablespoons finely grated lemon zest
- 1 teaspoon finely chopped fresh rosemary
- ¾ cup olive oil
- Salt and freshly ground black pepper

SALMON SALAD:

- 3 medium red bell peppers
- 2 pounds new potatoes, sliced ¼ inch thick
- 1 tablespoon olive oil
- ¾ pound fresh cremini or chanterelle mushrooms, thinly sliced
- Salt and freshly ground black pepper
- 3-pound skinless salmon fillet
- 1 tablespoon fresh thyme
- 1 teaspoon fennel seeds
- ½ teaspoon celery seeds
- 1 pound fresh young arugula, tough stems trimmed
- ¾-pound fresh fennel bulb—trimmed, cored, and very thinly sliced lengthwise
- 12 to 16 fresh cilantro sprigs

HEALTHY SEAFOOD

FAT: All seafood is extraordinarily low in saturated fat (the kind that contributes to heart disease). Most shellfish and white-fleshed fish and even some dark-fleshed fish have less total fat than any other form of animal protein. Crab, clams, lobster, and yellowfin tuna contain about 1 gram of fat per 3½ ounce serving. Scallops weigh in at only ¾ gram of fat per serving. Fish like salmon and swordfish are higher in total fat, delivering 6 grams or more per serving. But they also offer omega-3 fatty acids, which studies suggest raise the levels of HDL ("good") cholesterol.

CHOLESTEROL: To compare, look at skinless chicken breast, which has about 58 milligrams (mg) of cholesterol per serving. Clams have 34 mg per serving; scallops, 33; salmon and swordfish, 39. Lobster and shrimp are higher in cholesterol, at 95 and 152 mg respectively. But each contains less saturated fat—which is primarily responsible for raising blood cholesterol levels—than skinless chicken breast.

VITAMINS AND MINERALS: The milligram counts below are amounts per serving; the percentages, the proportion of the government's Daily Values for optimal health.

- Crab: 89 mg calcium (9%). Strengthens bones.
- Shrimp: 1.1 mg zinc (about 7%). Boosts the immune system.
- Swordfish: 9.7 mg niacin (about 50%). Improves blood circulation.
- Clams: 14 mg iron (78%). Prevents anemia.

SAFETY: Seafood is responsible for one illness per 250,000 servings; chicken is 10 times as risky. If you exclude bivalve mollusks that are eaten raw, fish causes one illness per 5,000,000 servings. Those are pretty good odds.

FRESHNESS: In a hot car, fish can spoil in an hour. If you shop on a warm day and won't be coming home directly, bring a cooler and some ice along for the ride. Most refrigerators run about 40°—not cold enough. Fill the vegetable bin with ice and bury the still-wrapped fish there, or sandwich between ice packs.—MARK BITTMAN

Potato and Smoked Salmon Lasagna

1. Make the vinaigrette: In a bowl, combine the vinegar, lemon juice, shallots, lemon zest, and rosemary. Whisk in the olive oil and season with salt and pepper. (MAKE AHEAD: The vinaigrette can be made up to 6 hours ahead; let stand at room temperature.)
2. Make the salmon salad: Roast the bell peppers directly over a gas flame or under the broiler as close to the heat as possible until charred all over. Transfer to a paper bag and let steam for 15 minutes. Scrape off the blackened skins and discard the stems, ribs, and seeds. Cut the peppers into ⅓-inch-thick strips.
3. Meanwhile, put the sliced potatoes in a medium saucepan of salted water and bring to a boil. Remove from the heat and let sit in the hot water until tender, about 18 minutes. Drain and transfer to a plate.
4. Heat the olive oil in a medium skillet. Add the mushrooms and cook over high heat, stirring occasionally, until softened, about 4 minutes. Season the mushrooms with salt and black pepper and transfer to a bowl.
5. Preheat the oven to 500°. Lay the salmon fillet, skinned side down, on a lightly oiled baking sheet and remove any stray bones with tweezers. Sprinkle the salmon with the thyme, fennel seeds, and celery seeds; season with salt and black pepper. Roast for about 10 minutes, until the salmon is opaque but still slightly rare in the center. Remove the salmon from the oven and preheat the broiler. Broil for about 1 minute, or until the top is browned. Break the salmon into large chunks.
6. In a large bowl, combine the arugula with the fennel, mushrooms, roasted red peppers, potatoes, and cilantro. Add three-quarters of the vinaigrette and toss. Arrange the salad on large plates or in shallow bowls and top with the chunks of salmon. Drizzle the remaining vinaigrette on the fish and serve.—BEN BARKER

POTATO AND SMOKED SALMON LASAGNA

Gary Danko serves this elegant lasagna at The Dining Room at The Ritz-Carlton in San Francisco.

🍷 *The ingredients in this dish all point to a rich, deep-flavored Chardonnay. Consider the 1994 Lindemans Bin 65 from Australia or the 1993 Arrowood Reserve Cuveé Michel Berthoud from California.*

6 TO 9 SERVINGS

- 2 tablespoons unsalted butter
- 1 medium leek, white and tender green, coarsely chopped
- ½ pound fresh wild mushrooms, such as chanterelles or shiitakes, stems removed and caps thinly sliced
- 1 garlic clove, minced
- 1 tablespoon finely chopped fresh flat-leaf parsley
- ¾ pound fresh spinach, tough stems discarded, leaves coarsely chopped
- Coarse salt
- 1 cup bottled clam juice
- ¾ cup heavy cream
- 2 teaspoons finely chopped fresh tarragon
- 3 pounds large red potatoes, peeled and sliced lengthwise ⅛ inch thick
- 6 ounces smoked salmon, coarsely or finely chopped

1. Preheat the oven to 350°. Melt the butter in a large heavy skillet. Stir in the leek. Cook over moderate heat, stirring occasionally, until just tender, about 5 minutes. Add the mushrooms and cook, stirring, until softened, about 6 minutes. Transfer to a large bowl and add the garlic and parsley.
2. Wipe out the skillet. Add the spinach and toss over moderately high heat until wilted, about 2 minutes. Stir the spinach into the mushrooms and season with coarse salt. In a small bowl, combine the clam juice, heavy cream, chopped tarragon, and 1 teaspoon coarse salt.
3. In a large bowl, rinse the potato slices in cold running water until the water runs clear. Drain the potato slices and pat dry. In a 9-by-13-inch nonreactive baking dish, arrange one-third of the potatoes, overlapping the slices. Spread half the spinach-mushroom mixture over the potatoes and sprinkle with half of the salmon. Repeat the process with another third of the potato slices and the remaining spinach-mushroom mixture and smoked salmon. Cover with the remaining potatoes and pour the cream mixture evenly over the top.
4. Cover the lasagna with foil and bake for 1 hour. Uncover and bake for about 30 minutes longer, or until the potatoes are tender and golden. (MAKE AHEAD: The lasagna can be made 1 day ahead; cover and refrigerate. Let return to room temperature, then rewarm in a 350° oven for about 30 minutes.)

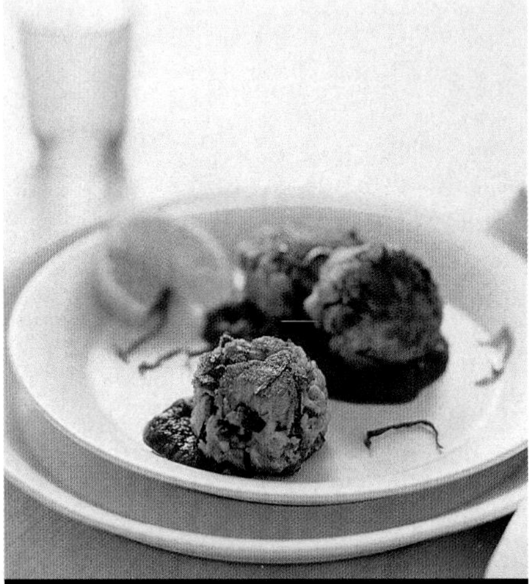

Alaska Salmon Cakes with Red Pepper Coulis

5. Preheat the broiler. Broil the lasagna for about 1 minute, until the potatoes are crisp. Allow the lasagna to cool slightly before serving.—GARY DANKO

ALASKA SALMON CAKES WITH RED PEPPER COULIS

The start of salmon fishing season, usually at the end of May, is a cause for celebration at the Riversong Lodge outside Anchorage, Alaska. Kirsten Dixon also hot-smokes the excess salmon to use after the season is over in early September. You can substitute two cups of flaked cooked salmon for the raw salmon; simply omit Step 2.

A full-flavored ale, such as Bass or Samuel Adams, is a good choice for these salmon cakes.

4 TO 6 SERVINGS

COULIS:

1 large red bell pepper
½ teaspoon rice vinegar
¼ teaspoon poppy seeds
¼ teaspoon salt

SALMON CAKES:

1 pound piece of skinless salmon fillet
Salt and freshly ground black pepper
¼ cup finely chopped red onion
¼ cup finely chopped red bell pepper
¼ cup fresh fine sourdough bread crumbs
1 tablespoon minced fresh basil plus 2 tablespoons shredded fresh basil
1 large egg
½ teaspoon Worcestershire sauce
¼ teaspoon hot pepper sauce
Lemon wedges, for serving

1. Make the coulis: Roast the bell pepper directly over a gas flame or under the broiler, turning often, until charred all over. Transfer to a paper bag and let steam for 10 minutes. Scrape off the skin and discard the stem, core, seeds, and ribs. Cut the pepper into 1-inch pieces. Transfer to a food processor and puree until smooth. Add the vinegar, poppy seeds, and salt, and pulse until blended. Transfer the *coulis* to a small bowl.
2. Make the salmon cakes: Preheat the oven to 400°. Season the salmon with salt and pepper and set it on a large piece of foil. Crimp the edges together to enclose the salmon and bake for about 25 minutes, or until cooked through. Let cool. Reduce the oven temperature to 350°.
3. Flake the cooked salmon into a bowl, discarding any bones. Add the red onion, red bell pepper, bread crumbs, and minced basil, and toss. In another bowl, beat the egg, Worcestershire, hot pepper sauce, 1 teaspoon salt, and ¼ teaspoon pepper. Add to the salmon and mix until blended.
4. Shape the salmon mixture into twelve 2½-inch cakes, about ½ inch thick. Set the salmon cakes on a lightly buttered baking sheet and bake for about 15 minutes, or until golden and cooked through. Arrange the salmon cakes on warmed plates, spoon the red pepper *coulis* around them, and sprinkle with the shredded basil. Serve with lemon wedges.—KIRSTEN DIXON

GRILLED TUNA WITH HERBED CREAM

To make two meals at once, cook extra tuna steaks and turn them into a salad for sandwiches (see Note).

4 SERVINGS

1 garlic clove, smashed
Salt
¼ cup mayonnaise
¼ cup chopped fresh basil
¼ cup minced fresh chives
Freshly ground black pepper
Pinch of cayenne pepper
Four 6-ounce tuna steaks, about ¾ inch thick
4 slices of a large tomato, cut about ⅓ inch thick
⅓ cup heavy cream

1. Light a grill or set a heavy grill pan over moderately high heat. On a work surface, using a fork, mash the garlic with ¼ teaspoon salt. In a small bowl, blend the garlic with the mayonnaise, basil, chives, ¼ teaspoon black pepper, and the cayenne.
2. Season the tuna steaks with salt and black pepper and lightly oil the grill or the pan. Grill the tuna for about 2½ minutes, then

turn the steaks and top each one with a tomato slice. Grill for 2 to 3 minutes for medium-rare, longer if desired. Transfer to plates.
3. While the fish is cooking, beat the cream until stiff and fold in the herbed mayonnaise. Serve the fish warm or at room temperature. Pass the sauce separately.
NOTE: Flake the extra cooked tuna into a bowl. Add finely diced celery, minced basil, mayonnaise, lemon juice, salt, and pepper. Serve on crusty peasant bread topped with thinly sliced onion and tomato, young greens, and strips of roasted bell pepper. You can also toast the bread, butter it, and rub each side with a garlic clove before making the sandwiches.—TRACEY SEAMAN

PAN-SEARED TUNA WITH SUMMER VEGETABLES

To preserve the bright green color of the fresh cilantro, blanch it first. Dice the skin and the firm, fleshy portions of the zucchini and yellow squash, discarding the seedy centers.

4 SERVINGS

- ½ cup fresh cilantro leaves
- ¼ cup olive oil
- 2 ounces *haricots verts* or thin green beans
- 1½ tablespoons unsalted butter
- 1 medium zucchini, cut into ⅓-inch dice
- 1 medium yellow squash, cut into ⅓-inch dice
- 2 cups fresh corn kernels (from 3 medium ears)
- 1 tablespoon finely chopped scallion
- Salt and freshly ground pepper
- Four 6-ounce tuna steaks, about 1 inch thick
- 2 teaspoons fresh lime juice

1. Bring a medium pot of salted water to a boil. Place 6 tablespoons of the fresh cilantro leaves in a small sieve. Immerse the sieve in the boiling water until the cilantro is wilted, 10 to 15 seconds. Refresh with cold water and squeeze dry; leave the water boiling on the stove. Combine the blanched cilantro and 3 tablespoons of the olive oil in a mini-food processor or mortar and process or pound until pureed. Shred the remaining 2 tablespoons fresh cilantro.
2. Add the *haricots verts* to the boiling water and cook until crisp-tender, about 3 minutes. Drain, refresh with cold water, and cut into ½-inch pieces.
3. Melt the butter in a large nonreactive skillet. Add the zucchini and yellow squash and sauté over moderately high heat until slightly softened, 2 to 3 minutes. Add the corn, scallion, 1 teaspoon salt, and ¼ teaspoon pepper, and sauté until the corn is crisp-tender, about 3 minutes. Add the *haricots verts* and cook, stirring once or twice, until the beans are heated through, about 1 minute longer; keep warm.
4. In a large heavy skillet, heat the remaining 1 tablespoon oil until very hot but not smoking. Season the tuna steaks generously on both sides with salt and pepper. Add them to the skillet and cook over high heat, turning once, until nicely seared on both sides but still rare within, 2 to 3 minutes per side. Transfer the tuna to individual plates.
5. Stir the lime juice and the shredded fresh cilantro into the warm vegetables and spoon them around the tuna steaks. Drizzle the cilantro oil over the fish and serve.—JUDITH SUTTON

Grilled Tuna with Herbed Cream

QUICK DINNER

FRESH LEMON-LIMEADE (P. 16)

GRILLED TUNA WITH HERBED CREAM (P. 218)

SUMMER GARDEN COUSCOUS SALAD (P. 81)

INSTANT ICE CREAM SANDWICHES (P. 460)

TIMETABLE:
- **Make and freeze the sandwiches.**
- **Make the lemon-limeade.**
- **Cook and dress the couscous, then prepare the vegetables for the salad.**
- **Prepare the cream and grill the tuna.**
- **Toss the vegetables with the dressed couscous and serve.**

SWORDFISH STEAKS WITH TAPENADE CRUST

🍷 *This dish demands a crisp white, such as the 1993 Preston Cuvée de*

Swordfish Steak with Tapenade Crust

Fumé from California or 1994 Rosemount Fumé Blanc from Australia.

4 SERVINGS

TAPENADE:

½ cup green olives, such as picholine, pitted
¼ cup fresh flat-leaf parsley leaves
2 anchovy fillets
1 tablespoon drained capers
1 small garlic clove
2 teaspoons extra-virgin olive oil
1 teaspoon red wine vinegar
Cayenne pepper
Salt and freshly ground black pepper

SWORDFISH AND VEGETABLES:

3 medium yellow squash, sliced ⅛ to ¼ inch thick on the diagonal
¼ cup plus 2 tablespoons extra-virgin olive oil, plus more for brushing
Salt and freshly ground pepper
2 tablespoons fresh lemon juice
2 medium fennel bulbs—trimmed, quartered, cored, and thinly sliced lengthwise
1 ripe plum tomato—peeled, seeded, and finely chopped
Four 6-ounce swordfish steaks, about 1 inch thick
3 tablespoons plain dry bread crumbs
¼ cup drained oil-packed sun-dried tomato halves, quartered lengthwise
Fresh rosemary, thyme, and cilantro sprigs, for garnish

1. Prepare the tapenade: In a food processor, combine the olives, parsley, anchovies, capers, and garlic, and pulse until coarsely chopped. With the machine on, add the oil and vinegar in a steady stream. Season with cayenne, salt, and black pepper. (MAKE AHEAD: The tapenade can be refrigerated, covered, for up to 1 week. Let return to room temperature before serving.)

2. Prepare the swordfish and vegetables: Heat a large grill pan or skillet. Lightly brush the squash with olive oil and season with salt and pepper. Cook over moderately high heat, turning once, until lightly browned and slightly softened, about 3 minutes. Transfer to a plate.

3. In a small bowl, gradually whisk the olive oil into the lemon juice and season well with salt and pepper. Pour 3 tablespoons of the dressing into a medium bowl, add the fennel, and toss to coat. Stir the chopped plum tomato into the remaining dressing.

4. Preheat the broiler. Brush the grill pan with olive oil and season the swordfish lightly with salt and pepper. Grill the swordfish over moderately high heat for 4 minutes. Turn the steaks over and spread the tapenade on top. Continue grilling until the fish is just firm to the touch, about 3 minutes longer. Sprinkle the tapenade with the bread crumbs and broil the fish for about 1 minute, until the bread crumbs are lightly browned.

5. To serve, fan the squash in the center of each of 4 large plates. Mound the dressed fennel on the squash and set the swordfish on top. Spoon the tomato dressing around the fish and garnish with the sun-dried tomatoes and the herb sprigs.—JOHN SCHENK

CRISP POTATO CANNELLONI WITH HALIBUT

Rather than using pasta dough, these halibut-filled cannelloni are made

with thinly sliced potatoes. Plastic mandolines with metal blades make an easy job of cutting potatoes into even slices.

6 SERVINGS

CANNELLONI:

- 5 tablespoons unsalted butter, melted
- Salt and freshly ground white pepper
- 4 very large Idaho potatoes, peeled and sliced lengthwise on a mandoline 1/16 inch thick
- 1/2 pound halibut fillet, cut into 1/4-inch dice
- 2 shallots, minced
- 2 tablespoons finely chopped chives
- 1 large egg, lightly beaten

TOMATOES AND SALAD:

- 1/3 cup extra-virgin olive oil
- 2 shallots, minced
- 10 plum tomatoes—peeled, seeded, and halved lengthwise
- 1 fresh thyme sprig
- 2 garlic cloves, lightly crushed
- 1 tablespoon finely shredded fresh basil
- 2 tablespoons clarified unsalted butter
- 2 cups loosely packed baby spinach leaves
- 1/2 cup fresh flat-leaf parsley leaves
- 2 shallots, minced
- 1 tablespoon fresh chives, cut into 2-inch lengths
- 2 tablespoons extra-virgin olive oil
- 1 teaspoon balsamic vinegar

1. Make the cannelloni sheets: Preheat the oven to 350°. Line 3 baking sheets with parchment paper. Brush the paper with some of the butter and sprinkle with salt and white pepper. Arrange the 36 largest potato slices in a single layer on the sheets. Brush the potatoes with butter and sprinkle with salt and white pepper. Cover the potatoes with another sheet of parchment paper and bake for about 10 minutes, or until just tender. (MAKE AHEAD: The potato slices can be baked up to 1 day ahead, covered with plastic wrap, and refrigerated. Bring to room temperature before proceeding.)

2. Make the filling: In a medium bowl, stir together the halibut,

Crisp Potato Cannelloni with Halibut

shallots, and chives. Season the mixture with ½ teaspoon salt and ¼ teaspoon pepper.

3. Lay an 8-inch piece of plastic wrap on a work surface. Place 2 potato slices lengthwise in the center of the plastic wrap, overlapping them slightly, to form a cannelloni wrapper with rounded edges that measures about 3-by-6 inches. Spoon 2 to 3 teaspoons of halibut filling along one short edge of the potato sheet and spoon a dab of the beaten egg at the other end as a sealer. Tightly roll up the cannelloni, using the plastic wrap to help. Wrap the cannelloni snugly in the plastic wrap and set it on a large plate. Repeat the process to make 17 more cannelloni. Refrigerate to firm up for at least 2 hours or overnight.

4. Prepare the tomatoes: Heat the olive oil in a nonstick medium skillet. Add the shallots and cook over moderately low heat, stirring, until softened, about 3 minutes. Add the plum tomatoes, the thyme sprig, and the crushed garlic. Increase the heat to moderate and cook until the tomatoes are tender but still hold their shape, about 4 minutes. Discard the garlic and the thyme sprig and stir in the shredded basil. Remove from the heat and set aside until serving time.

5. To fry the cannelloni and serve: Carefully unwrap the cannelloni. Meanwhile, heat the clarified butter in a large nonstick skillet. When the butter is hot, add half of the cannelloni to the pan and fry over moderate heat, turning gently with tongs, until the cannelloni are golden brown on all sides, about 10 minutes. Carefully transfer the cannelloni to a towel-lined baking sheet and keep warm in a low oven. Fry the remaining cannelloni.

6. Reheat the tomatoes. In a medium bowl, gently toss together the baby spinach, flat-leaf parsley, shallots, chives, olive oil, and balsamic vinegar. Season with salt and pepper. Spoon the tomatoes into 6 warmed shallow soup plates or bowls and arrange 3 cannelloni in a row in the center of each. Mound the spinach salad on top and serve immediately.—JOACHIM SPLICHAL

HALIBUT WITH ARTICHOKES IN RED WINE SAUCE

Artichoke trimmings are sautéed with prosciutto and aromatic vegetables to impart an incredibly rich flavor to the red wine sauce; be sure not to use the choke, or prickly center, as part of the trimmings.

🍷 *This dish, with the assertive sauce, would be ideal for pairing with an elegant red Bordeaux—except that artichokes alter the flavors of subtle wines. Instead, stick with straightforward young West Coast Merlots, such as the 1993 Covey Run from Washington State or the 1992 Gundlach-Bundschu from California.*

6 SERVINGS

¼ cup plus 1 tablespoon extra-virgin olive oil
3 ounces of prosciutto, cut into ¼-inch dice
8 fresh artichoke hearts (see "Preparing Artichoke Hearts," p. 83), cut into ¼-inch-thick slices, trimmings reserved
2 medium onions, coarsely chopped
2 medium carrots, thinly sliced
2 ounces mushrooms, coarsely chopped
6 scallions, thinly sliced
3 garlic cloves, minced
1 bottle (750 ml) Merlot or other full-bodied red wine
1 tablespoon tomato paste
6 fresh parsley stems
2 imported bay leaves
½ teaspoon thyme
6 black peppercorns
Salt
3¼ cups chicken stock or canned low-sodium broth
2 tablespoons brandy
2 tablespoons unsalted butter
2 medium shallots, minced
2 pounds halibut, orange roughy, or red snapper fillets
Freshly ground black pepper
2 tablespoons minced fresh flat-leaf parsley

1. Heat 3 tablespoons of the oil in a large nonreactive skillet. Add the prosciutto, artichoke trimmings, onions, carrots, mushrooms, scallions, and garlic, and cook over moderately high heat, stirring, until lightly browned, about 5 minutes. Add the wine and bring to a boil. Add the tomato paste, parsley stems, bay leaves, thyme, peppercorns, and 1 teaspoon salt, and boil until the liquid is reduced by half, about 15 minutes. Add the chicken stock, bring to a simmer, and cook until the liquid is reduced by half, about 30 minutes. Strain the red wine sauce through a fine strainer into a large measuring cup, pressing down on the solids.

2. Heat the remaining 2 tablespoons oil in the skillet. Drain the artichoke slices, pat dry, and add them to the skillet. Cook the artichoke slices over moderate heat, stirring, until they are lightly browned, about 10 minutes. Add the brandy and simmer until reduced to a glaze, about 1 minute. Add the red wine sauce and bring to a simmer, then lower the heat and simmer gently until the artichokes are just tender, about 15 minutes. Remove from the heat. (MAKE AHEAD: The red wine sauce can be made up to 1 day ahead; cover and refrigerate.)

3. Preheat the oven to 400°. Melt the butter in a large nonreactive baking dish. Add the shallots and cook over moderate heat, stirring, until softened, about 1 minute. Sprinkle the halibut with salt and pepper and arrange the fillets in the dish, overlapping any thinner pieces if necessary. Spoon the red wine sauce over and bring to a simmer over moderate heat. Cover and braise in the oven for 10 to 12 minutes, or until the halibut is opaque throughout. Transfer the halibut to a platter and cover loosely with foil. Bring the sauce to a boil over high heat, then lower the heat and simmer until slightly thickened, about 3 minutes. Stir in the minced parsley, then spoon the sauce over the fish and serve.—ANN CHANTAL ALTMAN

ROASTED COD WITH PROSCIUTTO AND FRESH SAGE

6 SERVINGS

- 2 carrots, cut into ½-inch dice
- 3 tablespoons vegetable oil
- 1 small yellow onion, finely diced
- ½ head of Savoy cabbage (about 1½ pounds), finely shredded
- 2 tablespoons chopped fresh flat-leaf parsley
- 1 tablespoon ground coriander
- Salt and freshly ground pepper
- Six 6-ounce pieces of fresh cod fillet, about 1½ inches thick
- 18 fresh sage leaves, 12 whole and 6 minced
- 6 paper-thin slices prosciutto di Parma
- 3 tablespoons all-purpose flour
- 1 cup dry white wine
- Juice and finely grated zest of 1 small lemon
- 1 cup chicken stock or canned low-sodium broth
- 3 tablespoons unsalted butter

1. Preheat the oven to 400°. In a small saucepan, boil the carrots in lightly salted water until just tender, about 2 minutes. Drain and rinse under cold water until cool. Set aside.

2. In a large skillet, heat 2 tablespoons of the oil. Add the onion and sauté over high heat until lightly browned, about 2 minutes. Add the cabbage and toss to coat with oil. Reduce the heat to moderate and cook, stirring occasionally, until softened, about 5 minutes. Stir in the parsley and coriander and season with salt and pepper. Keep warm over very low heat.

3. Pat the pieces of cod dry and place 2 whole sage leaves on top of each piece. Wrap a slice of prosciutto around each piece of fish and secure with a toothpick. Lightly dust the cod with flour and pepper.

4. Heat the remaining 1 tablespoon oil in a large nonstick skillet. Add the cod in batches and cook over moderately high heat until browned and crisp, about 2 minutes per side. Using a spatula, transfer the fish to a small baking sheet; make sure the pieces are not touching. Roast the cod in the oven for about 8 minutes, or until the fish is just cooked through.

5. Meanwhile, set the skillet in which the fish was seared over high heat. Add the wine, lemon juice, and lemon zest, and boil, scraping up any browned bits from the bottom of the pan until only a few tablespoons remain, about 7 minutes. Add the chicken stock, the butter, and the reserved cooked carrots and boil until reduced by half and thickened, about 5 minutes. Add the minced sage and season with salt and pepper.

6. Reheat the cabbage if necessary and bring the sauce back to a boil. Mound the heated cabbage in the center of 6 warmed dinner plates. Set a piece of cod

$60 DINNER PARTY

🍷1992 Kenwood Sauvignon Blanc

PUMPKIN RISOTTO (P. 295)

🍷 1992 Iron Horse Pinot Noir

ROASTED COD WITH PROSCIUTTO AND FRESH SAGE (P. 223)

PEAR AND DRIED CHERRY SCRUNCH (P. 423)

—CHARLIE PALMER

Roasted Cod with Prosciutto and Fresh Sage

on the cabbage and discard the toothpicks. Spoon the sauce over the fish and cabbage and serve.—CHARLIE PALMER

GRILLED BLACK BASS WITH SHALLOT-SAFFRON VINAIGRETTE

For the fish: Rub a cleaned 4-pound black bass (or red snapper) inside and out with smashed garlic and fresh thyme. Cut 4 or 5 deep diagonal slashes on each side of the fish. Rub the fish with olive oil, and season it with salt and pepper. Stuff the cavity with fresh fennel tops. Grill in a fish basket over hot coals for 15 to 18 minutes per side. Or roast on a rack in a 475° oven, without turning, for about 30 minutes.

For the vinaigrette: Soak a scant ½ teaspoon of saffron threads in 2 tablespoons of hot water for 20 minutes. In a nonreactive skillet, cook 2¼ cups slivered shallots and 6 slivered garlic cloves in ¾ cup extra-virgin olive oil until softened. Add the saffron water and ⅓ cup fresh lemon juice. Simmer 4 minutes. Season with 1 teaspoon salt, ¼ teaspoon each ground cumin and black pepper, and ⅛ teaspoon cayenne. Spoon some over the fish just before serving. Pass the rest at the table.—TODD ENGLISH

POACHED STRIPED BASS WITH TWO SAUCES

Any fish can be cooked in this manner, but striped bass, halibut, salmon, trout, and other firm-fleshed fish are the best choices. Have your fishmonger fillet your fish, but don't forget to ask for the bones to make a nice fish stock, which you can freeze for future use. You can serve the fish with one or both of the accompanying sauces.

🍷 *The fish may be mild, but the sauces are notably piquant. That narrows the choice to a tart white with lean, focused flavors that can act as a refreshing foil. A West Coast Sémillon, such as the 1992 Columbia Crest from Washington State, or the 1992 Clos Du Val from California, would work particularly well.*

4 TO 6 SERVINGS

- 1 large carrot, coarsely chopped
- 1 medium celery rib with leaves, coarsely chopped
- 1 medium onion, quartered
- 1 large unpeeled garlic clove, lightly crushed
- 4 fresh parsley sprigs
- 1½ tablespoons coarse salt
- 1 teaspoon whole black peppercorns
- 1 cup dry white wine
- 1 tablespoon red or white wine vinegar
- 1 large striped bass (about 4¼ pounds), filleted, with the skin left on (two 12-ounce fillets)

Extra-virgin olive oil
Watercress or escarole, for serving
Salsa Verde (recipe follows)
Salsa Rossa Cruda (recipe follows)

1. Pour 6 cups of water into a large nonreactive skillet. Add the carrot, celery, onion, garlic, parsley, salt, and black peppercorns. Stir in the wine and vinegar and bring to a boil. Simmer for 15 minutes.

2. Gently lower the fish fillets, skin side down, into the pan. Poach gently at a bare simmer until opaque throughout, about 10 minutes.

3. Using a large slotted metal spatula, transfer the fillets to a platter. Scrape off the skin while the fish is still warm, then brush the fillets with some olive oil. Let cool. (MAKE AHEAD: The fish can be prepared up to 1 day ahead; cover tightly and refrigerate. Let come to room temperature before serving.)

4. To serve, garnish the platter with watercress or escarole. Spoon half of either of the salsas over the fish and pass the rest of the salsas separately.

Salsa Verde

Translated from the Italian as green sauce, *this piquant oil-and-herb-based sauce also goes well with grilled shrimp or chicken or with potatoes of any kind.*

MAKES ABOUT 1½ CUPS

- ¼ cup fresh lemon juice
- 1 small garlic clove, finely chopped
- 1 tablespoon finely chopped fresh flat-leaf parsley
- 2 teaspoons finely chopped fresh chives or scallion
- 1 teaspoon small capers
- ½ cup extra-virgin olive oil

Salt and freshly ground pepper

In a small bowl, stir together the lemon juice, garlic, flat-leaf parsley, chives, and capers. Gradually

COOKING IN THE FIREPLACE

HELPFUL TIPS

• Use hardwoods, like fruitwoods or oak. Fruitwoods lend flavor to grilled foods. You can also add mesquite chips, alder, lemon branches, or grapevines to nonfruit woods for more flavor. Do not use pine (it produces resins), chemical logs (their petroleum content is dangerous), or lighter fluids.

• Build a fire in the conventional manner by layering kindling and paper, allowing room for air to circulate.

• Begin cooking only after the flames have died down and the embers have turned white and red.

• Have the chimney cleaned regularly if you cook in your fireplace often. Fat accumulation can cause fires. Keep a fire extinguisher nearby.

To make fireplace cooking neater, easier, and safer, you may want to purchase:

• A COVER FOR THE FIREPLACE SURROUND, because cooking in the fireplace will leave food and oil stains.

• AN L-SHAPED TUSCAN GRILL (available at The Gardener; 510-548-4545) to support pots and pans so that they are not resting directly on the wood.

• A DUTCH OVEN for cooking breads, stews, and soups.

• A NONSTICK FISH BASKET to facilitate turning fish and to keep it from sticking to the grill.—TODD ENGLISH

whisk in the oil. Season with salt and pepper. (MAKE AHEAD: The salsa can be made up to 2 days ahead; cover and set aside at room temperature.)

Salsa Rossa Cruda

"Uncooked tomato sauce" is out of this world made with vine-ripened plum tomatoes but almost as good made with tasty cherry tomatoes, which are widely available throughout the year. You can also use this sauce on pasta.

MAKES ABOUT 2 CUPS

- 1½ pounds ripe plum tomatoes—peeled, seeded, and coarsely chopped
- ⅓ cup imported brine-cured black olives, such as Niçoise, pitted and coarsely chopped
- ¼ cup torn or coarsely chopped fresh basil leaves
- ¼ cup extra-virgin olive oil
- 1 small garlic clove, finely chopped
- ½ teaspoon salt
- ¼ teaspoon freshly ground pepper

Place the tomatoes in a medium bowl. Stir in the olives, basil, oil, garlic, salt, and pepper. Cover and let sit for at least 1 and up to 3 hours before serving. (MAKE AHEAD: The salsa can be made and refrigerated up to 1 day ahead.)—JULIA DELLA CROCE

CASUAL DINNER FOR SIX

🍷 Serve this menu with a dry Riesling or fragrant Sauvignon Blanc.

CHESAPEAKE CRAB CAKES (P. 58)

ROSY FRUIT SALSA (P. 59)

TARTAR SAUCE (P. 59)

SORREL SOUP (P. 95)

GRILLED TROUT (P. 226)

AVOCADO AIOLI (P. 309)

ASPARAGUS WITH LEMON-GARLIC VINAIGRETTE (P. 309)

STRAWBERRY-RHUBARB SORBET (P. 419)

BUTTER COOKIES (P. 372)

—SHEILA LUKINS

GRILLED TROUT

A whole grilled fish has more flavor than boneless fillets. For tips on how to fillet any whole fish you're served, see "Boning a Trout" (opposite page).

6 SERVINGS

- 6 whole brook trout (about ¾ pound each), cleaned
- About ¼ cup olive oil
- Salt and freshly ground pepper
- 3 lemons, halved

1. Heat a grill to moderately high or preheat the broiler. Generously brush the trout with oil and season them inside and out with salt and pepper.

2. Grill the trout for about 5 minutes per side, or until the skin is browned and crisp and the flesh flakes easily when tested with a fork at the thickest part. Alternatively, arrange the trout on a heavy baking sheet and broil for about 5 minutes per side, turning the sheet as necessary for even cooking. Serve the grilled fish immediately with the lemon halves.—SHEILA LUKINS

TROUT WITH TOMATO-HERB SALAD AND ROASTED POTATOES

6 SERVINGS

BASIL MAYONNAISE:

- 2 cups packed fresh basil leaves
- ½ cup plus 2 tablespoons mayonnaise
- 1½ tablespoons fresh lime juice
- 1 teaspoon finely grated lime zest
- Salt and freshly ground pepper

SALAD:

- 3 large baking potatoes—peeled, halved crosswise, and each half cut into 8 wedges
- ½ cup plus 1 tablespoon olive oil
- Salt and freshly ground pepper
- 2 tablespoons Champagne or white wine vinegar
- 6 cups loosely packed mixed salad greens
- ¼ cup small fresh basil leaves
- ¼ cup 1-inch pieces of chives
- 2 tablespoons fresh tarragon leaves
- 6 medium tomatoes
- 1 pint cherry tomatoes or 4 medium plum tomatoes

TROUT:

- ⅓ cup all-purpose flour
- 2 teaspoons finely chopped fresh dill
- 1 teaspoon salt
- ½ teaspoon freshly ground pepper
- Six 6-ounce or twelve 3-ounce trout fillets
- 6 tablespoons clarified unsalted butter (see Note)

1. Make the basil mayonnaise: In a blender, combine the basil, mayonnaise, lime juice, and lime zest and blend until smooth. Scrape the mayonnaise into a small bowl and season with salt and pepper. Refrigerate until ready to use.

2. Make the salad: Preheat the oven to 425°. Spread the potato wedges on a baking sheet and drizzle 3 tablespoons of the olive oil over them; toss to coat evenly. Season with salt and pepper. Roast the potatoes on the bottom shelf of the oven for about 30 minutes, or until they are dark brown on the bottom and tender when pierced.

3. In a small bowl, whisk together the vinegar, ¾ teaspoon salt, and ¼ teaspoon pepper; whisk in the remaining 6 tablespoons olive oil. Set the vinaigrette aside. In a large bowl, combine the salad greens, basil, chives, and tarragon. Thinly slice the larger tomatoes, leaving the cherry tomatoes whole.

4. Prepare the trout: Preheat the oven to 300°. Set a large, 10-inch cast-iron skillet over low heat to warm up. On a large plate, mix the flour, chopped dill, salt, and pepper. Dredge half of the trout fillets in the seasoned flour and shake off the excess. Add 3 tablespoons of the clarified butter to the skillet and increase the heat to high. Add the flour-coated trout fillets, skin side down, and fry until browned and crisp on the bottom, 3 to 5 minutes. Lower the heat to moderate, flip the trout, and fry on the other side until the fish is just cooked through, about 2 minutes. Transfer the trout to a baking sheet. Wipe out the pan and cook the remaining fillets in the remaining 3 tablespoons clarified butter. When all the trout fillets have been fried, rewarm them briefly in the oven. Reheat the potatoes in the oven as well.

5. To serve, toss the greens and herbs with 6 tablespoons of the vinaigrette. Divide the salad among 6 large plates. Put one sliced tomato and a few cherry tomatoes on top of the greens. Drizzle about 1 teaspoon of the remaining vinaigrette over each portion and season the salads with salt and pepper. Arrange 8 potato wedges around each salad and put 1 large or 2 small trout fillets on top of the tomato slices. Dab 4 teaspoonfuls of the basil mayonnaise around each plate; reserve any remaining mayonnaise for another use. Serve the trout at once.

NOTE: Clarified butter can withstand high temperatures without

Grilled Trout, with Asparagus with Lemon-Garlic Vinaigrette (p. 309)

BONING A TROUT

1. Beginning at the tail end and using the bones as your guide, run the knife along the length of the top fillet to loosen it completely.

2. Lift off the fillet and cut the skin at the bottom to detach it completely.

3. Remove the central bone and discard it, along with the head and the tail. The fillets should be mostly clean now; any bones that remain can be discarded as you eat the trout.—SHEILA LUKINS

burning. To make 6 tablespoons of clarified butter, melt 1 stick (4 ounces) unsalted butter over low heat. Remove from the heat and skim off the foam. Slowly pour the butter into a bowl, leaving behind all of the milky sediment. Clarified butter will keep, refrigerated, for up to 2 weeks; melt before using.—ODESSA PIPER

CHEF'S MENU

ROASTED GARLIC AND YELLOW PEPPER SOUP (P. 92)

TROUT WITH TOMATO-HERB SALAD AND ROASTED POTATOES (P. 226)

CHEVRE COEUR A LA CREME WITH BERRIES (P. 440)

HICKORY NUT SHORTBREAD (P. 373)

—ODESSA PIPER

LOBSTER AMERICAINE WITH RICE AND HARICOTS VERTS LF

To make 4 cups of boiled long-grain rice, start with about 1½ cups raw rice.

The intense, savory flavors of the soup and the lobster sauce suggest a dry, crisp white. A 1993 California Sauvignon Blanc, such as Lakewood or Dry Creek, would do nicely.

4 SERVINGS

Two 1½-pound live lobsters
1 tablespoon olive oil
1 medium onion, coarsely chopped
1 small carrot, coarsely chopped
1 garlic clove, thinly sliced
¼ cup Cognac
¾ cup dry white wine
2 large Italian plum tomatoes, finely chopped
3 fresh flat-leaf parsley sprigs
1 fresh thyme sprig or ¼ teaspoon dried
1 bay leaf
Salt
Freshly ground pepper
¾ pound *haricots verts* or thin green beans
1 teaspoon unsalted butter
1½ teaspoons all-purpose flour
1 scant tablespoon minced fresh tarragon
1 tablespoon minced fresh chives
4 cups boiled long-grain rice, preferably jasmine*

*Available at Asian markets

Trout with Tomato-Herb Salad and Roasted Potatoes

1. Bring a large pot of salted water to a boil. Plunge in the lobsters head first, cover, and simmer over moderate heat for 17 minutes. Transfer the lobsters to a large bowl and let cool for about 1 hour.

2. Working over the bowl to catch the liquid, detach the lobster tails from the bodies. Using kitchen shears, snip through the soft underside of the tail shells and remove the meat. Twist off the claws, crack them open, and remove the meat. Pull out and discard the intestinal vein that runs down the tail. Cut the lobster meat into ½-inch pieces and add it to the bowl. Discard the sand sac behind the eyes and chop the shells and head into 1-inch pieces.

3. Heat the oil in a large, heavy, nonreactive saucepan. Add the onion and carrot and cook over moderately high heat, stirring occasionally, until lightly colored, about 3 minutes. Add the lobster shells and garlic and cook until fragrant, about 3 minutes longer. Add the Cognac and ignite with a match. Cook until the flame burns out, about 1 minute.

4. Add the wine, tomatoes, parsley, thyme, bay leaf, ¼ teaspoon salt, and 5 cups of water to the saucepan. Bring to a boil, cover, and simmer over moderately low heat, stirring occasionally, for 50 minutes. Pass the stock through a fine strainer into a large clean saucepan and discard the solids. Add any liquid from the lobster meat and boil over high heat until reduced to 1 cup, about 15 minutes. Season the stock with salt and pepper. (MAKE AHEAD: The recipe can be prepared to this point up to 4 hours ahead. Cover and let the lobster meat and stock stand separately at room temperature. Rewarm the stock before proceeding.)

5. In a medium saucepan of boiling salted water, cook the *haricots verts* over moderately high heat until tender, about 5 minutes. Drain and keep warm.

6. In a small bowl, work the butter into the flour to form a paste, then whisk the paste into the hot lobster stock. Bring to a boil over high heat, whisking constantly. Reduce the heat to low, add the lobster meat, tarragon, and half of the chives, and stir until warmed through.

7. To serve, arrange the rice in a ring on a platter. Spoon the lobster and sauce in the center. Arrange the *haricots verts* around the rice and garnish with the remaining chives.—DIANA STURGIS

Lobster Americaine with Rice and Haricots Verts

LOBSTER MEDALLIONS WITH DILL SAUCE

4 TO 6 BUFFET SERVINGS

Four 1- to 1½-pound boiled Maine lobsters
2 cups low-fat milk
1 tablespoon minced scallion, white part only
¼ cup low-fat sour cream
1 tablespoon finely chopped fresh dill
Salt and white pepper

1. Remove the lobster meat from the tails and claws. Cover and refrigerate.

2. Remove and discard the sand sac, roe, and tomalley from one of the lobster shells. Coarsely chop the shell and legs and place them in a medium saucepan. Add the milk and simmer gently over moderate heat until it is

LOW-FAT MENU

🍷 The intense, savory flavors of the soup and the lobster sauce suggest a dry, crisp white. A 1993 California Sauvignon Blanc, such as Lakewood or Dry Creek, would do nicely.

DOUBLE MUSHROOM SOUP WITH SAUTEED SHIITAKES (P. 95)

LOBSTER AMERICAINE WITH RICE AND HARICOTS VERTS (P. 228)

COFFEE CREME CARAMEL (P. 450)

Lobster Medallions with Dill Sauce

reduced to ½ cup, about 40 minutes. Strain and let cool to room temperature.

3. In a food processor, combine the reduced milk with ½ cup of small pieces of lobster meat and the scallion; puree until smooth. Transfer to a bowl and stir in the sour cream and 2 teaspoons of the dill. Season with salt and white pepper.

4. Cut the lobster tails into medallions and arrange on a platter with the claw meat. Decorate with the shells if desired. Garnish the sauce with the remaining dill and serve.—EDWARD SAFDIE

SHRIMP AND FETA CASSEROLE WITH DILL Q

The recipe can be made into individual servings by baking in four shallow gratin dishes, about five inches in diameter, for about 12 minutes.

4 SERVINGS

- 1 tablespoon olive oil
- 4 large scallions, minced
- 1 garlic clove, minced
- 1 pound medium shrimp, shelled and deveined
- 4 plum tomatoes—halved, seeded, and cut into ½-inch dice
- 4 ounces feta cheese, crumbled
- 2 large eggs, lightly beaten
- 1 tablespoon finely chopped fresh dill or 1 teaspoon dried
- ¼ teaspoon hot pepper sauce
- ¼ teaspoon salt
- ¼ teaspoon freshly ground black pepper
- ½ cup heavy cream
- 2 tablespoons freshly grated Parmesan cheese

1. Preheat the oven to 400°. Butter a shallow 10-cup enameled cast-iron or glass baking dish.

2. Heat the olive oil in a small frying pan. Add the minced scallions and cook over moderately high heat, stirring frequently, until softened, about 2 minutes. Add the garlic and cook, stirring, for 1 minute longer. Spread the mixture in the prepared baking dish and arrange the shrimp on top. Sprinkle with the tomatoes and feta cheese.

3. In a bowl, beat the eggs with the dill, hot pepper sauce, salt, and black pepper. Beat in the cream. Spoon the custard over the shrimp; the shrimp should be at least halfway covered with custard. Sprinkle with the Parmesan. Bake for about 17 minutes, until the custard is set and the shrimp are cooked through. Let the casserole stand for 5 minutes before serving.—BOB CHAMBERS

SPICY SHRIMP AND JACK CHEESE LASAGNA

At Park Avenue Cafe in New York City, David Burke makes his peppery, tangy lasagna with the unlikely combination of shrimp, Monterey Jack cheese, and barbecue sauce.

The tomato vinaigrette should not be prepared ahead, but it can be made easily while the lasagna bakes.

4 TO 6 SERVINGS

- 1 pound medium shrimp, shelled and deveined, shells reserved
- 2 large eggs
- ¼ cup barbecue sauce
- 2 teaspoons finely grated lemon zest

Salt and freshly ground pepper
¾ cup shredded Monterey Jack cheese (about 2½ ounces)
4 ounces fresh lasagna noodles

SHRIMP AND TOMATO VINAIGRETTE:
Reserved shrimp shells, coarsely chopped
½ cup tarragon vinegar
¾ cup tomato sauce
1 teaspoon minced fresh tarragon
½ cup olive oil

GARNISH:
1 teaspoon olive oil
4 ounces medium shrimp, shelled and deveined
Salt and freshly ground pepper

1. Preheat the oven to 350°. Lightly oil an 8-by-12-inch baking dish. Bring a large pot of water to a boil.

2. In a food processor, coarsely chop the shrimp. Add the eggs, the barbecue sauce, the lemon zest, 1 teaspoon salt, and 1 tablespoon freshly ground pepper, and process until the mixture is almost smooth, about 30 seconds. Transfer the mixture to a medium bowl and fold in the Monterey Jack cheese.

3. Add 1 teaspoon salt to the boiling water. Add the fresh lasagna noodles and cook them just until al dente, about 2 minutes. Drain the lasagna noodles; do not rinse them. Let the noodles cool slightly.

4. Arrange half of the lasagna noodles in the prepared baking dish. Spread the shrimp mixture evenly on top and cover with the remaining lasagna noodles, pressing down lightly. (MAKE AHEAD: The assembled lasagna can be covered and frozen for up to 1 month; see "Strategies for Freezing Lasagna," p. 263. Or refrigerate for up to 1 day. Freeze or refrigerate the shrimp shells separately. Allow the lasagna to return to room temperature before baking.)

5. Prepare the shrimp and tomato vinaigrette: In a small nonreactive saucepan, combine the reserved shrimp shells and the tarragon vinegar and bring to a boil over high heat. Reduce the heat to low and simmer until reduced by half, about 5 minutes. Strain the stock into a bowl and wipe out the saucepan. Return the stock to the saucepan. Whisk in the tomato sauce and the minced fresh tarragon and cook over low heat until heated through. Gradually whisk in the oil; keep the tomato vinaigrette warm.

6. Meanwhile, cover the lasagna with foil and bake for 25 minutes. Spread the vinaigrette over the lasagna and bake uncovered for about 10 more minutes, or until

QUICK DINNER

🍷 A refreshing 1993 California Sauvignon Blanc, such as Meridian or William Hill, would blend with the salty feta, briny shrimp, and the flavors of the cucumber salad.

SHRIMP AND FETA CASSEROLE WITH DILL (P. 230)

LEMONY CUCUMBER SALAD WITH BELL PEPPERS (P. 75)

BUTTERED ORZO

WALNUT-CARAMEL SUNDAES (P. 458)

TIMETABLE:

- **Bring the orzo water to a boil. Salt the cucumbers and bell peppers.**
- **Toast the walnuts and make the caramel sauce for the sundaes.**
- **Assemble and bake the Shrimp and Feta Casserole with Dill.**
- **Cook the orzo. Toss the salad.**
- **Prepare the Walnut-Caramel Sundaes just before serving.**

—BOB CHAMBERS

Shrimp and Feta Casserole with Dill

Shrimp Salad in Tortillas

the lasagna is heated through and lightly glazed on top.

7. Prepare the garnish: Heat the olive oil in a medium nonstick skillet. Season the shrimp with salt and pepper and cook over moderate heat, turning once, until opaque throughout, about 1½ minutes. Garnish the lasagna with the sautéed shrimp and pass the remaining tomato vinaigrette separately.—DAVID BURKE

SHRIMP SALAD IN TORTILLAS

🍷 *Cold shrimp, here accented by mayonnaise and Tabasco, calls for a crisp, light lager. Try a Japanese beer, such as Kirin or Sapporo.*

4 SERVINGS

- 2 teaspoons olive oil
- 1½ pounds medium-large shrimp—shelled, halved lengthwise, and deveined
- ¼ cup minced red onion
- 1 large celery rib, finely diced
- ½ cup mayonnaise
- 2½ tablespoons ketchup
- 1½ tablespoons finely chopped fresh tarragon
- 1 tablespoon fresh lime juice
- 1 teaspoon Tabasco or other hot pepper sauce
- Salt and freshly ground pepper
- Eight 7-inch flour tortillas
- 8 large spears of Belgian endive or small inner romaine lettuce leaves (optional)
- 1 package (3¼ ounces) alfalfa sprouts

1. Heat the olive oil in a large nonstick skillet. Add the shrimp and cook over moderately high heat, stirring, until just opaque throughout, 4 to 5 minutes. Transfer the shrimp to a plate and let cool.

2. Coarsely chop the shrimp. In a large bowl, toss the shrimp with the minced red onion and the diced celery. In a small bowl, combine the mayonnaise, ketchup, chopped fresh tarragon, lime juice, Tabasco, and ¼ teaspoon each of salt and pepper. Fold the mayonnaise dressing into the chopped shrimp. (MAKE AHEAD: The shrimp salad can be prepared up to 1 day ahead and refrigerated, covered.)

3. Preheat the oven to 350°. Wrap the flour tortillas in foil and warm them in the oven for about 5 minutes, until softened. Lay the tortillas out on a work surface. Place an endive spear in the center of each tortilla, spoon about ⅓ cup of the shrimp salad over the spears, and top with a packed ¼ cup of alfalfa sprouts. Roll up the tortillas and cut them in half crosswise if desired. Serve the shrimp-filled tortillas immediately or wrap 2 halves together in foil or plastic wrap for up to 3 hours.—TRACEY SEAMAN

MEDITERRANEAN RICE SALAD WITH SHRIMP

4 SERVINGS

- Salt
- 1½ cups arborio or long-grain white rice
- ¼ cup fresh lemon juice

¾ pound shrimp, shelled and deveined
4 to 5 tablespoons extra-virgin olive oil
4 ripe tomatoes, seeded and diced
1 large fennel bulb—halved, cored, and cut into ¼-inch dice
4 scallions, thinly sliced
¼ cup chopped fresh dill
1 garlic clove, minced
Crushed red pepper (optional)

1. In a large saucepan, bring 10 cups of water to a boil. Stir in 1 tablespoon of salt. Add the arborio or long-grain white rice and cook uncovered over moderate heat until al dente, about 15 minutes. Drain the cooked rice in a colander, rinse with cold water, and drain again. Place the rice in a large bowl.

2. Bring a saucepan of salted water to a boil and stir in 1 tablespoon of the fresh lemon juice. Add the shrimp and cook until opaque, about 1½ minutes. Transfer the cooked shrimp to a work surface. Chop the shrimp into small pieces.

3. Toss the cooked rice with ¼ cup of the extra-virgin olive oil and the remaining 3 tablespoons lemon juice. Add the chopped shrimp, the diced tomatoes and fennel, the sliced scallions, the chopped dill, and the minced garlic; toss. Add up to 1 tablespoon extra-virgin olive oil. Season with salt and crushed red pepper. Let stand for at least 20 minutes before serving. (MAKE AHEAD: The salad can be made 1 day ahead and refrigerated, covered. Serve at room temperature.) —ERICA DE MANE

FRIED OYSTERS WITH PANCETTA AND LEEKS

Using high-gluten flour in the coating helps form a crisp crust on the oysters; bread flour is best, or use unbleached all-purpose.

🍷 *Lager beer—such as Heineken—is one way to balance the bite of cayenne, vinegar, and arugula here; another is bubbles. California brut sparkling wine, such as Domaine Carneros or Scharffenberger, would be ideal for the purpose.*

4 SERVINGS

LEEK RAGOUT:

One 2-ounce slice of pancetta, cut into ¼-inch dice
¼ cup olive oil
2 medium leeks, white part only, halved and sliced ¼ inch thick
1 medium onion, thinly sliced
¼ cup chicken stock or canned low-sodium broth
2 tablespoons tarragon vinegar
¼ teaspoon crushed red pepper
Salt and freshly ground black pepper

OYSTERS AND SALAD:

Vegetable oil, for frying
1½ cups bread flour or unbleached all-purpose flour
½ cup yellow cornmeal
Cayenne pepper
Salt and freshly ground black pepper
24 shucked medium oysters, drained
6 ounces arugula, tough stems trimmed
⅓ cup Tarragon-Shallot Vinaigrette (p. 56)

1. Make the leek ragout: In a medium nonreactive saucepan, sauté the diced pancetta over moderately high heat until it is browned and crisp, about 4 minutes. Transfer the pancetta to paper towels to drain and wipe out the pan.

2. Heat the olive oil in the saucepan. Add the sliced leeks and onion and cook over moderate heat, stirring occasionally, until translucent, about 5 minutes. Add the chicken stock, the tarragon vinegar, the sautéed pancetta, and the crushed red pepper, and season with salt and black pepper. Cook until the vegetables are tender, about 12 minutes. (MAKE AHEAD: The leek ragout can be refrigerated, covered, for up to 2 days. Rewarm before serving.)

3. Make the oysters and salad: In a large skillet, heat about ½ inch of the vegetable oil to 375°. On a large plate, combine the flour and yellow cornmeal and season with cayenne pepper, salt, and freshly ground black pepper. Dredge the shucked oysters in the cornmeal mixture and let

Fried Oysters with Pancetta and Leeks

Calamari and Saffron Rice Salad

stand for 1 minute. Working in batches, fry the oysters in the hot oil, turning once, until golden and crisp, about 1 minute per side. Transfer the fried oysters to paper towels to drain and keep warm while you fry the remaining oysters.

4. In a medium bowl, toss the arugula with the Tarragon-Shallot Vinaigrette. Mound the arugula in the center of 4 salad plates. Spoon the leek ragout on the arugula and arrange the fried oysters on top. Serve the dish at once.—RICK ROBINSON

CALAMARI AND SAFFRON RICE SALAD

8 SERVINGS

1 tablespoon table salt
1½ cups arborio or long-grain white rice
Large pinch of saffron threads (about ½ teaspoon), crumbled and dissolved in ¼ cup warm water
¼ cup plus 2 tablespoons extra-virgin olive oil
2 tablespoons Champagne vinegar or white wine vinegar
½ pound fresh peas, shelled (about ¾ cup), or ½ pound sugar snap peas, strings removed
1½ pounds small squid, cleaned, bodies cut into thin rings and tentacles halved if large
¼ cup dry white wine
2 medium garlic cloves, finely diced
Coarse sea salt and freshly ground pepper
3 large ripe tomatoes—peeled, seeded, and cut into small dice
About 20 basil leaves, finely chopped
Leaves from 2 fresh thyme sprigs, coarsely chopped

1. In a large saucepan, bring 10 cups of water to a boil. Stir in the table salt. Add the arborio or long-grain white rice and cook uncovered over moderate heat until the rice is al dente, about 15 minutes. Drain the rice in a colander, rinse with cold water, and drain again.

2. Place the cooked rice in a large serving bowl and toss it with the saffron water. Stir in ¼ cup of the extra-virgin olive oil and the vinegar.

3. In a large saucepan of boiling salted water, blanch the peas for 1 minute. Drain the peas in a colander, rinse with cold water, and drain again.

4. In a large nonreactive skillet, heat the remaining 2 tablespoons olive oil over high heat until hot but not smoking. Add the squid and cook, stirring occasionally, just until opaque throughout, 2 to 3 minutes. Transfer the squid to a bowl with a slotted spoon. Add the white wine and the diced garlic to the skillet and boil until the liquid is reduced to ½ cup, about 3 minutes. Season with coarse sea salt and pepper and let cool.

5. Add the squid and its liquid, the peas, tomatoes, basil, and thyme to the rice and toss. Season with sea salt and pepper if desired. Let stand for at least 20 minutes before serving. (MAKE AHEAD: The salad can be made 1 day ahead and refrigerated, covered. Serve at room temperature.)—ERICA DE MANE

ADRIATIC FISH STEW WITH CLAMS, SQUID AND SHRIMP

In the Marches region, on Italy's eastern coast, it is said that a traditional brodetto *should be made with exactly thirteen different kinds of fish—and Adriatic fish at that. But here in the States we're not as fussy. Use fresh, firm-fleshed, non-oily fish, such as whiting, gray mullet, halibut, red snapper, sea bass, monkfish, and haddock, and you'll turn out a great, if nontraditional,* brodetto. *Skate wing, though, is essential, more for the texture that it imparts than the flavor. The addition of vinegar sets this recipe apart from other Italian fish stews.*

6 SERVINGS

CROUTONS:

Twelve ½-inch-thick slices of Italian bread
3 tablespoons olive oil
1 garlic clove, halved lengthwise

STEW:

½ pound cleaned small squid, cut into ¼-inch rings (about 4 small squid)
½ cup olive oil
1 large onion, thinly sliced
2 garlic cloves, crushed
5 pounds assorted non-oily fish—cleaned, filleted, and cut into 3-inch pieces; heads, bones, and tails reserved and cut into 3-inch pieces
½ pound medium shrimp, shelled and deveined, shells reserved
½ cup dry white wine
½ cup white wine vinegar
2 cups canned Italian peeled tomatoes, coarsely chopped, with their liquid
Salt and freshly ground pepper

½ pound cleaned skate wing
1 pound cherrystone clams, scrubbed
2 tablespoons minced fresh flat-leaf parsley

1. Make the croutons: Preheat the oven to 350°. Arrange the Italian bread slices on a baking sheet and brush them with the olive oil. Toast the bread for about 20 minutes, until lightly browned. Rub the croutons on one side with the garlic.

2. Make the stew: Bring a medium saucepan of water to a boil over moderately high heat. Add the squid, stir once, and drain immediately. Plunge the squid into a bowl of cold water and drain thoroughly.

3. Heat the olive oil in a large, high-sided nonreactive skillet. Add the sliced onion and the crushed garlic and cook over moderate heat, stirring, until the onion is translucent, about 7 minutes. When the garlic is golden, discard it. Transfer the onion to a bowl.

4. Add the fish heads, bones, and tails and the shrimp shells to the skillet and cook over high heat, stirring, for 5 minutes. Add ¼ cup of the wine and cook, stirring, until the liquid is slightly reduced, about 2 minutes. Stir in ½ cup of water and strain the mixture, pressing on the solids. Wipe out the skillet and return the liquid to it.

5. Add the cooked onion to the skillet with the remaining ¼ cup wine and the white wine vinegar and simmer over moderate heat until the liquid is reduced by half, about 3 minutes. Add the tomatoes with their liquid and season with salt and pepper. Simmer for 5 minutes, crushing the tomatoes with a wooden spoon. Cover and cook for 5 minutes, stirring occasionally.

6. Spread the firmest fish—skate, monkfish, and halibut—in the skillet in a single layer. Cook the fish over moderate heat for 2 minutes, then turn the pieces over. Add the more delicate fish—red snapper, sea bass, whiting, haddock, and gray mullet—and the shrimp to the skillet and top with the scrubbed cherrystone clams. The sauce should barely cover the fish; if necessary, add a little water. Cover and simmer over moderately low heat until the fish is cooked through and most of the clams have opened, about 10 minutes.

7. Transfer the fish, shrimp, and opened clams to a large warmed serving bowl and cover loosely with foil. Boil the broth over moderately high heat until it is reduced to about 4 cups, removing the clams as they open. Stir the squid into the broth to rewarm it. Pour the sauce and the squid over the seafood, sprinkle with the minced flat-leaf parsley, and serve the stew with the croutons.—G. FRANCO ROMAGNOLI

FISH STEW WITH SHRIMP, MUSSELS AND COUSCOUS

This preparation comes from the Italian shores closest to North Africa, where it's known as cuscusu cu 'a ghiotta 'e pisci *(*ghiotta *means gluttony). The cinnamon, saffron, and almonds, as well as the couscous, reflect the stew's Arabic influences. Make the stew with white fish, such as halibut, monkfish, red snapper, haddock, and grouper. If you like, you can use seven pounds of assorted whole small white-fleshed fish in place of the fish fillets and heads, bones, and tails called for in this recipe. Clean and fillet the fish, reserving the heads, bones, and tails.*

6 SERVINGS

BROTH:

1 medium onion, finely chopped
2 garlic cloves, minced
½ cup sliced blanched almonds, coarsely chopped
2 tablespoons finely chopped fresh flat-leaf parsley
¼ teaspoon cayenne pepper
¼ cup olive oil
½ cup dry white wine
2 cups drained canned Italian peeled tomatoes, coarsely chopped
2 teaspoons salt
4 pounds non-oily fish heads, bones, and tails
½ pound medium shrimp, shelled and deveined, shells reserved

COUSCOUS:

1 tablespoon olive oil
¼ teaspoon cinnamon
¼ teaspoon salt
⅛ teaspoon saffron threads, crushed
1½ cups couscous (10 ounces)
½ pound mussels, scrubbed and debearded
3 pounds firm-fleshed white fish fillets, cut into 2-inch pieces

1. Make the broth: In a food processor, combine the chopped onion, the minced garlic cloves, the blanched almonds, the flat-leaf parsley, and the cayenne pepper, and process to a coarse paste. ➤

Adriatic Fish Stew with Clams, Squid and Shrimp

2. Heat the oil in a large nonreactive saucepan. Add the almond paste and cook over moderately high heat, stirring, until golden, about 5 minutes. Stir in the white wine and cook until the liquid is reduced by half, about 2 minutes. Add the canned Italian peeled tomatoes and cook over high heat for 2 minutes, crushing the tomatoes with a wooden spoon. Add 4 cups of water and the salt and bring to a boil. Add the fish heads, bones, and tails and the shrimp shells, and bring back to a boil. Cover and simmer over moderately low heat for 25 minutes.

3. Strain the broth through a fine sieve or a colander lined with cheesecloth. Wipe out the saucepan, return the broth to it, and boil over high heat until reduced to about 4 cups. (MAKE AHEAD: The broth can be prepared up to 2 days ahead; cover and refrigerate.)

4. Make the couscous: In a medium saucepan, bring 1 cup of the fish broth, 1¼ cups of water, the olive oil, cinnamon, salt, and crushed saffron threads to a boil over high heat. Stir in the couscous and remove from the heat. Cover and let stand for at least 5 minutes.

5. Meanwhile, bring the remaining 3 cups fish broth to a boil. Add the mussels, cover, and cook over high heat until they open, about 4 minutes. Transfer the mussels to a platter.

6. Add the firmest fish—monkfish and halibut—to the saucepan, cover, and simmer over moderate heat until cooked through, about 4 minutes. Transfer to the platter. Add the more delicate fish—red snapper, haddock and grouper—and the shrimp to the saucepan, cover, and simmer until the fish are cooked through and the shrimp turn pink, about 2 minutes. Add to the platter.

Fish Stew with Shrimp, Mussels and Couscous

7. To serve, fluff the couscous and arrange it in a ring in 6 large shallow soup plates. Spoon the fish, shrimp, and mussels inside the couscous and ladle the broth over all.—G. FRANCO ROMAGNOLI

MINESTRONE OF MAINE LOBSTER WITH OLIVE CROUTONS

6 SERVINGS

Pinch of sea salt
½ teaspoon red wine vinegar
Five 1½-pound live lobsters
2 tablespoons extra-virgin olive oil
1 small white onion, finely chopped
2 garlic cloves, minced
1 quart Lobster Stock (recipe follows)
⅓ cup cooked white navy beans or rinsed canned beans
2 small bell peppers, 1 red and 1 green
1 medium zucchini, cut into ¼-inch dice
1 medium yellow squash, cut into ¼-inch dice
1 medium Japanese eggplant, cut into ¼-inch dice
2 plum tomatoes—peeled, seeded, and cut into ¼-inch dice
½ cup loosely packed finely shredded fresh basil
Salt and coarsely cracked white pepper
1 cup cooked (al dente) angel hair pasta
Olive Croutons, for serving (recipe follows)

1. Bring a large pot of water to a boil. Add the sea salt and vinegar. Plunge in the lobsters, head first, and cover the pot. Cook for 8 minutes. Using tongs, transfer the lobsters to a large bowl. When they are cool enough to handle, twist off the claws and the tail sections. (Reserve the bodies for making the Lobster Stock that follows.) Remove all the meat from the claws, knuckles, and tail. Slice the meat into ¾-inch pieces, cover, and refrigerate.
2. In a large saucepan, heat 1 tablespoon of the olive oil. Add the onion and cook over moderate heat, stirring, until softened, about 3 minutes. Add the garlic and stir for 1 minute more. Add 1⅓ cups of the Lobster Stock and the white beans and simmer for 15 minutes.
3. Meanwhile, roast the red and green bell peppers directly over a gas flame or under the broiler as close to the heat as possible, turning, until charred all over. Transfer the peppers to a paper bag and let steam for 5 minutes. Peel the peppers and discard the cores, seeds, and ribs. Cut the peppers into ¼-inch dice.
4. Heat the remaining 1 tablespoon olive oil in a large skillet. Add the zucchini, yellow squash, and eggplant, and cook over moderately high heat, stirring occasionally, until the vegetables are just tender, about 5 minutes. Stir these vegetables into the simmering stock in the saucepan. Add the remaining 2⅔ cups Lobster Stock, the tomatoes, basil, and roasted peppers. Season with salt and white pepper.
5. Bring the minestrone to a simmer and cook, stirring, until thickened slightly, about 5 minutes. Add the reserved lobster pieces and the cooked pasta and stir gently just until heated through. Ladle the soup into 6 large warmed soup plates or bowls and serve immediately with the warm Olive Croutons.

Lobster Stock

MAKES 1 QUART

Reserved bodies from the 5 cooked lobsters (see Minestrone of Maine Lobster with Olive Croutons, above)
1 cup dry white wine
¼ cup brandy
1 tablespoon unsalted butter
1 celery rib, chopped
1 small onion, chopped
1 small leek, chopped
1 medium carrot, chopped
2 garlic cloves, unpeeled
1 fresh parsley sprig
1 teaspoon tomato paste
1 plum tomato, coarsely chopped
1 fresh thyme sprig

1. Preheat the oven to 350°. Place a flameproof roasting pan in the oven to heat up. Chop the lobster bodies into small pieces. When the pan is hot, add the chopped lobster bodies and roast for 20 minutes, stirring once after 10 minutes.
2. Set the roasting pan over two burners set on moderately high heat. Slowly pour in the wine and the brandy. Stir well, scraping up any flavorful bits from the bottom of the pan. Set aside.
3. In a large saucepan, melt the butter over moderately high heat. Add the celery, onion, leek, carrot, garlic, and parsley, and cook, stirring often, until the vegetables are golden, about 8 minutes. Add the roasted lobster bodies with their liquid and cook

Salt Cod and Polenta Stew

until all the liquid evaporates, about 5 minutes. Add the tomato paste and cook, stirring, for 2 minutes. Add the tomato, thyme, and 8 cups of water and bring to a simmer. Skim the stock and reduce the heat to moderately low. Simmer until the stock has reduced to 1 quart, about 1½ hours. Strain and let cool, then refrigerate until ready to use.

Olive Croutons

MAKES 6 LARGE CROUTONS

18 peeled garlic cloves
2 tablespoons extra-virgin olive oil plus more for brushing
Salt and freshly ground white pepper
½ cup Niçoise olives, pitted and coarsely chopped (about 2½ ounces)
2 teaspoons fresh thyme leaves
Three ½-inch thick slices of country bread, halved on the diagonal and toasted

1. Preheat the oven to 350°. On a 12-inch square of foil, toss the garlic cloves with the 2 tablespoons olive oil and salt and pepper. Fold up the foil to make a neat package and roast for about 30 minutes, or until the garlic is soft.
2. Transfer the garlic to a food processor and add the olives and thyme. Process until a chunky puree forms. Arrange the toasts on a baking sheet and brush lightly with olive oil. Dollop the olive puree at the rounded end of each toast. Warm the croutons in the oven for 5 to 8 minutes before serving.—JOACHIM SPLICHAL

SALT COD AND POLENTA STEW

Polenta e baccalà *is a classic dish from the Veneto region of Italy. Its popularity is understandable: savory* baccalà, *or salt cod, in a tomato sauce and the creamy polenta are a match made in heaven. Start this dish one day before you plan to serve it to allow time for the salt cod to soak. To test the saltiness of the soaked cod, poach a small piece in simmering water, then taste it. If it's still very salty, continue soaking it. To save time, use instant polenta. Follow the package instructions, adding one-fourth more water than suggested since the polenta should be soft.*

🍷 *This rich mix of flavors needs a refreshing, fruity white. Italian Pinot Grigio, such as the 1992 Castello d'Albola or the 1992 Alois Lageder, is an obvious choice.*

4 SERVINGS

1 pound skinless, boneless center-cut salt cod
1 tablespoon golden raisins
3 tablespoons olive oil
2 garlic cloves, lightly crushed
1 small dried red chile
2 medium onions, thinly sliced
¼ cup dry white wine
2½ cups drained canned Italian peeled tomatoes, coarsely chopped
Pinch of sugar
1 tablespoon pine nuts
Salt and freshly ground pepper
Soft cooked polenta

1. Rinse the salt cod. In a bowl, cover the salt cod with cold water and allow it to soak in the refrigerator for at least 24 hours, changing the water 3 or 4 times. Drain the salt cod, pat it dry with paper towels, and remove any bones. Cut the salt cod into 3-inch pieces.
2. In a small bowl, cover the golden raisins with warm water and let them plump for 20 minutes. Drain well.
3. Heat the olive oil in a large nonreactive saucepan. Add the crushed garlic cloves and the dried red chile and cook over moderately high heat, stirring, until they are fragrant and lightly browned, about 3 minutes. Discard the garlic and chile.
4. Add the sliced onions to the saucepan and cook over moderately high heat, stirring occasionally, until the onions are translucent, about 5 minutes. Add the white wine and cook, stirring occasionally, until the liquid is almost evaporated, about 5 minutes. Add the canned Italian peeled tomatoes and a pinch of sugar, raise the heat to high, and cook, stirring and crushing the tomatoes with a wooden spoon, until the mixture is slightly thickened, about 10 minutes.

Stir in the plumped golden raisins and the pine nuts.

5. Add the salt cod to the tomato sauce, pushing the pieces of cod down so that they are partially submerged in the sauce. Bring the sauce to a bare simmer over moderately high heat. Lower the heat, cover, and cook gently until the salt cod is tender, about 10 minutes. Season the stew with salt and pepper.

6. To serve the stew, spoon the polenta into shallow soup plates and ladle the salt cod stew on top.—G. FRANCO ROMAGNOLI

CHAPTER 11

PASTA

Spinach Fettuccine with Leeks and Butternut Squash

SPINACH FETTUCCINE WITH LEEKS AND BUTTERNUT SQUASH

4 SERVINGS

3 tablespoons unsalted butter
4 medium leeks—halved lengthwise, thinly sliced crosswise, and well rinsed
1 medium butternut squash (1½ pounds)—quartered, seeded, peeled, and cut into ½-inch dice
¼ cup chicken stock, canned low-sodium broth, or water
1 cup heavy cream, preferably not ultrapasteurized
6 fresh sage leaves, finely chopped
1 pound fresh or dried spinach fettuccine
¼ cup freshly grated Parmesan cheese, plus more for serving
Salt and freshly ground pepper

1. Bring a large pot of water to a boil for the pasta. In a large skillet, melt the butter over moderate heat. Add the sliced leeks and cook for 5 minutes. Add the diced butternut squash and cook for 3 minutes longer. Add the chicken stock, cover the pan, and steam the vegetables until just tender, about 5 minutes. Stir in the heavy cream and the chopped sage until well mixed, and remove the skillet from the heat.
2. Salt the boiling pasta water. Add the fettuccine and cook until al dente, about 3 minutes for fresh and 10 minutes for dried. Drain the fettuccine and return it to the empty pot. Add the butternut squash sauce and the ¼ cup of Parmesan cheese and toss well. Season the pasta with salt and pepper.
3. Transfer the fettuccine to a large warmed bowl or platter and serve. Pass the extra Parmesan cheese separately.—ERICA DE MANE

SAFFRON PASTA WITH TOMATOES AND BLACK BEANS

Use as many varieties of tomatoes as possible, including cherry, pear, and currant (both red and yellow), and green grape tomatoes. Spinach or black pepper pasta can be substituted for the saffron pasta.

4 SERVINGS

1 tablespoon balsamic vinegar
Sea salt
½ teaspoon minced garlic
2 tablespoons plus 1 teaspoon olive oil
Freshly ground pepper
1½ pounds assorted tomatoes, cut into ⅓-inch wedges if large or medium; halved lengthwise or left whole if small
1 cup fresh basil leaves, shredded, plus whole sprigs, for garnish
½ pound fresh mozzarella, cut into ¼-inch cubes
2 cups cooked black beans, rinsed and drained if canned
1 pound fresh saffron fettuccine

1. Bring a large saucepan of water to a boil. In a large bowl, combine the balsamic vinegar and a pinch of salt. Whisk in the minced garlic and 2 tablespoons of the olive oil and season with pepper. Add the tomatoes and the shredded basil and toss with the vinaigrette. Add the mozzarella and the cooked black beans and toss gently.
2. Salt the boiling water. Add the fettuccine and cook, stirring occasionally, until al dente, 3 to 4 minutes. Drain, return the cooked fettuccine to the pot, and toss it with the remaining 1 teaspoon of olive oil.
3. Mound the fettuccine in the center of 4 large plates. Spoon the tomato and black bean mixture on top. Garnish the pasta with whole fresh basil sprigs and serve.—NORA POUILLON

LINGUINE WITH TOMATO PESTO

4 SERVINGS

½ cup sliced almonds (about 2 ounces)
4 garlic cloves, smashed
¼ cup plus 2 tablespoons olive oil
Salt

Linguine with Tomato Pesto

¼ teaspoon freshly ground pepper
1 pound ripe tomatoes, cut into 1-inch chunks
1½ cups fresh basil leaves, plus whole sprigs for garnish
1 pound dried linguine
Freshly grated Parmesan cheese, for serving

1. Bring a large pot of water to a boil. In a blender, combine 6 tablespoons of the sliced almonds, the smashed garlic cloves, the olive oil, 1¼ teaspoons salt, and the freshly ground pepper, and pulse until coarsely chopped. Add the tomato chunks and process to a puree. Add 1¼ cups of the basil leaves and process until smooth. Coarsely chop the remaining ¼ cup basil leaves by hand and set aside.

2. Meanwhile, add salt to the boiling water. Add the linguine and cook, stirring occasionally, until al dente, about 11 minutes. Drain the pasta, reserving ½ cup of the cooking water separately. Return the pasta to the pot, toss with the pesto, and let stand for 1 minute.

3. Toss the linguine with the reserved cooking water. Transfer the linguine to a large bowl or individual plates and garnish with the remaining sliced almonds, the chopped basil, and the basil sprigs. Serve the linguine immediately, passing the freshly grated Parmesan cheese separately at the table.—JUDITH SUTTON

QUICK DINNER

OLIVE AND CELERY ANTIPASTO (P. 53)

LINGUINE WITH TOMATO PESTO (P. 245)

CHILLED ORANGE-CANTALOUPE SOUP (P. 441)

TIMETABLE:

- **Make and chill the soup (speed up the process by refrigerating it in a stainless steel bowl rather than a glass one).**
- **Put the pasta water on to boil.**
- **Make the antipasto and let stand at room temperature.**
- **Make the pesto sauce while you cook the pasta.**

—JUDITH SUTTON

PENNE WITH EGGPLANT AND RICOTTA SALATA

Supermarket tomatoes will ripen a bit more if you leave them at room temperature for a couple of days.

🍷 *Eggplant, garlic, and tomatoes point to a red wine, but one with enough acidity to match the flavors and ingredients in this dish. An Italian Barbera, such as the 1992 Prunotto Fiulot or the 1991 Pio Cesare Barbera d'Alba, would be perfect.*

4 SERVINGS

¼ cup plus 2 tablespoons olive oil
1 large eggplant, cut into ½-inch dice
3 medium garlic cloves, minced
Finely chopped leaves of 1 small fresh rosemary sprig
Salt and freshly ground pepper
1 pint ripe cherry tomatoes
1 pound penne rigate
¼ pound *ricotta salata* cheese, crumbled

1. In a large pot, bring 4 quarts of water to a boil for the pasta. Meanwhile, in a large skillet, warm 3 tablespoons of the olive oil over moderately high heat. Add the diced eggplant and cook, stirring frequently, until it starts to soften and brown, about 10 minutes. Add half of the minced garlic cloves and all of the chopped rosemary and cook until the garlic is slightly golden, about 2 minutes. Season with salt and pepper.

2. In a medium nonreactive skillet, heat the remaining 3 tablespoons olive oil. Add the cherry tomatoes and cook over high heat, tossing, until slightly softened, about 3 minutes. Stir in the remaining minced garlic; season with salt and pepper.

3. Salt the boiling pasta water. Add the penne rigate and cook until al dente, about 13 minutes. Drain the pasta and return it to the empty pot. Add the *ricotta salata* cheese and toss. Add the eggplant and toss again. Add the cherry tomatoes to the pasta, cheese, and eggplant; toss gently. Transfer the pasta to a large warmed bowl or platter and serve immediately.—ERICA DE MANE

FUSILLI WITH VINEGAR-MARINATED ZUCCHINI

4 TO 6 SERVINGS

3 pounds very fresh, glossy zucchini
Salt
Vegetable oil, for frying
3 tablespoons red wine vinegar
1 teaspoon very finely chopped garlic
10 to 15 fresh mint leaves, torn by hand into small pieces

Penne with Eggplant and Ricotta Salata

Fusilli with Vinegar-Marinated Zucchini

MARINATED VEGETABLES

To prepare eggplant, carrots, or green beans *a scapece*, follow the directions for the zucchini in the recipe for Fusilli with Vinegar-Marinated Zucchini. Eggplant can be sliced into rounds, half-rounds, or sticks; carrots can be sliced into rounds or sticks, and trimmed green beans can be left whole. Fry the vegetables until they're just beginning to soften. Pack the vegetables and their marinade in a jar, cover completely with olive oil, and seal tightly. An Italian would be likely to keep vegetables *a scapece* in a kitchen cupboard, but you might prefer to refrigerate them. If you store the vegetables in the refrigerator, bring them to room temperature before serving.—MARCELLA HAZAN

⅓ cup extra-virgin olive oil
Freshly ground black pepper
1 pound fusilli

1. Soak the zucchini in a bowl of cold water for at least 20 minutes, then scrub vigorously under cold running water with a rough cloth or a stiff brush to remove any embedded grit. Trim away the ends and cut the zucchini into sticks about 2 inches long and ¼ inch thick.

2. Set a large colander over a bowl or in the sink and put the zucchini sticks in the colander. Sprinkle the zucchini with 2 tablespoons of salt and toss two or three times. Let the zucchini sticks stand for at least 45 minutes to allow them to release as much liquid as possible. (Salt is required to draw off water and concentrate flavor. Be sure to use only freshly picked zucchini, or the vegetable will not release sufficient liquid to rinse off excess salt.)

3. If you have a deep-fat fryer, pour in enough vegetable oil to reach about 4 inches up the side of the pan. If you are using a large skillet, the vegetable oil should be at least 1½ inches deep if possible. Turn the heat to moderately high.

4. When you are ready to begin frying, remove the zucchini sticks from the colander and blot them thoroughly dry in kitchen towels. As soon as the vegetable oil is hot, add as much of the zucchini as will fit comfortably in the pan without crowding and fry until it becomes light brown. Using a slotted spoon or wire skimmer, transfer the fried zucchini sticks directly to the bowl in which you will later toss and serve the pasta. Repeat with the remaining zucchini.

5. When all the zucchini sticks have been fried and added to the bowl, spoon the red wine vinegar over them and toss once or twice. Add the chopped garlic, torn mint leaves, olive oil, and a few grindings of black pepper. Season with salt if necessary.

6. Meanwhile, cook the fusilli in a large pot of boiling salted water until it is just tender but still firm to the bite. Drain the pasta, toss it immediately with the zucchini sticks, and serve. No cheese is required or desirable with this dish.—MARCELLA HAZAN

BUCATINI WITH ROASTED FENNEL AND TOMATO SAUCE

4 SERVINGS

2 large fennel bulbs (1½ pounds)—halved, cored, and thinly sliced crosswise, feathery fronds reserved

1 medium yellow onion, thinly sliced crosswise
2 medium garlic cloves, crushed
½ teaspoon fennel seeds, crushed
¼ cup extra-virgin olive oil
Salt and freshly ground pepper
One 28-ounce can of Italian peeled tomatoes, drained and lightly crushed
1 pound bucatini or perciatelli

1. Preheat the oven to 350°. In a nonreactive roasting pan, combine the fennel slices, yellow onion slices, crushed garlic, and fennel seeds. Drizzle the olive oil on top and season lightly with salt and pepper. Roast for 20 minutes, stirring once or twice, until the fennel is almost tender when pierced.
2. Stir the crushed tomatoes into the vegetables and bake for 30 minutes. Season the mixture with salt and pepper.
3. Meanwhile, in a large pot, bring 4 quarts of water to a boil for the pasta. Salt the water. Add the bucatini and cook until al dente, about 10 minutes. Drain the bucatini and add it to the fennel sauce in the roasting pan; toss well.
4. Transfer the pasta to a large warmed bowl or platter. Chop the feathery fennel fronds and scatter them on top. Serve immediately.—ERICA DE MANE

Bucatini with Roasted Fennel and Tomato Sauce

ORECCHIETTE WITH CAULIFLOWER, CURRANTS AND PINE NUTS

Cauliflower sautéed with anchovies, raisins, and pine nuts is a classic southern Italian combination. Here the mixture is tossed with the ear-shaped pasta from Apulia (and currants instead of raisins).

The saltiness of this pasta dish calls for a light, dry Italian white wine, such as the 1993 Antinori Galestro or the 1992 Santa Margherita Pinot Grigio.

4 SERVINGS

½ cup dried currants
¼ cup dry white wine
½ cup pine nuts (pignoli)
1 large head of cauliflower, cut into 1-inch florets
¼ cup extra-virgin olive oil
4 anchovy fillets

¼ teaspoon crushed red pepper
Salt
1 pound orecchiette
¼ cup dry bread crumbs
¼ cup grated Pecorino cheese, plus more for serving

1. In a large pot, bring 4 quarts of water to a boil for the pasta. Meanwhile, soak the dried currants in the wine until plumped, about 20 minutes.

2. In a small skillet, toast the pine nuts over moderately low heat, stirring occasionally, until golden and fragrant, about 7 minutes.

3. In a medium saucepan of boiling salted water, blanch the cauliflower florets until fork-tender but still firm, about 5 minutes. Drain.

4. In a large skillet, heat the olive oil. Add the anchovy fillets and cook over high heat for about 1 minute, mashing them with a wooden spoon. Add the blanched cauliflower florets and cook until just beginning to brown, about 3 minutes. Stir in the pine nuts, the currants with their liquid, and the crushed red pepper. Reduce the heat to moderate and simmer until the liquid has evaporated, about 5 minutes.

5. Salt the boiling pasta water. Add the orecchiette and cook until al dente, 18 to 30 minutes depending on the brand.

6. While the orecchiette is cooking, toast the bread crumbs in a small skillet over moderate heat, stirring until brown, about 2 minutes.

7. Drain the pasta, reserving ¼ cup of the cooking water. Return the pasta to the empty pot and toss with the cauliflower sauce, the reserved pasta water, and the ¼ cup of cheese.

8. Transfer the pasta to a large warmed bowl, sprinkle 2 tablespoons of the toasted bread crumbs on top, and serve immediately. Pass extra cheese and the remaining toasted bread crumbs separately.—ERICA DE MANE

Orecchiette with Cauliflower, Currants and Pine Nuts

FUSILLI WITH ONION AND RADICCHIO SAUCE

Traditionally an onion sauce is served without cheese, but I have had one served with Parmesan in Naples. Both ways are good.

4 SERVINGS

2 tablespoons unsalted butter
¼ cup olive oil
2 large yellow onions, thinly sliced crosswise
One-and-a-half 2-ounce cans of oil-packed anchovies, well drained
½ cup dry white wine
1 large head of radicchio (½ pound), cored and thinly sliced
Salt and freshly ground pepper
1 pound fusilli

1. In a large nonreactive skillet, melt the butter in the olive oil over moderate heat. Add the sliced onions and cook, stirring frequently with a wooden spoon, until soft and just starting to brown, about 30 minutes.

2. In a large pot, bring 4 quarts of water to a boil for the pasta. Stir the anchovies into the onions and cook until disintegrated, about 4 minutes. Add the white wine and cook until it evaporates, about 4 minutes. Add the radicchio and cook, stirring, until it starts to turn a dark wine color, 2 to 3 minutes. Season with salt and at least 1 teaspoon of freshly ground black pepper.

3. Salt the boiling pasta water. Add the fusilli and cook until al dente, about 12 minutes. Drain the pasta, reserving ½ cup of the cooking water. Return the pasta to the empty pot.

4. Toss the cooked fusilli with the onion sauce and add enough of the reserved pasta water to make a thick sauce. Transfer to a large warmed bowl or platter and serve immediately.—ERICA DE MANE

FARFALLE WITH CREMINI MUSHROOMS AND ESCAROLE

Cremini mushrooms are the least costly of the fancy varieties. They add a rich woodsy flavor.

4 SERVINGS

- 2 medium heads of escarole (1¾ pounds), coarsely chopped
- ¼ cup plus 2 tablespoons extra-virgin olive oil
- 6 medium garlic cloves, thinly sliced
- ¾ pound cremini mushrooms, stems trimmed, thinly sliced
- ½ teaspoon crushed red pepper
- Salt and freshly ground black pepper
- 1 pound farfalle
- ¼ cup freshly grated Parmesan cheese, plus more for serving

1. In a large saucepan of boiling water, blanch the escarole for 1 minute; drain very well. Bring a large pot of water to a boil for the pasta.

2. In a large skillet, heat ¼ cup of the olive oil. Add the thinly sliced garlic cloves and cook over low heat until the garlic is light brown and crisp, about 5 minutes. Using a slotted spoon, transfer the garlic to paper towels to drain.

3. Increase the heat to high, add the cremini mushrooms to the skillet, and cook, stirring, until browned and crisp, about 10 minutes. Drain the mushrooms on paper towels.

4. Add the remaining 2 tablespoons olive oil to the skillet. Stir in the escarole and crushed red pepper and cook over moderate heat for 2 minutes. Season with salt and black pepper.

5. Salt the boiling pasta water. Add the farfalle and cook until al dente, about 12 minutes. Drain, reserving ½ cup of the pasta cooking water.

6. Toss the pasta with the escarole, the ¼ cup of Parmesan, and as much of the reserved pasta

Farfalle with Cremini Mushrooms and Escarole

Orzo Salad with Wild Mushrooms and Asparagus

water as needed to moisten the pasta. Stir in the cremini mushrooms and transfer the pasta to a large warmed bowl or platter. Sprinkle the garlic on top and serve. Pass extra Parmesan cheese separately.—ERICA DE MANE

ORZO SALAD WITH WILD MUSHROOMS AND ASPARAGUS

MAKES 50 BUFFET SERVINGS

- 6 medium red or yellow bell peppers
- 1½ cups olive oil
- 2 pounds fresh shiitake mushrooms, stems discarded, caps sliced ⅓ inch thick
- Salt and freshly ground black pepper
- 2 pounds white mushrooms, sliced ⅓ inch thick
- 1 pound fresh chanterelles, sliced ⅓ inch thick
- 3 pounds thin asparagus, cut into 2½-inch lengths
- 4 medium leeks, white and tender green, split lengthwise and sliced crosswise 1 inch thick
- 4 pounds orzo
- ¼ cup fresh lemon juice
- 1 cup finely chopped fresh flat-leaf parsley

1. Bring a large stockpot of water to a boil. Meanwhile, roast the bell peppers directly over gas flames or under a broiler, turning often, until charred all over. Transfer the bell peppers to a paper bag and allow them to steam for 15 minutes. Discard the blackened skins, stems, seeds, and ribs. Chop the roasted peppers into 1-inch pieces.

2. Heat 2 tablespoons of the olive oil in a large nonstick skillet. Add half of the shiitake mushrooms and cook over high heat, stirring, until browned, about 10 minutes. Season the mushrooms with salt and pepper and transfer them to a large platter. Repeat the process with the remaining shiitakes, the white mushrooms, and the chanterelles, adding 2 tablespoons of olive oil for each batch; cook the white mushrooms in 2 batches and the chanterelles in 1 batch.

3. Add 1 tablespoon of olive oil to the skillet. Add the asparagus, season with salt and pepper, and cook over moderately high heat, stirring often, until browned and tender but still slightly firm, about 5 minutes. Transfer the asparagus to the platter with the mushrooms. Add 1 more tablespoon of olive oil to the skillet. Add the leeks, season with salt and pepper, and cook, stirring often, until wilted and beginning to brown, about 7 minutes. Add the leeks to the other vegetables.

4. Add 2 tablespoons salt to the boiling water. Add the orzo and cook, stirring often, until al dente, about 10 minutes. Drain, rinse with cold water, and drain again thoroughly. Transfer the orzo to a very large bowl. Add all the vegetables and toss. In a small bowl, combine the lemon juice, the chopped flat-leaf parsley, and the remaining ¾ cup olive oil. Pour the dressing over the orzo and toss again. Season with salt and pepper. (MAKE AHEAD: The orzo salad can be prepared up to 2 days ahead; cover and refrigerate. Let the salad return to room temperature before serving.) —GRACE PARISI

RAVIOLI OF SPRING GREENS

If you have a ravioli mold, by all means use it for this recipe. If not, the ravioli can be shaped free-form just as well.

8 SERVINGS

FOR THE PASTA DOUGH:

- 2½ cups unbleached flour
- 1 teaspoon salt
- 4 large whole eggs, lightly beaten
- 2 large egg yolks
- 1 tablespoon olive oil

FOR THE FILLING:

- 1½ pounds leafy greens, such as Swiss chard, beet, or turnip greens, or spinach, stemmed
- ½ cup heavy cream
- ¼ cup freshly grated Parmesan cheese
- 2 tablespoons fine dry bread crumbs
- ¾ teaspoon salt
- A few gratings of fresh nutmeg

- 1 egg, beaten with 2 tablespoons water
- Flour or cornmeal, for dusting

FOR SERVING:

6 large plum tomatoes—peeled, halved lengthwise, and seeded
Tomato Butter Sauce (recipe follows)
¼ cup snipped chives

1. Make the pasta dough: In a food processor, blend the flour with the salt. With the machine on, add the eggs, egg yolks, and olive oil, and process until the dough comes together. Scrape the dough out onto a work surface and knead until smooth. Flatten the dough into a 6-inch disk and cover with plastic wrap. Refrigerate for at least 1 hour or overnight.

2. Make the filling: Blanch the greens in a large saucepan of boiling salted water until bright in color and slightly tender, about 2 minutes. Drain the greens and transfer them immediately to a large bowl of very cold water. Drain the greens and squeeze them dry. Finely chop the greens and transfer to a bowl; toss the greens to loosen them. Mix in the heavy cream, the grated Parmesan cheese, the bread crumbs, salt, and nutmeg.

3. Cut the pasta dough into 8 pieces and cover them with plastic wrap. Using a pasta machine, roll 1 piece of the pasta dough through successively narrower settings until you reach the thinnest setting and the pasta sheet measures about 14 inches in length. Lay the pasta sheet on a ravioli mold or on a lightly floured work surface and cover it with a towel. Roll out a second piece of pasta dough.

4. Place 2 rounded teaspoons of the greens filling into each ravioli pocket. Alternatively, spoon the greens filling directly onto the pasta sheet, leaving about ½ inch between the mounds. Brush the exposed pasta dough with the beaten egg. Cover with the second sheet of pasta and press lightly around the ravioli to release any air bubbles. If you are using a mold, run a rolling pin over the top to cut the ravioli; if not, cut the ravioli with a knife. Put the ravioli on a baking sheet dusted with flour. Repeat to make 3 more batches of ravioli. Cover the ravioli tightly with plastic wrap and refrigerate for up to 1 day.

5. Shortly before serving, bring a large saucepan of water to a boil and add salt. Meanwhile, cut the tomato halves into ½-inch strips, then cut the strips into small diamonds. Rewarm the Tomato Butter Sauce, if necessary, whisking it very gently over low heat.

6. Add the ravioli to the boiling water and cook until tender, about 4 minutes. Drain the ravioli and arrange 5 or 6 in each shallow bowl. Spoon the Tomato Butter Sauce over the ravioli and garnish with the tomato diamonds and the snipped chives. Serve at once. ➤

Ravioli of Spring Greens

Tomato Butter Sauce

MAKES ABOUT 2 CUPS

- 2 cups dry white wine
- ¼ cup sherry vinegar
- 1 cup coarsely chopped fresh plum tomatoes
- 3 large shallots, chopped
- 1½ teaspoons whole black peppercorns
- 1½ teaspoons whole coriander seeds
- ½ cup heavy cream
- 2 sticks (½ pound) cold unsalted butter, cut into tablespoons
- Salt and freshly ground pepper

1. In a large nonreactive saucepan, combine the white wine, sherry vinegar, plum tomatoes, shallots, whole black peppercorns, and coriander seeds, and boil over high heat until reduced by three-quarters, about 30 minutes. Add the heavy cream and boil for a few minutes to thicken slightly. (MAKE AHEAD: The tomato butter sauce can be prepared to this point up to 1 day ahead. Let cool, then strain and refrigerate. Return to a simmer before proceeding.)

Roasted Vegetable Ravioli on Yellow Pepper Mole Sauce

2. Reduce the heat to low and start whisking in the butter, a few pieces at a time, adding more before the last batch is fully incorporated. Remove the saucepan from the heat the moment all the butter is incorporated; overheating will cause the sauce to separate.

3. Pass the tomato butter sauce through a fine strainer into a clean nonreactive pan. Season the sauce with salt and pepper. Keep the sauce in a warm place until serving.—DAVID WALTUCK

ROASTED VEGETABLE RAVIOLI ON YELLOW PEPPER MOLE SAUCE LF

6 SERVINGS

RED PEPPER CONFIT:

- 1 medium red bell pepper, cut into ¼-inch-thick strips
- 2 tablespoons fresh lime juice
- 2 tablespoons white wine
- 2 teaspoons sugar
- Kosher salt

RAVIOLI:

- ½ pound butternut squash, peeled and finely diced
- ½ pound rutabaga, peeled and finely diced
- 1 small Japanese eggplant, finely diced
- 1 large celery rib, finely diced
- 1 small zucchini, finely diced
- ½ small onion, finely diced
- 1 small garlic clove, minced
- 1½ teaspoons balsamic vinegar
- 1½ teaspoons tomato paste
- 1 teaspoon Dijon mustard
- Kosher salt and freshly ground pepper
- About 1 tablespoon cornstarch, for dusting
- 12 egg roll wrappers
- Yellow Pepper Mole Sauce (recipe follows)
- 2 tablespoons crumbled soft goat cheese
- ¼ cup fresh cilantro leaves

1. Make the red pepper confit: In a small saucepan, combine the red bell pepper strips, lime juice, white wine, and sugar. Bring just to a boil over moderately high heat and simmer until the liquid has thickened, about 15 minutes. Season with salt.

2. Make the ravioli: Preheat the oven to 500°. Warm a roasting pan in the oven for 5 minutes. Add the butternut squash, rutabaga, Japanese eggplant, celery, zucchini, and onion, and roast for about 30 minutes, stirring, until tender. Stir in the garlic, balsamic vinegar, tomato paste, and Dijon mustard, and season with salt and pepper. Let cool. (MAKE AHEAD: The recipe can be prepared to this point up to 2 days ahead; cover and refrigerate the red pepper confit and the roasted vegetables separately. Let both return to room temperature before proceeding.)

3. Dust a baking sheet with cornstarch. Spoon ¼ cup of the roasted vegetables in a 3-inch mound on 6 of the egg roll wrappers. Brush the edges of the wrappers with water and set the remaining 6 wrappers on top, pressing down on the edges to seal. Transfer to the prepared baking sheet, cover with plastic, and refrigerate until chilled, for up to 3 hours.

4. Bring a large saucepan of salted water to a boil. Add the ravioli and cook over moderately high heat until tender, about 3 minutes. Carefully drain them. Slide each ravioli into a shallow bowl and add ⅓ cup of the Yellow Pepper Mole Sauce. Garnish with 1 tablespoon of red pepper confit, 1 teaspoon of goat cheese, and the cilantro.

Yellow Pepper Mole Sauce

MAKES ABOUT 2 CUPS

- 2 large yellow bell peppers
- 4 tomatillos—husked, rinsed, cored, and halved
- 1 small onion, coarsely chopped
- 3 garlic cloves, coarsely chopped
- One 6-inch yellow corn tortilla
- ¼ teaspoon cumin seeds
- ¼ teaspoon coriander seeds
- Pinch of aniseed
- 1 cup vegetable stock, canned vegetable broth, or water
- 1 teaspoon moderately hot pure chile powder, such as japone or New Mexico
- Pinch of ground allspice
- Salt and freshly ground black pepper

1. Preheat the oven to 450°. Roast the yellow bell peppers on a baking sheet for about 20 minutes, until they are charred all over. Let cool. Peel the roasted peppers and discard the stems, ribs, and seeds. Cut the peppers into large pieces.

2. Meanwhile, roast the tomatillos and onion in a small baking dish for about 15 minutes, or until tender and golden. Stir in the garlic and roast for 5 minutes longer. Bake the tortilla on the oven rack for about 4 minutes until crisp. Let cool slightly, then break into small pieces.

3. In a skillet, toast the cumin seeds, coriander seeds, and aniseed over moderately high heat until fragrant, about 30 seconds. Transfer to a mortar or spice grinder and grind to a powder.

4. In a blender or food processor, combine the roasted peppers, the tomatillo mixture, the tortilla pieces, the ground spices, the vegetable stock, the chile powder, and the ground allspice. Puree until smooth and transfer the mixture to a small saucepan. Bring to a boil over moderate heat and simmer, stirring, until slightly thickened, about 20 minutes. Season the mole sauce with salt and pepper. (MAKE AHEAD: The sauce can be made up to 1 day ahead; cover and refrigerate.) —CHARLES WILEY

LASAGNA WITH RADICCHIO AND SHIITAKES

At Il Cantinori in New York City, Frank Minieri serves his delicious vegetarian lasagna with a creamy tomato sauce.

🍷 *Sautéed shiitakes could be matched to a number of wines, but the bitter hint of the radicchio here suggests that a wine with some acerbic tannins would balance the dish best. A medium-bodied 1991 California Cabernet Sauvignon, such as the Kenwood or the Alexander Valley Vineyards, would be ideal.*

8 TO 10 SERVINGS

WHITE SAUCE:

- 1 quart milk
- 1 stick (4 ounces) unsalted butter
- ¼ cup plus 2 tablespoons all-purpose flour
- ½ teaspoon salt

TOMATO SAUCE:

- 1 tablespoon olive oil
- 1 medium onion, finely chopped
- One 28-ounce can Italian peeled tomatoes, drained and coarsely chopped
- Salt and freshly ground pepper
- 3 tablespoons finely chopped flat-leaf parsley

- 4 large heads of radicchio—halved, cored, and sliced ½ inch thick
- ½ cup plus 1 tablespoon olive oil

ELEGANT LOW-FAT DINNER

This vegetarian menu is impressive without being difficult. The succotash is dressed up with simple chile-baked phyllo rounds, and the ravioli is made with store-bought egg roll wrappers instead of labor-intensive fresh pasta.

🍷 Set off these flavors with an herby-fruity 1993 California Sauvignon Blanc, such as the Quivira or Cakebread. A Late Harvest Johannisberg Riesling, such as the 1992 Hogue Cellars from Washington State, would add a grace note to the dessert.

FAVA BEAN SUCCOTASH WITH CRISP PHYLLO ROUNDS (P. 43)

ROASTED VEGETABLE RAVIOLI ON YELLOW PEPPER MOLE SAUCE (P. 254)

ORANGE ANGEL FOOD CAKE WITH WARM BERRY COMPOTE (P. 395)

—CHARLES WILEY

Rice Noodles with Stir-Fried Cabbage and Peanuts

Salt and freshly ground pepper
- 2 pounds fresh shiitake mushrooms, stems removed and caps sliced ½ inch thick
- 1 pound fresh lasagna noodles
- 1 cup freshly grated Parmesan cheese (about 3 ounces)
- ½ pound mozzarella, preferably fresh, cut into ¼-inch-thick slices
- ¼ cup milk (if preparing the lasagna ahead)

1. Make the white sauce: In a medium saucepan, bring the milk just to a boil over moderately high heat; keep warm. Melt the butter in another medium saucepan. Add the flour and stir over moderate heat for 1 minute. Gradually whisk in the milk until the mixture is smooth. Raise the heat to high and whisk the sauce until it boils and thickens, about 3 minutes. Reduce the heat to moderately low and simmer, whisking often, until no floury taste remains, about 10 minutes. Stir in the salt, pour into a bowl, and let cool; cover the surface with plastic wrap.

2. Make the tomato sauce: Heat the olive oil in a nonreactive medium saucepan. Add the onion and cook over moderate heat, stirring, until softened, about 4 minutes. Add the tomatoes and simmer, stirring often, until the sauce is thick, about 20 minutes. Season with salt and pepper and stir in the parsley. Transfer the tomato sauce to a bowl and let cool slightly. Stir in 1 cup of the white sauce and season with salt and pepper.

3. Preheat the broiler. Bring a large saucepan of water to a boil. Spread the sliced radicchio on a large baking sheet and toss with 3 tablespoons of the olive oil. Season with salt and freshly ground pepper and broil for about 6 minutes, stirring often with tongs, until the radicchio is lightly browned and tender. Transfer the radicchio to a large bowl. Turn the oven to 350°.

4. Heat 2 more tablespoons of the olive oil in a large skillet until almost smoking. Add one-third of the shiitake mushrooms, season with salt and pepper, and cook over high heat without stirring, until the mushrooms are golden brown on the bottom, about 3 minutes. Stir the mushrooms and continue cooking until tender and browned all over, 3 to 4 minutes longer. Add the mushrooms to the radicchio. Repeat the process 2 more times with the remaining olive oil and shiitake mushrooms. Stir 2½ cups of the white sauce into the vegetables and season with salt and pepper.

5. Add salt to the boiling water. Working in batches, cook the lasagna noodles for 1 minute. Carefully transfer the cooked lasagna noodles to a bowl of cold water to cool, then drain them on paper towels.

6. Lightly butter a 9-by-13-inch nonreactive baking dish. Arrange one-fifth of the lasagna noodles in the prepared dish. Spread one-quarter of the radicchio mixture over the lasagna noodles and sprinkle with ¼ cup of the Parmesan cheese. Repeat this layering process 3 more times and cover with the remaining lasagna noodles. Spread the remaining ½ cup of white sauce over the noodles and arrange the sliced mozzarella on top. (MAKE AHEAD: The assembled lasagna can be covered and frozen for up to 1 month; see "Strategies for Freezing Lasagna," p. 263. Or refrigerate the lasagna for up to 2 days. Freeze or refrigerate the tomato-white sauce separately. Let the lasagna return to room temperature before baking, then pour the milk around the sides of the lasagna.)

7. Cover the lasagna loosely with foil and bake for 1 hour. Remove the foil and continue baking for about 20 minutes more, or until the lasagna is bubbling and the mozzarella cheese is melted and beginning to brown. Let stand for 10 minutes before serving. Meanwhile, reheat the tomato-white sauce in a small saucepan over moderately low heat. Season the sauce with salt and pepper and serve it with the lasagna.—FRANK MINIERI

RICE NOODLES WITH STIR-FRIED CABBAGE AND PEANUTS

4 TO 6 SERVINGS

- 1 pound dried medium-width rice noodles
- ¼ cup hoisin sauce
- ¼ cup soy sauce
- 3 tablespoons dry white wine
- 2 teaspoons cider vinegar
- 2 teaspoons Asian sesame oil
- 1½ teaspoons sugar
- 1½ teaspoons salt
- ¼ teaspoon freshly ground white pepper
- ½ cup peanut oil
- 1 large onion, thinly sliced
- 2 tablespoons finely chopped fresh ginger
- 3 large garlic cloves, minced
- 1 to 2 medium jalapeño chiles, halved lengthwise and thinly sliced crosswise
- 1 large red bell pepper, thinly sliced lengthwise
- 2 pounds napa cabbage, cut crosswise into 1-inch-thick strips
- 3 ounces snow peas, thinly sliced lengthwise
- 1 cup mung bean sprouts
- ½ cup coarsely chopped unsalted peanuts (about 3 ounces)
- 2 medium scallions, thinly sliced on the diagonal
- ¼ cup shredded fresh basil
- Lemon or lime wedges, for serving

1. Bring a large saucepan of water to a boil. In a large bowl, cover the rice noodles with cold water and let soak until pliable, about 20 minutes. Drain the rice noodles in a colander, then add them to the boiling water and cook for 1 minute, stirring once. Drain the rice noodles, return them to the saucepan, and add cold water to cover, swirling the noodles around. Drain and repeat the process once more, leaving the rice noodles in the colander; handle the noodles as little as possible.

2. In a bowl, combine the hoisin sauce, soy sauce, white wine, cider vinegar, sesame oil, sugar, salt, and pepper.

3. Heat a large wok. Add the peanut oil and heat until shimmering. Add the onion and cook over high heat, stirring occasionally, until browned and crisp, about 5 minutes. Using a slotted spoon, transfer the onion to paper towels to drain.

4. Pour off all but 3 tablespoons of the oil and set the wok over high heat. Add the ginger and stir-fry for 1 minute. Add the garlic and jalapeño and stir-fry for 1 minute. Add the red bell pepper and stir-fry for 2 minutes. Add the napa cabbage and stir-fry until wilted, about 4 minutes. Add the snow peas and stir-fry for 1 more minute.

5. Rinse the rice noodles under very hot water to loosen them. Add the rice noodles to the stir-fried vegetables and gently toss over high heat using 2 large spoons; do not overmix. Add the hoisin mixture and toss until the sauce is bubbling and the rice noodles are heated through, about 2 minutes.

6. Transfer the rice noodles to a platter, garnish with the mung bean sprouts, onions, chopped peanuts, scallions, and shredded basil, and serve the noodles with lemon wedges.—MARCIA KIESEL

HERBED SPAETZLE *LF*

6 SERVINGS

- 1 large egg
- 1 large egg white
- 2¼ cups all-purpose flour
- 1 tablespoon finely chopped fresh chives
- 1 tablespoon finely chopped fresh parsley
- ½ teaspoon finely chopped fresh thyme
- 1¼ teaspoons salt
- ½ recipe warm Three-Mushroom Gravy (p. 152)

1. In a medium bowl, lightly beat the egg and the egg white with ¾ cup of water. Stir in the flour, chives, parsley, thyme, and salt just until a sticky dough forms. (MAKE AHEAD: The dough for the spaetzle can be refrigerated, covered, for up to 4 hours.)

2. Bring a large pot of salted water to a simmer. Pat one-third of the spaetzle dough into a 3-inch square on a small cutting board with a handle, or on the back of a square cake pan. Using a moistened metal spatula or chef's knife, cut off a ¼-inch-thick strip of spaetzle dough and scrape it into the simmering water. Working quickly over the pot, slice the remaining spaetzle dough into the simmering water, moistening the spatula or knife if it sticks to the dough. Stir the spaetzle and cook them over moderate heat until the dumplings float to the surface and are just cooked through, about 2 minutes. Using a slotted spoon, transfer the cooked spaetzle to a bowl and keep them warm. Repeat the process with the remaining spaetzle dough. ➤

3. Add the Three-Mushroom Gravy to the cooked spaetzle and toss gently to combine. Serve at once.—GRACE PARISI

ORECCHIETTE WITH LEMON-PARMESAN CREAM

4 SERVINGS

Salt
½ pound orecchiette or farfalle
2 tablespoons unsalted butter
2 tablespoons fresh lemon juice
⅔ cup heavy cream
½ cup freshly grated Parmesan cheese (about 1½ ounces)
¼ cup minced fresh chives
2 teaspoons finely grated lemon zest
Freshly ground pepper

1. Bring a large saucepan of water to a boil. Add salt and then the orecchiette to the water and cook, stirring often, until the pasta is al dente, about 11 minutes. Drain and return the pasta to the saucepan.
2. Meanwhile, in a small nonreactive saucepan, melt the butter in the lemon juice and heavy cream over moderately low heat. Reduce the heat to very low and cook until the cream is barely simmering, about 10 minutes.
3. Just before serving, stir the cream sauce into the pasta. Add the Parmesan, chives, and lemon zest, season with salt and pepper, and toss.—TRACEY SEAMAN

SHEEP'S-MILK-RICOTTA RAVIOLI

The bite of the pesto and the acidity of the tomato confit require a crisp, tart, lean white. A California Sauvignon Blanc, such as the 1993 Kenwood or the 1993 Sterling, would balance the tastes nicely.

4 SERVINGS

8 medium plum tomatoes—peeled, halved, and seeded
Salt
¾ cup olive oil
2 large garlic cloves, smashed
1 fresh rosemary sprig
1 pound Fresh Pasta Dough (recipe follows) or 80 gyoza skins,* thawed but cold
1 pound sheep's-milk-ricotta cheese or other fresh ricotta
2 tablespoons Basil Pesto (recipe follows)
2 tablespoons freshly grated Parmesan cheese
Freshly ground pepper
1 large egg, lightly beaten
¾ cup pine nuts (4 ounces)
1 large bunch of arugula, tough stems removed
1 tablespoon extra-virgin olive oil
1 teaspoon balsamic vinegar

*Available at Asian markets

1. Put the plum tomatoes in a colander, sprinkle with ½ teaspoon salt, and let drain for 30 minutes; pat dry. Lightly pack the tomatoes in a nonreactive medium saucepan and pour in the olive oil. Push the garlic and rosemary into the oil and bring to a gentle simmer over moderate heat. Reduce the heat to low and cook until the tomatoes are meltingly tender but not broken down, about 40 minutes. (MAKE AHEAD: The tomato confit can be refrigerated, covered, for up to 1 day.)
2. Working with 1 sheet at a time, spread the Fresh Pasta Dough on a work surface. Using a biscuit cutter or a large sharp knife, cut the pasta into eighty

Sheep's-Milk-Ricotta Ravioli

3-inch rounds or squares. Layer in kitchen towels.

3. In a large bowl, stir together the ricotta, the Basil Pesto, and the Parmesan cheese. Season with salt and pepper and stir in the egg. Lay 20 pasta rounds or gyoza skins out on a work surface and brush lightly with water. Mound a generous teaspoon of the filling on half of the rounds, then cover with the remaining rounds, moistened sides down. Press around the edges to seal. Repeat with the remaining pasta rounds and filling to make 40 ravioli. Layer the ravioli on a baking sheet between sheets of wax paper dusted with flour. (MAKE AHEAD: The ravioli can be frozen for up to 2 weeks.)

4. Bring a large pot of salted water to a boil. In a small dry skillet, toast the pine nuts over moderate heat, shaking the pan, until golden, about 4 minutes. Transfer to a plate to cool.

5. Working in batches, cook the ravioli in the boiling water until tender, 4 to 5 minutes. Using a medium strainer, carefully transfer the cooked ravioli to a colander to drain.

6. Meanwhile, rewarm the tomato confit over moderately low heat. In a large bowl, toss the arugula with the extra-virgin olive oil and balsamic vinegar. Season with salt and pepper.

7. Arrange the sheep's-milk-ricotta ravioli on individual plates. Spoon the tomato confit in the center, reserving the oil. Arrange the dressed arugula on top of the ravioli. Sprinkle with the toasted pine nuts and drizzle with the reserved oil from the tomato confit.

Fresh Pasta Dough

MAKES 1 POUND

2 cups unbleached flour
Pinch of salt
4 large eggs, lightly beaten
1 teaspoon olive oil

1. In a food processor, pulse the flour with the salt to sift. With the machine on, add the eggs and olive oil and process just until the dough comes together. Transfer the pasta dough to a lightly floured surface and knead until smooth and elastic, about 6 minutes. Cover with a towel and let rest at room temperature for 15 to 30 minutes.

2. Cut the pasta dough into quarters; work with one piece at a time, and keep the remaining pieces covered. Work the dough through a pasta machine on consecutively narrower settings until you reach the next to last setting. If the dough becomes too long to handle, cut it in half crosswise. Lay the pasta on kitchen towels and let dry for 20 minutes before cutting into shapes.

Basil Pesto

MAKES ABOUT ¾ CUP

¼ cup pine nuts or walnuts
8 medium garlic cloves, coarsely chopped
4 cups packed fresh basil leaves
¼ cup olive oil

1. In a small dry skillet, toast the pine nuts over moderate heat, shaking the pan, until the nuts are lightly browned, about 5 minutes. Let cool.

2. In a food processor, finely chop the garlic. Add the toasted pine nuts and the basil leaves and pulse until finely chopped, scraping down the sides as necessary. With the machine on, add the olive oil in a steady stream until it is incorporated. (MAKE AHEAD: The basil pesto can be refrigerated, covered, for up to 1 week.) —TERRANCE BRENNAN

FETTUCCINE WITH CREAMY CHICKEN AND SPINACH Q

To make this quick dish even quicker, use ten ounces of thawed, drained frozen spinach in place of the fresh.

This rich pasta dish requires a big, full white that will not be overwhelmed by the strong-flavored beans with garlic. Oak-aged California Chardonnay is the answer. Try deep, round examples, such as the 1991 Hess Collection or the 1990 Dry Creek Reserve.

4 SERVINGS

4 tablespoons unsalted butter
4 skinless, boneless chicken breast halves (about 4 ounces each), cut diagonally into 1-by-½-inch strips

SPICY VARIATION

Punch up Fettuccine with Creamy Chicken and Spinach by using black pepper fettuccine (available at many supermarkets and specialty food stores) and a large pinch of crushed red pepper, which can be added to the cream sauce with the tomatoes. Alternatively, add a peppery bite to the dish by replacing the spinach with arugula.—NANCY VERDE BARR

1 pound fresh spinach, stemmed and coarsely chopped
Salt and freshly ground pepper
¼ teaspoon freshly grated nutmeg
1 cup drained canned Italian peeled tomatoes, coarsely chopped
1 cup heavy cream
¾ pound dried fettuccine
⅓ cup freshly grated Parmesan cheese (about 1 ounce) plus more for serving

1. In a large covered pot, bring 4 quarts of water to a boil. Meanwhile, melt the butter in a large heavy skillet. Add the strips of boneless chicken breast and sauté over moderately high heat just until lightly browned all over and cooked through, 1 to 2 minutes. Transfer the chicken strips to a plate.

2. Add the spinach to the skillet, season with salt, pepper, and nutmeg, and cook over moderately high heat, stirring occasionally, until the spinach is wilted, about 2 minutes. Add the canned Italian tomatoes and cook, stirring, until heated through, about 3 minutes. Stir in the heavy cream in a steady stream and simmer the sauce until slightly thickened, about 4 minutes. Season with salt and pepper.

3. Add 1 tablespoon salt to the boiling water. Add the fettuccine and cook uncovered until the pasta is al dente, about 7 minutes. Drain the fettuccine and return it to the pot.

4. Add the chicken strips to the cream sauce and stir over moderate heat until warmed through. Add the chicken and cream sauce to the fettuccine with the ⅓ cup Parmesan cheese and toss to coat. Serve immediately and pass additional Parmesan at the table.—NANCY VERDE BARR

Fettuccine with Creamy Chicken and Spinach

FRESH TAGLIATELLE WITH CARROTS AND PROSCIUTTO

Look for prosciutto di Parma, which is available at specialty food markets. It is less salty than other kinds.

4 SERVINGS

2 tablespoons unsalted butter
¼ cup extra-virgin olive oil
1 medium white onion, finely chopped (about ⅔ cup)
6 medium carrots, shaved into ribbons with a vegetable peeler
⅓ pound thinly sliced prosciutto, cut crosswise into ⅛-inch strips
6 gratings of fresh nutmeg
About ⅔ cup chicken stock, canned low-sodium broth, or water
Salt and freshly cracked black pepper
1 pound fresh egg tagliatelle or fettuccine
¼ cup freshly grated Grana Padano or Parmesan cheese, plus more for serving

1. In a large pot, bring 4 quarts of water to a boil for the pasta. In a large skillet, melt 1 tablespoon of the butter in 2 tablespoons of the olive oil over moderately high heat. Add the onion and cook, stirring, until translucent, about 3 minutes. Add the carrots and the strips of prosciutto and cook until the carrots start to brown and the prosciutto strips become crisp, about 10 minutes. Stir in the nutmeg, then stir in ⅔ cup of the chicken stock and simmer for 5 minutes. Season with salt and cracked pepper.

2. Salt the boiling pasta water, add the tagliatelle, and cook until the pasta is al dente, about 3 minutes. Drain the tagliatelle and return it to the pot. Toss with the remaining 1 tablespoon butter and 2 tablespoons olive oil and the ¼ cup of cheese. Pour the carrot sauce over the pasta and toss. If the pasta seems dry, add a bit more stock. Transfer the pasta to a large warmed bowl and serve. Pass extra cheese separately.—ERICA DE MANE

LASAGNA VERDE

If you don't have the time or inclination to make your own pasta for this rich, meaty dish, Roberto Donna, of Galileo in Washington, D.C., recommends substituting 12 ounces of fresh lasagna noodles—cook them in batches for 1 minute.

8 TO 10 SERVINGS

SPINACH PASTA:

6 ounces fresh spinach, tough stems discarded
1½ cups all-purpose flour
Salt
2 large eggs

WHITE SAUCE:

2½ cups milk
Salt and freshly ground pepper
Pinch of ground nutmeg
4 tablespoons unsalted butter
¼ cup plus 2 tablespoons all-purpose flour

Bolognese Sauce (recipe follows)
½ cup freshly grated Parmesan cheese (about 1½ ounces)
½ tablespoon unsalted butter, cut into small pieces

1. Prepare the spinach pasta: In a medium saucepan of boiling water, blanch the fresh spinach until it is wilted, about 1 minute. Drain and rinse with cold water. Squeeze the spinach dry, then finely chop it.

2. In a food processor, pulse the flour with ½ teaspoon salt. Add the spinach and pulse until incorporated. With the machine on, add the eggs and process until the dough forms a ball. Transfer to a work surface and knead briefly until smooth. Flatten the dough into a disk and wrap in plastic wrap; let it stand for 30 minutes.

3. Divide the dough into 4 pieces. Working with one piece at a time and keeping the remaining pieces covered, pass the dough through consecutively narrower settings of a pasta machine, ending at the last setting; lightly flour the dough if it begins to stick. Drape the lasagna sheet over a rack or the back of a chair while you roll out the remaining dough. Cut each sheet in half crosswise so that you have 8 lasagna noodles, each about 12 by 4 inches.

4. Bring a large pot of water to a boil. Add salt to the boiling water and cook the lasagna noodles, 2 sheets at a time, for 1 minute. Carefully transfer the cooked noodles to a bowl of cold water to cool, then drain them on paper towels.

5. Prepare the white sauce: In a small saucepan, combine the milk with ½ teaspoon salt, ¼ teaspoon pepper, and the nutmeg, and bring just to a boil over moderately high heat; keep warm. Melt the butter in a medium saucepan. Add the flour and stir over moderate heat for 1 minute. Gradually whisk in the milk until smooth. Raise the heat to high and whisk the sauce until it boils and thickens, about 3 minutes. Reduce the heat to moderately low and simmer, whisking often, until no floury taste remains, about 10 minutes. Season the sauce with salt and pepper. Pour the sauce into a bowl and allow it to cool slightly; press a piece of plastic wrap directly on the surface.

6. Preheat the oven to 350°. Lightly butter an 8-by-12-inch nonreactive baking dish. Arrange 2 lasagna noodles in the dish, draping any excess dough

QUICK DINNER

FETTUCCINE WITH CREAMY CHICKEN AND SPINACH (P. 259)

ROASTED GREEN BEANS WITH GARLIC (P. 317)

RIPE BARTLETT OR ANJOU PEARS

BISCOTTI

CAPPUCCINO OR ESPRESSO

TIMETABLE:

- **Preheat the oven and put the pasta water on to boil before assembling the ingredients.**
- **Wash and trim the beans. Start roasting them while you grate the cheese.**
- **Cook the chicken and the spinach and make the sauce.**
- **Stir the pasta into the boiling water. Add the chicken to the sauce and rewarm while the pasta is cooking.**

—NANCY VERDE BARR

Orzo Risotto with Cockles and Spicy Sausage

over the sides. Spoon ½ cup of the white sauce over the pasta, then spread 1 cup of the Bolognese Sauce on top. Sprinkle with 2 tablespoons of Parmesan. Repeat the process 2 more times and cover with the remaining lasagna noodles. Fold the overhanging dough back over the top of the lasagna. Spread the remaining ½ cup white sauce on top, sprinkle on the remaining 2 tablespoons Parmesan, and dot with the butter. (MAKE AHEAD: The assembled lasagna can be covered and frozen for up to 1 month; see "Strategies for Freezing Lasagna," right. Or refrigerate for up to 2 days. Let return to room temperature before baking.)

7. Cover the lasagna with foil and bake for about 50 minutes, or until hot and bubbling. Raise the oven temperature to 400° and remove the foil from the dish. Bake the lasagna in the upper third of the oven for about 20 more minutes until golden brown on top. Let stand for 10 minutes before cutting.

Bolognese Sauce

This rich sauce featuring five kinds of meat makes an excellent topping for wide noodles like fettuccine.

MAKES ABOUT 3 CUPS

- 2 tablespoons unsalted butter
- 2 ounces pancetta, finely chopped
- 2 small carrots, finely chopped
- 2 medium celery ribs, peeled and finely chopped
- 1 small onion, finely chopped
- 3 ounces ground pork
- 3 ounces ground chuck
- 3 ounces prosciutto, finely chopped
- 1 cup chicken stock or canned low-sodium broth
- ¼ cup canned tomato puree
- 3 ounces chicken livers, trimmed and finely chopped
- ½ cup heavy cream

Salt and freshly ground pepper

Melt the butter in a nonreactive medium saucepan. Add the pancetta, carrots, celery, and onion, and cook over moderate heat, stirring occasionally, until the vegetables are softened, about 5 minutes. Add the pork, chuck, and prosciutto, and cook, stirring often, until lightly browned, about 12 minutes. Add the chicken stock and tomato puree to the saucepan and simmer over moderately low heat, stirring once or twice, until the sauce is slightly thickened, about 15 minutes. Stir in the chicken livers and simmer until thickened, about 5 minutes. Pour in the heavy cream and simmer the sauce until heated through, about 3 minutes. Season with salt and pepper. (MAKE AHEAD: The sauce can be refrigerated, covered, for up to 3 days.) —ROBERTO DONNA

ORZO RISOTTO WITH COCKLES AND SPICY SAUSAGE

At the Ajax Tavern in Aspen, Nick Morfogen makes his spicy risotto with cockles, but small clams are a great, readily available alternative. Any small pasta shape, such as tubettini or acini de pepe, *can be the basis for the risotto, though oval orzo is a particularly good choice. If you substitute another size or shape of pasta, the cooking time and amount of liquid might vary. Just be sure to use pasta that's made only with hard durum wheat.*

STRATEGIES FOR FREEZING LASAGNA

- UNDERCOOK THE PASTA SLIGHTLY, **since it will absorb moisture from the sauce while it sits in the freezer.**
- MAKE SURE THE LASAGNA COMPONENTS ARE COOL **before freezing the unbaked lasagna so that it will chill quickly. This prevents ice crystals from forming on the food.**
- PLACE A LAYER OF PLASTIC WRAP DIRECTLY ON THE LASAGNA **to protect it from the dry air in the freezer, then tightly wrap the dish in foil.**
- **To freeze the lasagna without losing the use of your baking dish,** ASSEMBLE THE LASAGNA IN A BAKING DISH LINED WITH FOIL, **allowing a two-inch overhang at each end. Cover with another piece of foil and fold the edges together. Freeze the lasagna until firm, about eight hours. Remove the wrapped lasagna from the dish, label it, and return to the freezer.**
- THAW THE LASAGNA IN THE REFRIGERATOR FOR A DAY BEFORE BAKING **to ensure good texture. You can also thaw the frozen lasagna in a microwave oven according to the manufacturer's instructions before baking it.**

🍷 *A fresh, crisp, uncomplicated Italian or Spanish white, such as the 1993 Antinori Orvieto Campogrande or the 1992 Torres Viña Sol, is all that's needed to provide a crisp counterpoint to the salty clams and spicy sausage in this risotto.*

Linguine with Shrimp

SIMPLE PASTA DINNER

LINGUINE WITH SHRIMP (P. 265)

BROCCOLI WITH BLACK OLIVES (P. 309)

BAKED PEARS (P. 420)

—SARAH FRITSCHNER

4 SERVINGS

- ½ pound hot Italian sausage
- ¼ cup plus 3 tablespoons olive oil
- 5 large garlic cloves, minced
- 1 tablespoon finely chopped fresh basil
- 1 tablespoon finely chopped fresh oregano
- 2 pounds cockles or small clams, scrubbed
- ¼ cup dry vermouth
- 1 medium tomato—peeled, seeded, and finely chopped
- 1½ cups bottled clam juice
- 1 medium onion, finely chopped
- 1 cup orzo (about 6 ounces)
- ½ cup dry white wine
- 3 tablespoons unsalted butter
- ½ cup freshly grated Parmesan cheese (about 1½ ounces)

Freshly ground pepper

1. Preheat the broiler. Split the sausage lengthwise and arrange on a broiler pan. Broil for about 4 minutes per side, turning once, until cooked through. Let cool, then cut into ¼-inch dice. (MAKE AHEAD: The sausage can be prepared up to 1 day ahead; cover and refrigerate.)

2. Heat 3 tablespoons of the olive oil in a large nonreactive saucepan. Add the sausage dice and cook over high heat, stirring occasionally, until the sausage is well browned, 4 to 5 minutes. Add two-thirds of the minced garlic and cook, stirring, until golden, about 2 minutes. Stir in the basil and oregano and transfer the sausage mixture to a small bowl.

3. Add the cockles to the saucepan and stir to coat with the oil remaining in the pan. Add the vermouth and bring to a boil over high heat. Cover and cook until the cockles open, about 4 minutes, removing them to a bowl as they open. Cover the cockles with foil and keep warm. Add the chopped tomato and ¼ cup of the clam juice to the saucepan and boil over high heat until the liquid is reduced by half, 3 to 4 minutes. Stir in the sausage mixture.

4. Heat the remaining ¼ cup olive oil in a medium nonreactive saucepan. Add the onion and the remaining minced garlic and cook over moderate heat, stirring occasionally, until translucent, about 4 minutes. Add the orzo and stir until the pasta is well coated. Pour in the white wine and simmer, stirring occasionally, until absorbed.

5. In a large measuring cup, combine the remaining 1¼ cups clam juice with 1 cup plus 2 tablespoons of water. Add one-third of the diluted clam juice to the orzo and cook over moderate heat, stirring constantly, until absorbed. Stir in the sausage mixture and half the remaining diluted clam juice and cook, stirring, until absorbed. Add the remaining diluted clam juice and stir until absorbed, about 25 minutes total cooking time. The orzo should be al dente and have a creamy consistency; add up to ¼ cup more water and continue cooking if necessary. Remove

SOUL SEASONING

Fish sauce (*nuoc mam*) is essential to Vietnamese cooking. Although it is not always detectable in a dish, the depth of flavor that fish sauce provides would be sorely missed if it were left out. It also happens to be very rich in protein and B vitamins. Fish sauce should be purchased in glass bottles only. Golden Boy, Squid, and Lobster are all excellent brands.

from the heat and stir in the butter and Parmesan. Season with pepper.

6. Divide the orzo risotto among warmed shallow bowls or soup plates. Spoon the cockles on top and serve.—NICK MORFOGEN

LINGUINE WITH SHRIMP

This garlicky shrimp dish calls for a crisp, dry white with enough assertiveness to stand up to the strongly flavored accompaniment of broccoli with black olives. A West Coast Sauvignon Blanc, such as the 1994 Robert Pecota or the 1994 Hogue Cellars Fumé Blanc, would be ideal.

4 SERVINGS

Salt
12 ounces linguine
¼ cup olive oil
3 garlic cloves, minced
1 pound medium shrimp, shelled and deveined
1 lemon, zest finely grated, juice squeezed
½ teaspoon freshly ground black pepper
½ cup minced fresh parsley

1. Bring a large pot of water to a boil. Add salt and the linguine and cook, stirring often, until tender but still firm to the bite, about 8 minutes. Drain in a colander.

2. Meanwhile, heat the olive oil in a large nonreactive skillet. Add the garlic and cook over moderate heat, stirring, for 1 minute; do not let it brown. Add the shrimp, lemon zest, ½ teaspoon salt, and the pepper, and stir well. Add ¼ cup of water and the lemon juice and cook for 1 minute. Add the parsley and simmer until the shrimp are just cooked, about 2 minutes longer.

3. Put the linguine in a large bowl. Add the shrimp and its sauce, toss well, and serve.—SARAH FRITSCHNER

VIETNAMESE NOODLES WITH SHRIMP AND PEANUTS

4 TO 6 SERVINGS

1 pound dried rice sticks or rice vermicelli
¼ cup fresh lime juice
2 tablespoons fish sauce (*nuoc mam*)
1 large garlic clove, minced
2 teaspoons sugar
½ teaspoon finely grated lime zest
Salt
1 pound medium shrimp—shelled, deveined, and halved lengthwise
⅓ unpeeled European cucumber—halved lengthwise, seeded, and cut into 2-by-¼-inch matchsticks
3 tablespoons small fresh mint leaves
2 tablespoons small fresh coriander (cilantro) leaves
Crispy Shallots (recipe follows) or ¼ cup packaged fried red onions
3 tablespoons coarsely chopped roasted unsalted peanuts

1. Bring a large saucepan of water to a boil. Meanwhile, put the rice noodles in a large bowl and cover with hot water. Stir to separate the strands and let soak until the noodles are softened, about 20 minutes. In a small bowl, combine the lime juice, fish sauce, garlic, sugar, and lime zest.

2. Add salt to the boiling water. Stir in the shrimp and boil over high heat until they curl up and

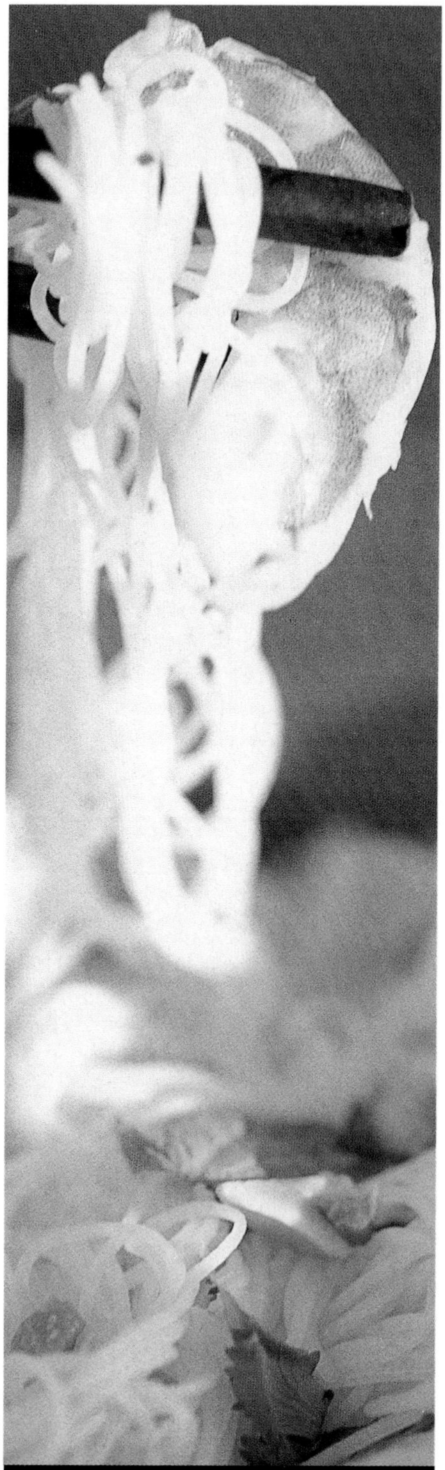

Vietnamese Noodles with Shrimp and Peanuts

Pasta with Fresh Tuna and Tomatoes

LOW-FAT MENU

PASTA WITH FRESH TUNA AND TOMATOES (P. 266)

ZUCCHINI, MINT AND LEMON SALAD (P. 73)

STRAWBERRY SORBET (P. 419)

are just cooked through, about 2 minutes. Using a slotted spoon, transfer the shrimp to a plate. Set aside ½ cup of the shrimp cooking liquid.

3. Bring the remaining cooking liquid back to a boil over high heat. Drain the rice noodles and add them to the boiling liquid. Cook, stirring, until slightly tender but still chewy, about 2 minutes. Drain the noodles and return them to the pan. Add cold water to cover, stir to separate the noodles, and drain in a colander. Repeat the process, then let the noodles stand in the colander for 5 minutes, lifting occasionally to help them dry.

4. Transfer the noodles to a large bowl. Add the reserved shrimp cooking liquid and toss well. Add the shrimp, the cucumber, and the lime juice mixture, and toss to combine. Add the mint, coriander, and Crispy Shallots, and toss again. Transfer to shallow bowls, sprinkle with the peanuts, and serve at once.

Crispy Shallots

Roasted shallot slices make a crisp garnish to the Vietnamese Noodles with Shrimp and Peanuts; prepare them while the rice noodles are soaking. They also make a wonderful textural garnish for noodle soups, salads, and stir-fries.

MAKES ABOUT ¼ CUP

6 large shallots, thinly sliced
2 tablespoons vegetable oil
Salt

Preheat the oven to 400°. Toss the shallot slices on a baking sheet to separate them, then spread in an even layer. Drizzle on the vegetable oil and stir to coat. Bake the shallots in the center of the oven for about 15 minutes, stirring occasionally, until the shallots are evenly browned and crisp. Season the shallots lightly with salt and allow them to cool completely. (MAKE AHEAD: The crispy shallots can be refrigerated, covered, for up to 10 days. Rewarm in a 350° oven.) —MARCIA KIESEL

PASTA WITH FRESH TUNA AND TOMATOES LF

To save time and keep your kitchen cool, you can substitute one cup of drained, jarred roasted red peppers for the peppers roasted in the recipe. Coarsely chop them and proceed from Step 2.

🍷 *A tangy, dry French white, such as the 1993 Sauvion Château du Cléray Muscadet, or a lean, oaky California Pinot Blanc, such as the 1993 Mirassou or the 1993 Chalone Estate, would play off against the savory flavors in this main-dish pasta.*

4 SERVINGS

2 medium red bell peppers
Olive oil cooking spray
¾ cup coarse fresh bread crumbs
1½ teaspoons finely chopped fresh rosemary
½ pound fresh tuna steak, ½ inch thick
Salt and freshly ground black pepper
½ cup finely chopped red onion
6 medium plum tomatoes, seeded and finely chopped

WHAT'S THE BEST TUNA?

Unless it comes swimming in a can of oil, tuna is already low in fat. You can reduce the fat even further by selecting the right variety. YELLOWFIN **has very little total fat, only .3 grams for each ounce of raw fish. On the other end of the scale,** BLUEFIN **has almost five times as much fat, coming in at 1.4 grams an ounce.**

- 1 large garlic clove, minced
- 2 tablespoons drained capers, coarsely chopped
- 2 tablespoons extra-virgin olive oil
- 2 tablespoons red wine vinegar
- 1/8 teaspoon crushed red pepper
- 3/4 pound farfalle or orecchiette

1. Roast the bell peppers directly over a gas flame or under the broiler, as close to the heat as possible, or until charred all over. Transfer to a paper bag and let steam for 15 minutes. Peel the charred skin and discard the cores, ribs, and seeds. Finely chop the peppers.
2. Lightly coat a small nonstick skillet with olive oil cooking spray. Add the bread crumbs and stir over moderately high heat until toasted, about 2 minutes. Add the rosemary and cook, stirring, for 1 more minute. Transfer to a small bowl.
3. Wipe out the skillet and lightly coat with more cooking spray. Season the tuna with 1/2 teaspoon each of salt and pepper and cook over high heat, turning once, until nicely browned but still pink inside, about 2 minutes per side. Transfer the tuna to a plate and let cool.
4. In a serving bowl, combine the roasted peppers, red onion, tomatoes, garlic, capers, oil, red wine vinegar, and crushed red pepper. Let stand for at least 10 minutes or up to 4 hours. Break the tuna into 1-inch chunks and stir it into the tomato mixture. Season with salt and pepper.
5. Meanwhile, bring a large pot of water to a boil. Add salt to the boiling water. Add the farfalle and cook over high heat, stirring occasionally, until the pasta is al dente, about 7 minutes. Drain the farfalle and add to the bowl with the tomato sauce. Toss well and sprinkle with the bread crumbs. Serve the pasta warm or at room temperature.—JEAN GALTON

CHAPTER 12

POTATOES

Roasted Garlic Mashed Potatoes

ROASTED GARLIC MASHED POTATOES

Octavio Becerra serves many variations on the mashed potato theme at Pinot Bistro in Studio City, California, but this roasted garlic version is the most popular. For a more intense garlic flavor, squeeze the roasted garlic cloves from their skins and stir them into the potatoes after you've added the warmed cream mixture.

4 SERVINGS

20 unpeeled garlic cloves
2 teaspoons olive oil
Pinch of thyme
¼ cup heavy cream
¼ cup milk
4 tablespoons unsalted butter, cut into small pieces
2 pounds large Idaho potatoes, peeled and cut into 2-inch chunks
Kosher salt
Freshly ground white pepper

1. Preheat the oven to 350°. Set the garlic on a large piece of foil, drizzle with the oil, and sprinkle with the thyme. Wrap the garlic in the foil and roast for about 1 hour, until the garlic is very tender. Let cool slightly.
2. Work the garlic through a coarse strainer set over a small saucepan. Add the cream, milk, and butter. Warm over moderate heat, stirring occasionally, until the butter melts; keep warm.
3. In a medium saucepan, cover the potatoes with water and add 1 teaspoon kosher salt. Bring to a boil over high heat and cook until tender, about 15 minutes. Drain the potatoes. Return them to the saucepan and shake over high heat for about 30 seconds to dry them out.
4. Pass the potatoes through a ricer or food mill into a medium bowl. Stir in the garlic cream and season with salt and white pepper. Serve hot.—OCTAVIO BECERRA

CHILE-CORN MASHED POTATOES

Red chile powder and yellow corn kernels color these southwestern-style potatoes, served at Star Canyon in Dallas. Any pure (not blended) chile powder can be used. Choices include ancho chile powder and New Mexico mild or hot powder, depending on the level of spiciness you like.

4 SERVINGS

2 pounds large Idaho potatoes, peeled and cut into 1-inch chunks
Salt
3 tablespoons unsalted butter
½ cup milk
1½ cups fresh or frozen corn kernels (about ½ pound)
4 garlic cloves, smashed
2 teaspoons pure chile powder*
1 teaspoon honey
1 teaspoon finely chopped fresh coriander

*Available at specialty food stores and Latin American markets

1. In a medium saucepan, cover the potatoes with water and add 1 teaspoon salt. Bring to a boil over high heat and cook until tender, about 12 minutes. Drain the potatoes. Return them to the

Chile-Corn Mashed Potatoes

saucepan and shake over high heat for about 30 seconds to dry them out.

2. Meanwhile, in a small skillet, melt the butter in the milk over moderate heat and bring to a simmer. Add the corn and garlic and simmer over low heat until the corn is tender, about 3 minutes for fresh and 1 minute for frozen. Stir in the chile powder and pass the mixture through a coarse strainer. Discard the garlic and reserve the corn and cooking liquid separately.

3. Using an electric mixer on low speed, whip the potatoes with the cooking liquid. Fold in the corn kernels, honey, and chopped fresh coriander, and season with salt. Serve hot.—STEPHAN PYLES

Wasabi Mashed Potatoes

WASABI MASHED POTATOES

Powdered Japanese horseradish, called wasabi, *adds a pale green hue and tingling heat to these potatoes from The Little Nell Restaurant in Aspen, Colorado.*

6 SERVINGS

- 3 pounds medium Idaho potatoes, peeled and cut into 1-inch chunks
- Salt
- ¼ cup wasabi powder*
- 7 tablespoons unsalted butter
- 1½ cups heavy cream
- Freshly ground white pepper

*Available at Asian markets

1. In a large saucepan, cover the potatoes with water and add 2 teaspoons salt. Bring to a boil over high heat and cook until tender, about 12 minutes. Drain the potatoes. Return to the saucepan and shake over high heat for about 30 seconds to dry out.

2. Meanwhile, in a small bowl, stir the wasabi powder with ¼ cup of hot water until smooth. Cover with a plate and let stand for 5 minutes.

3. In a small saucepan, melt the butter in the heavy cream over moderately low heat. Stir in the wasabi paste.

4. Pass the potatoes through a ricer or food mill into a medium bowl. Stir in the wasabi cream and season the potatoes with salt and pepper. Serve the potatoes hot.—GEORGE MAHAFFEY

Red-Skinned Mashed Potatoes

RED-SKINNED MASHED POTATOES

Yukon Gold potatoes can replace the red-skinned ones used in these chunky mashed potatoes from Fog City Diner in San Francisco.

6 TO 8 SERVINGS

- 3½ pounds medium red-skinned potatoes—unpeeled, halved lengthwise, and sliced crosswise ¼ inch thick

Salt
- 4 tablespoons unsalted butter, cut into small pieces
- 1 cup half-and-half
- 1 teaspoon freshly ground white pepper

1. In a large saucepan, cover the potatoes with water and add 2 teaspoons salt. Bring to a boil over high heat and cook until tender, about 12 minutes. Drain the potatoes. Return them to the saucepan and shake over high heat for about 30 seconds to dry them out.
2. Meanwhile, in a small saucepan, melt the butter in the half-and-half over moderate heat. Stir in 1¼ teaspoons salt and the white pepper and keep warm.
3. Using a stiff whisk or potato masher, mash the potatoes, gradually adding the half-and-half; the potatoes should be fairly lumpy. Serve hot.—ROBERT CUBBERLY

Country-Style Mashed Potatoes

COUNTRY-STYLE MASHED POTATOES

Mike Fennelly sometimes adds finely chopped roasted Anaheim chiles to flavor and spice up the coarsely mashed, sour cream-enriched potatoes that he serves at Mike's on the Avenue in New Orleans.

6 SERVINGS

- 3 pounds large Idaho potatoes, peeled and cut into 2-inch chunks

Kosher salt
- 1 stick (8 tablespoons) unsalted butter, at room temperature
- 1 cup heavy cream, at room temperature
- ½ cup sour cream
- 3 large scallions, finely chopped

Several dashes of Tabasco
Freshly ground pepper

1. In a large saucepan, cover the potatoes with water and add 1 teaspoon salt. Bring to a boil over high heat and cook until tender, about 20 minutes. Drain the potatoes. Return to the saucepan and shake over high heat for about 30 seconds to dry out.
2. Using a potato masher, mash the potatoes with the butter, leaving in some small lumps. Stir in the heavy cream, sour cream, and scallions. Season with Tabasco, salt, and pepper.—MIKE FENNELLY

POBLANO AND CHIPOTLE MASHED POTATOES

At Patria in New York City, Douglas Rodriguez uses a combination of roasted poblano and smoky chipotle for a double dose of chiles in his mashed potatoes. Poblanos have thin skins, so be sure not to roast them for too long, or the flesh will burn. The potatoes can be whipped or mashed, depending on your preference; just be sure not to overwhip them, or they'll be gummy.

6 SERVINGS

- 3 pounds red-skinned or all-purpose potatoes, peeled and cut into 2-inch chunks
- 1 dried chipotle chile—split lengthwise, stem and seeds discarded
- 2 quarts milk

Salt
- 1 large poblano chile
- 6 tablespoons unsalted butter, cut into 6 pieces

Freshly ground black pepper

1. In a large saucepan, cover the potatoes and chipotle with the milk and add 2 teaspoons salt. Bring to a boil over high heat, then lower the heat and simmer until the potatoes and chipotle are tender, about 20 minutes. Drain, reserving 1½ cups of the milk. Finely chop the chipotle and set aside. Return the potatoes to the saucepan and shake over high heat for about 30 seconds to dry them out.
2. While the potatoes cook, roast the poblano directly over a gas flame or under the broiler as close to the heat as possible, turning often, until blackened all over. Transfer to a paper bag and let steam for 5 minutes. Peel the poblano, discard the stem, seeds, and ribs, and cut the chile into ⅓-inch dice.
3. Using a potato masher or electric mixer on low speed, mash or whip the potatoes, gradually adding the butter and the reserved milk. The potatoes can be lumpy or smooth, according to your preference. Stir in the chopped poblano and chipotle chiles and season with salt and black pepper. Serve hot.—DOUGLAS RODRIGUEZ

MASHED POTATOES WITH REAL MUSHROOM GRAVY

6 SERVINGS

5 tablespoons unsalted butter, softened
2 tablespoons finely chopped fresh flat-leaf parsley
¼ teaspoon fresh lemon juice
Salt
3½ pounds medium Yukon Gold potatoes, peeled and halved crosswise
1 cup milk
Freshly ground pepper
Real Mushroom Gravy (recipe follows)

1. In a small bowl, combine 2 tablespoons of the butter with the chopped parsley. Stir in the lemon juice and season with salt.
2. In a large saucepan, cover the potatoes with water and add 2 teaspoons salt. Bring to a boil over high heat and cook until tender, about 18 minutes. Drain, return to the saucepan, and shake over high heat for about 30 seconds to dry them out.
3. In a small saucepan, warm the milk over moderate heat. Using a potato masher, mash the potatoes, gradually adding the remaining 3 tablespoons butter and the milk; the potatoes should be slightly lumpy. Season with salt and pepper. Top with the parsley butter and Real Mushroom Gravy.

Real Mushroom Gravy

This is an excellent addition to almost all the mashed potato recipes offered here. (The wasabi and the chile-corn potatoes are best served plain.)

MAKES ABOUT 2½ CUPS

½ ounce dried porcini mushrooms
¾ pound white mushrooms—stems removed and reserved, caps sliced ¼ inch thick
4 ounces fresh shiitake mushrooms—stems removed and reserved, caps sliced ¼ inch thick
About 2 teaspoons fresh lemon juice
1½ tablespoons olive oil
Salt and freshly ground pepper
2 tablespoons unsalted butter, softened
3 shallots, thinly sliced
½ teaspoon finely chopped fresh thyme
1 garlic clove, minced
1½ tablespoons all-purpose flour
1 teaspoon Dijon mustard

1. In a small bowl, soak the porcini in 1½ cups of hot water until softened, about 20 minutes. Rinse the mushrooms in the soaking liquid to remove any grit, then thinly slice them. Set the porcini and soaking liquid aside separately.
2. In a small saucepan, combine the white and shiitake mushroom stems with 1½ cups of water. Bring to a boil over high heat and boil for 10 minutes. Strain, discarding the stems; you should have about 1¼ cups of mushroom liquid.
3. In a medium bowl, toss the white mushrooms with 2 teaspoons of the lemon juice. In a large nonreactive skillet, heat 1 tablespoon of the olive oil until almost smoking. Add the white mushrooms in an even layer and season with salt and pepper. Cook over high heat, without stirring, until the exuded liquid evaporates and the bottoms are browned, about 8 minutes. Stir and continue cooking until browned all over, 3 to 4 minutes. Transfer to a plate.
4. Add the remaining ½ tablespoon oil to the skillet. Add the shiitake mushrooms in an even layer and season with salt and pepper. Cover and cook over high heat, without stirring, until the bottoms are browned, about 2 minutes. Stir, cover, and continue cooking until browned all over, about 2 minutes. Add the shiitakes to the white mushrooms. ➤

Poblano and Chipotle Mashed Potatoes

5. Melt ½ tablespoon of the butter in the skillet. Add the shallots and thyme and cook over low heat, stirring, until softened, about 4 minutes. Add the garlic and cook, stirring occasionally, for 2 more minutes. Stir in the white and shiitake mushrooms and the porcini. Add the mushroom liquid and the porcini soaking liquid, stopping when you reach the grit at the bottom.

6. In a small bowl, combine the remaining 1½ tablespoons butter with the flour to make a paste. Whisk the paste into the mushroom mixture over high heat and bring to a boil. Lower the heat and cook, whisking, until the gravy is thickened, about 5 minutes. Remove from the heat, stir in the mustard, and season with salt, pepper, and lemon juice. (MAKE AHEAD: The gravy can be made up to 1 day ahead; cover and refrigerate. Rewarm gently before serving.) —MARCIA KIESEL

ALABASTER

Mashed potatoes turn luminous from the addition of white turnips in this classic Shaker preparation.

8 SERVINGS

3 pounds Idaho potatoes, peeled and quartered

Roasted Potatoes with Lavender and Mint

Salt
2½ pounds medium white turnips, peeled and quartered
1 stick (4 ounces) unsalted butter, cut into tablespoons
¾ cup milk
Freshly ground white pepper
¼ cup fresh flat-leaf parsley leaves

1. In a large saucepan, cover the potatoes with water and bring to a boil over high heat. Stir in 2 teaspoons of salt and boil for 5 minutes. Add the white turnips and boil until the potatoes and turnips are tender when pierced, about 15 minutes. Drain the vegetables in a colander.
2. Return the potatoes and turnips to the saucepan and, using a potato masher or a large spoon, mash with the butter and milk. Season with salt and white pepper. Transfer the mashed vegetables to a large, shallow, heatproof serving dish. (MAKE AHEAD: This dish can be made up to 1 day ahead. Let cool, then cover and refrigerate. Return the vegetables to room temperature, then rewarm in a 400° oven. If necessary, stir in extra milk, then dot with extra butter.) Decorate the border with the parsley and serve.—CASSANDRA DOOLEY

OVEN-ROASTED RED POTATOES WITH ROQUEFORT

2 SERVINGS

1 tablespoon olive oil
½ pound small red potatoes, halved
¼ teaspoon salt
¼ teaspoon freshly ground pepper
⅔ cup crumbled Roquefort or other blue cheese

1. Preheat the oven to 450°. Brush the olive oil on a nonstick baking sheet. Arrange the red potatoes, cut sides up, on the baking sheet. Sprinkle with the salt and pepper and turn the potatoes over.
2. Roast the potatoes for about 20 minutes, until browned on the bottom. Turn them over and keep warm. Leave the oven on.
3. Five minutes before serving, sprinkle the cheese on the potatoes. Bake about 3 minutes until the cheese starts to melt. Don't overcook or the cheese will melt off the potatoes.—BOB CHAMBERS

ROASTED POTATOES WITH LAVENDER AND MINT

Lavender, used judiciously in cooking, lends a delicate flavor. You can use any small new potatoes in this recipe from the Herbfarm in Fall City, Washington. Fingerlings (so-called because of their fingerlike appearance) are a terrific choice.

4 TO 6 SERVINGS

2 pounds small new potatoes
1 tablespoon distilled white vinegar
2 teaspoons salt
6 fresh lavender sprigs or 2 teaspoons dried lavender buds
¼ cup olive oil
3 medium garlic cloves, minced
1 tablespoon chopped fresh spearmint
Salt and freshly ground pepper

1. Preheat the oven to 400°. Put the small new potatoes in a large nonreactive saucepan, and add enough water to cover. Add the vinegar, salt, and half the lavender. Boil over high heat until the potatoes can be easily pierced with a knife, about 12 minutes. Drain and let the potatoes cool. Discard the lavender. Slice the potatoes ½ inch thick.
2. Put the potato slices in a medium bowl. Remove the buds from the remaining lavender sprigs and add them to the potatoes (or add the remaining dried buds). Add the olive oil, garlic, and spearmint, and toss well. Season with salt and pepper.
3. Spread the potatoes in a single layer on a large baking sheet. Bake the potatoes for about 40 minutes, or until golden brown. Serve warm.—JERRY TRAUNFELD

ROAST POTATO WEDGES

4 SERVINGS

4 unpeeled baking potatoes, washed and cut into wedges
2 tablespoons olive oil
1 teaspoon coarse salt
½ teaspoon black pepper
Large pinch of cayenne pepper

Preheat the oven to 425°. On a large baking sheet, toss the potato wedges with the oil. Sprinkle with the salt, black pepper, and cayenne. Bake for about 25 minutes, or until tender and golden. Serve hot.—SARAH FRITSCHNER

ASIAGO AND SAGE SCALLOPED POTATOES

Wisconsin produces very good versions of Asiago, the hard cheese with a slightly sharper flavor than Parmesan. Chef Sanford D'Amato recommends the Stella brand. An inexpensive

Potato and Mushroom Galette

plastic mandoline, available at many kitchenware stores, is ideal for slicing the potatoes evenly.

8 SERVINGS

- 2 tablespoons unsalted butter
- 2 medium onions, thinly sliced
- 1½ teaspoons finely chopped garlic
- 2 imported bay leaves
- ¼ teaspoon freshly grated nutmeg
- Coarse salt and freshly ground pepper
- 1¼ cups heavy cream
- ½ cup milk
- 1 cup freshly grated Asiago cheese (about 3 ounces), preferably aged
- 1 cup plain dry bread crumbs
- 2 tablespoons extra-virgin olive oil
- 2½ tablespoons finely shredded fresh sage leaves
- 2½ pounds medium Idaho potatoes, peeled and sliced lengthwise ⅛ inch thick

1. Preheat the oven to 400°. Melt the butter in a large heavy saucepan. Add the onions and cook over high heat, stirring, until golden, about 8 minutes. Add the garlic, bay leaves, nutmeg, 1 tablespoon coarse salt, and ¾ teaspoon pepper, and cook for 30 seconds. Add the heavy cream and milk, and bring to a boil. Remove from the heat, cover, and let stand for 5 minutes.

2. In a medium bowl, toss the cheese with the bread crumbs, olive oil, ½ tablespoon of the sage, ¼ teaspoon coarse salt, and ¼ teaspoon pepper.

3. Remove the bay leaves from the onion mixture and stir in the remaining 2 tablespoons sage. Put the sliced potatoes in a large bowl, add the onion mixture, and toss gently. Spread half of the potatoes and liquid in a 2-quart nonreactive baking dish and sprinkle ⅔ cup of the cheese bread crumbs over the top. Cover with the remaining potato slices and press firmly to pack them down. Spoon the remaining liquid over the potatoes and cover with the remaining cheese bread crumbs.

4. Bake in the middle of the oven for about 1 hour, or until the potatoes are tender and the top is golden; if they brown too quickly, loosely cover the dish with foil. (MAKE AHEAD: The scalloped potatoes can be baked up to 5 hours ahead; let stand at room temperature. Rewarm the potatoes in the oven before serving.) —SANFORD D'AMATO

CURRIED POTATOES AND BABY LIMA BEANS

4 SERVINGS

- 3 tablespoons vegetable oil
- 2 teaspoons cumin seeds
- 1 large garlic clove, minced
- 1 fresh serrano or jalapeño chile, minced
- 1 teaspoon ground coriander
- 1 tablespoon curry powder
- 2 teaspoons tomato paste
- 4 Idaho potatoes, peeled and cut into 1-inch cubes
- 2 cups frozen baby lima beans (from a 10-ounce package)
- Salt and freshly ground black pepper

1. Heat the vegetable oil in a nonreactive medium saucepan. Add the cumin seeds and cook over moderately high heat until fragrant and dark, about 1 minute. Add the garlic and fresh chile and cook, stirring, for 1 minute. Add the ground coriander and curry powder and stir until fragrant, about 2 minutes.

2. Add the tomato paste and cook until it sticks to the pan and starts to caramelize, about 2 minutes. Add the cubed potatoes and 1½ cups of water. Stir to blend, scraping the bottom of the pan to loosen any browned bits. Reduce the heat to low, cover, and cook until the potatoes are almost tender, about 8 minutes. Add the frozen baby lima beans, cover, and cook until the potatoes are done, about 5 minutes more. Season with salt and freshly ground black pepper. (MAKE AHEAD: This recipe can be made up to two days ahead and refrigerated, covered.) —MARCIA KIESEL

GIANT POTATO PANCAKE Q

4 SERVINGS

- 2 pounds medium all-purpose potatoes, peeled
- 1 small onion
- 1 teaspoon salt
- ¼ teaspoon freshly ground pepper
- ¼ cup olive oil

1. In a large saucepan, cover the potatoes with water. Cover the saucepan and bring the water to a boil over moderately high heat. Uncover and parboil the potatoes for 5 minutes.
2. Drain the potatoes and rinse with cold water. Coarsely shred the potatoes and the onion in a food processor fitted with a shredding disk or on a box grater. Transfer the potato mixture to a large bowl and toss with the salt and pepper.
3. Heat 2 tablespoons of the olive oil in a 12-inch nonstick skillet. Spread the shredded potatoes evenly in the skillet, patting them down with a spatula. Cook the potato pancake over moderately high heat until deep golden brown on the bottom, about 10 minutes.
4. Hold a cookie sheet or a large upside-down platter directly over the skillet and, using pot holders, carefully invert the pancake onto it. Heat the remaining 2 tablespoons olive oil in the skillet. Slide the pancake back into the skillet, uncooked side down, and cook until the bottom is nicely browned, about 10 minutes more. Slide the potato pancake onto a large cutting board, cut it into 4 even wedges, and serve immediately.—SUSAN SHAPIRO JASLOVE

POTATO AND MUSHROOM GALETTE

This galette is easier than most because you don't have to turn it during cooking. If you prefer a potato cake that's crisp on both sides, invert the galette onto a large plate after you've browned the bottom, then slide the cake back into the pan and continue cooking until browned. Shiitakes, yellow chanterelles, and hen of the woods are good substitutes for the mushrooms below.

6 SERVINGS

- 1 pound assorted fresh wild mushrooms, such as hedgehogs, red and green russulas, and *Lactarius volemus*
- 1½ tablespoons unsalted butter
- 2½ tablespoons canola oil
- Salt
- ½ teaspoon freshly ground pepper
- 2½ pounds all-purpose potatoes
- 1½ tablespoons extra-virgin olive oil

1. Rinse the mushrooms thoroughly in cool water. Lift the mushrooms from the water and drain well. Slice the mushrooms ½ inch thick.
2. In a large nonstick skillet, melt the butter in 1 tablespoon of the canola oil. Add the sliced mushrooms, ½ teaspoon salt, and the freshly ground pepper, and cook over high heat, stirring occasionally, until the exuded liquid has evaporated and the mushrooms begin to brown, about 10 minutes. Transfer the mushrooms to a bowl. Wipe out the skillet.
3. Peel the potatoes and shred them in a food processor or on a box grater. Rinse the strips of potato and pat dry.
4. Heat the olive oil and the remaining 1½ tablespoons canola oil in the skillet. Add the potatoes and ½ teaspoon salt, toss, and sauté over high heat until lightly browned, about 5 minutes. Transfer one-third of the potatoes to a bowl. Press down on the remaining potatoes in the skillet to create a thin, firm "bed." Spoon the mushrooms over the potato bed, then spread the reserved potatoes on top so that they cover most of the mushrooms; press down lightly to compress the galette.
5. Cover and cook the galette over moderate heat, shaking the pan occasionally, until browned on the bottom, about 10 minutes. Remove the pan from the heat and let rest for 5 minutes. Invert the galette onto a round platter, cut it into wedges, and serve.—JACQUES PEPIN

POTATO PANCAKE TIPS

• Choose medium rather than large potatoes for the Giant Potato Pancake to reduce the parboiling time. Cover the pot when bringing the potatoes to a boil. Or use leftover boiled potatoes if you have them on hand to eliminate the parboiling time altogether.
• Using a box grater rather than a food processor to grate the cooked potatoes will keep them from falling apart in the shredding process.—SUSAN SHAPIRO JASLOVE

CRISP PARMESAN POTATOES

Patting the potato slices dry keeps them from sticking to the pan.

4 SERVINGS

2 tablespoons vegetable oil
4 medium Yukon Gold potatoes—scrubbed, sliced ¼ inch thick, and patted dry
Salt and freshly ground pepper
3 tablespoons freshly grated Parmesan cheese

Heat the vegetable oil in a large heavy skillet. Add the potatoes, season with salt and pepper, and cook over moderately high heat, turning occasionally, until golden, 5 to 7 minutes. Reduce the heat to moderately low, cover partially, and cook, stirring occasionally, until the slices are lightly browned and tender, 10 to 12 minutes longer. Sprinkle the Parmesan over the potatoes and toss. Cover and cook until the cheese is melted, about 1 minute. Serve hot.—JUDITH SUTTON

PAN-FRIED DICED POTATOES

4 SERVINGS

1½ pounds waxy boiling potatoes
Vegetable oil
Salt

1. Peel the potatoes and cut them into ½-inch dice. Wash them in two changes of cold water and pat dry.
2. Choose a skillet that can loosely accommodate all the potatoes. Pour in ½ inch of vegetable oil and turn the heat to moderately high. When the oil sizzles if you drop in a piece of potato, add all the diced potatoes and lower the heat to moderate. Cook the potatoes until tender when pierced but still pale, not having yet formed a crust. Remove from the heat. Using a slotted spoon, remove the potatoes to a plate and allow them to cool completely. Leave the oil in the pan. (MAKE AHEAD: The potatoes can be prepared to this point up to 2 hours ahead.)
3. Shortly before serving, set the skillet with the vegetable oil over high heat. When the oil is very hot, return the potatoes to the pan and cook until light brown and crusty on all sides. Transfer the potatoes to a warm platter, sprinkle with salt, and serve at once.—MARCELLA HAZAN

POTATO AND CORN RISOTTO WITH CARROT JUICE

Hans Röckenwagner's vibrantly colored risotto, served at Röckenwagner in Santa Monica, uses sweet carrot juice as the cooking liquid and diced potatoes in place of rice. This risotto is on the soupy side.

4 SERVINGS

2 teaspoons olive oil
4 scallions, cut into 4-inch lengths
2 large russet or other baking potatoes, peeled and cut into ¼-inch dice
1 cup fresh or frozen corn kernels
2 cups fresh carrot juice*
¼ teaspoon cayenne pepper
1 tablespoon fresh lemon juice
2 tablespoons heavy cream
4 tablespoons unsalted butter, cut into small pieces
¼ cup freshly grated Parmesan cheese
1 teaspoon salt
¼ teaspoon freshly ground white pepper
8 sprigs of fresh chervil or flat-leaf parsley

*Available at health food stores, juice bars, and specialty food shops

1. Heat the olive oil in a medium nonstick skillet. Add the scallions and cook over high heat, stirring occasionally, until softened and well browned, about 3 minutes. Transfer to a paper towel-lined plate, cover with foil, and keep warm.
2. In a medium nonreactive saucepan, combine the potatoes, corn kernels, fresh carrot juice, and cayenne pepper. Bring to a boil over moderately high heat and cook, stirring occasionally, until the potatoes are just tender and the liquid is reduced by half, about 15 minutes. Raise the heat to high, add the lemon juice, and bring to a boil. Add the heavy cream and lower the heat to moderate. Stir in the butter, the Parmesan cheese, the salt, and the white pepper.
3. Ladle the potato risotto into warmed shallow bowls or soup plates, garnish with the fried scallions and chervil, and serve at once.—HANS ROCKENWAGNER

SWEET POTATO BAKE

4 SERVINGS

2 pounds orange sweet potatoes or yams
1 teaspoon sugar
½ teaspoon ground allspice

Potato and Corn Risotto with Carrot Juice

¼ teaspoon cayenne pepper, or more to taste
¼ teaspoon salt
½ cup whole milk or unsweetened coconut milk
2 eggs, beaten

1. Preheat the oven to 375°. Roast the sweet potatoes on a baking sheet for 30 to 45 minutes, or until soft. Let cool slightly, then peel.
2. In a bowl, mash the sweet potatoes to a smooth puree with the sugar. Season with the allspice, cayenne, and salt. (MAKE AHEAD: The recipe can be prepared to this point up to 2 days ahead and refrigerated. Bring to room temperature before proceeding.)
3. Preheat the oven to 375°. Stir the milk and eggs into the sweet potatoes, blending well. Scrape the mixture into a 4-cup soufflé dish or 9-inch square glass baking dish and bake until set, about 30 minutes.
4. To serve, dip one soup spoon into the sweet potatoes and use another spoon to shape the mixture into large ovals; gently push the sweet potato ovals onto a plate. Serve 2 sweet potato ovals per person.—MARCIA KIESEL

ASIAN-CARIB PLATE

This vegetable plate reflects the many ethnic groups that coexist in the Caribbean. Chinese, African, Indian, Spanish, and French influences are evident in the ingredients. The Mixed Roasted Peppers and Allspice-Pickled Onions can be warmed together in a skillet and served alongside the plantains.

SWEET POTATO BAKE (P. 280)
ALLSPICE-PICKLED ONIONS (P. 354)
MIXED ROASTED PEPPERS (P. 311)
FRIED PLANTAINS (P. 332)
CHAYOTE SALAD (P. 69)
COCONUT RICE AND PEAS (P. 297)

SWEET POTATO OVEN FRIES

4 SERVINGS

4 medium sweet potatoes, peeled and cut lengthwise into 8 wedges each
2 tablespoons vegetable oil
Salt and freshly ground pepper

Preheat the oven to 375°. On a baking sheet, toss the sweet potato wedges with the vegetable oil. Lay the potato wedges on their side, season with salt and freshly ground pepper, and roast for about 25 minutes, turning once, until the potatoes are tender and lightly browned. (MAKE AHEAD: The roasted sweet potatoes can stand at room temperature for up to 3 hours; recrisp in a 500° oven before serving.) —JESSICA B. HARRIS

SWEET POTATO AND MUSHROOM HASH

12 SERVINGS

½ cup walnuts (about 2 ounces)
3 tablespoons unsalted butter
3 tablespoons olive oil
2 pounds assorted fresh mushrooms, such as chanterelles, cremini, and stemmed shiitakes, sliced ⅓ inch thick
3 medium shallots, finely chopped
2 garlic cloves, finely chopped
1 teaspoon finely chopped fresh thyme
Kosher salt and freshly ground pepper
2 pounds Yukon Gold potatoes, peeled and cut into ½-inch cubes
2 pounds sweet potatoes, peeled and cut into ½-inch cubes
¼ cup peanut oil
1 large red onion, finely chopped
½ teaspoon finely grated orange zest
Pinch of ground nutmeg

1. Preheat the oven to 375°. Spread the walnuts on a baking sheet and toast for about 7 minutes, or until fragrant. Let cool slightly, then coarsely chop the walnuts.
2. Melt 1 tablespoon of the butter in 1 tablespoon of the olive oil in a large skillet. Add one-third of the sliced mushrooms and sauté over high heat until golden and all the exuded liquid has evaporated, about 8 minutes. Transfer to a large plate and repeat the process with the remaining butter, olive oil, and mushrooms.
3. Add the shallots and garlic to the skillet and cook over moderately high heat, stirring occasionally, until the shallots are translucent, 2 to 3 minutes. Stir in the mushrooms and thyme and season with kosher salt and pepper. (MAKE AHEAD: The mushrooms can be refrigerated for up to 1 day; the toasted walnuts can stand at room temperature.)

4. Bring 2 medium saucepans of salted water to a boil. Cook the potatoes and sweet potatoes separately until just tender, about 3 minutes. Drain and transfer all the potatoes to a large bowl.

5. Heat half of the peanut oil in a large nonstick skillet. Add the red onion and cook over moderately high heat, stirring frequently, until softened, about 5 minutes. Add half of the potatoes and cook over high heat, stirring occasionally, until tender and browned, about 10 minutes. Transfer to a very large bowl. Repeat with the remaining peanut oil and potatoes; add them to the bowl. Stir in the orange zest and season with kosher salt, pepper, and nutmeg. Add the mushrooms and walnuts and mix gently. Transfer the hash to a large serving bowl or platter. (MAKE AHEAD: The hash can stand at room temperature for up to 3 hours. Rewarm in the oven before serving.) —PATRICK CLARK

CHAPTER 13

RICE & GRAINS

Lebanese Couscous Risotto with Carrots and Snow Peas

LEBANESE COUSCOUS RISOTTO WITH CARROTS AND SNOW PEAS

Gary Danko's risotto, served at The Dining Room at The Ritz-Carlton in San Francisco, features Lebanese couscous and brightly colored vegetables; it is less creamy than most.

6 SERVINGS

- 1 medium red bell pepper
- ½ cup fresh or frozen baby lima beans
- ½ pound thin asparagus, trimmed and cut into 1-inch lengths
- 2 medium carrots, thinly sliced
- 2 ounces *haricots verts* or thin green beans, trimmed and cut into 1-inch lengths
- 3 ounces snow peas, strings removed
- 1 quart Chicken Stock (p. 289) or canned low-sodium broth
- 2 tablespoons olive oil
- ¼ cup minced red onion
- 1 cup (about ½ pound) Lebanese couscous (see "New Couscous," right)
- ¼ cup dry white wine
- 2 tablespoons unsalted butter
- ¼ cup freshly grated Parmesan cheese plus more for serving
- 2 tablespoons finely chopped fresh flat-leaf parsley

Salt and freshly ground pepper

1. Roast the red bell pepper directly over a gas flame or under a broiler, as close to the heat as possible, turning often, until charred all over. Transfer the roasted bell pepper to a paper bag and let steam for 10 minutes. Scrape off the blackened skin from the pepper and remove the stem, seeds, and ribs. Cut the pepper into ¼-inch dice.

2. Bring a medium saucepan of salted water to a boil. Add the lima beans and blanch over moderately high heat until just tender, about 6 minutes for fresh and 3 minutes for frozen. Using a slotted spoon, transfer to a colander, rinse with cold water, and drain thoroughly; transfer to a bowl. Repeat the process with the asparagus, carrots, *haricots verts*, and snow peas, cooking each until tender, about 3 minutes for the asparagus, carrots, and *haricots verts* and 2 minutes for the snow peas. (MAKE AHEAD: The recipe can be prepared to this point up to 6 hours ahead; cover the vegetables and let stand at room temperature.)

3. Bring the Chicken Stock just to a boil in a medium saucepan; keep warm. Heat the olive oil in a large nonreactive saucepan. Add the red onion and cook over moderate heat, stirring, until translucent, about 4 minutes. Add the couscous and stir to coat. Add the wine and simmer until evaporated, about 2 minutes. Add ½ cup of the warm stock and cook, stirring occasionally, until absorbed, about 4 minutes. Continue adding the stock ½ cup at a time, stirring occasionally until it is absorbed before adding more. The couscous is done when it is tender but still slightly chewy, about 55 minutes total cooking time.

4. Add the blanched vegetables and roasted red pepper to the couscous and stir over moderate heat until warmed through. Remove from the heat, stir in the butter, ¼ cup Parmesan, and the flat-leaf parsley, and season with salt and pepper.

5. Spoon the couscous risotto into warmed shallow bowls or soup plates. Serve at once, passing additional Parmesan at the table.—GARY DANKO

ISRAELI COUSCOUS RISOTTO PRIMAVERA WITH MORELS

From Picholine in New York City, this spring vegetable risotto is made with Israeli couscous and is dotted with luxurious morel mushrooms. One-half pound of fresh morels can be substituted for the reconstituted dried ones; trim them and cut any large mushrooms in half.

🍷 *The spring vegetables in this dish would ordinarily be paired with an equally herbaceous white, but the pungent, meaty morels call for a red—something fresh and lively, such*

NEW COUSCOUS

Two new-to-us kinds of couscous are turning up on restaurant menus across the country. Both are made from the same processed semolina as Moroccan couscous and are toasted and round—the Israeli version is the size of peppercorns; the larger, Lebanese couscous, also sold as *Mograbeyeh* or *Moughrabiye*, is the size of petite peas. (Israeli couscous can be mislabeled as *Mograbeyeh*, so check the size when buying.) Both can be found at Middle Eastern groceries or mail-ordered from Kalustyan in New York City (212-685-3451).

as the 1993 Domaine Brusset Cairanne Côtes du Rhône-Villages, or fruity California Rhône-style blends, like the 1993 Preston Faux or the 1993 Zaca Mesa Z Cuvée.

6 SERVINGS

- 2 ounces dried morels, rinsed
- 2 pounds fresh fava beans, shelled, or 1 cup fresh or frozen green peas
- ½ pound medium asparagus, trimmed
- ¾ pound baby leeks or ramps, trimmed, or thin medium leeks, white and tender green portion only
- 4 tablespoons unsalted butter
- 2 large shallots, minced
- Salt and freshly ground pepper
- 3¾ cups Chicken Stock (p. 289) or canned low-sodium broth
- 2 tablespoons olive oil
- 1 medium onion, finely chopped
- 1 tablespoon finely chopped garlic
- 2 cups (about 10 ounces) Israeli couscous (see "New Couscous," p. 287)
- ½ cup freshly grated Parmesan cheese plus 1½ ounces shaved Parmesan, for garnish
- ¼ cup finely chopped fresh flat-leaf parsley
- 4 fresh chives, coarsely chopped

Israeli Couscous Risotto Primavera with Morels

1. In a medium bowl, cover the dried morels with hot water. Let stand until softened, about 15 minutes. Drain well and rinse the morels to remove any grit.

2. Bring a medium pot of salted water to a boil. Add the fava beans or green peas and blanch over high heat just until tender, about 3 minutes for fava beans or fresh peas and 1 minute for frozen peas. Using a slotted spoon, transfer the fava beans or peas to a colander, rinse, and drain thoroughly. Peel off and discard the fava bean skins and transfer the fava beans or peas to a bowl.

3. Add the asparagus to the boiling water and blanch just until tender, about 4 minutes. Transfer the asparagus to the colander, rinse, and drain well. Cut the asparagus into 1½-inch pieces and add to the fava beans.

4. Add the leeks or ramps to the boiling water and blanch just until tender, about 3 minutes for baby leeks or ramps and 7 minutes for medium leeks. Transfer the leeks or ramps to the colander, rinse, and drain. Cut the baby leeks or ramps into 1-inch pieces; cut the medium leeks into ½-inch slices and add them to the fava beans.

5. Melt 1 tablespoon of the butter in a large saucepan. Add the shallots and cook over moderately high heat, stirring, until translucent, about 2 minutes. Add the morels and cook, stirring, until tender, about 5 minutes. Season with salt and pepper. Add ¼ cup of the stock and boil until evaporated, about 3 minutes. Add to the vegetables in the bowl. (MAKE AHEAD: The recipe can be prepared to this point up to 6 hours ahead; cover and let stand at room temperature.)

6. Heat the olive oil in the large saucepan. Add the onion and a pinch of salt and cook over moderate heat, stirring, until translucent, about 4 minutes. Stir in the garlic and cook for 1 more minute. Add the couscous and 2½ cups of the stock and cook, stirring occasionally, until the stock is absorbed, about 12 minutes. Add the remaining 1 cup stock and cook, stirring, until absorbed, about 5 minutes. Stir the couscous vigorously to release the starch and make the risotto creamier. Season with salt and pepper.

7. Add the blanched vegetables and morels to the couscous and cook over moderate heat, stirring frequently, until heated through, about 1 minute. Stir in the remaining 3 tablespoons butter, the grated Parmesan, and the parsley.

8. Spoon the couscous risotto into warmed shallow bowls or soup plates. Garnish the risotto with the chives and the shaved Parmesan cheese and serve at once.—TERRANCE BRENNAN

BARLEY RISOTTO WITH ROASTED TOMATOES AND NICOISE OLIVES

Heavy cream enhances the texture and flavor of this earthy risotto, popular at The French Laundry in Napa Valley, but it can be omitted for a lighter dish.

8 SERVINGS

- 3 large tomatoes, halved crosswise
- 1 tablespoon olive oil
- 1 small onion, finely chopped
- 2 cups pearl barley (about 14 ounces)
- 2 cups Chicken Stock (recipe follows) or canned low-sodium broth
- 5 cups of boiling water
- 2 teaspoons salt
- 2 tablespoons unsalted butter
- ½ cup freshly grated Parmesan cheese (about 1½ ounces)
- 2 tablespoons heavy cream (optional)
- ¼ cup coarsely chopped pitted Niçoise olives

1. Preheat the oven to 300°. Line a baking sheet with parchment paper. Set the tomatoes, cut sides up, on the baking sheet and roast for about 2 hours, or until leathery but still moist. Let cool, then cut the tomatoes into ½-inch pieces. (MAKE AHEAD: The tomatoes can be prepared up to 1 day ahead; cover and let stand at room temperature.)

2. Heat the olive oil in a medium saucepan. Add the onion and cook over moderate heat, stirring, until softened, about 3 minutes. Add the barley and stir to coat. Pour in the stock, reduce the heat to moderately low, and cook, stirring occasionally, until absorbed, about 7 minutes. Add half the boiling water and cook, stirring frequently, until absorbed. Add the remaining boiling water and the salt and cook, stirring often, until the barley is tender and creamy, about 55 minutes total cooking time; add more boiling water if the risotto is dry. Stir vigorously to release the starch and make the texture creamier. Stir in the butter, Parmesan cheese, heavy cream, and three-quarters each of the tomatoes and olives.

3. Spoon the barley risotto into warmed shallow bowls or soup plates. Garnish with the remaining roasted tomatoes and olives and serve.—THOMAS KELLER

Chicken Stock

MAKES ABOUT 2 QUARTS

- 7 pounds chicken backs and wings
- 2 medium onions, quartered
- 3 celery ribs, halved

1. In a stockpot, combine all the ingredients with 3 quarts of water. Bring to a boil over high heat. Lower the heat, cover partially, and simmer for 2 hours.

2. Strain the stock into a large bowl, pressing down on the solids to extract all the liquid. (MAKE AHEAD: The stock can be refrigerated for up to 3 days or frozen for up to 1 month. Discard the fat before using or freezing.) —F&W TEST KITCHEN

BARLEY RISOTTO WITH LOBSTER AND BASIL

At March in New York City, Wayne Nish has been making risotto based on unusual ingredients for more than three years. He often finishes the dish with a little cream and uses the Japanese herb shiso *in place of the basil.*

🍷 *Look for a round, oak-laced California Chardonnay, such as the 1992 Fisher Coach Insignia or the 1992 Acacia Carneros.*

6 SERVINGS

- Two 1½-pound live lobsters
- ½ cup kosher salt
- 4 quarts of ice water
- 1 tablespoon olive oil
- 1 quart Chicken Stock (left) or canned low-sodium broth
- 1 cup pearl barley (about 7 ounces)
- 2½ cups of boiling water
- Table salt and freshly ground pepper
- 2 large ripe plum tomatoes—peeled, seeded, and coarsely chopped

Barley Risotto with Lobster and Basil

1 tablespoon finely chopped fresh basil plus 2 tablespoons finely shredded basil, for garnish
¼ teaspoon fresh lemon juice

1. In a large pot of boiling salted water, cook the lobsters, covered, over moderate heat for 17 minutes. Meanwhile, in a large bowl, dissolve the kosher salt in the ice water. Transfer the lobsters to the ice water and let cool for 1 minute. Drain and let cool for 1 hour.
2. Working over a bowl to catch the juices, detach the lobster tails from the bodies. Snip through the soft underside of the tail shells and remove the meat. Discard the intestinal vein that runs down the tail. Crack open the claws and remove the meat. Cut the lobster meat into 1-inch pieces and add it to the bowl. Discard the sand sac behind the eyes; the green tomalley and any coral from the bodies can be discarded or reserved for another use. Chop the shells and heads into 2-inch pieces.
3. Heat the olive oil in a large heavy saucepan. Add the lobster shells and heads and cook over high heat, stirring, until fragrant, 1 to 2 minutes. Add 2 cups of the Chicken Stock and 5 cups of water and bring to a boil. Lower the heat to moderate, cover, and cook for 15 minutes. Uncover and boil gently, stirring occasionally, until the lobster stock is reduced to about 1½ cups, about 45 minutes. Strain the stock into a small saucepan and boil over high heat until reduced to ½ cup, about 5 minutes. Stir in the juices from the lobster meat.
4. In a medium nonreactive saucepan, combine the pearl barley with the remaining 2 cups of Chicken Stock. Cook over moderately low heat, stirring occasionally, until the liquid is absorbed, about 10 minutes. Add ½ cup of the boiling water and simmer, stirring occasionally, until absorbed. Continue adding the remaining boiling water, ½ cup at a time, stirring occasionally until it is absorbed before adding more, about 40 minutes total cooking time.
5. Add the reduced lobster stock to the pearl barley and cook over moderate heat, stirring frequently, until the barley is tender and creamy, about 10 minutes longer; add more boiling water if the risotto is dry. Stir vigorously to release the starch and make the risotto creamier, and season with salt and pepper. Stir in the lobster meat, tomatoes, chopped basil, and lemon juice.
6. Spoon the barley risotto into warmed shallow bowls or soup plates, top with the shredded basil, and serve.—WAYNE NISH

ZUCCHINI AND LEMON RISOTTO *LF*

4 SERVINGS

2 cups chicken stock or canned low-sodium broth, skimmed of fat
1 tablespoon plus 1 teaspoon olive oil
2 pounds zucchini, cut into ½-inch chunks
1 large onion, finely chopped
3 large garlic cloves, minced
Salt
2 cups arborio rice (about 14 ounces)
½ cup dry white wine
3 tablespoons finely chopped fresh flat-leaf parsley
1 tablespoon finely grated lemon zest
1 tablespoon fresh lemon juice
Freshly ground pepper

1. In a medium saucepan, combine the chicken stock and 4 cups of water. Bring just to a boil over high heat; lower the heat and keep warm.
2. Heat 2 teaspoons of the olive oil in a large nonstick skillet. Stir in the zucchini, onion, garlic, and ½ teaspoon salt and cook over high heat, stirring frequently, until the vegetables are softened, about 5 minutes. Add 1 cup of the diluted chicken stock, lower the heat, and simmer until the zucchini is very tender, about 8 minutes.
3. Heat the remaining 2 teaspoons olive oil in a nonreactive medium saucepan. Add the arborio rice and cook over moderate heat, stirring, until coated, about 1 minute. Stir in the wine and cook until absorbed. Add the zucchini mixture with its liquid and cook, stirring, until the liquid is absorbed.
4. Add 1 cup of the diluted chicken stock to the rice and cook over moderately high heat, stirring constantly, until absorbed. Continue adding the chicken stock, ½ cup at a time, stirring until it is absorbed before adding more. Cook until the rice is tender but still firm, about 18 minutes. Stir in the chopped flat-leaf parsley, the lemon zest, and the lemon juice; season with salt and freshly ground pepper and serve at once.—JEAN GALTON

Caramelized Onion Risotto with Corn and Bacon

CARAMELIZED ONION RISOTTO WITH CORN AND BACON

🍷 *An Oregon Pinot Noir, such as the 1992 Yamhill or the 1993 Knudsen-Erath, is the ideal light red to pair with this dish—there's enough ripe fruit flavor to chime in with the sweet onions and corn and enough depth to stand up to the bacon and Parmesan.*

6 TO 8 SERVINGS

- 3 medium ears of corn, preferably Silver Queen, silk discarded, husks left on (see Note)
- 7 tablespoons unsalted butter
- 3 large sweet onions, such as Vidalia, thinly sliced
- 4 ounces slab bacon, cut into 2-by-¼-inch strips
- About 8 cups chicken stock or canned low-sodium broth
- 1 medium onion, coarsely chopped
- 1 small carrot, coarsely chopped
- 1 small celery rib, coarsely chopped
- 2 cups arborio rice
- 1 cup dry white wine
- ¼ cup freshly grated Parmesan cheese (about ¾ ounce)
- Salt and freshly ground pepper
- Fresh chervil sprigs, for garnish

1. Light a grill or preheat the oven to 350°. Grill or roast the corn in the middle of the oven for about 15 minutes, turning occasionally, until the kernels are tender. Let cool slightly, then remove the husks and cut the kernels off the cob into a bowl; reserve the cobs.

2. Melt 3 tablespoons of the unsalted butter in a large nonreactive saucepan. Add the sliced onions and cook over high heat,

CHEF'S MENU

CARAMELIZED ONION RISOTTO WITH CORN AND BACON (P. 291)

BARBECUED SQUAB WITH BALSAMIC SAUCE AND BROCCOLI RABE

SWEET POTATO GNOCCHI

BLACKBERRY-POLENTA BREAD PUDDING (P. 431)

or

SPICY PECAN ICE CREAM (P. 460)

—**SCOTT HOWELL**

stirring frequently, until caramelized, about 25 minutes. Add to the corn kernels. Add the bacon to the saucepan and cook over high heat, stirring, until browned and crisp, about 3 minutes. Transfer to paper towels to drain. Pour off all but 2 tablespoons of the fat.

3. In another large saucepan, bring the chicken stock and corn cobs just to a boil; keep warm. Meanwhile, heat the bacon fat. In a food processor, finely chop the onion, carrot, and celery. Add to the bacon fat and cook over moderately high heat, stirring, until softened, about 3 minutes. Add the rice and stir until evenly coated with fat. Add the white wine and stir constantly until almost all the liquid has been absorbed, about 2 minutes. Stir in the corn, sliced onions, and bacon.

4. Add 1 cup of the chicken stock to the rice and cook over moderate heat, stirring constantly, until absorbed. Continue adding stock, about ½ cup at a time, stirring constantly until absorbed before adding more. Cook until the rice is just tender, about 25 minutes. Stir in the remaining 4 tablespoons butter and the Parmesan cheese and season with salt and pepper. If the risotto is too sticky, add a little more chicken stock. Serve, garnished with chervil sprigs.

NOTE: To prepare corn for grilling, pull back the husks and remove the silk. Pull the husks back up over the corn and soak briefly.—SCOTT HOWELL

TOMATO RISOTTO *LF*

A combination of red and yellow tomatoes makes this dish especially pretty.

6 SERVINGS

- 1 large sweet onion, coarsely chopped
- 1 tablespoon olive oil
- 3 cups tomato juice
- 2½ cups defatted chicken stock or canned low-sodium broth
- 2 medium shallots, minced
- 1½ cups arborio rice
- 1 cup dry white wine
- 1 pound assorted cherry and pear tomatoes, halved or quartered if large
- Salt and freshly ground pepper
- ⅓ cup finely shredded fresh basil
- 2 tablespoons freshly grated Pecorino Romano cheese

1. Preheat the oven to 375°. On a baking sheet, toss the onion with 1 teaspoon of the olive oil; spread out on the sheet. Roast for about 20 minutes, stirring, until lightly browned.

2. In a medium nonreactive saucepan, bring the tomato juice and chicken stock to a boil over moderately high heat; keep warm. Heat the remaining 2 teaspoons olive oil in a large nonreactive saucepan. Add the shallots and cook over moderate heat, stirring, until translucent, about 2 minutes. Add the rice and cook, stirring, for 1 minute. Add the wine and cook, stirring, until almost completely absorbed, about 7 minutes.

3. Add 1 cup of the hot tomato broth to the rice and simmer over moderate heat, stirring constantly, until almost all of the broth is absorbed. Add 1 more cup of broth and stir constantly until absorbed. (MAKE AHEAD: See below.) Continue adding broth to the risotto, 1 cup at a time, stirring constantly until absorbed before adding more. The rice is done when it's al dente and lightly bound with creamy cooking liquid, about 25 minutes total cooking time. Stir in the tomatoes and roasted onion until heated through. Season the risotto with salt and pepper,

MAKE-AHEAD RISOTTO

Here's a chef's tip for making risotto in advance. Stir the first 2 cups of liquid into the rice as directed. Spread the risotto out on a baking sheet and let cool, then refrigerate for up to 1 day; refrigerate the remaining broth separately. Before proceeding, reheat the liquid. Return the risotto to the saucepan, set the pan over the heat, and continue with the recipe.—MATTHEW KENNEY

garnish with the basil and Pecorino Romano cheese, and serve at once.—MATTHEW KENNEY

SAFFRON AND SHRIMP RISOTTO

6 SERVINGS

- ½ teaspoon saffron threads
- ¼ cup dry white wine
- 1 pound medium shrimp, shelled and deveined, shells reserved
- 2 tablespoons unsalted butter
- 1 small onion, finely chopped
- 1½ cups arborio rice
- 2 ripe plum tomatoes, cut into ½-inch dice

Salt and freshly ground pepper

1. In a small nonreactive saucepan, warm the saffron and wine over moderate heat for 1 minute. In a medium saucepan, boil the shrimp shells with 6½ cups of water over high heat for 5 minutes. Strain the stock into a medium saucepan; keep hot over moderately low heat. In a large nonreactive saucepan, melt 1½ tablespoons of the butter over high heat. Add the shrimp and cook, stirring, until just opaque, about 3 minutes; transfer to a plate. Add the remaining ½ tablespoon butter and the onion to the pan and cook over moderately high heat until the onion is translucent, about 2 minutes. Stir in the rice. Add the saffron liquid and boil it until almost completely evaporated.
2. Add 1 cup of the hot shrimp stock or just enough to form a thin veil over the rice. Gently boil the rice, stirring, until the liquid is absorbed. Repeat this procedure, adding the hot stock 1 cup at a time, until it is all used and the rice is tender but firm. Add the shrimp and cook just to warm through. Fold in the plum tomatoes and season the risotto with salt and freshly ground black pepper. Serve the risotto at once.—MARCIA KIESEL

SHRIMP AND FENNEL RISOTTO LF

A simple white—a Chilean Chardonnay, for example—would provide a refreshing backdrop to the savory, aromatic flavors in this shrimp dish. Consider the 1993 Caliterra or the 1992 Los Vascos.

4 SERVINGS

- 2 medium fennel bulbs
- ½ pound medium shrimp—shelled, deveined, and halved lengthwise, shells reserved
- 2 small onions—1 coarsely chopped and 1 finely chopped
- 1 medium carrot, thinly sliced
- 1 tablespoon fennel seeds
- 1 bay leaf

Salt

- ¼ teaspoon saffron threads
- ½ cup dry white wine
- 1 tablespoon olive oil
- 3 medium plum tomatoes, seeded and finely diced
- 2 large garlic cloves, minced
- 2 cups arborio rice (about 14 ounces)
- 2 tablespoons finely chopped fresh flat-leaf parsley

Freshly ground pepper

1. Trim the fennel bulbs, reserving the stems and the fronds. Coarsely chop the fennel stems and fronds; set aside 1 tablespoon of the chopped fennel fronds for garnish. Halve the

Shrimp and Fennel Risotto

fennel bulbs lengthwise and cut out the cores. Cut the fennel bulbs into ⅓-inch dice.
2. In a large saucepan, combine the chopped fennel stems and fronds, the shrimp shells, the coarsely chopped onion, the carrot, fennel seeds, bay leaf, and 1½ teaspoons salt. Cover with 9 cups of water and bring to a boil over high heat. Lower the heat and simmer for 30 minutes. Strain the fennel stock and return it to the saucepan. You should have about 7 cups of fennel stock; add water if necessary. Keep warm over low heat.
3. Meanwhile, crumble the saffron into the wine in a small bowl. Heat the olive oil in a medium nonreactive saucepan. Add the diced fennel bulbs, the finely chopped onion, and ½ teaspoon salt and cook over moderately high heat, stirring occasionally, until the vegetables are lightly

Savoy Cabbage and Lentil Risotto

browned and the fennel is softened, about 8 minutes. Stir in the plum tomatoes and minced garlic and cook for 1 minute. Add the arborio rice and cook, stirring, until coated, about 1 minute. Pour in the saffron-wine mixture and stir until absorbed.

4. Add 1 cup of the fennel stock to the rice and cook over moderately high heat, stirring constantly, until it is absorbed. Continue adding stock, about ½ cup at a time, stirring constantly until the stock is absorbed before adding more. Cook until the rice is just tender, about 18 minutes. Add the shrimp and parsley and continue stirring just until the shrimp are cooked through and the rice is tender but still firm, about 2 minutes longer. Season with salt and pepper, sprinkle with the reserved fennel fronds, and serve at once.—JEAN GALTON

SAVOY CABBAGE AND LENTIL RISOTTO *LF*

4 SERVINGS

- 2 cups chicken stock or canned low-sodium broth, skimmed of fat
- ⅓ cup brown or green lentils (about 2 ounces), rinsed and picked over
- 1 teaspoon olive oil
- 1 medium carrot, finely chopped
- 1 small onion, finely chopped
- 2 ounces pancetta, trimmed of fat and coarsely chopped
- Salt
- 2 large garlic cloves, minced
- 1 pound Savoy cabbage, finely shredded
- 1½ cups arborio rice (about 10½ ounces)
- 3 tablespoons freshly grated Parmesan cheese
- Freshly ground pepper

1. In a large measuring cup, combine the chicken stock with 5 cups of water. In a small saucepan, combine the lentils with 1 cup of the diluted chicken stock. Bring the lentils to a boil over high heat, then lower the heat, cover, and simmer for 20 minutes longer.

2. In a medium saucepan, bring the remaining diluted stock just to a boil over high heat. Lower the heat and keep warm.

3. In a large heavy saucepan, combine the olive oil, carrot, onion, pancetta, and ¾ teaspoon salt. Cook over moderately high heat, stirring occasionally, until the vegetables are softened, about 3 minutes. Stir in the garlic and cook for 1 minute. Add three-quarters of the cabbage and cook over low heat, stirring occasionally, until wilted, about 5 minutes. Add the rice and cook, stirring, until coated, about 1 minute. Stir in the lentils and any cooking liquid.

4. Add 1 cup of the diluted chicken stock to the rice and cook over moderately high heat, stirring constantly, until absorbed. Continue adding the chicken stock, about ½ cup at a time, stirring until it is absorbed before adding more. Cook until the rice is just tender, about 15 minutes. Stir in the remaining cabbage and continue cooking until the rice is tender but still firm, about 2 minutes longer. Stir in the Parmesan cheese, season with salt and pepper, and serve the risotto at once.—JEAN GALTON

PUMPKIN RISOTTO

6 SERVINGS

- 2 tablespoons olive oil
- ½ pound fresh pumpkin or butternut squash, peeled and cut into ¾-inch dice (1⅓ cups)
- 2 medium white onions, finely diced
- ¾ cup dry Riesling
- 1½ teaspoons freshly grated nutmeg
- About 1 teaspoon freshly ground white pepper
- 1 teaspoon salt
- 7 cups Vegetable Stock for Risotto (recipe follows) or canned low-sodium chicken broth
- 5 tablespoons unsalted butter
- 1½ cups arborio rice (about 11 ounces)
- 3 tablespoons finely chopped fresh flat-leaf parsley (optional)
- ½ cup freshly grated Parmesan cheese, plus more for serving

1. Heat the olive oil in a nonreactive medium saucepan. Add the diced pumpkin and half of the onions and cook over moderately high heat, stirring frequently, until the pumpkin is just tender, about 7 minutes. Stir in the wine, nutmeg, white pepper, and salt, and cook, stirring occasionally, until most of the liquid has evaporated, about 12 minutes. Remove the saucepan from the heat and let the mixture cool slightly.

2. In a food processor, puree the pumpkin mixture until smooth. Transfer to a small bowl.

3. In a medium saucepan, bring the Vegetable Stock for Risotto to a boil over moderate heat. Reduce the heat to low and keep the stock hot.

4. In a nonreactive medium saucepan, heat 2½ tablespoons of the butter until it begins to sizzle. Add the arborio rice and the remaining onions and cook over moderately high heat, stirring with a wooden spoon, until the onions are translucent, about 7 minutes. Immediately stir in 1 cup of the hot Vegetable Stock and cook, stirring constantly, until all of the liquid has been absorbed, about 2 minutes.

5. Reduce the heat to moderate and gradually add 3 more cups of the hot Vegetable Stock, 1 cup at a time, stirring and cooking until each cup is almost absorbed before adding the next, about 15 minutes. Stir in the pumpkin puree. Continue adding the remaining 3 cups of Vegetable Stock, 1 cup at a time, stirring and cooking as above, until the rice is tender, about 10 minutes longer. The risotto will be quite loose. Stir in the parsley and the remaining 2½ tablespoons butter.

6. Spoon the risotto into 6 warmed soup plates and sprinkle the Parmesan on top. Serve the risotto immediately.

Vegetable Stock for Risotto

MAKES 7 CUPS

- 4 medium carrots, coarsely chopped
- 4 medium onions, quartered
- 6 medium celery ribs, coarsely chopped
- 2 medium shallots, quartered
- 1 small white turnip, peeled and coarsely chopped
- 2 fresh thyme sprigs or ½ teaspoon dried thyme
- 1 bay leaf
- 1 garlic clove, smashed

In a large nonreactive saucepan, combine all of the ingredients

LOW-FAT RISOTTO TIP

For a standard risotto, the rice is sautéed in a generous amount of fat to seal the grains and keep them separate. If you want to adapt a risotto recipe to make it low fat, cook the grains of rice in a small amount of fat. They won't be as well sealed and therefore will absorb a larger amount of stock, so be sure to increase the amount of stock used by at least one cup.—JEAN GALTON

Pumpkin Risotto

with 11 cups of water and bring to a boil over high heat. Reduce the heat to moderately low and simmer for 50 minutes. Remove from the heat and strain the stock into a clean saucepan. (MAKE AHEAD: The stock can be made up to 3 days ahead; cover and refrigerate. Or freeze for up to 1 week.)—CHARLIE PALMER

RISOTTO CAKES WITH WILD MUSHROOMS AND SALSIFY

Salsify, a root vegetable, discolors quickly, so be sure to add it to water mixed with lemon juice as soon as it is peeled.

6 SERVINGS

- 9 cups Vegetable Stock (recipe follows)
- About 7½ tablespoons unsalted butter
- 1 small onion, finely chopped
- 2 cups arborio rice (about 14 ounces)
- ¼ cup dry white wine
- ½ cup freshly grated Parmesan cheese (about 1½ ounces)
- 1 tablespoon fresh lemon juice
- 1 pound medium salsify
- 4 garlic cloves—2 crushed and 2 minced
- 2 fresh thyme sprigs plus additional sprigs, for garnish
- 1 fresh marjoram sprig
- 1½ pounds assorted fresh wild mushrooms, such as shiitakes, cremini, and cèpes, stemmed and sliced ¼ inch thick
- 2 medium tomatoes—peeled, seeded, and coarsely chopped
- About 1½ tablespoons olive oil

1. In a medium saucepan, bring 5½ cups of the stock to a boil; keep warm over low heat.

2. Melt 3 tablespoons of the butter in a large nonreactive saucepan. Add the onion and cook over moderate heat, stirring, until softened, about 3 minutes. Add the rice and stir until coated, about 1 minute. Add ½ cup of the hot Vegetable Stock and cook, stirring constantly, until the stock has been absorbed by the rice. Continue adding hot stock, about ½ cup at a time, stirring constantly until it is absorbed before adding more. The rice is done when it is just cooked through and creamy, about 35 minutes total cooking time. Add the wine and cook, stirring constantly, for 2 more minutes. Stir in the cheese and spread the risotto in a medium baking dish. Cover and refrigerate until firm, at least 4 hours or overnight.

3. Stir the lemon juice into a medium bowl of water. Scrub the salsify and trim the ends. Peel the salsify, cut it into 3-inch lengths, and immediately drop it into the bowl of acidulated water. Drain the salsify and transfer it to a medium saucepan. Add the remaining 3½ cups Vegetable Stock, the crushed garlic, and the thyme and marjoram sprigs. Bring to a simmer over moderate heat and cook until the salsify is tender, about 15 minutes. Drain the salsify and pat dry; reserve the stock for later use.

4. Melt 2 more tablespoons of the butter in a large nonstick skillet. Add the minced garlic and cook over moderate heat, stirring, until fragrant, about 1 minute. Add the mushrooms and sauté over moderately high heat until tender and lightly browned, about 8 minutes. Add the tomatoes and cook, stirring, for 1 more minute; keep warm.

5. Meanwhile, in another skillet, heat 1 more tablespoon of the butter. Add the salsify pieces and cook over moderately high heat, stirring occasionally, until lightly browned, about 2 minutes; keep warm.

6. Using your hands, shape the chilled risotto into twelve ½-inch-thick disks. In a large nonstick skillet, melt ½ tablespoon of the butter in ½ tablespoon of the oil. Working in batches, cook the risotto cakes over moderately high heat, turning once, until golden brown, about 2 minutes per side. Transfer to a baking sheet and keep warm in a low oven. Wipe out the skillet and repeat with the remaining butter, oil, and risotto cakes.

7. Arrange 2 risotto cakes on each of 6 large plates, and spoon the sautéed mushrooms and salsify alongside. Garnish with thyme sprigs and serve immediately.

Vegetable Stock

MAKES ABOUT 9 CUPS

- 1 tablespoon olive oil
- ½ pound mushrooms, coarsely chopped
- 2 large celery ribs, coarsely chopped
- 1 large onion, coarsely chopped
- 1 medium leek, coarsely chopped
- 1 medium tomato, coarsely chopped
- 2 large garlic cloves, coarsely chopped
- 2 fresh thyme sprigs

2 fresh parsley sprigs
1 bay leaf
6 whole black peppercorns
1 teaspoon salt

Heat the olive oil in a stockpot. Add the mushrooms, celery, onion, leek, tomato, and garlic, and cook over high heat, stirring frequently, until the vegetables begin to wilt, about 5 minutes. Add the thyme, parsley, bay leaf, peppercorns, salt, and 3 quarts of water and bring to a boil. Lower the heat and simmer for 1¼ hours. Strain the stock. (MAKE AHEAD: The stock can be frozen for 1 month or refrigerated for up to 3 days.)—TOM COLICCHIO

COCONUT RICE AND PEAS

4 SERVINGS

2 teaspoons vegetable oil
1 small onion, finely chopped
2 teaspoons minced fresh ginger
½ teaspoon salt
1 cup long-grain rice, rinsed
1 cup cooked red, pinto, or black beans
1 15-ounce can unsweetened coconut milk

1. Preheat the oven to 375°. Heat the vegetable oil in a 9-by-5-inch flameproof baking dish. Add the chopped onion and cook over moderate heat, stirring, until the onion is softened, about 2 minutes. Add the minced ginger and cook for 1 minute longer. Add the salt and the long-grain rice and mix well. Stir in the beans and the unsweetened coconut milk and bring to a simmer.
2. Remove from the heat and cover with foil. Bake the rice in the oven for 15 minutes. Let stand, covered, for 5 minutes before removing the foil. Serve hot.—MARCIA KIESEL

WHITE AND WILD RICE PILAF

8 SERVINGS

1 tablespoon olive oil
½ cup wild rice (about 3 ounces), well rinsed
3 medium garlic cloves, minced
1 large shallot, minced
Salt and freshly ground pepper
3¾ cups chicken stock or canned low-sodium broth
1½ cups long-grain white rice (10½ ounces)
2 tablespoons finely chopped fresh flat-leaf parsley

1. In a small, heavy, nonreactive saucepan, heat the oil. Add the wild rice, garlic, and shallot, and cook over moderate heat until the shallot is slightly softened, about 2 minutes. Season with ½ teaspoon salt and ¼ teaspoon pepper. Stir in 1 cup of the chicken stock and bring to a boil over moderately high heat. Reduce the heat to low, cover tightly, and cook until the rice has burst open and all the chicken stock is absorbed, about 1 hour. If any liquid remains, increase the heat and boil it away. (Sometimes wild rice takes longer to cook through and open; if all of the chicken stock has been absorbed before this happens, add a few tablespoons of water, cover, and cook over low heat for another 10 minutes or so.)
2. Meanwhile, in a heavy medium saucepan, place the remaining 2¾ cups chicken stock and season with salt to taste. Add the white rice and bring to a boil over moderately high heat. Reduce the heat to low, cover tightly, and cook for 20 minutes. Remove from the heat and let sit, covered, for 15 to 20 minutes. Then fluff the rice with a fork and transfer to a large warmed serving bowl.
3. Using a large metal spoon, fold the wild rice and parsley into the white rice and season with additional salt and pepper. Serve warm.—JOAN AND DICK ERATH

MUNG BEANS AND RICE WITH SPICY GREENS AND YOGURT

This meatless main dish is a variation of kedgeree, *the nourishing Indian lentil-and-rice porridge. Leftovers are delicious browned in a skillet until a crust forms. In summer, tomatoes make an ideal garnish, but in winter use cooked spinach or mustard greens and add lime juice to give the greens a lively edge.*

🍷 *Asian spices lend heat to this dish, and the yogurt adds tartness. Choose a simple white that will stand up to all the spice and bite, such as the 1992 Alsace Sylvaner from Domaine Weinbach or Hugel.*

SERVES 4 TO 6

MUNG BEANS AND RICE:

¾ cup dried green mung beans, picked over and rinsed well
¼ cup finely chopped fresh coriander (cilantro)
3 medium garlic cloves
1 tablespoon minced fresh ginger
1 teaspoon garam masala*
½ teaspoon turmeric
¼ teaspoon cayenne pepper

- 2 tablespoons ghee (see Note), melted unsalted butter, or vegetable oil
- 1 medium onion, finely diced
- 2 jalapeño chiles—seeded, deribbed, and finely diced
- 2 tablespoons chopped fresh dill or 1 teaspoon dill seeds
- ½ teaspoon cumin seeds
- 1½ teaspoons salt
- 1 cup basmati rice, rinsed

YOGURT AND SPICY GREENS:

- 2 cups plain yogurt
- 3 large bunches of spinach or 2 bunches of mustard greens (about 3 pounds), thoroughly rinsed
- 1½ tablespoons unsalted butter
- 1 jalapeño chile, finely diced
- ½ teaspoon cumin seeds
- ½ teaspoon dill seeds
- Salt
- Juice of 2 limes
- Chopped fresh coriander (cilantro) or dill, for garnish

*Available at Indian markets

1. Make the mung beans and rice: In a large bowl, cover the mung beans with water and let soak for at least 6 hours or overnight. (Alternatively, in a large saucepan, cover the beans with water and boil over moderately high heat for 2 minutes. Remove from the heat, cover, and let soak for 1 hour.) Drain off the soaking liquid and rinse the mung beans.

2. Using a mortar and pestle, pound the fresh coriander with the garlic, ginger, garam masala, turmeric, and cayenne to make a rough paste. Stir in 1 tablespoon of water to thin it.

Mung Beans and Rice with Spicy Greens and Yogurt

3. Heat the ghee in a large saucepan. Add the onion, jalapeño chiles, dill, and cumin seeds, and cook over moderate heat, stirring frequently, until the onion starts to brown, 8 to 10 minutes. Add the spice paste and cook for 3 minutes longer. Stir in the mung beans, salt, and 3½ cups of water and bring to a boil. Reduce the heat to moderately low, cover, and simmer for 15 minutes. Add the basmati rice, cover, and cook until the water is absorbed and the mung beans are tender but not mushy, about 18 minutes. Remove from the heat and let stand, covered, for 10 minutes.

4. Meanwhile, **make the yogurt and spicy greens:** Put the yogurt in a fine stainless steel sieve set over a bowl and let stand for 20 minutes to let the whey drain. Discard the whey and transfer the yogurt to a bowl.

5. Trim off the spinach or mustard stems and coarsely chop the leaves. Melt the butter in a large nonreactive skillet. Add the jalapeño, cumin seeds, and dill seeds, and cook over moderate heat, stirring briskly, until the cumin seeds start to brown, 1 to 2 minutes. Stir in the spinach, season with salt, and cook until tender, stirring frequently so that the spices don't burn, about 2 minutes for spinach and 5 minutes for mustard greens. Stir in the lime juice.

6. To serve, spoon the mung beans and rice onto plates and top with the spicy cooked greens and a sprinkling of fresh coriander. Generously dollop each serving with the yogurt and serve at once, passing the remaining yogurt separately.

NOTE: Ghee, a type of clarified butter with a wonderful nutty taste, is available at Indian markets. It is also easy to make yourself: in a small saucepan, melt 1 pound of unsalted butter over low heat and simmer, skimming off the froth, until the milky solids fall to the bottom of the pan and brown slightly. Strain the clear butter through cheesecloth into a jar. (MAKE AHEAD: Clarified butter can be refrigerated for up to 2 months.) —DEBORAH MADISON

ROASTED VEGETABLE PAELLA

Serve this rice and vegetable combination as a vegetarian main course or as a side dish.

8 TO 10 SERVINGS

2 tablespoons vegetable oil
1 large Spanish onion, ¼ finely diced and ¾ cut into 1-inch pieces
2 cups long-grain white rice, such as Carolina
4 cups Vegetable Stock (recipe follows), chicken stock, or water
1 large pinch of saffron
1 medium carrot, sliced crosswise ½ inch thick
2 medium celery ribs, sliced crosswise ½ inch thick
8 plum tomatoes, quartered
1 medium red bell pepper, cut into 1-inch pieces
1 medium green bell pepper, cut into 1-inch pieces
1 small eggplant, cut into 1-inch chunks
1 medium zucchini, cut into 1-inch chunks
10 garlic cloves, finely chopped
3 tablespoons olive oil
Salt and freshly ground black pepper
1 cup fresh or frozen green peas

1. Preheat the oven to 425°. Heat the vegetable oil in a large saucepan. Add the diced onion and cook over moderately high heat, stirring, until translucent, about 4 minutes. Stir in the rice. Add the Vegetable Stock and saffron. Cover and bring to a boil over high heat, then reduce the heat to low and cook until the liquid evaporates, about 20 minutes. Remove from the heat; keep covered.

2. While the rice is cooking, in a medium saucepan, steam the carrot and celery over simmering water until slightly tender, about 5 minutes.

3. In a large bowl, toss together the carrot, celery, tomatoes, bell peppers, eggplant, zucchini, garlic, olive oil, and the remaining onion. Season with salt and black pepper. Spread the vegetables out on a baking sheet and roast in the oven for about 25 minutes, until brown on the edges. Lower the oven temperature to 400°.

4. In a small saucepan, steam the peas over simmering water until just tender but still firm, about 4 minutes.

5. Toss the roasted vegetables with the cooked rice and place in a casserole. Gently stir in the peas. Cover with foil and bake in the oven for 15 minutes, or until heated through. (MAKE AHEAD: The paella can be made 1 day ahead. In that case, do not bake the paella. Instead, let cool, then cover and refrigerate. To reheat, bring to room temperature and preheat the oven to 400°. Bake, uncovered, for 5 minutes. Stir gently, then drizzle ¼ cup hot water on top and stir in gently. Cover with foil and bake until heated through, about 15 minutes.) —NEUMAN & BOGDONOFF

Vegetable Stock

This flavorful meatless stock can be prepared up to five days in advance and kept in the refrigerator.

MAKES 7 CUPS

1 pound green or Chinese cabbage, cored and cut into large pieces
2 large carrots, coarsely chopped
2 large celery ribs, coarsely chopped
1 large onion, cut into 8 wedges
10 garlic cloves
1 bunch of flat-leaf parsley
4 fresh thyme sprigs or 1 teaspoon dried thyme

1. In a stockpot, combine all the ingredients. Cover with 16 cups of cold water. Bring to a boil over high heat, then lower the heat and simmer, uncovered, for 1½ hours.

2. Strain the stock through a fine-mesh sieve, pressing lightly on the vegetables with the back of a spoon to extract any excess liquid. Discard the solids and set the stock aside to cool at room temperature. —F&W TEST KITCHEN

WILD MUSHROOM POLENTA WITH GRILLED VEGETABLES

🍷 *A full-bodied California Chardonnay, such as the 1992 Simi or the 1993*

Beringer, would tie together the flavors of the grilled vegetables and the rich, earthy polenta.

4 SERVINGS

GRILLED VEGETABLES:

1 large fennel bulb—trimmed, halved, and sliced lengthwise ¼ inch thick
2 small eggplants, sliced lengthwise ¼ inch thick
2 small zucchini, sliced diagonally ¼ inch thick
2 small yellow squash, sliced diagonally ¼ inch thick
1 small red onion, sliced crosswise ½ inch thick
¼ cup olive oil
Salt and freshly ground pepper

TOMATO SAUCE:

2 tablespoons olive oil
1 medium onion, finely chopped
1 large garlic clove, smashed
½ cup dry white wine
1½ pounds ripe medium tomatoes, coarsely chopped
Salt and freshly ground pepper
¼ cup shredded fresh basil

POLENTA:

½ cup dried porcini mushrooms (about ½ ounce)
1 cup yellow cornmeal
4 ounces Fontina cheese, cut into ½-inch cubes
Salt

1. Prepare the grilled vegetables: Light a grill or preheat the oven to 450°. In a large bowl, toss the fennel, eggplants, zucchini, squash, and red onion with the olive oil and season with salt and pepper. If grilling, grill the vegetables in batches, allowing about 3 minutes per side for the fennel and onion and 1½ minutes per side for the eggplants, zucchini, and squash. If roasting, spread the vegetables in a large, lightly oiled roasting pan and roast for about 20 minutes, tossing occasionally, until lightly browned and tender. If necessary, roast the fennel and onion for a little longer.

2. Make the tomato sauce: Heat the olive oil in a medium nonreactive skillet. Add the onion and garlic and cook over moderately high heat, stirring, until softened, about 5 minutes. Add the white wine and tomatoes, crushing them against the sides of the pan, and season with salt and pepper. Cover and cook until the tomatoes are softened, about 10 minutes. Pass the sauce through a strainer, pressing down on the solids. (MAKE AHEAD: The recipe can be prepared to this point up to 2 days ahead; cover and refrigerate the vegetables and sauce separately. Rewarm both before serving.)

3. Make the polenta: In a small bowl, cover the porcini with ½ cup of very hot water. Let soak until softened, about 20 minutes. Drain the porcini, reserving the soaking liquid. Finely chop the mushrooms.

4. Meanwhile, bring 4½ cups of water to a boil in a large saucepan. Gradually whisk in the cornmeal over high heat. Lower the heat to moderately high and cook, stirring frequently, until the polenta is thick and creamy, about 25 minutes. Pour in the mushroom liquid, stopping when you reach the grit at the bottom. Stir in the chopped porcini and Fontina just until combined. Season with salt.

5. Spoon the polenta into individual bowls. Stir half of the shredded fresh basil into the tomato sauce and spoon over the polenta. Top with the grilled vegetables, garnish with the remaining basil, and serve.—GRACE PARISI

LAYERED POLENTA WITH TOMATO AND MOZZARELLA

In Italian this dish is called maritata, *which means married and signifies that the components are well suited to each other.*

🍷 *Tomato and cheese dominate here, which points to a tart, dry red as an attractive match. An Italian red, such as the 1988 Prunotto Barbaresco or the 1990 Chianti Classico Riserva, would showcase the flavors of the dish nicely.*

8 SERVINGS

POLENTA:

1 tablespoon salt
2 cups polenta or coarse cornmeal

TOMATO SAUCE:

3 tablespoons extra-virgin olive oil
4 large garlic cloves, peeled and lightly crushed
5 pounds ripe plum tomatoes, coarsely chopped, or two 28-ounce cans Italian peeled tomatoes, drained and chopped
Salt and freshly ground pepper

10 ounces mozzarella, shredded
3 tablespoons coarsely chopped fresh basil

1. Lightly oil 2 baking sheets or a large work surface.

2. Make the polenta: In a large heavy saucepan, combine 7 cups of water with the salt and bring to a boil. Very gradually sprinkle in the cornmeal, stirring in one direction to prevent lumps. Cook over moderate heat, stirring constantly, until the mixture is thick, creamy, and pulls away from the sides of the pan, about 25 minutes. If the polenta is quite thick but not pulling away easily from the pan, add a little more hot water and continue to stir and cook.

3. Scrape the hot polenta directly onto the prepared work surface. Using a large spreading spatula or rubber spatula dipped in water, spread the polenta to an even thickness of about ½ inch. Let set until firm, about 30 minutes.

4. Meanwhile, **make the tomato sauce:** In a large nonreactive saucepan, warm the extra-virgin olive oil over moderate heat. Add the garlic and stir until golden, about 2 minutes. Stir in the tomatoes. Bring to a simmer and cook for 25 minutes. Remove from the heat and let cool slightly, then pass the sauce through a food mill. Season with salt and pepper.

5. Lightly oil a 9-by-13-inch nonreactive baking dish. Cut the cooled polenta into 3-inch squares. Cover the bottom of the prepared dish with half of the polenta squares. Ladle half of the tomato sauce on top, then

Wild Mushroom Polenta with Grilled Vegetables

sprinkle with half of the cheese and basil. Cover with the remaining polenta squares. Spoon the remaining sauce on top and sprinkle with the remaining cheese and basil. (MAKE AHEAD: The casserole can be made to this point up to 1 day ahead; cover and refrigerate. Let sit at room temperature for at least 1 hour before baking.)

6. Preheat the oven to 400°. Bake the polenta casserole in the middle of the oven for about 40 minutes, or until the cheese is melted and the sauce is bubbling. Let sit for 15 minutes before cutting the casserole into squares. Serve hot.—JULIA DELLA CROCE

LAYERED POLENTA AND CURRIED VEGETABLES

Nick Morfogen at Ajax Tavern in Aspen adds semolina flour to his polenta for a smooth, creamy texture. If you don't care about having distinct layers, make the lasagna with soft polenta just out of the saucepan.

🍷 *The tart tomatoes, sharp cheese, and pungent mushrooms could be accompanied with a medium-bodied red with an attractive bite of its own, such as Chianti Classico—look for the 1991 Badia a Coltibuono—or California Sangiovese, such as the 1992 Atlas Peak.*

6 TO 8 SERVINGS

VEGETABLES:

- ⅓ cup extra-virgin olive oil
- 1¼ teaspoons curry powder
- 1 pound fresh mushrooms, such as shiitakes or cremini, stems removed and caps cut into ⅓-inch dice
- 1 tablespoon coarsely chopped fresh oregano
- Salt and freshly ground black pepper
- 1 medium leek, white and tender green, halved lengthwise and sliced crosswise ¼ inch thick
- 2 medium zucchini, cut into ⅓-inch dice
- 2 medium red bell peppers, cut into ¼-inch dice
- 1 small butternut squash (about 1¼ pounds)—quartered, seeded, peeled, and cut into ¼-inch dice
- 2 tablespoons minced garlic
- 1 tablespoon finely chopped fresh ginger
- 2 pounds fresh plum tomatoes—peeled, seeded, and coarsely chopped, with their juices, or 2½ cups canned Italian peeled tomatoes, coarsely chopped
- 1 tablespoon coarsely chopped fresh mint
- ¼ cup freshly grated Pecorino Romano cheese (about ¾ ounce)

POLENTA:

- 3 cups vegetable stock (see Note), canned vegetable broth, or water
- 3 cups half-and-half
- ¾ cup semolina*
- ¾ cup polenta, preferably coarse
- ¾ cup freshly grated Pecorino Romano cheese (about 2½ ounces)
- Coarse salt and freshly ground white pepper

*Available at specialty food stores and some supermarkets

1. Prepare the vegetables: Heat 1 tablespoon of the olive oil in a large nonstick skillet. Stir in ½ teaspoon of the curry powder and cook over moderately high heat for 30 seconds. Add the mushrooms, 1 teaspoon of the oregano, 1 teaspoon salt, and ½ teaspoon black pepper and cook, stirring, for 1 minute. Lower the heat to moderate and cook, stirring occasionally, until the mushrooms are tender, about 5 minutes. Transfer to a large bowl.

2. Wipe out the skillet, add 1 tablespoon of the olive oil, and heat. Stir in ½ teaspoon of the curry powder and cook over moderate heat for 30 seconds. Add the sliced leek and cook, stirring occasionally, until wilted, about 1 minute. Add the diced zucchini, 1 teaspoon of the oregano, ½ teaspoon salt, and ¼ teaspoon black pepper, and cook for 5 minutes, stirring occasionally. Raise the heat to moderately high. Add the red bell peppers and cook, stirring occasionally, until all the vegetables are tender, about 5 minutes. Add to the mushrooms.

3. Wipe out the skillet, add 2 more tablespoons of the olive oil, and heat. Stir in the remaining ¼ teaspoon curry powder and cook over moderate heat for 30 seconds. Add the butternut squash, the remaining 1 teaspoon oregano, ½ teaspoon salt, and ¼ teaspoon black pepper, and cook, stirring, for 2 minutes. Stir in 3 tablespoons of water and cook, stirring, until the squash is tender and the water has evaporated, about 5 minutes. Add to the vegetables.

4. Wipe out the skillet, add the remaining 4 teaspoons olive oil, and heat. Add the garlic and ginger and cook over moderate heat, stirring, until softened, 1 to 2 minutes. Add the plum tomatoes, mint, ½ teaspoon salt, and a pinch of black pepper, and cook, stirring, until the tomatoes are softened but still juicy, about 5 minutes. Add to the cooked vegetables and stir in the Pecorino.

5. Prepare the polenta: In a large heavy saucepan, bring the vegetable stock and half-and-half to a boil over moderate heat. Gradually whisk in the semolina and then the polenta. Reduce the heat to low and cook, stirring constantly with a wooden spoon, until the polenta is soft and creamy, about 15 minutes. Remove the pan from the heat. Stir in ½ cup of the Pecorino and season with coarse salt and white pepper. Immediately spoon the polenta onto a large baking sheet and spread it out to a ½-inch-thick layer. Let cool, then cover the polenta and refrigerate until chilled. (MAKE AHEAD: The recipe can be prepared to this point 1 day ahead; cover and refrigerate the polenta and vegetables separately.)

6. Preheat the oven to 425°. Generously oil 2 large baking sheets and heat them in the oven for 5 minutes. Cut the polenta into 8 equal rectangles. Transfer the polenta rectangles to the heated baking sheets and bake for about 20 minutes, or until firm on top. Lower the oven temperature to 350°.

7. Lightly oil an 8-by-12-inch nonreactive baking dish. Arrange 4 of the polenta rectangles in the prepared baking dish and spread half of the cooked vegetables on top. Cover with the remaining polenta squares and top with the remaining vegetables. (MAKE AHEAD: The lasagna can be assembled up to 1 day ahead; cover and refrigerate. Let stand at room temperature for 2 hours before baking.)

8. Sprinkle the lasagna with the remaining ¼ cup Pecorino. Cover loosely with foil and bake for 30 minutes. Remove the foil and continue baking for about 30 minutes longer, or until the lasagna is heated through. Serve the lasagna hot.

NOTE: You can make a simple vegetable stock with the trimmings from the vegetables: use the leek greens, zucchini and bell pepper trimmings, and shiitake stems. In a medium saucepan, combine 3 cups of the vegetable trimmings with 1 bay leaf and 5 cups of water. Bring to a boil and simmer over moderately low heat for 40 minutes. Strain the stock; you should have about 3 cups. If necessary, boil to reduce it to 3 cups.—NICK MORFOGEN

JALAPENO GRITS IN RED PEPPER CUPS

If you want to tone down the spicy heat of this dish, remove the seeds and ribs from the jalapeño chile.

8 SERVINGS

- 4 medium red bell peppers
- Olive oil
- 1 cup old-fashioned or medium-ground organic grits
- 4 tablespoons unsalted butter
- 1 medium jalapeño chile, minced
- 1 cup heavy cream
- Salt and freshly ground black pepper
- ½ cup plain dry bread crumbs

1. Preheat the broiler. Halve the bell peppers crosswise. Remove and discard the stems, seeds, and ribs. Using your hands, lightly rub the peppers with olive oil. Place them cut side down on a lightly greased baking sheet and broil, turning once, until lightly charred. (Alternatively, grill the pepper cups on a hot grill, turning, until lightly charred.)

2. In a large saucepan, bring 4 cups of lightly salted water to a boil over high heat. Gradually whisk in the grits. Reduce the heat to low, cover, and simmer gently, stirring occasionally, until the grits are tender, smooth, and thick, about 20 minutes.

3. Meanwhile, melt the butter in a small nonreactive skillet over moderately high heat. Add the jalapeño and cook, stirring, until slightly softened, about 2 minutes. Stir the butter and jalapeño into the grits along with the heavy cream. Season well with salt and black pepper.

4. Preheat the oven to 375°. Sprinkle half of the bread crumbs in the bottom of the 8 red pepper cups. Divide the grits among the red pepper cups, mounding them slightly. Sprinkle the remaining crumbs on top. (MAKE AHEAD: The recipe can be made to this point up to 3 hours ahead. Cover and refrigerate. Let stand at room temperature for 30 minutes before proceeding.) Bake in the oven for about 15 minutes until hot. Serve at once.—KATHY CARY

CREAMED HOMINY

8 SERVINGS

- 2 tablespoons unsalted butter
- 1 medium onion, finely diced

- ½ yellow bell pepper, finely diced
- 2 garlic cloves, minced
- ½ teaspoon hot or mild pure chile powder
- 5 cups drained, canned yellow or white hominy (from about three 16-ounce cans)

Creamed Hominy

Bulgur, Green Lentil and Chickpea Salad

- ½ cup chicken stock or canned low-sodium broth
- ½ teaspoon chopped fresh thyme
- ¾ cup heavy cream
- ½ cup finely chopped fresh cilantro
- 2 teaspoons fresh lemon juice
- ½ teaspoon salt
- ¼ teaspoon freshly ground black pepper
- ¼ cup milk

1. In an 11-by-8-inch nonreactive flameproof baking dish, melt the butter over moderate heat. Add the onion and bell pepper and cook until softened, about 6 minutes. Add the garlic and cook, stirring, for 3 minutes. Stir in the chile powder and cook for 1 minute. Stir in the hominy until well coated. Add the chicken stock and thyme and simmer until the stock has reduced slightly, about 4 minutes. Stir in the cream and bring just to a simmer. Remove from the heat and stir in the cilantro, lemon juice, salt, and black pepper. (MAKE AHEAD: The dish can be made 1 day ahead; let cool to room temperature, then cover and refrigerate. Return to room temperature before proceeding.)
2. Preheat the oven to 375°. Stir the milk into the hominy, cover with foil, and bake about 20 minutes, stirring a few times, until bubbling. Season the hominy with salt and black pepper and serve.—MARCIA KIESEL

BULGUR, GREEN LENTIL AND CHICKPEA SALAD

You'll recognize the flavors of tabbouleh here, but this version has the additional textures and tastes of lentils and chickpeas. The dish is a snap to make, particularly if you use canned chickpeas, in which case it shouldn't take any longer than the 25 minutes the lentils need to cook. Of all the beans that are canned, chickpeas hold up best because their texture remains firm.

MAKES 4 SERVINGS

- ¾ cup dried chickpeas, picked over and rinsed well, or one 19-ounce can of chickpeas
- ½ cup lentils, preferably French green (Le Puy) lentils, picked over and rinsed well
- 1 bay leaf
- Salt
- ¾ cup fine bulgur
- 2 cups boiling water
- About ½ cup fresh lemon juice
- 5 medium scallions, white plus 3 inches of green, thinly sliced crosswise
- 2 medium garlic cloves, minced
- 2 teaspoons finely grated lemon zest
- 1 teaspoon paprika, plus more for garnish
- ½ cup extra-virgin olive oil
- 1½ cups minced fresh flat-leaf parsley
- 1 tablespoon crushed dried mint

1. If using dried chickpeas, place in a large bowl, cover with water, and let soak for at least 6 hours or overnight. (Alternatively, in a large saucepan, cover the chickpeas with water and boil over moderately high heat for 2 minutes. Remove from the heat, cover, and let soak for 1 hour.) Drain off the soaking liquid and rinse the chickpeas well.
2. In a large saucepan, cover the dried chickpeas with 2 to 3 inches

of water, cover the pan, and simmer over moderate heat until tender but not mushy, 50 to 60 minutes. Skim the foam off the surface as necessary; taste the chickpeas often to test for doneness. Let them cool slightly in their liquid, then drain and transfer to a bowl. Alternatively, drain and thoroughly rinse the canned chickpeas and put them in a bowl.

3. In a medium saucepan, combine the lentils, bay leaf, and ½ teaspoon of salt. Cover with 3 cups of water and bring to a boil. Lower the heat and simmer until the lentils are tender but still firm, 20 to 25 minutes; drain well. Discard the bay leaf and add the lentils to the chickpeas.

4. Meanwhile, in a heatproof bowl, cover the bulgur with the 2 cups boiling water and set aside to swell for 15 minutes. Drain and press out as much water as you can with the back of a spoon. (MAKE AHEAD: The recipe can be made to this point up to 4 days ahead; tightly cover the legumes and the bulgur separately and refrigerate.)

5. In a large serving bowl, whisk together 6 tablespoons of the lemon juice, the scallions, garlic, lemon zest, 1 teaspoon paprika, and 1 teaspoon of salt. Whisk in the olive oil.

6. Add the chickpeas, lentils, bulgur, parsley, and mint, and toss gently and thoroughly. Season with up to 2 more tablespoons of lemon juice and more salt. Serve warm or at room temperature. Sprinkle with paprika just before serving.—DEBORAH MADISON

CHAPTER 14

VEGETABLES

Broccoli with Black Olives

BROCCOLI WITH BLACK OLIVES

4 SERVINGS

Salt
1 medium head of broccoli, cut into florets, stems peeled and sliced crosswise 1 inch thick
2 tablespoons unsalted butter
12 imported black olives, pitted and chopped
Freshly ground pepper

Bring a large saucepan of water to a boil. Add salt and the sliced broccoli stems and cook for 1 minute. Add the broccoli florets and cook until just tender, about 4 minutes. Drain well in a colander and shake dry. Return the broccoli stems and florets to the saucepan and toss with the butter. Add the olives, season with salt and pepper, and toss again. Spoon the broccoli into a dish and serve.—SARAH FRITSCHNER

ASPARAGUS WITH LEMON-GARLIC VINAIGRETTE

Asparagus fares well with the assertive flavors of lemon and garlic. Mincing garlic with salt enhances the underlying sweetness of this potent member of the lily family. Peeling medium-size stalks of asparagus removes the tough fibers and makes them more attractive; however, it's a purely personal choice, and some cooks prefer just snapping off the tough ends.

6 SERVINGS

2 small garlic cloves
½ teaspoon coarse salt
3 tablespoons fresh lemon juice
2 teaspoons Dijon mustard
¼ cup plus 2 tablespoons extra-virgin olive oil
¼ cup plus 2 tablespoons mild olive oil
½ teaspoon sugar
Fine salt and freshly ground pepper
2 pounds asparagus
2 tablespoons chopped fresh flat-leaf parsley

1. Using a large heavy knife, mince the garlic with the coarse salt. Scrape into a bowl. Whisk in the lemon juice and mustard. Slowly drizzle in the extra-virgin and mild olive oils and whisk constantly until thickened. Season with the sugar and salt and pepper. (MAKE AHEAD: The vinaigrette can be refrigerated, covered, for up to 1 day. Let return to room temperature before serving.)
2. Bring a large nonreactive skillet of salted water to a boil. Add the asparagus in small batches and cook just until crisp-tender, 1 to 2 minutes. Remove each batch with tongs and refresh immediately under cold running water. Transfer to a kitchen towel and gently pat dry. Cover and refrigerate if desired.
3. Just before serving, arrange the asparagus on a platter and drizzle with half the vinaigrette. Sprinkle the parsley on the asparagus. Serve the remaining vinaigrette on the side.—SHEILA LUKINS

GLAZED CARROTS AND ASPARAGUS

8 SERVINGS

1½ pounds small spring carrots, tops trimmed to 1 inch
1½ pounds asparagus, tips trimmed to 3 inches (reserve the stems for soup)
2 tablespoons unsalted butter
Salt and freshly ground pepper

1. In a large saucepan of boiling salted water, cook the carrots until tender, about 5 minutes. With a slotted spoon, transfer the carrots to a plate to cool. Add the asparagus tips to the boiling water and cook until just tender, about 3 minutes. Drain the asparagus and rinse with very cold water until cool. (MAKE AHEAD: The vegetables can be prepared to this point up to 1 day ahead. Cover and refrigerate.)
2. Shortly before serving, melt 1 tablespoon of the butter in a large skillet. Add the carrots, cover, and cook over moderate heat until warmed through. Season with salt and pepper. Transfer to a plate and cover to keep warm. Add the remaining 1 tablespoon butter to the skillet and reheat the asparagus similarly. Season with salt and pepper and serve with the carrots.—DAVID WALTUCK

AVOCADO AIOLI

For a splash of spring, nothing is more dramatic or satisfying than a platter of the season's finest young vegetables. Aïoli *is the Provençal name for the garlicky mayonnaise that is the centerpiece for a meal of assorted seasonal vegetables and often seafood. With the use of uncooked egg yolks so widely disputed, a prejudice against fresh mayonnaise and, alas, aioli, has developed. It's impossible to reproduce aioli's velvety texture with other ingredients, but I've begun with the best alternative I could think of, a creamy, ripe avocado. Olive oil and fresh lime juice help to create the illusion of the classic sauce.*

6 TO 8 SERVINGS

VEGETABLES:
1 lemon, halved
12 baby artichokes

Avocado Aioli

AVOCADO TIP

Q: How can I keep avocados from turning brown when I have to prepare them ahead of time?

A: Chris Schlesinger, chef and co-owner of East Coast Grill in Cambridge, Massachusetts, removes the skin and pit from the avocado, then wraps it in a cloth that has been soaked with lime or lemon juice. The avocados will remain bright green for several hours.

This technique also works very well with other fruits. Slice or cube each piece of fruit and wrap it in the saturated cloth.—ARLENE FELTMAN-SAILHAC

- 1 pound young carrots, tops trimmed to 1 inch
- ½ pound thin green beans (*haricots verts*)
- ½ pound sugar snap peas
- 12 small red-skinned new potatoes
- 12 small beets

AVOCADO AIOLI:

- 2 ripe Hass avocados (about ½ pound each)
- 2 tablespoons fresh lime juice
- 1 large garlic clove, minced
- 2 tablespoons extra-virgin olive oil
- ¼ cup chopped fresh coriander (cilantro) or flat-leaf parsley

Salt and freshly ground pepper

- 6 hard-cooked eggs, halved lengthwise
- 2 tablespoons coarsely chopped fresh flat-leaf parsley

1. Cook the vegetables: Squeeze the lemon halves into a medium bowl and fill with water. Trim the artichoke stems and cut about ½ inch off the tops. Remove any tough outer leaves at the base and snip the points from the remaining leaves with scissors. Toss the artichokes into the acidulated water.

2. Bring a large pot of water to a boil. Add the artichokes and boil until tender when pierced, 15 to 20 minutes. Remove with a slotted spoon and drain well. In the same pot, boil the remaining vegetables, one at a time, until just tender; remove each batch with a slotted spoon as it's done.

3. Make the Avocado Aioli: Halve the avocados. Scoop the flesh into a bowl. Mash with the lime juice and garlic. Scrape into a food processor and puree. With the machine on, drizzle in the oil.

4. Scrape the puree into a bowl. Fold in the coriander and season with salt and pepper. Refrigerate for up to 2 hours.

5. To serve, arrange the vegetables and eggs on a large platter. Sprinkle the parsley over all. Spoon the aioli into a bowl and serve alongside.—SHEILA LUKINS

SUGAR SNAP PEAS WITH WALNUTS

MAKES 50 BUFFET SERVINGS

- 2 cups walnut halves (about ½ pound)
- 8 pounds sugar snap peas, strings removed
- ½ cup walnut oil or extra-virgin olive oil

Salt and freshly ground pepper

1. Preheat the oven to 350°. Bring a large stockpot of salted water to a boil. Toast the walnuts on a large baking sheet for about 7 minutes, or until golden and fragrant. Let cool slightly, then finely chop the nuts. (MAKE AHEAD: The walnuts can be prepared up to 2 days ahead; store at room temperature in an airtight container.)

2. Working in 2 or 3 batches, add the peas to the stockpot and boil until tender but still slightly crunchy, about 5 minutes. Using a large skimmer, transfer the peas to a bowl of cold water, then drain them thoroughly. Let stand for up to 6 hours.

3. In a large serving bowl, toss the peas with the oil. Season generously with salt and pepper. Add the toasted walnuts and toss to combine.—GRACE PARISI

STIR-FRIED SNOW PEAS AND BEAN SPROUTS WITH SLICED SCALLIONS

4 SERVINGS

1 tablespoon vegetable oil
4 ounces bean sprouts
½ pound snow peas, strings removed
3 scallions, thinly sliced
1 teaspoon rice wine vinegar
Soy sauce
Salt and freshly ground pepper

Heat the oil in a wok or large nonreactive skillet over high heat until almost smoking. Add the bean sprouts, snow peas, and scallions, and stir-fry over moderately high heat just until tender, about 3 minutes. Sprinkle in the vinegar, season with the soy sauce, salt, and pepper, and toss. Serve at once.—KENNETH WAPNER

MIXED ROASTED PEPPERS

4 SERVINGS

4 large poblano chiles
4 large jalapeño chiles
2 red bell peppers
8 hot Italian cherry peppers
Olive oil
Salt and freshly ground black pepper

Roast all the chiles and peppers directly over a gas flame, turning, just until the skins are blistered and charred all over. Put the peppers in a paper bag and let steam for 5 minutes. Open the bag and, working over it, remove the charred skins and the stems, cores, and seeds. Cut the chiles and peppers into 2-inch strips and put them in a bowl. Drizzle with a little olive oil and season with salt and black pepper.—MARCIA KIESEL

Chinese Charred Peppers and Zucchini

CHINESE CHARRED PEPPERS AND ZUCCHINI

This side dish is composed of succulent vegetables seasoned with Asian flavorings.

4 SERVINGS

1 large red bell pepper, cut into ¾-inch dice
1 large yellow bell pepper, cut into ¾-inch dice
2 medium zucchini, sliced ¼-inch thick
2 teaspoons salt
2 tablespoons soy sauce
1 tablespoon plus 1 teaspoon red wine vinegar
1 teaspoon chili oil
1 teaspoon sugar
2 tablespoons peanut oil

1. Layer the bell peppers and the zucchini in a large bowl, sprinkling the salt between the layers. Let rest for 1 hour. Then rinse, drain, and pat the vegetables dry.
2. Meanwhile, in a small bowl, whisk together the soy sauce, vinegar, chili oil, and sugar.
3. Heat a wok or large heavy skillet over moderately high heat until barely smoking. Add 1 tablespoon of the peanut oil to

the wok and swirl with a wooden spatula to coat. Add half of the peppers and zucchini. Cook, turning occasionally and pressing down with the spatula, until nicely charred, about 5 minutes. Transfer to a bowl. Repeat the procedure with the remaining 1 tablespoon peanut oil and vegetables. Return the first batch of vegetables to the wok.

4. Give the reserved sauce a stir and pour it over the vegetables. Cook over moderately high heat, stirring, until the liquid evaporates, 1 to 2 minutes. Transfer to a bowl, let cool to room temperature, and serve. (MAKE AHEAD: The recipe can be made up to 2 days ahead; cover and refrigerate. Bring to room temperature before serving.) —KAREN LEE

Vegetable Pan Roast

VEGETABLE PAN ROAST

8 SERVINGS

- 1/3 cup plus 2 tablespoons olive oil
- 16 small-to-medium parsnips (about 1½ pounds), peeled
- 2 large orange sweet potatoes (1½ pounds), peeled and cut lengthwise into 4 wedges
- 2 large red onions (1½ pounds), peeled and each cut lengthwise into 8 wedges with root ends intact
- Salt and freshly ground black pepper
- 1 large eggplant (1 pound)—trimmed and quartered, then each piece halved crosswise
- 2 large red bell peppers
- 2 large yellow bell peppers
- 4 fresh rosemary sprigs
- 4 fresh thyme sprigs
- 2 tablespoons dry white wine

1. Preheat the oven to 375°. Pour 1/3 cup of the oil into a very large, wide roasting pan (or divide between two smaller roasting pans). Add the parsnips, sweet potatoes, and onions, and turn to coat evenly with oil; season with salt and black pepper. Roast in the oven for about 1 hour, until nicely browned and almost tender. Remove the roasting pan from the oven and increase the temperature to 450°.

2. Using a metal spatula, push the cooked vegetables to the side and add the eggplant, bell peppers, and the remaining 2 tablespoons oil. Turn the eggplant and bell peppers in the oil to coat; season with salt and black pepper. Scatter the rosemary and thyme sprigs in the pan and roast for about 40 minutes, until the peppers are blistered and browned and the other vegetables are tender. (MAKE AHEAD: The recipe can be made to this point up to 1 day ahead. Let the vegetables cool to room temperature, then cover and refrigerate. Return to room temperature before proceeding.)

3. Preheat the oven to 350°. Drizzle the vegetables with the wine, cover with foil, and bake on the bottom shelf of the oven for about 20 minutes, until hot. Increase the temperature to 450°.

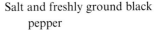

Uncover the vegetables and roast for about 15 minutes longer, until the juices in the pan have browned and glazed the vegetables. Season with salt and black pepper, arrange on a platter, and serve.—MARCIA KIESEL

LIME-GRILLED VEGETABLES

4 SERVINGS

- 4 medium potatoes, sliced crosswise ½ inch thick
- 3 large carrots, sliced diagonally ¼ inch thick
- ⅓ cup olive oil
- 1 tablespoon fresh lime juice
- 2 tablespoons finely grated onion
- ½ teaspoon ground cumin
- ½ teaspoon salt
- ¼ teaspoon freshly ground pepper
- 2 large zucchini, sliced diagonally ¾ inch thick

1. Bring a medium saucepan of water to a boil. Add the potatoes and carrots and parboil over high heat for 10 minutes. Drain and set aside.
2. Light a grill or preheat the broiler. In a large bowl, combine the oil, lime juice, onion, cumin, salt, and pepper. Add the potatoes, carrots, and zucchini. Toss to coat. Let stand up to 15 minutes.
3. Grill or broil the vegetables about 3 minutes per side, turning once, until nicely browned and tender. Serve hot.—CHATA DUBOSE

SAUTEED ZUCCHINI WITH THYME

Zucchine al Timo

The zucchini is sautéed in a mild flavor base of onion and parsley cooked in olive oil and butter. In this recipe, you will need two skillets with all the ingredients split equally between them.

12 SERVINGS

- ½ cup extra-virgin olive oil
- 4 tablespoons unsalted butter
- ⅔ cup finely chopped onion
- ⅔ cup chopped fresh parsley
- 3 pounds firm, fresh zucchini—soaked in water for 20 minutes, patted dry, and cut into 3-by-½-inch sticks
- 2 beef bouillon cubes, crumbled
- 4 teaspoons thyme
- Salt and freshly ground pepper

1. In 2 large skillets, combine the olive oil, butter, onion, and parsley. Cook over moderate heat, stirring occasionally, until the onion is softened but not browned.
2. Add the zucchini, bouillon, thyme, and a pinch of salt and pepper. Stir gently but thoroughly. Cover and cook, stirring occasionally, until the zucchini is tender, 20 to 30 minutes. Serve hot or lukewarm.—MARCELLA HAZAN

STUFFED ZUCCHINI

8 SERVINGS

- 6 cups ½-inch cubes of white bread (from 1 Italian loaf)
- Eight 6-inch-long zucchini or 4- to 5-inch pattypan squash (6 to 8 ounces each)
- Coarse salt and freshly ground pepper
- 4 thick slices of smoked bacon
- 5½ tablespoons unsalted butter
- 1 medium onion, finely diced
- 2 tart apples, such as Winesap, Greening, or Granny Smith, peeled and finely diced
- 3 tablespoons finely chopped fresh flat-leaf parsley
- 2 teaspoons finely chopped fresh thyme
- 2 large eggs, beaten

1. Preheat the oven to 325°. Spread the bread cubes on a large baking sheet and bake for about 30 minutes, or until crisp but not brown. Let cool.
2. Bring a large saucepan of salted water to a boil. Halve the zucchini lengthwise. Using a spoon, scrape out the seeds, creating a hollow channel down the center of each half. (If using pattypan squash, cut a 2-inch-round piece from the stem end of each squash and discard. Using a spoon, scoop out the center of each squash to remove the seeds and create a substantial hollow.) Boil the squash until just tender, about 8 minutes. Using tongs, transfer the squash to paper towels to drain. Pat the insides dry. Let cool completely. Season the insides with coarse salt and pepper.
3. In a large skillet, fry the bacon over moderate heat until crisp, about 4 minutes per side. Drain the bacon on paper towels, then coarsely chop.
4. Pour off the bacon fat from the skillet. Add 4 tablespoons of the butter. Add the onion; cook over moderate heat until softened, about 6 minutes. Add the apples and cook until almost tender, about 3 minutes. Let cool slightly.
5. In a large bowl, toss the bread cubes with the bacon, onion, apples, parsley, and thyme. In a small bowl, beat the eggs with 1 cup water, 1 teaspoon coarse salt, and ½ teaspoon pepper. Add to the stuffing and mix well. Firmly pack the stuffing into the squash, mounding it slightly. Place the

squash on a large baking sheet. (MAKE AHEAD: The recipe can be made to this point up to 1 day ahead; cover the squash and refrigerate. Return to room temperature before proceeding.)

6. Preheat the oven to 375°. Dot the stuffing with the remaining 1½ tablespoons butter. Bake on the top rack of the oven for about 30 minutes, until hot and crusty. Serve at once.—MARCIA KIESEL

SPICY CORN FRITTERS

These fritters can accompany grilled salmon, pork, or chicken.

6 TO 8 SERVINGS

- 1 cup unbleached all-purpose flour
- 1¾ teaspoons salt
- 1¼ teaspoons baking powder
- ¾ cup milk
- 1 large egg
- 2 tablespoons unsalted butter, melted

- 4 cups fresh corn kernels (from 5 to 6 medium ears)
- ¼ cup plus 2 tablespoons minced scallions (white and tender green)
- ¼ cup finely diced red bell pepper
- 1 to 2 medium jalapeño chiles, minced
- Few drops of Tabasco (optional)
- Vegetable oil, for panfrying

1. In a large bowl, stir together the flour, the salt, and the baking powder. In a medium bowl, combine the milk, egg, and unsalted butter, and stir the mixture into the dry ingredients until well blended. Fold in the corn kernels, minced scallions, diced bell pepper, minced jalapeño chiles, and Tabasco until incorporated.

2. In a large heavy skillet, preferably cast iron, heat ¼ inch of vegetable oil until almost smoking, about 5 minutes. Add heaping tablespoons of the fritter batter to the skillet without crowding and fry over moderately high heat until golden brown on the bottom, about 4 minutes. Turn the fritters carefully and continue frying until golden all over, about 4 minutes longer. Using a slotted spoon, transfer the fritters to paper towels to drain. Mound the fritters on a plate, cover loosely with foil, and keep warm. Fry the remaining fritters, adding more vegetable oil to the pan if necessary; be sure that the oil is very hot before adding another batch to the pan or the fritters will be soggy. Serve immediately.—JUDITH SUTTON

Stuffed Zucchini

KNOW YOUR ONIONS

The onion comes from the large lily family and the extensive *Allium* genus. How can you identify one? If you crush it and you cry, it's an allium. Sulfur compounds concentrated in the tissue of the onion are responsible for this notorious reaction.

Of the several hundred alliums in the world, most are wild species that have from time to time been gathered and eaten. The cultivated alliums—the ones sold in our markets—need no further introduction. They are onions, leeks, shallots, garlic, and chives; and they each belong to a different species. Onions alone make up a species called *cepa*.

Eat an onion and you will consume no fat, very few calories, a jolt of vitamin C, and enough fiber to do your digestive system some good.—FRED AND LINDA GRIFFITH

CORN CUSTARD SOUFFLE

If the corn kernels are large, sauté them briefly in a little butter before adding to the soufflé base. Serve this dish with a green salad to make a meal.

4 SERVINGS

- 8 medium tomatoes—peeled, seeded, and finely chopped
- 2 tablespoons finely chopped fresh basil
- Salt and freshly ground pepper
- 1 tablespoon unsalted butter
- 1 tablespoon finely chopped shallot

1 tablespoon all-purpose flour
1 cup heavy cream
5 large eggs, separated
4 cups fresh corn kernels (from about 6 medium ears)
Pinch of freshly grated nutmeg
Freshly grated Parmesan cheese (optional)

1. In a medium bowl, toss the chopped tomatoes with the fresh basil and season with salt and pepper.
2. Preheat the oven to 400°. Butter a 2-quart oval gratin dish. Melt the butter in a heavy medium saucepan. Add the shallot and cook over moderate heat for 1 minute. Add the flour and cook, stirring, until the mixture is lightly colored, about 2 more minutes. Pour in the cream and simmer, whisking constantly, until thickened, about 4 minutes longer. Transfer the mixture to a large bowl and beat in the egg yolks one at a time, beating well after each addition. Stir in the corn and season with salt, pepper, and nutmeg.
3. In a large bowl, beat the egg whites with a pinch of salt until stiff peaks form. Gently fold the whites into the corn base. Spoon the soufflé mixture into the prepared dish and bake for about 20 minutes, or until set and browned on top. Serve the soufflé at once, with the tomatoes and the Parmesan cheese.—PARKER BOSLEY

FIRE-ROASTED CORN WITH SPICY RED PEPPER PUREE LF

When pulled back, the husks become a natural handle for the corn, making the ears easier to hold while cooking and eating.

6 SERVINGS
2 medium red bell peppers
2 medium oil-packed sun-dried tomatoes, patted dry and coarsely chopped
1 chipotle chile packed in *adobo* sauce*
1 shallot, coarsely chopped
1 garlic clove, coarsely chopped
1 tablespoon light brown sugar
Vegetable oil cooking spray
6 large ears of corn, husk pulled back but not removed and corn silk discarded
Kosher salt and freshly ground black pepper

*Available at Latin American food stores and specialty food stores

1. Roast the bell peppers over a gas flame or under the broiler, turning often, until charred all over. Transfer to a paper bag

TYPES OF CORN

As you stand before piles of fresh corn at the local market, you're probably thinking about two things: whether you should get white or yellow and how you're going to prepare what you buy. The recipes here will give you plenty of delicious ideas for using fresh corn. As for white or yellow, remember one thing: all of the corn you're looking at, regardless of color, is officially classified as sweet corn (other common types include field corn—which is used for feed, flour, oil, and syrup—and popcorn, used for just that).

THREE KINDS **(or, more correctly, genotypes) of sweet corn dominate the market, and they are distinguished by the amount of sugar they contain. In ascending order of sweetness, they are normal sugary, sugary enhanced, and shrunken gene supersweet. These are hybrids that were developed in the Thirties to appeal to America's sweet tooth. There are white, yellow, and bicolor varieties of all three, but it is the genotype, not the color, that determines the sweetness of the corn. Normal sugary and sugary enhanced have traditional corn taste and are best when eaten within a day of picking (the corn loses a significant amount of sugar within 24 hours). Supersweets can be kept longer because they have two to three times as much sugar and will retain much of their sweetness for up to 48 hours, but their taste is not considered a true corn taste.**

WHEN BUYING CORN, **your primary consideration should be freshness; get the corn as close to the time it was picked as possible. Here are some common varieties you will see on the market: Normal sugary—Golden Jubilee (yellow), Silver Queen (white), Harmony (bicolor). Sugary enhanced—Bodacious (yellow), Argent (white), Peaches and Cream (bicolor). Supersweet—Jupiter (yellow), Starbrite (white), Honey 'n Pearl (bicolor).**

Corn and Fava Bean Succotash

and let steam for 10 minutes. Peel the roasted peppers, discarding the stems, ribs, and seeds, and coarsely chop them. Transfer to a blender or food processor along with the tomatoes, chile, shallot, garlic, and brown sugar, and blend to a puree.

2. Light a grill or preheat the oven to 500°. Spray six 9-inch-long pieces of foil with the vegetable oil cooking spray. Spread the roasted red pepper puree all over the ears of corn and season with salt and pepper. Wrap the ears of corn in the prepared foil. Grill over a low fire or roast in the middle of the oven for about 45 minutes, or until the corn is tender.—CHARLES WILEY

CHILE-PIMENTO CORN

8 SERVINGS

- 4 large scallions, halved crosswise
- 4 large fresh thyme sprigs
- 1 to 2 Scotch bonnet chiles, halved
- ¼ cup salt
- 2 tablespoons allspice berries

16 large ears of corn, husked, with a thin layer of corn silk left on

In a very large stockpot, combine the scallions, thyme, chiles, salt, and allspice with 8 quarts water. Cover and bring to a boil over high heat. Simmer 20 minutes. Add the corn, cover, and cook until tender, about 25 minutes. Drain and serve hot.—PAUL CHUNG

CORN AND FAVA BEAN SUCCOTASH

This rich, bacon-studded dish is good with grilled meats and poultry.

4 SERVINGS

- 2 pounds young fava beans, shelled
- 3 thick slices of bacon, cut crosswise into ½-inch strips
- 1 tablespoon unsalted butter
- 2 cups fresh corn kernels (from 3 medium ears)
- ¼ cup heavy cream
- ¼ teaspoon salt
- ⅛ teaspoon freshly ground pepper

1. In a medium pot of boiling water, blanch the beans for 1 minute. Drain and rinse with cold water. Peel off and discard the tough skins. (MAKE AHEAD: The beans can be refrigerated, covered, for up to 1 day.)
2. In a large heavy skillet, cook the bacon over moderate heat until golden brown and just crisp, about 3 minutes. Drain on paper towels. Pour off the fat and wipe out the skillet.
3. In the same skillet, melt the butter. Add the corn and cook over moderate heat, stirring, until crisp-tender, 3 to 5 minutes. Add the cream and bring to a simmer. Add the beans, salt, and pepper. Reduce the heat to low and simmer until the beans are tender and warmed through, 1 to 2 minutes. Stir in the bacon and serve hot.—JUDITH SUTTON

CORN: PICKING THE BEST

- **Look for ears of corn that are tightly closed with bright green husks.**
- **The ends of the corn silk should be golden brown, not pale, an indication that it was picked too early.**
- **The stem end of the corn should be pale green and moist, not woody.**
- **Don't peel back the husk. If you do, the corn will dry out. Instead, feel through the husk for plump, resilient kernels.**

DILLED STRING BEANS Q

4 SERVINGS

- 1 pound string beans, trimmed
- 1 tablespoon unsalted butter
- 2 teaspoons minced fresh dill
- 1 tablespoon fresh lemon juice
- Salt and freshly ground pepper

1. Bring a nonreactive saucepan of salted water to a boil. Add the beans and cook over moderate heat until crisp-tender, about 5 minutes; drain.
2. Melt the butter in the saucepan. Add the beans and dill and sauté over moderately high heat until lightly browned, about 3 minutes. Sprinkle with the lemon juice, season with salt and pepper, and serve.—JESSICA B. HARRIS

CUTTING THE CORN OFF THE COB

- **To remove corn kernels, stand an ear on its end in a bowl and slice off the kernels with a sharp, thin-bladed knife.**
- **Grating corn removes all the kernels from the cob, and juices and "purees" the corn kernels in the process. Use the large holes of a box grater set inside a bowl or a flat grater placed across the top of a bowl.**

ROASTED GREEN BEANS WITH GARLIC Q

4 SERVINGS

- 1 pound green beans, stemmed, with tender tips left on
- 3 garlic cloves, smashed
- 3 fresh thyme sprigs, coarsely chopped
- ¼ cup extra-virgin olive oil
- Salt and freshly ground pepper
- 3 anchovy fillets, mashed
- 2 to 3 teaspoons fresh lemon juice
- Finely grated zest of 1 lemon

1. Preheat the oven to 450°. In a large baking dish, toss the beans with the garlic, thyme, and oil, and season with salt and pepper. Spread the beans and seasonings in a single layer and roast for about 15 minutes, tossing occasionally, until the beans are tender and lightly browned. Discard the thyme sprigs.
2. Transfer the beans to a bowl. Add the anchovies, lemon juice,

and lemon zest, and toss well to coat. Serve warm or at room temperature.—NANCY VERDE BARR

FARMERS' MARKET VEGETABLE STEW

This stew can be quite a colorful jumble of vegetables when you mix the squash (try baby yellow pattypans with baby green zucchinis) and the beans (try flat Romanos with plump Blue Lakes). The flavors improve if the stew sits for a few hours.

6 TO 8 SERVINGS

- 1½ pounds tomatoes
- 3 tablespoons safflower or canola oil plus more for rubbing the tomatoes
- 2 medium onions, cut into ½-inch dice
- 3 large garlic cloves, thinly sliced
- 2 teaspoons ground cumin
- 2 teaspoons ground New Mexico chile or 1 tablespoon hot paprika
- 1½ teaspoons dried oregano
- 1½ teaspoons salt
- 12 ounces mixed summer squash, cut into 1-inch chunks if large
- ½ pound mixed summer beans, cut into 2-inch lengths
- 3 bell peppers, preferably red, yellow, and orange, cut into 1-inch squares
- 2½ cups corn kernels (from 4 ears of corn)
- ¼ cup each finely chopped fresh flat-leaf parsley and fresh cilantro
- Green Chile and Goat Cheese Quesadillas (recipe follows)

1. Preheat the broiler or light a grill. Rub the tomatoes with a little oil, then place in a cast-iron skillet and broil or grill until shriveled and blackened in places, about 12 minutes. Transfer the tomatoes to a food processor and puree—burned skins and all.

2. While the tomatoes are broiling, heat the oil in a large, heavy, nonreactive casserole. Add the onions and garlic and stir to coat. Cook over moderate heat, stirring occasionally, until softened and lightly colored, about 5 minutes.

3. Stir the cumin, chile, oregano, and salt into the onions. Pour in the pureed tomatoes and 2 cups of water. Add the squash, beans, and bell peppers, and bring to a simmer. Cover the casserole and cook over moderate heat for 15 minutes. Stir in the corn, cover, and continue cooking until all the vegetables are tender, about 5 minutes longer. (MAKE AHEAD: The stew can be made up to 8 hours in advance; cover and refrigerate. Rewarm over moderately low heat.)

4. To serve the stew, stir in the chopped herbs. Ladle the stew into bowls. Serve with the quesadillas.

Green Chile and Goat Cheese Quesadillas

These cheese-filled tortillas are a great partner for the vegetable stew; they're also terrific on their own.

8 SERVINGS

- 3 large green chiles, such as Anaheims or poblanos
- Eight 8-inch white or whole wheat tortillas
- 4 to 6 ounces soft, fresh goat cheese
- 4 scallions, thinly sliced crosswise
- ⅓ cup chopped fresh cilantro

1. Roast the chiles directly over a gas or grill flame or under the broiler as close to the heat as possible, turning often until charred all over. Transfer the chiles to a bag and set aside to steam for 5 minutes. Using a small sharp knife, scrape off the blackened skins. Remove the stems, seeds, and ribs. Chop coarsely.

2. In a large ungreased skillet, warm 1 tortilla over moderate heat until softened and lightly toasted. Flip the tortilla and toast for a minute on the other side. Remove from the pan and repeat with the remaining tortillas. Evenly distribute the chiles, cheese, scallions, and cilantro over 4 of the tortillas, and top

CHEF'S MENU

🍷 The spicy tastes in this menu need a fruity, ripe, round Chardonnay, such as the 1993 Lindemans Bin 65 from Australia or the 1993 Meridian from California.

EGGPLANT-TOMATO CROSTINI (P. 30)

CUCUMBER, ONION AND PURSLANE SALAD (P. 76)

ZUCCHINI AND SQUASH-BLOSSOM FRITTATA (P. 64)

FARMERS' MARKET VEGETABLE STEW (P. 318)

GREEN CHILE AND GOAT CHEESE QUESADILLAS (P. 318)

PLUM-APRICOT UPSIDE-DOWN CAKE (P. 423)

—DEBORAH MADISON

each one with another tortilla, pressing firmly to make sandwiches. (MAKE AHEAD: The recipe can be made to this point up to 1 day ahead; wrap and refrigerate.)

3. Working in batches, cook the quesadillas in the hot skillet over moderate heat until the cheese melts, a minute or so on each side. (Keep the first ones in a warm oven until the rest are done.)

4. Slide each quesadilla onto a cutting board and cut into quarters.—DEBORAH MADISON

MUSHROOMS IN CREAM

These sautéed mushrooms make a lovely first course spooned over thick slices of toast. Or omit the bread and serve the mushrooms as an accompaniment to roasted meat or poultry.

A good substitute here is the domestic white mushroom. Use older ones (identifiable by their dark gills) if you can find them; they have more flavor than younger ones.

6 SERVINGS

- 1½ pounds *rosé* (meadow) mushrooms
- 2 tablespoons unsalted butter
- 2 medium shallots, finely chopped
- ½ cup heavy cream
- 1 teaspoon salt
- ½ teaspoon freshly ground pepper
- 1 teaspoon potato starch or arrowroot, dissolved in 1 tablespoon of water
- 2 teaspoons Cognac or other brandy
- 1 tablespoon minced fresh chives
- Toasted slices of country bread, for serving

1. Rinse the mushrooms thoroughly in cool water. Lift the mushrooms from the water and drain well. Cut the larger mushrooms into 2-inch pieces.

2. Melt the butter in a large nonreactive saucepan. Add the shallots and sauté over moderately high heat until translucent, about 1 minute. Add the mushrooms and sauté until tender, 6 to 8 minutes; there will be about 1 cup of mushroom liquid remaining in the pan. Add the

MUSHROOM TIPS

If foraging for mushrooms isn't in your future, you can certainly find an increasing number of varieties at supermarkets, specialty food shops, and farmers' markets. Cremini (which look like a brown variant of common white button mushrooms), Portobellos, shiitakes, and enoki are among the most readily available, but oyster mushrooms, chanterelles, cèpes (porcini), black trumpets, morels, hen of the woods, chicken of the woods, hedgehog, and lobster mushrooms are just a few of the types you'll be seeing more of.

BUYING AND STORING:

- **Whether you're looking for cultivated mushrooms or wild mushrooms, choose firm, fresh-looking, unblemished specimens with intact gills or pores.**
- **If you have trouble finding mushrooms in your area, the following sources can ship a wide selection of cultivated and seasonally foraged mushrooms to your door year-round: Aux Délices des Bois (800-666-1232), Gourmet Mushrooms (707-823-1743), and Hans Johansson's Mushrooms and More (914-232-2107).**
- **Store fresh mushrooms unwashed in the refrigerator in a paper bag.**

COOKING:

- **Do not clean mushrooms until you are ready to cook them.**
- **To prepare mushrooms for cooking, trim off any blemishes and tough stems or stem ends. Wipe the mushrooms clean with a moist cloth if they're not dirty; wash thoroughly in cool water if they are. Washing is a controversial issue. Many people claim that you should not do it, but I disagree. It may add a little water to the mushrooms, but that water will evaporate during cooking.**
- **Cook all wild mushrooms thoroughly (for at least 15 to 20 minutes). Some types, such as morels, can cause a severe reaction if they're undercooked.**
- **I sometimes dry sliced wild mushrooms on a wire rack in the hot sun or in a 150° oven, then pack them in airtight containers or sturdy plastic bags and store them in the cupboard.**
- **To freeze quantities of wild mushrooms, I first cut them into pieces and roast them in a 400° oven for 45 minutes. Then I pack them with their juices in small, sturdy plastic bags, squeeze out the air, and freeze them. The liquid can be used in soups and stews, and the drained mushrooms can be sautéed with herbs, garlic, and onion.—JACQUES PEPIN**

BEST-SELLING VEGETARIAN COOKBOOKS

Ellen Rose, owner of Cook's Library in Los Angeles, estimates that vegetarian cookbooks account for about 15 percent of her sales. Here are her 10 best-sellers (in no particular order): *The Greens Cookbook* and *The Savory Way*, both by Deborah Madison; *Fields of Green* by Annie Somerville; *Almost Vegetarian* by Diana Shaw; *Friendly Foods* by Brother Ron Pickarski; *Verdura* by Viana La Place; *Moosewood Cookbook* (revised) by Mollie Katzen; *Quick Vegetarian Pleasures* by Jeanne Lemlin; *Fast Vegetarian Feasts* by Martha Rose Shulman; and *Classic Indian Vegetable and Grain Cooking* by Julie Sahni.

cream, salt, and pepper, and bring to a boil. Stir in the dissolved potato starch and simmer just until thickened, about 2 minutes. Stir in the Cognac and chives.

3. Arrange the toasted bread on individual plates. Spoon the mushrooms and cream on top and serve.—JACQUES PEPIN

SAUTE OF MIXED MUSHROOMS

6 SERVINGS

- 1½ pounds assorted fresh wild mushrooms, such as red and black chanterelles and cèpes (porcini)
- 3 tablespoons unsalted butter
- 2 tablespoons extra-virgin olive oil
- 3 medium shallots, minced
- 3 large garlic cloves, minced
- 1 teaspoon salt
- ½ teaspoon freshly ground pepper
- ½ cup coarsely chopped assorted fresh herbs, such as flat-leaf parsley, oregano, and chives
- Crusty French bread, for serving

1. Rinse the mushrooms thoroughly in cool water. Lift the mushrooms from the water and drain well. Cut the larger mushrooms into 1-inch pieces.

2. Melt the butter in the oil in a large saucepan. Add the mushrooms and sauté over high heat until the exuded liquid has evaporated and the mushrooms are browned all over, about 20 minutes. Add the shallots, garlic, salt, and pepper, and sauté for 1 minute. Sprinkle the herbs on the mushrooms and serve with bread.—JACQUES PEPIN

COUSCOUS-STUFFED ARTICHOKES

4 SERVINGS

- 1¼ cups instant couscous
- 1¼ cups boiling water
- 4 large artichokes
- 3½ tablespoons unsalted butter
- 1½ tablespoons olive oil
- 3 large garlic cloves, minced
- 3 large shallots, minced
- ⅛ teaspoon cayenne pepper
- 2 tablespoons tomato paste
- ½ cup frozen baby peas
- 2 teaspoons fresh lemon juice
- 1 tablespoon chopped fresh thyme
- 1 teaspoon salt
- ¼ cup freshly grated Parmesan cheese

1. Put the couscous in a large bowl and pour the boiling water on top. Cover and set aside for about 10 minutes, or until the water is absorbed and the couscous is tender but firm. Fluff up with a fork.

2. With a serrated stainless steel knife, cut off the top third of each artichoke. Trim the stems so that the artichokes will sit upright. Put the artichokes in a steamer basket, cover, and steam over moderate heat until the bottoms can be easily pierced with a fork, about 30 minutes.

3. Pull out the small center leaves from each artichoke until you reach the chokes. Scoop out the chokes with a spoon.

4. Preheat the oven to 375°. In a medium skillet, melt 1 tablespoon of the butter in the oil over moderately low heat. Add the garlic and shallots, cover, and cook, stirring once or twice, until translucent, about 5 minutes. Uncover, add the cayenne, and cook for 30 seconds. Add the tomato paste and cook, stirring, for 1 minute. Off the heat, add the peas, lemon juice, and thyme. Scrape this mixture into the couscous and mix well. Season with the salt and add 3 tablespoons of the Parmesan and more cayenne pepper if desired.

5. To stuff the artichokes with the couscous, gently open the leaves a bit to make room. Fill the cavities and use a small spoon to stuff the couscous in between the leaves. Put the artichokes in a baking dish that holds them snugly. Dot the top of each artichoke with the remaining 2½ tablespoons butter and sprinkle with the remaining 1 tablespoon Parmesan. Bake for about 25 minutes, or until heated through and lightly crusted. Serve hot or warm.—MARCIA KIESEL

SAUTEED SPINACH SALAD WITH TOASTED SESAME SEEDS Q

4 SERVINGS

2 teaspoons sesame seeds
1 pound fresh spinach, stemmed
1 teaspoon fresh lemon juice
½ teaspoon soy sauce
Pinch of sugar
Pinch of salt
2 teaspoons sesame oil

1. Bring a medium saucepan of lightly salted water to a boil. In a small heavy skillet, toast the sesame seeds over moderate heat, shaking the pan occasionally, until the seeds are fragrant, about 4 minutes.
2. Add the spinach to the boiling water and blanch for 1 minute. Drain, rinse with cold water, and drain again thoroughly; squeeze the spinach dry. Coarsely chop the spinach and transfer to a medium bowl.
3. In a small bowl, combine the lemon juice, soy sauce, sugar, and salt. Stir in the sesame oil. Pour this sesame dressing over the spinach and toss to coat. Let stand at room temperature until ready to serve.
4. Divide the blanched spinach and its sesame dressing among 4 small bowls or plates, sprinkle with the toasted sesame seeds, and serve.—KENNETH WAPNER

SAUTEED SPINACH WITH GARLIC AND ORANGE Q

2 SERVINGS

1 small navel orange
1 tablespoon unsalted butter
1 garlic clove, minced
¾ pound fresh spinach, stemmed
Salt and freshly ground pepper

1. Using a knife, peel the orange, removing all the white pith. Cut between the membranes to release the segments; halve them crosswise.
2. Melt the butter in a medium nonreactive saucepan. Add the garlic and cook over moderately

Sauté of Mixed Mushrooms

Couscous-Stuffed Artichoke

high heat, stirring, until fragrant, about 2 minutes. Add the spinach and toss to coat. Cover and cook until the spinach is wilted, about 2 minutes. Drain off any liquid and season with salt and freshly ground pepper. Stir in the orange segments and serve.—BOB CHAMBERS

CHOPPING METHODS

Q: Does the method used to slice or chop food affect its taste? For instance, do tomatoes that are pureed in a food mill taste different from those processed in a blender?

A: Yes and yes. You release the flavor of fruits and vegetables when you slice, chop, or crush them. The action cuts the plant cells, which have different chemical substances sealed off in different sections. When you cut a cell, compounds freed from one part of the cell mix with substances in other parts to produce different tastes. The flavor changes according to how many times you tear the cells. This process is easy to demonstrate with something strong, such as garlic. A whole clove has a mild flavor when cooked; a slightly crushed clove has more flavor, a sliced one even more, and a chopped one the most.

Equipment that produces greater or lesser degrees of cell damage will yield different results. A food mill crushes fewer cells than a blender or food processor, giving a somewhat milder taste to foods such as your tomatoes.—SHIRLEY CORRIHER

CREAMED SPINACH AND WATERCRESS

8 SERVINGS

- 1 tablespoon unsalted butter
- ½ pound shallots, finely chopped (about 1 cup)
- 2½ pounds spinach, large stems trimmed, thoroughly washed
- 2 large bunches of watercress, stems trimmed, washed
- 1 cup heavy cream
- Salt and freshly ground pepper
- 4 to 5 tablespoons freshly grated Parmesan cheese

1. Melt the butter in a large, heavy, nonreactive saucepan. Add the shallots and cook over moderate heat, stirring occasionally, until softened, about 5 minutes.

2. Add the spinach and watercress to the pan with only the water that clings to their leaves. Cover and cook over moderately high heat, stirring once, until wilted and tender, about 5 minutes. Drain the greens and finely chop. Rinse the pan.

3. Add the cream and bring to a boil over moderate heat. Boil until reduced to ¾ cup, about 2 minutes. Remove from the heat, stir in the greens, and season with salt and pepper. Spread the mixture in an oval gratin dish. (MAKE AHEAD: The recipe can be made to this point up to 1 day ahead; let the greens cool, then cover and refrigerate. Return to room temperature before proceeding.)

4. Preheat the oven to 375°. Sprinkle the greens with the Parmesan cheese and bake for about 20 minutes, or until bubbling and the cheese is melted. Serve at once.—DIANA STURGIS

KALE WITH SHERRY VINEGAR

8 SERVINGS

- 3 pounds kale, stems trimmed
- 2 tablespoons peanut oil
- 3 large garlic cloves, minced
- ¼ teaspoon crushed red pepper
- 2½ tablespoons sherry vinegar
- 2 tablespoons soy sauce
- 2 teaspoons Asian sesame oil
- Kosher salt and freshly ground black pepper
- 1 tablespoon sesame seeds

1. Bring a large saucepan of salted water to a boil. Add the kale by the handful, pressing down with tongs or a spoon as the kale wilts into the water. When all of the kale has been added, stir well and boil over high heat until tender, about 5 minutes. Drain the kale in a colander, lightly pressing with a spoon to extract some of the excess moisture. When the kale is cool enough to handle, chop it into 2-inch pieces. Transfer to a large glass or ceramic baking dish or a heatproof serving dish.

2. Heat the peanut oil in a small nonreactive skillet. Add the garlic and crushed red pepper and cook over moderately high heat, stirring, until fragrant, about 2 minutes. Remove the pan from the heat and stir in the vinegar, soy sauce, and sesame oil. Pour the dressing over the kale and mix well. Season with kosher salt and black pepper.

3. In a small skillet, toast the sesame seeds over moderate heat, shaking the pan often, until golden brown, about 4 minutes. Transfer the seeds to a plate to cool. (MAKE AHEAD: The recipe can be made to this point up to 1 day ahead. Cover the kale and refrigerate; cover the cooled sesame seeds and set aside at room temperature.)
4. Preheat the oven to 400°. Sprinkle 3 tablespoons of water over the kale. Cover tightly with foil. Bake the kale for about 20 minutes, or until heated through.
5. If necessary, season the kale with a few drops of vinegar, soy sauce, and sesame oil. Sprinkle the sesame seeds all over the top and serve at once.—MARCIA KIESEL

SAUTEED LEAFY GREENS

Look for the freshest greens in your market and create your own combination for this side dish.

8 SERVINGS

2 pounds bok choy, stem ends trimmed
1 pound escarole, stem ends trimmed
½ pound kale, tough stems trimmed
Salt
2 tablespoons olive oil
3 medium garlic cloves, minced
1 tablespoon minced fresh ginger
Freshly ground pepper

1. Using a large sharp knife, cut the bok choy crosswise ½ inch thick. Keep the white stalks and green leaves separate. Slice the escarole and kale crosswise into ½-inch strips.
2. Bring a large saucepan of water to a boil; add salt to taste. Add the bok choy stalks and cook for 30 seconds. Add the escarole and kale to the pan and cook for 2 minutes. Drain well. (MAKE AHEAD: The recipe can be made to this point up to 4 hours ahead.)
3. In a wok or large heavy skillet, heat the oil until hot but not smoking. Add the garlic and ginger and cook over moderate heat for 1 minute. Add the uncooked bok choy leaves and the drained greens and toss over moderately high heat until the bok choy is just tender, about 3 minutes. Season with salt and pepper. Serve hot.—JOAN AND DICK ERATH

BRAISED MIXED GREENS WITH GLAZED RUTABAGAS

Chunks of butter-glazed rutabaga make a sweet and colorful contrast with the slightly bitter greens, which are flavored with bacon in the traditional Southern style. Try using an assortment of greens, including collards, mustard greens, turnip greens, and kale.

12 SERVINGS

2 large rutabagas (about 2 pounds each), peeled and cut into 1-inch cubes
1½ tablespoons unsalted butter
1½ teaspoons finely chopped fresh thyme
Salt and freshly ground black pepper
4 ounces thick-sliced smoked bacon, cut into ½-inch-wide strips
2 small onions, thinly sliced
2 garlic cloves, minced
1 teaspoon crushed red pepper
6 pounds assorted greens, large stems removed, greens cut into 1-inch strips
2 teaspoons sugar (optional)

1. In a large saucepan, combine the rutabagas with the butter, thyme, 1 teaspoon salt, ½ teaspoon pepper, and 6 cups of water. Bring to a boil over high heat. Lower the heat to moderate and cook, stirring occasionally, until tender, 25 to 30 minutes. Using a slotted spoon, transfer the rutabagas to a bowl. Boil the cooking liquid over high heat until reduced to about ¾ cup, 10 to 15 minutes. Gently stir in the rutabagas and keep warm.
2. In a large saucepan, cook the bacon over moderately high heat, stirring often, until crisp, about 5 minutes. Add the onions, garlic, and crushed red pepper, and cook, stirring often, until the onion is tender, about 5 minutes. Add the greens in batches, stirring each batch to wilt slightly before adding more. Cover and

Kale with Sherry Vinegar

cook, stirring often, until wilted, about 15 minutes. Add the sugar, 2 teaspoons salt, and 1½ teaspoons pepper. Lower the heat to moderate, cover partially, and cook until the greens are completely tender, about 15 minutes longer. (MAKE AHEAD: The rutabagas and greens can be refrigerated separately for up to 1 day. Reheat before proceeding.)

3. Drain the greens, reserving the liquid, and transfer to a platter. Boil the reserved liquid over moderately high heat, until reduced to ¼ cup, about 5 minutes, then stir into the greens. Add the rutabagas and stir gently to combine. Serve hot.—PATRICK CLARK

USING YOUR ONIONS

- **Onions should feel firm when pressed and should not be covered with a powdery gray mold.**
- **When cutting onions, use a stainless steel knife. A carbon steel blade will sometimes discolor the onions.**
- **There is a greater concentration of the irritating sulfur compound in the root, so cut from top to bottom, leaving the root end intact for as long as possible.**
- **To peel pearl and boiling onions, blanch them in a pot of boiling water for one minute, then drain and plunge them into ice water. Using a small sharp knife, cut off both the root and stem ends and remove the skin.**
- **Chop onions in a food processor only when using in a soup or very runny sauce. It bruises the pieces, and they will disintegrate during cooking.—FRED AND LINDA GRIFFITH**

A MESS O' GREENS

Collard greens are cooked with a bit of pork, then served with a cruet of hot pepper vinegar, which you can make yourself by replacing one-fourth of the vinegar in a bottle with whole or sliced hot peppers. Set the vinegar aside for one week before using.

A mess of greens is usually about 12 plants, weighing about 8 pounds. They can be cooked several days in advance and reheated.

12 SERVINGS

- ¾ pound smoked pork neck bones or ham hocks
- 8 pounds collard greens
- 2 dried hot peppers (optional)
- Hot pepper vinegar, for serving

1. Put the pork bones in a large nonreactive pot, add 1 gallon of water, and boil over moderately high heat for 30 minutes.

2. Meanwhile, clean the greens by pulling off the leaves and rinsing them thoroughly under running water. Discard any yellowish or wilted leaves and any thick stalks. Cover the greens with water and continue filling the sink with as much water as it will hold. Gently shake the greens around in the water so that any dirt falls to the bottom of the sink. Lift out the greens. Repeat the rinsing process as many times as necessary until the greens are completely free of grit.

3. Tear the greens into pieces about the size of your palm and add them to the pot with the hot peppers, if using. Simmer the collard greens over moderate heat until they are very tender, or done to your liking. They can take as little as 45 minutes and as long as 2 hours. Serve the greens straight from the pot with a slotted spoon. Pass the hot pepper vinegar at the table so that guests can season their greens to taste.—JOHN MARTIN TAYLOR

SLICING ONIONS

Q: How can I prevent my eyes from tearing when I slice an onion?

A: Jean Marie Josselin, chef and owner of A Pacific Cafe in Kauai, Hawaii, halves an onion and sets it in ice water for a couple of minutes before slicing, and he never cries.—ARLENE FELTMAN-SAILHAC

GREENS WITH MUSTARD SEEDS

4 SERVINGS

- 1 pound collard greens or 1½ pounds spinach, stemmed
- 1 teaspoon mustard seeds
- 1 tablespoon olive oil
- 1 garlic clove, minced
- Salt and freshly ground pepper

1. In a large saucepan of boiling salted water, cook the collard greens until just tender, 10 to 15 minutes. If using spinach, blanch the leaves in boiling water for about 1 minute. Drain the greens well and chop them coarsely.

2. In a large skillet, toast the mustard seeds over moderately high heat until slightly darkened, about 1 minute. Transfer the seeds to a plate. In the same skillet, heat the oil. Add the garlic and cook over moderately high heat until fragrant, about 1 minute. Add the greens and cook, tossing to blend the greens with the garlic. Season with salt and pepper, transfer to plates or a bowl, and sprinkle with the toasted mustard seeds.—MARCIA KIESEL

CAULIFLOWER AND RED LENTIL DAL

Dal is a classic Indian dish of spicy stewed lentils. Tiny red or orange lentils cook quickly and simmer down to a golden puree.

4 SERVINGS

- 2 tablespoons vegetable oil
- 1 small onion, finely chopped
- 2 large garlic cloves, minced
- 1 tablespoon minced fresh ginger
- 3 tablespoons chopped fresh coriander (cilantro) stems
- ⅛ to ¼ teaspoon cayenne pepper
- 1 teaspoon turmeric
- ¾ cup red lentils (about 5 ounces), rinsed
- 1 head of cauliflower (about 2 pounds), cored and separated into large clusters
- Salt
- Fresh lemon juice
- Fresh coriander (cilantro) leaves, for garnish

1. In a medium saucepan, heat the oil over moderately high heat. Add the onion and cook, stirring, for a minute or so. Add the garlic and ginger and stir until fragrant, about 2 minutes. Add the coriander stems, cayenne, and turmeric, and stir over moderate heat to cook the spices, 2 to 3 minutes.

2. Add the lentils and coat them with the flavoring mixture. Add the cauliflower and stir a few times. Pour in 2½ cups of water and bring to a boil. Reduce the heat to low, cover, and simmer for 15 minutes, or until the cauliflower is just tender and the lentils are cooked. Season with salt and lemon juice to taste. (MAKE AHEAD: The recipe can be prepared to this point 1 day ahead and refrigerated, covered. Reheat before serving.) Garnish with coriander leaves.—MARCIA KIESEL

LEMON AND GARLIC ROASTED BEETS LF

6 SERVINGS

- 1 pound medium beets—peeled, halved, and sliced ¼ inch thick
- 4 medium garlic cloves, thinly sliced
- 2 tablespoons fresh lemon juice
- ¼ teaspoon finely grated lemon zest
- ½ teaspoon olive oil
- ¼ teaspoon sugar
- Salt and freshly ground pepper

Preheat the oven to 375°. In an 8-inch square nonreactive baking dish, toss the beets with the garlic, lemon juice, lemon zest, oil, and sugar. Season with salt and pepper and spread the beets in a single layer. Spray an 8-inch piece of parchment paper lightly with olive oil cooking spray and set it oiled-side down on the beets. Cover tightly with foil and roast, shaking the pan occasionally, for about 40 minutes, until the beets are tender. (MAKE AHEAD: The beets can be prepared up to 1 day ahead; cover and refrigerate. Rewarm before serving.) Serve the beets warm or hot.—GRACE PARISI

LEMON-LACQUERED RADISHES, SHALLOTS AND BRUSSELS SPROUTS

8 SERVINGS

- 1½ pounds medium brussels sprouts, trimmed and bottoms scored with an "x"
- ¼ cup sugar
- ⅓ cup fresh lemon juice
- 1 tablespoon finely grated lemon zest
- 1 pound medium shallots, peeled
- 1 pound medium radishes, ¼ inch of the green tops left on
- 3 tablespoons unsalted butter

QUICK DINNER

This colorful plate was inspired by the many vegetable preparations and fragrant spice mixtures in the Indian repertoire. In the East, a flatbread such as puri or naan would be served to scoop up the little stews. You can use warmed pita bread or flour tortillas, or you can make your own Roti, a flatbread similar to puri.

CAULIFLOWER AND RED LENTIL DAL (P. 325)

CURRIED POTATOES AND BABY LIMA BEANS (P. 278)

CUCUMBER-POPPY SEED RAITA (P. 355)

GREENS WITH MUSTARD SEEDS (P. 324)

ROTI (P. 339)

¼ teaspoon ground cardamom
Coarse salt and freshly ground pepper

1. Bring a large saucepan of salted water to a boil. Add the brussels sprouts and cook over moderately high heat until crisp-tender, about 3 minutes. Plunge the sprouts into a bowl of ice water to cool, then drain.

Lemon-Lacquered Radishes, Shallots and Brussels Sprouts

Brussels Sprouts with Sun-Dried Tomatoes

2. In a large nonstick skillet, combine the sugar, lemon juice, and lemon zest. Cook over moderate heat, stirring occasionally, until the sugar turns golden brown, about 7 minutes. Add the shallots and radishes. Stir in 1 tablespoon of the butter, the cardamom, and 1½ cups of water, and season with 1¼ teaspoons coarse salt and ¼ teaspoon pepper. Cover and cook over moderate heat for 5 minutes, tossing frequently. Uncover and boil over moderately high heat until the vegetables are crisp-tender and glazed, about 7 minutes. Transfer to a bowl. (MAKE AHEAD: The recipe can be prepared to this point up to 1 day ahead; cover and refrigerate the glazed vegetables and the brussels sprouts separately. Let them return to room temperature before serving.) —SANFORD D'AMATO

BRUSSELS SPROUTS WITH SUN-DRIED TOMATOES

8 SERVINGS

2 pounds brussels sprouts
¼ cup drained and coarsely chopped oil-packed sun-dried tomatoes plus 1½ tablespoons of their oil
1 tablespoon unsalted butter, softened
1 tablespoon Dijon mustard
1 teaspoon fresh lemon juice
Kosher salt and freshly ground pepper

1. Bring a large saucepan of salted water to a boil. Meanwhile, using a small, sharp knife, trim the brussels sprouts and score the root ends with an "x". Cook over high heat until crisp-tender and bright green, about 5 minutes. Drain in a colander and refresh under cold water. Halve each of the brussels sprouts and arrange them all in a single layer in a large baking dish or heatproof serving dish.

2. In a medium bowl, combine the sun-dried tomatoes and their oil with the butter, mustard, lemon juice, and 1 teaspoon kosher salt. Mix until thoroughly combined. Dab the tomato mixture evenly all over the brussels sprouts. (MAKE AHEAD: The recipe can be made to this point up to 1 day ahead; cover and refrigerate the brussels sprouts. Return the dish to room temperature before proceeding.)

3. Preheat the oven to 400°. Add 2 tablespoons of water to the baking dish, cover with foil, and bake the brussels sprouts for about 20 minutes, until piping hot. Season the brussels sprouts lightly with kosher salt and pepper and serve.—MARCIA KIESEL

GLAZED CARROTS Q

4 SERVINGS

1¼ pounds thin carrots, peeled and cut into 1-inch lengths
1 tablespoon unsalted butter
1 tablespoon dark or light brown sugar
Salt
¼ teaspoon freshly grated nutmeg
Pinch of cinnamon

Put the carrots in a large saucepan. Add the butter, brown sugar, ½ teaspoon salt, the nutmeg, cinnamon, and 1 cup of water. Bring to a boil over high heat. Lower the heat to moderate and simmer, shaking the pan occasionally, until the carrots are tender and lightly glazed, 20 to 25 minutes; if necessary, continue cooking over moderately high heat to evaporate any remaining liquid. Season the carrots with salt.—SUSAN SHAPIRO JASLOVE

GINGER AND DATE GLAZED CARROTS

8 SERVINGS

- 2 pounds carrots, sliced crosswise ¼ inch thick
- 4 tablespoons unsalted butter
- 1 tablespoon minced fresh ginger
- 1 teaspoon sugar
- Salt and freshly ground pepper
- ½ cup coarsely chopped dried dates (about 10 dates)
- ¼ cup finely chopped fresh flat-leaf parsley

1. In a medium saucepan, combine the carrots, butter, ginger, sugar, 1 teaspoon salt, ½ teaspoon pepper, and 1½ cups of water. Bring to a boil over high heat. Reduce the heat to low and cover. Simmer until tender, about 15 minutes. Transfer to a medium bowl with a slotted spoon.
2. Boil the carrot liquid over moderate heat until syrupy, about 3 minutes. Add the dates and cook until tender, about 2 minutes. Remove from the heat, pour the glaze over the carrots, and toss. (MAKE AHEAD: The recipe can be made to this point up to 1 day ahead. Let the carrots cool to room temperature, cover, and refrigerate. Before proceeding, bring the carrots to a simmer in a large covered saucepan over moderately low heat. Add a tablespoon or two of water if all the liquid has evaporated.)
3. Season the carrots with salt and pepper and transfer to a serving dish. Sprinkle with the parsley and serve.—PATSY A. MADDEN

JERUSALEM ARTICHOKE GRATIN

Topinambur Gratinati

12 SERVINGS

- Salt
- 3 pounds smooth, ungnarled Jerusalem artichokes
- Unsalted butter
- Freshly ground pepper
- ¾ cup freshly grated Parmigiano-Reggiano cheese (about 2½ ounces)

1. Preheat the oven to 400°. Bring 3 quarts of water to a boil in a large saucepan and add salt. Meanwhile, peel the artichokes.
2. Add the larger artichokes to the water first, followed by the smaller ones. Cook them until tender when pierced with a fork; begin testing 10 minutes after the water returns to a boil and check frequently because they go from firm to very soft within minutes. Drain well. As soon as they're cool enough to handle, slice them ½ inch thick.
3. Generously butter a large baking dish. Arrange the sliced artichokes in the dish in overlapping rows, seasoning each layer with salt and pepper. Sprinkle the grated cheese on top and dot with butter. Bake the gratin on the top rack of the oven for about 35 minutes, or until a light golden crust begins to form. Let settle for a few minutes before serving.—MARCELLA HAZAN

TIME-SAVING TIPS

Buy packaged peeled baby carrots, available in many supermarkets, to reduce the prep time for peeling and cutting regular carrots for the Glazed Carrots.

RUTABAGA IN ROASTED GARLIC SAUCE

8 SERVINGS

- 40 garlic cloves, peeled (from about 3 heads)
- 4½ tablespoons unsalted butter, 1½ tablespoons melted
- 1 tablespoon olive oil
- 2 large rutabagas (3¼ pounds)—quartered, peeled, and sliced lengthwise ¼ inch thick
- 1 teaspoon cumin seeds
- 1¼ cups chicken stock or canned low-sodium broth
- Kosher salt and freshly ground pepper
- 1 medium red onion, halved lengthwise and sliced crosswise
- 1 cup fine fresh white bread crumbs
- ¼ cup freshly grated Pecorino Romano cheese

1. Preheat the oven to 350°. In a large, shallow glass or ceramic baking dish, toss the garlic with 2 tablespoons of the butter and the olive oil. Cover with foil and bake for about 30 minutes, until the garlic is tender and golden brown.
2. Meanwhile, bring a large saucepan of salted water to a boil. Add the slices of rutabaga and return to a boil. Cook the

rutabaga over high heat until tender, about 8 minutes. Drain in a colander.

3. In a small skillet, toast the cumin seeds over moderately high heat until fragrant, about 30 seconds. Transfer the toasted seeds to a mortar and let cool, then pound the seeds to a coarse powder. Alternatively, finely chop the toasted cumin seeds with a large sharp knife.

4. Using a fork, mash the garlic to a coarse puree in the baking dish. Add the cumin and chicken stock and stir to make a smooth liquid. Season the sauce with kosher salt and pepper.

5. In a large skillet, melt 1 tablespoon of the butter. Add the red onion slices and cook over moderate heat, stirring, until wilted, about 5 minutes. Using a rubber spatula, stir the red onion and the rutabaga into the garlic sauce in the baking dish and blend well. Season with kosher salt and pepper.

6. In a small bowl, combine the bread crumbs with the 1½ tablespoons melted butter, cheese, ½ teaspoon kosher salt, and ¼ teaspoon pepper. (MAKE AHEAD: The recipe can be made to this point up to 1 day ahead; cover the rutabagas and the bread crumb mixture separately and refrigerate. Return to room temperature before proceeding.)

7. Preheat the oven to 425°. Sprinkle the bread crumb mixture over the red onion and rutabaga mixture and bake in the upper third of the oven for approximately 25 minutes, until the topping is bubbling and richly browned. Serve the rutabagas at once.—MARCIA KIESEL

SQUASH GRATIN WITH ROASTED TOMATO-GARLIC SAUCE

Both butternut and banana squash are good choices here since they're so easy to peel. The roasted tomato sauce, spiced with paprika and cayenne, contrasts nicely with the natural sweetness of the squash.

4 SERVINGS

ROASTED TOMATO SAUCE:

2½ tablespoons vegetable oil
5 unpeeled medium garlic cloves
1¼ pounds ripe plum tomatoes
¼ cup finely diced onion
1 teaspoon sweet paprika
Pinch of cayenne pepper
Salt and freshly ground black pepper
Pinch of sugar (optional)

2½ to 3 pounds butternut or banana squash—peeled, halved, seeded, and sliced crosswise ⅓ inch thick
½ cup all-purpose flour
About ¾ cup olive oil, for frying
Salt and freshly ground black pepper
4 ounces Fontina cheese, thinly sliced
2 tablespoons finely chopped assorted fresh herbs such as flat-leaf parsley, sage, and thyme

1. Make the roasted tomato sauce: Heat ½ tablespoon of the vegetable oil in a small skillet. Add the garlic, cover, and cook over low heat, shaking the pan occasionally, until the skins are charred and the garlic is softened, about 20 minutes. Let cool slightly, then remove the skins.

2. Meanwhile, heat a large heavy skillet. In a large bowl, toss the tomatoes with 1 tablespoon of the vegetable oil to coat. Add the tomatoes to the skillet and cook over moderately high heat, turning occasionally, until the skins are blistered and slightly charred, about 8 minutes. Transfer the unpeeled tomatoes to a food processor, add the peeled garlic, and puree until smooth.

3. Heat the remaining 1 tablespoon vegetable oil in the large skillet. Add the onion and cook over moderately high heat, stirring occasionally, until translucent, about 5 minutes. Add the pureed tomatoes, paprika, and cayenne, and cook over moderate heat, stirring occasionally, until the sauce thickens, about 15 minutes. Season the sauce with salt, black pepper, and the sugar. (MAKE AHEAD: The sauce can be made up to 3 days ahead; cover and refrigerate.)

4. Preheat the oven to 375°. Lightly oil a 3-quart shallow gratin or glass baking dish. In a large bowl, toss the squash slices in the flour, shaking to remove the excess.

5. Heat ¼ cup of the olive oil in the large skillet. Working in three batches, fry one-third of the squash slices in a single layer over moderately high heat, turning once, until lightly browned and just tender, about 4 minutes per side. Transfer to paper towels to drain and season with salt and black pepper. Fry the remaining batches of squash slices in the remaining olive oil.

6. Spread the roasted tomato sauce evenly in the bottom of the prepared gratin dish. Arrange the fried squash slices on top and tuck the cheese slices among the squash slices. Cover the gratin dish with foil and bake for about 25 minutes, or until the cheese is melted and the gratin is thoroughly heated. Remove the gratin from the oven and preheat the broiler. Uncover the gratin and broil until nicely browned on top. Sprinkle the fresh herbs all over the top of the gratin and serve at once.—DEBORAH MADISON

BUTTERNUT SQUASH COINS WITH CILANTRO SALSA

Try to choose a butternut squash with a long slender neck so the "coins" cut from it will be small and attractive.

6 SERVINGS

One 3-pound butternut or delicata squash (see Note)
About ¼ cup plus 2 tablespoons olive oil, for frying
Salt and freshly ground pepper
Cilantro Salsa (recipe follows)

1. Cut the neck of the butternut squash from the round base; reserve the base for soups, stocks, or purees. Stand the squash neck on its end and, using a sharp knife, slice downward with sure, even strokes to remove the skin in 5 or 6 long pieces and to create the base for many-sided coins. (For rounder coins, use a vegetable peeler instead of a knife to remove the skin.) Slice the squash neck crosswise ¼ inch thick.

2. Heat 3 tablespoons of the olive oil in a large skillet. Working in batches, add the squash coins in a single layer and fry over moderately high heat, turning once, until lightly browned, about 5 minutes. Drain on paper towels and keep warm in a low oven while you fry the rest of the squash in the remaining olive oil. Season with salt and pepper.

3. Transfer the squash coins to a platter or individual plates, drizzle with a little of the Cilantro Salsa, and serve with the remaining salsa alongside.

NOTE: An oval-shaped delicata squash makes attractive round squash coins. Trim the ends, peel off the skin with a vegetable peeler, and remove the seeds from the center using a long-handled spoon. Cut the squash into ⅓-inch-thick rings and proceed as for Step 2, frying them until lightly browned and tender.

Cilantro Salsa

This spicy condiment goes wonderfully with many vegetables—grilled eggplant, baked tomatoes, chilled beets, as well as chickpeas and white beans. You can leave the seeds in the chile for a hotter salsa.

MAKES ABOUT 1⅓ CUPS

1 large bunch of fresh cilantro, coarsely chopped
½ cup fresh mint leaves, coarsely chopped
3 medium garlic cloves, peeled
Fresh ginger, 2-inch piece, peeled and coarsely chopped
1 serrano chile, coarsely chopped
½ cup extra-virgin olive oil
⅓ cup fresh lime juice
1 tablespoon sweet paprika
1 teaspoon ground cumin
½ teaspoon ground coriander
¼ teaspoon salt

In a food processor, combine the cilantro, mint, garlic, ginger, chile, and ¼ cup of water, and puree until a smooth sauce forms. Add the oil, lime juice, paprika, cumin, coriander, and salt, and pulse to combine. (MAKE AHEAD: The salsa can be prepared up to 4 hours ahead; cover and let stand at room temperature.)—DEBORAH MADISON

ROASTED BUTTERCUP SQUASH AND BAKED APPLES

Richly flavored orange- and yellow-fleshed winter squash such as buttercup, butternut, and turban need no fancy treatment; slowly roasted with a little olive oil and herbs, these dense, buttery squash are delicious with baked apples. A small dollop of Spicy Thickened Yogurt (p. 355) makes a nice topping for this dish.

4 SERVINGS

One 4-pound buttercup squash, halved crosswise, seeds scraped out
Olive oil
Fresh thyme leaves
Salt and freshly ground pepper
4 large Cortland apples, cored

Butternut Squash Coins with Cilantro Salsa

1. Preheat the oven to 375°. Rub the cut sides of the squash with olive oil. Sprinkle with thyme leaves and season with salt and pepper. Put the squash halves cut sides down on a baking sheet and bake until tender, about 40 minutes.

PREPARING SQUASH

A pound of squash yields about 1¾ cups cooked meat.
TO CUT **a small winter squash, knock off the dried stem by pressing it firmly against the counter. Then, with a whack, sink the blade (not the tip) of a large chef's knife or cleaver into the squash, and press down on it heavily or tap it with a mallet, using a rocking motion to help the knife work its way through.**
TO PEEL **squash whose surfaces are warty or convoluted, first steam the cut and seeded pieces until tender, at least 20 minutes. Or brush squash pieces with oil and bake, cut side down, at 350° for about 30 minutes, until the skin is soft when pressed. Then slice off the skin.**
TO BAKE **whole squash, pierce it in several places with a knife, then set it in a baking dish and bake at 350° for one hour, or until tender. Halve the squash, remove the seeds, season, and eat (you can roast and salt the seeds for great out-of-hand eating). Or scoop out the meat to use for a puree, pie, soup, or other dish.—DEBORAH MADISON**

2. Meanwhile, stand the apples in a glass or ceramic baking dish big enough to hold them comfortably. When the squash has baked for 15 minutes, put the apples on the middle shelf of the oven and bake for about 25 minutes, or until soft and puffed up. Turn the apples as necessary during baking so they will cook evenly.
3. To serve, transfer the apples to plates with a spatula and spoon the juices on top. Halve each piece of squash again and serve alongside the apples.—MARCIA KIESEL

CURRIED VEGETARIAN STEW WITH WINTER SQUASH AND TOFU

This is a true Buddhist vegetarian stew, made without any meat or fish. Soy sauce is used in place of fish sauce; garlic and scallions are omitted. Firm tofu cakes add texture.

4 TO 6 SERVINGS

- 2 tablespoons vegetable oil
- 2 large leeks, split lengthwise and thinly sliced crosswise
- 2 tablespoons minced fresh ginger
- ½ Thai, or bird, chile or 1 serrano chile, minced
- 1 tablespoon curry powder
- 1 medium butternut squash (about 2 pounds)—quartered, seeded, peeled, and cut into 1-inch cubes
- 1 teaspoon sugar
- 1-inch piece of cinnamon stick
- 2 tablespoons soy sauce
- 1 cup unsweetened coconut milk
- 10 ounces firm tofu (bean curd), cut into 1-inch cubes
- Salt
- About 6 cups steamed long-grain white rice, preferably jasmine (see "Cooking Rice," p. 105)
- ½ cup roasted unsalted peanuts (about 2 ounces), coarsely chopped
- ¼ cup fresh coriander (cilantro) leaves

QUICK FIXES FOR SQUASH

ROAST SQUASH: **Cut unpeeled squash into chunks if large; halves if small. Brush with olive oil. Season and bake at 375° for 40 minutes.**
SAUTEED SQUASH: **Peel and grate into long shreds. Sauté in olive oil with onions. Add salt, pepper, toasted pecans, minced garlic, and sage.**
SQUASH GRATIN: **Cube peeled squash and toss in flour. Toss the squash with parsley, sage, and garlic. Place in a gratin dish, drizzle with oil, and bake at 350° for about 1½ hours.—DEBORAH MADISON**

1. Heat the oil in a medium dutch oven or enameled cast-iron casserole. Add the leeks and cook over moderately high heat, stirring, until wilted, about 3 minutes. Add the ginger and chile. Cook, stirring, until fragrant, about 1 minute. Stir in the curry powder and cook until fragrant, about 2 minutes. Add the squash, sugar, cinnamon, soy sauce, and 3 cups of water. Bring to a boil. Cover and cook over moderately low heat until the squash is just tender, about 15 minutes. (MAKE AHEAD: The recipe can be made to this point up to 1 day ahead; cover and refrigerate. Rewarm and proceed.)
2. Stir the coconut milk and the tofu into the stew and bring to a

WINTER SQUASH

ACORN SQUASH, one of the most familiar on the American table, is mild in flavor. It's difficult to peel because of its hard, ridged exterior, but lends itself well to stuffing; halve, then fill the cavity. To bring out its subtle nutty flavor, bake with a sprinkling of butter, brown sugar, and spices on top.

AUSTRALIAN BLUE SQUASH, OR AUSTRALIAN QUEENSLAND PUMPKIN, gets its name from its blue-gray-green exterior. It has a mild flavor and soft texture that is best suited for soups and baked goods.

BANANA SQUASH, which can tip the scales at as much as 40 pounds, is often sold in pieces weighing a pound or so. It's a good, basic, easy-to-peel squash, with pale pinkish-orange flesh. Leave it in large pieces, or cut it into smaller "steaks" and roast.

BLACK FOREST, BUTTERCUP, HOKKAIDO (ALSO CALLED RED KURI), AND HONEY DELIGHT SQUASH are moderate-sized varieties, averaging about five pounds. They are prized for their rich, sweet, dense, fine-grained flesh, which is most often a deep orange. They make flavorful soups, silky purees, and exceptional pies. They can also be worked into batters for delicious muffins, waffles, breads, and cakes.

BUTTERNUT SQUASH, buckskin-colored with a long neck and bulbous bottom, is the workhorse of winter squash. It tastes good and is readily available; its smooth, thin skin is easily peeled; and its slender neck, which is free of seeds, is easy to cut into pieces. Grill or roast butternut, or use for gratins.

DELICATA, JACK-BE-LITTLE, AND MUNCHKIN SQUASH are good if you're cooking for one. Small and sweet, the oblong delicata is cream-colored with dark green stripes on the outside and deep orange-yellow inside. It is great stuffed. Jack-Be-Little and Munchkin are miniature pumpkins. Their sweet flesh makes fine eating—and, being small, they don't take long to cook.

GREEN STRIPED CUSHAW SQUASH is a prolific producer on the vine. It's fine for baking but doesn't stand too well on its own. Its large seeds, however, make a tasty snack if roasted.

HUBBARD SQUASH are goofy-looking, old-fashioned varieties with blue, orange, or green skin that's often covered with wartlike bumps. Large ones weigh 40 pounds or more, with tough skins that resist most cutting implements; you might be tempted to use a chainsaw. Fortunately the Baby Blue Hubbards and Golden Hubbards come in the 5- to 10-pound range. If you can't slice the squash with a knife or cleaver, bake it until softened and divide into pieces. Hubbards have dense, sweet, flavorful flesh, and they're great for stuffing or pureeing.

PUMPKINS come in many varieties, but the small orange Sugar Pumpkin has long set the standard for pie pumpkins. It can be carved, but is sweeter and finer than most jack-o'-lantern types. Some surprising newcomers, among them the ghostly Lumina, have white skins, but inside you'll find the same familiar orange flesh.

SWEET DUMPLING SQUASH resembles a squat round version of the oblong delicata. It has the same green-striped, cream-colored skin, but very sweet, tender orange flesh. Hollowed out, it makes an attractive miniature soup container and takes well to stuffing.

ROUGE D'ETAMPES SQUASH, a French pumpkin variety, is marvelously curvaceous—as shapely as Cinderella's golden coach—and luscious to eat, proving that you can use a large pumpkin without sacrificing flavor. Of all the pumpkins suitable for cooking, this is the best. It has fine-grained, flavorful flesh. Hollow one out and fill it with milk, cream, layers of bread, and Gruyère cheese to make a *penade*, or bread soup, baked in the shell. Or use the squash in tagines and stews.

SPAGHETTI SQUASH breaks all the rules and somehow wins. What we usually want in a squash is flesh that is fine-grained, dense, and sweet. Spaghetti squash is just the opposite: stringy and only marginally sweet. It's terrific, all the same. Bake it, then pull the flesh apart with a fork into spaghetti-like strands. Treat it like pasta: sauce with tomato; toss with parsley, garlic and cheese; or serve with a vegetable sauté.—DEBORAH MADISON

simmer over moderate heat, stirring gently. Season with salt.

3. Divide the rice among 4 to 6 individual bowls and ladle the stew on top. Sprinkle with the peanuts and coriander. Serve at once.—MARCIA KIESEL

CHAYOTE IN OYSTER SAUCE

4 SERVINGS

- ½ tablespoon vegetable oil
- 2 medium shallots, thinly sliced
- 2 large chayote—halved lengthwise, pitted, and sliced lengthwise ¼ inch thick
- 1 tablespoon oyster sauce
- ½ teaspoon Oriental sesame oil
- Salt and freshly ground pepper

Heat the vegetable oil in a large skillet. Add the shallots and cook over moderate heat, stirring occasionally, until translucent, about 4 minutes. Add the chayote. Cook, stirring, until heated through, about 2 minutes. Add ¼ cup of water, cover, and simmer until the chayote is translucent, about 4 minutes. Uncover and boil until the liquid evaporates and forms a light coating on the chayote. Stir in the oyster sauce and sesame oil. Season with salt and pepper and serve.—MARCIA KIESEL

Cheese and Sweet Pepper Sandwiches

CASUAL VEGETARIAN SUPPER

CHEESE AND SWEET PEPPER SANDWICHES (P. 332)
ROAST POTATO WEDGES (P. 277)
CHERRY TOMATO SALAD (P. 75)

SIMPLE SHORTBREAD (P. 373)

—SARAH FRITSCHNER

CHEESE AND SWEET PEPPER SANDWICHES

A sandwich like this calls for beer. Pick one with depth of flavor, such as Beck's, Grolsch, or St. Pauli Girl.

4 SERVINGS

- 2 tablespoons olive oil
- 1 red bell pepper, sliced lengthwise into ½-inch strips
- 1 yellow bell pepper, sliced lengthwise into ½-inch strips
- 1 medium onion, thinly sliced
- 1 teaspoon dried thyme
- Hot pepper sauce
- Salt and freshly ground black pepper
- 4 ounces cheese, such as softened goat cheese or thinly sliced sharp Cheddar or Monterey Jack
- 4 long sandwich buns, sliced open lengthwise

1. Heat the oil in a large skillet. Add the bell peppers. Cook over moderate heat, stirring occasionally, until wilted, about 6 minutes. Add the onion. Cook until all the vegetables are softened, about 15 minutes. Stir in the thyme. Season with hot pepper sauce and salt and pepper to taste.

2. Spread or layer the cheese on the bottom half of the buns. Heap the vegetables on top. Close the sandwiches, transfer to plates, and serve.—SARAH FRITSCHNER

FRIED PLANTAINS

Yellow-skinned plantains mottled with brown and black are far sweeter than their green counterparts.

Figure on one large yellow plantain for two small appetites or one hearty one. Peel and slice crosswise ⅓ inch thick. Heat a thin film of vegetable or fresh peanut oil in a large skillet and fry the plantains over moderately high heat until browned, about 1 minute on each side.—MARCIA KIESEL

SMOKY BLACK BEANS

The beans must soak overnight, so plan accordingly. For best flavor, make them a day or two before serving.

4 SERVINGS

- 1½ cups dried black beans
- ¾ cup dried mushrooms,* such as Polish or porcini
- 2 dried chipotle chiles
- 1 large onion, chopped
- 8 fresh thyme sprigs or 1 teaspoon dried
- 2 bay leaves
- Salt and freshly ground black pepper
- Thinly sliced scallions and minced fresh red chile, for garnish
- Hot sauce, for serving

*Available at specialty food shops and large supermarkets

1. Put the beans in a large bowl. Cover with cold water. Let soak overnight at room temperature.
2. Put the dried mushrooms and chipotles in a bowl and add 2 cups of hot water. Cover and set aside to soften for about 30 minutes.
3. Remove the chipotles from the water, trim off the tops, and halve the chiles lengthwise. Scrape out the seeds and cut the chiles into ½ inch pieces. Rinse the mushrooms in their soaking liquid and transfer to paper towels to drain. Coarsely chop them, discarding any tough bits. Reserve the soaking liquid.
4. Drain the beans and put in a large saucepan or small dutch oven. Cover with 10 cups of water and add the chipotles and mushrooms. Pour in their reserved soaking liquid, stopping before you reach the grit at the bottom. Add the onion, thyme, and bay leaves, and bring to a boil over high heat. Reduce the heat to low and simmer, skimming occasionally, until the beans are very tender but still intact, 3 to 5 hours. Add water as necessary if the beans begin to look dry.
5. Discard the thyme sprigs and bay leaves. Season the beans with salt and black pepper. Transfer to plates or a bowl. Garnish with the scallions and chile. Pass hot sauce at the table.—MARCIA KIESEL

RED BEANS WITH PARSLEY AND POMEGRANATE

4 TO 6 SERVINGS

- 2 cups small red beans (about 1 pound)—picked over, rinsed, and soaked overnight in 6 cups of water
- 2 teaspoons coriander seeds
- 3 tablespoons extra-virgin olive oil
- 6 garlic cloves, minced
- Scant 2 tablespoons pomegranate syrup
- ⅓ cup red wine vinegar
- 1½ cups loosely packed flat-leaf parsley leaves, coarsely chopped
- Salt

1. In a large saucepan, cover the beans with 8 cups cold water and bring to a boil over high heat. Reduce the heat to moderately high and cook until very tender, 1½ to 2 hours. Drain and set aside. (MAKE AHEAD: The beans can be refrigerated up to 3 days or frozen for up to 1 month.)
2. In a small dry skillet, toast the coriander over moderately high heat, stirring often, until darkened and fragrant, about 1½ minutes. Transfer to a spice grinder or a mortar and grind to a powder.
3. Heat the oil in a large heavy skillet. Add the garlic and stir-fry over moderately high heat until just beginning to color. Stir in the ground coriander and then the drained beans. Cook over moderate heat, stirring gently, until warmed through.
4. Meanwhile, whisk the pomegranate syrup with the vinegar. Stir into the beans and remove from the heat. Fold in the parsley until evenly distributed and season with salt. Serve warm or at room temperature.—JEFFREY ALFORD AND NAOMI DUGUID

FIRESIDE PINTO BEAN AND CHILE STEW LF

If you can't find nopal cactus pads in the produce section of your supermarket, green beans are a good substitute.

6 SERVINGS

- 1 cup dried pinto beans (about 6 ounces), picked over and rinsed
- 12-ounce bottle full-bodied beer
- 1½ teaspoons olive oil
- 1 large celery rib, peeled and cut into ¾-inch dice
- 1 medium red onion, cut into ¾-inch dice
- 1 medium carrot, cut into ¾-inch dice
- 1½ tablespoons minced garlic
- 1 ancho chile, seeded and coarsely crumbled
- 1 cup dry white wine

BLACK BEAN PLATE

This plate evolved from a desire to fill the house with the wonderful scent of baking apples. Dark, rich, and smoky black bean stew is a hearty, aromatic complement to the baked apples and roasted butternut squash. Spaghetti squash, usually served hot and often overcooked, is boiled until still crisp and served as a tangy refreshing salad dressed simply with lemon and olive oil.

The tart milkiness of the yogurt—not to mention the lemon-dressed salad—makes this menu hard to match with wine. The answer? A rich flavorsome ale, such as Samuel Adams or Bass.

SMOKY BLACK BEANS (P. 332)
SPICY THICKENED YOGURT (P. 355)
SPAGHETTI SQUASH SALAD WITH LEMON DRESSING (P. 69)
ROASTED BUTTERCUP SQUASH AND BAKED APPLES (P. 329)
ROTI (P. 339)

Spinach and Portobello Spirals

1 teaspoon cumin seeds
2 medium fresh Anaheim chiles, preferably red, or poblano chiles, seeded and cut into ½-inch dice
½ medium green bell pepper, cut into ¾-inch dice
½ medium yellow bell pepper, cut into ¾-inch dice
2 large pads of nopal cactus, dethorned and cut into ¾-inch dice, or 4 ounces green beans, trimmed and cut into ¾-inch lengths
1 large tomato, seeded and cut into ¾-inch dice
2 tablespoons cider vinegar
1 tablespoon tomato paste
1 tablespoon unsulphured molasses
Kosher salt
About ¼ cup coarsely chopped fresh cilantro, for serving (optional)

1. In a medium saucepan, bring the beans, beer, and 5 cups water to a boil over moderately high heat. Reduce the heat to moderately low. Simmer gently until the beans are tender, about 1½ hours.
2. Heat the oil in a large saucepan. Add the celery, onion, and carrot, and cook over moderately high heat, stirring often, until golden, about 5 minutes. Add the garlic and ancho chile, and stir for 1 minute more. Pour in the wine and cook, stirring, until reduced by half, about 5 minutes.
3. Toast the cumin in a small dry skillet over moderate heat, tossing, until fragrant, about 3 minutes. Transfer to a mortar or spice grinder and grind to a powder.
4. Add the ground cumin to the vegetables along with the Anaheims, green and yellow peppers, the cactus, tomato, cider vinegar, tomato paste, and molasses. Add the beans and their cooking liquid. Cook, stirring occasionally, until the vegetables are tender and the mixture is slightly thickened, 20 to 30 minutes. Season well with salt. (MAKE AHEAD: The stew can be made up to 1 day ahead; cover and refrigerate. Rewarm before serving.) Sprinkle with cilantro.—CHARLES WILEY

SPINACH AND PORTOBELLO SPIRALS

4 SERVINGS

VINAIGRETTE:
¼ cup plus 2 tablespoons red wine vinegar
1 tablespoon plus 1 teaspoon finely grated lemon zest
2 small garlic cloves, minced
2 teaspoons coarsely chopped fresh thyme
2 teaspoons fresh lemon juice
1 teaspoon Dijon mustard
⅔ cup olive oil
Salt and freshly ground pepper

4 large Portobello mushrooms (about 1¼ pounds), stems removed
One 14-ounce package of lavash (shepherd's flatbread)
1 pound sliced lean bacon
4 ounces Roquefort cheese, crumbled
1 pound fresh flat-leaf spinach—stemmed, well washed, and spun dry

1. Make the vinaigrette: In a large bowl, whisk the vinegar with the lemon zest, garlic, thyme, lemon juice, and mustard. Gradually whisk in the oil in a fine stream until incorporated. Season with at least 1 teaspoon salt and ½ teaspoon pepper. Pour ¼ cup of the vinaigrette into a salad bowl; reserve the remainder in the large bowl.
2. With a small sharp knife, trim the dark brown gills from the undersides of the Portobellos. Add the mushroom caps to the vinaigrette in the large bowl and turn to coat.
3. Preheat the oven to 350°. Unwrap the lavash. Separate the two pieces; do not unfold the breads or they will break. Place one on top of the other and wrap loosely in foil. Warm in the oven 10 to 15 minutes to soften. Take out of the oven but do not unwrap.
4. Meanwhile, in a large skillet, fry the bacon over moderate heat until crisp. Drain on paper towels.
5. Light a grill or preheat the broiler. Remove the Portobellos from the vinaigrette and grill or broil for about 8 minutes, turning once or twice, until nicely browned and tender. Fill the concave side of the caps with the crumbled Roquefort and cover with foil to melt the cheese. Let cool, then slice ¼ inch thick.
6. Add the spinach leaves to the reserved dressing and toss well.
7. To assemble the spirals, unfold the sheets of lavash on a work surface. Evenly top them with the spinach, bacon, and Portobellos; arrange the mushrooms and bacon in horizontal rows in a single layer. Beginning at the edge closest to you, roll up the lavash snugly. With a large serrated knife, trim the ends of the rolls and cut each roll diagonally into 5 pieces. Serve immediately or wrap in wax paper for up to four hours.—TRACEY SEAMAN

CHAPTER 15

BREADS

Flatbread with Salad

FLATBREAD WITH SALAD

You can wash the greens a day ahead and store them in a lettuce spinner or a perforated plastic bag.

MAKES 6 SANDWICHES

BREAD:

1 cup lukewarm water
2 teaspoons active dry yeast
2¾ cups all-purpose flour
1¼ teaspoons salt
Olive oil, for greasing

SALAD:

1 large bunch arugula
1 cup (lightly packed) fresh coriander (cilantro) leaves
½ cup (lightly packed) fresh flat-leaf parsley leaves
½ cup (lightly packed) fresh basil leaves
¼ cup (lightly packed) fresh mint leaves
1½ tablespoons extra-virgin olive oil
1 tablespoon fresh lemon juice
1 small garlic clove, minced
Salt and freshly ground pepper

1. Make the bread: In a large bowl, stir together the lukewarm water and yeast. Stir in 1 cup of the flour. Let sit in a draft-free place until the mixture starts to bubble, about 15 minutes. Stir in the salt and 1 more cup of flour until a loose dough forms.

2. Turn out the dough onto a work surface. Knead in up to ¾ cup more flour as necessary until the dough is smooth, elastic, and slightly tacky, about 8 minutes. (Alternatively, mix and knead the dough in a standing electric mixer fitted with a dough hook.)

3. Lightly grease a large bowl with oil, add the dough, and turn to coat. Cover and let the dough rise in a warm place until it is doubled in bulk, 1 to 1½ hours. (MAKE AHEAD: You can make the dough and refrigerate overnight. The next day, let it sit at room temperature until it loses its chill, about 30 minutes, then proceed.)

4. Preheat the oven to 450°. Place a pizza stone or baking tiles on the bottom rack of the oven. Punch down the dough and press with your hands or roll out with a rolling pin into a 9-inch round. Using a fork, prick the dough in 5 places. Place on a floured pizza peel or baking sheet without sides. Slide the dough off the peel or baking sheet onto the pizza stone with a quick jerk. Bake for 12 to 16 minutes, until golden brown. Transfer to a rack to cool completely. (MAKE AHEAD: The bread can be baked up to 1 day ahead; wrap in foil and store in a dry place. Rewarm slightly in a moderate oven before serving.)

5. Just before serving, **make the salad:** Using a large sharp knife, coarsely chop the arugula, coriander, parsley, basil, and mint. Place in a large bowl. In a small bowl, whisk the oil, lemon juice, and garlic. Season with salt and pepper. Dress the salad. Toss well.

6. Using a long serrated knife, split the flatbreads horizontally. Evenly distribute the salad on the bottom halves, then cover with the top halves. Cut into 6 wedges and serve.—JOANNE WEIR

ROTI

This Caribbean flatbread is fashioned after the puri of India.

MAKES 8 FLATBREADS

4 cups all-purpose flour
2¼ teaspoons baking powder
2 teaspoons salt
8 tablespoons unsalted butter, 4 cut into small pieces and 4 melted
1¼ cups ice water plus a bit more if needed
Vegetable oil, for the pan

1. Working over a large bowl, sift the flour with the baking powder and salt. Using a pastry blender or two knives, cut in the small pieces of butter until the mixture resembles coarse meal. Pour in the 1¼ cups ice water and blend with a fork until a dough forms. If the dough seems dry, add 1 or 2 tablespoons more ice water. Flatten the dough into a disk and wrap it in wax paper. Let the dough relax at room temperature for at least 30 minutes before rolling it out. (MAKE AHEAD: The dough can be made up to 1 day in advance and refrigerated.)

2. Cut the dough into 8 equal pieces. Roll each piece into an 8-inch round about ¼ inch thick. Brush each piece with melted butter and fold in half and then in half again, forming a triangle. Set the folded pieces aside to rest for about 15 minutes.

3. Roll out the triangles to 8-inch circles, then pull them into very thin, 10- to 12-inch rounds.

4. Preheat a cast-iron skillet or griddle over low heat for at least 5 minutes. Lightly oil the skillet. Working with 1 piece of dough at a time, cook the roti over moderately high heat until it starts to bubble up from underneath, about 1 minute. Flip the roti, brush it with melted butter, and cook until the underside begins to brown, about 2 minutes. Flip the roti again, brush with melted butter, and cook another minute. Flip and cook one more time for about 1 minute, then transfer the roti to a work surface.

5. Lightly crack the roti all over with the back of a knife, then wrap it in a clean towel to keep warm. Repeat the process to make the remaining roti, oiling the pan occasionally and adjusting the heat to moderate when the pan becomes too hot.—MARCIA KIESEL

GARLIC BREAD IN A BAG Q

If you don't want to use a bag, toast the bread halves separately on an oven rack, buttered sides up, until golden. Using salted butter saves seasoning the bread, but you can use unsalted butter and a large pinch of salt.

4 SERVINGS

- 1 large garlic clove, minced
- 2 tablespoons salted butter, softened
- 1 loaf of Italian bread, preferably semolina, halved lengthwise
- 2 tablespoons freshly grated Parmesan cheese

Preheat the oven to 450°. In a small bowl, blend the garlic with the butter. Spread each bread half with 1 tablespoon of the garlic butter and sprinkle with 1 tablespoon of the Parmesan. Sandwich the bread halves together and put the loaf in a paper bag. Fold the top closed and bake in the center of the oven for about 8 minutes, or until the bag darkens slightly and the bread feels crisp when pressed through the bag.—MARCIA KIESEL

BREAD BAGS

Baking garlic bread in a paper bag might sound odd, but the paper absorbs the moisture created in the bag and produces a dry heat that yields an extra-crisp crust and a hot, moist center. Use the brown or white paper bag that the loaf comes in (but only if it is unwaxed), or substitute one of the narrow, brown-paper bags found at liquor stores.

BUTTERMILK-SCALLION BISCUITS LF

These biscuits can also be made in a 10-inch dutch oven or cast-iron skillet; the cooking time will be the same. The biscuits will run together but can easily be separated.

6 SERVINGS

- Vegetable oil cooking spray
- 1¼ cups unbleached all-purpose flour
- ¼ cup yellow cornmeal
- 2 teaspoons baking powder
- 2 teaspoons sugar
- ½ teaspoon salt
- 1½ teaspoons unsalted butter
- 4 medium scallions, finely chopped
- 1 cup low-fat (1.5%) buttermilk

1. Preheat the oven to 375°. Lightly spray a large baking sheet with the cooking spray. In a large bowl, toss the flour, cornmeal, baking powder, sugar, and salt. Using your fingertips, work in the butter until blended. Toss in the scallions, then stir in the buttermilk just until the mixture comes together.

2. Spoon the dough onto the prepared baking sheet in 6 equal mounds, spacing them about 2 inches apart. Bake for about 25 minutes, or until golden. Transfer to a rack and let cool slightly. Serve warm.—CHARLES WILEY

Johnnycakes

JOHNNYCAKES

These rich panfried biscuits are a Jamaican favorite. Other versions of johnnycakes may be baked or boiled.

MAKES ABOUT 26 CAKES

- 4 cups unbleached all-purpose flour
- 1 tablespoon plus 1 teaspoon baking powder
- 1½ teaspoons salt
- 4 tablespoons unsalted butter, melted
- Vegetable oil, for frying

1. Sift the flour, baking powder, and salt into a large bowl. Using a wooden spoon, stir in the melted butter and 1 cup of water. When the dough becomes too stiff to stir, use your hands to mix the dough and form a smooth ball; add a few more tablespoons of water if necessary to make a stiff (but not dry) dough.

2. Transfer the dough to a lightly floured surface and knead briefly, then roll out to a 12-by-

8-inch rectangle, about ½ inch thick. Cut into 2-inch squares. In the palm of your hand, shape each square into a flattened 3-inch disk. Fold the edges into the center to shape the dough into balls, pinching the bottom.

3. In a 10-inch cast-iron skillet, heat ¼ inch of the vegetable oil over moderately low heat until hot but not smoking. Add enough johnnycakes to fill the pan, leaving about 1 inch between them to allow for rising. Cook the johnnycakes in the gently bubbling oil, turning once, until puffed and golden brown, about 5 minutes per side. Transfer the cakes to paper towels to drain; keep warm. Repeat the process with the remaining dough.—PAUL CHUNG

CHEDDAR CHEESE CORN BREAD

The batter can also make about 36 cornsticks. Bake for 25 minutes.

MAKES ONE 8-INCH CORN BREAD

- 1 cup yellow cornmeal
- ½ cup unbleached all-purpose flour
- 1 teaspoon baking powder
- ½ teaspoon baking soda
- 1¼ teaspoons salt
- 1¼ cups buttermilk
- 2 large eggs, lightly beaten
- 3 tablespoons unsalted butter, melted
- 1½ cups fresh corn kernels (from 2 medium ears)
- 1 cup grated sharp Cheddar cheese (about 3½ ounces)
- ¼ cup finely shredded fresh basil leaves

Preheat the oven to 400°. Generously butter an 8-inch-square baking pan. In a large bowl, stir together the cornmeal, flour, baking powder, baking soda, and salt. Mix in the buttermilk, eggs, and melted butter. Stir in the corn kernels, cheese, and basil, and scrape the batter into the prepared pan. Bake for 35 to 40 minutes, or until golden and a cake tester inserted in the center comes out clean. Let cool slightly in the pan, then cut into squares and serve.—JUDITH SUTTON

CINNAMON-RAISIN STICKY BUNS LF

These sticky buns are best served warm straight out of the oven.

MAKES 9 BUNS

- ¾ cup lukewarm skim milk (100° to 110°)
- 1 envelope active dry yeast
- 2 tablespoons dark brown sugar
- 1¾ cups unbleached all-purpose flour
- ¾ cup raisins
- 2 tablespoons finely chopped walnuts
- ⅓ cup plus 2 tablespoons pure maple syrup
- 3 tablespoons fresh orange juice
- 1 tablespoon cinnamon
- 1 teaspoon finely grated orange zest
- ½ teaspoon ground cardamom
- 2 tablespoons unsalted butter

1. In a medium bowl, stir the milk, yeast, and sugar together. Let stand in a warm place until bubbly, about 10 minutes.

2. Stir 1 cup of the flour into the yeast mixture; cover the bowl with a dish towel and let stand in a warm place for 30 minutes.

3. Coat a 9-inch square baking pan and a bowl with vegetable oil cooking spray. Stir the remaining ¾ cup flour into the dough. Turn it out onto a lightly floured surface and knead until smooth and elastic, about 7 minutes. Transfer to the prepared bowl, cover with a dish towel, and let rise in a warm place for 1 hour.

4. In a small bowl, combine the raisins and chopped walnuts. In another bowl, combine the syrup, orange juice, cinnamon, orange zest, and cardamom. Pour all but 3 tablespoons of the syrup mixture into the prepared pan and tilt to evenly coat the bottom.

5. Lightly knead the dough to knock out the excess air. On a lightly floured surface, roll out the dough to a 10-by-12-inch rectangle. Sprinkle the raisins and walnuts evenly on top of the dough, leaving a ¼-inch border on all sides. Starting from a short end, roll up the dough into a tight cylinder. Cut into 9 even slices and arrange the slices cut sides down in the baking pan with the sides touching. Cover and let the buns rise in a warm place until almost doubled in volume, about 30 minutes. Alternatively, cover the buns and let rise overnight in the refrigerator. ➤

Cinnamon-Raisin Sticky Bun

Cinnamon Coffee Ring

6. Preheat the oven to 350°. In a small saucepan, melt the butter in the reserved 3 tablespoons of the syrup mixture over moderate heat. Drizzle the mixture over the buns. Bake for 25 to 30 minutes, or until the buns are browned on top and spring back slightly when pressed. Let cool in the pan for 5 minutes, then invert onto a plate and separate them. Drizzle any remaining syrup from the pan over the buns and serve warm.—MARY CARROLL

CINNAMON COFFEE RING

To make this coffee cake recipe, you'll need a standing electric mixer with the paddle and dough hook attachments.

MAKES TWO 9-INCH COFFEE CAKES

DOUGH:

- ¼ cup plus 1 tablespoon lukewarm water (about 110°)
- 6 tablespoons plus 1 teaspoon sugar
- 1 tablespoon active dry yeast
- 4 large eggs, at room temperature, lightly beaten
- 3 cups bread flour
- 1 teaspoon salt
- 2½ sticks (10 ounces) unsalted butter, at room temperature

CINNAMON FILLING:

- ¾ cup sugar
- 2½ tablespoons cinnamon
- 4 tablespoons unsalted butter, melted

TOPPING:

- 1 large egg yolk beaten with 1 tablespoon water
- 1 cup pecan halves
- ¼ cup apricot jam or 2 tablespoons currant or apple jelly
- ¼ cup confectioners' sugar
- 1½ tablespoons heavy cream or milk

1. Make the dough: In the large bowl of a standing electric mixer, combine the water and 1 teaspoon of the sugar. Sprinkle the yeast on top and set aside in a warm spot until foaming, about 10 minutes.
2. Using the paddle on the mixer, gently beat the eggs and remaining 6 tablespoons sugar into the yeast. Add the flour and salt and mix at low speed until incorporated. Switch to the dough hook and knead at medium speed for 5 minutes until stiff. Let the dough rest for 30 minutes.
3. Switch back to the paddle and beat in the butter in 2 additions, mixing well after each, until a shaggy dough forms. Transfer to a clean bowl and cover with plastic wrap. (MAKE AHEAD: You can make the dough to this point and refrigerate it overnight. The next day, let the dough return to room temperature, then proceed.) Let the dough rise in a warm place until doubled in bulk, about 2 hours.
4. Make the cinnamon filling and form the coffee ring: In a small bowl, combine the sugar and cinnamon. Halve the dough and

cover one piece with a towel. On a well-floured work surface, dusted with flour as necessary, roll the other piece of dough into an 8-by-20-inch rectangle about ¼ inch thick. Generously brush with half of the melted butter. Sprinkle half of the cinnamon-sugar evenly on top in a thick dry layer. Beginning at one long side, roll up the dough jelly-roll fashion. Tuck one end of the cylinder into the other end to form a 6-inch ring. Place the ring in a 9-inch pie pan. Repeat the procedure to form the second ring. Cover the rings with towels and let rise in a warm place until doubled in bulk, 1½ to 2 hours. Meanwhile, preheat the oven to 350°.

5. Make the topping: Brush the rings with the egg wash. Arrange the nuts on top, pressing them lightly to adhere. Bake the rings for about 30 minutes, or until browned. Transfer the pans to racks to cool, remove the rings from the pans, and let cool completely. (MAKE AHEAD: The rings can be baked 1 week ahead; wrap in foil and freeze. Reheat in a moderate oven for 20 minutes.)

6. Just before serving, melt the jam or jelly in a nonreactive saucepan. If using jam, strain it. Brush the jam or jelly all over the rings.

7. In a small bowl, mix the confectioners' sugar and cream. Drizzle over the rings. Slice and serve.—NEUMAN & BOGDONOFF

CRANBERRY-SPICE BREAD LF

MAKES 12 SLICES

- 1¼ cups unbleached all-purpose flour
- 1 teaspoon baking powder
- ¾ teaspoon cinnamon
- ½ teaspoon ground cardamom
- ½ teaspoon freshly grated nutmeg
- ½ teaspoon baking soda
- ½ teaspoon salt
- ½ cup shredded bran cereal
- ½ cup coarsely chopped pitted dates (about 3 ounces)
- ¾ cup low-fat (1%) buttermilk
- ⅓ cup pure maple syrup
- 1 large egg, lightly beaten
- 2 tablespoons unsweetened applesauce
- 2 tablespoons canola oil
- ½ cup fresh or frozen cranberries

1. Preheat the oven to 400°. Lightly coat an 8-by-3-inch nonstick loaf pan with cooking spray, then flour the pan.

2. In a large bowl, stir together the flour, baking powder, cinnamon, cardamom, nutmeg, baking soda, and salt. Stir in the bran cereal and dates.

3. In another bowl, whisk the buttermilk with the syrup, egg, applesauce, and oil. Stir in the cranberries. Fold in the dry ingredients. Spoon into the loaf pan. Bake for about 50 minutes, until golden and a cake tester inserted in the center comes out clean. Let cool in the pan for 5 minutes, then unmold onto a rack and let cool completely. (MAKE AHEAD: The bread can be wrapped in plastic and kept at room temperature for 1 day or frozen for up to 1 month. Let return to room temperature before serving.)—MARY CARROLL

Orange-Date Muffin (p. 344) and Cranberry-Spice Bread

Basic Crêpes

ORANGE-DATE MUFFINS LF

MAKES 12 MUFFINS

- 1 large navel orange
- ½ cup low-fat (1%) buttermilk
- 1 large egg, lightly beaten
- 3 tablespoons honey
- 3 tablespoons finely grated orange zest
- 2 tablespoons unsweetened applesauce
- 2 tablespoons canola oil
- ½ cup coarsely chopped pitted dates (about 3 ounces)
- 1½ cups unbleached all-purpose flour
- 1 teaspoon baking powder
- 1 teaspoon baking soda

1. Preheat the oven to 400°. Lightly coat a 12-cup nonstick muffin tin with cooking spray. Using a small sharp knife, peel the orange, removing all the bitter white pith. Cut between the membranes to release the sections.

2. In a food processor, combine the orange sections, buttermilk, egg, honey, zest, applesauce, and canola oil, and process until thoroughly blended. Add the dates and process just until combined.

3. In a large bowl, sift together the flour, baking powder, and baking soda. Stir in the orange mixture just until incorporated. Spoon into the muffin cups, filling them about three-quarters full. Bake about 15 minutes, or until the tops are golden and spring back slightly when pressed. Let cool in the pan for 5 minutes. Unmold, transfer to a wire rack, and let cool. Serve warm or at room temperature. (MAKE AHEAD: The muffins can be made 1 day ahead and kept in an airtight container, or frozen for up to 1 month. Rewarm in a 350° oven before serving.)—MARY CARROLL

ABOUT CREPES

The only tricky part about making crêpes is cooking them, but once you get the hang of it, you'll see how easy it is. The most important thing to remember is that the batter cooks almost instantly upon contact with the hot pan. Thus it is imperative that the pan be tilted the moment the batter is added to ensure thin and even distribution over the entire base of the pan. As long as the batter isn't too thick (it should resemble heavy cream in texture), the thinness of the crêpe will be determined by the speed with which the batter is spread. Under the very best conditions—if the batter is liquid enough and is spread quickly enough—the edge of the crêpe will have a lacy look. Experienced cooks will be able to spread the batter evenly over the bottom of the pan, while novices may make crêpes with holes. It is better to add too little batter at first than too much; you can always fill in any holes with drops of additional batter. And don't worry if your finished crêpes are slightly thicker than ideal; the crêpes will still taste very good.

Because I like large crêpes, I suggest making them in an eight- to nine-inch nonstick skillet. If you prefer smaller ones, by all means use a nonstick crêpe pan (most are five to seven inches across the base). If you will be making the crêpes in advance, stack them on a plate, with the nicely browned side down, and cover the crêpes with plastic wrap.—JACQUES PEPIN

BASIC CREPES

These versatile crêpes can be used with any sweet or savory fillings. If

HOW TO FLIP A CREPE

For an experienced hand, flipping a crêpe is a simple matter of dexterity. Until you master the skill, just lift the edge of the crêpe with a fork, then grab it with your thumb and forefinger and flip it over.—JACQUES PEPIN

you are making savory crêpes, omit the sugar in the batter.

MAKES 12 TO 16 CREPES

- ⅔ cup all-purpose flour
- 2 large eggs
- ½ teaspoon sugar
- ⅛ teaspoon salt
- ¾ cup skim milk
- 1 tablespoon corn or canola oil, plus more for greasing the pan

1. In a medium bowl, whisk together the flour, eggs, sugar, salt, and ¼ cup of the milk; the batter will be thick and lumpy, but keep whisking until smooth. (Because the mixture is so thick, the wires of the whisk will break up all the floury lumps in the batter.)
2. Whisk in the remaining ½ cup milk and the 1 tablespoon oil; if the batter is thicker than heavy cream, thin with up to 1 tablespoon more water.
3. Lightly grease an 8-inch nonstick skillet and set it over moderately high heat until hot. Pour in 3 tablespoons of the batter and quickly tilt the skillet in a circular motion to spread the batter evenly over the bottom. Cook for about 45 seconds on one side, then flip and cook for about 20 seconds on the other. If not eating immediately, slide onto a plate. Repeat to make the remaining crêpes.—JACQUES PEPIN

CARAMELIZED APPLE FRENCH TOAST WITH WARM BLUEBERRY AND MANGO COMPOTE LF

4 SERVINGS

- 1 teaspoon unsalted butter
- ¼ cup dark brown sugar
- 1 cup low-fat (1%) milk
- 2 large eggs
- ¼ cup plus 2 tablespoons unsweetened applesauce
- ¼ cup granulated sugar
- 2 tablespoons dark rum
- 1 teaspoon pure vanilla extract
- ⅜ teaspoon ground cardamom
- Pinch of salt
- Eight ½-inch-thick slices white bread
- Warm Blueberry and Mango Compote (recipe follows)

1. Preheat the oven to 375°. Lightly grease a large nonstick baking sheet with the butter. Press the brown sugar through a strainer onto a medium plate to remove any lumps and then sprinkle 2 tablespoons evenly over the prepared baking sheet.
2. In a shallow bowl, whisk the milk with the eggs, applesauce, granulated sugar, rum, vanilla, cardamom, and salt. Add the bread slices and turn to coat, until thoroughly moistened. Arrange the slices on the prepared baking sheet and sprinkle evenly with the remaining 2 tablespoons brown sugar. Bake about 20 minutes, turning once, until the toast is lightly browned and the sugar is caramelized. Transfer to warm individual plates and serve with the compote.

Warm Blueberry and Mango Compote

This fruity compote can also be served with pancakes or waffles, or even as a topping for angel food cake. If mangoes are unavailable, substitute nectarine or peeled peach slices. Be sure to taste the compote before serving; you may need to stir in a little more sugar, depending on the ripeness of the fruit.

Caramelized Apple French Toast with Warm Blueberry and Mango Compote

4 SERVINGS

- 1 medium mango
- ½ cup fresh or frozen blueberries
- 3 tablespoons sugar
- 1 teaspoon fresh lemon juice
- ½ teaspoon finely chopped candied ginger
- ¼ teaspoon finely grated lemon zest

1. Peel half the mango and cut ½-inch-thick lengthwise slices down to the pit. Cut crosswise to release the slices. Repeat the process with the other half, then cut the mango slices into ½-inch dice.
2. In a small nonreactive saucepan, combine the mango, blueberries, sugar, lemon juice, candied ginger, and lemon zest with ¼ cup of water. Bring to a boil over high heat. Lower the heat and simmer until the fruit is softened and the liquid thickened, about 15 minutes. Let cool slightly. (MAKE AHEAD: The compote can be prepared up to 3 days ahead; cover and refrigerate. Rewarm before serving.) —GRACE PARISI

CHAPTER 16

SAUCES, MARINADES & CONDIMENTS

Clockwise from top left: Curry Powder (p. 356); Bouquet Garni (p. 355); Cranberry, Ginger and Pear Chutney (p. 354); and Spicy Thickened Yogurt (p. 355), with Smoky Black Beans (p. 332) and Roti (p. 339)

SWEET-AND-SOUR CARROT DRESSING *LF*

Serve this dressing with watercress, raw spinach, Boston or romaine lettuce, or cabbage slaw.

MAKES ABOUT ¾ CUP

3 cups fresh carrot juice
1 tablespoon fresh lemon juice
2 tablespoons rice wine vinegar
1½ teaspoons soy sauce
1½ teaspoons vegetable oil
3 drops of hot chili oil
Salt
2 tablespoons minced scallion

In a small nonreactive saucepan, bring the carrot juice and lemon juice to a boil over moderately high heat. Cook until the solids separate from the liquid, about 5 minutes, then strain into a bowl. Return the juice to the pan. Boil over moderately high heat until reduced to ⅔ cup, about 20 minutes. Transfer to a bowl and let cool slightly. Whisk in the vinegar, soy sauce, vegetable oil, and chili oil, and season with salt. (MAKE AHEAD: The dressing can be refrigerated, covered, for up to 3 days.) Whisk in the scallion just before serving.—GRACE PARISI

ROASTED POBLANO DRESSING *LF*

Serve with raw spinach, romaine, steamed potatoes, or tomatoes.

MAKES ABOUT 2¼ CUPS

4 medium poblano chiles
2 medium scallions, coarsely chopped
2 garlic cloves, coarsely chopped
½ cup fresh cilantro leaves, coarsely chopped
2 tablespoons fresh lime juice
1 cup low-fat (1.5%) buttermilk
¼ cup plus 2 tablespoons olive oil
Large pinch of sugar
Salt and freshly ground pepper

1. Roast the poblanos over a gas flame or under the broiler until charred all over. Transfer to a small bowl, cover with plastic wrap, and let stand until cool.
2. Peel the blackened skin from the poblanos. Discard the cores, seeds, and ribs. Coarsely chop the poblanos and transfer them to a blender or food processor. Add the scallions, garlic, cilantro, and lime juice, and blend until roughly chopped. Add the buttermilk, oil, and sugar, and puree until smooth. Season with salt and pepper. (MAKE AHEAD: The dressing can be refrigerated, covered, for up to 1 day.) —GRACE PARISI

SMOKED TOMATO DRESSING *LF*

Serve with watercress, raw spinach, steamed potatoes, or grilled white-fleshed fish.

MAKES ABOUT 2 CUPS

1 pound plum tomatoes
1 teaspoon minced garlic
2 tablespoons extra-virgin olive oil
2 tablespoons balsamic vinegar
1 teaspoon Worcestershire sauce
1 teaspoon Dijon mustard
Salt and freshly ground pepper
1 tablespoon minced fresh flat-leaf parsley

1. Preheat a rangetop grill or heat a large grill pan or cast-iron skillet. Add the tomatoes, cover with a metal bowl or pot lid, and cook over high heat, turning once, until the skins are charred, about 10 minutes. Remove from the heat and let stand, covered, for 30 minutes.
2. Discard the tomato skins and transfer the tomatoes to a food processor. Add the garlic, 2 tablespoons of water, the olive oil, vinegar, Worcestershire sauce, and mustard, and process until smooth. Transfer to a bowl and season with salt and pepper. Let the dressing stand at room temperature for 3 to 5 hours. (MAKE AHEAD: The dressing can be refrigerated, covered, for up to 3 days.) Stir in the parsley just before serving.—GRACE PARISI

From top: Tangy Goat Cheese Dressing, Sweet-and-Sour Carrot Dressing, Roasted Poblano Dressing, and Smoked Tomato Dressing

TANGY GOAT CHEESE DRESSING *LF*

Serve with arugula, Boston lettuce, watercress, or pear slices; omit the

SKINNY SALAD DRESSINGS

Although it's easy to find low-fat salad dressings at your supermarket, it's almost impossible to find one that tastes good but doesn't substitute preservatives, stabilizers, and massive amounts of sugar for oil.

The solution: make your own. Simply cutting down on the oil is not the answer; the result would be too mouth-puckeringly acid. By using the following techniques, you can whip up wonderful low-fat dressings.

TECHNIQUE NO. 1: REDUCTIONS

Reducing fresh vegetable juices, as in Sweet-and-Sour Carrot Dressing (p. 349), or fruit juices, as in Orange-Fennel Dressing, intensifies their sweetness, providing a good balance for whatever acid the dressing contains.

TECHNIQUE NO. 2: VEGETABLE PUREES

Roasting (see Roasted Poblano Dressing, p. 349) or smoking (Smoked Tomato Dressing, p. 349) vegetables concentrates their flavor so that it counteracts the acidity of the dressing. Pureeing the cooked vegetables adds body to the dressing.

TECHNIQUE NO. 3: INTENSELY FLAVORED INGREDIENTS

A little of a strongly flavored, rich-tasting ingredient, such as miso or the goat cheese in Tangy Goat Cheese Dressing (p. 349), balances the tart edge in a low-fat dressing.—GRACE PARISI

minced scallions if serving the dressing with fruit.

MAKES ABOUT 1 CUP

4 ounces soft goat cheese, at room temperature
2 teaspoons white wine vinegar
1 teaspoon Dijon mustard
Pinch of superfine sugar
2 tablespoons low-fat (1.5%) buttermilk
Salt and freshly ground white pepper
1 tablespoon minced scallion

In a small bowl, stir the goat cheese, vinegar, mustard, and sugar until smooth. Stir in the buttermilk and 2 tablespoons water until smooth; if necessary, stir in more water. Season with salt and pepper. (MAKE AHEAD: The dressing can be refrigerated, covered, up to 3 days.) Stir in the scallion just before serving.—GRACE PARISI

ORANGE-FENNEL DRESSING LF

Serve with arugula, mesclun, raw spinach, cabbage slaw, or fennel slaw.

MAKES ABOUT 1¼ CUPS

1 teaspoon fennel seeds
2½ cups fresh orange juice
1 large fennel bulb with feathery tops—halved, cored, and thinly sliced lengthwise
8 crushed saffron threads
1 teaspoon arrowroot
2 tablespoons olive oil
2 tablespoons fresh lemon juice
2 teaspoons Dijon mustard
Salt and freshly ground white pepper
2 teaspoons minced fresh basil

1. In a nonreactive medium saucepan, toast the fennel seeds over moderately high heat, shaking the pan, until fragrant, about 2 minutes. Add the orange juice, sliced fennel, and saffron, and bring to a boil. Lower the heat to moderate and simmer until the juice has reduced to 1 cup, about 20 minutes. Strain the juice into a bowl, pressing down on the cooked fennel; reserve the fennel.

2. Return the juice to the saucepan and bring to a simmer over moderate heat. In a small bowl, mix the arrowroot with 2 tablespoons of water, then whisk into the juice and cook just until thickened, about 30 seconds. Remove from the heat, stir in the cooked fennel, and let stand at room temperature until cool. Strain the mixture into a medium bowl and whisk in the oil, lemon juice, and mustard. Season with salt and white pepper. (MAKE AHEAD: The dressing can be refrigerated, covered, for up to 3 days.) Stir in the basil just before serving.—GRACE PARISI

BASIC ASIAN DRESSING

This dressing is ideal for leafy greens, steamed vegetables, and cold meats.

MAKES ⅓ CUP

2 tablespoons distilled white vinegar
1½ tablespoons soy sauce
1 tablespoon plus 1 teaspoon granulated sugar
1½ teaspoons Asian sesame oil
½ teaspoon finely grated fresh ginger
1 tablespoon finely chopped fresh coriander
A few drops of hot chili oil

In a small bowl, whisk together the vinegar, soy sauce, sugar, sesame oil, and ginger. Just before serving, stir in the coriander and the chili oil.—JOYCE JUE

MOREL CREAM SAUCE

Serve this sauce on top of buttered toast, over mashed potatoes, or with fettuccine, roast chicken, veal, or pan-fried trout.

MAKES ABOUT 1⅓ CUPS

- 1 ounce dried morels
- 1 cup boiling water
- 1 tablespoon unsalted butter
- 1 large minced shallot
- Salt and freshly ground pepper
- 1 cup heavy cream
- ½ teaspoon finely chopped fresh thyme
- 1 teaspoon fresh lemon juice

Cover the morels with the boiling water and let soften for 30 minutes. Rub the morels in the liquid to remove grit. Transfer them to a bowl; cut any large ones in half. Reserve the liquid. In a saucepan, melt the butter over moderate heat. Add the shallot and cook until translucent, about 1 minute. Stir in the morels and season with salt and pepper. Pour in the mushroom liquid, stopping when you reach the grit. Boil over high heat to reduce by half, about 6 minutes. Add the cream and thyme, then simmer over moderately high heat until reduced by a third, about 5 minutes. Season with salt, pepper, and the lemon juice.—MARCIA KIESEL

YOGURT MARINADE

To make enough marinade for one pound of fish: Combine 1 tablespoon olive oil, ½ cup yogurt, 1 tablespoon lemon juice, 2 tablespoons minced mint or cilantro, salt and freshly ground black pepper to taste, ¼ teaspoon minced garlic, and 1 teaspoon curry powder (optional). Stir and let sit for at least 10 minutes.—MARK BITTMAN

SOY MARINADE

To marinate one pound of fish: Combine ¼ cup soy sauce with 1 tablespoon dark sesame oil, 1 teaspoon minced garlic, 1 tablespoon minced or grated ginger, and ½ teaspoon sugar. Marinate

MARINATING AND SMOKING GUIDE

POULTRY:

- Marinate a whole chicken (6 to 7 pounds) or turkey breast (5 pounds) overnight, then smoke to an internal temperature of 180°, 4 hours for the chicken, 7 hours for the turkey.
- Marinate skinless, boneless chicken breasts for about 20 minutes (coat the breasts lightly with oil before applying a dry rub), then smoke for 25 to 30 minutes.
- Steam 5-ounce duck breasts for about 15 minutes (to release some of the fat), then marinate for 2 hours and smoke for 45 to 60 minutes.

MEAT:

- Marinate a 6- to 7-pound bone-in Boston butt (pork shoulder) or beef brisket overnight, then smoke for 1¼ to 1½ hours per pound.
- Marinate 14-ounce strip steaks, 1-inch-thick sirloin steaks and loin lamb chops, and ¾-inch pork chops for 2 hours. Sear on both sides in a skillet and smoke for about 1 hour.
- Marinate a beef tenderloin or boneless center-cut pork loin for at least 4 and up to 12 hours, sear on all sides in a skillet, and then smoke for about 1 hour per pound to an internal temperature of 145° for beef (medium rare), 155° for pork.

FISH AND SHELLFISH:

- Marinate 1 pound of peeled, deveined large shrimp or a 1-pound center-cut salmon fillet for 30 minutes, then smoke for 20 to 30 minutes for shrimp, 30 to 45 minutes for salmon. (Note: You can also smoke shrimp in their shells. Snip down the backs with scissors and remove the veins before marinating.)
- Marinate 1-inch-thick steaks of tuna, salmon, or swordfish for 30 minutes, sear both sides in a hot skillet, then smoke for 25 minutes.
- Parboil whole lobsters or large crabs for 3 to 4 minutes; drain, cool, and crack all over (make knife incisions on the underside of the lobster tail and knuckles.) Marinate for about 2 hours and smoke for 1½ hours for lobster, 55 minutes for crab.

CHEESE:

Coat 1 pound of firm cheese (mozzarella, Monterey Jack, Cheddar, Mexican asadero) with 1 to 3 tablespoons of marinade. Place in a shallow baking dish and smoke for 1 to 1¼ hours, or until the cheese is evenly melted.—CHERYL ALTERS JAMISON AND BILL JAMISON

the fish for 10 minutes to 2 hours.—MARK BITTMAN

PACIFIC RIM MARINADE

This mixture is an excellent mate for duck, tuna, shrimp, and lobster.

MAKES ABOUT 2½ CUPS

¾ cup soy sauce
6-ounce can of frozen orange juice concentrate, thawed
½ cup strong brewed tea
¼ cup dry sherry
3 tablespoons rice vinegar or 2 tablespoons distilled white vinegar
2 tablespoons peanut oil or Oriental sesame oil
2 tablespoons honey
2 teaspoons five-spice powder
3 garlic cloves, minced

Blend all the ingredients in a food processor or blender. (MAKE AHEAD: The marinade will keep in an airtight jar, refrigerated, for 5 days.) —CHERYL ALTERS JAMISON AND BILL JAMISON

Chicken with All-Purpose Dry Rub

BARBECUE RUBS, PASTES, AND MARINADES

Generally, three tablespoons of rub or paste and one-half to one cup liquid marinade per pound of meat or fish is ample. Cover and refrigerate (see "Marinating and Smoking Guide," p. 351). For poultry, rub or pour the mixture under the skin as well as over. Use high-quality spices such as those available by mail from Penzey's Spice House Ltd. (414-574-0277) or Vanns Spice Ltd. (410-583-1643). Spice Islands is an excellent supermarket brand.

ALL-PURPOSE DRY RUB

This rub is great with ribs, Boston butt, beef brisket, a whole chicken, and boneless, skinless chicken breasts. Or try it with Monterey Jack, medium sharp Cheddar, or Mexican asadero cheese. After the cheese is smoked, spoon it onto flour or corn tortillas and garnish with chopped tomatoes and scallions.

MAKES ABOUT ½ CUP

2 tablespoons freshly ground black pepper
2 tablespoons paprika
2 tablespoons onion powder
1 tablespoon brown sugar
1 tablespoon chili powder
1 tablespoon coarse salt
½ teaspoon ground sage
½ teaspoon ground nutmeg
¼ teaspoon cayenne pepper (optional)

Mix the spices together in a small bowl. (MAKE AHEAD: The blend will keep in an airtight container up to 8 weeks. Store in a cool, dark place.)—CHERYL ALTERS JAMISON AND BILL JAMISON

STEAK AND CHOP RUB

This blend is tailored to tender cuts of meat like New York strip steaks, sirloin steaks, beef tenderloin, and pork chops, tenderloin, or loin.

MAKES ABOUT 1 CUP

5 tablespoons coarsely ground or cracked pepper
3 tablespoons onion powder
2½ tablespoons coarse salt
2 tablespoons garlic powder
1 tablespoon Worcestershire powder (see Note)
2 teaspoons ground ginger
2 teaspoons dry mustard
1 teaspoon sugar

Mix the spices together in a small bowl. (MAKE AHEAD: The blend will keep in an airtight container for up to 8 weeks. Store in a cool, dark place.) **NOTE:** Look for the La Chateau brand in supermarkets or specialty stores.—CHERYL ALTERS JAMISON AND BILL JAMISON

THYME AND BAY LEAF RUB

This simple mix of herbs is based on a marinade used to cure duck for confit. More subtle than most spice rubs, it's delicious on pork, beef, or veal, as well as duck. If you're a garlic lover, combine this mix with minced garlic and equal parts lemon juice and olive oil, and rub the paste on the meat.

MAKES ABOUT ⅓ CUP

2 bay leaves, crumbled
2 tablespoons thyme
1 tablespoon whole black peppercorns
2 teaspoons coarse salt
1 whole clove

Using a spice grinder or a mortar and pestle, coarsely crush all of the spices together until blended.—JAN NEWBERRY

MUSTARD AND CORIANDER RUB

This tangy rub complements chicken, pork, even burgers. For an extra kick, brush the meat with prepared mustard before rubbing in the spices.

MAKES ABOUT ⅓ CUP

- 2 tablespoons yellow mustard seeds
- 1 tablespoon coriander seeds
- 1 tablespoon coarse salt
- 1 teaspoon ground ginger
- 1 teaspoon cayenne pepper

1. Set a small heavy skillet over moderately high heat for 2 minutes. Add the mustard and coriander seeds and cook, stirring frequently, until fragrant and beginning to brown, about 5 minutes. Transfer to a plate to prevent further cooking.
2. Using a spice grinder or a mortar and pestle, finely crush all of the spices together until blended.—JAN NEWBERRY

TROPICAL PASTE

Try this zesty paste with shrimp, salmon fillet, whole chicken, center-cut pork loin, pork butt, and beef brisket.

MAKES ABOUT 1 CUP

- 8 medium scallions, coarsely chopped
- One 1-inch chunk of peeled fresh ginger, coarsely chopped
- 1 small fresh or dried hot green or red chile, such as serrano, cayenne, or de arbol, stemmed and seeded
- ¼ cup brown sugar
- 2 tablespoons tamarind concentrate or paste*
- 2 tablespoons fresh lime juice
- 2 tablespoons coarse salt
- 1 tablespoon tomato paste
- 2 teaspoons curry powder
- 1 teaspoon ground allspice

*Available at Asian and Latin markets

In a blender or food processor, mince the scallions, ginger, and chile. Scrape down the sides of the processor. Add the remaining ingredients and process until a paste forms. (MAKE AHEAD: The paste will keep in an airtight jar, refrigerated, for 2 days.)—CHERYL ALTERS JAMISON AND BILL JAMISON

GARLIC-HERB PASTE

Don't be daunted by the quantity of garlic in this blend; it mellows during smoking, leaving a distinct but not overpowering flavor. The paste works wonders with loin lamb chops.

MAKES ABOUT 1 CUP

- 1 head of garlic, separated into peeled cloves
- ½ cup coarsely chopped fresh mint or flat-leaf parsley
- ¼ cup coarsely chopped fresh herbs, such as sage, thyme, and rosemary
- 2 tablespoons coarsely ground pepper
- 2 tablespoons capers plus 1 tablespoon juice
- 1 tablespoon coarse salt
- ½ cup olive oil

In a food processor, combine the garlic, mint, herbs, pepper, capers and caper juice, and the salt. Process until the herbs are finely chopped. With the machine on, add the oil in a slow stream until a thick paste forms. (MAKE AHEAD: The paste will keep in an airtight jar, refrigerated, for 2 days.)—CHERYL ALTERS JAMISON AND BILL JAMISON

Mango Pickle

FRUITY HOT SAUCE

This sauce can be made with underripe, overripe, or perfectly ripe melons. It makes about 2 cups. Brush on pork ribs, chicken, and vegetables before grilling or roasting, or serve as a condiment.

Combine 4 cups of 1-inch cubes of peeled cantaloupe or orange-fleshed honeydew, 3 chopped shallots, 1 chopped Scotch Bonnet chile, and 2 tablespoons sugar in a medium nonreactive saucepan. Boil over high heat until most of the liquid has evaporated, about 8 minutes. Transfer to a blender and add 2½ tablespoons white wine vinegar and ¾ teaspoon salt. Blend until smooth. Let cool, then refrigerate in a glass jar for up to 2 weeks.—MARCIA KIESEL

MANGO PICKLE

This wonderful condiment gets a boost of heat from fresh ginger, dried

chiles, and black peppercorns. It's great as an accompaniment to rice-based dishes.

MAKES ABOUT 1 QUART

- 1 large firm mango, peeled and sliced ⅓ inch thick
- ¼ cup sugar
- 10 thin slices of fresh ginger
- 2 dried red chiles, pricked a few times with the tip of a small knife
- 1 garlic clove, halved lengthwise
- ½ teaspoon whole black peppercorns, coarsely cracked
- ½ teaspoon salt
- ¼ cup white wine vinegar

Pack the mango slices into a 1-quart jar. In a small nonreactive saucepan, combine the sugar, ⅔ cup water, the ginger, chiles, garlic, peppercorns, and salt. Simmer over moderately high heat just until the sugar dissolves. Remove from the heat and stir in the vinegar. Pour the mixture over the mango slices in the jar. Let cool to room temperature, then cover and refrigerate for up to 4 days.—MARCIA KIESEL

ALLSPICE-PICKLED ONIONS

MAKES ABOUT 2 CUPS

- 2 medium onions, sliced crosswise ½ inch thick
- 1 cup white wine vinegar
- 2 teaspoons sugar
- 1 teaspoon salt
- 15 whole allspice berries, crushed

In a nonreactive medium saucepan, cover the onion slices with the vinegar and 1 cup of water. Add the sugar, salt, and allspice and bring to a boil over moderate heat. Simmer for a few minutes, then remove from the heat. Cover and set aside until cool. Drain and serve. (MAKE AHEAD: The pickled onions can be prepared up to a week ahead of time; after draining, cover and refrigerate.) —MARCIA KIESEL

CRANBERRY, GINGER AND PEAR CHUTNEY

MAKES ABOUT 3½ CUPS

- 1 cup plus 2 tablespoons light brown sugar
- ⅓ cup red wine vinegar
- 2 ounces fresh ginger, peeled and cut into ⅛-by-1-inch strips
- ¼ teaspoon cayenne pepper
- Pinch of salt
- 2 pounds firm pears, such as Bosc, peeled and cut into ⅓-inch dice
- ¾ pound fresh cranberries (about 3½ cups), picked over

1. Combine the sugar, red wine vinegar, ginger, cayenne, and salt in a nonreactive medium saucepan, and bring to a boil over moderate heat. Add the diced pears, cover, and cook until they are crisp-tender, about 10 minutes. Strain and transfer the pears to a bowl. Return the liquid to the pan.

2. Add the cranberries to the liquid. Cover and cook over moderate heat until the cranberries just begin to pop, about 3 minutes. Strain into a bowl and add the cranberries to the pears. Return the liquid to the pan and boil over moderately high heat until reduced to ½ cup, about 5 minutes. Stir in the cranberry mixture and let cool. (MAKE AHEAD: The chutney can be refrigerated, covered, for up to 3 days.) Serve chilled or at room temperature.—SANFORD D'AMATO

FIG AND APPLE CHUTNEY

This sweet fruity condiment gets even tastier as it sits. If there's any chutney left over, Chef Patrick Clark chops it fine, mixes in a little mayonnaise, and spreads it on sliced pork or turkey sandwiches.

MAKES ABOUT 4 CUPS

- 6 dried mission figs, thinly sliced
- 2 tablespoons sugar
- 1 cup ruby port
- ½ cup red wine vinegar
- 2 teaspoons mustard seeds
- ½ teaspoon cinnamon
- ½ teaspoon ground allspice
- 2 whole cloves
- ¼ teaspoon cayenne pepper
- ¼ teaspoon salt
- 1 medium red onion, finely chopped
- 2½ pounds tart green apples, such as Granny Smith or greening—peeled, cored, and cut into ½-inch pieces
- 1 teaspoon finely grated orange zest
- 1 teaspoon finely grated lemon zest
- 1 teaspoon fresh lemon juice

1. Combine the sliced figs, sugar, ruby port, red wine vinegar, mustard seeds, cinnamon, allspice, cloves, cayenne pepper, and salt in a nonreactive medium saucepan. Bring to a boil over high heat, then lower the heat to moderate and simmer, stirring occasionally, until the figs are soft, 10 to 15 minutes. Add the onion and cook until tender, about 10 minutes longer.

2. Stir in the apples and simmer over moderate heat, stirring often, until the chutney is thick and chunky, about 30 minutes. Stir in the orange zest, lemon zest, and lemon juice, and cook for 2 minutes longer. Transfer to a bowl and let cool. (MAKE AHEAD: The chutney can be refrigerated for up to 3 days. Let return to room temperature before serving.) —PATRICK CLARK

CUCUMBER-POPPY SEED RAITA

4 SERVINGS

- 2 teaspoons poppy seeds
- 1 small garlic clove, minced
- 1 cup plain yogurt or Spicy Thickened Yogurt (recipe follows)
- 1 large cucumber—peeled, halved lengthwise, seeded, and sliced ¼ inch thick
- 1 small red onion, halved lengthwise and thinly sliced crosswise
- 2 scallions, thinly sliced
- Salt and freshly ground pepper

1. In a small skillet, toast the poppy seeds over high heat until they darken slightly, about 40 seconds. Transfer the seeds to a plate to cool.

2. In a medium bowl, combine the garlic with the yogurt. Fold in the cucumber, red onion, and scallions, and season with salt and pepper. Let stand at room temperature until the cucumber softens, 2 to 4 hours. Just before serving, sprinkle the raita with the toasted poppy seeds.

Spicy Thickened Yogurt

MAKES ABOUT ¾ CUP

- 1 cup plain yogurt
- ½ teaspoon pure chile powder
- ½ teaspoon ground coriander
- 1 teaspoon pure maple syrup
- ¼ teaspoon salt

1. Put the yogurt in a stainless steel strainer set over a bowl and let drain for 2 to 4 hours at room temperature.

2. In a small skillet, toast the chile powder and coriander over moderately high heat, stirring with a metal spatula until slightly darkened and fragrant, about 40 seconds. Scrape the spices into a small bowl to cool. Stir in the drained yogurt, maple syrup, and salt. (MAKE AHEAD: The yogurt will keep in the refrigerator for up to 1 week. Stir well and bring to room temperature before serving.) —MARCIA KIESEL

BOUQUET GARNI

- 3 sprigs fresh parsley
- 1 sprig fresh thyme
- 1 dried or fresh bay leaf

Optional Additions: 1 sprig celery leaf, fennel frond, or marjoram

Bouquet garni is the traditional French seasoning for stews and other slowly cooked meat dishes. Fresh herbs are tied together in a bouquet with plain white kitchen string, or enclosed in cheesecloth to make a sachet. Remove the bundle after cooking, before the food is served. Instead of using only with meat dishes, experiment: add the garni to a savory white bean casserole.—BECKY SUE EPSTEIN AND HILARY DOLE KLEIN

FINES HERBES

- 1 sprig fresh parsley, minced
- 1 sprig fresh tarragon, minced
- 1 sprig fresh chervil, minced
- 1 fresh chive, minced

Fines herbes is a time-honored French seasoning composed of four delicate chopped, fresh green herbs. It is often used in omelets, on grilled meats, and in marinades. The blend is used raw or added toward the end of cooking. Try mixing *fines herbes* into mayonnaise, sour cream, cottage cheese, cream cheese, or butter as a spread for sandwiches or hors d'oeuvres.—BECKY SUE EPSTEIN AND HILARY DOLE KLEIN

QUATRE-EPICES

- ½ teaspoon freshly ground black or white pepper (½ teaspoon whole black or white peppercorns)
- ½ teaspoon freshly grated nutmeg (½ of a whole nutmeg)
- ½ teaspoon ground ginger
- ½ teaspoon ground cloves (18 whole cloves) or cinnamon (a 2-inch piece of cinnamon stick)

Quatre-épices is a mixture of four ground spices (*quatre-épices* is French for four spices) traditionally used in charcuterie. Allspice, also known as "Jamaican pepper," is a common substitute. This four-spice blend, used in almost every country of the world, has taken on a life of its own, with chefs incorporating many other spices to get the flavor just right on their palates. Use *quatre-épices* to add a more aromatic nuance to all meats, particularly game, or to add a lovely Caribbean piquance to grilled or stewed meat or vegetable dishes.—BECKY SUE EPSTEIN AND HILARY DOLE KLEIN

GARAM MASALA

1 tablespoon ground cardamom (2 teaspoons cardamom seeds)
2½ teaspoons ground coriander (2 teaspoons coriander seeds)
2 teaspoons ground cumin (1½ teaspoons cumin seeds)
1 teaspoon ground black pepper (1 teaspoon peppercorns)
½ teaspoon ground cloves (a heaping ½ teaspoon whole cloves)
½ teaspoon ground cinnamon (a 2-inch piece of cinnamon stick)
½ teaspoon ground nutmeg (½ whole nutmeg, cut into chunks)

Traditionally used in northern Indian cuisine, *garam masala* means literally "warm spice blend" because its spices are supposed to heat the body. It is stirred into curries, pilafs, and *biryanis* toward the end of cooking. Try substituting garam masala for cinnamon and nutmeg in oatmeal cookies. Dry-roast the whole spices in a hot pan over low heat before grinding them.—BECKY SUE EPSTEIN AND HILARY DOLE KLEIN

CURRY POWDER

2 teaspoons ground coriander (1½ teaspoons coriander seeds)
2 teaspoons ground cumin (1½ teaspoons cumin seeds)
2 teaspoons pure red chile powder
2 teaspoons turmeric
2 teaspoons ground ginger
Optional Additions: allspice, black pepper, cardamom, cinnamon, cloves, fennel seeds, fenugreek seeds, mace, black (also called brown) or red mustard seeds, poppy seeds, saffron, or sesame seeds

An Indian curry usually consists of eggs, fish, chicken, lamb, or vegetables cooked in a highly seasoned sauce, the spices for which have varied infinitely for

UMBELLIFER HERBS

Going to seed can be a good thing—at least when it comes to the Umbelliferae family of herbs. Though herbs are generally grown for their fresh, green leaves, this group provides a bonus: fragrant seeds that will last long after the growing season is over.

Umbellifers are distinguished by hollow stems and umbels, fine pinnate clusters of flowers that resemble dainty parasols and hold the pungent seeds. Family members include common herbs like parsley, dill, coriander, chervil, cumin, caraway, and fennel, and less-familiar ones like lovage, angelica, anise, and sweet cicely.

Umbellifers are EASY TO GROW because they're hardy and don't require much attention (they attract beneficial pollinating insects and butterflies to boot). Just let nature take its course, and the tasseled seed heads will emerge. The plants produce green berries, which will ripen into brown seeds, a process that can take up to 10 days. When the seeds are ready, pick them off and store them in an airtight container; they will keep for up to a year.

Umbellifer seeds, which contain oils that give them a deeper, stronger flavor than the leaves, have A MULTITUDE OF USES. You can steep them in the liquid of your favorite pickles (cucumber, okra, onion, artichoke, or carrot). You can add dill seeds to the dough for potato bread and rolls. And you can use fennel seeds for sweet biscotti and savory cheese crackers, or as a seasoning for pork roast.

Try making a FLAVORED OIL with dill, fennel, coriander, caraway, and cumin. Toast the seeds in a dry skillet, lightly crush them with the flat side of a knife, and infuse in olive oil with black pepper and dried hot chile for one to three days. Brush the flavored oil on focaccia before baking, on pizza fresh from the oven, and on fish during grilling, or use it as a dip for peasant bread.

The same combination of umbellifers makes a tasty SEASONED SALT. Grind the umbellifer seeds in a mortar with a pestle, combine them with kosher salt, and set aside for a few days. Use as an overnight dry rub for beef, pork, chicken, or duck; sprinkle on meat right before roasting; add a generous amount to water for a crab or crayfish boil; or serve at the table for spicing up corn on the cob.—MARCIA KIESEL

thousands of years. The word itself comes from the south Indian word *kari*, which means sauce. For something different, try adding a little curry powder to a fresh carrot soup or to a mayonnaise sauce for fish. To maximize flavor, dry-roast the whole spices in a hot pan over low heat before grinding them.—BECKY SUE EPSTEIN AND HILARY DOLE KLEIN

FIVE-SPICE POWDER

- 1 teaspoon ground star anise (3 whole star anise)
- 1 teaspoon ground fennel seeds (¾ teaspoon whole fennel seeds)
- 1 teaspoon ground Szechwan or white pepper (1 teaspoon whole Szechwan or white peppercorns)
- ½ teaspoon ground cassia or cinnamon (a 2-inch piece of cinnamon stick)
- ½ teaspoon ground cloves (a heaping ½ teaspoon whole cloves)

Sometimes called five-fragrance powder, five perfumes, or five heavenly spices, this traditional Chinese blend has a powerful anise flavor. It is used throughout southern China and Vietnam in stir-fries and in marinades involving pork, beef, chicken, or duck. Five-spice powder makes a wonderful addition to barbecued ribs or leeks braised in butter.—BECKY SUE EPSTEIN AND HILARY DOLE KLEIN

HERBES DE PROVENCE

- 1 teaspoon minced fresh or dried thyme
- 1 teaspoon minced fresh or dried summer savory
- ½ teaspoon minced fresh or dried lavender
- ¼ teaspoon minced fresh or dried rosemary

Optional Additions: ¼ teaspoon minced fresh fennel fronds, ¼ teaspoon minced fresh basil, ½ teaspoon minced fresh or dried oregano, or ¼ teaspoon minced fresh or dried sage

Herbes de Provence, literally "herbs from Provence," consists of the herbs commonly found growing in that southern region of France. The mixture varies according to the availability of the herbs. Although it is most often used with roasted or grilled meat or poultry dishes, it also makes a wonderful flavoring for a pizza.—BECKY SUE EPSTEIN AND HILARY DOLE KLEIN

CHAPTER 17

COOKIES

Palm Springs Lemon Squares and Creole Pecan Praline Bars

PALM SPRINGS LEMON SQUARES WITH DATES

A layer of sliced dates lies between the shortbread on the bottom and the tart lemon custardy topping. The topping has a tendency to stick, so I use cooking oil spray, even though the pan has also been buttered and floured. The squares cut best when frozen, and they also taste great frozen (or cold).

MAKES 32 BARS

SHORTBREAD CRUST:

1 stick (8 tablespoons) unsalted butter plus ½ tablespoon for the pan
1 cup plus 3 tablespoons sifted unbleached flour plus more for the pan
¼ cup (firmly packed) light brown sugar
Pinch of salt

LEMON TOPPING:

¼ cup plus 1 teaspoon sifted unbleached flour
½ teaspoon baking powder
⅛ teaspoon salt
2 large eggs
1 cup granulated sugar
⅓ cup fresh lemon juice
Finely grated zest of 2 cold and firm lemons
Cooking oil spray
1 loosely packed cup pitted dates (4 ounces), sliced crosswise ¼ inch thick
Confectioners' sugar, for sifting

1. Preheat the oven to 350° and position a rack in the bottom third of the oven. Turn a 9-inch square baking pan upside down. Press a 12-inch square of foil, shiny side down, onto the pan, shaping it to the sides and corners with your hands. Remove the foil. Run some tap water into the pan to wet it all over. Pour out all but about 1 tablespoon of the water, then place the shaped foil in the pan and press it gently against the bottom and sides to adhere. Put the ½ tablespoon butter in the pan and melt in the oven. Using a piece of crumpled plastic wrap, spread the melted butter all over the foil. Freeze until set, then dust with flour, tapping out the excess; freeze again.

2. Make the shortbread crust: In a food processor, combine the 1 cup plus 3 tablespoons flour, the brown sugar, and the salt. Pulse a few times to mix. Cut the remaining 1 stick butter into six pieces and add it to the processor. Mix for about 30 seconds until the dough holds together. Turn the dough out of the bowl.

3. Using your hands, break off teaspoon-size pieces of dough and place them all over the bottom of the prepared pan. Flour your fingertips and press the dough evenly over the bottom of the pan; reflour your fingertips as necessary. Bake for 28 minutes, or until lightly browned.

4. Meanwhile, **make the lemon topping:** In a medium bowl, sift together the flour, baking powder, and salt. In a medium bowl, beat the eggs with the granulated sugar and lemon juice. Beat in the dry ingredients until well mixed. Stir in the lemon zest.

5. When the crust is done, remove it from the oven and lower the oven temperature to 325°. Spray the sides and corners of the foil thoroughly with cooking oil spray. Arrange the dates in 1 layer all over the crust. Pour the topping over the dates and press them down to submerge them.

6. Bake the cake for 35 minutes, or until lightly golden and a little crusty. Transfer to a rack to cool completely.

7. To slice, cover the pan with a flat board or a cookie sheet and invert. Remove the pan and peel off the foil (be careful around the sides). Cover the bottom of the cake with a piece of parchment or wax paper and then another board or cookie sheet and invert again so that the cake is right side up. Freeze for at least 1 hour and up to 4 days.

8. Using a large, heavy, serrated knife, cut the cake into quarters, then halve each quarter. Now you have 8 strips; cut each strip crosswise into 4 squares. Using a fine strainer, sift confectioners' sugar over the squares.—MAIDA HEATTER

CREOLE PECAN PRALINE BARS

This is a very old recipe from New Orleans. The thin bars have a crisp, brown sugar shortbread base that's completely covered with a solid pecan praline topping.

MAKES 32 BARS OR 64 BITE-SIZE PIECES

SHORTBREAD LAYER:

1 stick (8 tablespoons) unsalted butter, at room temperature
1 cup (packed) light brown sugar
¼ teaspoon salt
2 cups sifted unbleached flour
2½ cups large pecan halves (9 ounces)

PRALINE TOPPING:

1½ sticks (12 tablespoons) unsalted butter
⅓ cup (packed) light brown sugar

1. Preheat the oven to 350° and position a rack in the center. Turn a 9-by-13-by-2-inch baking pan upside down. Press a 17-inch length of foil, shiny side down, onto the pan, shaping it to the sides and corners with your hands. Remove the foil. Run tap water into the pan to wet it all over. Pour out all but about 1 tablespoon of the water, then place the shaped foil in the pan and press it against the bottom and sides to adhere.

2. Make the shortbread layer: In a medium bowl, using an electric mixer, beat the butter at medium-high speed until soft. Add the sugar and salt and beat to mix. Add the flour and beat at low speed for 1 or 2 minutes until the ingredients form tiny crumbs that hold together when pinched.

3. Turn out the dough into the prepared pan. Using your fingertips, spread the dough to form an even layer, then press down firmly with the palm of your hand. Place the pecan halves, flat sides down, in one direction—they should be touching each other—to cover the dough.

4. Make the praline topping: In a small saucepan, melt the butter and brown sugar over high heat. Stir with a wooden spatula until the mixture comes to a rolling boil; continue to stir for 30 seconds. Remove the pan from the heat and pour the caramel over the nuts, coating the entire surface as much as possible.

5. Bake the cake for 22 minutes. Transfer to a rack to cool, then refrigerate for at least 1 hour and up to 2 days before slicing.

6. To slice, cover the pan with a flat board or a cookie sheet and invert. Remove the pan and peel off the foil. Cover with another board or cookie sheet and invert again so that the cake is right side up.

7. Using a large, heavy, serrated knife, cut the cake crosswise into quarters, then cut each strip crosswise into 8 bars, each about 3¼ inches by 1 inch (or halve the bars to make pieces about 1⅔ inches by 1 inch). Serve at room temperature.—MAIDA HEATTER

WALNUT PASSION

These bars are divine: a shallow, dense chocolate cookie layer on the bottom topped with caramel loaded with walnuts. You can substitute pecans, but be sure to toast them first. You will need a candy thermometer for testing the caramel.

MAKES 32 BARS

CHOCOLATE LAYER:

- 6 tablespoons unsalted butter plus more for the pan
- ½ cup (firmly packed) light brown sugar
- 1 large egg
- ½ teaspoon pure vanilla extract
- ⅛ teaspoon salt
- ¼ cup unsweetened cocoa powder, preferably Dutch process
- ¼ cup sifted unbleached flour

WALNUT TOPPING:

- ⅓ cup heavy cream
- 1 tablespoon dark rum or Cognac
- 6 tablespoons unsalted butter
- 1½ cups (firmly packed) light brown sugar
- ¼ cup dark corn syrup
- Scant ¼ teaspoon salt
- 7 ounces walnut halves or pieces (2 cups)

1. Preheat the oven to 375° and position a rack in the bottom third. Turn a 9-inch square baking pan upside down on a work surface. Press a 12-inch square of foil, shiny side down, onto the pan, shaping it to the sides and corners with your hands. Remove the foil. Run some tap water into the pan to wet it all over. Pour out all but about 1 tablespoon of water, then place the shaped foil in the pan and press it gently against the bottom and sides to adhere. Put a piece of butter in the pan and melt in the oven. Then, using a piece of crumpled plastic wrap, spread the butter all over the bottom and sides of the foil.

2. Make the chocolate layer: In a small saucepan, melt the 6 tablespoons butter over moderate heat. Pour into a medium bowl and add the brown sugar, egg, vanilla, and salt. Beat with an electric mixer at medium speed to mix. At low speed, beat in the cocoa powder and the flour. Pour the batter into the prepared pan and, using a metal spoon, spread in an even layer.

3. Bake the layer for about 15 minutes, or until it begins to come away from the sides of the pan. Remove from the oven. Leave the oven on.

4. Make the walnut topping: In a cup, combine the heavy cream and rum. In a heavy medium saucepan, melt the butter over moderate heat. Using a wooden spoon, stir in the brown sugar, dark corn syrup, and salt. Continue stirring until the mixture comes to a full boil. Place a candy thermometer in the saucepan and boil, stirring the mixture

Left to right: Heath Bar Brownies (p. 364), Walnut Passion

a few times, until the temperature reaches 250°, about 2 minutes; do not overcook.

5. Remove from the heat and quickly stir in the heavy cream; the mixture will bubble up. Stir in the walnuts. Pour the hot caramel over the chocolate layer. Using a metal spoon or a fork, spread the nuts evenly; don't miss the corners.

6. Bake the cake for 25 minutes. Remove and let cool completely.

7. To slice, cover the pan with a flat board or a cookie sheet and invert. Remove the pan and peel off the foil. Cover with another board or cookie sheet and invert again so that the cake is right side up. Using a large, heavy, serrated knife, cut the cake into quarters, then halve each of the quarters. Now you have 8 strips; cut each strip crosswise into 4 bars. Serve the bars at room temperature.—MAIDA HEATTER

HEATH BAR BROWNIES

In the immortal words of Mae West, "Too much of a good thing can be wonderful." In this recipe, the chocolate-toffee candy bars called Heath bars—a lot of them—are cut up and mixed into the brownie batter.

The brownies can be served at room temperature or refrigerated; I like them best cold.

MAKES 24 SMALL BROWNIES

- 1 stick (8 tablespoons) unsalted butter, plus more for the pan
- ¾ cup pecan halves or pieces (2½ ounces)
- Five 1¼-ounce Heath candy bars or 20 miniature Heath candy bars (6¼ ounces)
- 2 ounces unsweetened chocolate
- 2 large eggs
- ¾ cup sugar
- ½ teaspoon pure vanilla extract
- ¼ teaspoon salt
- 1 cup sifted unbleached flour

1. Preheat the oven to 350° and position a rack in the bottom third. Turn an 8-inch square baking pan upside down. Press a 12-inch square of foil, shiny side down, onto the baking pan, shaping it to the sides and corners with your hands. Remove the foil. Run tap water into the baking pan to wet it all over. Pour out all but about 1 tablespoon of the water, then place the shaped foil in the baking pan and press it gently against the bottom and sides to adhere. Put a piece of butter in the pan and melt in the oven. Using a piece of crumpled plastic wrap, spread the melted butter all over the foil.

2. Spread the pecans in a shallow pan and toast them in the oven for about 12 minutes, or until the nuts are very hot and fragrant. Set aside.

3. Using a large sharp knife, cut the Heath bars crosswise ¼ to ⅓ inch thick; you will have about 1½ cups. Chop a scant ¼ cup of the Heath bars into smaller pieces and reserve.

4. In a small double boiler, melt the unsweetened chocolate and the stick of butter over warm water, stirring occasionally. Set the melted chocolate aside to cool slightly.

5. In a medium bowl, using an electric mixer, beat the eggs, sugar, vanilla, and salt at medium speed until mixed. Add the melted chocolate and beat only to mix. Then add the flour and beat at low speed just until incorporated. Using a wooden spoon, stir in the toasted pecans and all but the reserved ¼ cup of the Heath bars. Pour the batter into the prepared pan and spread smooth. Sprinkle the remaining Heath bars on top.

6. Bake the brownies for 28 minutes, or until a toothpick inserted in the center comes out just barely clean. Transfer the brownies to a rack to cool.

7. To slice, cover the pan with a flat board or a cookie sheet and invert. Remove the pan and peel off the foil. Cover the cake with a piece of parchment or wax paper, then with another board or cookie sheet, and invert again so that the cake is right side up. Refrigerate for about 1 hour.

8. Using a large, heavy, serrated knife, cut the cake into quarters, then halve each of the quarters. Now you have 8 strips; cut each of the strips crosswise into 3 brownies, each about 2 by 1⅓ inches.—MAIDA HEATTER

MACADAMIA NUT COCONUT BARS

In this recipe, a buttery brown sugar layer is covered with a moist and chewy topping that is loaded with gorgeous, whole macadamia nuts and shredded coconut. It creates the most tempting kitchen aroma ever.

MAKES 32 BARS OR
64 BITE-SIZE PIECES

BROWN SUGAR LAYER:

- 1 stick (8 tablespoons) unsalted butter, at room temperature, plus 1 tablespoon for the pan
- ½ cup (firmly packed) light brown sugar
- 1 large egg

¼ teaspoon salt
1¼ cups sifted unbleached flour

MACADAMIA TOPPING:
1½ cups salted macadamia nuts (about 7 ounces)
2 tablespoons sifted unbleached flour
½ teaspoon baking powder
Pinch of salt
2 large eggs
1 cup (firmly packed) light brown sugar
1 teaspoon pure vanilla extract
6 ounces shredded unsweetened coconut (about 2 cups)

1. Preheat the oven to 350° and position a rack in the center. Turn a 9-by-13-by-2-inch baking pan upside down. Press a 17-inch length of foil, shiny side down, onto the baking pan, shaping it to the sides and the corners with your hands. Remove the foil. Run tap water into the baking pan to wet it all over. Pour out all but about 1 tablespoon of the water, then place the shaped foil in the baking pan and press it gently against the bottom and sides to adhere. Put 1 tablespoon of the butter in the baking pan and melt in the oven. Using a piece of crumpled plastic wrap, spread the melted butter all over the foil. Place the baking pan in the freezer.
2. Make the brown sugar layer: In a medium bowl, using an electric mixer, beat the stick of butter at medium-high speed until it is soft. Beat in the light brown sugar. Beat in the egg and the salt, then beat in the sifted unbleached flour at low speed until it is just incorporated.
3. Using a spoon, dollop the dough all over the bottom of the cold baking pan. With floured fingertips, pat the dough evenly to cover the bottom of the pan (it will be necessary to reflour your fingertips frequently). Bake this brown sugar layer for about 14 minutes, or until set. Remove from the oven and let stand. Leave the oven on.
4. Meanwhile, **make the macadamia topping:** Shake the macadamia nuts gently in a coarse strainer to remove any excess salt. Sift together the unbleached flour, the baking powder, and the salt, and set aside.
5. In a medium bowl, using an electric mixer, beat the eggs, light brown sugar, and vanilla extract at medium speed until mixed. Beat in the sifted dry ingredients at low speed. Using a wooden spoon, stir in the macadamia nuts and two-thirds of the shredded coconut. Using a tablespoon, dollop the mixture evenly on top of the brown sugar layer and spread to form a smooth layer. Sprinkle the remaining shredded coconut on top.
6. Bake for 25 minutes, rotating the pan once, until the top is richly browned and a toothpick inserted in the middle comes out clean. Transfer to a rack to cool completely.
7. To slice, cover the pan with a flat board or a cookie sheet and invert. Remove the pan and peel off the foil. Cover with another board or cookie sheet and invert again so that the cake is right side up. Refrigerate or freeze the cake for 1 hour.
8. Using a large, heavy, serrated knife, cut the cake crosswise into quarters, then cut each strip crosswise into 8 bars, each about 3¼ inches by 1 inch (or halve these bars crosswise again to make pieces about 1⅔ inches by 1 inch).—MAIDA HEATTER

BRANDIED FRUIT BARS

These bars are almost solid brandied fruit with just barely enough batter to hold them together. This recipe came about quite by accident when I was doing too many things at once and unintentionally left the butter out of a recipe I was following.

You can use any combination of dried fruits. I have been using dates, prunes, apricots, figs, raisins, and sour cherries. (Wonderful dried cherries—as well as dried cranberries—are available from American Spoon Foods, 800-222-5886.) Even though the fruits marinate for at least three hours, it is still important to start with soft, moist fruit.

MAKES 32 BARS

1½ pounds dried fruits (3 firmly packed cups), large fruits cut with scissors into ¼- to ½-inch pieces
½ cup brandy, Cognac, or dark rum
1 tablespoon unsalted butter, for the pan
3 tablespoons plain dry bread crumbs, for the pan
2 cups pecan halves (7 ounces)
1 cup sifted unbleached flour
½ teaspoon baking powder
¼ teaspoon salt
3 large eggs
1 cup sugar

1. In a large jar or glass bowl, combine the dried fruits and the brandy. Cover and let stand for at least 3 hours or indefinitely

Miami Beach Peanut Flats

(the longer they soak the better); stir occasionally.

2. Preheat the oven to 350° and position a rack in the center. Turn a 9-by-13-by-2-inch baking pan upside down. Press a 17-inch length of foil, shiny side down, onto the baking pan, shaping it to the sides and corners with your hands. Remove the foil. Run tap water into the baking pan to wet it all over. Pour out all but about 1 tablespoon of the water, then place the shaped foil in the baking pan and press it gently against the bottom and sides to adhere. Put the butter in the baking pan and melt in the oven. Using a piece of crumpled plastic wrap, spread the melted butter all over the foil. Let stand until cool, then dust all over with the bread crumbs, shaking out any excess.

3. Spread the pecans in a shallow pan and toast in the oven, shaking the pan a few times, for about 10 minutes, just until they are very hot and fragrant. Set aside to cool.

4. In a medium bowl, sift together the flour, baking powder, and salt. In the large bowl of an electric mixer, beat the eggs at medium speed just to mix. Beat in the sugar and then add the dry ingredients; beat at medium-low speed only until mixed. Using a large wooden spoon, stir in the soaked fruits and their liquid and the pecans. Turn out the batter into the prepared pan and smooth the top.

5. Bake the cake for 45 minutes, rotating the pan once, until the top of the cake is richly browned and springs back when gently pressed. Transfer to a rack to cool completely.

6. To slice, cover the pan with a flat board or a cookie sheet and invert. Remove the pan and peel off the foil (be careful around the sides). Cover the bottom of the cake with another board or cookie sheet and invert again so that the cake is right side up. Freeze for 1 hour.

7. Using a large, heavy, serrated knife, cut the cake crosswise into quarters, then cut the strips crosswise into 8 bars, each about 3¼ inches by 1 inch.—MAIDA HEATTER

MIAMI BEACH PEANUT FLATS

These thin and tender bar cookies are loaded with chopped salted peanuts. The combination of salted peanuts in a sweet, brown sugar cookie is surprisingly good.

MAKES 32 COOKIES

- 1 stick (8 tablespoons) unsalted butter plus 1 tablespoon for the pan
- 1⅓ cups salted cocktail peanuts (6 ounces)
- 1 cup sifted unbleached flour
- ½ teaspoon cinnamon
- ¼ teaspoon baking soda
- Pinch of salt
- 1 teaspoon pure vanilla extract
- ½ cup (firmly packed) light brown sugar
- 1 large egg

1. Preheat the oven to 325° and position a rack in the center. Turn a 15½-by-10½-by-1-inch jelly-roll pan upside down. Press a 17½-inch length of foil, shiny side down, onto the jelly-roll pan, shaping it to the sides and corners with your hands. Remove the foil. Run tap water into the jelly-roll pan to wet it all over. Pour out all but about 1 tablespoon of the water, then place the shaped foil in the jelly-roll pan and press it gently against the bottom and sides to adhere. Put the 1 tablespoon butter in the pan and melt in the oven. Using a piece of crumpled plastic wrap, spread the melted butter all over the foil. Place the pan in the freezer.

2. Place the cocktail peanuts in a coarse strainer and shake vigorously to remove some of the salt. Place the peanuts in a food processor and pulse 7 times. Some of the peanuts will be fine, and some of them will still be whole.

3. Sift together the flour, cinnamon, baking soda, and salt, and set aside. In a medium bowl, using an electric mixer, beat the remaining 1 stick butter at medium-high speed until soft. Beat in the vanilla extract and then the light brown sugar. In a small cup, beat the egg lightly only until mixed but not foamy. Add 2 tablespoons of the egg to the butter (reserve the remaining egg for the top). Beat to mix, then beat in the dry ingredients on low speed just until incorporated. Using a wooden spoon, stir in half of the peanuts.

4. This next step requires patience. First, dollop the dough by small spoonfuls all over the pan. Then, with well-floured fingertips, pat the dough to cover the pan in an even layer. It will be a very, very thin layer, and it will be necessary to reflour your fingertips very often. You will think there is not enough dough, but there is.

5. Pour the reserved beaten egg onto the dough and spread it all over with the palm of your hand and your fingertips. Sprinkle the reserved chopped peanuts all over. Cover with a piece of parchment paper, wax paper, or plastic wrap, and press all over with your palms to be sure the nuts adhere. Place something flat—a cookie sheet or a telephone book—on the layer and press to level the dough. Discard the paper.

6. Bake the cookie layer for 25 to 30 minutes, or until the top is uniformly deep golden brown. Transfer to a rack to cool slightly.

7. To slice, cover the pan with a flat board or a cookie sheet and invert. Remove the pan and peel off the foil. Cover the cookie layer with another board or cookie sheet and invert again so that the layer is right side up. Using a large, heavy, serrated knife, cut the cookie layer crosswise into quarters, then cut each of these strips crosswise into 8 bars, each one about 4 by 1⅓ inches.—MAIDA HEATTER

GANACHE-FILLED BROWN SUGAR BARS

These miniature cakes, or bar cookies, are particularly easy to transport because their "topping" of chocolate ganache (a rich mixture of melted chocolate and heavy cream) is actually inside.

BAR COOKIE TIPS

- TO GET BAR COOKIES OF EXACTLY THE SAME SIZE, **remove the baked cake from the pan in one piece, use a ruler, and insert toothpicks along the edge to mark the cake before slicing.**
- FOR EASY SLICING, **use a large, heavy, serrated knife. Cut with a sawing motion.**
- TO STORE BAR COOKIES, **place them in an airtight container with wax paper between the layers. Or wrap the bars individually in clear cellophane, wax paper, or aluminum foil. They will keep for up to four days in an airtight container and up to two months in the freezer.**—MAIDA HEATTER

MAKES 32 BARS

1¾ cups all-purpose flour
¼ teaspoon salt
2 sticks (½ pound) unsalted butter, at room temperature
1⅔ cups packed dark brown sugar
2 large eggs, at room temperature
1½ teaspoons pure vanilla extract
½ cup heavy cream
½ pound bittersweet chocolate, coarsely chopped

1. Preheat the oven to 350°. Lightly butter the bottom of a 10-by-15-inch baking pan. Line the baking pan with wax paper, then butter and flour the paper and the sides of the baking pan, tapping out excess flour.

2. In a small bowl, whisk the all-purpose flour with the salt. In a large bowl, using an electric mixer, beat the butter and the dark brown sugar at medium speed until light and fluffy, about 3 minutes. Beat in the eggs 1 at a time, beating well after each addition. Beat in the vanilla. On low speed, beat in the flour in 3 additions. The batter will be fairly stiff.

3. Using a long metal spatula, spread the batter evenly in the prepared pan. Bake in the middle of the oven for 18 to 20 minutes, or until a cake tester inserted in the center comes out clean but not dry; do not overbake. Transfer the pan to a rack to cool completely.

4. In a small saucepan, bring the heavy cream to a boil over moderate heat. In a food processor, finely grind the chopped bittersweet chocolate. With the machine on, add the heavy cream to the bittersweet chocolate and process until completely smooth. Scrape the chocolate ganache into a medium bowl and let stand to firm up for 30 minutes to 1 hour.

5. Cover the pan of brown sugar cake with a large wire rack and invert. Remove the pan and peel off the wax paper. Invert the cake again onto a large cutting board. Using a large serrated knife, cut the cake in half crosswise. Using a large metal icing spatula, spread the chocolate ganache evenly on one half of the brown sugar cake to within ⅛ inch of the edge. Carefully set the other half of the cake on top, matching up the cut edges. Cover and refrigerate until the chocolate ganache is set, at least 2 hours or up to 2 days.

6. To slice, using a large, heavy, serrated knife, trim the uncut edges of the cake. Cut the cake lengthwise into 4 strips, then cut each of these strips crosswise into 8 rectangles. Serve the bar cookies chilled or at room temperature.—JUDITH SUTTON

DOUBLE DATE BARS LF

MAKES 20 BARS

Vegetable oil cooking spray
1 cup all-purpose flour
½ teaspoon baking powder
½ teaspoon baking soda
½ teaspoon cinnamon
½ teaspoon salt
Pinch of ground nutmeg
1½ cups pitted dates (about ½ pound)
⅔ cup dark brown sugar
1 large egg
2 tablespoons vegetable oil
1 teaspoon pure vanilla extract
¼ cup coarsely chopped walnuts (about 1 ounce)

1. Preheat the oven to 350°. Lightly coat an 8-inch-square baking pan with vegetable oil cooking spray. In a medium bowl, stir together the flour, baking powder, baking soda, cinnamon, salt, and nutmeg.

2. Coarsely chop ¼ cup of the dates. In a food processor, combine the remaining dates with ⅓ cup of water and process until smooth. Add the brown sugar, egg, vegetable oil, and vanilla extract, and process until blended. Fold the date puree into the dry ingredients. Fold in the chopped dates and the walnuts and spread the batter in the prepared pan. Bake for about 25 minutes, or until the center springs back when it is lightly pressed. Let the cake cool on a rack. Cut into 20 bars.—MICHELE SCICOLONE

FROSTED BUTTERSCOTCH BLONDIES

If you're pressed for time, or would prefer something less indulgent, these blondies are also good without the German chocolate cake topping.

MAKES 48 BARS

BLONDIES:
1½ cups all-purpose flour
½ teaspoon baking powder
¼ teaspoon salt
2 sticks (½ pound) unsalted butter, at room temperature
1¾ cups (packed) light brown sugar
3 large eggs, at room temperature
1½ teaspoons pure vanilla extract

CARAMEL FROSTING:
¾ cup pecans
¾ cup heavy cream
½ cup (packed) light brown sugar
¼ cup granulated sugar
4 large egg yolks, at room temperature
6 tablespoons unsalted butter, cut into pieces, at room temperature
Pinch of salt
1 teaspoon pure vanilla extract
1 cup sweetened flaked coconut

1. Make the blondies: Preheat the oven to 350°. Butter and flour a 9-by-13-inch baking pan. In a small bowl, whisk together the all-purpose flour, the baking powder, and the salt.

2. Using an electric mixer, beat the butter and brown sugar at medium speed until light and fluffy, about 3 minutes. Add the eggs 1 at a time, beating well after each addition. Beat in the vanilla. At low speed, mix in the dry ingredients in 3 additions until just blended.
3. Using a rubber spatula, spread the batter evenly in the prepared baking pan. Bake the blondies in the center of the oven for 35 to 40 minutes, or until they are golden and a cake tester inserted in the center comes out clean. Transfer the pan to a rack to cool completely.
4. Make the caramel frosting: Spread the pecans on a baking sheet and toast in the oven for about 8 minutes, or until fragrant and brown. Transfer the toasted nuts to a work surface to cool, then chop coarsely.
5. In a heavy medium saucepan, combine the heavy cream, light brown sugar, granulated sugar, egg yolks, butter, and salt. Cook over moderate heat, stirring constantly with a wooden spoon, until the sugar dissolves and the mixture thickens (the spoon will start to leave a track), about 12 minutes; do not boil. Strain the mixture into a large bowl, pressing it through a sieve with a rubber spatula. Stir in the vanilla. Stir in the coconut and toasted pecans and let cool.
6. Using the rubber spatula, spread the caramel frosting evenly over the cooled blondies. Cover the baking pan and refrigerate the blondies for 30 minutes. Cut the blondies into 48 small bars and serve them cold or at room temperature. (MAKE AHEAD: The blondies can be made up to 2 days in advance and refrigerated.) —JUDITH SUTTON

CHOCOLATE CHIP COOKIES THREE DIFFERENT WAYS

Here are three variations on the basic chocolate chip cookie recipe. The first is a thin, crisp cookie. Since it contains butter, which melts quickly, it spreads easily. A little corn syrup is added for crispness and color, and all-purpose flour, which doesn't absorb much liquid, is used to encourage spreading. The second, a soft, puffy cookie, contains cake flour (instead of all-purpose flour), baking powder (instead of baking soda), shortening (instead of butter, and a little less than usual), and a slightly reduced amount of sugar to help limit spreading. It is made with an egg, which lifts and puffs the dough. The third, an intermediate cookie, contains half butter for tenderness and half shortening to limit spreading. An egg and a little corn syrup add body, crispness, and color.

MAKES ABOUT 2½ DOZEN COOKIES

FOR THIN/CRISP COOKIES:

- 1 cup coarsely chopped nuts and 2 tablespoons unsalted butter
- 1½ cups all-purpose flour
- ¾ teaspoon salt
- ¾ teaspoon baking soda
- 10 tablespoons unsalted butter
- ½ cup granulated sugar plus ⅓ cup light brown sugar plus 3 tablespoons light corn syrup
- 2 tablespoons milk
- 1 tablespoon pure vanilla extract
- 1 cup semisweet chocolate chips

FOR PUFFED/SOFT COOKIES:

- 1 cup coarsely chopped nuts and 2 tablespoons unsalted butter
- 1½ cups cake flour
- ¾ teaspoon salt
- 1½ teaspoons baking powder
- 9 tablespoons shortening
- 1 cup minus 1 tablespoon light brown sugar
- 1 large egg
- 1 tablespoon pure vanilla extract
- 1 cup semisweet chocolate chips

INTERMEDIATE:

- 1 cup coarsely chopped nuts and 2 tablespoons unsalted butter
- 1½ cups cake flour
- ¾ teaspoon salt
- 1½ teaspoons baking powder
- 5 tablespoons unsalted butter plus 5 tablespoons shortening
- ¾ cup light brown sugar plus 2 tablespoons light corn syrup
- 1 large egg
- 1 tablespoon pure vanilla extract
- 1 cup semisweet chocolate chips

1. Preheat the oven to 350°. On a large baking sheet, roast the nuts for about 10 minutes. Remove from the oven and immediately stir in the 2 tablespoons butter. Increase the oven temperature to 375°.
2. In a medium bowl, sift together the flour, salt, and baking soda or baking powder.
3. In a large bowl, using a handheld electric mixer, cream the butter or shortening and the sugar at medium-high speed until

light and fluffy. Beat in the corn syrup if using. Beat in the milk or egg thoroughly. Beat in the vanilla. On low speed, gradually beat in the dry ingredients until thoroughly combined. Scrape down the sides once with a rubber spatula. Add the roasted nuts and the chocolate chips and beat on low speed for about 5 seconds. Using the rubber spatula, mix until the chips and nuts are thoroughly incorporated.

4. Spray cookie sheets lightly with cooking oil spray. Drop slightly heaping tablespoons of the cookie dough about 2 inches apart on the prepared sheets. Bake the cookies for 12 minutes, or until the edges are just beginning to brown. Transfer the cookie sheets to racks and let cool for 3 minutes, then transfer the cookies to the racks to cool completely.—SHIRLEY CORRIHER

COOKIE Q&A

Q: How do I keep my cookies from spreading?

A: Here are three ways.

- **Refrigerate the dough before you form the cookies. A chilled dough limits spreading as the cookies bake.**
- **Decrease the sugar a little; it encourages spreading.**
- **Substitute shortening for some of the butter. Shortening maintains a more solid texture than butter over a wider temperature range. This suggestion best applies to cookies made with chocolate, spices, nuts, and other flavorings (see Chocolate Chip Cookies Three Different Ways, p. 369) rather than a simple butter cookie whose pure flavor might be compromised.—SHIRLEY CORRIHER**

OLD-FASHIONED OATMEAL-CHOCOLATE CHIP COOKIES

These plain-looking cookies are just the sort that seem made for keeping in an old-fashioned cookie jar. The rolled oats lend a pleasant nutty flavor and a slightly nubby texture.

MAKES ABOUT 3 DOZEN COOKIES

1 cup all-purpose or unbleached flour
½ teaspoon baking soda
½ teaspoon baking powder
¼ teaspoon salt
10 tablespoons unsalted butter, slightly softened
Scant 1 cup (packed) dark brown sugar
1 large egg, lightly beaten
2 teaspoons pure vanilla extract
2⅓ cups old-fashioned rolled oats
1⅓ cups mini chocolate chips
2 to 3 tablespoons granulated sugar, for flattening cookies

1. Preheat the oven to 350°. Generously grease several cookie sheets. In a small bowl, thoroughly stir together the flour, the baking soda, the baking powder, and the salt.

2. In a large bowl, using an electric mixer, beat the butter at medium speed until light. Add the dark brown sugar and beat until the mixture is fluffy and smooth. Beat in the egg and the vanilla extract. Beat in the flour mixture. Using a large wooden spoon, stir in the oats and the mini chocolate chips until incorporated.

3. Break off tablespoon-size portions of dough and roll between your palms into generous 1½-inch balls. Place the balls about 2½ inches apart on the prepared cookie sheets.

4. Lightly grease the bottom of a large drinking glass. Place the granulated sugar in a shallow bowl. Dip the bottom of the glass into the sugar and use to flatten the cookies into 2-inch rounds; dip the glass into the sugar again between cookies.

5. Bake the cookies 1 sheet at a time in the upper part of the oven for about 13 minutes, or until the cookies are lightly colored and just slightly darker at the edges. Rotate the cookie sheet halfway through baking to ensure even browning.

6. Transfer the cookie sheet to a cooling rack and let the cookies firm up slightly, 2 to 3 minutes. Using a metal spatula, transfer the cookies to racks to cool completely. (MAKE AHEAD: The cookies will keep for up to 10 days in an airtight container at room temperature or for up to 2 months wrapped airtight and frozen.) —NANCY BAGGETT

CRANBERRY OATMEAL COOKIES

These crunchy, bumpy cookies have lacy edges that are almost candylike in texture. The dried cranberries are a holiday twist, but you can stick to the traditional raisins if you prefer.

MAKES ABOUT 4 DOZEN COOKIES

⅔ cup all-purpose flour
½ teaspoon salt

- ½ teaspoon baking soda
- ½ cup old-fashioned rolled oats
- 1½ sticks (6 ounces) unsalted butter, softened
- ⅔ cup granulated sugar
- ⅔ cup light brown sugar
- 1 large egg, lightly beaten
- 1 teaspoon pure vanilla extract
- 2 cups pecan pieces (about 8 ounces)
- ⅔ cup dried cranberries (about 4 ounces)

1. Preheat the oven to 350°. In a small bowl, whisk together the all-purpose flour, the salt, and the baking soda. Stir in the old-fashioned rolled oats. In a medium bowl, using an electric mixer, cream the butter with the granulated sugar and the brown sugar until the mixture is light and fluffy. Add the egg and beat until thoroughly incorporated. Scrape down the bowl with a rubber spatula and beat for another 30 seconds. Beat in the vanilla extract. Using a rubber spatula, fold in the flour mixture until completely incorporated. Mix in the pecan pieces and the dried cranberries. The batter will be very soft.

2. Line 2 cookie sheets with parchment paper. Form the mixture into balls about 1¼ inches in diameter. Place the balls about 3 inches apart on the prepared cookie sheets.

3. Bake the cookies for 10 to 12 minutes, or until they are golden brown and lacy. Let the cookies cool completely on the cookie sheets. Using a metal spatula, preferably an icing spatula, transfer the cookies to a plate. (MAKE AHEAD: The cookies will keep for up to 1 week in an airtight container and for up to 1 month in the freezer.)—PEGGY CULLEN

BUTTER-PECAN SANDIES

Pecans, brown sugar, and butter—a combination favored by Southern bakers—team up in these crisp cookies. For optimal results, be sure to use fresh, top-quality pecans.

MAKES ABOUT 3½ DOZEN COOKIES

- 1½ cups pecan halves (about 6 ounces)
- ½ cup (packed) light brown sugar
- 2½ cups all-purpose flour
- ½ teaspoon baking powder
- Scant ½ teaspoon salt
- ¼ teaspoon baking soda
- 10 tablespoons plus 2 teaspoons unsalted butter, softened slightly
- ¼ cup corn oil or other vegetable oil
- 1¼ cups confectioners' sugar, sifted
- 1 large egg
- 1½ teaspoons pure vanilla extract

1. Preheat the oven to 350°. Grease several cookie sheets and set them aside. Spread the pecan halves in a roasting pan and toast in the oven for about 8 minutes, stirring frequently, until the nuts are nicely darkened and fragrant. Transfer to a plate to cool completely.

2. Measure out ¾ cup of the toasted pecans. Using a large, sharp knife, chop the nuts finely and evenly.

3. Transfer the remaining toasted pecan halves and the light brown sugar to a food processor. Pulse to coarsely chop the pecans. Then process continuously until the pecans form a slightly dry paste, 3 minutes longer; scrape down the sides and bottom of the bowl several times during processing.

Old-Fashioned Oatmeal-Chocolate Chip Cookies

4. Sift together the flour, baking powder, salt, and baking soda. In a large bowl, using an electric mixer, beat the butter and oil at medium speed until well blended and lightened. Add the pecan paste and the confectioners' sugar and beat until fluffy and smooth. Beat in the egg and the vanilla extract until well blended. Beat or stir in the dry ingredients and ¼ cup of the reserved chopped pecans until thoroughly mixed; reserve the remaining nuts for garnish.

5. Halve the cookie dough and, using your hands, flatten each piece of dough into a disk. Place each disk between long sheets of

Simple Shortbread

wax paper. Roll out each piece of dough ¼ inch thick, smoothing out any wrinkles that form in the paper. Transfer the paper and the cookie dough to large baking sheets and freeze until the dough is firm, at least 45 minutes or up to 24 hours (if the dough is frozen, allow it to sit at room temperature to thaw slightly before continuing).

6. Preheat the oven to 350°. Peel off 1 sheet of wax paper from 1 of the dough layers (to loosen it), then replace the wax paper and flip over the dough layer. Peel off the top sheet of wax paper and discard.

7. Using a 2-inch round cookie cutter or juice glass, cut out the cookies. Using a metal spatula, place the cookies about 1½ inches apart on the prepared cookie sheets. Garnish the center of each cookie with a generous pinch or two of the reserved chopped pecans. Lightly pat down the nuts to adhere. Repeat the procedure with the second piece of dough. Combine the dough scraps and roll out again (freeze for a few minutes if the dough is soft). Then continue cutting out cookies until all of the dough has been used; place the cookies on the cookie sheets and garnish with the pecans, as above.

8. Bake the cookies 1 sheet at a time in the upper part of the oven for 9 to 12 minutes, or until they are just tinged with brown and slightly darker around the edges. Rotate the cookie sheet halfway through baking to ensure even browning.

9. Transfer the cookie sheet to a cooling rack and let the cookies firm up slightly, 2 to 3 minutes. Using a metal spatula, carefully transfer the cookies to racks to cool completely. (MAKE AHEAD: The cookies will keep for up to 10 days in an airtight container at room temperature or for up to 2 months wrapped airtight and frozen.) —NANCY BAGGETT

BUTTER COOKIES

To my mind, there is no first bite as luxurious as that of a butter cookie. When baked just right, the cookie melts in your mouth. A dusting of confectioners' sugar just before serving adds a touch of elegance.

MAKES ABOUT 2 DOZEN COOKIES

- 2 sticks (½ pound) unsalted butter, at room temperature
- ⅔ cup superfine sugar, plus more for sprinkling
- 1 teaspoon pure vanilla extract
- ¼ teaspoon salt
- 2 cups all-purpose flour
- ¼ cup confectioners' sugar, for dusting

1. In a medium bowl, using an electric mixer, cream the butter with the superfine sugar, vanilla extract, and salt. Do not overmix; the butter should not be fluffy. Using a wooden spoon or a rubber spatula, stir in the flour in two batches. Mix just until the flour is incorporated.

2. Shape the cookie dough into a log. Cover well with plastic wrap and refrigerate until firm, at least 2 hours or overnight.

3. Preheat the oven to 350°. Line two baking sheets with parchment

COOKIE Q&A

Q: How do I prevent my favorite cookies from breaking and crumbling?

A: Here are two suggestions.

• Substitute one egg for one to three tablespoons of liquid in the cookie dough recipe. The proteins in the egg will cook and set to hold the cookies together.

• If the recipe has no liquid, switch to a high-protein flour, such as unbleached or bread, which will form more gluten than the lower-protein all-purpose and cake flours. Gluten forms bonds in the dough and helps it hold together. (Another way to develop the gluten is to mix a few tablespoons of water with the flour before combining it with the other ingredients.)—SHIRLEY CORRIHER

or wax paper. Remove the dough from the refrigerator and let it soften slightly before rolling.

4. Cut the cookie dough into four pieces. On a well-floured work surface, roll out one piece of dough ¼ inch thick. Run a long metal spatula under the dough to loosen it from the work surface. Using a 3-inch cookie cutter, cut out shapes as close together as possible. Transfer the shapes to one of the prepared baking sheets with a spatula, leaving about 1 inch between them. Repeat with the remaining pieces of dough. Gather up all of the scraps and roll them out to make more cookies.

5. Sprinkle the shapes with superfine sugar and bake for 15 to 20 minutes, or until the edges are just barely golden brown. Remove from the oven and let the cookies cool on the baking sheets for 10 minutes. Transfer to a wire rack with a metal spatula and let them cool completely. (MAKE AHEAD: The cookies can be stored in an airtight container for up to 2 days.) Sift confectioners' sugar over the cookies just before serving.—SHEILA LUKINS

BUTTER COOKIES WITH CLOVES

MAKES 4 DOZEN COOKIES

- 2 sticks (½ pound) unsalted butter, softened
- 1 cup confectioners' sugar
- 2 cups bleached all-purpose flour
- About 2 tablespoons whole cloves

1. Preheat the oven to 250°. In a large bowl, cream the softened butter. Gradually beat in the sugar, then beat in the flour, ¼ cup at a time. Knead lightly to form a smooth dough.

2. Divide the dough in half and roll each piece into a 12-inch log. Cut each log into 24 even slices and roll the slices into balls. Arrange the balls 1 inch apart on 2 large cookie sheets and flatten slightly. Gently press a clove in the center of each cookie.

3. Bake the cookies for about 1 hour, or until they are still pale but cooked through. Let the cookies cool on the sheets. (MAKE AHEAD: The cookies can be stored in an airtight container in a cool place for up to 1 week.) —FATIMA HAL

SIMPLE SHORTBREAD

MAKES 27 COOKIES

- 1½ sticks (6 ounces) unsalted butter, softened
- ½ cup sugar
- 1 large egg, separated
- 1¾ cups all-purpose flour
- ½ teaspoon ground cloves
- ⅛ teaspoon ground mace

1. Preheat the oven to 325°. In a medium bowl, cream the softened butter. Add the sugar and stir to blend. Beat in the egg yolk and then the all-purpose flour, ground cloves, and ground mace. Press the dough into a 9-inch-square baking pan.

2. Beat the white of the egg and brush it over the shortbread dough. Bake for 45 minutes, or until the shortbread is golden. Cut the warm shortbread into 3-by-1-inch pieces. Allow it to cool in the baking pan before serving.—SARAH FRITSCHNER

HICKORY NUT SHORTBREAD

These cookies pair well with Chèvre Coeur à la Crème with Berries (p. 440). If you have trouble finding hickory nuts, order them by mail from American Spoon Foods, 800-222-5886.

MAKES ABOUT 28 COOKIES

- ½ cup hickory nut or pecan pieces (about 3 ounces)
- 1½ teaspoons granulated sugar
- 1 stick (4 ounces) unsalted butter, softened
- ½ cup confectioners' sugar plus more for dusting
- ½ teaspoon pure vanilla extract
- 1 cup all-purpose flour
- ¼ teaspoon salt

1. Preheat the oven to 300°. Line a cookie sheet with parchment paper. In a food processor, pulverize the nuts with the granulated sugar to a coarse meal. Do not overprocess or the nuts will turn to paste. ➤

COOKIE Q&A

Q: Is there a tidy and handy way to dust with confectioners' sugar or cocoa powder?

A: George Morrone, former chef of Aqua in San Francisco, makes his own sugar shaker. To follow his example, take a clean paper coffee cup and fill it with confectioners' sugar or cocoa powder. Cover the top with a piece of cheesecloth and tie it on with string. You're now ready to decorate your dessert.—ARLENE FELTMAN-SAILHAC

Sugar Cookies

2. In a standing electric mixer, beat the butter, confectioners' sugar, and vanilla extract until light and fluffy. Add the flour, salt, and ground nuts, and mix just until blended. Turn out the dough onto a lightly floured surface and roll it out to a ¼-inch thickness. Using a 2-inch heart, quarter-moon, or other cookie cutter, cut out the cookies.
3. Working in batches, place the cookies ½ inch apart on the prepared cookie sheet. Bake in the center of the oven until the cookies are set but not browned, about 25 minutes. Transfer the cookies to a rack to cool slightly. Dust with confectioners' sugar while still warm. (MAKE AHEAD: The cookies will keep overnight in an airtight container, or wrap well and freeze for up to 1 month.) —ODESSA PIPER

CHOCOLATE-DRIZZLED SHORTBREAD

These buttery shortbread cookies are delicious with or without the chocolate drizzle.

MAKES ABOUT 2 DOZEN COOKIES

- 1½ sticks (6 ounces) unsalted butter, at room temperature
- ¼ cup plus 2 tablespoons sugar
- 1 teaspoon finely grated orange zest
- ½ teaspoon pure vanilla extract
- 1¾ cups plus 2 tablespoons all-purpose flour
- ½ teaspoon salt
- 4 ounces semisweet chocolate

1. In a large bowl, using an electric mixer, beat the butter at medium speed until creamy. With the mixer at low speed, gradually beat in the sugar until light and fluffy. Beat in the orange zest and vanilla. Gradually beat in the flour and salt, stirring in the last half cup with a wooden spoon or your hand to make a smooth firm mixture. Form the dough into a smooth 7-inch disk. Wrap in wax paper and refrigerate for 30 minutes. (MAKE AHEAD: The recipe can be made to this point up to 1 day ahead. Let the shortbread dough soften at room temperature for about 20 minutes before rolling out.)
2. Preheat the oven to 275° and position a rack in the center. On a lightly floured surface, roll out the shortbread dough evenly into a 12-inch round. Using a heart-shaped cookie cutter or any other cutter that measures 2 to 2½ inches at its widest point, cut out the cookies. Re-roll the scraps once to a scant ⅜ inch thick and cut out the remainder. Using a metal spatula, transfer the cookies to an ungreased cookie sheet and bake for 30 to 35 minutes, or until very lightly colored but not brown. Let cool slightly, then transfer to a rack to cool completely.
3. In a small heavy saucepan, melt the chocolate over very low heat. Pour the melted chocolate into a pastry bag fitted with a small writing tip, or pour it into a small plastic bag and snip a tiny opening in one corner. Drizzle the chocolate decoratively over one side of the cookies. Alternatively, using a long metal spatula, spread half of each cookie with the chocolate. Let the cookies sit briefly until the chocolate hardens, then serve. (MAKE AHEAD: The cookies will keep for up to 1 week in an airtight container.) —JOAN AND DICK ERATH

COOKIE DECORATOR'S TOOL KIT

- **Chopsticks or bamboo skewers to make eyes, details, holes for hanging**
- **Large needle and ribbon, ⅜ inch wide or less, for hanging cookies or making borders**
- **Rubber stamps, butter molds, or biscuit stamps to make impressions in dough**
- **Stencils (soft acetate, stencil paper, or hard plastic) and doilies**
- **Pastry bags with decorating tips**
- **Food coloring**
- **Cocoa, confectioner's sugar, and gold or silver dust or leaf for stenciling and dusting**
- **Serrated pastry wheel to cut decorative edges**
- **Sugar glitter**
- **Silver or gold dragées**
- **Garlic press to make dough hair for gingerbread people**
- **Pastry or paintbrushes for moistening dough and applying icing**
- **Palette for mixing icing colors**
- **Surgical gloves to prevent staining your hands when mixing colors**

FOR SPECIALTY SUPPLIES, CALL:

- **King Arthur Flour Baker's Catalogue; 800-827-6836**
- **N.Y. Cake & Baking Distributors; 800-942-2539**

—PEGGY CULLEN

SUGAR COOKIES

This dough is ideal for cutting into shapes and decorating with Royal

COOKIE DECORATING TIPS

You don't have to be an artist to make cookies that are almost too pretty to eat. First, prepare the dough for the Gingerbread Cookies or the Sugar Cookies. Then whip up some Royal Icing (p. 378) and try the decorating suggestions that follow.

PAINTING AND PIPING

- **To pipe filigree patterns, stripes, or other designs on baked or unbaked cookies, stir in sifted confectioners' sugar to stiffen the icing, then use a homemade parchment-paper cone or a pastry bag fitted with a writing tip.**
- **To make flowers on baked cookies, add even more sugar to the icing; pipe with a pastry bag and a decorative tip.**
- **Pipe outlines on baked or unbaked cookies using moderately stiff icing, then fill in the shapes by brushing on thinned icing of a different color.**

EMBOSSING AND STENCILING

- **Dip rubber stamps, biscuit stamps, or butter molds (or any item with an interesting surface) into flour, tap off the excess, and press the mold into raw dough.**
- **Firmly press an acetate or hard plastic stencil into the dough. Paint the raised areas with Royal Icing. Clean the stencil after each use. The embossed pattern can also be painted with icing after the cookie is baked.**
- **To make a snowflake, place a doily facedown on a work surface and center a round of raw dough on top; press so that the doily adheres. Flip the dough onto a lightly floured surface. Brush the exposed areas with thinned white Royal Icing. Carefully remove the doily.**
- **Place a stencil on raw dough. Dust the dough with confectioners' sugar, cocoa powder, or edible gold dust.**
- **Place a flexible stencil (or a homemade one cut from stencil or butcher paper) on a baked cookie. With a paintbrush, fill in with Royal Icing or cooled melted white or dark chocolate.**

APPLYING TOPPINGS

- **To use nuts, seeds, or dried fruit, lightly moisten a pastry brush with water and brush the raw dough. Gently press the topping into the dough.**
- **To make hair for gingerbread people, mermaids, or animals, knead a little extra flour into some dough, then squeeze it through a garlic press.**
- **Paint or pipe icing onto the cookies; before the icing dries, sprinkle the cookie with sugar glitter or dragées, or dust with confectioners' sugar or powdered food coloring.**

MAKING HANGING ORNAMENTS

- **Pierce unbaked cookies with the blunt end of a bamboo skewer. Repierce after baking while still warm.**
- **To make a ribbon border, punch holes around the edge of an unbaked cookie with a chopstick. Repierce the cookie after baking. Weave a ribbon through the holes after the cookie has cooled.**—PEGGY CULLEN

Icing (p. 378). It's also delicious simply sprinkled with cinnamon sugar, which is made with two to three teaspoons of cinnamon per ¼ cup granulated sugar.

MAKES ABOUT 6 DOZEN 2½-INCH COOKIES

3¾ cups all-purpose flour
2 teaspoons baking powder
½ teaspoon salt
2 sticks (½ pound) unsalted butter, softened
1⅔ cups sugar
2 large eggs, at room temperature, lightly beaten
2 teaspoons pure vanilla extract
Cinnamon sugar, for sprinkling

1. In a medium bowl, whisk together the flour, baking powder, and salt.
2. In a large bowl, using an electric mixer, cream the butter and sugar until light and fluffy. Add the eggs one at a time, beating well after each addition until thoroughly incorporated. Scrape down the bowl with a rubber spatula and beat for a few more seconds. Beat in the vanilla. On low speed, mix in half the dry ingredients; stir in the remainder with the spatula or your hands.
3. Turn out the dough onto a lightly floured work surface and cut it in half. Pat the dough into 2 disks and wrap them in plastic wrap. Refrigerate the dough until it is firm, at least 4 hours or overnight.
4. Preheat the oven to 350°. Line 2 cookie sheets with parchment paper. On a lightly floured surface, roll out the cookie dough about 3/16 inch thick. Cut the dough with cookie cutters and

sprinkle generously with cinnamon sugar if desired. Transfer the cookies to the cookie sheets.

5. Bake the cookies for 10 minutes, or until the edges just begin to turn golden. Let cool on the sheet until firm, then transfer to a rack to cool completely. (MAKE AHEAD: The cookies will keep for up to 1 week in an airtight container and for up to 1 month in the freezer.) —PEGGY CULLEN

GINGERBREAD COOKIES

These cookies make a perfect canvas for Royal Icing (recipe follows). The decorated cookies make great Christmas tree ornaments (see "Cookie Decorating Tips," opposite page).

MAKES ABOUT 7 DOZEN 2½-INCH COOKIES

- 4 cups all-purpose flour
- 2 tablespoons unsweetened cocoa powder
- 5 teaspoons ground ginger
- 2 teaspoons cinnamon
- 1 teaspoon ground cloves
- 1 teaspoon baking soda
- 1 teaspoon salt
- 2 sticks (½ pound) unsalted butter, softened
- 1 cup sugar
- 1 egg, at room temperature, lightly beaten
- ½ cup unsulphured molasses

Gingerbread Cookies

COOKIE Q&A

Q: Is there anything I can do to make pale cookies browner?

A: Yes, there are at least five things you can do.

• SUBSTITUTE AN EGG OR EGG YOLK, which is primarily protein, for up to three tablespoons of liquid called for in the recipe. Protein makes baked goods browner. For the same reason, using a high-protein flour like bread flour will make for browner cookies, too.

• INCREASE THE AMOUNT OF SUGAR in the recipe slightly, because sugar, like protein, causes a chemical reaction that results in browning.

• SUBSTITUTE UP TO FOUR TABLESPOONS OF CORN SYRUP for an equivalent amount of granulated sugar. Since corn syrup browns at a lower temperature than sugar, your cookies will brown faster. You don't need much: by replacing just one tablespoon of sugar, you will get a noticeably browner and crisper cookie.

• SWITCH TO LIGHT OR DARK BROWN SUGAR, which by its very color, darkens a dough.

• Acid inhibits browning, so ADD A LITTLE BAKING SODA to neutralize the acidity that exists naturally in many cookie ingredients, including sugar, chocolate, even cake flour. You can use up to one teaspoon baking soda per cup of flour.—SHIRLEY CORRIHER

1. In a large bowl, sift together the all-purpose flour, unsweetened cocoa powder, ground ginger, cinnamon, ground cloves, baking soda, and salt. Whisk together to combine.

2. In a large bowl, using an electric mixer, cream the butter with the sugar until light and fluffy. Beat in the egg until incorporated, then gradually beat in the unsulphured molasses. Scrape down the bowl with a rubber spatula and mix again for a few seconds. On low speed, gradually beat in the dry ingredients until thoroughly combined.

3. Turn out the cookie dough onto a lightly floured surface and knead it gently a few times. Divide the dough into 4 equal pieces and flatten each piece into a 6-inch disk. Cover each piece of dough with plastic wrap and refrigerate for at least 4 hours or overnight.

4. Preheat the oven to 350°. Line 2 cookie sheets with parchment paper. On a lightly floured surface, using a floured rolling pin, roll out 1 piece of the dough ⅛ inch thick for cookies or ½ inch thick for ornaments. Cut with cookie cutters. Using a long, wide metal spatula, transfer the cookies to the prepared cookie sheets. Repeat with the remaining pieces of dough. Reroll all the dough scraps and cut out more cookies.

5. Bake the thin gingerbread cookies for 10 minutes and the thick ones for 20 minutes, or until the edges just begin to brown. Let the gingerbread cookies cool on the cookie sheets until firm, then transfer them to a rack to cool completely. (MAKE AHEAD: The gingerbread cookies will keep for up to 1 week in an airtight container and for up to 1 month in the freezer.) —PEGGY CULLEN

Royal Icing

This easy-to-make icing hardens as it dries, so it's ideal for decorating. It can be brushed or piped onto the Sugar Cookies (p. 375) or Gingerbread Cookies (above) before or after baking.

MAKES 2 CUPS

- 2 large egg whites, at room temperature
- About 1 pound confectioners' sugar, sifted
- ¼ teaspoon cream of tartar
- 1 tablespoon fresh lemon juice
- Liquid, paste, or powdered food coloring

1. In a large bowl, combine all the ingredients except the food coloring. Using a hand-held electric mixer, beat at high speed until fluffy, thick, and shiny, 2 to 3 minutes.

2. Divide the icing into small batches and adjust the consistency as needed. To thin for painting, beat in water; for a stiffer icing that holds its shape, add more confectioners' sugar. Tint the icing with food coloring. Cover tightly with plastic wrap to prevent the icing from drying out. (MAKE AHEAD: The icing can be refrigerated in an airtight container and kept for up to 1 week.) —PEGGY CULLEN

LEMON PAPER THINS

Spreading the dough for these delicate wafers is a little tricky, but definitely worth the effort. You'll need a metal icing spatula, preferably offset, which is available at kitchenware stores. You can cut the cookies into any shape, but I prefer the look of diamonds.

If you like, flavor the sugar with a seasoning other than lemon, such as orange zest or ground cinnamon. Make the flavored sugar a day ahead.

MAKES ABOUT 5 DOZEN COOKIES

- ½ cup granulated sugar
- 2 tablespoons finely grated lemon zest
- 1 stick plus 2 tablespoons (5 ounces) unsalted butter, softened
- ¾ cup plus 2 tablespoons confectioners' sugar, sifted
- 1 teaspoon pure vanilla extract
- 1½ cups all-purpose flour, sifted
- ½ cup milk

1. In a small bowl, stir together the granulated sugar and lemon zest. Leave uncovered overnight to dry out, stirring once or twice. The next day sift the flavored sugar with your fingers to break up any lumps.
2. Preheat the oven to 325°. Using a pastry brush, spread 2 tablespoons of the softened unsalted butter on two 16-by-14-inch unrimmed cookie sheets. Refrigerate the cookie sheets while you make the dough.
3. In a medium bowl, using an electric mixer, cream the remaining 1 stick butter with the confectioners' sugar. Beat in the vanilla extract. Stir in the flour alternately with the milk, beginning and ending with the flour. Beat for a few seconds until the dough is completely smooth and has the consistency of soft mashed potatoes.
4. Divide the dough in half. Using a metal icing spatula, preferably offset, spread half the dough on one of the chilled cookie sheets in a thin, even layer, covering the sheet completely; take care to make the edges as thick as the center. Sprinkle the dough with half of the lemon-sugar. Repeat with the remaining dough and lemon-sugar.
5. Using a blunt table knife, score parallel vertical lines 2 inches apart from one edge of the dough to the other, wiping the knife clean between each cut. Then cut another set of parallel lines, also 2 inches apart, at a 45° angle to the first set of lines, to form diamonds.
6. Bake the cookies for 18 to 20 minutes, turning the cookie sheets once (and switching them if the cookies are coloring unevenly), until the cookies are golden; do not let them get too dark. Remove the cookie sheets from the oven and, working quickly, use a large sharp knife to recut the diamonds. (If you wait too long, the cookies will harden and break.) Using a metal spatula, transfer the cookie diamonds to a rack to cool. (MAKE AHEAD: The lemon cookies will keep for up to 1 week in an airtight container and for up to 1 month in the freezer.) —PEGGY CULLEN

BITTERSWEET CHOCOLATE WAFERS

You will need a pastry bag to pipe out this dough, which you can make into cookies of any size, from little chocolate dots to rounds big enough to make sandwiches with ice cream, ganache, or buttercream filling. You can also layer the wafers with whipped cream and refrigerate for a soft, cakey dessert. Here, each of the wafers is topped with a nut for a simple, elegant look.

Clockwise from left: Ukrainian Jam Swirls (p. 382), Cranberry Oatmeal Cookies (p. 370), and Bittersweet Chocolate Wafers

MAKES ABOUT 4 DOZEN 2-INCH COOKIES

- ¾ cup all-purpose flour
- ½ teaspoon baking soda
- 1 stick (4 ounces) unsalted butter, softened
- ⅔ cup dark brown sugar
- ½ teaspoon salt
- ¼ cup plus 2 tablespoons unsweetened cocoa powder, sifted
- 1 teaspoon pure vanilla extract
- 2 large egg whites, at room temperature
- About 2 ounces assorted nuts, such as walnut and pecan halves, pine nuts, and whole almonds

1. Preheat the oven to 325°. In a small bowl, sift the flour and baking soda; whisk to combine. In a medium bowl, using an electric mixer, cream the butter,

COOKIE Q&A

Q: My cookie recipe says "do not grease the pan" but the cookies stick. How can I prevent this?

A: Transfer the cookies from the baking sheet to a cooling rack when they are just firm enough to hold together. With most recipes this window of opportunity is from one to three minutes. If they are removed from the pan too soon, the cookies will be soft and will tear apart. If they're removed too late, the cookies will be nothing short of welded to an ungreased baking sheet.

I believe in spraying pans with cooking oil spray, which leaves a nice light coating, regardless of recipe directions; it's a good safeguard against sticking. Lining a cookie sheet with parchment paper or greased foil solves the sticking problem too.—SHIRLEY CORRIHER

brown sugar, and salt until light and fluffy. Beat in the unsweetened cocoa powder and the vanilla extract. Scrape down the bowl with a rubber spatula. Add the egg whites one at a time, beating well after each addition. Stir in the sifted dry ingredients.

2. Line 2 cookie sheets with parchment paper. Fit a pastry bag with a tip approximately 3/8 inch in diameter. Pipe thick 1¼-inch mounds about 2 inches apart on the prepared cookie sheets. Place 1 large nut or 4 to 5 pine nuts in the center of each of the mounds.

3. Bake the cookies for 15 to 20 minutes, or until the centers spring back somewhat when they are gently pressed. Let the cookies cool for about 10 minutes on the cookie sheets, then transfer the cookies to racks to cool completely. (MAKE AHEAD: The chocolate wafers will keep for up to 1 week in an airtight container and for up to 1 month in the freezer.) —PEGGY CULLEN

LEMON-PEPPER BISCOTTI

MAKES ABOUT 120 BISCOTTI

- 4½ cups all-purpose flour
- 1 tablespoon baking powder
- 2½ teaspoons coarsely cracked black pepper
- ½ teaspoon salt
- 2 sticks (½ pound) unsalted butter, at room temperature
- 1½ cups granulated sugar
- 4 large eggs
- 2½ tablespoons finely grated lemon zest
- 2 tablespoons orange-flavored liqueur or brandy
- 2 teaspoons pure vanilla extract
- About 3 tablespoons confectioners' sugar, for sprinkling

1. Preheat the oven to 325°. Line 2 large baking sheets with parchment paper and set aside.

2. In a large bowl, whisk together the flour, baking powder, pepper, and salt. In a standing electric mixer fitted with the paddle, beat the butter with the granulated sugar until combined. Add the eggs, lemon zest, orange liqueur, and vanilla, and beat until combined. Beat in the dry ingredients on low speed.

3. Divide the dough into 6 equal pieces. On a work surface sprinkled with confectioners' sugar, shape each piece of dough into a 12-inch log about 1½ inches wide. Transfer the logs to the prepared baking sheets, arranging them about 3 inches apart. Bake them in the upper and lower thirds of the oven for about 25 minutes, switching the pans halfway through baking, until the logs are golden and the tops spring back when lightly touched. Let cool on the baking sheets for 5 minutes. Leave the oven on.

4. Carefully transfer one of the logs to a cutting board. Using a serrated knife, cut the log diagonally into ½-inch slices. Arrange the slices on the baking sheet, cut sides down; repeat with the remaining logs.

5. Bake the biscotti for about 20 minutes, turning them once after 10 minutes, until dry and golden. Let cool completely on the baking sheets. (MAKE AHEAD: The biscotti can be frozen for up to 1 month in airtight containers. Let return to room temperature before serving.) Arrange the biscotti on large plates.—GRACE PARISI

CHOCOLATE-ALMOND BISCOTTI

MAKES ABOUT 150 BISCOTTI

- 1½ cups slivered almonds (about 6 ounces)
- 2⅔ cups sifted all-purpose flour
- ½ cup unsweetened cocoa powder, preferably Dutch process, plus 2 tablespoons, for sprinkling

2 tablespoons plus 1 teaspoon instant espresso powder
1½ teaspoons baking soda
½ teaspoon salt
6 ounces bittersweet chocolate, finely chopped
4 large eggs
1½ tablespoons coffee-flavored liqueur or brandy
1½ teaspoons pure vanilla extract
1½ cups granulated sugar
About 3 tablespoons confectioners' sugar, for sprinkling
6 ounces semisweet chocolate

1. Preheat the oven to 325°. Line 2 large baking sheets with parchment paper. Toast the almonds on a small baking sheet for about 6 minutes, or until golden. Leave the oven on.

2. In a medium bowl, sift the flour with ½ cup of the cocoa, the espresso powder, baking soda, and salt. Transfer 1 scant cup to a food processor, add the bittersweet chocolate, and process to a fine powder. Add the remaining dry ingredients and pulse until combined.

3. In a standing electric mixer fitted with the paddle, beat the eggs, coffee liqueur, and vanilla extract until combined. Add the bittersweet chocolate mixture and the granulated sugar and mix on low speed just until blended; the dough will be very stiff. Mix in the toasted almonds.

4. In a small bowl, stir the confectioners' sugar with the remaining 2 tablespoons cocoa and sprinkle the mixture on a work surface. Divide the dough into 6 equal pieces. On the work surface, shape each piece of dough into a 12-inch log about 1½ inches wide. Transfer to the prepared baking sheets, arranging the logs about 3 inches apart. Bake in the upper and lower thirds of the oven for about 35 minutes, switching the pans halfway through baking, until the tops spring back when lightly touched. Let cool on the baking sheets for 15 minutes. Lower the oven temperature to 300°.

5. Carefully transfer one of the logs of dough to a cutting board. Using a serrated knife, cut the log diagonally into ½-inch slices. Arrange the slices on the baking sheet, cut sides down, and repeat with the remaining logs. Bake the biscotti for about 17 minutes, switching the pans halfway through baking, until dry; the slices don't need to be turned. Let cool completely on the baking sheets.

6. In a small bowl set over a saucepan of simmering water, melt the semisweet chocolate. Using a fork, drizzle the chocolate over the biscotti. Press parchment or wax paper gently on the surface of the cookies and freeze until the chocolate is set. (MAKE AHEAD: The biscotti can be frozen for up to 1 month in airtight containers. Peel off the wax paper and let return to room temperature before serving.) Arrange the biscotti on large plates.—GRACE PARISI

PISTACHIO-ORANGE BISCOTTI

MAKES ABOUT 120 BISCOTTI

1½ cups shelled unsalted pistachios (about 6 ounces)
4½ cups all-purpose flour
1 tablespoon baking powder
½ teaspoon salt
2 sticks (½ pound) unsalted butter, softened
1¾ cups granulated sugar
4 large eggs, lightly beaten
1 tablespoon plus 1 teaspoon finely grated orange zest
2 teaspoons pure vanilla extract
3 tablespoons confectioners' sugar, for sprinkling

1. Preheat the oven to 325°. Line 2 baking sheets with parchment paper.

2. In a food processor, finely chop ½ cup of the pistachios.

COOKIE Q&A

Q: What causes a cookie to be too dry and hard?

A: Overbaking. Cookies are thin and cook—usually at 350 degrees to 375 degrees Fahrenheit—in a short time. Therefore, a few degrees and a few minutes matter. Check your oven temperature with a good oven thermometer to make sure it's calibrated properly and use a reliable timer.

It's difficult to tell when cookies are done. They may look undercooked when, in fact, they are perfect. I have had to train myself to take them out even though they look underbaked. Watch for browning on the edges, which is an indication that the cookies are finished baking. —SHIRLEY CORRIHER

Add the remaining pistachios and pulse 4 times, leaving some of the nuts coarsely chopped.

3. In a medium bowl, whisk together the flour, baking powder, and salt. In a standing electric mixer fitted with the paddle, beat the butter with the granulated sugar until combined. Add the eggs, orange zest, and vanilla, and beat until combined. Beat in the dry ingredients on low speed. Fold in the pistachios.

4. Divide the dough into 6 equal pieces. On a work surface sprinkled with the confectioners' sugar, shape each piece of dough into a 12-inch log about 1½ inches wide. Transfer to the prepared baking sheets, arranging the logs about 3 inches apart. Bake in the upper and lower thirds of the oven for about 30 minutes, switching the pans halfway through baking, until golden and the tops spring back when lightly touched. Let cool on the baking sheets for 10 minutes. Lower the oven temperature to 300°.

5. Carefully transfer one of the logs to a cutting board. Using a serrated knife, cut the log diagonally into ½-inch slices. Arrange the slices on the baking sheet, cut sides down, and repeat with the remaining logs. Bake the biscotti for about 20 minutes, switching the pans halfway through baking, until golden and dry; the slices don't need to be turned. Let cool completely on the baking sheets. (MAKE AHEAD: The biscotti can be frozen for up to 1 month in an airtight container. Let return to room temperature before serving.) Arrange the biscotti on large plates.—GRACE PARISI

UKRAINIAN JAM SWIRLS

Like biscotti, these logs are baked, sliced, and baked again, but only for a short period of time so that they won't be too crunchy. They are made with a soft buttery dough that is rolled up with jam. Kept tightly wrapped, they're even better the second day.

MAKES 5 DOZEN COOKIES

- 5 cups all-purpose flour
- 2 teaspoons baking powder
- 1 teaspoon salt
- 2 sticks (½ pound) unsalted butter, softened
- 2 cups plus 4 teaspoons sugar
- 3 large eggs, at room temperature, lightly beaten
- 1 teaspoon pure vanilla extract
- ⅔ cup apricot preserves
- ⅔ cup raspberry preserves
- ¼ teaspoon cinnamon

1. In a medium bowl, whisk together the flour, baking powder, and salt. In a large bowl, using an electric mixer, cream the butter with the 2 cups of sugar just until combined. Beat in the eggs one at a time until incorporated; don't overbeat. Scrape down the bowl with a rubber spatula. Beat in the vanilla. Stir in the dry ingredients; when the stirring becomes too difficult, use your hands to combine the ingredients. The dough should be soft but not sticky; knead it gently a few times to bring it together. Cover with plastic wrap and refrigerate for at least 4 hours or overnight.

2. Preheat the oven to 400°. Line 2 cookie sheets with parchment paper. Put the apricot and raspberry preserves into small bowls and stir gently to break them up a little, especially the apricot. In a cup, combine the remaining 4 teaspoons of sugar with the cinnamon.

3. Roll the chilled dough into a smooth cylinder and cut it into 4 even pieces. Rewrap 3 of the pieces and refrigerate them. On a lightly floured surface, pat the remaining piece of dough into a 6-by-4-inch rectangle. Place a large sheet of plastic wrap on the work surface and dust it with flour; set the dough in the center and cover with another large sheet of plastic wrap. Using a rolling pin, roll the dough between the sheets of plastic wrap into a 12-by-7-inch rectangle, flipping the whole piece once and rolling on the other side to keep the dough even. Flip the whole piece back so that the floured side is on the bottom again.

4. Peel off the top sheet of plastic wrap. Using a spatula, spread ⅓ cup of one kind of the preserves evenly over the dough, leaving a ½-inch border all around. Fold in the ½-inch border on the two short edges. Beginning with the long edge closest to you, lift the plastic wrap to roll up the dough jelly-roll fashion. Cradling the log in the plastic wrap, transfer it to the prepared cookie sheet, positioning it seam side down and leaving room for another log. Remove and discard the plastic wrap. Repeat the procedure with the remaining pieces of dough and preserves, putting 2 logs spaced evenly apart on each cookie sheet.

5. Lightly brush the tops of the logs with water. Sprinkle each log with 1 teaspoon of the cinnamon-sugar.

6. Bake the logs of dough for 30 to 35 minutes, or until the tops are golden. A few cracks may appear along the length of the logs; this is not a problem. Remove from the oven and let cool for 15 minutes.

7. Using a large sharp knife, trim a thin slice from each end; then slice each log crosswise into 15 equal pieces, cleaning off the knife between cuts; the tops may crack a little.

8. Line the cookie sheets with clean parchment paper. Arrange the cookies cut side up on the prepared cookie sheets. Bake for another 10 minutes. Using a metal spatula, transfer the cookies to a rack to cool completely. (MAKE AHEAD: The cookies will keep for up to 1 week in an airtight container and for up to 1 month in the freezer.) —PEGGY CULLEN

CHAPTER 18

CAKES

Hot Chocolate Torte

HOT CHOCOLATE TORTES

The batter for these dense chocolate cakes, from Vincent Guerithault on Camelback in Phoenix, must be refrigerated for four hours to prevent it from overflowing during baking.

6 SERVINGS

- ½ pound bittersweet chocolate, finely chopped
- 1 stick (8 tablespoons) unsalted butter, cut into small pieces
- 4 large eggs, separated
- ¾ cup plus 2 tablespoons granulated sugar
- 1 teaspoon confectioners' sugar
- Unsweetened whipped cream, for serving (optional)

1. Preheat the oven to 375°. Butter and flour a baking sheet. Butter the insides of 6 metal rings that measure 3 inches wide and 2 inches high (see Note). Dip the rings in flour and set them on the prepared baking sheet.

2. In a medium bowl set over a saucepan of barely simmering water, melt the chocolate and butter, stirring occasionally, until smooth, about 5 minutes. Let cool slightly.

3. In another bowl, lightly beat the egg yolks. Using a rubber spatula, stir in the chocolate until blended.

4. In a large bowl, using an electric mixer, beat the egg whites until soft peaks form. Gradually beat in the granulated sugar until the whites are firm and glossy. Gently fold the chocolate mixture into the whites just until no white streaks remain. Cover and refrigerate for 4 hours.

5. Spoon the mixture into the prepared rings and bake for about 18 minutes until the tops are firm and a knife inserted between the inside of a ring and the cake comes out clean. Using a wide metal spatula, transfer the tortes to individual plates and remove the rings. The tortes will sink slightly and crack. Sift the confectioners' sugar over the tops and serve at once with whipped cream.

NOTE: Metal cake rings are available at kitchen supply stores. They must be at least 2 inches high. Alternatively, 8-ounce pineapple cans with the tops and bottoms removed or similarly sized cans can be used.—VINCENT GUERITHAULT

SWISS TRUFFLE CAKE

This rich, solid chocolate dessert is one that can easily be called "killer."

MAKES TWO 5-BY-9-INCH CAKES (12 SERVINGS EACH)

GANACHE:

2 cups heavy cream
4 tablespoons unsalted butter
4 tablespoons light corn syrup
1½ pounds semisweet chocolate, finely chopped

CAKE:

7 ounces semisweet chocolate, finely chopped
1½ sticks (6 ounces) unsalted butter, at room temperature
¾ cup sugar
8 large eggs, separated, at room temperature
7 ounces blanched or natural almonds, finely ground
⅔ cup fine dry bread crumbs
1 tablespoon unsweetened Dutch process cocoa powder

1. Make the ganache: In a medium saucepan, bring the cream, butter, and corn syrup to a boil over moderate heat. Remove from the heat, add the chocolate, stir once, and let stand for 5 minutes. Whisk until smooth and strain into a bowl. Refrigerate until thickened, about 2 hours.

2. Make the cake: Preheat the oven to 350° and position a rack in the middle. Butter a 10½-by-15½-inch jelly-roll pan and line the bottom with parchment paper. Butter the paper. In a small bowl set over a saucepan of hot but not simmering water, melt the chocolate, stirring occasionally. Let cool.

3. In a large bowl, using an electric mixer, cream the butter with half of the sugar. Beat in the chocolate; then beat in the egg yolks 1 at a time. Combine the almonds and bread crumbs and stir them into the batter.

4. In another large bowl, whip the egg whites until they hold very soft peaks. Gradually beat in the remaining sugar until the whites hold firm peaks. Stir one-quarter of the whites into the batter, then fold in the remaining whites with a rubber spatula.

5. Spread the batter evenly in the prepared pan. Bake for 20 minutes, or until the cake is firm and no longer sticky when touched lightly in the center.

6. Let the cake cool in the pan for 2 minutes, then loosen the sides with the tip of a knife. Invert the cake onto a rack and

Swiss Truffle Cake

peel off the paper. Cover the cake with another rack and turn it right side up. Let cool to room temperature. (MAKE AHEAD: The cake can be covered and kept at room temperature overnight.)

7. To assemble the 2 cakes, halve the layer crosswise. Cut each half crosswise into thirds, each about 3½ by 7¾ inches. Cut 2 pieces of stiff cardboard about ¼ inch larger than the layers. Place 1 cake rectangle on each cardboard.

8. Gently whisk the ganache to a spreading consistency. Using a long metal spatula, spread each of the 2 cake rectangles with about 3 tablespoons ganache. Cover with 2 more layers of cake and ganache. Generously frost the sides of the 2 cakes with ganache.

9. To finish, spoon the remaining ganache into a pastry bag fitted with a ½-inch plain tip and pipe thick diagonal strips on top of the cakes. Refrigerate the cakes to set, about 2 hours. (MAKE AHEAD: Refrigerate the cakes loosely covered overnight. Or freeze until firm, wrap in plastic, and freeze for up to 1 month; unwrap and defrost in the refrigerator. Let the cakes return to room temperature.) Just before serving, dust the tops of the cakes with cocoa powder.—NICK MALGIERI

TRUFFLE CAKE TIPS

Here are a half-dozen hints that will make baking the Swiss Truffle Cake go smoothly.

TO PREPARE THE PAN: **Use a brush to coat the entire pan with soft, but not melted, butter. Cut a piece of parchment or wax paper to fit the bottom of the pan. (It is not necessary to line the sides of the pan; the cake will detach easily.) Butter the paper to ensure that it will pull away from the baked cake.**

TO MELT THE CHOCOLATE: **A microwave oven is handy for this purpose. Cut the chocolate into chunks no larger than ½ inch and place in a heatproof bowl. Microwave on half power for 20 seconds at a time, stirring between zaps, until melted; this will probably require about four zaps. Or follow the conventional method in the recipe.**

TO GRIND THE ALMONDS: **Place the whole almonds in a food processor fitted with the metal blade and pulse the machine repeatedly to finely grind the almonds, about 20 pulses, each a second long. Scrape the bottom of the work bowl with a spatula to incorporate all the almonds, then pulse again to blend. Do not overprocess, or the nuts will become pasty.**

TO MIX THE BATTER: **Be sure your ingredients are at room temperature. If the room you are working in is cold, the batter of butter, sugar, chocolate, and eggs may stiffen. If that happens, before proceeding, soften the mixture by placing it over a bowl of warm tap water and stirring until the batter is creamy.**

TO SPREAD THE GANACHE FILLING: **Allow enough time for the filling to come to room temperature; if it is too cold, it won't spread easily. Just before using, whisk the ganache to bring it to a good spreading consistency. Using a metal icing spatula, put a dab of ganache on each corner of the cake and spread it away from the corners toward the center of the cake. If you spread the ganache toward the corners, the spatula will lift off the cream.**

TO SERVE: **Use a thin, sharp knife to cut the truffle cakes into at least 12 slices. They should be quite thin because the cake is rich.—NICK MALGIERI**

CRISPY CHOCOLATE SOUFFLE CAKES

At Chanterelle in New York City, these incredibly rich and chocolatey soufflés are baked in paper-thin crêpes that are only available commercially. We found thin lumpia *or spring roll (but not egg roll) wrappers to be the best substitute. The soufflé mixture can also be baked on its own. Be sure to use a sturdy muffin tin with four-ounce cups.*

8 SERVINGS

6 ounces bittersweet chocolate, chopped
6 tablespoons unsalted butter, cut into 12 pieces
3 large eggs, separated
⅔ cup sugar
Eight 7½- to 9-inch *lumpia* or spring roll wrappers*
Confectioners' sugar and unsweetened cocoa
Vanilla ice cream, for serving

*Available at Asian markets

1. Preheat the oven to 400°. Butter eight 4-ounce cups in a sturdy muffin tin. Combine the chocolate and butter in a double boiler and place over simmering water. Stir occasionally until almost melted. Remove from the heat and set aside for several minutes, then stir until smooth.
2. In a large bowl, whisk the egg yolks with ⅓ cup of the sugar until blended. Whisk in the melted chocolate mixture.
3. In another bowl, beat the egg whites until fluffy. Gradually beat in the remaining ⅓ cup sugar, then beat until the whites hold soft peaks. Fold the whites into the chocolate mixture in 2 batches.
4. Place a *lumpia* wrapper in front of you on a work surface. Scoop a level ⅓ cup of the chocolate soufflé mixture onto the center of the wrapper. Pick up all four corners of the wrapper to form a purse and place it inside a buttered muffin cup; the edges of the wrapper should stand straight up. Repeat with the remaining *lumpia* wrappers and chocolate soufflé mixture. (MAKE AHEAD: The soufflé cakes can be assembled up to 3 hours ahead and kept at room temperature.)
5. Bake the soufflé cakes for about 12 minutes, or until the wrappers are nicely browned and the filling feels firm. Let rest in the pan for 5 minutes. (The center of the soufflés will be slightly runny.)
6. To serve, sift a dusting of confectioners' sugar and cocoa all over 8 plates. Place a scoop of ice cream and a chocolate soufflé cake on each plate and serve immediately.—DAVID WALTUCK

CHOCOLATE CAKE LF

9 SERVINGS

Vegetable oil cooking spray
¾ cup pastry or cake flour plus more for dusting
⅓ cup unsweetened cocoa powder, preferably Dutch process
1½ teaspoons baking powder
2 tablespoons unsalted butter
1 cup (packed) light brown sugar
3 large egg whites
1 large egg
1 cup plain nonfat yogurt
1 teaspoon pure vanilla extract
1 ounce semisweet chocolate, coarsely chopped
1 tablespoon skim milk

1. Preheat the oven to 350°. Spray an 8-inch square cake pan with the vegetable oil cooking spray and dust lightly with flour. In a medium bowl, sift the cake flour, unsweetened cocoa powder, and baking powder.
2. In a bowl, combine the butter and brown sugar. Beat in the egg whites, egg, nonfat yogurt, and vanilla. Gradually beat in the

Crispy Chocolate Soufflé Cake

flour mixture until incorporated. Pour the batter into the prepared pan and bake 35 to 40 minutes, or until a cake tester inserted in the center comes out clean. Let the cake cool in the pan. (MAKE AHEAD: The cake can be made up to 4 hours ahead. Cover and let stand at room temperature.)

3. In a small bowl, melt the chopped semisweet chocolate in the skim milk in a microwave or over a saucepan of barely simmering water. Let cool slightly. Invert the cake onto a platter and spread with the melted chocolate. Cut the cake into 9 squares and serve.—CHARLES WILEY

LOW-FAT CHOCOLATE CAKE LF

10 SERVINGS

Vegetable oil cooking spray
1¼ cups cake flour
½ cup unsweetened Dutch-process cocoa plus 1 teaspoon for dusting
1 teaspoon baking soda
1½ cups granulated sugar
½ ounce unsweetened chocolate, coarsely chopped
4 tablespoons unsalted butter
1 cup low-fat (1.5%) buttermilk
1 tablespoon pure vanilla extract
2 large eggs
1 large egg white
1 teaspoon confectioners' sugar

1. Preheat the oven to 350°. Spray a 9-by-2-inch round cake pan with vegetable oil cooking spray and line the bottom with parchment or wax paper. In a bowl, sift the cake flour with the ½ cup unsweetened cocoa and the baking soda.

2. In a small saucepan, combine the granulated sugar, unsweetened chocolate, and ½ cup of water. Cook over moderate heat, stirring occasionally, until the sugar dissolves and the chocolate melts, about 4 minutes. Transfer the mixture to a large bowl and stir in the butter until melted. Stir in the buttermilk and vanilla. Beat in the eggs and the egg white and then the flour mixture until combined. Pour the batter into the prepared cake pan.

3. Bake the chocolate cake for about 35 minutes, or until a cake tester inserted in the center of the cake comes out clean. Set the pan on a rack and let cool for 20 minutes. Invert the cake onto a large platter and let cool completely. (MAKE AHEAD: The cake can be kept, covered, at room temperature for 1 day.) Just before serving, garnish the cake by sifting the confectioners' sugar and the remaining 1 teaspoon unsweetened cocoa evenly over the top.—DIANA STURGIS

Low-Fat Chocolate Cake and Fresh Fruit Cake (p. 393)

LOW-FAT BAKING TIPS

Fat plays such an important role in baking that it's not easy to reduce the amount and maintain the flavor and texture that it supplies. Here, however, are some tricks for replacing some of the fat normally used in baking.

- **Substitute cocoa for most of the unsweetened chocolate in a recipe. The Low-Fat Chocolate Cake recipe uses unsweetened cocoa plus buttermilk and some butter in place of about three ounces of unsweetened chocolate.**
- **Use egg whites for some of the whole eggs. Fresh Fruit Cake (p. 393) calls for two egg whites instead of a third whole egg.**
- **Replace some of the butter or oil with mashed or pureed fruit, such as bananas or dates. In the Banana Cake recipe (p. 396), fruit puree takes the place of about 50 percent, or four tablespoons, of butter.**
- **Punch up the flavor of diced or sliced fresh fruit that's added to the batter by tossing it with a little cinnamon-sugar.**
- **Add low-fat buttermilk instead of cream or whole milk; use it also in place of some of the butter and oil.**

DIPLOMATICO

This homey dessert, made with store-bought pound cake, can be assembled in less than half an hour.

6 TO 8 SERVINGS

RUM-AND-ESPRESSO SOAK:

1¼ cups strong espresso (see "Diplomatico Tips," right)
5 tablespoons rum
5 teaspoons sugar
One 16-ounce pound cake, cut into ¼-inch slices (see "Diplomatico Tips," right)

CHOCOLATE FILLING:

4 large eggs, separated
1 teaspoon sugar
6 ounces semisweet chocolate, coarsely chopped

FROSTING AND GARNISH:

1 cup very cold heavy cream
1 teaspoon sugar
Fresh berries or walnut halves and candied fruit

1. Make the rum-and-espresso soak: In a small bowl, combine the espresso, rum, sugar, and 5 tablespoons of water.

2. Moisten a sheet of cheesecloth large enough to line a 9-by-5-by-3-inch glass loaf pan with plenty of overhang. Line the loaf pan with the cheesecloth. Dip the pound cake, slice by slice, in the rum-and-espresso soak, then use the slices to line the bottom and sides of the loaf pan. (Dip the pound cake slices very quickly, or else they'll become too soggy to handle; allow any excess liquid to drip from each slice before using it to line the pan.) Leave no gaps, patching where necessary with additional pieces of soaked pound cake.

3. Make the chocolate filling: In a large bowl, beat the yolks of the eggs with the sugar until the yolks turn pale yellow, about 4 minutes.

4. Melt the chopped semisweet chocolate in a double boiler over gently simmering water. Gradually pour the melted chocolate over the beaten egg yolks, mixing quickly with a rubber spatula until smoothly combined.

5. In a medium bowl, beat the whites of the eggs until they form stiff peaks. Stir a rounded tablespoon of the beaten egg whites into the semisweet chocolate mixture to loosen it, then gently fold in the remaining beaten whites.

6. Spoon the chocolate filling into the cake-lined loaf pan. Cover the filling with more slices of rum-and-espresso-soaked pound cake. (You may have some slices of pound cake left over.) Fold the moistened cheesecloth over the top of the cake. Refrigerate the *diplomatico* for at least one day and up to a week.

7. When you take the *diplomatico* out of the refrigerator, unfold the cheesecloth and pull it away from the top of the cake. Invert the loaf pan onto a platter and shake it firmly to free the cake. Peel off the cheesecloth.

8. Make the frosting and garnish the diplomatico: In a very well-chilled bowl, using chilled beaters, whip the cold heavy cream with the sugar until stiff. Frost the top and sides of the *diplomatico* with the whipped cream. Garnish the *diplomatico* with fresh berries, or with a simple arrangement of walnuts and candied fruit.—MARCELLA HAZAN

Diplomatico

DIPLOMATICO TIPS

- **Strong brewed espresso is very important for the flavor of Diplomatico, and using an extra-strong cup of regular coffee in its place just will not do. If you don't have an espresso machine, simply buy some espresso at your local coffee bar on your way home.**
- **Some pound cakes absorb too much liquid, become too soggy to handle, and break apart. Look for the cheapest brands, made with little or no butter; these cakes remain firmer and are easier to work with.—MARCELLA HAZAN**

VANILLA-SOUR CREAM BUNDT CAKE

A velvety yet moist crumb, fine buttery flavor, and excellent keeping properties make this Bundt cake a hit. It is delicious plain or with whipped cream. It also goes well with fruit or ice cream. A standing electric mixer is needed for this recipe.

12 TO 15 SERVINGS

3 cups cake flour
1⅔ cups granulated sugar
2½ teaspoons baking powder
¾ teaspoon salt
½ cup sour cream
⅓ cup milk
3 large whole eggs
2 large egg yolks
1 tablespoon pure vanilla extract
2½ sticks (10 ounces) unsalted butter, softened
Confectioners' sugar, for dusting

1. Preheat the oven to 350°. Generously grease and flour a 12-cup Bundt pan or tube pan. Tap out any excess flour.
2. Sift the cake flour, granulated sugar, baking powder, and salt into the bowl of a standing electric mixer.
3. In a medium bowl, using a fork, beat together the sour cream, milk, whole eggs, egg yolks, and vanilla until very well blended and smooth.
4. Add the butter and half of the egg mixture to the dry ingredients. Beat at low speed just until thoroughly incorporated. Increase the speed to high and beat the mixture for 1 minute; do not overmix. Add the remaining egg mixture and beat at medium-high speed until the batter is fluffy and smooth, about 1 minute longer.
5. Scrape the batter into the prepared Bundt pan. Rap the pan on the counter several times to remove air bubbles. Bake the cake in the middle of the oven for 50 to 60 minutes, or until it is well browned, pulls away from the pan sides, and a toothpick inserted in the thickest part comes out clean. Transfer to a rack to cool completely.
6. Run a thin knife around the pan edges to loosen the cake, then invert onto a serving plate. Using a small strainer, sift a little confectioners' sugar over the cake if desired. (MAKE AHEAD: The cake will keep for up to 5 days covered at room temperature or up to 2 weeks wrapped airtight and frozen.) —NANCY BAGGETT

Vanilla-Sour Cream Bundt Cake

Lemon Pound Cake with Berries in Pomegranate Syrup

LEMON POUND CAKE WITH BERRIES IN POMEGRANATE SYRUP

The moist, lemony pound cake, also good on its own, can be made in five 9-by-4½-by-2-inch loaf pans rather than the six disposable pans used in Step 1. You can substitute cranberry juice for the pomegranate juice in the syrup, but it lacks the latter's tangy, intense flavor. You can also use any combination of fresh berries to replace those specified here; you should have about 12 pints.

MAKES 50 BUFFET SERVINGS

POUND CAKE:

3½ sticks (14 ounces) unsalted butter, softened
5 cups granulated sugar
10 large eggs, lightly beaten
3 tablespoons finely grated lemon zest
7½ cups sifted all-purpose flour
1¼ teaspoons baking powder
1¼ teaspoons baking soda
1¾ teaspoons salt
3 cups plus 2 tablespoons buttermilk
1½ tablespoons pure vanilla extract

ACCOMPANIMENTS:

4 cups pomegranate juice*
¼ cup grenadine (optional)
2 cups granulated sugar
Zest of ½ medium orange, cut into thick strips
5 cups heavy cream, chilled
¼ cup plus 3 tablespoons confectioners' sugar
¼ cup brandy or rum

10 pints hulled strawberries, halved if large
1½ pints raspberries

*Available at health food stores and Middle Eastern markets

1. Prepare the pound cakes: Preheat the oven to 325°. Butter and flour six 8-by-4-by-2¼-inch disposable foil loaf pans with butter and coat with flour, discarding the excess.
2. In a large bowl, using an electric mixer, cream the butter and granulated sugar on medium speed until light and fluffy. Mix in the eggs on low speed until blended. Add the lemon zest. The mixture may look curdled, but it won't affect the cake.
3. In a medium bowl, sift together the all-purpose flour, the baking powder, the baking soda, and the salt. In another medium bowl, combine the buttermilk and the vanilla extract. On low speed, beat the dry ingredients into the butter mixture, alternating with the buttermilk, beginning and ending with the dry ingredients; mix just until combined. Spoon the pound cake batter into the prepared loaf pans and smooth the tops.
4. Bake the pound cakes in the upper and lower thirds of the oven for about 50 minutes, switching the pans halfway through baking, until the tops are golden and a cake tester inserted in the center comes out clean. Let the cakes cool in the pans for 5 minutes. Remove the cakes from the pans and let cool completely on cake racks. (MAKE AHEAD: The pound cakes can be made up to 1 month ahead and frozen; wrap them well in plastic, then in foil. Allow them to return to room temperature before serving.) Slice the pound cakes up to 3 hours before serving, arrange the cake slices on platters, and cover them with plastic.
5. Prepare the accompaniments: In a medium nonreactive saucepan, combine the pomegranate juice, grenadine, granulated sugar, and orange zest. Bring to a boil over moderately high heat, stirring, just until the sugar dissolves. Reduce the heat to moderately low and simmer until reduced to 2 cups, about 35 minutes. Discard the orange zest and let the pomegranate syrup cool completely. (MAKE AHEAD: The syrup can be prepared up to 2 weeks ahead; cover tightly and refrigerate.)
6. No more than 1 hour before serving, beat the heavy cream to soft peaks. Add the confectioners' sugar and brandy and continue beating until firm. Transfer the whipped cream to a large serving bowl. In another large serving bowl, toss the strawberries and raspberries with the pomegranate syrup. Serve the cream and berries alongside the cake.—GRACE PARISI

FRESH FRUIT CAKE *LF*

The inspiration for this cake comes from my mother-in-law's German apple kuchen and a fruit cake I once tasted made by the wonderful baker Jim Dodge.

10 SERVINGS

Vegetable oil cooking spray
1 large firm ripe pear, preferably Bosc, peeled and cut into ¾-inch dice
1 large tart green apple, peeled and cut into ¾-inch dice
6 ounces fresh or thawed frozen cranberries (1½ cups)
1 cup plus 2 tablespoons sugar
2 teaspoons cinnamon
5 tablespoons unsalted butter, softened
⅓ cup low-fat (1.5%) buttermilk
2 large eggs
2 large egg whites
2 cups cake flour
2 teaspoons baking powder

1. Preheat the oven to 350°. Lightly spray a 9-by-2-inch round cake pan with vegetable oil cooking spray. Line the bottom of the cake pan with parchment or wax paper. Lightly spray the paper with vegetable oil cooking spray and sprinkle the sides of the cake pan with sugar.
2. In a medium bowl, combine the diced pear and apple with the cranberries. Add 1 tablespoon of the sugar and the cinnamon and toss to coat.
3. In a large bowl, beat the butter until creamy. Gradually beat in 1 cup of the sugar and the low-fat buttermilk. Beat in the eggs and the egg whites until combined, then beat in the cake flour and the baking powder. Stir in the fruit. Spoon the batter into the prepared cake pan and sprinkle the top with the remaining 1 tablespoon sugar.
4. Bake the fruit cake for about 1 hour, or until golden and a cake tester inserted in the center comes out clean. Set the cake pan on a rack and let the cake cool for 20 minutes. Invert the

Upside-Down Mango Corn Cake

cake onto a plate and peel off the paper. Invert the cake again onto a large plate or platter and allow it to cool completely. (MAKE AHEAD: The fruit cake can be kept, covered, at room temperature for 1 day.) —DIANA STURGIS

UPSIDE-DOWN MANGO CORN CAKE

6 TO 8 SERVINGS

TOPPING:

- 2 tablespoons unsalted butter
- 3 tablespoons light brown sugar
- 2 large mangoes, peeled and sliced ½ inch thick

CAKE:

- ½ cup coarse yellow cornmeal, preferably stone-ground
- ½ cup all-purpose flour
- 1 teaspoon baking powder
- ¼ teaspoon cinnamon
- Pinch of salt
- 6 tablespoons unsalted butter, softened
- ⅓ cup (lightly packed) light brown sugar
- 2 large eggs
- 2 large egg yolks
- ¼ teaspoon pure vanilla extract

1. Preheat the oven to 350°. **Make the topping:** In a 9-inch cast-iron skillet, melt the butter over moderate heat. Stir in the brown sugar until it is melted. Arrange the mango slices in the skillet in a tight pinwheel, filling in with scraps. Continue cooking until the mangoes are tender and lightly caramelized, about 10 minutes.

2. Meanwhile, **make the cake:** Sift the yellow cornmeal, all-purpose flour, baking powder, cinnamon, and salt into a small bowl. If any large pieces of cornmeal remain in the sifter, dump them into the bowl.

3. In a medium bowl, using an electric mixer, beat the butter until light and fluffy. Beat in the light brown sugar until fluffy. Beat in the whole eggs and the eggs yolks one at a time, blending well after each addition. Beat in the vanilla extract. Using a rubber spatula, fold in the dry ingredients a handful at a time, mixing lightly but thoroughly. Drop dollops of the cake batter evenly over the pinwheel of mango slices and gently spread the batter to within 1 inch of the edge of the skillet.

4. Bake the cake in the middle of the oven for about 20 minutes,

HOW TO SLICE AND DICE A MANGO

Peel half of the mango lengthwise, preferably using a sturdy peeler. Then cut lengthwise slices down to the pit of the mango. Cut crosswise to release the slices. Repeat the process with the other half of the mango. The slices can then be diced if desired.

or until the top springs back when lightly touched. Remove the cake from the oven and let settle for 1 minute. Invert a large plate over the skillet. Hold the skillet handle with an oven mitt and with a quick motion, flip the cake onto the plate. Allow the cake to cool for about 10 minutes, then cut it into wedges and serve.—MARCIA KIESEL

ORANGE ANGEL FOOD CAKE WITH WARM BERRY COMPOTE LF

12 SERVINGS

CAKE:

- 2 cups sugar
- 1⅓ cups cake flour
- 2 cups egg whites (from about 16 large eggs)
- ½ teaspoon cream of tartar
- ⅛ teaspoon salt
- 1 tablespoon finely grated orange zest
- ¼ teaspoon pure vanilla extract

BERRY COMPOTE:

- 1 teaspoon cornstarch
- 2 pints strawberries, hulled and quartered
- 2 tablespoons orange-flavored liqueur
- 1 tablespoon sugar
- 1 pint blueberries

1. Make the cake: Preheat the oven to 375°. In a large bowl, sift ¾ cup of the sugar and the cake flour 3 times. Using a standing electric mixer, whip the egg whites at medium speed until foamy, about 1 minute. Add the cream of tartar and the salt and whip the whites for 1 minute more. Increase the speed to high and gradually beat in the remaining 1¼ cups sugar until the egg whites are stiff and smooth; do not overbeat.

2. Scrape the beaten egg whites over the dry mixture and fold them together with a large rubber spatula just until incorporated. Add the grated orange zest and the vanilla extract and fold until blended. Scrape the angel food cake batter into a 10-inch tube pan with a removable bottom, smoothing the top. Run a knife through the center of the batter to remove any large air bubbles. Bake for about 45 minutes, or until the top of the cake springs back when it is lightly pressed and a tester inserted in the center comes out clean. Invert the tube pan over a narrow-necked bottle and allow the cake to cool completely.

3. Run a thin sharp knife around the sides and center of the pan to loosen the cake. Remove the pan, cutting around the bottom of the cake to loosen it. Set the cake bottom side up. (MAKE AHEAD: The angel food cake can be prepared up to eight hours ahead; cover and let stand at room temperature.)

4. Make the berry compote: In a small bowl, dissolve the cornstarch in ¼ cup of water. Heat a medium nonreactive skillet over moderate heat. Add the quartered strawberries, the orange-flavored liqueur, and the sugar. Stir in the cornstarch mixture and cook until the liquid is slightly thickened, about 2 minutes. Fold in the blueberries. Serve the berry compote warm with the orange angel food cake.—CHARLES WILEY

GINGERED APPLE CAKE

This tender apple cake is best served the same day it is made.

6 SERVINGS

- 3 tart apples, such as Granny Smith, Winesap, or Baldwin (about 1½ pounds)
- ¾ cup dry white wine
- ⅓ cup plus 2½ tablespoons sugar
- Zest of 1 lemon
- 1 tablespoon finely chopped fresh ginger
- ½ cup all-purpose flour, sifted
- ½ teaspoon baking powder
- 3 large eggs, separated
- 1½ cups heavy cream, 1 cup chilled
- 1 tablespoon unsalted butter, melted
- 2 teaspoons Calvados or other apple brandy

1. Preheat the oven to 375°. Set a shallow baking pan on the lowest

Orange Angel Food Cake with Warm Berry Compote

Banana Cake

shelf of the oven and fill it with water. Butter the bottom and sides of a baking dish that is 8 inches square and 2 inches deep, preferably glass. Peel, halve, and core the apples.

2. In a large nonreactive saucepan, simmer the wine, ⅓ cup of the sugar, the lemon zest, and the ginger for five minutes. Add the apples, cover, and poach over moderate heat, turning once, until tender, about 10 minutes. Remove from the heat. Using a slotted spoon, place the apples, cut sides down, in the baking dish. Place the saucepan over low heat and cook the poaching liquid until slightly reduced, about 4 minutes. Pour the liquid over the apples.

3. In a small bowl, sift the flour with the baking powder. In a medium bowl, beat the egg yolks with 1 tablespoon sugar until thickened and light colored. Stir in the ½ cup unchilled heavy cream and the melted butter. Stir in the flour.

4. In a clean bowl, beat the egg whites with 1 tablespoon sugar until stiff but not dry. Fold a little of the egg yolk mixture into the whites, then fold the whites into the remaining yolk mixture and blend until there are no streaks of white left. Pour the batter over the apples.

5. Bake the apple cake in the middle of the oven for about 25 minutes, or until golden brown. Meanwhile, in a small chilled bowl, whip the 1 cup of chilled heavy cream, the remaining ½ tablespoon sugar, and the Calvados until soft peaks form. Refrigerate the whipped cream until ready to serve. Transfer the apple cake to a rack to let it cool slightly.

6. Serve the cake warm with the whipped cream.—ANN AMERNICK

BANANA CAKE *LF*

9 SERVINGS

Vegetable oil cooking spray
- 4 tablespoons unsalted butter, softened
- ¾ cup light brown sugar
- ½ cup low-fat (1.5%) buttermilk
- 2 large eggs
- 2 large egg whites
- 2 large overripe bananas plus 1 large ripe banana
- 2 teaspoons finely grated lemon zest
- 2 tablespoons fresh lemon juice
- 2 cups cake flour
- 1½ teaspoons baking soda
- 1 tablespoon granulated sugar

1. Preheat the oven to 350°. Lightly spray an 8-by-12-inch baking dish with vegetable oil cooking spray. In a large bowl, beat the softened butter until creamy. Beat in the light brown sugar and the low-fat buttermilk until combined. Beat in the eggs and the egg whites.

2. In a large measuring cup, mash the overripe bananas with a fork; you should have 1 cup of puree. Halve the ripe banana lengthwise, then cut it crosswise into ½-inch chunks and add the chunks to the puree. Stir in the lemon zest and the fresh lemon juice. Fold the banana mixture into the cake batter, then fold in the cake flour and the baking soda just until no white streaks remain. Spoon the cake batter into the prepared baking dish and sprinkle the top with the granulated sugar.

3. Bake the banana cake for about 30 minutes until golden and the top springs back when lightly pressed in the center. Let the banana cake cool completely in the pan before cutting it into pieces.—DIANA STURGIS

CHRISTMAS FRUITCAKE

MAKES A 9-BY-5-INCH LOAF

CANDIED FRUIT MIXTURE:
- 1 thin-skinned grapefruit
- 1 tangerine
- 1 lime
- 1 lemon
- ¾ cup sugar
- ½ cup diced (¼ inch) dried apricots (2½ ounces)
- ⅓ cup diced (¼ inch) dried pears (1½ ounces)
- ⅓ cup diced (¼ inch) dried peaches (1¼ ounces)

- ⅓ cup dark raisins (about 2 ounces)
- ⅓ cup dark rum

CAKE:

- 2½ sticks (10 ounces) unsalted butter, softened to room temperature
- 1 cup sugar
- 5 large eggs, at room temperature
- 3 tablespoons fresh orange juice
- 2 cups all-purpose flour
- ½ cup cake flour
- ¼ teaspoon salt

1. Prepare the candied fruit mixture: For each of the citrus fruits, cut the peels in wedge-shaped sections from the blossom to the stem end using a small sharp paring knife. Peel the fruits. Cut all the peels into ¼-inch dice. (Reserve the citrus fruits for another use.)

2. Put the diced peels in a nonreactive medium saucepan, add 3 cups of water, and bring to a boil over high heat. Boil for 1 minute. Drain the peels in a colander and rinse under cold running water for a few seconds. Rinse out the saucepan. Repeat the boiling, draining, and rinsing process one more time to remove bitterness from the peels before candying them. Rinse the saucepan again and return the blanched peels to it.

3. Add the sugar and 1½ cups of water to the saucepan and boil the blanched peels over high heat until the liquid in the pan is reduced to a few syrupy tablespoons, 15 to 20 minutes. Remove the saucepan from the heat and stir in the dried apricots, pears, peaches, and raisins, and the rum. Let cool completely, then transfer to a jar and refrigerate if desired.

4. Make the cake: Preheat the oven to 350°. Cut a strip of parchment paper to an 18-by-5-inch rectangle. Butter a 9-by-5-by-3-inch loaf pan and the parchment paper. Line the loaf pan with the paper, allowing some to extend at either end; this will help to unmold the finished cake. ➤

Christmas Fruitcake

BAKING POWDER AND BAKING SODA

Q: What's the difference between baking powder and baking soda?

A: Baking soda and baking powder are both CHEMICAL LEAVENING AGENTS. These fast-acting gas sources create a reaction between acidic and alkaline elements to produce the carbon dioxide bubbles that help all baked goods rise.

The alkaline component in the equation is sodium bicarbonate, otherwise known as BAKING SODA. It can be used alone for leavening if the recipe also calls for an acidic ingredient. Buttermilk, sour cream, yogurt, brown sugar, molasses, and certain kinds of chocolate are some of the naturally acidic ingredients often used in baking.

BAKING POWDER is baking soda plus a mild acid. It also contains cornstarch to absorb moisture and keep the soda and acid dry. Because it contains the exact amount of acid needed to neutralize the soda, baking powder is often preferred to the less precise combination of baking soda and an acidic ingredient.

Another advantage of most baking powders available in supermarkets today is that they are DOUBLE-ACTING. This means they contain one acid (like cream of tartar, tartaric acid, or monocalcium phosphate monohydrate) that dissolves in liquid and produces gas immediately, and another acid (such as sodium aluminum sulfate or anhydrous monocalcium phosphate) that does not dissolve until the batter is baked. In other words, these baking sodas produce a small amount of leavening right after they are mixed, followed by a maximum amount of leavening in the oven.

SOME RECIPES CALL FOR BOTH baking powder and baking soda. The baking powder is there because of its raising reliability, and the baking soda because of its ability to neutralize acidic ingredients, and also to mellow their flavor.—SHIRLEY CORRIHER

Caramel-Glazed Spice Cake

5. In a standing electric mixer fitted with the paddle, cream the butter with the sugar. Add the eggs, orange juice, all-purpose flour, cake flour, and salt, and beat just until blended. Using a large rubber spatula, gently fold in the candied fruit mixture until evenly distributed.

6. Scrape the fruitcake batter into the prepared loaf pan and smooth the surface. Set the loaf pan on a baking sheet and bake the fruitcake for 45 minutes. Lower the oven temperature to 325° and continue baking for about 45 minutes longer, or until the fruitcake is evenly browned and a tester inserted in the center comes out clean. Let the cake cool in the pan before unmolding.—JACQUES PEPIN

CARAMEL-GLAZED SPICE CAKE

This easy cake is great for serving a crowd. It keeps well and actually mellows overnight. It's also delicious for breakfast.

12 SERVINGS

CAKE:

1 cup pecans or walnuts
3 cups all-purpose flour
2 teaspoons baking powder
1 teaspoon baking soda
1½ teaspoons cinnamon
1 teaspoon ground ginger
½ teaspoon ground allspice
⅜ teaspoon ground mace
¼ teaspoon ground cloves
1 teaspoon salt
2½ sticks (10 ounces) unsalted butter, at room temperature
1 cup (packed) dark brown sugar
1 cup granulated sugar
4 large eggs, at room temperature
2 teaspoons pure vanilla extract
1 cup milk
⅓ cup sour cream

GLAZE:

½ cup (packed) dark brown sugar
4 tablespoons unsalted butter
¼ cup heavy cream

1. Make the cake: Preheat the oven to 350°. Generously butter and flour a 12-cup Bundt pan. Spread the pecans or walnuts on a baking sheet and toast them in the oven for about 8 minutes, or until the nuts are fragrant and brown. Transfer the toasted nuts to a plate to cool, then coarsely chop them.

2. In a large bowl, whisk the all-purpose flour with the baking powder, the baking soda, the cinnamon, the ground ginger, allspice, mace, and cloves, and the salt. In another large bowl, using an electric mixer, beat the butter, the dark brown sugar, and the granulated sugar at medium speed until the mixture is light and fluffy, 3 to 5 minutes. Beat in the eggs 1 at a time, beating after each addition and stopping to scrape the bowl. Beat in the vanilla extract. Reduce the speed to low, then beat in about one-quarter of the dry ingredients. Beat in half of the milk, then beat in the remaining dry ingredients in 3 additions, alternating with the remaining milk and the sour cream. Fold in the chopped toasted nuts.

3. Pour the cake batter into the prepared Bundt pan and smooth the top. Bake in the center of the oven for 50 to 55 minutes, or until a cake tester inserted in the center of the cake comes out clean. Transfer the Bundt pan to a rack and let the cake cool for about 15 minutes.

4. Run a thin sharp knife around the center tube of the Bundt pan and invert the spice cake onto the rack. (If the cake doesn't release from the Bundt pan immediately, allow it to sit for about 1 minute, then lift off the Bundt pan.) Let the cake cool completely. (MAKE AHEAD: The spice cake will keep, well wrapped, at room temperature for up to 2 days and can be frozen for up to 2 weeks.)

5. Make the glaze: In a small, deep, heavy saucepan, bring the dark brown sugar, the unsalted butter, and the heavy cream to a boil over moderately high heat, stirring to dissolve the sugar. Boil, stirring occasionally, until the mixture thickens slightly, 3 to 5 minutes. Let cool just until thickened but still pourable, about 10 minutes.

6. Set the spice cake and the rack on a baking sheet. Slowly pour the caramel glaze over the top of the cake, letting the glaze run down the sides of the cake. Slide the glazed cake onto a serving plate and let sit at room temperature for at least 15 minutes or overnight. Slice the cake with a serrated knife.—JUDITH SUTTON

CAKE PAN SIZES

Q: I have a cake recipe that calls for two 9-inch round pans. Can I use a 9-by-13-inch rectangular pan and get the same results?

A: Yes, if you're careful. Substituting one pan for another in baking is always risky business, but it can be done. The key is to know the volume of the respective pans, i.e. the pan the recipe calls for and the one you want to use. To check, fill each pan with water, then measure the liquid in a measuring cup.

Each 9-inch round pan (1½ inches deep) holds about 7 cups of liquid, a total of 14 cups. A 9-by-13-inch pan (2 inches deep) holds about 15 cups—close enough. You can bake your cake in the rectangular pan.

One caveat: if you change the pan size, you may also need to change the baking time. If your batter is spread over a greater surface than it would have been in the original pan, your cooking time will be shorter; conversely, if your batter fills a deeper pan, the time will be longer.—SHARON TYLER HERBST

CHAPTER 19

PIES

Hazelnut Tart

HAZELNUT TART

The sweet pastry recipe makes enough for two 11-inch tarts. The extra pastry can be wrapped and frozen as a handy timesaver.

8 TO 10 SERVINGS

PASTRY:

2 sticks (½ pound) unsalted butter, at room temperature
½ cup sugar
1 large egg, at room temperature
½ teaspoon pure vanilla extract
2¾ cups all-purpose flour

HAZELNUT FILLING:

1⅔ cups shelled hazelnuts (about ½ pound)
1½ tablespoons unsalted butter
4 large eggs
1 large egg yolk
¾ cup sugar
½ cup dark corn syrup
2 tablespoons cider vinegar
1 teaspoon pure vanilla extract
⅛ teaspoon salt

Lightly sweetened whipping cream, for serving

1. Make the pastry: In a medium bowl, beat the butter and sugar until light and creamy. Beat in the egg and vanilla. Stir in the flour just until combined. Shape the dough into a ball and cut it in half. Flatten each piece into a 6-inch disk and wrap separately in plastic wrap. Refrigerate one half until chilled, for at least 1 hour or overnight; reserve the other half in the freezer for up to 1 month for future use.

2. On a lightly floured sheet of parchment paper, roll out the chilled dough to a 13-inch round; if the pastry becomes too soft, slide the paper onto a cookie sheet and refrigerate for 10 minutes. Invert the pastry onto an 11-inch tart pan with a removable bottom and peel off the paper. Press the pastry into the pan and trim the edges. Refrigerate the pastry for 30 minutes.

3. Preheat the oven to 350°. Line the tart shell with a large piece of foil and fill it with pie weights, dried beans, or rice. Bake the pastry on the bottom rack of the oven for 15 minutes. Remove the foil and weights. Bake for about 15 minutes longer, or until the pastry is golden. Let cool in the tart pan. Leave the oven on.

4. Make the hazelnut filling: Spread the hazelnuts on a baking sheet and toast for about 15 minutes, or until the skins are blistered. Rub the nuts together in a towel to remove as much of the skin as possible. Let the nuts cool, then coarsely chop them. (MAKE AHEAD: The recipe can be prepared to this point up to 1 day ahead; let the tart shell and nuts stand separately at room temperature.)

5. In a small saucepan, cook the butter over moderate heat until browned, about 1 minute. In a medium bowl, whisk together the eggs, egg yolk, and sugar until light and fluffy. Whisk in the corn syrup, vinegar, browned butter, vanilla, and salt, and stir in the hazelnuts. Pour the filling into the prebaked tart shell, spreading it evenly. Bake on the bottom rack of the oven for about 30 minutes, or until the filling is set. Let cool for at least 1 hour or up to 8 hours. Serve the tart warm or at room temperature with whipped cream.—SANFORD D'AMATO

CHOCOLATE BOURBON-PECAN TART

8 TO 10 SERVINGS

4 large eggs
¾ cup (packed) dark brown sugar
½ cup light corn syrup
¼ cup bourbon
3 tablespoons unsulphured molasses
1 teaspoon pure vanilla extract
1 teaspoon finely grated orange zest
½ teaspoon salt
3 tablespoons unsalted butter, melted
2½ cups pecans (10 ounces), coarsely chopped
1 Pastry Crust (recipe follows)
2 ounces bittersweet chocolate

1. Preheat the oven to 325°. In a large bowl, lightly beat the eggs. Beat in the sugar, corn syrup, bourbon, molasses, vanilla, zest, and salt. Stir in the butter and then the nuts. Pour into the crust. Bake for about 40 minutes, or just until set. If the top browns too quickly, lower the temperature to 300° for the last 10 minutes. Let the tart cool completely.

2. Melt the chocolate over a double boiler. Cool for 1 minute. With a fork, drizzle the chocolate over the tart and let stand until set. Cut the tart into wedges and serve.

Pastry Crust

The second crust can be frozen for up to one month.

MAKES TWO 11-INCH TART SHELLS

2¼ cups sifted all-purpose flour
1 stick plus 6 tablespoons unsalted butter, softened

6 tablespoons sugar
1 large egg
Pinch of salt

1. Mound the flour on a work surface and make a well in the center. Put the butter, sugar, egg, and salt in the well and mix until smooth. Work in the flour just until the dough holds together; knead lightly. Shape the dough into 2 disks, wrap separately in plastic, and refrigerate for at least 2 hours or overnight. Let stand at room temperature for 5 minutes before rolling out.
2. On a floured work surface, roll out one disk to a 14-inch round. Transfer the dough to an 11-inch tart pan with a removable bottom, pressing it evenly into the pan. Trim off any overhanging pastry. Refrigerate until ready to fill and bake.—WALTER ROYAL

CHOCOLATE-CARAMEL TART

Caramel is used both as a flavoring and a garnish for this two-layer tart.

8 TO 10 SERVINGS

PASTRY:
1⅓ cups all-purpose flour
3 tablespoons light brown sugar
2 tablespoons granulated sugar
⅛ teaspoon salt
1 stick (4 ounces) cold unsalted butter, cut into ½-inch dice
1 large egg yolk
2 to 2½ tablespoons ice water

GANACHE LAYER:
¾ cup heavy cream
4½ ounces bittersweet chocolate, coarsely chopped

CARAMEL CREAM:
½ cup granulated sugar
1¼ cups heavy cream
3 tablespoons unsalted butter, cut into 6 pieces, at room temperature
2 large egg whites, at room temperature
Pinch of salt
2 tablespoons superfine sugar

Chocolate Bourbon-Pecan Tart

1. Make the pastry: In a food processor, combine the flour, brown sugar, granulated sugar, and salt, and pulse to blend. Scatter the butter on top and pulse 10 to 15 times, until the mixture resembles coarse meal. Add the egg yolk and pulse just to blend. Drizzle 2 tablespoons of the ice water on top and pulse until the dough just comes together, adding up to ½ tablespoon more ice water if necessary. Using your hands, shape and pat the dough into a disk, wrap well, and refrigerate for at least 1 hour and up to 2 days.
2. Roll out the dough between 2 sheets of wax paper to a 13-inch round. Peel off the top sheet of wax paper and invert the dough into a 10-inch fluted tart pan with a removable bottom. Peel off the remaining paper and fit the dough into the pan without stretching. Using a small sharp knife, trim the excess dough. Refrigerate the shell for 30 minutes.
3. Preheat the oven to 375°. Line the shell with foil and fill it with pie weights or dried beans. Bake for 18 minutes. Remove the foil and weights. Bake about 15 minutes longer, or until golden brown and cooked through. Let cool.
4. Make the ganache layer: In a small saucepan, bring the heavy cream to a boil over moderate heat. Meanwhile, in a food processor, finely grind the chocolate. With the machine on, add the hot cream to the chocolate and process until completely smooth. Scrape the ganache into a medium bowl. Refrigerate, stirring occasionally with a rubber spatula, until the ganache is cold to the touch but not set, 1 to 1½ hours.
5. Using an electric mixer, beat the ganache on low speed just until it lightens in color and holds soft peaks, about 1 minute. Do not overbeat. Scrape the ganache into the cooled tart shell, spreading it evenly. Cover and refrigerate the tart while you prepare the caramel cream. (MAKE AHEAD: The tart can be prepared to this point up to 1 day ahead.)
6. Make the caramel cream: In a small, deep, heavy saucepan, bring the granulated sugar and 3 tablespoons of water to a boil over moderately high heat, stirring to dissolve the sugar. Wash down the sides of the pan with a wet pastry brush. Boil without stirring until the caramel turns a golden amber color, 5 to 8 minutes. Remove from the heat and immediately add ½ cup of the cream; stand back to avoid spatters. Cook over low heat, stirring, until completely smooth,

about 1 minute. Remove from the heat, add the butter, and stir until melted. Transfer the caramel to a large bowl and let cool to room temperature. (MAKE AHEAD: The caramel can be made up to 1 day ahead; cover and refrigerate. Bring to room temperature before proceeding.)

7. Transfer 3 tablespoons of the caramel to a small saucepan and set aside. In a medium bowl, beat the remaining ¾ cup heavy cream until it holds soft peaks; do not overbeat. In a large bowl, using an electric mixer, beat the egg whites and salt at medium speed until soft peaks form. Gradually beat in the superfine sugar. Increase the speed to high and beat until the whites are stiff and glossy. Stir 3 tablespoons of the whites into the caramel in the bowl. Fold in the remaining whites, then fold in the whipped cream. Spread the cream over the chilled ganache. Refrigerate while you proceed.

8. Rewarm the reserved caramel over low heat, stirring, until it begins to liquefy and is barely warm, not hot, about 30 seconds. Using a fork, drizzle the caramel over the top of the tart. Refrigerate the tart for at least 2 and up to 6 hours. Cut into wedges and serve.—JUDITH SUTTON

CHOCOLATE SILK PIE

Use a standing electric mixer and beat well. This will give the filling its rich, silky-smooth texture. A handheld electric mixer will also do the job.

8 SERVINGS

PASTRY:

- 1⅓ cups all-purpose flour
- 3 tablespoons granulated sugar
- ⅛ teaspoon salt
- 1 stick (8 tablespoons) cold unsalted butter, cut into ½-inch pieces
- 3 to 3½ tablespoons ice water

FILLING:

- 2 ounces bittersweet chocolate, coarsely chopped
- 2 ounces unsweetened chocolate, coarsely chopped
- 1½ sticks (6 ounces) unsalted butter, at room temperature
- 1 cup superfine sugar
- 2 teaspoons bourbon
- 1½ teaspoons pure vanilla extract
- 3 large eggs, at room temperature

TOPPING:

- 1 cup heavy cream
- 1 tablespoon superfine sugar
- ½ teaspoon pure vanilla extract

1. Make the pastry: In a food processor, combine the flour, granulated sugar, and salt and pulse to blend. Scatter the butter pieces over the flour mixture and pulse 10 to 15 times, until the mixture resembles coarse meal. Drizzle 3 tablespoons of the ice water on top and pulse until the dough just comes together, adding up to ½ tablespoon more ice water if necessary. Using your hands, shape the dough into a disk, wrap well, and refrigerate for at least 1 hour or overnight.

2. On a lightly floured surface, roll out the dough into a 13-inch round. Fit the dough into a 9-inch pie pan. Trim the overhang to ½ inch. Fold under the overhanging dough and crimp the edge decoratively. Refrigerate the pie shell for 30 minutes.

Chocolate-Caramel Tart

3. Preheat the oven to 375°. Line the shell with foil and fill it with pie weights or dried beans. Bake for 15 minutes. Remove the foil and weights and bake for 10 to 12 minutes longer, or until golden brown. Let cool.

4. Make the filling: In a small heatproof bowl set over a saucepan of barely simmering water, melt the bittersweet and unsweetened chocolates, stirring occasionally, until smooth. Let cool slightly.

5. In a large bowl, using an electric mixer, beat the butter and superfine sugar until light and fluffy, about 3 minutes. Beat in the bourbon and vanilla, then beat in the melted chocolate. Beat in the eggs 1 at a time, beating for 5 minutes after each addition and scraping down the bowl several times.

6. Scrape the filling into the pie shell and smooth the top with a rubber spatula. Refrigerate until set, at least 4 hours or overnight.

7. Shortly before serving, **make the topping:** In a medium bowl, beat the heavy cream with the superfine sugar and vanilla until stiff. Using a long metal spatula, spread the whipped cream over the top of the pie. (Alternatively, spoon the topping into a pastry bag fitted with a large star tip. Pipe a border of rosettes around the edge of the pie.) Cut into wedges and serve.—JUDITH SUTTON

WHITE CHOCOLATE MACADAMIA NUT TARTS

Susan Molzan, of The Ruggles Grill in Houston, prefers using a walnut liqueur, such as Nocello, to flavor the filling of these sweet tartlets, but hazelnut liqueur works just as well. If you don't have a five-inch round pastry cutter, use a small saucer or a cardboard circle.

8 SERVINGS

PASTRY:

- 3 cups all-purpose flour
- 1 tablespoon sugar
- 1½ teaspoons salt
- 2 sticks (½ pound) unsalted butter, cut into small pieces
- ¼ cup plus 1 tablespoon ice water

FILLING:

- 2½ tablespoons unsalted butter
- 1 vanilla bean, split
- 1 cup macadamia nuts (about 5 ounces), halved
- ½ pound white chocolate, cut into small chunks
- 1¼ cups light corn syrup
- ¾ cup (packed) light brown sugar
- 3 large eggs, lightly beaten
- ¼ cup walnut or hazelnut liqueur
- Vanilla ice cream, for serving

1. Make the pastry: In a bowl, stir together the flour, sugar, and salt. Using a pastry cutter or your fingers, cut in the butter until it resembles coarse crumbs. Sprinkle the ice water on top and stir just until combined. Shape the dough into a ball and pat out to an 8-inch disk. Wrap in wax paper and refrigerate for at least 1 hour or overnight.

2. On a lightly floured surface, roll out the dough to a 16-by-18-inch rectangle, about ¼ inch thick. Using a 5-inch round pastry cutter, cut out 8 circles. Press the circles into eight 4-inch tartlet pans with removable bottoms. Trim the tops of the pastry shells and refrigerate them.

3. Make the filling: Preheat the oven to 375°. In a small saucepan, melt the butter with the vanilla bean over low heat. Remove the saucepan from the heat and, using a small knife, scrape the seeds from the vanilla bean into the melted butter. Discard the vanilla bean or reserve it for another use.

4. Set the pastry shells on a large baking sheet and divide the macadamia nuts and white chocolate chunks evenly among them. In a medium bowl, mix the corn syrup with the brown sugar and the eggs. Stir in the vanilla butter and the walnut liqueur and pour the mixture over the nuts and chocolate to fill the tartlet shells. Bake the tartlets in the center of the oven for about 40 minutes, or until the tops are puffed and lightly browned. Let the tartlets cool slightly on a rack. (MAKE AHEAD: The tartlets can be kept at room temperature for up to 4 hours. They can be rewarmed gently in a 300° oven.) Remove the sides of the tartlet pans. Serve the tartlets warm or at room temperature with vanilla ice cream.—SUSAN MOLZAN

WHITE CHOCOLATE BANANA CREAM PIES

Deliciously rich, this festive dessert features white chocolate in the filling and the topping. The shavings are easily made with a piece of room-temperature white chocolate and a vegetable peeler. If the pie dough gets too soft during rolling, refrigerate it to firm it up.

MAKES TWO 9-INCH PIES

PIE SHELLS:

- 2 cups all-purpose flour
- ½ teaspoon salt
- ½ cup plus 1 tablespoon shortening
- 4 tablespoons unsalted butter, cut into 1-inch pieces
- About 3 tablespoons of ice water

FILLING:

- 4 cups milk
- 1 vanilla bean, split
- 1¼ cups granulated sugar
- Pinch of salt
- 5 large egg yolks
- ½ cup cornstarch, sifted
- 5 ounces white chocolate, coarsely chopped
- 6 medium bananas, sliced ¼ inch thick

TOPPING:

- 4 ounces white chocolate, coarsely chopped, plus about 2 ounces of white chocolate shavings for garnish
- 3 cups heavy cream, chilled
- ¼ cup confectioners' sugar

1. Make the pie shells: In a large bowl, sift together the flour and salt. Using your fingers, rub in the shortening and butter until the mixture resembles coarse meal. Stir in the ice water to form a soft dough. Divide the dough in half and shape into two 6-inch disks. Wrap each disk in plastic and refrigerate until well chilled, at least 1 hour or up to 2 days.

2. Preheat the oven to 350°. On a lightly floured surface, roll out each disk of dough to a 12-inch round. Transfer each round to a 9-inch pie pan and press the dough into the corners. Fold in the edge of each pie shell and crimp the rim of each with a fork. Prick the bottoms with the fork and bake in the middle of the oven for about 30 minutes, or until golden brown. Let cool.

3. Make the filling: In a medium saucepan, combine 3 cups of the milk with the vanilla bean, ½ cup of the sugar, and the salt. Bring just to a boil over high heat. Remove from the heat, cover, and set aside for 15 minutes.

4. In a medium bowl, whisk the egg yolks with the remaining 1 cup milk and ¾ cup sugar and the cornstarch until smooth. Whisk in 1 cup of the warm milk. Bring the remaining warm milk just to a boil over moderately high heat and whisk in the egg yolk mixture in a steady stream. Cook, whisking constantly, until the custard is thickened and starts to bubble around the edge, about 10 minutes. Remove from the heat and strain into a bowl. Stir in the chopped white chocolate and let cool. (MAKE AHEAD: The custard can be refrigerated overnight; let the pie shells stand at room temperature.)

5. Arrange the sliced bananas in the baked pie shells, covering the bottoms. Spoon the custard over the bananas. Set a lightly buttered round of wax paper directly on the filling of each pie and refrigerate until chilled, about 2 hours.

White Chocolate Banana Cream Pie

6. Make the topping: Melt the chopped white chocolate in the top of a double boiler, stirring occasionally, until smooth. Let cool to tepid. In a large bowl, beat the cream with the sugar until soft peaks form. Gently whisk one-third of the whipped cream into the melted white chocolate. Fold the white chocolate mixture into the remaining whipped cream just until combined.

7. Discard the wax paper from the pies. Using a spatula, swirl the whipped cream over the filling. Garnish with the white chocolate shavings.—PATRICK CLARK

APPLE AND WALNUT CREAM TART

A layer of ground walnuts adds a fresh nutty flavor to this elegant dessert, served at The Inn at Little Washington in Washington, Virginia.

🍷 *The warm fruit and nut flavors are the perfect foil for a classic sweet Sauternes. Look for a 1988, such as Château Clos Haut-Peyraguey or Château Doisy-Védrines.*

8 SERVINGS

PASTRY:

About 1⅓ cups sifted all-purpose flour
Pinch of sugar
Pinch of salt
4 tablespoons cold unsalted butter, cut into ½-inch pieces
¼ cup cold vegetable shortening
3 tablespoons ice water

FILLING:

¾ cup walnuts (about 3 ounces)
4 tablespoons unsalted butter, at room temperature
⅓ cup plus 2 tablespoons sugar
1 large egg

- 1 tablespoon dark rum
- 1 tablespoon all-purpose flour
- 3 large Granny Smith apples
- 1 tablespoon fresh lemon juice
- ¼ teaspoon cinnamon
- ¼ teaspoon freshly ground nutmeg
- 2 tablespoons apple jelly or apricot jam

1. Make the pastry: In a bowl, stir the 1⅓ cups flour with the sugar and salt. Using your fingers, rub the butter and shortening into the flour until the mixture resembles coarse crumbs. Sprinkle the ice water on top and stir until just combined. If the dough is sticky, work in 1 more tablespoon of flour. Shape the dough into a ball and pat it out to a 6-inch disk. Wrap in wax paper and refrigerate for at least 1 hour or overnight.

2. Preheat the oven to 400°. On a lightly floured surface, roll out the dough to a 13-inch circle. Transfer the dough to an 11-by-1-inch tart pan with a removable bottom. Trim the overhang flush with the rim and prick the bottom all over with a fork. Butter a large piece of foil, set it buttered side down on the dough, and fill with rice or pie weights. Bake for about 20 minutes, or until the

Apple and Walnut Cream Tart

edges are golden. Remove the foil and weights and bake for about 5 minutes longer until the bottom is just cooked through. Let cool slightly. Lower the oven temperature to 375°.

3. Meanwhile, **make the filling:** In a food processor, pulse the walnuts until finely ground but not pasty. In a medium bowl, beat the butter with ⅓ cup of the sugar. Beat in the egg, rum, and flour until blended. Fold in the ground walnuts; the mixture may look curdled, but it won't affect the tart.

4. Peel, halve, and core the apples, and cut them lengthwise into ⅛-inch slices. Transfer to a medium bowl and toss with the lemon juice, cinnamon, and nutmeg.

5. Spread the walnut mixture evenly in the tart shell. Arrange the apple slices on top in concentric circles and sprinkle with the remaining 2 tablespoons sugar. Bake the tart for about 35 minutes, or until the apples are browned at the edges and tender when pierced with a knife. Let cool slightly on a rack.

6. In a small saucepan, melt the apple jelly over low heat, stirring, until smooth. (If using apricot jam, strain it after melting.) Brush the apples with the jelly. (MAKE AHEAD: The tart can be kept at room temperature for up to 4 hours. It can be rewarmed gently in a 325° oven.) Remove the sides of the pan and serve the tart warm.—PATRICK O'CONNELL

APPLE TARTLETS WITH CARAMEL SAUCE

Use a high-quality commercial puff pastry, such as Dufour, which is available in the freezer section of specialty food markets. Or purchase puff pastry from your local French bakery.

MAKES FOUR 5-INCH TARTLETS

CARAMELIZED APPLES:

4 Granny Smith apples (about 2 pounds)
2 tablespoons fresh lemon juice
⅓ cup granulated sugar
3 tablespoons unsalted butter

ALMOND CREAM AND CARAMEL SAUCE:

2 ounces whole blanched almonds (⅓ cup) or 2 ounces blanched almond meal (available at health food stores)
¼ cup plus 2 tablespoons confectioners' sugar
4 tablespoons unsalted butter
½ teaspoon finely grated lemon zest
⅛ teaspoon pure almond extract
⅛ teaspoon pure vanilla extract
½ cup heavy cream

12 ounces puff pastry
3 tablespoons granulated sugar
Vanilla ice cream, for serving

1. Make the caramelized apples: Peel, quarter, and core the apples; cut into 12 wedges each. In a large bowl, toss the apples with the lemon juice. In a large nonreactive skillet, cook the granulated sugar over high heat until it turns dark brown, about 3 minutes. Using a wooden spoon, stir in the butter until blended. Add the apples and cook, turning occasionally, until golden brown but still firm, 5 to 8 minutes. Transfer the apples to a colander set over a bowl to catch the juices. Refrigerate the apples and reserve the juices at room temperature while you proceed.

2. Make the almond cream: In a food processor, pulsing the machine, finely chop the almonds for about 1 minute. Add the confectioners' sugar and process until combined, scraping down the sides of the bowl.

3. Add the butter, lemon zest, and almond and vanilla extracts, and pulse, scraping down the bowl occasionally, until thoroughly mixed. Refrigerate until chilled, at least 2 hours and up to 4 days.

4. Make the caramel sauce: In a small, heavy, nonreactive saucepan, cook the reserved apple juices over moderately high heat, stirring occasionally, until thick and syrupy, about 4 minutes. Add the heavy cream and cook, stirring, until reduced by half, about 5 minutes.

5. To assemble the tartlets: On a lightly floured work surface, roll out the puff pastry ⅛ inch thick. Using a small saucer as a template, cut out four 5- to 6-inch rounds. Place the pastry rounds on a baking sheet lined with parchment paper, prick them all over with a fork, and freeze until firm, about 10 minutes.

6. Place 2 tablespoons of the almond cream in a mound in the center of the rounds. Place the apple wedges in an overlapping ring on top of the cream, leaving a ½-inch border of pastry all around. (The center will be rather tall, but sinks a bit during baking.) Freeze until firm, about 10 minutes.

7. Meanwhile, preheat the oven to 350°. Sprinkle the tartlets with the sugar and bake for 25 to 30 minutes, or until the pastry is

Apple Tartlet with Caramel Sauce

brown and crisp. Serve each apple tartlet warm with vanilla ice cream and a drizzle of the caramel sauce.—LISSA DOUMANI

ORANGE TARTLETS MADE OUT OF APPLES

This recipe appears in Book of Tarts *(Morrow) by Maury Rubin.*

MAKES EIGHT 4-INCH TARTS

PASTRY:

- 13 tablespoons (6½ ounces) unsalted butter, cut into ½-inch pieces and slightly softened
- ⅓ cup confectioners' sugar
- 1 large egg yolk
- ¾ cup unbleached all-purpose flour, sifted
- ¾ cup bread flour, sifted

APPLE FILLING:

- ½ cup plus 3 tablespoons granulated sugar
- 2 tablespoons finely grated orange zest
- ¾ cup plus 1 tablespoon heavy cream
- 5 medium Granny Smith or Mutsu apples (about 2¼ pounds)

1. Make the pastry: In a medium bowl, using an electric mixer, beat the butter and confectioners' sugar on medium speed for 2 minutes. Beat in the egg yolk, scraping down the bowl with a rubber spatula. Using a wooden spoon, stir in half of the all-purpose and bread flours until combined. Mix in the remaining flour to form a soft, sticky dough. Scrape the dough onto wax paper and pat into a disk. Wrap and refrigerate until firm, at least 2 hours or overnight.

2. On a lightly floured surface, cut the cold dough into 1-inch pieces. Using the heel of your hand, knead the pieces together until the dough is smooth but still cool; use a pastry scraper or metal spatula to scrape up the dough. Form the dough into a 12-inch log and cut into 8 equal pieces. Transfer to a plate, cover with plastic wrap, and refrigerate until cold, about 20 minutes.

3. Line a baking sheet with parchment paper. Place eight 4-inch flan rings or 4½-inch fluted tartlet pans with removable bottoms on the baking sheet. Remove 1 piece of dough from the refrigerator and, on a lightly floured surface, roll it into a 5½-inch round. Ease the pastry into one of the flan rings and, using your thumbs, gently but firmly press the dough into the ring to form a close fit around the base. Using a small knife, trim the dough flush with the rim. Prick the dough all over with a fork. Repeat with the remaining dough and flan rings. Freeze the rings on the baking sheet until the pastry is firm, about 15 minutes. (MAKE AHEAD: You can freeze the flan rings overnight; cover them with foil. Before proceeding, let the flan rings sit at room temperature for 10 minutes, then uncover.)

4. Meanwhile, preheat the oven to 375°. Bake the tart shells on the baking sheet for about 12 minutes, or until golden. (If the dough puffs up, tap it with a spoon; do not prick it.) Remove the tart shells from the oven and let cool on the baking sheet. Leave the oven on.

5. Make the apple filling: In a small, heavy, nonreactive saucepan, combine the granulated sugar and orange zest. Using the back of a spoon, mash the zest into the sugar. Stir in the heavy cream and cook over moderately high heat, stirring, just until the sugar dissolves, about 3 minutes. Let the cream sit for 10 minutes to infuse the flavors. Strain the orange cream into a large bowl and discard the orange zest.

6. Peel, quarter, and core the apples; cut them into 12 wedges each. Add the apple wedges to the orange cream and toss to coat. Divide the apples evenly among the tart shells and pour in the orange cream.

7. Bake the tartlets for about 25 minutes, or until the apples are golden and the orange cream is bubbling around the edges. Let rest for 1 minute on the baking sheet before removing the rings.

Using a metal spatula, gently transfer the tartlets to a rack and let them cool completely before serving.—MAURY RUBIN

MANGO PIE

While you're waiting for peaches to come into season, treat yourself to a slice of this exotic peachlike pie.

MAKES ONE 9-INCH PIE

PIE DOUGH:

- 2 cups all-purpose flour, sifted
- ½ teaspoon salt
- 1 stick (8 tablespoons) cold unsalted butter, cut into small pieces
- ½ cup cold vegetable shortening
- About 5 tablespoons ice water

FILLING:

- 3 large ripe mangoes—peeled and cut into ¼-inch slices
- ⅓ cup sugar, plus more for sprinkling
- 2 tablespoons instant tapioca
- 1½ tablespoons fresh lemon juice
- Large pinch of cinnamon
- Milk or heavy cream, for brushing

1. Make the pie dough: In a medium bowl, combine the flour and salt. Using a pastry blender or 2 knives, cut in the butter until the mixture resembles coarse meal. Cut in the vegetable shortening until blended. Dribble in 4 tablespoons of the ice water, mixing lightly with a fork until the pie dough begins to cohere. Gather the pie dough into a ball; if the dough seems dry, add the remaining 1 tablespoon ice water. Pat the pie dough into a disk, wrap the disk in wax paper, and refrigerate for at least 30 minutes or overnight.

2. Divide the pie dough in half. On a lightly floured surface, roll out 1 piece of the pie dough into a 12-inch round about ¼ inch thick. Fold the round of dough in half and transfer it to a 9-inch glass pie dish; unfold the pie dough and gently press it to fit the pie dish comfortably without stretching. Trim the overhanging dough to ¼ inch. Freeze the pie shell for about 20 minutes to firm it up.

3. Preheat the oven to 375°. Bake the pie shell on the bottom shelf of the oven for 10 minutes. Transfer to a rack to cool. Leave the oven on.

4. Meanwhile, **prepare the filling:** In a large bowl, toss the mango slices with the sugar, instant tapioca, fresh lemon juice, and cinnamon. Let the mixture stand for about 5 minutes to soften the tapioca.

5. On a lightly floured surface, roll out the second piece of pie dough as you did the first. With a slotted spoon, transfer the mango slices to the baked bottom pie crust. Spoon just enough of the juices over the fruit to moisten.

6. Dampen the rim of the bottom pie crust with water. Drape the rolled-out dough over the mango filling and press all around the rim to seal. Trim off any excess pie dough. Make a decorative border with a fork by pressing the tines all around the rim of the pie. Cut 3 long narrow crescents in the top crust, brush the pie with milk or heavy cream, and then sprinkle generously with sugar.

7. Bake the pie on the bottom shelf of the oven for about 45 minutes, or until the crust is golden brown and juices are bubbling through the steam vents. Transfer the pie to a rack and let cool for a few hours before serving. Serve warm or at room temperature.—MARCIA KIESEL

CHOOSING A MANGO

- **There are about 40 varieties of mangoes, but only six are readily available in American markets. They can be either round or flat, depending on the variety. The flatter fruits tend to be more fibrous, though the flavor can be spicier and more complex.**
- **Like those of most fruits, the skins of unripe mangoes are green; splashes of yellow, orange, and red appear as the mango ripens.**
- **A ripe mango will have firm, deep orange flesh that yields when pressed lightly.**
- **Push aside the little nub at the stem end and sniff; ripe fruit will give off a spicy peachlike aroma.**
- **Soft spots or wrinkled skin indicate overripeness.**

CHAPTER 20

FRUIT DESSERTS

Frozen Pineapple and Coconut Parfait

FROZEN PINEAPPLE AND COCONUT PARFAITS

6 SERVINGS

- 46 ounces pineapple juice, well chilled
- ⅔ cup sweetened cream of coconut, such as Coco Lopez, at room temperature
- 1 ripe medium pineapple (about 3½ pounds)
- ½ cup light brown sugar
- 1 tablespoon unsalted butter
- Coconut Tuiles (recipe follows)

1. Set a 2-quart container and 6 parfait glasses in the freezer. In a medium bowl, stir together the pineapple juice and the cream of coconut. Working in 2 batches, freeze the mixture in an ice cream machine according to the manufacturer's instructions. Transfer the sorbet to the chilled container, cover tightly, and freeze.

2. Using a long sharp knife, remove the skin from the pineapple. Cut the pineapple in half lengthwise and remove the core. Cut one pineapple half into ¼-inch dice. Cut three ⅓-inch thick crosswise slices from the other pineapple half, then cut 2 neat triangles from each slice. Reserve the remaining pineapple for another use.

3. In a large, heavy, nonreactive skillet, combine the brown sugar and butter with 1 tablespoon of water and stir over moderately high heat until bubbling. Add the 6 pineapple triangles and cook until golden brown, 3 to 4 minutes per side. Transfer the triangles to a plate to cool.

4. Add the diced pineapple to the skillet and cook until the juices evaporate, about 5 minutes. Transfer the pineapple to a bowl and let cool. (MAKE AHEAD: The pineapple can be prepared up to 4 hours ahead.)

5. Place a scoop of slightly softened sorbet in each of the 6 chilled parfait glasses. Cover the sorbet with half of the diced pineapple. Make a second layer with another scoop of sorbet and the remaining diced pineapple. Top the parfaits with the remaining sorbet. (MAKE AHEAD: The parfaits can be assembled up to 30 minutes ahead and held in the freezer.) Just before serving, garnish each of the parfaits with a caramelized pineapple triangle and a Coconut Tuile. Pass the remaining Coconut Tuiles separately.

Coconut Tuiles

MAKES ABOUT 1½ DOZEN COOKIES

- ¼ cup plus 2 tablespoons clarified butter
- 2 cups unsweetened shredded coconut
- ⅔ cup sugar
- ½ cup egg whites
- ⅓ cup all-purpose flour

1. Preheat the oven to 350°. Line 2 large cookie sheets with parchment paper and brush with 2 tablespoons of the clarified butter.

2. In a medium bowl, thoroughly mix together the shredded coconut, sugar, egg whites, all-purpose flour, and the remaining ¼ cup clarified butter.

3. Drop about 1½ tablespoons of the coconut mixture onto a prepared cookie sheet. With dampened fingers, pat the mixture into a thin, flat, 6-by-3-inch triangle. Repeat with the remaining coconut mixture.

4. Bake 1 sheet of cookies at a time for 12 to 15 minutes, or until the tuiles are golden. Let the tuiles cool completely on the pan. (MAKE AHEAD: The tuiles can be made up to 3 days ahead and stored in an airtight container.) —ANNE ROSENZWEIG

OLD-FASHIONED MERINGUES WITH PEACH ICE CREAM

8 SERVINGS

MERINGUES:

- 4 large egg whites
- ¼ teaspoon cream of tartar
- ¼ teaspoon salt
- 1 cup sugar
- ¼ teaspoon pure vanilla extract

ICE CREAM:

- 2 pounds peaches—peeled, pitted, and sliced ¼ inch thick
- 1 cup sugar
- ⅛ teaspoon salt
- 2 cups milk
- 4 large egg yolks, lightly beaten
- 1 cup heavy cream
- ¼ teaspoon pure vanilla extract

TOPPING:

- 6 peaches—peeled, pitted, and sliced ¼ inch thick (about 4½ cups)
- 2 tablespoons peach liqueur or Amaretto di Saronna

1. Make the meringues: Preheat the oven to 275°. Line a large cookie sheet with parchment paper. In a large bowl, using a balloon whisk or a handheld electric mixer, beat the egg whites until thick and foamy. Beat in the cream of tartar and salt and beat until firm peaks form. Gradually beat in the sugar and vanilla until the mixture is satiny.

2. Using a large spoon, drop eight 4-inch mounds of meringue, evenly spaced, onto the prepared cookie sheet. Moisten the back of a medium spoon and make a depression in the center of each mound. Bake for about 1 hour, until the meringues are lightly colored and almost dry. Let cool on the pan. (MAKE AHEAD: The meringues will keep overnight in an airtight container.)

3. Make the ice cream: In a medium bowl, toss the peach slices with half of the sugar and the salt and let the peaches macerate until the sugar dissolves, about 30 minutes.

4. Meanwhile, in a medium saucepan, combine the remaining ½ cup sugar and the milk and cook over moderately low heat, stirring with a wooden spoon, until the sugar dissolves. Whisk in the egg yolks and cook, stirring constantly, until the custard thickens to the consistency of cream and coats the back of the spoon, about 20 minutes. Do not let the custard boil. Strain the custard immediately through a sieve set over a bowl. Stir in the heavy cream and vanilla extract. Set the bowl in a larger bowl full of ice water and chill, stirring, for 20 minutes. (Alternatively, cover and refrigerate until cold, at least 2 hours.)

5. In a food processor, puree the peaches and their liquid.

6. Transfer the chilled custard to an ice cream machine and freeze according to the manufacturer's instructions. When it is halfway churned and frozen, add the peach puree.

7. Make the topping: Place the sliced peaches in a bowl and toss with the liqueur.

8. Place the meringues on individual serving plates. Top with the ice cream and peaches and serve.—KATHY CARY

CHUNKY MANGO SAUCE WITH COCONUT ICE CREAM

Use very ripe mangoes to impart an intense flavor to the sauce. This luxurious ice cream laced with shredded coconut contains no eggs.

4 TO 6 SERVINGS

SAUCE:

2 very ripe mangoes, peeled
4 to 5 tablespoons sugar, depending on the ripeness of the fruit
3 tablespoons fresh lime juice

ICE CREAM:

1-inch piece of vanilla bean, split lengthwise
One 14-ounce can unsweetened coconut milk
½ cup sugar
1 teaspoon pure vanilla extract
½ cup sweetened shredded coconut
Pinch of salt

1. Make the sauce: Cut the mango flesh from the pits in large pieces. Cut 1 mango into ¼-inch dice. Coarsely chop the second mango and put it in a food processor. Add the sugar and the lime juice and puree until smooth. Scrape the mango puree into a bowl and stir in the diced mango. (MAKE AHEAD: The sauce can be refrigerated, covered, for up to 1 week.)

2. Make the ice cream: Using a small knife, scrape the vanilla bean seeds into a bowl. Whisk in the coconut milk, sugar, and vanilla. Pour the mixture into an ice cream maker, add the shredded coconut and salt, and freeze according to the manufacturer's instructions. Pack the ice cream into an airtight container and freeze for at least 4 hours and up to 3 days. Let the ice cream soften slightly before serving.

3. To serve, layer small scoops of ice cream and sauce in parfait glasses. Or simply spoon the sauce over the ice cream in small bowls.—MARCIA KIESEL

HOW TO CHUNK A MANGO

Cut off half the fruit lengthwise, just above the pit. Turn the mango over and cut off the other half, also just above the pit. Cut the flesh down to, but not through, the peel in a crosshatch pattern. Push the peel inside out so that the chunks separate; then cut off the chunks.

WARM RASPBERRY-MARSALA SUNDAES

4 SERVINGS

3 tablespoons unsalted butter
3 tablespoons light brown sugar
¼ cup plus 2 tablespoons sweet Marsala or Madeira
Pinch of cinnamon
½ pint raspberries (about 5 ounces)
Vanilla or coffee ice cream, for serving

From left: **Warm Raspberry-Marsala Sundae, Candied Ginger Plum Sundae, Lemon-Blueberry Sundae**

Melt 2 tablespoons of the butter in a medium nonreactive skillet. Add the brown sugar and stir occasionally over moderately high heat until melted. Stir in the Marsala and cinnamon and boil for 1 minute. Remove the pan from the heat and stir in the remaining 1 tablespoon butter. Fold in the raspberries and let cool slightly before serving over the ice cream.—TRACEY SEAMAN

LEMON-BLUEBERRY SUNDAES

For a quick upside-down version of blueberry pie à la mode, add a buttery cookie to the sauce-topped ice cream.

4 TO 6 SERVINGS

- 2 tablespoons unsalted butter
- 3 tablespoons sugar
- 2 teaspoons fresh lemon juice
- 1 teaspoon finely grated lemon zest
- 1 pint blueberries (about 10 ounces)

Vanilla ice cream, for serving

Melt the butter in a medium nonstick skillet. Add the sugar, lemon juice, lemon zest, and ⅓ cup of water, and bring to a boil over moderately high heat, stirring occasionally, until the sugar is dissolved. Stir in the blueberries and cook, smashing some of the berries against the pan, until the fruit is soft and the sauce is thickened, about 4 minutes. Let cool slightly before serving over the ice cream.—TRACEY SEAMAN

CANDIED GINGER PLUM SUNDAES

Tart plums, such as Santa Rosas, add a pleasant tang to the sauce.

4 SERVINGS

- 1 tablespoon unsalted butter
- 2½ tablespoons sugar
- 1 pound tart red or purple plums, pitted and sliced ⅓ inch thick
- ¼ cup fresh orange juice

Pinch of ground allspice
3 tablespoons coarsely chopped candied ginger
Vanilla or strawberry ice cream, for serving

Melt the butter in a medium nonreactive skillet. Add the sugar and stir over moderately high heat until melted. Add the plum slices, orange juice, and allspice, and toss occasionally until the plums soften and the liquid becomes syrupy, about 2 minutes. Remove from the heat and stir in the candied ginger. Let cool slightly before serving over ice cream.—TRACEY SEAMAN

SOUR CHERRY-WALNUT SUNDAES

4 SERVINGS

2 tablespoons unsalted butter
2 cups fresh, dark, sweet cherries (about ¾ pound), pitted
¼ cup sugar
¼ cup coarsely chopped walnuts
1 teaspoon cinnamon
¼ teaspoon cornstarch
Vanilla, chocolate, or vanilla-fudge ice cream, for serving

Sautéed Berries with Zabaglione Ice Cream

Melt the butter in a large nonreactive skillet. Add the cherries, sugar, walnuts, and cinnamon, and bring to a boil over moderately high heat. In a small bowl, dissolve the cornstarch in 2 tablespoons of water and stir the mixture into the cherries. Continue cooking until the sauce is thickened, about 3 minutes. Let cool slightly before serving over ice cream.—TRACEY SEAMAN

STRAWBERRY-BALSAMIC SUNDAES

Aged balsamic vinegar, also known as aceto balsamico, *can be found at specialty food stores. Although it makes an especially smooth-tasting sauce, any balsamic will be fine.*

4 TO 6 SERVINGS

3 tablespoons unsalted butter
⅓ cup (packed) light brown sugar
2 pints strawberries (1 pound), hulled and halved
2 teaspoons balsamic vinegar
2 fresh mint sprigs
Vanilla, chocolate, or strawberry ice cream, for serving

Melt the butter in a large nonstick skillet. Add the light brown sugar and stir over moderately high heat until dissolved, about 2 minutes. Add the strawberries and cook, stirring occasionally, until the berries begin to release their juices, about 1 minute. Using a slotted spoon, transfer the strawberries to a bowl. Boil the sauce until thickened, 1 to 2 minutes. Pour the sauce over the strawberries and stir in the balsamic vinegar and the mint sprigs. Let stand for 2 minutes, then discard the mint sprigs. Stir the sauce and serve it over ice cream.—TRACEY SEAMAN

SAUTEED BERRIES WITH ZABAGLIONE ICE CREAM

6 TO 8 SERVINGS

ZABAGLIONE ICE CREAM:

1 cup plus 2 tablespoons heavy cream
1 cup half-and-half
6 large egg yolks
½ cup plus 1 tablespoon sugar
⅛ teaspoon salt
¼ cup plus 2 tablespoons dry Marsala

SAUTEED BERRIES:

2 tablespoons unsalted butter
4½ cups mixed fresh berries, such as blueberries, blackberries, and sliced strawberries
2 tablespoons sugar
Few splashes of balsamic vinegar
Freshly ground pepper

1. Make the zabaglione ice cream: In a large saucepan, bring the heavy cream and the half-and-half just to a boil over moderate heat. Meanwhile, in a large bowl, whisk the egg yolks with the sugar and salt. Gradually whisk in the hot cream, then return the mixture to the saucepan. Cook over moderate heat, stirring constantly, until the custard thickens slightly and coats the back of a spoon, about 3 minutes. Strain the custard into a bowl and let cool.

2. Stir the Marsala into the cooled custard. Freeze the mixture in an ice cream maker according to the manufacturer's instructions. Transfer the ice cream to a chilled container. (MAKE

AHEAD: The ice cream can be frozen, covered, for up to 3 days.)

3. Make the sautéed berries: Melt the butter in a medium nonreactive skillet. Add the mixed fresh berries and the sugar, and sauté over moderately high heat until heated through and the berries have released some of their juices, about 4 minutes. Sprinkle with balsamic vinegar and season with pepper. Spoon the sautéed berries into goblets or individual bowls and top with a generous scoop of the zabaglione ice cream.—BEN BARKER

APPLE SORBET WITH CARAMELIZED APPLES

You will need a juice extractor to make this refreshing dessert.

6 SERVINGS

- 7 Golden Delicious apples or 10 medium McIntosh apples (about 3 pounds)
- ¼ cup fresh lemon juice (from 1 large lemon)
- ½ cup plus 1 tablespoon granulated sugar
- 3 Granny Smith apples (about 1½ pounds)
- 1 tablespoon confectioners' sugar

1. Peel, halve, and core the Golden Delicious or McIntosh apples. Toss them with 2 tablespoons of the lemon juice to coat. Crush the apples in a juice extractor, reserving the juice and pulp separately.

2. Stir 5 tablespoons of the granulated sugar into the apple juice. Pour the syrup into an ice cream maker and freeze according to the manufacturer's instructions until the sorbet is firm but not grainy, about 20 minutes. Transfer the sorbet to a freezer container and freeze while you proceed or for up to 4 hours.

3. Meanwhile, in a medium nonreactive saucepan, combine the reserved apple pulp and the remaining 2 tablespoons lemon juice and 4 tablespoons granulated sugar with 1½ cups of water. Bring to a boil over moderately high heat and cook, stirring, until smooth, about 2 minutes. Strain the liquid into a medium heatproof bowl and let cool.

4. Peel, quarter, and core 2 of the Granny Smith apples; cut lengthwise into very thin slices. Add them to the strained liquid.

5. Preheat the oven to 325°. Peel and core the remaining Granny Smith apple. Slice it crosswise into ⅛-inch rings. Place the rings on a nonstick baking sheet or a baking sheet lined with parchment paper and bake for about 8 minutes, or until lightly browned. Sprinkle the rings with the confectioners' sugar, place under the broiler, and broil for about 30 seconds, or until the sugar melts. Let the caramelized apples cool completely, then transfer to the freezer while you proceed.

6. To serve, scoop some of the thinly sliced Granny Smith apples with their liquid into chilled dessert bowls; dollop the sorbet on top. Garnish with the caramelized apple rings.—JACQUES TORRES

STRAWBERRY SORBET LF

4 SERVINGS

- ½ cup sugar
- 2 pints fresh strawberries, hulled, or 4 cups thawed frozen strawberries

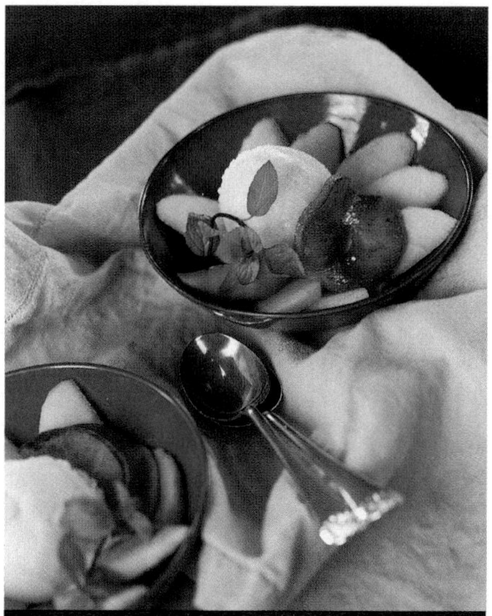

Apple Sorbet with Caramelized Apples

- 2 tablespoons fresh lemon juice
- 1 tablespoon framboise or cassis liqueur

1. In a small saucepan, bring the sugar and ⅓ cup of water to a simmer over high heat and cook until the sugar has dissolved. Let cool.

2. In a food processor or blender, puree the strawberries until smooth. With the machine on, add the sugar syrup, lemon juice, and framboise until incorporated. Pour the strawberry mixture into a metal 8-inch square or round cake tin. Freeze until set, about 4 hours. Break the sorbet into chunks with a fork and puree in the food processor until smooth. Serve the sorbet at once in individual bowls.—JEAN GALTON

STRAWBERRY-RHUBARB SORBET

The stalks of early spring rhubarb are not the deep, rich red of summer's established crop, but they are tender

Strawberry-Rhubarb Sorbet

and delicious all the same. Be sure to discard the leaves of the rhubarb because they're toxic.

6 SERVINGS

1¼ pounds rhubarb stalks, sliced ¾ inch thick (4 cups)
1¼ cups sugar
1 pint ripe strawberries, hulled and halved
¾ cup fresh orange juice

1. Combine the rhubarb with the sugar and ½ cup of water in a nonreactive medium saucepan and bring to a boil over high heat. Reduce the heat to moderately low and simmer gently until the rhubarb is very tender, about 20 minutes.
2. Transfer the rhubarb to a food processor and puree until smooth. Scrape the puree into a large bowl.
3. Add the strawberries and orange juice to the processor and puree. Stir the strawberry puree into the rhubarb; let the puree cool to room temperature.
4. Transfer the puree to an ice cream maker and freeze according to the manufacturer's instructions. Firmly pack the sorbet into a container. Cover tightly and freeze for at least 3 hours or up to 1 day.—SHEILA LUKINS

BAKED PEARS

4 SERVINGS

4 firm but ripe Bartlett pears
3 tablespoons light brown sugar
2 tablespoons chopped candied ginger (optional)
1 tablespoon unsalted butter
¼ cup pecan pieces
Vanilla ice cream or frozen yogurt, for serving

Preheat the oven to 350°. Peel and halve the pears. With a small spoon or melon baller, scoop out the seeds from the pear halves. Lightly butter a 9-by-13-inch baking dish and put in the pear halves, cut sides up. Sprinkle the pears with the brown sugar and the candied ginger if using. Dot with the butter and scatter the pecan pieces on top. Bake the pears on the top shelf of the oven until hot and bubbling, about 20 minutes. Serve immediately with ice cream.—SARAH FRITSCHNER

GRILLED BANANAS WITH SWEETENED CREAM Q

4 SERVINGS

1 cup sour cream
½ teaspoon pure vanilla extract
1 tablespoon light brown sugar
2 large firm bananas, sliced diagonally ½ inch thick
2 tablespoons unsalted butter, melted
½ teaspoon cinnamon
Fresh mint sprigs, for garnish

1. Light a grill, if using. In a small bowl, stir together the sour cream, vanilla extract, and light brown sugar until the sugar is dissolved.
2. In a medium bowl, sprinkle the banana slices with the melted butter and cinnamon. Grill the bananas or panfry them in a large nonstick skillet over moderately high heat, turning, until golden, about 2 minutes per side. Transfer the bananas to individual plates, spoon the sweetened cream on top, and garnish with the mint.—CHATA DUBOSE

Baked Pear

RASPBERRY GRATIN WITH SAUTERNES SABAYON

If you don't have 8 shallow gratin dishes for this dessert, simply assemble it in a larger gratin dish and serve at the table with a spoon.

8 SERVINGS

RASPBERRY COULIS:
½ pound fresh raspberries or 2 cups frozen unsweetened raspberries, thawed
About 2½ tablespoons sugar

SABAYON:
⅓ cup sweet white wine, such as Sauternes or Late-Harvest Riesling
2 large egg yolks
2 tablespoons plus 2 teaspoons sugar
⅓ cup heavy cream

1 pint fresh raspberries

1. Make the coulis: In a food processor, puree the raspberries with 2 tablespoons of the sugar. Pass the puree through a fine stainless steel strainer into a bowl. Stir in up to ½ tablespoon more sugar if desired. (MAKE AHEAD: The *coulis* can be refrigerated, covered, for up to 1 day. Bring to room temperature before using.) ➤

2. Make the sabayon: In a double boiler, combine the white wine, the egg yolks, and the sugar. Using a handheld electric mixer, beat the mixture at medium speed over simmering water until hot and fluffy, about 5 minutes. Remove from the heat and set the pan in an ice-water bath. Using a rubber spatula, gently fold the sabayon until cool, about 1 minute.

3. Using clean beaters and a clean bowl, whip the heavy cream until it holds a shape well. Fold in the sabayon until blended.

4. Spoon the *coulis* into 8 shallow gratin dishes that measure about 5 inches in diameter. Tilt and tap the dishes to coat the bottoms with *coulis*. Spoon the sabayon into each dish and spread it to ¾ inch from the rim. (MAKE AHEAD: The gratins can be assembled to this point and refrigerated for up to 3 hours before serving.)

5. When ready to serve, preheat the broiler. Evenly sprinkle the whole raspberries over the sabayon. Set 4 of the gratin dishes on a baking sheet and broil for about 2 minutes, turning as necessary, until the sabayon is lightly browned. Broil the 4 remaining gratins and serve immediately.—DAVID AND KAREN WALTUCK

SPICED RHUBARB-RASPBERRY COBBLER

Like asparagus, rhubarb is among the harbingers of spring. And a cobbler is a great way to show off the plant's distinctive, pleasantly astringent taste. (Be sure, though, to use only the stalks; the leaves are toxic and must be discarded.) This tart cobbler—similar to a deep-dish pie—combines rhubarb and raspberries with cinnamon, ginger, and cardamom. Add a tablespoon or two more sugar for a slightly sweeter version. You can substitute individually quick-frozen rhubarb pieces if you can't find fresh or want a taste of spring in winter. Plan to serve the cobbler with generous scoops of vanilla ice cream.

6 SERVINGS

FILLING:

- 1 cup sugar
- 2½ tablespoons cornstarch
- 1 teaspoon cinnamon
- 1 teaspoon finely grated fresh ginger
- ¼ teaspoon ground cardamom
- 1½ pounds fresh rhubarb, cut into ¾-inch pieces (5 cups)
- ½ tablespoon unsalted butter
- 12 ounces fresh or unsweetened frozen raspberries (3 cups)

DOUGH:

- 1¼ cups all-purpose flour
- 3 teaspoons granulated sugar
- 1 teaspoon baking powder
- Pinch of salt
- 5 tablespoons unsalted butter, cut into small pieces, chilled
- ⅔ cup buttermilk

1. Preheat the oven to 375°. **Make the filling:** In a large nonreactive saucepan, thoroughly stir together the sugar, cornstarch, cinnamon, ginger, and cardamom. Add the rhubarb, stirring until coated with the sugar mixture. Add the butter. Bring to a simmer over moderate heat and cook, stirring occasionally, until the rhubarb exudes its juices and the mixture thickens, about 5 minutes. Immediately remove the pan from the heat. Gently stir in the raspberries. Turn the mixture into a round 9½-by-1¾-inch casserole or baking dish.

2. Make the dough: In a medium bowl, stir together the flour, 2 teaspoons of the sugar, the baking powder, and salt. Using your fingertips, a pastry blender, or 2 knives, cut in the butter until the mixture resembles coarse meal. Stir all but 1 tablespoon of the buttermilk into the dry ingredients, tossing with a fork just until evenly incorporated. Pat the dough gently into a ball and flatten into a disk.

3. Place the disk between 2 sheets of wax paper and roll it into a 9-inch round. Peel off the top sheet of wax paper. If desired, using lightly greased fingertips, flute the edges of the dough. Invert the dough over the fruit mixture. Peel off the wax paper.

4. Make 5 or 6 slashes, about 2½ inches long by ¼ inch wide, that radiate from the center of the dough. Brush the dough evenly with the reserved 1 tablespoon buttermilk and sprinkle the remaining 1 teaspoon sugar on top.

5. Bake the cobbler in the middle of the oven for 30 minutes. Lower the temperature to 350° and bake for 15 to 20 minutes longer, or until the top is nicely browned, the fruit filling is bubbling around the edges, and a cake tester inserted in the center of the dough comes out clean. Transfer the cobbler to a rack and let cool for 15 minutes before serving. (MAKE AHEAD: The cobbler can be made up to 5 hours ahead; set aside at room temperature. To serve, reheat the cobbler for 15 minutes in a warm oven.) —NANCY BAGGETT

PEACH AND BLACKBERRY CRISP LF

6 SERVINGS

5 medium peaches, peeled and cut into 1-inch chunks
1 pint blackberries
3 tablespoons honey
2 teaspoons finely grated lemon zest
1 teaspoon instant tapioca
2 tablespoons unsalted butter, cut into thin slices
1¾ cups old fashioned rolled oatmeal
⅓ cup light brown sugar
1 teaspoon cinnamon

1. Preheat the oven to 400°. In a medium baking dish, toss the peaches and blackberries with the honey, lemon zest, and tapioca. Cover with foil and bake for 20 minutes. Stir once, cover, and bake for 10 more minutes, until the fruit is tender and the juices are slightly thickened.
2. In a bowl, work the butter into the oatmeal. Mix in the brown sugar and cinnamon. Pour the mixture into a heavy skillet and stir over moderate heat until the oatmeal is toasted and the sugar hardens into clumps, about 7 minutes. Remove from the heat and stir for 3 more minutes.
3. Spoon the warm fruit into individual bowls. Sprinkle the oatmeal topping over the fruit and serve.—CHARLES WILEY

PLUM-APRICOT UPSIDE-DOWN CAKE

If you can't find decent fresh apricots, drained canned apricots work beautifully here. Serve with softly whipped cream flavored with almond extract or orange zest, or with honey ice cream.

8 SERVINGS

1 stick (4 ounces) plus 2 tablespoons unsalted butter, at room temperature
¾ cup lightly packed brown sugar
8 to 12 Italian prune plums, halved and pitted
8 small apricots, halved and pitted
¾ cup granulated sugar
1 teaspoon pure vanilla extract
¼ teaspoon pure almond extract
3 large eggs, at room temperature
⅔ cup blanched almonds, finely ground
1 cup all-purpose flour
1 teaspoon baking powder
¼ teaspoon salt

1. Preheat the oven to 375°. In a 10-inch cast-iron skillet, combine the 2 tablespoons butter and the brown sugar and cook over moderate heat, stirring, until melted. Remove the skillet from the heat and arrange the plums and apricots, cut sides up, snugly and attractively in a single layer in the melted brown sugar.
2. In a large bowl, using a handheld electric mixer or a wooden spoon, beat together the remaining 1 stick butter and the granulated sugar until light and fluffy. Beat in the vanilla and almond extracts, then add the eggs 1 at a time, beating until smooth after each addition. Stir in the almonds, then the flour, baking powder, and salt. Spoon the batter over the fruit and smooth it out with a rubber spatula.
3. Bake the cake in the center of the oven for about 35 minutes, or until lightly browned and springy when pressed with a fingertip. Transfer to a rack and let cool for a few minutes, then invert onto a cake plate and carefully remove the skillet. Serve the cake warm or at room temperature.—DEBORAH MADISON

PEAR AND DRIED CHERRY SCRUNCH

6 TO 8 SERVINGS

8 firm, ripe pears, such as Anjou or Bosc (about 4 pounds)—peeled, cored, and cut into 1-inch dice
1 cup dried sour cherries (about 4 ounces)
½ cup light brown sugar
3 tablespoons fresh orange juice
2 tablespoons fresh lemon juice
1 teaspoon finely grated lemon zest
1 teaspoon cinnamon
4 tablespoons unsalted butter, cut into small pieces

TOPPING:
1 cup all-purpose flour
1 cup quick-cooking oatmeal
1 cup chopped walnuts (4 ounces)
½ cup light brown sugar
1 stick (8 tablespoons) unsalted butter, cut into small pieces
Whipped cream, crème fraîche, or vanilla ice cream, for serving

1. Preheat the oven to 350° and butter a 9-by-13-inch baking dish or a 3-quart oval gratin dish.
2. In a large bowl, toss the pears with the dried sour cherries, brown sugar, orange juice, lemon juice, lemon zest, and cinnamon. Transfer the fruit to the prepared dish, making sure that

Pear and Dried Cherry Scrunch

the cherries are evenly distributed. Dot with the butter.

3. Make the topping: In a medium bowl, combine the flour, oatmeal, walnuts, brown sugar, and butter. Rub the mixture between your fingers to form large crumbs. Sprinkle the topping evenly over the fruit, lightly pressing it down.

4. Bake the scrunch for about 50 minutes, or until the fruit is bubbling and tender when pierced and the top is crisp and browned. (If after 40 minutes or so the top looks nicely browned, cover loosely with foil to finish cooking.) Let the scrunch rest uncovered for at least 15 minutes before serving. Serve warm or at room temperature with a dollop of whipped cream or crème fraîche, or a scoop of vanilla ice cream.—CHARLIE PALMER

CINNAMON CRUNCH SHORTCAKES WITH MIXED BERRIES

These individual shortcake biscuits are dipped in butter and then coated with cinnamon sugar to create a crunchy topping. Don't use a knife to split biscuits; it will crush their flaky layers. Use your fingers to open them.

8 SERVINGS

Biscuit Dough (recipe follows), patted into a rectangle
2 cups raspberries
1½ cups blackberries
2 cups blueberries
⅔ cup plus ½ cup sugar
1 stick (4 ounces) unsalted butter
2 teaspoons cinnamon
Ginger Whipped Cream (p. 427), for serving

1. Preheat the oven to 450°. On a lightly floured surface, roll out the Biscuit Dough ½ to ¾ inch thick. Using a heart-shaped or any other biscuit cutter that measures 3 inches at its widest point, cut out 5 shortcakes as close together as possible. Press the cutter straight down; don't twist it. If the cutter sticks to the dough, dip it in flour between cuts. Gather the scraps together and press or roll out as before. Cut out 2 more shortcakes. Press the remaining scraps into a ball, flatten, and cut out the last shortcake. (Alternatively, on a lightly floured surface, pat the dough into an 8-inch round. Halve the round, then cut each half into 3 wedges for a total of 6 triangular shortcakes.) Place the shortcakes on an ungreased baking sheet, cover with the plastic wrap, and refrigerate.

2. In a medium bowl, gently toss the raspberries and blackberries to combine. In a medium nonreactive saucepan, gently toss the blueberries with ⅔ cup of the sugar and 2 teaspoons of water. Cover and cook over moderate heat, stirring once or twice and brushing down the sides of the pan, just until the blueberries start to pop and release their juices, about 5 minutes. If the sugar hasn't dissolved, stir in a few more drops of water. Remove the pan from the heat and add the raspberries and blackberries. Do not stir. Transfer the berries to the bowl.

3. Bake the shortcakes in the middle of the oven for about 15 minutes, or until golden brown.

4. Meanwhile, melt the butter in a small saucepan. In a small bowl, combine the remaining ½ cup sugar and the cinnamon.

5. Immediately after removing the shortcakes from the oven, dip them in the butter and cinnamon sugar as follows. Holding a shortcake right side up, dip the bottom in the melted butter. Place the shortcake, buttered side down, in the cinnamon sugar and shake the bowl so that the sugar adheres to and completely covers the bottom. Then turn the shortcake over and dip the top in the butter and cinnamon sugar in the same manner. Place the shortcake right side up on a plate. Continue with the remaining shortcakes. (If the level of the butter is too low for dipping the last shortcake, use a pastry brush to generously brush the butter on the top and bottom of the biscuit.)

6. Using your fingers, gently split open the shortcakes. Spoon about ½ cup of the mixed berries over the bottom of each shortcake. Cover the berries with the shortcake tops and spoon a dollop of the Ginger Whipped Cream alongside. Serve the mixed berry shortcakes at once.

Biscuit Dough

MAKES 8 SHORTCAKE BISCUITS

- 2 cups all-purpose flour
- 1 tablespoon baking powder
- ½ teaspoon salt
- 1 stick (4 ounces) cold unsalted butter, cut into ½-inch dice
- ¾ cup cold milk

1. In a food processor, pulse the all-purpose flour, the baking powder, and the salt until mixed. Add the butter and pulse until the mixture resembles coarse meal with particles the size of peas and lentils, about 40 times.

2. Drizzle the milk evenly over the dry ingredients and pulse a few times, just until incorporated and the dough forms small clumps.

3. Turn out the dough onto a work surface and knead once or twice to gather it into a mass; do not overwork the dough. Gently pat the dough into a disk or rectangle, as needed. (MAKE AHEAD: The dough can be made up to 2 hours ahead; wrap tightly and refrigerate.) —PEGGY CULLEN

STRAWBERRY SPIRAL PIE

This makes a great breakfast dish as well as a wonderful summer dessert served warm with vanilla ice cream.

6 TO 8 SERVINGS

- 1½ pounds strawberries—hulled, washed, and drained (4½ cups)
- ⅔ cup strawberry jam
- 1 tablespoon unsalted butter
- 1 tablespoon cornstarch
- 1 tablespoon quick-cooking tapioca
- ½ teaspoon ground ginger
- ¼ teaspoon cinnamon
- ⅛ teaspoon nutmeg
- ⅓ to ½ cup sugar, according to the sweetness of the berries
- Biscuit Dough (left), patted into a rectangle

1. Preheat the oven to 450° and line the oven floor with foil to catch any drips.

2. Spread the strawberries on paper towels to dry. In a small bowl, stir the jam to loosen it. In a saucepan, melt the butter and keep warm.

3. In a large bowl, whisk together the cornstarch, tapioca, ginger, cinnamon, nutmeg, and sugar. Halve any very large berries. Gently toss the berries with the dry ingredients.

4. On a lightly floured surface, roll out the Biscuit Dough into a 10-by-18-inch rectangle. Square off the corners. Brush the dough lightly with about half of the melted butter. Using an icing spatula, spread the strawberry jam over the rectangle, leaving a ½-inch border on one long side. Starting at the opposite long side, roll up the dough jelly-roll fashion and pinch the seam closed. Roll the log so that it is an even diameter, exactly 18 inches long; turn the log seam side down.

5. Using a large sharp knife, quarter the log, then cut each quarter into 3 equal pieces so that there will be 12 spiraled biscuits in all. ➤

STRAWBERRY SUBSTITUTE

You can use any fresh fruit and any flavor of jam in place of the strawberries in the Strawberry Spiral Pie. Follow this guide for a basic fruit filling: sweeten 6 cups of fruit with about ⅔ cup of sugar and thicken with 3 tablespoons of either cornstarch or tapioca. Use spices judiciously. Let the mixture sit for 15 minutes to soften the starch. Meanwhile, make the Biscuit Dough, and you are ready to assemble the pie.—PEGGY CULLEN

MAKING PERFECT BISCUITS

The basic recipe for biscuits hasn't changed since pioneers made them on the prairie. Back then, harsh circumstances required improvisation. Water, for instance, would sometimes stand in for milk, or 'coon fat would replace butter. Or the biscuits would be baked on a shovel over a campfire instead of in an oven. While edible in any case, the choice of ingredients, as well as tender handling of the dough, will make the difference between a decent biscuit and one that is sublime.

FIVE ESSENTIAL INGREDIENTS

- FLOUR: When it comes to flour, what's good for bread is bad for biscuits. High-protein flour is great for forming the strong elastic bonds of gluten that give bread its structure. But it makes for a tough little biscuit. So choose low-protein flour with no more than 12 grams of protein per cup. Usually, nationally available all-purpose flours fill the bill, but check the label on the package. If the protein content is more than 12 grams, use two parts all-purpose and one part cake flour, which is very low in protein. If you can, use a Southern all-purpose flour made from soft wheat, favored throughout the South for producing a tender, cakey texture.

- FAT: Chunks of fat serve as "spacers" in dough. As the fat melts in the oven, the cavities created fill with steam and gas from the leavening; this causes the dough to expand and push upward, creating a flaky structure.

Butter, shortening, or lard can all make a great biscuit dough, but in fruit desserts I prefer butter for its incomparable flavor. You may have heard that shortening and lard yield a flakier biscuit than butter. It is true that their melting point is higher than butter's, which means that the fat stays intact longer during baking, keeping the layers of dough from collapsing before they're set. However, as long as butter is kept cold and left in small pieces, it too will create spaces and produce a flaky biscuit.

- LIQUID: Milk is the most common liquid used in biscuit dough. To my taste it adds the right amount of color and flavor to the finished product, and it gives the crust a little crunch. But there are other liquids you can use. Heavy cream, because of its extra fat, yields a tender but denser texture. The acid in buttermilk, sour cream, and yogurt helps to tenderize the dough and also adds a slight tang.

The amount of liquid affects the dough's consistency. The thicker the liquid, the more you need to make a soft, moist dough. For example, you use a lot more sour cream than milk for the same quantity of flour.

Rolling a dough flattens the butter and creates more noticeable layers. A wet dough, which can be dropped from a spoon, produces biscuits that are fluffy and tender but not flaky.

- LEAVENING: Too much leavening can cause a dough to become heavy. One tablespoon of baking powder is more than enough to raise a standard dough made with two cups of flour.

You may want to consider making your own baking powder. It gives better lift than the commercial product, which sometimes adds a slightly bitter flavor to baked goods. The recipe couldn't be easier: mix one part baking soda with two parts cream of tartar.

- SALT AND OTHER FLAVORINGS: Salt, which enhances the flavors of other ingredients, is not optional in the Biscuit Dough recipe (p. 425). Other ingredients, however, are. For example, by adding different flavorings, you can produce a variety of biscuits. Up to one tablespoon of sugar per two cups of flour will supply just the right light touch of sweetness. Or after cutting in the fat, add herbs, spices, or grated citrus zest. Or try mixing cocoa with the dry ingredients to make chocolate biscuits.

THE DOUGH

The technique of cutting cold fat into flour accounts for a biscuit's delicate flaky layers. The easiest method is to pulse the two ingredients in a food processor until the mixture resembles coarse meal with pieces that vary from the size of a lentil to the size of a pea. Then pour the liquid over the mixture all at once and pulse briefly until it forms curdlike pieces. Dump the biscuit dough out on a lightly floured surface and knead it a few times very gently to form a unified mass.—PEGGY CULLEN

6. Using a rubber spatula, fold the strawberry filling once to remix. Spoon the filling into a 9-inch glass pie plate and smooth the top. Arrange 8 biscuits around the perimeter of the pie and the remaining 4 biscuits in the center. Don't push the biscuits down into the strawberries.
7. Bake the pie for 20 minutes, or until the top is golden brown and the strawberry filling is bubbling. Lower the oven temperature to 350°, loosely cover the pie with foil, and bake for 15 minutes longer. Transfer the pie to a rack to cool for 30 minutes before serving.—PEGGY CULLEN

PLUM POT PIES

You can make these individual pies with any fruit. If you have only one-cup dishes, that's fine. You'll be able to make eight portions instead of six.

6 SERVINGS

- ¾ cup plus 2 tablespoons sugar
- 2 tablespoons cornstarch
- 1 tablespoon quick-cooking tapioca
- ¼ teaspoon plus ¾ teaspoon ground ginger
- ¼ teaspoon cinnamon
- 2 pounds red or black plums, pitted and sliced ⅜ inch thick (6 cups)
- Biscuit Dough (p. 425), patted into any shape
- 1 tablespoon unsalted butter, melted
- Vanilla ice cream or Ginger Whipped Cream (recipe follows), for serving

1. Preheat the oven to 450°. In a large bowl, whisk together ¾ cup of the sugar, the cornstarch, the tapioca, ¼ teaspoon of the ground ginger, and the cinnamon. Add the plum slices and toss gently to coat.
2. Lightly butter the inside rim of six 1½-cup ovenproof ramekins or baking cups. In a small bowl, combine the remaining 2 tablespoons sugar and ¾ teaspoon ground ginger.
3. On a lightly floured surface, roll out the Biscuit Dough ⅛ inch thick. Using a round cutter that is ½ inch larger than the ramekins, cut out 6 rounds of dough. Cut small decorative shapes from the dough scraps for appliqués if desired.
4. Stir the plum slices and spoon them and their juice evenly into the ramekins; the ramekins should be about three-quarters full. Place a round of Biscuit Dough over each ramekin, tucking the excess inside the rim. Press the dough gently to adhere to the rim.
5. Brush the top of the Biscuit Dough with the melted butter. If using, affix the appliqués on the top of the pot pies and brush the appliqués with butter. Sprinkle the top of each pot pie with about 1 teaspoon of the ginger-sugar. Using the tip of a sharp knife, slice a few vents in the Biscuit Dough.
6. Place the ramekins on a baking sheet, making sure they don't touch one another. Bake the pot pies for 20 minutes, then lower the temperature to 350° and bake for 15 minutes longer, or until the tops are nicely browned and the plum filling is bubbling. Transfer the ramekins to a rack to cool for 30 minutes. Serve the pot pies warm with ice cream or Ginger Whipped Cream.

Ginger Whipped Cream

MAKES ABOUT 3 CUPS

- 1 cup heavy cream
- 3 tablespoons confectioners' sugar
- 1 teaspoon ground ginger

In a medium bowl, combine all the ingredients. Beat until soft peaks form. Refrigerate until ready to use. (MAKE AHEAD: The whipped cream will keep, tightly covered, overnight. Rewhip briefly before using.)—PEGGY CULLEN

CHERRY LATTICE COBBLER

Without a doubt, the best cherries to use here are fresh sour cherries. If all you can find are sweet cherries, cut the sugar back to ⅔ cup. Don't let the cherries macerate in the sugar more than 15 minutes, or too much liquid will seep out. Out of season, you can use frozen sour cherries. Spread them in a single layer on a baking sheet and let defrost for about 30 minutes.

6 TO 8 SERVINGS

- ¾ cup plus 1 tablespoon sugar
- 1½ tablespoons cornstarch
- 1 tablespoon quick-cooking tapioca
- 1½ pounds sour cherries, pitted (6 cups)
- 1 teaspoon pure almond extract
- Biscuit Dough (p. 425), patted into a rectangle
- 1 tablespoon unsalted butter, melted

1. Preheat the oven to 450° and line the oven floor with foil to catch any drips. In a large bowl, whisk ¾ cup of the sugar with the cornstarch and tapioca. Add the cherries and the almond extract and fold gently with a rubber spatula to incorporate.

2. Choose a 6-cup ovenproof glass or ceramic baking dish or a 10-inch glass pie plate. On a lightly floured surface, roll out the Biscuit Dough ⅛ inch thick and at least as large as the baking dish you are using. Lift the Biscuit Dough frequently as you roll and lightly reflour the surface to prevent the dough from sticking. Using a fluted pastry wheel, cut the Biscuit Dough into 1½-inch-wide strips.

3. Gently stir the cherries. Spoon the cherries and their juice into the baking dish and spread the fruit evenly with a rubber spatula. Lay about half the strips of Biscuit Dough, spaced evenly apart, across the pie without stretching. Allow the extra dough to hang over the sides of the dish. Weave in the remaining strips of dough (see "Weaving a Lattice Top"). Using a small sharp knife and a swift downward motion, trim the overhanging dough flush with the edge of the baking dish.

4. Brush the lattice top with the melted butter (you may not need to use all of it) and sprinkle the remaining 1 tablespoon sugar on the dough. Bake the cobbler for 20 minutes or until the top is beginning to brown. Lower the oven temperature to 350° and bake for 30 minutes. If the edge is browning too quickly, cover it with foil. Transfer the cobbler to a rack to cool for at least 30 minutes. Serve warm or at room temperature.—PEGGY CULLEN

WEAVING A LATTICE TOP

It's easy to weave biscuit dough into a lattice top for a cobbler. Be sure the dough is rolled thin enough—⅛ inch is perfect. If the dough is too thick, the underside of the dough will still be raw when the fruit filling is cooked. The wider you cut the strips, the easier they are to work with.

To start, lay half the strips, spaced evenly, across the pie without stretching the dough. Fold back every other strip to its midway point. Starting at the fold, place a new strip at a 90° angle over the unfolded strips. Unfold the folded strips, crossing the new one. Now fold back the strips that alternate with the first ones you folded. Place another new strip of dough parallel to and evenly spaced from the first. Continue in this fashion until you reach the edge of the pie, half of which is now latticed.

Then repeat the process on the other half of the pie. Don't worry about overhanging dough. Just cut it off flush with a sharp paring knife in a quick downward motion.—PEGGY CULLEN

SUMMER FRUIT "PIZZA"

Any fruit can be used for this very colorful free-form tart. Alternatively, you can make small individual pizzas. Roll the dough into a log and slice crosswise into equal pieces. Then roll each piece into a round and top with the fruit as described.

MAKES ONE 9-INCH PIZZA

- ½ recipe of Biscuit Dough (p. 425), patted into a disk
- 2 tablespoons unsalted butter, melted
- 1 small plum, pitted and sliced ¼ inch thick
- ½ peach, pitted and sliced ¼ inch thick
- ½ cup raspberries
- ½ cup small strawberries, halved
- ½ cup blackberries or blueberries
- 3½ tablespoons sugar
- Ginger Whipped Cream (p. 427), for serving

1. Preheat the oven to 450°. On a lightly floured surface, roll out the Biscuit Dough into a 9-inch round; do not roll it any larger. Fold the round of Biscuit Dough in half and transfer it to a heavy ungreased baking sheet. Unfold the Biscuit Dough and smooth the edges.

2. Using a pastry brush, lightly coat the Biscuit Dough with some of the melted butter. Arrange the plum and peach slices, the raspberries, strawberries, and blackberries in a decorative overlapping pattern all the way to the edge of the dough, fanning the plum and peach slices and clustering the berries. Dab the fruit with the remaining melted butter. Sprinkle 2½ tablespoons of the sugar over the fruit.

3. Bake the fruit "pizza" for 20 minutes, or until the bottom is golden brown. Remove the pizza from the oven and turn on the broiler. Sprinkle the remaining 1 tablespoon of sugar over the fruit. Broil the pizza for about 1 minute, watching carefully, until

Summer Fruit "Pizza"

the fruit begins to bubble and brown. Slide the pizza onto a rack to cool slightly. Serve the pizza warm with the Ginger Whipped Cream.—PEGGY CULLEN

DRIED CHERRY AND PEACH STEAMED PUDDING

To make the chopping of the dried peaches a little easier, rub your knife with vegetable oil so that the fruit doesn't stick to it. You'll need to start the cherry and peach pudding at least one day before you plan to serve it to allow time for the fruit to macerate in the beer and bourbon.

8 SERVINGS

- ½ pound dried sour cherries
- ½ pound dried peaches, finely chopped
- ½ cup dark beer
- ⅓ cup plus 2 teaspoons bourbon
- 14 tablespoons (7 ounces) unsalted butter, at room temperature
- 1 cup dark brown sugar
- 2 large eggs, at room temperature
- 1 tablespoon finely grated orange zest
- 2 teaspoons finely grated lemon zest
- 1 cup all-purpose flour
- ½ teaspoon baking powder
- 1 teaspoon ground cinnamon
- ½ teaspoon ground cardamom
- ½ teaspoon ground cloves
- ½ teaspoon ground nutmeg
- 2½ cups fine brioche bread crumbs (4 ounces)
- 2 tablespoons confectioners' sugar
- Mint sprigs (optional) and lightly sweetened whipped cream, for serving

1. In a medium bowl, combine the cherries, peaches, beer, and

⅓ cup of the bourbon. Cover and let macerate overnight.

2. Butter a 1½-quart steamed pudding mold or soufflé dish. Using a standing mixer fitted with a paddle or a hand-held electric mixer, beat the butter and brown sugar on moderate speed until light and creamy. Add the eggs one at a time, beating well after each addition. On low speed, add the grated orange and lemon zest. Sift in the flour, baking powder, cinnamon, cardamom, cloves, and nutmeg, and blend just until smooth. Add the brioche crumbs and macerated dried fruit and its liquid and mix just until combined.

3. Bring 2 inches of water to a boil in a large enameled cast-iron casserole. Scrape the batter into the prepared mold. Cover with foil and tie with string to hold the foil in place. Set the pudding in the casserole, cover with a lid, and steam over moderate heat until the pudding is set and a skewer inserted in the center comes out clean, about 1¼ hours. Transfer to a rack and let cool for ½ hour. (MAKE AHEAD: The pudding can be steamed up to 8 hours ahead; let stand at room temperature. Reheat in the water bath in the casserole for about 20 minutes.)

4. Run a knife around the sides of the mold to loosen the pudding, then invert the pudding onto a large serving plate. In a small bowl, whisk the confectioners' sugar with the remaining 2 teaspoons bourbon until smooth. Spoon the icing into a small sturdy plastic bag and cut off a very small corner of the bag. Drizzle the icing in a crisscross pattern over the top of the pudding. Garnish the pudding with mint sprigs and serve warm with whipped cream.—SANFORD D'AMATO

Dried Cherry and Peach Steamed Pudding

CARAMEL APPLE PUDDING

This sweet dessert is great as is or when served with a simple berry coulis.

4 SERVINGS

- 4 apples, such as McIntosh or Jonathan (1¾ pounds)
- 1⅔ cups sugar
- 1 vanilla bean, split
- 1 teaspoon finely grated lemon zest
- ⅛ teaspoon salt
- 1 stick (4 ounces) unsalted butter, softened
- 1 tablespoon all-purpose flour
- 3 large eggs, lightly beaten
- 2 tablespoons fresh lemon juice
- Crème fraîche, for serving

1. Peel, quarter, and core the apples. Slice them lengthwise ⅛ inch thick. In a large nonreactive saucepan, cook the apples, ⅔ cup of the sugar, the vanilla bean, the lemon zest, and the salt over moderate heat until the apples can be mashed with a spoon, about 20 minutes. (If the apples start to brown, cover the saucepan with a lid.) Preheat the oven to 350°.

2. Transfer the apple mixture to a bowl, discard the vanilla bean, mash well, and let cool. Beat in the butter, the flour, and the eggs, blending well after each addition.

3. In a small, heavy, nonreactive saucepan, stir together the remaining 1 cup sugar, 2 tablespoons of water, and the lemon juice, and cook over moderate heat until the caramel turns a rich golden brown, about 7 minutes. Very carefully pour a small amount of caramel into a 6-ounce ramekin and rotate quickly to cover the bottom and sides of the dish lightly with the caramel. Pour any excess back into the pan. Repeat with 3 more ramekins (use any extra caramel for another use).

4. Spoon the apple mixture evenly into the ramekins. Put them in a baking pan and fill the pan with enough hot water to reach halfway up the sides of the ramekins. Bake the puddings in the oven for about 45 minutes, or until set. Remove the ramekins from the water bath and let stand for 10 minutes before serving. (MAKE AHEAD: The puddings can be made up to 4 hours ahead; leave at room temperature. Reheat the puddings in a 350° oven for about 5 minutes before serving.)

5. To serve, run a knife around the inside of each ramekin and unmold the caramel apple puddings onto dessert plates. Dollop each of the puddings with crème fraîche and serve.—EMILY LUCHETTI AND HOLLYCE SNYDER

BLACKBERRY-POLENTA BREAD PUDDING

At Nana's, Scott Howell serves this rich dessert with a lemon curd sauce; he often uses blueberries in place of the blackberries.

4 TO 6 SERVINGS

POLENTA BREAD:

- ¾ cup all-purpose flour
- ⅔ cup yellow cornmeal
- 1 tablespoon baking powder
- Pinch of salt
- 2 sticks (½ pound) unsalted butter, at room temperature
- 1 cup plus 1 tablespoon sugar
- 4 large eggs, separated
- 2 large egg yolks

BLACKBERRY CUSTARD:

- 1 vanilla bean, split
- 4 cups heavy cream
- 10 large egg yolks
- 1 cup sugar
- 1 pint fresh blackberries plus additional berries for garnish

1. Make the polenta bread: Preheat the oven to 325°. Butter a 9-by-5-inch loaf pan. In a bowl, combine the flour, cornmeal, baking powder, and salt. In another bowl, cream the butter with the sugar until light and fluffy. Beat in the 6 egg yolks in 3 batches. Fold in the dry ingredients in 3 batches just until incorporated.

2. In another bowl, beat the egg whites until firm but not dry. Stir one-third of the egg whites into the batter, then fold in the remaining whites. Spread the batter in the prepared pan and bake for about 50 minutes, or until a cake tester inserted in the center comes out clean. Let cool in the pan on a wire rack. Leave the oven on. (MAKE AHEAD: The polenta can be prepared 1 day ahead; cover and let stand at room temperature.)

3. Make the blackberry custard: In a medium saucepan, scrape the seeds from the vanilla bean into the heavy cream and add the bean. Bring just to a simmer over moderately high heat. Meanwhile, in a bowl, whisk the egg yolks with the sugar. Gradually whisk in the hot cream. Strain the mixture into a medium bowl and let cool. Stir in the fresh blackberries.

4. Butter a 9-by-13-inch baking dish. Cut the polenta bread into ½-inch-thick slices and spread them on a baking sheet. Toast the slices in the oven for about 7 minutes, or until the polenta is lightly browned. Let cool. Leave the oven on.

5. Tear the slices of toasted polenta bread into ¾-inch-thick strips and spread them in the prepared baking dish. Pour the blackberry custard over the polenta bread, evenly distributing the blackberries. Set the baking dish in a larger pan and add enough hot water to the pan to reach halfway up the sides of the baking dish. Cover the blackberry-polenta bread pudding with foil and bake until the blackberry custard is set, about 2 hours. Let cool slightly. Serve the bread pudding garnished with fresh blackberries.—SCOTT HOWELL

Blackberry-Polenta Bread Pudding

BREAD PUDDING WITH DRIED CRANBERRIES, VANILLA AND MINT

6 SERVINGS

- 1 cup dried cranberries (about 5 ounces)
- 1½ cups milk
- 1½ cups heavy cream
- ½ teaspoon finely grated lemon zest
- ¼ teaspoon finely grated orange zest
- 5 fresh mint sprigs
- 1 vanilla bean, split
- ¾ cup sugar
- 1½ envelopes of unflavored gelatin
- Six 2½-inch rounds of challah bread
- ½ cup seedless raspberry jam

1. Put the dried cranberries in a small bowl and cover with ½ cup of warm water. Set aside to plump for about 20 minutes.

2. Preheat the oven to 325°. In a medium saucepan, combine the milk, heavy cream, lemon zest, orange zest, and 4 of the mint

Bread Pudding with Dried Cranberries, Vanilla and Mint

sprigs. Scrape the seeds from the vanilla bean into the milk and add the bean to the saucepan. Bring to a boil over moderate heat. Remove from the heat and stir for a few minutes to cool slightly. Whisk in the sugar and the gelatin and set aside for 3 minutes, then whisk again. Strain the mixture into a heat-proof measuring cup.

3. Drain the cranberries and divide them among six ½-cup ramekins set on a baking sheet. Stir the milk mixture once and pour it over the cranberries, filling the ramekins. Top each with a challah round. Bake the puddings for 20 minutes, or until the custard is bubbling and still wobbly. Remove from the oven.

4. Preheat the broiler. Broil the puddings for about 30 seconds just to toast the bread rounds. Let the custards cool, then refrigerate until completely set, at least 4 but not more than 6 hours.

5. Just before serving, melt the raspberry jam in a small nonreactive skillet over low heat. Run a knife around the inside of each ramekin to loosen the bread puddings, and invert them onto dessert plates. Spoon a little of the raspberry jam over and around them. Garnish each plate with a few mint leaves from the remaining sprig.—DANIEL BOULUD

BITTERSWEET CHOCOLATE CREME BRULEE WITH CARAMELIZED BANANAS

Crème brûlée crusts need to be caramelized quickly. Since most home broilers aren't as hot as those in restaurants, Hubert Keller of Fleur de Lys in San Francisco suggests setting ramekins in a baking dish half filled with ice water. This will keep the crème brûlées cool while the tops are becoming crisp.

6 SERVINGS

- ¼ cup (packed) light brown sugar
- 1½ cups heavy cream
- ½ cup plus 2 tablespoons milk
- 3½ ounces bittersweet chocolate, finely chopped
- 5 large egg yolks
- ⅓ cup plus 1 teaspoon granulated sugar
- 2 ripe medium bananas

1. Sift the brown sugar onto a plate in an even layer and let stand at room temperature for at least 6 hours or overnight to dry. Sift the sugar again to break up any lumps.

2. Preheat the oven to 300°. In a medium saucepan, bring the heavy cream and milk to a boil over moderate heat. Remove from the heat, stir in the chocolate, and let stand until melted, about 5 minutes.

3. In a medium bowl, whisk the egg yolks with the granulated sugar until blended. Whisk in the chocolate mixture. Strain the custard into a large measuring cup and pour it into six 4-ounce ramekins.

4. Set the ramekins in a baking dish and add enough hot water to the dish to reach halfway up the sides of the ramekins. Bake for about 40 minutes, or until the custards are set. Remove from the water bath and let cool. Cover and refrigerate for at least 6 hours or overnight.

5. Preheat the broiler. Slice the bananas ⅛ inch thick and arrange 5 or 6 overlapping slices in a circle on top of each custard. Sprinkle the dried brown sugar evenly over the bananas and custard and broil as close to the heat as possible for about 20 seconds, or until the sugar melts.—HUBERT KELLER

CREME CARAMEL WITH STRAWBERRIES

If you're transporting this dessert, leave it in its pan and unmold it at your destination.

8 SERVINGS

- 1¼ cups sugar
- ½ teaspoon light corn syrup
- 1¼ cups half-and-half
- 1 cup heavy cream
- 6 large egg yolks
- Boiling water
- 1 pint ripe strawberries, hulled
- 2 tablespoons strawberry or raspberry liqueur
- Fresh mint sprigs

1. Preheat the oven to 300°. In a small nonreactive saucepan, combine ¾ cup of the sugar with the corn syrup and ⅓ cup of water. Bring to a boil over moderately high heat, stirring to dissolve the sugar. Wash down the side of the pot with a wet pastry brush. Boil without stirring until the caramel reaches an amber color, about 8 minutes.

2. Immediately pour the hot caramel into a 4-cup ring (savarin) mold and swirl to coat as much of the inside of the pan as possible. After about a minute, when the caramel starts to thicken, brush it all over the inside of the mold to thoroughly coat. Let the caramel set.

3. In a medium saucepan, combine the half-and-half, the heavy cream, and the remaining ½ cup sugar. Bring almost to a boil over moderate heat, then immediately remove the saucepan from the heat.

4. In a medium bowl, using an electric mixer, beat the egg yolks at medium speed for 1 minute. Gradually whisk in the hot cream until well blended. Strain the custard into a clean bowl, then skim off the foam. Pour the custard into the caramel-lined mold.

5. Set a kitchen towel folded in quarters in the bottom of a 9-by-13-inch baking pan. Set the caramel-lined ring mold on top. Pour enough boiling water into the pan to reach two-thirds of the way up the outside of the mold. Place in the oven and bake for 1 hour, or until the custard feels set when pressed with a finger. Transfer the mold to a rack to cool completely. Cover with plastic wrap and refrigerate overnight.

6. Up to 3 hours before serving, toss the strawberries with the liqueur and refrigerate.

7. To serve, unmold the custard onto a round rimmed platter. (If the caramel resists unmolding, hold the mold in an inch of hot water for about 30 seconds, then wipe dry and try again.) Toss the strawberries again and arrange them in the center of the ring. Garnish the crème caramel with fresh mint sprigs.—LYDIE MARSHALL

LEMON FLANS WITH LEMON SAUCE AND CANDIED ZEST

Jamie Shannon, of Commander's Palace in New Orleans, likes to serve these luxurious, tangy, and sweet lemon flans at room temperature so that they resemble cheesecake. Alternatively, you can chill the flans for a denser, creamier texture that's more like that of custard. Clarifying the butter for the phyllo helps the pastry crisps brown evenly during baking.

8 SERVINGS

FLANS:

- 1 pound cream cheese, at room temperature
- 1 cup sugar
- 5 large eggs
- ¾ cup fresh lemon juice
- ¼ cup white rum

LEMON SAUCE:

- 5 large egg yolks
- ⅔ cup sugar
- ⅓ cup fresh lemon juice
- 3 tablespoons white rum

CANDIED LEMON ZEST:

- 6 medium lemons
- 1½ cups sugar
- Fresh mint leaves, for garnish (optional)

PASTRY CRISPS:

- 4 tablespoons unsalted butter
- 4 sheets of phyllo dough
- 2½ tablespoons sugar
- ¼ teaspoon cinnamon

1. Make the flans: Preheat the oven to 250°. Butter eight 4-ounce ramekins and sprinkle them with sugar. In a large bowl, beat the cream cheese with the sugar until smooth. In a medium bowl, beat the eggs with the lemon juice and rum. Gradually beat the eggs into the cream cheese. Strain into a large measuring cup.

2. Pour the lemon mixture into the prepared ramekins. Set the ramekins in a baking dish and add enough hot water to the dish to reach halfway up the sides of the ramekins. Bake for about 1 hour, or until the flans are set. Let cool in the water bath for about 2½ hours. Raise the oven temperature to 325°.

3. Make the lemon sauce: In a heavy, medium, nonreactive saucepan, combine the egg yolks, sugar, and lemon juice. Whisk over low heat until slightly thickened, about 5 minutes; do not let boil. Remove from the heat and stir in the rum. Pour the sauce into a medium bowl, set it in a larger bowl of ice water and let

Crème Caramel with Strawberries

Lemon Flan with Lemon Sauce and Candied Zest

cool, stirring occasionally. As the mixture cools, gradually stir in 2 to 3 tablespoons of cold water until the sauce has a pourable consistency.

4. Make the candied lemon zest: Using a lemon zester, strip the zest from the lemons. In a small saucepan of boiling water, blanch the zest for 1 minute; drain. Repeat the blanching process two more times to remove the bitterness. Transfer the zest to paper towels and pat dry.

5. In a heavy medium saucepan, combine 1 cup of the sugar with ¼ cup of water. Stir over moderate heat to dissolve the sugar, then boil the syrup until it reaches 238° on a candy thermometer, about 7 minutes. Remove from the heat and stir in the lemon zest. Drain the zest and transfer to a bowl. Toss the zest with the remaining ½ cup sugar until coated. (MAKE AHEAD: The recipe can be prepared to this point up to 1 day ahead. Cover and refrigerate the flans and the lemon sauce separately. Cover the lemon zest and let stand at room temperature.)

6. Make the pastry crisps: Line a small baking sheet with parchment paper. In a small saucepan, melt the butter over low heat. Pour the butter into a small bowl, leaving the milky residue behind.

7. Spread 1 sheet of the phyllo dough on a work surface; keep the remaining sheets covered with a damp towel. Lightly brush the phyllo with the melted butter. Lay another sheet of phyllo on top and brush with butter. Repeat the process with the remaining phyllo and butter.

8. In a small bowl, combine the sugar and cinnamon. Using a 3-inch round pastry cutter or a glass, cut out 8 circles from the phyllo dough and transfer them to the prepared baking sheet. Sprinkle the circles with the cinnamon sugar and cover them with another sheet of parchment paper. Bake the phyllo circles for about 25 minutes until crisp and golden. Remove the top layer of parchment paper and let the circles cool on the baking sheet for up to 2 hours.

9. Assemble the dessert: Run a knife around the inside of each ramekin and invert the lemon flans onto plates. Top each of the lemon flans with a pastry crisp, sugared side up. Spoon the lemon sauce around the lemon flans and garnish each flan with the candied lemon zest and fresh mint leaves.—JAMIE SHANNON

APPLE CREPE SOUFFLE

These crêpes are filled with both apple puree and fluffy vanilla soufflé. Since crêpes keep very well, you can make them ahead. Wrap them tightly and refrigerate for up to two days or freeze for up to two months. You can also double the crêpe recipe to have extras on hand.

8 SERVINGS

CREPES:

- ½ cup plus 2 tablespoons milk
- 1 large egg, beaten
- ½ cup plus 2 tablespoons all-purpose flour, sifted
- 2 tablespoons unsalted butter, melted
- 1½ teaspoons sugar
- Pinch of salt
- 1 tablespoon vegetable oil

APPLE FILLING AND CALVADOS SAUCE:

- 2 Granny Smith, Mutsu, or Baldwin apples (about 1 pound)
- ¼ cup plus 2 tablespoons sugar
- 3 tablespoons unsalted butter
- 1½ teaspoons honey
- ⅛ teaspoon pure vanilla extract
- 1 teaspoon fresh lemon juice
- 2 tablespoons Calvados or other apple brandy

SOUFFLE FILLING:

- ¾ cup milk
- 3½ tablespoons sugar
- 4 tablespoons unsalted butter
- 3 tablespoons all-purpose flour
- 3 large eggs, separated
- ¼ teaspoon pure vanilla extract

- 2 tablespoons confectioners' sugar

1. Make the crêpes: In a medium bowl, whisk together the milk, egg, flour, butter, sugar, and salt until smooth. Let the batter rest at room temperature for 1 hour.

2. Heat a 6- or 7-inch crêpe pan or nonstick skillet over moderately high heat. Lightly coat the pan with some of the vegetable oil, wiping out any excess oil with a paper towel. Pour 2 tablespoons of batter into the center of the pan and, working quickly, tilt and rotate the pan to swirl the batter all around and coat the bottom evenly. Cook on 1 side until golden brown, about 2 minutes. Then flip the crêpe and cook the other side just until set, about 30 seconds. Transfer the crêpe to a baking sheet lined with wax paper. Continue making crêpes with the remaining batter, oiling the pan only when necessary. Transfer the crêpes to the baking sheet.

3. Make the apple filling: Peel, quarter, and core the apples. Cut them into ¼-inch dice (about 2 cups). In a medium bowl, sprinkle the diced apples with 2 tablespoons of the sugar and toss to coat. In a large, heavy, nonreactive skillet, melt 1 tablespoon of the butter over high heat until it begins to sizzle. Add the apples, honey, and vanilla, and cook, shaking the pan and stirring occasionally with a wooden spoon, until the apples turn a dark brown color, about 7 minutes. Transfer the mixture to a plate to cool slightly.

4. Meanwhile, **make the Calvados sauce:** In a small, heavy, nonreactive saucepan, combine the remaining ¼ cup sugar with the lemon juice and cook over moderately high heat, stirring occasionally, until the sauce turns a dark amber color, about 3 minutes. Immediately remove from the heat and, using a wooden spoon, stir in the remaining 2 tablespoons butter until well blended. Stir in the Calvados; be careful of splatters.

5. Make the soufflé filling: In a small saucepan, scald the milk and 2 tablespoons of the sugar over high heat. In another medium saucepan, melt the butter over moderately high heat. Using a whisk, stir in the flour and cook until golden and nutty, about 2 minutes. Whisk in the hot milk and stir until thick, about 1 minute. Remove from the heat.

6. In a medium bowl, stir the egg yolks just to mix. Stir a small amount of the flour mixture into the egg yolks, then add to the remaining flour mixture in the saucepan, stirring constantly until combined. Cook the soufflé base over moderate heat, stirring, until it thins slightly, just 1 minute. Remove from the heat and stir in the vanilla.

7. In a copper bowl, using a balloon whisk (or using an electric mixer) beat the egg whites into soft peaks. Add the remaining 1½ tablespoons sugar and beat until glossy, about 30 seconds longer. Stir one-third of the egg whites into the soufflé base, mixing well. Using a rubber spatula, gently fold the mixture into the remaining egg whites.

8. To assemble: Preheat the oven to 400°. Place the crêpes flat on a work surface with the paler sides facing up. Using a spoon, spread some of the apple filling down the center of each crêpe. Spread 2 rounded tablespoons of the soufflé mixture over the apple filling and roll up the crêpes. Place the rolled crêpes, seam side down, on a nonstick baking sheet. Sprinkle with confectioners' sugar and bake until lightly golden and puffed, about 7 minutes. Transfer the crêpes to dessert plates.

9. Rewarm the sauce over low heat and drizzle over the crêpes. Serve at once.—DIETER G. SCHORNER

LEMON SOUFFLE

4 TO 6 SERVINGS

- ½ cup granulated sugar
- 4 tablespoons unsalted butter
- ⅓ cup fresh lemon juice
- 4 large egg yolks
- 1 tablespoon finely grated lemon zest
- 5 large egg whites, at room temperature
- Confectioners' sugar, for dusting

1. In a medium nonreactive saucepan, combine ¼ cup of the granulated sugar, the butter, and the lemon juice, and cook over moderate heat, stirring, until the sugar and butter are melted. Remove from the heat and stir in the egg yolks one at a time, mixing well after each addition. Add the lemon zest and cook over moderately low heat, stirring, until slightly thickened, about 2 minutes. Do not boil or the lemon curd will curdle. (MAKE AHEAD: The recipe can be prepared to this point up to 4 hours ahead; press plastic wrap directly on the surface of the lemon curd and let stand at room temperature.)

2. Preheat the oven to 425°. Butter a 5-cup soufflé dish and freeze until set. Butter the dish again and coat with granulated sugar. Rewarm the lemon curd over moderately low heat, stirring, just until hot to the touch.

3. Meanwhile, in a medium bowl, beat the egg whites until soft peaks form. Add the remaining ¼ cup granulated sugar and continue beating until the whites are glossy and firm, about 1 minute longer. Stir one quarter of the egg whites into the lemon curd, then fold the mixture into the remaining whites just until combined.

4. Spoon the soufflé mixture into the prepared dish and smooth the surface. Run your thumb around the inside edge of the dish. Bake the soufflé in the lower third of the oven for about

Lemon Soufflé

13 minutes, until puffed, nicely browned on top, and set around the edges. Dust with confectioners' sugar and serve immediately.—ANNE WILLAN

HAZELNUT-PEAR SOUFFLE

4 TO 6 SERVINGS

- ½ cup hazelnuts (about 2½ ounces)
- 1 ripe medium pear
- 1 teaspoon fresh lemon juice
- ⅔ cup milk
- 2 large egg yolks
- 3 tablespoons granulated sugar
- 2 tablespoons all-purpose flour
- 4 large egg whites, at room temperature

Confectioners' sugar, for dusting

1. Preheat the oven to 350°. Spread the hazelnuts on a baking sheet and toast for about 12 minutes, until the skins are blistered. Wrap the hazelnuts in a dish towel and rub vigorously to remove the skins. Let cool completely. Transfer the hazelnuts to a food processor and pulse until the nuts are finely ground but not a paste. Increase the oven temperature to 425°.

2. Peel, quarter, and core the pear. Rub the quarters with the lemon juice, transfer them to the food processor, and puree until smooth.

3. Bring the milk just to a boil in a medium saucepan; keep warm. In a medium bowl, whisk the egg yolks with 1½ tablespoons of the granulated sugar until thick and pale, 1 to 2 minutes. Whisk in the flour. Whisk in half of the hot milk, then whisk the mixture back into the remaining milk. Cook over moderate heat, whisking constantly, until thickened, 1 to 2 minutes. Continue cooking this pastry cream, stirring, until it thins slightly (indicating that the flour is cooked), about 2 minutes longer. Let cool slightly, then stir in the hazelnuts and the pear puree. (MAKE AHEAD: The recipe can be prepared to this point up to 4 hours ahead; press plastic wrap directly on the surface of the hazelnut mixture and let stand at room temperature.)

4. Brush a 5-cup soufflé dish with butter and freeze until set. Butter the dish again. Rewarm the hazelnut mixture over moderately low heat, stirring, just until hot to the touch.

5. Meanwhile, in a medium bowl, beat the egg whites until soft peaks form. Add the remaining 1½ tablespoons granulated sugar and continue beating until the whites are glossy and firm, about 1 minute longer. Whisk one quarter of the egg whites into the hazelnut mixture, then fold the mixture into the remaining whites just until combined.

6. Spoon the hazelnut-pear soufflé mixture into the prepared dish and smooth the surface. Run your thumb around the inside edge of the soufflé dish. Bake the soufflé in the lower third of the oven for about 18 minutes, until it is puffed, nicely browned on top, and set around the edges. Dust the soufflé with confectioners' sugar and serve immediately. —ANNE WILLAN

BEATING SOUFFLES

The bowl and beater you use will affect the volume and texture of the whipped egg whites. A copper bowl and a balloon whisk will produce optimal results: six egg whites whipped with a balloon whisk will yield about six cups of whipped whites, about one cup more than if whipped in a stainless bowl with an electric mixer. (Copper helps stabilize the egg whites during beating, and the high circular motion of a balloon whisk incorporates more air.) Be sure the equipment you use is clean and dry.—ANNE WILLAN

ROASTED WHOLE PINEAPPLE

Here, a whole ripe pineapple studded with vanilla beans is roasted in a caramel syrup infused with vanilla, rum, and banana. The roasted pineapple is equally delicious served hot or cold. The halved vanilla beans used to stud the pineapple can be rinsed, dried, and reused.

8 SERVINGS

CARAMELIZED VANILLA SYRUP:

- ⅔ cup sugar
- 2 Tahitian vanilla beans, split lengthwise and halved crosswise
- 6 thin slices of fresh ginger
- 3 whole allspice berries, freshly ground
- 3 tablespoons pureed ripe banana
- 2 tablespoons dark rum

- 1 ripe pineapple (3 pounds)
- 5 Tahitian vanilla beans, halved crosswise

Vanilla ice cream, for serving

1. Make the caramelized vanilla syrup: Put the sugar in a small heavy saucepan or casserole and cook over low heat, undisturbed, until a deep amber caramel forms, about 25 minutes. Add the quartered Tahitian vanilla beans, the slices of fresh ginger, and the allspice to the caramel; 5 seconds later, pour in 1 scant cup of water to stop the caramel from cooking further. Stir to dissolve the caramel, then bring the syrup to a boil and remove the saucepan from the heat.

2. Stir 1 tablespoon of the caramel syrup into the banana puree, then mix the puree into the syrup in the pan along with the dark rum. Stir well, then pour the syrup into a glass jar, cover, and refrigerate. (MAKE AHEAD: The syrup can be made up to 3 days ahead.)

3. Preheat the oven to 450°. Peel the pineapple with a sharp knife. Make 10 angled incisions all around the fruit and insert the halved Tahitian vanilla beans, leaving about 1 inch protruding. Set the pineapple on its side in a small glass baking dish and strain the chilled vanilla syrup over it.

4. Roast the pineapple in the oven for about 1 hour, turning and basting it with the vanilla syrup every 15 minutes. The pineapple is done when it feels tender when pierced. Remove the roasted pineapple from the oven and let cool slightly.

5. To serve, slice the roasted pineapple crosswise ½ inch thick. Spoon the caramelized vanilla syrup over the fruit and serve on its own or with vanilla ice cream.—PIERRE HERME

PINEAPPLE WITH GINGER SYRUP LF

6 SERVINGS

- ½ cup sugar
- 18 nickel-size peeled rounds of fresh ginger
- 1-inch strips of lemon zest from ½ lemon
- ¼ cup plus 1 tablespoon sweet white dessert wine, such as Late Harvest Riesling
- 1 large ripe pineapple—peeled, quartered lengthwise, cored, and sliced crosswise ½ inch thick
- 2 teaspoons coarsely chopped fresh mint

In a nonreactive saucepan, combine the sugar, the fresh ginger rounds, the lemon zest, ¼ cup of the sweet white dessert wine, and 1 cup of water, and boil over moderately high heat until the liquid is reduced to ⅔ cup, about 5 minutes. Let the ginger syrup cool for 20 minutes, then strain it into a bowl and add the pineapple slices. Refrigerate until chilled, at least 1 hour or up to 8 hours. Spoon the pineapple and the ginger syrup into tall glasses. Drizzle with the remaining 1 tablespoon wine and garnish with chopped mint.—MATTHEW KENNEY

ORANGE-GLAZED PINEAPPLE LF

4 SERVINGS

- 4 fresh pineapple rings, ½ inch thick
- ¼ cup sugar
- ½ cup strained fresh orange juice
- ⅛ teaspoon pure vanilla extract
- 1 pint nonfat vanilla frozen yogurt

1. Preheat the broiler or heat a cast-iron grill pan over moderately high heat. Sprinkle each pineapple ring with 1 teaspoon of sugar and broil or grill, sugared side toward the heat, for about 3 minutes, until nicely browned and the sugar is bubbling. Transfer to a plate.

2. Mix the orange juice with the remaining sugar in a small nonreactive saucepan. Bring to a boil over moderate heat and cook until the liquid is reduced by half, about 5 minutes. Stir in the vanilla extract. Spoon 1 teaspoon of the glaze over each pineapple ring and let stand at room temperature for at least 1 hour or up to 4 hours.

3. Shortly before serving, rewarm the pineapple rings under the broiler until hot and bubbly. Transfer to individual plates. Reheat the remaining orange glaze and spoon over the pineapple rings. Serve warm with frozen yogurt.—MARGE POORE

Pineapple with Ginger Syrup

CHEVRE COEUR A LA CREME WITH BERRIES

This classic French dessert is traditionally made with a cream or curd cheese. It is formed in a heart-shaped porcelain mold that has perforations on the bottom for draining excess moisture. There is not a significant amount of drainage in this recipe, so you can substitute regular ramekins. Here fresh goat cheese adds a subtle tang. Try to find a low-salt variety at the farmers' market. Be sure to allow enough time to let the cheese firm up overnight.

6 TO 8 SERVINGS

½ cup heavy cream, well chilled
6 ounces cream cheese, softened
6 ounces fresh low-salt goat cheese, softened
2 tablespoons confectioners' sugar
Raspberry Sauce (recipe follows)
1 pint assorted fresh berries, such as strawberries, blueberries, and red currants, for garnish
Mint sprigs, for garnish

1. Line six or eight ½-cup *coeur à la crème* molds or ramekins with dampened cheesecloth. In a medium bowl, beat the heavy cream to firm peaks.
2. In a large bowl, blend the softened cream cheese and goat cheese and the confectioners' sugar. Using a rubber spatula, fold in the whipped cream. Spoon the mixture into the prepared *coeur à la crème* molds and press gently; smooth the tops with the rubber spatula and fold the cheesecloth over the tops. Put the molds on a baking sheet and refrigerate overnight.
3. To serve, unmold each *coeur à la crème* onto a plate. Spoon 2 tablespoons of the Raspberry Sauce around each heart and garnish with berries and mint.

Raspberry Sauce

MAKES ABOUT 1 CUP

1½ pints raspberries
¼ cup sugar

In a food processor, puree the raspberries with the sugar. Scrape the mixture into a small nonreactive saucepan and bring to a boil over high heat, stirring often. Pass the sauce through a fine strainer to remove the seeds. Cool and refrigerate the sauce until needed. (MAKE AHEAD: The sauce can be made up to 1 day ahead.) —ODESSA PIPER

SLICED CANTALOUPE WITH COCONUT-PEACH CREAM

An orange-fleshed honeydew can be substituted for the cantaloupe.

4 TO 6 SERVINGS

1 ripe medium peach—peeled, pitted, and coarsely chopped
2 tablespoons sugar
⅔ cup unsweetened coconut milk
¼ cup sweetened shredded coconut
1 medium cantaloupe (about 2½ pounds)

1. In a food processor or blender, puree the peach with the sugar. Add the coconut milk and process until smooth. Refrigerate until chilled for at least 2 hours or overnight.
2. Preheat the oven to 400°. Spread the shredded coconut on a baking sheet and toast in the middle of the oven for about 5 minutes, stirring a few times, or until golden brown. Transfer to a plate and let cool.
3. Cut the cantaloupe in half crosswise and scrape out the seeds. Set the cantaloupe halves cut sides down and peel the skin with a sharp knife. Halve each

PICKING A RIPE MELON

Unlike most other fruits, a melon can't be judged by its appearance alone. Here are four tips to help you choose a ripe one:

- **PRESS IT—the flesh at the stem end should yield only slightly.**
- **SMELL IT—the fragrance at the stem end should be pleasant without being too strong.**
- **HOLD IT—the heavier the melon, the juicier the flesh.**
- **SHAKE IT—nothing should rattle; if you sense seeds or juices moving, the melon is overripe.**

It's easier to judge the ripeness of a cut melon. Look for:

- **Flesh that smells FRAGRANT.**
- **Flesh that is MOIST.**
- **Flesh that has a RICH UNIFORM COLOR. Streaks of green near the rind mean that the melon isn't ripe enough; watery or translucent streaks indicate that it is overripe.**
- **SEEDS THAT ARE INTACT. If the seeds have fallen off and clump together, the melon is probably over the hill.**

half, then slice the quarters ¼ inch thick. Arrange the cantaloupe on a large plate or platter. Stir the coconut-peach cream and drizzle it over the melon. Sprinkle the toasted coconut on top.—MARCIA KIESEL

ORANGE HONEYDEWS FILLED WITH RED WINE SYRUP

4 SERVINGS

2 cups full-flavored red wine, such as Côtes du Rhône or Zinfandel
½ cup sugar
3-inch piece of cinnamon stick
2 medium orange-fleshed honeydew melons or cantaloupes (about 2½ pounds each)

1. In a medium nonreactive saucepan, combine the wine, sugar, and cinnamon. Bring to a boil over high heat and cook until reduced by half, about 12 minutes. Remove the cinnamon and let the syrup cool to room temperature. (MAKE AHEAD: The syrup can be refrigerated, covered, for up to 1 week.)
2. Halve the melons crosswise and discard the seeds. Cut a thin slice from the bottom of each melon half so that it sits upright and set each half on a plate. Pour the red wine syrup into the melon halves and serve with large spoons.—MARCIA KIESEL

GINGER-SPICED MELONS WITH SPARKLING WINE

Casaba melons make a fragrant alternative to Crenshaws and provide the same colorful contrast to the honeydew cubes.

6 SERVINGS

1 vanilla bean, split
2 tablespoons finely chopped fresh ginger
3 tablespoons honey
½ medium Crenshaw melon
½ medium honeydew melon
1 bottle (750 ml) sparkling wine or brut Champagne

1. In a small saucepan, combine the vanilla bean, ginger, and 2 cups of water, and bring to a boil over high heat. Cover, remove from the heat, and let steep for 15 minutes. Strain the liquid into a small bowl and stir in the honey until it is dissolved. Let the syrup cool to room temperature. (MAKE AHEAD: The syrup can be refrigerated, covered, for up to 3 days.)
2. Peel the Crenshaw melon and cut it into ½-inch slices. Cut the slices into ½-inch dice; you should have about 3 cups. Repeat the process with the honeydew. In a large bowl, combine the diced melons, pour in the syrup, and let macerate in the refrigerator for 10 to 20 minutes.
3. To serve, spoon the melon cubes and syrup into 6 long-stemmed glasses. Fill the glasses with the sparkling wine and serve.—MARCIA KIESEL

CHILLED ORANGE-CANTALOUPE SOUP Q

4 SERVINGS

2 ripe medium cantaloupes—peeled, seeded, and cut into large chunks
¼ cup plus 2 tablespoons superfine sugar
¼ cup plus 2 tablespoons fresh orange juice
½ teaspoon finely grated orange zest
2 tablespoons slivered fresh mint
Sugar cookies (optional), for serving

In a blender, working in batches, combine the cantaloupes, superfine sugar, fresh orange juice, and grated orange zest, and blend

MELON VARIETIES

In the United States, melons are generally divided into three categories: MUSKMELONS, or melons with netted skin, such as American cantaloupes; WINTER MELONS (so-called because they ripen into the winter), which include honeydews, Crenshaws, and casabas; and, believe it or not, in a category by themselves, WATERMELONS. While muskmelons and winter melons have a hollow in the center that houses the seeds, watermelons are solid with seeds scattered throughout their flesh.

America's most popular melons are cantaloupes, honeydews, and watermelons. But because melons are easy to crossbreed, newer hybrids in an extensive range of sizes and shapes are entering the American marketplace. These melons include orange-fleshed honeydews, light green-fleshed Santa Claus melons, and yellow-fleshed Orchid Sweet watermelons.

until smooth. Transfer to a large bowl and refrigerate until chilled for at least 45 minutes. Serve the cantaloupe soup in shallow bowls or large cups, garnished with the mint and accompanied with the cookies.—JUDITH SUTTON

MELON SALAD

Using a long sharp knife, cut small pineapples in half lengthwise through the green leafy crowns and the fruit. With a paring knife, cut out the pineapple flesh; reserve it for another use. Scoop out balls of green honeydew and seedless watermelon with a melon baller. Toss with chopped fresh mint and mound in the pineapple halves. Garnish with more mint and strips of lemon zest.—GENE MEYER

ORANGE SALAD WITH CINNAMON

6 SERVINGS

- 4 medium navel oranges
- 1 tablespoon sugar
- ½ teaspoon cinnamon
- 1 tablespoon orange flower water*
- ½ cup coarsely chopped walnuts or almonds
- Fresh mint leaves, for garnish

*Available at Middle Eastern markets and specialty food stores

Using a small sharp knife, peel the oranges, removing all the bitter white pith. Slice the oranges crosswise about ⅓ inch thick. Arrange them in a shallow serving bowl and sprinkle with the sugar, cinnamon, and orange flower water. Garnish the fruit salad with the chopped nuts and mint leaves.—FATIMA HAL

ORANGES IN CARAMEL SYRUP

Light and refreshing, this fruit dessert is simple yet elegant enough for company—and it contains no fat.

8 SERVINGS

- ⅔ cup plus ½ cup sugar
- 8 large or 10 medium seedless oranges
- Mint sprigs, for garnish

1. Lightly oil a baking sheet. In a small, deep, heavy saucepan, bring ½ cup of the sugar and 3 tablespoons of water to a boil over moderately high heat, stirring with a wooden spoon to dissolve the sugar. Wash down the sides of the pan with a wet pastry brush. Boil without stirring until the caramel turns a golden amber color, about 5 minutes. Immediately pour the caramel onto the oiled baking sheet and tilt the baking sheet to spread it as thin as possible. (Use a pot holder; the caramel will heat the baking sheet very quickly.) Let cool thoroughly.

2. Using any handy utensil, break up the cooled caramel into 1- to 2-inch pieces. (Be careful, the shards will be sharp.) In a food processor, pulse the caramel shards until they are finely chopped; do not overprocess. Store the caramel chips in an airtight container until ready to use or for up to 1 week. (If the caramel chips stick together, you can shake the container to break them up.)

3. Using a small sharp knife, peel the oranges, removing all of the bitter white pith. Working over a heatproof bowl, cut between the membranes to release the orange sections. Measure out ½ cup of the orange juice.

4. Bring the remaining ⅔ cup sugar and ¼ cup of water to a boil in a small, deep, heavy saucepan over moderately high heat, stirring to dissolve the sugar. Wash down the sides of the pan with a wet pastry brush. Boil without stirring until the caramel turns a golden amber color, 5 to 7 minutes.

5. Remove the caramel from the heat and add the reserved ½ cup orange juice; stand back to avoid spatters. Stir the mixture with a wooden spoon, then cook over low heat, stirring, until smooth. Remove from the heat and let cool slightly. Pour the caramel sauce over the orange sections, cover, and refrigerate for at least 2 hours or overnight, stirring occasionally.

6. To serve, arrange the orange slices in dessert bowls. Spoon some of the juices over the oranges and sprinkle the caramel chips on top. Garnish with mint sprigs.—JUDITH SUTTON

MACERATED MIXED FRESH FRUIT

Macedonia di Stagione

If you will be using the maraschino liqueur called for below, reduce the lemon juice to 1 tablespoon.

12 SERVINGS

- 1½ cups fresh orange juice
- 2 or 3 tablespoons fresh lemon juice
- Grated zest of 1 lemon
- 2 apples
- 2 pears

Oranges in Caramel Syrup

Taboulleh with Ratatouille of Fresh Fruit

2 bananas
2 pounds other seasonal fruit, such as seedless grapes, mangoes, and pineapple, in as varied an assortment as possible
⅓ to ½ cup sugar
½ cup maraschino liqueur (optional)
3 tablespoons toasted walnuts or blanched almonds, coarsely chopped (optional)

In a large serving bowl, combine the orange juice, lemon juice, and lemon zest. Peel and core or pit the fruit, as applicable, and cut it into ½-inch cubes; add each fruit to the bowl as it is cut. (If using berries of any sort, don't add them until shortly before serving.) Add the sugar and the maraschino liqueur to the fruit and toss gently but thoroughly. Cover and refrigerate for at least 4 hours but no longer than 8 hours. To serve, toss the fruit salad several times and garnish with the toasted nuts.—MARCELLA HAZAN

TABBOULEH WITH RATATOUILLE OF FRESH FRUIT

In this refreshingly light and playful fat-free dessert, the couscous soaks up juice just as bulgur soaks up water in traditional tabbouleh salads.

6 SERVINGS

TABBOULEH:

- ¾ cup instant couscous
- 1 cup guava nectar or passion fruit juice, at room temperature
- 2 tablespoons superfine sugar, or more to taste
- ½ cup fresh orange juice, strained

MANGO AND RASPBERRY COULIS:

- 1 ripe mango—peeled, fruit sliced off the pit, and chopped
- 3 tablespoons granulated sugar
- 2 tablespoons plus 1 teaspoon fresh lemon juice
- ½ cup fresh or unsweetened frozen raspberries

FRESH FRUIT RATATOUILLE:

- 3 kiwi fruits, peeled and cut into ¼-inch dice
- 1 cup finely diced cantaloupe (¼ inch)
- 1 cup finely diced strawberries (¼ inch)
- 1 cup finely diced pineapple (¼ inch)

1. Make the tabbouleh: In a medium bowl, stir the couscous with the guava nectar and sugar. (If using passion fruit juice, you may need to add a bit more sugar.) Cover and set aside until all the juice has been absorbed by the couscous, about 2 hours. Stir in the orange juice and let stand until absorbed, about 20 minutes longer.

2. Make the mango and raspberry coulis: In a food processor, puree the mango with 1½ tablespoons of the sugar and 2 tablespoons of the lemon juice. Pass the puree through a fine strainer. Clean the processor bowl and add the raspberries along with the remaining 1½ tablespoons sugar and 1 teaspoon lemon juice. Puree the berries and pass the sauce through a fine strainer. (MAKE AHEAD: The recipe can be prepared to this point up to 1 day ahead. Cover and refrigerate the couscous and the two *coulis* separately.)

3. Set six 2-inch-deep 3½-inch ring molds or six 8-ounce pineapple cans with tops and bases removed on a stainless steel baking sheet. Lightly fluff up the couscous and spoon it evenly into the 6 ring molds. Press the couscous down at an angle so there is a higher side and a very low side about ¼ inch tall.

4. Make the ratatouille and assemble the dessert: In a medium bowl, toss all of the diced fruits together. Spoon the fresh fruit ratatouille on top of the couscous in each mold, pressing to form an even layer.

5. Use a wide spatula to transfer each of the ring molds to a dessert plate. Carefully lift off the ring molds so that the ratatouille-topped couscous is freestanding. Spoon the mango *coulis* around the base of the couscous on each of the plates. Dot the mango *coulis* with raspberry *coulis* and serve.—JOACHIM SPLICHAL

CHAPTER 21

OTHER DESSERTS

Chocolate Crème Caramel

CHOCOLATE CREME CARAMEL

Since this dessert must be refrigerated overnight, you'll have to make it the day before serving. Be sure to scrape the delicious caramel sauce from the bottom of the ramekins when you unmold these custards.

8 SERVINGS

- 1 cup plus 2 tablespoons sugar
- 6 ounces bittersweet chocolate, finely chopped
- 2 cups milk
- ½ vanilla bean, split
- 3 large eggs, at room temperature
- 3 large egg yolks, at room temperature

1. Preheat the oven to 325°. In a small, deep, heavy saucepan, bring ½ cup plus 2 tablespoons of the sugar and 3 tablespoons of water to a boil over moderately high heat, stirring occasionally with a wooden spoon to dissolve the sugar. Wash down the sides of the pan with a wet pastry brush. Boil without stirring until the caramel turns a dark golden amber color, 6 to 8 minutes.

2. Immediately pour the hot caramel into eight 6-ounce ramekins and swirl to coat the bottoms of the dishes evenly. Place the ramekins in a baking pan large enough to hold them without touching.

3. Put the chocolate in a medium heatproof bowl. Pour the milk into a medium saucepan. Scrape the seeds from the vanilla bean into the milk, add the pod and whisk to combine. Bring the milk just to a boil over moderate heat; remove the vanilla bean pod and reserve for another use.

CARAMEL KNOWLEDGE

Essentially, caramel is sugar that is cooked until it liquefies and begins to color. This sounds simple, but since cooking sugar can be tricky, it's best to know a few things before you begin working.

COMBINE SUGAR AND WATER. **Although you can make caramel by heating and stirring sugar until it melts, this "dry" version cooks unevenly and is likely to burn. Instead, dissolve the sugar in a little water and then cook the mixture until the liquid evaporates and the sugar caramelizes.**

USE THE RIGHT POT. **A heavy saucepan will heat more evenly, and the deeper the pot the better: The high sides will help shield you from the boiling sugar. Caramel is extremely hot—between 320° and 375°—and it will stick to your skin, so use caution, especially when adding a liquid, such as heavy cream or fruit juice, to make a sauce. Stand back to avoid spatters.**

AVOID CRYSTALLIZATION. **When you start cooking, melt the sugar thoroughly, stirring occasionally with a wooden spoon (a metal one will be too hot to hold). You can tell when the sugar is dissolved—you will no longer hear a gritty sound as you stir. Watch carefully: a single undissolved granule can cause an entire batch of syrup to crystallize, or turn into sugary lumps, as it cooks. After the syrup comes to a boil, carefully wash down the sides of the pan with a pastry brush dipped in warm water to dissolve any sugar crystals that may still be clinging there. Then cook without stirring until the syrup begins to caramelize. If you see a build-up of syrup on the inside of the saucepan, wash down the sides again as necessary. Don't overdo it, though. Not only will you be lowering the temperature of the cooked syrup, but also adding moisture just when you're trying to make it evaporate.**

WATCH THE COLOR. **Once the syrup begins to color, it will darken rapidly. Because the caramel is hotter around the edges than in the center, it will darken unevenly. Swirl the pan to even out the color. When the caramel reaches the cooking stage you desire (see "Three Stages of Caramel," p. 461), remove from the heat at once. You can use a candy thermometer (available at kitchenware stores) to determine the correct temperature for each stage, but it's easier to go by color. If you use a light-colored pan, you can see the color easily. If you use a copper sugar pot or other dark pan, you may want to spoon a very small amount of the syrup onto a white heatproof plate to gauge doneness. The caramel will continue to cook off the heat, so err on the light side. Sometimes the choice between medium or dark is simply a matter of taste—caramel ice cream, for example, can be made with either. Don't let the caramel get too dark, though, or it will be inedibly bitter. Use the caramel at once, or stop the cooking by plunging the pan into a bowl of ice water.**—JUDITH SUTTON

Pour the hot milk over the chocolate and let sit for 30 seconds. Whisk until smooth.
4. In a large bowl, whisk the whole eggs and egg yolks with the remaining ½ cup sugar until well blended. Gradually whisk in the melted chocolate. Strain the custard into a large measuring cup, then pour the custard into the caramel-lined ramekins.
5. Set the baking pan in the lower third of the oven and pour enough hot water into the pan to reach about halfway up the sides of the ramekins. Bake for 30 to 35 minutes, or until the custards are just set; the centers of the custards should still wiggle slightly when touched. Transfer the ramekins to a rack to cool. Cover with plastic wrap and refrigerate overnight.
6. To serve, fill a heatproof bowl with hot water. Run a thin knife around each custard and dip the bottom of each ramekin in the hot water. Invert the custards onto plates. Scrape any caramel remaining in the ramekins over the custards.—JUDITH SUTTON

COFFEE CREME CARAMEL *LF*

4 SERVINGS

- 1 cup sugar
- 2 large eggs
- 3 large egg whites
- One 12-ounce can evaporated skim milk
- ¼ cup coarsely ground coffee beans
- ¼ cup heavy cream
- ½ teaspoon pure vanilla extract

1. Preheat the oven to 350°. Line a baking sheet with parchment paper.
2. In a small heavy saucepan, cook ⅔ cup of the sugar over moderately low heat without stirring until it is melted and deep golden, about 12 minutes. Working quickly, pour about 1 tablespoon of the caramel into each of four ⅔-cup ramekins. Drizzle the remaining caramel over the parchment paper on the baking sheet and let stand at room temperature to harden.
3. In a bowl, whisk the eggs with the egg whites and the remaining ⅓ cup sugar until combined. In a small saucepan, warm the evaporated skim milk and the ground coffee beans over moderate heat until steaming, about 3 minutes. Let stand for 1 minute. Whisk the steamed milk into the egg mixture, then whisk in the heavy cream and the vanilla extract.
4. Strain the coffee custard, then pour it into the ramekins and set them in a baking dish. Add enough cold water to the dish to reach three-quarters of the way up the sides of the ramekins. Bake for about 35 minutes, or until the custards are almost set. Allow the custards to cool in the water bath. Cover and refrigerate the coffee crème caramels until they are chilled, for at least 2 hours or overnight. (MAKE AHEAD: The caramel pieces can stand at room temperature, covered, overnight.)
5. To serve, dip the bottom of each ramekin in hot water, then run a knife around each of the coffee crème caramels and invert them onto individual plates. Break the hardened caramel into large pieces and arrange the pieces decoratively around the custards.—DIANA STURGIS

VANILLA TAPIOCA PUDDING

6 SERVINGS

- One 14-ounce can unsweetened coconut milk
- 1 vanilla bean, split
- 2½ cups milk
- 1½ cups sugar
- ¼ cup quick-cooking tapioca
- ¼ teaspoon salt
- 2 large eggs

1. Put the can of coconut milk in the refrigerator until well chilled, about 30 minutes. In a medium saucepan, cook the vanilla bean in the milk over moderate heat, stirring, until hot, about 5 minutes. Stir in the sugar, the quick-cooking tapioca, and the salt. Cover the saucepan and remove from the heat. Let stand for 5 minutes. Uncover and bring to a boil over moderate heat, stirring frequently.
2. Meanwhile, in a medium bowl, whisk the eggs. Whisk in 1 cup of the hot milk. Pour the egg mixture into the saucepan and bring to a simmer, whisking constantly. Pour the pudding into a medium heatproof bowl and let it stand, stirring, until it is slightly cooled, about 10 minutes. Remove the vanilla bean, scraping the seeds from each half into the pudding; stir to incorporate. Rinse the vanilla bean and save for another use.
3. Open the can of chilled coconut milk and, without stirring it, spoon off ½ cup of the thick cream that has risen to the top; save the remaining coconut milk for another use. Stir the coconut cream into the pudding until it is thoroughly incorporated. Spoon the pudding into six ½-cup

ramekins, cups, or glasses. Refrigerate the puddings overnight; if desired, cover the tops with plastic wrap to prevent a skin from forming.—MARCIA KIESEL

RICH CHOCOLATE MOUSSE Q

4 SERVINGS

- 4 ounces imported bittersweet chocolate, coarsely chopped
- 1 cup plus 2 tablespoons heavy cream
- 2 tablespoons Kahlúa or other coffee liqueur

1. Melt the chocolate in a small bowl set over a pan of barely simmering water, stirring until smooth. Remove the pan from the heat and let cool to tepid.
2. In a medium bowl, whip the heavy cream with the Kahlúa just until soft peaks form. Stir about 3 tablespoons of the whipped cream into the melted bittersweet chocolate, then fold in the remaining whipped cream, reserving ¼ cup for garnish; do not overwork, or the mousse will be grainy. Cover and refrigerate the chocolate mousse and remaining whipped cream until chilled, at least 30 minutes.
3. Spoon the mousse into bowls and garnish each serving with a dollop of the reserved whipped cream.—JUDITH SUTTON

CHESTNUT-CHOCOLATE PUREE WITH WHIPPED CREAM

Monte Bianco

On days when Milan's veil of gray miraculously dissolves, the eye is irresistibly drawn up to the perpetually white summit of Mont Blanc, gleaming like a frosty mirage in the northern sky. Monte Bianco, *as the mountain is called in Italian, has this namesake dessert, which appears on Milanese tables in the fall.*

12 SERVINGS

- 2 pounds fresh chestnuts
- About 2½ cups milk
- Salt
- 10 ounces imported semisweet chocolate, chopped
- ¼ cup rum
- 3 cups very cold heavy cream
- 1 tablespoon sugar

1. Wash the fresh chestnuts in cold water, then soak them in lukewarm water for 20 minutes to soften their shells. Using a sharp paring knife, make a shallow horizontal slash across the rounded side of each of the chestnuts.
2. Put the chestnuts in a medium saucepan and cover amply with water. Cover the saucepan and bring the water to a boil over high heat; boil for 25 minutes. Scoop the chestnuts out of the hot water a few at a time and peel them while they are still very warm; make sure you remove both the outer shell and the wrinkled inner skin. (Don't worry about keeping the nuts whole; you'll be pureeing them later.)
3. Put the peeled chestnuts in a clean saucepan with just enough milk to cover and a pinch of salt. Simmer steadily over moderate heat until all of the milk has been absorbed, about 20 minutes. Meanwhile, in a double boiler, melt the chopped semisweet chocolate.
4. Pass the peeled chestnuts through the large holes of a food mill into a bowl. Stir in the melted semisweet chocolate and the rum. Cover the bowl with plastic wrap and refrigerate until the chocolate chestnut puree is chilled, at least 1 hour. (MAKE AHEAD: The chocolate chestnut puree can be refrigerated for up to 1 day.)
5. Pass the chocolate chestnut puree through the food mill fitted with the same disk (or through a ricer), letting it drop onto a round serving platter. As the puree piles up, move the food mill so that you end up with a spiraled mound of puree. Do not pat or shape the mound of puree in any way.
6. In a chilled bowl and using a chilled whisk, beat the cream with the sugar until it holds its shape. Spoon half of the whipped cream onto the chestnut mound; it should reach about two-thirds of the way down and have a natural, "snowed-on" look. Serve the remaining whipped cream on the side. (MAKE AHEAD: The Monte Bianco can be refrigerated, uncovered, for up to 6 hours. Also refrigerate the remaining whipped cream.)—MARCELLA HAZAN

Chestnut-Chocolate Puree with Whipped Cream

BREAD PUDDING WITH WHISKEY SAUCE

This Southern classic can be served hot or warm from the oven, or it can be made early in the day and served at room temperature. The whiskey sauce, however, must be warm.

12 SERVINGS

BREAD PUDDING:

- ½ cup raisins
- ¼ cup bourbon
- 8 cups torn bite-size pieces of French bread (from 1 or 2 baguettes with a total weight of 1 pound)
- 5 cups milk
- 1 cinnamon stick
- 1 teaspoon pure vanilla extract
- 6 large eggs
- 1 cup sugar

WHISKEY SAUCE:

- 1 large egg
- ½ cup sugar
- 1 stick (8 tablespoons) unsalted butter, melted
- Reserved bourbon from soaking the raisins, plus more if needed

1. Make the bread pudding: Soak the raisins in the bourbon for at least 30 minutes or overnight if possible.

2. Preheat the oven to 350°. Butter a 3-quart baking dish, such as a 9-by-13-inch rectangular glass dish. Put the torn bite-size pieces of French bread in a large bowl. Drain the raisins and add them to the bread; reserve the bourbon soaking liquid for making the whiskey sauce.

3. In a medium saucepan, combine the milk, the cinnamon stick, and the vanilla extract, and cook over moderate heat until bubbles just begin to break the surface.

4. Beat the eggs with the sugar until well blended, then gradually stir in the scalded milk. Pour the mixture over the bread pieces and the raisins, and discard the cinnamon stick. Let the bread soak for 10 minutes.

5. Fill the baking dish with the soaked bread pieces, patting them even. Set the baking dish inside a larger roasting pan and pour enough hot water into the pan to reach 1 inch up the sides of the baking dish. Bake the pudding for about 45 minutes, or until a knife inserted in the center comes out clean.

6. Meanwhile, **make the whiskey sauce:** In a medium heatproof bowl set over simmering water, whisk the egg with the sugar until very light and nearly doubled in volume, about 3 minutes. Whisk in the melted butter, a little at a time, then whisk in the reserved bourbon (if you don't have ¼ cup, add enough to make up for what was absorbed by the raisins). Remove the pan from the heat but keep the sauce warm over the water.

7. To serve, rewarm the whiskey sauce in the double boiler if necessary. Cut the bread pudding into 12 pieces and transfer the pudding pieces to dessert plates. Drizzle the warm whiskey sauce on top.—JOHN MARTIN TAYLOR

Parfait Marquise

PARFAIT MARQUISE

6 SERVINGS

- 1 pint fresh strawberries, hulled and sliced
- 1 pint fresh raspberries
- 5 tablespoons confectioners' sugar
- 4 ounces fresh goat cheese, softened
- 4 ounces cream cheese, softened
- 2 tablespoons vanilla yogurt

1. Toss the strawberries and the raspberries with 2 tablespoons of the confectioners' sugar and set aside for 45 minutes.

2. In a bowl, combine the softened goat cheese and cream cheese. Add the vanilla yogurt and the remaining 3 tablespoons sugar and mix well. Drain the

Bread Pudding with Whiskey Sauce

Candied Ginger Cannoli Sandwiches

strawberries and raspberries and beat the juices into the cheese mixture. Layer the berries with the cheese mixture in stemmed glasses.—ANGELE PARLANGE

Cranberry-Orange Cheesecake

CANDIED GINGER CANNOLI SANDWICHES

At Mesa Grill in New York City, Wayne Harley Brachman uses the unlikely combination of flour tortillas, mascarpone, and candied ginger to create a deliciously rich and surprisingly easy dessert. If you don't have a four-inch round pastry cutter, use a large can or a wide glass.

4 SERVINGS

Four 8- or 9-inch flour tortillas
2 tablespoons granulated sugar
1 teaspoon cinnamon
Vegetable oil, for frying
1 cup mascarpone (about ½ pound), at room temperature
⅓ cup plus 1 teaspoon confectioners' sugar
2 ounces candied ginger, finely chopped
½ teaspoon pure vanilla extract

1. Using a 4-inch round pastry cutter, cut out 2 circles from each tortilla. In a small bowl, combine the granulated sugar and cinnamon.

2. In a medium skillet, heat ¾ inch of vegetable oil over moderate heat until very hot but not smoking. Add 2 or 3 tortilla rounds and fry, pressing them down in the oil with a slotted spoon, for 20 seconds. Let the rounds rise to the surface and cook until lightly golden on the bottom, about 1 minute. Turn the rounds over and cook until golden, about 30 seconds longer. Transfer to paper towels and generously sprinkle the tops with some of the cinnamon sugar. Repeat with the remaining tortilla rounds and cinnamon sugar.

3. In a medium bowl, combine the mascarpone, ⅓ cup of the confectioners' sugar, the candied ginger, and the vanilla extract. (MAKE AHEAD: The recipe can be prepared to this point up to 4 hours ahead. Cover and refrigerate the mascarpone filling. Let the tortilla rounds stand at room temperature.)

4. Arrange 4 tortilla rounds, sugared sides down, on a work surface. Spoon one-quarter of the filling on each round and top with the remaining rounds, sugared sides up. Sift the remaining 1 teaspoon confectioners' sugar on top and transfer to individual plates.—WAYNE HARLEY BRACHMAN

CRANBERRY-ORANGE CHEESECAKE

The tart bite of the fruit perfectly balances this creamy cheesecake. The cake is easier to cut when chilled.

12 TO 16 SERVINGS

1 cup dried cranberries (about 4 ounces)
1 cup fresh orange juice
3 pounds cream cheese, at room temperature

1½ cups sugar
1 vanilla bean, split
3 large eggs
1 cup sour cream
2 teaspoons finely grated orange zest

1. In a small bowl, cover the dried cranberries with hot water and let soak until softened, about 20 minutes; drain the cranberries well. Meanwhile, in a small nonreactive saucepan, bring the orange juice to a boil over moderately high heat. Cook until reduced to ¼ cup, about 20 minutes. Let cool.
2. Preheat the oven to 300°. Generously butter a 10-by-3-inch springform pan and coat thoroughly with sugar. Wrap the outside of the pan with foil to make it watertight.
3. Using a standing mixer fitted with a paddle or a hand-held electric mixer, beat the cream cheese on medium speed until light and fluffy. Add the sugar and, using a small knife, scrape in the seeds from the vanilla bean; reserve the bean for another use. Beat until thoroughly combined, then beat in the eggs one at a time, beating well after each addition. On low speed, beat the sour cream, reduced orange juice, drained cranberries, and orange zest into the batter and mix until incorporated.
4. Pour the batter into the prepared pan. Set the pan in a large roasting pan and pour enough hot water into the roasting pan to reach halfway up the sides of the cheesecake. Bake for about 1½ hours, or until the cake pulls away from the sides of the pan, the center is set, and the top is golden. Remove the pan from the water bath and let the cheesecake cool to room temperature. Cover and refrigerate overnight.
5. Remove the sides of the springform pan and transfer the cheesecake to a large serving plate. Serve chilled or at room temperature.—PATRICK CLARK

PETITS PAINS AU CHOCOLAT

Use a high-quality commercial all-butter puff pastry, such as Dufour, which is available in the freezer section of specialty food markets. Or purchase puff pastry dough from your local French bakery.

MAKES 16 PASTRIES

One 14- or 16-ounce package of cold puff pastry dough
12 ounces imported bittersweet or semisweet chocolate, broken into 3-by-1½-inch pieces
1 large egg, beaten

Preheat the oven to 425°. Line 2 baking sheets with parchment paper. Lightly roll out the puff pastry ⅛ inch thick if using 14 ounces of dough or ¼ inch thick if using 16 ounces of dough. Cut the pastry into sixteen 3½-by-4½-inch rectangles. Place a piece of chocolate in the center of each rectangle and fold the long sides over the chocolate like a business letter. Seal the exposed edge with some of the beaten egg. Repeat with the remaining dough rectangles, chocolate, and egg wash. Arrange 8 pastries on each baking sheet. Refrigerate 1 sheet of pastries and bake the other in the center of the oven for 10 minutes. Reduce the heat to 375° and bake for about 15 minutes longer, or until golden brown and cooked through. Transfer the *pains au chocolat* to a rack to cool slightly. Repeat with the remaining pastries. Serve slightly warm.—MARCIA KIESEL

CARAMELIZED FLAKY PASTRIES

This is one of Pierre Hermé's versions of a traditional pastry from Brittany called kouign amann *(queen-yaman), which literally means "bread and butter" in the local dialect. The rich, croissant-like dough is usually layered with sugar and baked as a large flat cake. To provide more caramelized sugar crunch, Hermé makes miniatures and bakes them in muffin tins. Everyone who has tasted them says they're irresistible.*

MAKES 24 PIECES

1 envelope (¼ ounce) active dry yeast
1½ cups warm water (115°F)
3½ cups bread flour
1 tablespoon coarse sea salt
3 sticks (¾ pound) cold unsalted butter plus 3½ tablespoons melted butter
1¾ cups granulated sugar for the dough plus more for sprinkling

1. In a small bowl, sprinkle the yeast into the warm water and stir to dissolve. In a large bowl, combine the flour and salt. Add the yeast mixture and stir rapidly to blend. Turn the dough out onto a floured work surface and knead until smooth, 2 to 3 minutes. Place the dough in a lightly oiled bowl and cover with plastic wrap. Set aside in a warm spot until the dough has risen slightly, about 30 minutes.

2. Meanwhile, on a large work surface, place the 3 sticks of butter side by side between 2 large pieces of wax paper. Using a rolling pin, press and roll them into a solid 7-inch square block.
3. On a lightly floured surface, roll out the dough into a 14-by-7½-inch rectangle about ½ inch thick. Set the block of butter in the center. Fold the short sides of the dough over the butter to completely enclose it (as if you were folding a business letter). Cover and let rest in the refrigerator for 20 minutes.
4. Return the dough to the floured work surface, seam side down. Roll out the dough to form the same size rectangle and fold it again, as above. Wrap the dough in plastic wrap and refrigerate for 1 hour.
5. Sprinkle ⅔ cup of the sugar on the work surface and set the dough on top, seam side down. Roll out again to a 14-by-7½-inch rectangle. Sprinkle some of the remaining sugar on top and fold the dough like a business letter, as above. Repeat the rolling and folding operation once more, sprinkling the remaining sugar over the work surface and the dough as you roll; refrigerate the dough for a few minutes at a time if the butter becomes too soft at any point during the process. Cover and refrigerate the dough for 30 minutes.
6. Lightly butter two 12-cup standard size muffin tins. On a lightly floured work surface, roll out the dough to a 12-by-10-inch rectangle about ½ inch thick. Using a sharp knife, cut the dough into twenty-four 3⅓-by-1½ inch rectangles.
7. Set each piece of dough in a muffin cup; the ends of the rectangles will reach up the sides of the muffin cups slightly. Brush lightly with the melted butter and sprinkle each rectangle with ¼ teaspoon sugar. Let the dough rise at room temperature until almost doubled in bulk, about 1½ hours.
8. Preheat the oven to 350°. Bake the mini *kouign amanns* for 30 to 40 minutes, or until they are golden brown. Unmold them at once and let cool on wire racks.—PIERRE HERME

WALNUT BAKLAVA

Though baklava is not a typical Moroccan dessert, versions do exist. This one comes from Fatima Hal's hometown of Oujda, where it was brought by the Turks.

MAKES ABOUT 40 PIECES

- 1 pound walnuts (about 4½ cups)
- 2 sticks (½ pound) unsalted butter, melted
- ¾ cup sugar
- 3 tablespoons rosewater* (optional)
- ½ teaspoon cinnamon
- 10 sheets of phyllo dough
- 40 whole blanched almonds (about 3½ ounces)
- 1 cup honey

*Available at Middle Eastern markets

1. Preheat the oven to 425°. Generously butter a baking dish, about 13-by-10½-inches. In a food processor, pulse the walnuts until coarsely chopped; do not overprocess to a paste. Transfer to a large bowl and stir in half the melted butter, the sugar, rosewater, and cinnamon.
2. Cover half of the phyllo sheets with a damp towel. Generously brush the remaining 5 phyllo sheets with melted butter and layer them in the prepared baking dish. Spread the walnut mixture on top. Butter the remaining phyllo sheets and layer them over the walnut filling; fold any overhanging phyllo over the top. Brush the top with any remaining melted butter.
3. Using a serrated knife and a gentle sawing motion, slice the baklava on the diagonal into 1½-inch-wide strips. Then slice on the diagonal in the opposite direction to form diamond shapes; you should have 40 diamonds. Top each of the diamonds with a whole almond. Bake the baklava in the center of the oven for about 25 minutes,

Walnut Baklava

Butter-Bourbon Sundae and Mexican Chocolate Sundae

or until the phyllo dough is crisp and golden brown.

4. Meanwhile, in a small saucepan, warm the honey gently over low heat. As soon as the baklava comes out of the oven, drizzle the warm honey all over the top and let the baklava cool to room temperature. (MAKE AHEAD: The baklava can be stored in an airtight container for up to 2 weeks.) —FATIMA HAL

WALNUT-CARAMEL SUNDAES

Heat the cream while the caramel cooks so that it can be added as soon as the caramel is removed from the heat; otherwise the sauce may burn.

4 SERVINGS

- ⅔ cup walnut halves
- ½ cup sugar
- ½ cup heavy cream
- Pinch of salt
- 1 pint vanilla ice cream

1. Preheat the oven to 400°. Toast the walnut halves for about 5 minutes, until they are fragrant. Coarsely chop the toasted walnuts.

2. In a heavy medium saucepan, bring the sugar and ¼ cup of water to a boil over high heat. Cook without stirring until the caramel turns a deep brown, about 7 minutes. Immediately remove from the heat.

3. Meanwhile, in a small saucepan, bring the heavy cream and the salt just to a boil over moderate heat. Slowly pour the hot cream into the caramel and stir gently until combined; be careful because the caramel may spatter. Stir in the chopped toasted walnuts and let cool.

4. Scoop the vanilla ice cream into 4 tall glasses or small bowls. Spoon the walnut-caramel sauce on top.—BOB CHAMBERS

BUTTER-BOURBON SUNDAES

4 SERVINGS

- 2 tablespoons light corn syrup
- 1 teaspoon fresh lemon juice
- 1 cup sugar
- 4 tablespoons unsalted butter
- 2 tablespoons bourbon
- ¼ teaspoon pure vanilla extract
- Vanilla, cookies-and-cream, vanilla-fudge, or coffee ice cream

1. In a medium nonreactive saucepan, combine the corn syrup, the fresh lemon juice, and 2 tablespoons of water. Stir in the sugar and bring to a boil over moderately high heat. Cook without stirring until the sauce turns golden amber, about 8 minutes; do not let the sauce get too dark. Immediately remove the saucepan from the heat and stir in the butter.

2. In a small bowl, combine the bourbon, the vanilla extract, and 3 tablespoons of water. Stir the mixture into the butterscotch sauce and let cool slightly before spooning over the ice cream and serving.—TRACEY SEAMAN

MEXICAN CHOCOLATE SUNDAES

This rich sauce, made with almond- and cinnamon-flavored sweet Mexican chocolate, can be combined instead with vanilla ice cream and soda water to make an ice cream soda.

4 SERVINGS

- 6 ounces Mexican chocolate,* such as Ibarra, coarsely chopped
- 2 tablespoons unsalted butter
- ¾ cup heavy cream
- Vanilla, coffee, or chocolate ice cream, for serving

*Available at specialty food stores and many supermarkets

In a medium bowl set over a saucepan of simmering water, melt the chopped Mexican chocolate and the butter in the heavy cream, stirring occasionally, until smooth. Do not let the sauce boil. Serve the sauce warm or at room temperature, with the ice cream.—TRACEY SEAMAN

PEANUT BUTTER-CHOCOLATE FUDGE SUNDAES

4 SERVINGS

- 6 ounces bittersweet chocolate, finely chopped
- ½ cup heavy cream
- 1 tablespoon light corn syrup
- ⅓ cup creamy peanut butter
- Vanilla, coffee, or cookies-and-cream ice cream, for serving

In a small bowl set over a small saucepan of simmering water, melt two-thirds of the chopped bittersweet chocolate in the heavy cream, stirring occasionally, until smooth. Remove the bowl from the heat. Add the remaining chocolate and the corn syrup and stir occasionally until the sauce is smooth. Stir in the peanut butter and serve the sauce over the ice cream.—TRACEY SEAMAN

CARAMEL SAUCE

For a delicious caramel sauce, you need only two ingredients, sugar and water, cooked to a medium caramel color (see "Three Stages of Caramel," p. 461). This sauce is naturally fat free. Add one more ingredient, cream, and you have a sauce that is richer but almost as simple.

MAKES ABOUT 1 CUP

- 1 cup sugar

1. In a small, deep, heavy saucepan, bring the sugar and ⅓ cup of water to a boil over moderately high heat, stirring occasionally to dissolve the sugar. Wash down the sides of the saucepan with a wet pastry brush. Boil without stirring until the caramel turns a golden amber color, 5 to 8 minutes.

2. Immediately remove the saucepan from the heat and add ½ cup of water; stand back to avoid spatters. Stir with a wooden spoon, then set the saucepan over low heat and cook, stirring, until the sauce is completely smooth, about 5 minutes. (For a thicker sauce, bring to a gentle boil and cook until slightly syrupy.) Remove from the heat and let cool. Serve the sauce warm or at room temperature. (MAKE AHEAD: The sauce will keep for up to 1 week; cover and refrigerate. Rewarm over low heat, stirring occasionally.)

FOR CREAMY CARAMEL SAUCE: Follow the recipe for Caramel Sauce, but add 1 cup heavy cream instead of the ½ cup water in Step 2. This will make about 1½ cups of Caramel Sauce. For a thinner sauce, increase the amount of cream by ½ cup; for a thicker sauce, decrease the cream by ¼ cup.—JUDITH SUTTON

HAZELNUT ICE CREAM

Buy the freshest hazelnuts you can get your hands on.

MAKES ABOUT 1½ QUARTS

- ½ cup hazelnuts (about 2½ ounces)
- 2 cups milk
- 2 large eggs, at room temperature
- ¾ cup sugar
- 2 cups heavy cream

Hazelnut Ice Cream, with Chocolate-Drizzled Shortbread (p. 375)

One 8-ounce jar of hazelnut butter,* at room temperature
1 teaspoon pure vanilla extract

*Available at health food stores

Instant Ice Cream Sandwiches

Spicy Pecan Ice Cream

Caramel-Swirl Ice Cream

1. Preheat the oven to 425°. Spread the hazelnuts on a baking sheet and toast in the middle of the oven for about 8 minutes, or until fragrant. Wrap the hot nuts in a kitchen towel and rub them vigorously together to remove most of the skins. Let cool, then coarsely chop.

2. In a heavy medium saucepan, heat 1 cup of the milk until it is steaming, about 4 minutes.

3. Meanwhile, in a medium bowl, whisk the eggs with the sugar until thickened and light in color, about 2 minutes. Gradually whisk in the hot milk. Pour the custard mixture into the saucepan and cook over moderate heat, stirring constantly with a wooden spoon, until the custard thickens enough to coat the back of the spoon and reaches 170° on an instant-read thermometer, about 7 minutes; do not let it boil. Strain the custard into a medium heatproof bowl and chill in a larger bowl of ice water, stirring occasionally, or refrigerate for up to 2 days with plastic wrap pressed to the surface.

4. Stir the heavy cream, hazelnut butter, vanilla, and the remaining 1 cup milk into the chilled custard until thoroughly combined.

5. Working in 2 batches, pour half the custard into an ice cream maker and freeze according to the manufacturer's instructions. When the ice cream is almost the right consistency, stir in half the chopped hazelnuts, then freeze completely. Transfer the ice cream to a chilled airtight freezer container. Repeat with the remaining custard and hazelnuts. Freeze at least 2 hours and up to 1 week.—JOAN AND DICK ERATH

INSTANT ICE CREAM SANDWICHES

MAKES 8 SANDWICHES

½ pint vanilla ice cream, softened
16 store-bought crisp chocolate wafer cookies
⅓ cup finely chopped peppermint candies or Heath bars

Spoon a heaping tablespoon of ice cream onto half of the cookies. Cover with the remaining cookies and press gently. Pat the chopped candies onto the ice cream. Wrap the sandwiches in pairs in wax paper and freeze until ready to eat.—TRACEY SEAMAN

SPICY PECAN ICE CREAM

Serve the ice cream on its own or with plain pound cake.

MAKES ABOUT 3 CUPS

½ vanilla bean, split
1½ cups heavy cream
½ cup half-and-half
5 large egg yolks
¾ cup sugar
2 tablespoons dark rum
4 tablespoons unsalted butter
½ cup pecan halves (about 2 ounces)
¼ teaspoon cayenne pepper
Pinch of salt

1. In a medium saucepan, scrape the seeds from the vanilla bean into the heavy cream and half-and-half and add the bean. Bring just to a simmer over moderately high heat. Meanwhile, in a bowl, whisk the egg yolks with ½ cup of the sugar. Gradually whisk in the hot cream. Pour the mixture back into the saucepan and cook over moderately high heat, stirring constantly, until the custard thickens and coats the back of a spoon, about 5 minutes. Strain into a bowl and let cool. Stir in the rum.

2. In a small skillet, melt the remaining ¼ cup sugar over moderately high heat until golden brown, about 5 minutes. Stir in the butter and the pecan halves and cook, stirring constantly, until the pecans are thoroughly coated. Spread the nuts on a plate and let cool. Sprinkle with the cayenne and salt.

3. Break the spiced pecans into small pieces and stir them into the custard. Freeze in an ice cream maker according to the manufacturer's instructions. Transfer the ice cream to a chilled container. (MAKE AHEAD: The ice cream can be frozen, covered, for up to 3 days.) —SCOTT HOWELL

CARAMEL-SWIRL ICE CREAM

This ice cream is made with a very dark caramel (see "Three Stages of Caramel," right) for an intense but not-too-sweet taste. You could make just the caramel ice cream, but the rich swirl makes it really special.

MAKES ABOUT 1½ PINTS

- 2 cups sugar
- 2 cups plus 2 tablespoons heavy cream
- 1½ cups milk
- 6 large egg yolks

1. In a small, deep, heavy saucepan, bring ¾ cup of the sugar and ¼ cup of water to a boil over moderately high heat, stirring occasionally to dissolve the sugar. Wash down the sides of the pan with a wet pastry brush. Boil without stirring until the caramel turns a golden amber color, 5 to 8 minutes. Remove from the heat and immediately add ½ cup plus 2 tablespoons of the heavy cream; stand back to avoid spatters. Stir with a wooden spoon, then cook over low heat, stirring, until smooth, about 1 minute. Remove from the heat and let cool. Transfer the caramel to a bowl, cover, and refrigerate until cold, at least 1 hour and up to 2 days.

2. Meanwhile, in a large heavy saucepan, bring the milk and the remaining 1½ cups heavy cream just to a boil over moderate heat. In a large bowl, whisk the egg yolks with ¾ cup of the sugar until smooth.

3. Gradually whisk the hot cream into the egg yolks. Pour the custard into the saucepan. Cook over moderate heat, stirring constantly with a wooden spoon, until the mixture thickens slightly and coats the back of the spoon, or until it registers about 180° on a candy thermometer, about 7 minutes. Do not boil. Immediately strain the custard into a large heatproof bowl and set aside.

4. In a small, deep, heavy saucepan, bring the remaining ½ cup sugar and 3 tablespoons of water to a boil over moderately high heat, stirring to dissolve the sugar. Wash down the pan with a wet pastry brush. Boil without stirring until the caramel turns a deep amber color, about 7 minutes. Remove from the heat and add 2 tablespoons of cold water; stand back to avoid spatters. Stir until smooth.

5. Whisk the hot caramel into the custard, making sure the caramel doesn't get on the whisk as you pour. Let cool to room temperature, stirring once or twice, then cover and refrigerate until cold, at least 2 hours or overnight.

6. Pour the custard into an ice cream maker and freeze according to the manufacturer's instructions. Transfer the ice cream to a chilled container and freeze until partially set but not hard, about 1 hour.

7. Spoon one-third of the ice cream into a chilled freezer container. Spoon one-third of the chilled caramel on top; it does not have to be an even layer. Top with a layer of ice cream. Continue layering, ending with caramel. Stir once; do not overmix, or the caramel will melt into the ice cream. Cover and freeze for at least 3 hours or up to 2 days.—JUDITH SUTTON

THREE STAGES OF CARAMEL

- LIGHT CARAMEL, **about 320°, has just a hint of color and little flavor; it is used for coating nuts or fruit and for making spun sugar and caramel cages.**
- MEDIUM CARAMEL, **about 345°, is cooked to a golden amber; it has a strong, sweet taste and is used in sauces, candies, and many caramel-based desserts.**
- DARK CARAMEL, **about 375°, is a deep amber-mahogany; less sweet than medium caramel, it is used in sauces, to line crème caramel molds, and for flavoring other desserts.—JUDITH SUTTON**

Individual Chocolate Soufflés

INDIVIDUAL CHOCOLATE SOUFFLES

If you're using a copper bowl and balloon whisk, you can make up to eight soufflés. You'll incorporate less air with an electric beater and stainless bowl and therefore get fewer servings.

6 TO 8 SERVINGS

- 4 ounces good-quality bittersweet chocolate, finely chopped
- ½ cup heavy cream
- 3 large egg yolks
- ½ teaspoon pure vanilla extract
- 5 large egg whites, at room temperature
- ¼ cup granulated sugar

Confectioners' sugar, for dusting

1. In a medium-size saucepan, melt the chocolate in the cream over moderately low heat, stirring, until perfectly smooth, about 3 minutes. Remove from the heat and whisk in the egg yolks, one at a time, mixing well after each addition. Stir in the vanilla. (MAKE AHEAD: The recipe can be prepared to this point up to 4 hours before baking; press plastic wrap directly on the surface of the chocolate mixture to prevent the formation of a skin and let stand at room temperature.)

2. Preheat the oven to 425°. Butter six to eight ⅔-cup ramekins. Put them in the freezer for a few minutes to set the butter quickly. Butter the ramekins again. Rewarm the chocolate mixture over moderately low heat, stirring, just until hot to the touch.

3. Meanwhile, in a medium bowl, beat the egg whites until they hold soft peaks. Add the granulated sugar and continue beating until the egg whites are glossy and hold stiff peaks, about 1 minute longer. Stir one quarter of the egg whites into the chocolate mixture to lighten it. The chocolate mixture and the egg whites should be close to the same density. Then fold the chocolate mixture into the remaining whites just until they are combined.

4. Scrape the soufflé mixture into the prepared ramekins, smooth the surfaces, and run your thumb around the inside rim of each ramekin. Set the ramekins on a baking sheet and bake the soufflés in the middle of the oven for about 8 minutes, until puffed and set around the edges. Dust the soufflés with confectioners' sugar and serve at once.—ANNE WILLAN

FOLDING SOUFFLES

Folding is key to the success of a soufflé. Fold the base into the beaten egg whites as gently as possible with a rubber spatula. Use the spatula to cut through the center of the mixture, then scoop around and under, turning the mixture over in a rolling motion. At the same time, revolve the bowl in the opposite direction. Fold just until the whites are combined with the base. If the mixture begins to look sloppy, it's an indication that the egg whites are losing air. Stop folding at once; a few streaks of white will not affect the outcome of the soufflé.—ANNE WILLAN

SOUFFLE TIPS

- **Soufflé dishes vary in size, and so they are measured by volume.** TO DETERMINE THE VOLUME OF A DISH, **just see how many cups of water are required to fill the dish to the top.**
- **Butter the soufflé dish twice** TO ENSURE THAT THE SOUFFLE RISES WITHOUT STICKING **to the sides. For an additional layer of coating, use dried bread crumbs for savory soufflés and sugar for sweet ones.**
- TO GET MAXIMUM VOLUME WHEN BEATING EGG WHITES, **use whites that are at room temperature.**
- TO STABILIZE THE EGG WHITES **when making savory soufflés, add a pinch of salt or cream of tartar as you start to whisk them. If you're making a sweet soufflé, beat in sugar when the whites start to stiffen, to make a light but sturdy meringue.**
- **Fill the soufflé dish to within three eighths of an inch of the top for the best results.** FOR EVEN RISING, **run your thumb around the inside edge of the filled soufflé dish before baking the soufflé to loosen the batter from the rim.**
- **If your oven heats unevenly, turn the soufflé during baking** SO THAT IT BROWNS UNIFORMLY **and isn't lopsided. Be careful when opening the oven door, since soufflés are extremely sensitive to drafts.**—ANNE WILLAN

INDIVIDUAL GINGER-CHOCOLATE SOUFFLES

Hidden inside each of these soufflés is a surprise: a small scoop of chocolate ice cream that melts during baking to make a rich sauce.

6 SERVINGS

- 1 cup milk
- 3 large egg yolks
- 2 tablespoons sugar
- 2 tablespoons all-purpose flour
- 2 tablespoons finely chopped candied ginger
- ¾ teaspoon ground ginger
- 4 large egg whites, at room temperature
- Six 1-tablespoon scoops of chocolate ice cream, frozen

1. Bring the milk just to a boil in a small saucepan; keep warm. In a medium bowl, whisk the egg yolks with 1 tablespoon of the sugar until thick and pale, about 2 minutes. Stir in the all-purpose flour. Whisk in half of the hot milk, then whisk the mixture back into the remaining hot milk. Cook over moderate heat, whisking constantly, until the mixture is thickened, about 4 minutes. Continue cooking this pastry cream, stirring, until it thins slightly (indicating that the flour is cooked), about 2 minutes longer. Let the pastry cream cool slightly, then stir in the chopped candied ginger and the ground ginger. (MAKE AHEAD: The recipe can be prepared to this point up to 4 hours ahead; press plastic wrap directly on the surface of the ginger mixture and let stand at room temperature.)

2. Preheat the oven to 425°. Butter six ⅔-cup ramekins and freeze until set. Butter the ramekins again. Rewarm the ginger mixture over moderately low heat, stirring, just until it is hot to the touch.

3. Meanwhile, in a medium bowl, beat the egg whites until soft peaks form. Add the remaining 1 tablespoon sugar and beat until the egg whites are glossy and firm, about 1 minute longer. Stir one quarter of the egg whites into the ginger mixture, then fold the ginger mixture into the remaining egg whites just until combined.

4. Half fill the prepared ramekins with the ginger soufflé mixture. Put a scoop of chocolate ice cream in the center of each ramekin, gently pushing it down. Cover the scoop of ice cream with the remaining soufflé mixture. Smooth the surfaces and run your thumb around the inside edge of each ramekin. Set the ramekins on a baking sheet and bake the soufflés in the middle of the oven for about 12 minutes, until they are puffed, nicely browned on top, and set around the edges. Serve the soufflés immediately.—ANNE WILLAN

Chewy Caramels

CHEWY CARAMELS

High humidity is a factor when making caramel. These chewy caramels may not set up properly on a damp day; if that's the case, try another caramel dessert and wait for a drier day to make the candy. You will need a candy thermometer to make this recipe. Colored or clear cellophane for wrapping the caramels can sometimes be found in rolls where wrapping paper is sold, and it's often available at florist shops. If you can't find it, wax paper works fine.

MAKES 90 CANDIES

- 2 cups sugar
- 2 cups heavy cream
- 1¾ cups light corn syrup
- 2 sticks (½ pound) unsalted butter
- Pinch of salt
- 2 teaspoons pure vanilla extract

1. Lightly butter the bottom of a 9-by-13-inch baking pan. Line the pan with foil, pressing it evenly into the corners. Lightly butter the foil.

2. Butter the sides of a heavy 4-quart saucepan. Add the sugar, 1 cup of the heavy cream, the corn syrup, butter, and salt, and cook over moderate heat, stirring with a wooden spoon, until the butter has melted and the sugar has completely dissolved, about 5 minutes. Wash down the sides of the pan with a wet pastry brush. Bring the mixture to a boil. Wash down the pan again and set a candy thermometer in the pan. Continue cooking at a moderate boil, without stirring, until the temperature reaches 242°, 25 to 30 minutes.

3. Slowly pour in the remaining 1 cup cream, letting the mixture continue to boil; stir it with a wooden spoon. Boil without stirring until the temperature reaches 246°, about 20 minutes. Remove the pan from the heat. Add the vanilla and stir just to blend. Pour the caramel into the prepared baking pan. Do not scrape the caramel from the bottom of the saucepan. Set the baking pan on a rack to cool, then cover with plastic wrap and let sit at room temperature for at least 4 hours or overnight.

4. Invert the caramel slab onto a cutting board and peel off the foil. Using a sharp heavy knife, cut the caramel lengthwise into 9 strips, then cut each strip crosswise into 10 caramels. Wrap each candy in cellophane and store at room temperature for up to 1 week, refrigerate for up to 2 weeks, or freeze for up to 1 month.—JUDITH SUTTON

INDEX

Page numbers in **boldface** indicate photographs

C

D

E

F

G

H

N

O

P

Q

R

S

T

CONTRIBUTORS

Jeffrey Alford and Naomi Duguid are location food photographers and the authors of *Flatbreads & Flavors* (William Morrow) and a forthcoming book about rice.
Ann Chantal Altman is the executive chef for Joseph E. Seagram & Sons and a cooking instructor at Peter Kump's School of Culinary Arts in New York City.
Ann Amernick is a pastry chef in Chevy Chase, Maryland. She is the author of *Special Desserts* and co-author of *Soufflés* (both from Clarkson N. Potter).
John Ash is the culinary director at Fetzer Vineyards in Redwood Valley, California, and co-author of *American Game Cooking* (Addison Wesley).
Nancy Baggett is a cooking teacher and the author of *100% Pleasure: The Lowfat Cookbook for People Who Love to Eat* (Rodale) and *The International Cookie Cookbook* (Stewart, Tabori & Chang).
Ben Barker is the chef/owner of Magnolia Grill in Durham, North Carolina.
Nancy Verde Barr is the author of *We Called It Macaroni* (Knopf) and was assistant writer to Julia Child on her book *In Julia's Kitchen with Master Chefs* (Knopf).
Octavio Becerra is the executive chef at Pinot Bistro in Studio City, California.
Richard Benz is the executive chef at Upper Line in New Orleans.
Mark Bittman is the author of *Fish: The Complete Guide to Buying and Cooking* and *Leafy Greens* (both from Macmillan).
Parker Bosley is the chef/owner at Parker's in Cleveland.
Daniel Boulud is the chef/owner of Daniel in New York City and the author of *Cooking with Daniel Boulud* (Random House).
Philippe Boulot is the chef at The Heathman Hotel in Portland, Oregon.
Wayne Harley Brachman is the executive pastry chef at Mesa Grill and Bolo in New York City and the author of *Cakes and Cowpokes: New Desserts from the Old Southwest* (William Morrow).
Terrance Brennan is the chef/owner at Picholine in New York City.
David Burke is chef/owner at the Park Avenue Café in New York City and owner of the restaurant's Chicago branch. He is the author of *Cooking with David Burke of the Park Avenue Café* (Knopf).
Capers Catering is located in Chicago.
Mary Carroll is a cookbook author and syndicated columnist based in Minneapolis. Her books include *Healthy Cooking* and *The New Gourmet* (both from CCA) and *The No Cholesterol (No Kidding!) Cookbook* (Rodale).
Kathy Cary is the chef/owner of Lilly's and La Pêche in Louisville, Kentucky.
Bob Chambers is the executive chef at Lâncome-L'Oréal in New York City.
Julia Child is the country's foremost television cooking teacher and the doyenne of French cooking in America. Her books include *Mastering the Art of French Cooking, The Way to Cook*, and *In Julia's Kitchen with Master Chefs* (all from Knopf).
Paul Chung, an enthusiast of ethnic cuisine, specializes in the recipes of his Jamaican-Chinese heritage.
Patrick Clark is the executive chef at Tavern on the Green in New York City.
Tom Colicchio is the chef of Gramercy Tavern in New York City.
Shirley Corriher is a food writer, teacher, and consultant, and the author of a forthcoming book on food science, including recipes, from William Morrow.
Creative Edge Parties is a catering company in New York City.
Robert Cubberly is the executive chef at Fog City Diner in San Francisco.
Peggy Cullen is a baker, writer, and candymaker living in New York City.
Charles Dale is the executive chef at Renaissance in Aspen, Colorado.
Sanford D'Amato is a cooking teacher and the chef/owner of Sanford Restaurant in Milwaukee.
Gary Danko is chef of The Dining Room at San Francisco's Ritz-Carlton Hotel.
Robert Del Grande is the chef/owner of Cafe Annie in Houston.
Julia Della Croce is a cooking teacher and the author of *The Vegetarian Table: Italy, Antipasti: The Little Dishes of Italy, The Pasta Book: Recipes in the Italian Tradition*, and *Pasta Classica: The Art of Italian Pasta Cooking* (all from Chronicle Books). She is currently working on two more books about Italian cooking.
Erica De Mane is a chef and food writer. She is working on a book about improvisational Italian cooking.
Traci Des Jardins is the executive chef at Rubicon in San Francisco.
Kirsten Dixon is the chef/owner of Riversong Lodge in Anchorage, Alaska, and author of *The Riversong Lodge Cookbook: World-Class Cooking in the Alaska Bush* (Alaska Northwest Books) and a forthcoming volume, *North Country Cuisine*.
Roberto Donna is the chef/owner of Galileo in Washington, D.C., and owner of five more establishments, including a bakery, a fish store, and a spaghetteria.
Cassandra Dooley is a freelance food writer and caterer based in New York City.
Tom Douglas is the chef/owner of Dahlia Lounge in Seattle.
Lissa Doumani is the pastry chef and co-owner of Terra in St. Helena, California.
Chata DuBose specializes in Mexican cuisine and teaches cooking at Le Panier and Sheldon's, both in Houston.
Todd English is the chef/co-owner of Olives in Charlestown, Massachusetts, and the author of the forthcoming *Olive's Kitchen*.
Becky Sue Epstein and Hilary Dole Klein are food writers and the authors of *Substituting Ingredients: An A to Z Kitchen Reference* (Globe Pequot).
Joan and Dick Erath are winemakers and owners of Erath Vineyards in Dundee, Oregon, and cooking enthusiasts.
Serge Falesitch is the chef/owner of Eclipse in West Hollywood, California.
Arlene Feltman Sailhac is the owner/director of the "DeGustibus at Macy's Great Cooks Program." She is also the author of *DeGustibus Presents the Great Cooks* cookbook series (Black Dog & Leventhal) and *Trucs of the Trade* (HarperCollins).
Mike Fennelly is the chef/co-owner of Mike's on the Avenue in New Orleans and the author of *East Meets Southwest* (Chronicle Books).
Flavors Catering & Carryout is located in New York City.
Susanna Foo is a cookbook author and the chef/owner of Susanna Foo Chinese Cuisine in Philadelphia.
Margaret Fox is the chef/owner of Cafe Beaujolais in Mendocino, California, and the author of *Cafe Beaujolais Morning Food* (Ten Speed Press).
Sarah Fritschner is the food editor of the Louisville *Courier-Journal* and the author of *Express Lane Cookbook* (Chapters).

Jean Galton is a food writer and cooking teacher based in Seattle. She is the author of the forthcoming *Lasagne* (Harper Collins) as well as co-author of the forthcoming *365 Great Soups and Stews* (Collins S.F.)

Fred and Linda Griffith are the authors of *Onions Onions Onions* (Chapters). In addition, Linda is a cooking teacher and Fred is the host of a daily TV show, "The Morning Exchange."

Vincent Guerithault is the chef/owner of Vincent Guerithault on Camelback in Phoenix. He is also the author of *Vincent's Cookbook* (Ten Speed Press).

Fatima Hal is the chef/owner of Mansouria in Paris, France.

Jessica B. Harris is the author of *A Kwanzaa Keepsake* (Simon & Schuster).

Marcella Hazan is the owner of the cooking school Master Class in Classic Italian Cooking in Venice, Italy, and a renowned author, most recently of *Essentials of Classic Italian Cooking* (Knopf).

Maida Heatter is the author of seven classic dessert cookbooks, including *Maida Heatter's Brand New Cookies* (Random House).

Sharon Tyler Herbst is the author of eight books, including *The Food Lover's Tiptionary* (William Morrow).

Pierre Hermé is a pastry chef at Fauchon in Paris, France.

Scott Howell is the chef/owner of Nana's and Pop's in Durham, North Carolina.

Jackson & Co. is a catering business in Houston.

Cheryl Alters Jamison and Bill Jamison are food and travel writers and the authors of several cookbooks, including *Smoke & Spice* and *The Border Cookbook* (both from Harvard Common Press).

Susan Shapiro Jaslove is a food writer and recipe developer. She is currently working on a cookbook about baking with children.

Bill Jones is a chef and the proprietor of Magnetic North Cuisine, a food industry consulting service in Vancouver, British Columbia. He has edited a book on mushrooms and is currently at work on a series of Northwestern cookbooks based on regional natural resources.

Joyce Jue is a food consultant, cooking teacher, and lecturer on Asian cuisine. She wrote *Asian Appetizers* (Harlow-Ratner) and the forthcoming *The Far-East Café* (Weldon-Owen), and co-wrote *The Cooking of Singapore* (Harlow-Ratner).

Hubert Keller is the chef/owner at Fleur de Lys in San Francisco.

Thomas Keller is the chef/owner of The French Laundry restaurant in Yountville, California.

Matthew Kenney is the chef/owner of Matthew's in New York City and is currently working on a cookbook.

Marcia Kiesel is the associate director of FOOD & WINE magazine's test kitchen and co-author of *Simple Art of Vietnamese Cooking* (Prentice Hall).

Christopher Kump is executive chef at Cafe Beaujolais in Mendocino, California, and currently at work on a cookbook to be published by Ten Speed Press.

Christer Larsson is the chef/owner of Christer's in New York City.

Karen Lee is a caterer, a cooking teacher, and the owner of Karen Lee's Cooking School in New York City. She is also the author of *The Occasional Vegetarian* (Warner Books).

Emily Luchetti and Hollyce Snyder are former pastry chefs of Stars in San Francisco. Luchetti is working on a book, *Emily's Desserts,* and Snyder is production manager for Whole Foods bakehouse.

Sheila Lukins is the food editor of *Parade* magazine and the author of *Sheila Lukins All Around the World* and co-author of *The Silver Palate Cookbook*, *The New Basics*, and *The Silver Palate Good Times Cookbook* (all from Workman).

Stephanie Lyness, a food writer and recipe developer based in New York City, is the author, with Jacques Manière, of *Cuisine à la Vapeur: The Art of Cooking with Steam*, as well as the forthcoming *Cooking with Steam* (both from William Morrow).

Patsy A. Madden is a freelance recipe tester based in Bronxville, New York.

Deborah Madison is a cooking teacher as well as a former chef and restaurateur. She is the author of *The Greens Cookbook* and *The Savory Way* (both from Bantam) and *The Vegetarian Taste* (Chronicle Books). She is at work on another vegetarian cookbook to be released in 1997.

George Mahaffey is the executive chef at The Little Nell in Aspen, Colorado.

Nick Malgieri is the vice president/director of baking programs at Peter Kump's School of Culinary Arts in New York City and the author of several books, including *How to Bake* (HarperCollins).

Tony Mantuano is the executive chef at Tuttaposto in Chicago.

Lydie Marshall is a cooking teacher and the owner of A la Bonne Cocotte cooking school in New York City. She is the author of *Chez Nous* and *A Passion for Potatoes* (both from HarperCollins).

Harold McGee is the author of *On Food & Cooking: The Science & Lore of the Kitchen* (Charles Scribner's Sons) and *The Curious Cook: More Kitchen Science & Lore* (Collier).

Steve Mellina is the executive chef at Doubles/Sherry Netherlands Hotel in New York City.

Gene Meyer is a New York fashion and tableware designer.

Mark Militello is the chef/owner of Mark's Place in North Miami, Florida. He is working on a fish cookbook.

Frank Minieri is the general manager at Il Cantinori in New York City.

Susan Molzan is the baker and co-owner of The Ruggles Grill in Houston.

Nick Morfogen is the chef at the Ajax Tavern in Aspen, Colorado.

Pamela Morgan is a food writer and the owner of Flavors Catering & Carryout in New York City.

Neuman & Bogdonoff is a takeout shop and catering company in New York City. Paul Neuman and Stacy Bogdonoff are the owners and Steven Podol is the chef.

Jan Newberry is the managing editor of *Fine Cooking* magazine.

Wayne Nish is the chef/co-owner of March Restaurant in New York City.

Patrick O'Connell is the co-owner and chef of The Inn at Little Washington in Washington, Virginia.

Pascal Oudin is the executive chef at The Grand Café at the Grand Bay Hotel in Coconut Grove, Florida.

Charlie Palmer is the chef/owner of Aureole in New York City. He is the author of the forthcoming *Great American Food* (Random House).

Angèle Parlange is a New Orleans-based designer of fabric, fashion, home accessories, and furniture.

Grace Parisi is recipe tester-developer for FOOD & WINE magazine.

Jacques Pépin is a famed cooking teacher and the author of numerous cookbooks, the most recent of which are *Jacques Pépin's Simple and Healthy Cooking* (Rodale) and *Jacques Pépin's Table* (KQED Books).

Odessa Piper is the executive chef/owner of L'Etoile Restaurant in Madison, Wisconsin. She is working on a cookbook.

Marge Poore is a culinary tour leader, cooking teacher, and the author of *The Complete Chicken Breast Cookbook* (Prima Publishing) and *365 Easy Mexican Recipes* (HarperCollins).

Nora Pouillon is the chef/owner at Restaurant Nora in Washington, D.C.

Stephan Pyles the chef/owner of Star Canyon in Dallas. He is the author of *The New Texas Cuisine* (Doubleday) and a forthcoming book about tamales.

Anne Quatrano and Clifford Harrison are chef/owners of Bacchanalia in Atlanta.

Miguel Ravago is the chef/owner at Fonda San Miguel in Austin, Texas.

Gary Regan writes about spirits and is the author of *The Bartender's Bible* (HarperCollins) and co-author, with his wife, Mardee Haidin Regan, of *The Book of Bourbon and Other Fine American Whiskeys* (Chapters).

Eric Ripert is the executive chef at New York City's Le Bernardin.

Rick Robinson is the chef/owner, in partnership with his wife, Millie, of Mondo Bistro in Chapel Hill, North Carolina.

Hans Rockenwagner is the chef/owner of Rockenwagner in Santa Monica, California, and is at work on *The Rockenwagner Cookbook*.

Douglas Rodriguez is the chef/owner of Patria in New York City and the author of *Nuevo Latino* (Ten Speed Press) as well as the forthcoming *Latin Ladels*.

G. Franco Romagnoli is the author of several cookbooks, including *The Romagnolis' Italian Fish Cookbook* (Henry Holt).

Anne Rosenzweig is chef/owner of Arcadia and The Lobster Club, both in New York City. She is the author of *The Arcadia Seasonal Mural and Cookbook* (Abrams).

Walter Royal is the executive chef and teaches cooking at The Inn at Bonnie Brae in Durham, North Carolina.

Maury Rubin is the chef/owner of The City Bakery in New York City and author of *Book of Tarts* (William Morrow).

David Ruggerio is the chef/owner of Le Chantilly Restaurant and Nonna Restaurant in New York City. He is working on a book about New York's Little Italy.

Edward Safdie is the author of *Spa Food* and *New Spa Food* (both from Crown).

Sage & Swift is a catering company in Durham, North Carolina.

John Schenk is the executive chef at the Monkey Bar in New York City.

Dieter G. Schorner is a pastry chef and the owner of Patisserie Cafe Didier in Washington, D.C.

Michele Scicolone is a cooking teacher and the author of *La Dolce Vita* and *The Antipasto Table* (both from William Morrow). She is working on a new book about Italian Cooking.

Tracey Seaman is a cookbook author and the test kitchen director for *Woman's Day*.

Jamie Shannon is the executive chef at Commander's Palace in New Orleans.

Susan Simon is a caterer and the author of *Visual Vegetables* (Clarkson N. Potter) as well as a work in progress about Nantucket cooking.

Annie Somerville is the executive chef at Greens Restaurant in San Francisco. She is the author of *Fields of Greens* (Bantam).

Greg Sonnier is the executive chef at Gabrielle in New Orleans.

Joachim Splichal is the chef/owner of Patina in Los Angeles and the author of *Joachim Splichal's Patina Cookbook: Spuds, Truffles and Wild Gnocchi* (Collins Publishers).

Tanya Wenman Steel writes frequently for *The New York Times*.

Diana Sturgis is the test-kitchen director of FOOD & WINE magazine.

Allen Susser is the executive chef of Chef Allen's Restaurant in Miami.

Judith Sutton is a food writer and editor and has worked as a cook and pastry chef at Sign of the Dove and other New York City restaurants.

John Martin Taylor is the owner of Hoppin' John's, a culinary bookstore in Charleston, South Carolina, and the author of *Hoppin' John's Low Country Cooking* and *The New Southern Cook* (both from Bantam). He is working on two new cookbooks.

Jacques Torres is the pastry chef at Le Cirque in New York City. He teaches at several cooking schools, including The French Culinary Institute.

Jerry Traunfeld is chef at The Herb Farm in Fall City, Washington. He is the author of *Seasonal Favorites from the Herbfarm* (Sasquatch Books).

The Upper Crust is a catering company in New York City.

David Waltuck is the chef/owner of Chanterelle in New York City.

Kenneth Wapner is a poet and freelance writer with a special interest in food.

Joanne Weir is a cooking teacher and the author of *From Tapas to Meze* (Crown). She is currently at work on *Seasonal Celebrations*, a series of four books that will be published in 1997 by Williams Sonoma.

Charles Wiley is executive chef of Carefree Resorts, including The Boulders Resort in Carefree, Arizona, the Inn at Telluride in Telluride, Colorado, and Carmel Valley Ranch in Carmel, California. He is at work on a book to be titled *Carefree Cuisine*.

Anne Willan teaches cooking at La Varenne in Burgundy and La Varenne at the Greenbrier. She is the author of *In and Out of the Kitchen in 15 Minutes or Less* (Rizzoli), *La Varenne Pratique* (Crown), and the 17-volume Look & Cook series (Dorling Kindersley). She is working on a new book, *Cooked to Perfection*.

Robert Waggoner is the chef at Nashville's Wild Boar Restaurant and the winner of FOOD & WINE's 1995 Reader's Choice Award.

Hallman Woods III is the executive chef at Le Rosier in New Iberia, Louisiana.

Word of Mouth is a catering company in New York City.